T0375326

Value Added Tax

This book integrates legal, economic, and administrative materials about the value added tax (VAT) to present a comparative approach to the study of VAT law. The comparative presentation of this volume offers an analysis of policy issues relating to tax structure and tax base as well as insights into how cases arising out of VAT disputes have been resolved. Its principal purpose is to provide comprehensive teaching tools – laws, cases, analytical exercises, and questions drawn from the experience of countries and organizations around the world.

This second edition includes new VAT-related developments in Europe, Asia, Africa, and Australia and adds new chapters on VAT avoidance and evasion and on China's VAT. Designed to illustrate, analyze, and explain the principal theoretical and operating features of value added taxes, including their adoption and implementation, this book will be an invaluable resource for tax practitioners and government officials.

Alan Schenk is a distinguished professor at Wayne State University Law School. He has taught VAT at other universities in the United States and abroad. Schenk is the author of numerous articles and several books on value added tax and goods and services tax, in addition to the first edition of this book, which was coauthored with the late Oliver Oldman. For the past eighteen years, he served as a technical adviser for the IMF's legal department, drafting VAT laws and regulations. He has consulted for foreign governments, testified before the U.S. Congress, and served as an expert in arbitrations involving VAT.

Victor Thuronyi served as lead counsel (taxation) in the IMF's legal department until 2013, where he coordinated the department's program of technical assistance in tax law, focusing on drafting new tax laws or on substantial revision of existing ones, as well as continuing to teach. He is the author of *Comparative Tax Law* (2003) and numerous articles and book chapters on tax law and policy, and he is the editor of and a contributing author to *Tax Law Design and Drafting* (2000).

Wei Cui is an associate professor in the Faculty of Law at the University of British Columbia. Prior to 2013, he taught and practiced law in Beijing and assisted Chinese government agencies on a variety of tax legislative and regulatory matters involving business and individual income taxation, the VAT, and tax administration. He served as senior tax counsel for the China Investment Corporation between 2009 and 2010, and he is a current member of the Permanent Scientific Committee of the International Fiscal Association.

CAMBRIDGE TAX LAW SERIES

Tax law is a growing area of interest, as it is included as a subdivision in many areas of study and is a key consideration in business needs throughout the world. Books in this series will expose the theoretical underpinning behind the law to shed light on the taxation systems, so that the questions to be asked when addressing an issue become clear. These academic books, written by leading scholars, will be a central port of call for information on tax law. The content will be illustrated by case law and legislation. The books will be of interest to those studying law, business, economics, accounting and finance courses.

SERIES EDITOR

Dr Peter Harris, *Law Faculty, University of Cambridge, Director of the Centre for Tax Law*

Dr Harris brings a wealth of experience to the series. He has taught and presented tax courses at a dozen different universities in nearly as many countries and has acted as an external tax consultant for the International Monetary Fund for more than a decade.

Value Added Tax

A Comparative Approach

Second Edition

Alan Schenk
Wayne State University School of Law

Victor Thuronyi
International Monetary Fund Legal Department (retired)

Wei Cui
University of British Columbia, Faculty of Law

CAMBRIDGE
UNIVERSITY PRESS

CAMBRIDGE
UNIVERSITY PRESS

32 Avenue of the Americas, New York NY 10013-2473, USA

Cambridge University Press is part of the University of Cambridge.

It furthers the University's mission by disseminating knowledge in the pursuit of education, learning and research at the highest international levels of excellence.

www.cambridge.org
Information on this title: www.cambridge.org/9781107042988

© Cambridge University Press 2007, 2015

This publication is in copyright. Subject to statutory exception and to the provisions of relevant collective licensing agreements, no reproduction of any part may take place without the written permission of Cambridge University Press.

First published 2007
Second edition 2015

A catalogue record for this publication is available from the British Library

Library of Congress Cataloguing in Publication data
Schenk, Alan, author.
Value added tax : a comparative approach / Alan Schenk, Victor Thuronyi, Wei Cui. – Second edition.
pages cm – (Cambridge tax law series)
Includes bibliographical references and index.
ISBN 978-1-107-04298-8 (hardback) – ISBN 978-1-107-61762-9 (paperback)
1. Value-added tax – Law and legislation. 2. Spendings tax – Law and legislation. 3. Taxation of articles of consumption – Law and legislation. I. Thuronyi, Victor author. II. Cui, Wei, 1970– author. III. Title.
K4573.S337 2014
336.2′714–dc23 2014027840

ISBN 978-1-107-04298-8 Hardback
ISBN 978-1-107-61762-9 Paperback

Cambridge University Press has no responsibility for the persistence or accuracy of URLs for external or third-party internet websites referred to in this publication, and does not guarantee that any content on such websites is, or will remain, accurate or appropriate.

To
Sophia
AS

Jie
WC

Contents

List of Tables and Charts

List of Cases

Cases listed by name of the taxpayer or, for action by the European Commission, the country. Cases in boldface are main textual cases.

Preface to the Second Edition

Thanks to our students at Wayne State, Duke, Michigan, and Sydney law schools for their contributions to the revision of this book. Thanks to Deans Robert Ackerman and Jocelyn Benson and Wayne State University Law School and to Virginia Thomas, Director of the Wayne Law Library, and her staff, particularly Michael Samson, for the support that made this revision possible. Thanks to Richard Ainsworth and the two anonymous readers who made helpful suggestions on how we could improve this edition of the book. Thanks to Yimin Kou for discussions of the material in Chapter 14. Thanks to Zainab Sabbagh Hazimi for her helpful research assistance. Thanks to Olive Hyman for her assistance with various aspects of the manuscript. Thanks to John Berger, our editor at Cambridge University Press, and our project manager, Nishanthini Vetrivel, for their help in the process of converting our manuscript to final text.

The cutoff date for this book generally was December 31, 2013, although we have included some material published after that date. In particular, we included some European VAT Directives and Court of Justice cases. This book is not intended to be exhaustive. It therefore does not include all significant cases in all countries or even all English-speaking countries. It is designed to illustrate, analyze, and explain the principal theoretical and operating features of value added taxes, including their adoption and implementation.

The European Union continues to revise its 2006 VAT Directive, which includes the principles that all member countries must adopt as part of their value added taxes. Some of the material from the first edition (omitted from this edition) may be of interest to researchers, in particular the discussion of transition rules (pp. 241–246), proposals for a U.S. Tax on Consumption (Chapter 14), and Commonwealth of New Vatopia Value Added Tax (Appendix B).

1 Introduction

I. Scope of Book

The value added tax (VAT) has spread around the world more quickly than any other new tax in modern history.[1] This book covers value added tax and, in some parts, other consumption taxes in use or proposed in developing and developed countries.

Tax on consumption generally refers to a tax on final consumption, consisting mainly of goods and services acquired by individuals for their personal use or satisfaction. It generally does not include business inputs (goods and services used by business in the production or distribution of goods or in the rendition of services).

It is difficult for a business to operate internationally without considering the implications of sales tax or value added tax, whether or not the company's country of residence has a broad-based tax on consumption. For example, the United States does not have a sales tax or value added tax, except at the state and local levels of government. Nevertheless, a U.S. business operating in, shipping goods or transferring intellectual property or providing or receiving services to and from other countries must consider the VAT implications of exports to or imports from those countries.

This book explores value added and other consumption tax principles from a comparative perspective. We hope that this study may lead to suggestions for improving existing VAT systems and designing new ones. We discuss VAT in the Member States of the European Union (EU), and explain major departures from the EU model in non-European countries (especially in New Zealand, China, Japan, and South Africa).

[1] See Appendix, listing the countries with VATs and sales taxes.

II. Development of Taxes on Consumption – A Brief Review of History

Most early forms of taxation were levies on land or on the produce from land.[2] The tax on land in early civilizations was payable in kind with the produce from the land.[3] The tithe in Egyptian kingdoms was imposed as a proportion of agricultural produce.[4] In the days of the city-states of Athens and Rome, while there were taxes in the form of rents from state-owned land (including taxes on natural resources extracted from these lands), the rulers supplemented revenue from land with indirect taxes.[5] Customs duties were imposed at the ports and taxes were extracted at the markets for goods that arrived by land.[6] In the third century AD, Diocletian imposed fees (or taxes) on the monopolies that he granted for the production and sales of goods.[7]

During the late thirteenth century, England imposed taxes on its wool exported by the Italian merchants who were granted the monopoly on this export. This "Ancient Custom," as it was known, later was expanded to cover all exports of goods from England.[8] In the late Middle Ages, in Italy and elsewhere, goods produced by artisans were taxed by taxing the guilds. The guilds raised the needed funds by taxing their members.[9]

The taxation of goods changed as firms were organized to produce goods and sell them through distributors to retailers. It became common, especially in Europe, to impose tax on business turnover (gross receipts). Thus, a cascading turnover tax was imposed every time goods were transferred in the process of production and distribution to the final consumer. The tax cascaded because the business purchaser, who could not reclaim the tax, increased the price of its output to cover the tax. Thus, "the tax component of the price of goods becomes larger and larger the more stages there are between producer and consumer – with obvious distortionary effects as between highly integrated enterprises and other enterprises."[10] For example, assume that a lumber mill sells lumber to a carpenter for a pretax price of $1,000. With a 1% turnover tax, the mill adds $10 tax and charges a tax-inclusive price of $1,010. The carpenter fashions the lumber into tables and sells the tables to a retailer. To its $5,010 pre-turnover-tax

[2] Land, as a representation of wealth, was a favorite subject of taxation because it was visible and the tax was collectible.

[3] C. Webber & A. Wildavsky, *A History of Taxation and Expenditure in the Western World* 44 (Simon & Schuster 1986). In the early civilizations of the Sumer city-states, tax payable in grain was transported to the ruler's storehouses. *Id.* at 43.

[4] *Id.* at 71.

[5] *Id.* at 107.

[6] *Id.*

[7] *Id.* at 112.

[8] *Id.* at 197.

[9] *Id.* at 149.

[10] See J. Owens, "The Move to VAT," 2 *Intertax* 45 (1996) [hereinafter Owens, The Move to VAT].

TABLE 1.1. Turnover tax for nonintegrated and vertically integrated business

	Nonintegrated	*Vertically integrated*
Mill sale to carpenter	$10	
$1,000 × 1%		
Carpenter sale to retailer	50	
$5,010 × 1%		
Retailer sale to consumers	101	
$10,060 × 1%		
Carpenter sales directly to consumers		$100
$10,000 × 1%		
Total tax imposed and collected	$161	$100

price (including the $10 tax on the lumber), the carpenter adds $50 tax for a tax-inclusive price of $5,060 (the numbers are rounded to dollars). The retailer sells the tables to consumers for a pretax price of $10,060. The retailer adds $101 tax for a tax-inclusive price of $10,161. The government collects a total tax of $161 (10 + 50 + 101).

To take an extreme comparison, assume that the carpenter operates the carpenter's own mill and sells crafted tables directly to consumers. If there were no turnover tax on the mill's purchase of trees, and if the carpenter sells the tables to consumers for pretax prices of $10,000 (because the carpenter would not bear the $60 tax imposed by the multiple turnovers), the carpenter would add a turnover tax of $100, for tax-inclusive prices totaling $10,100. This comparison made in Table 1.1 illustrates some of the deficiencies of the turnover tax – the cascading of taxes and the incentive to integrate a business vertically.

When businesses must pay turnover tax on business inputs, at each subsequent turnover of goods (i.e., sale), the values previously taxed are again subjected to tax in a process often referred to as pyramiding or cascading. In the earlier example, the carpenter charges $50 tax on the $5,010 sales price, which includes the $10 tax buried in the carpenter's $1,010 cost for the milled lumber (or, to put it differently, the carpenter collects a total of $60 tax from the retailer, of which the $50 tax charged on the sale is paid to the government and the $10 buried in the pretax $5,010 price is paid to the carpenter's lumber supplier).

As indicated, the cascading tax element in retail sales is reduced if the carpenter vertically integrates. The classic example of a vertically integrated American business was the Ford Motor Company's River Rouge complex (in Dearborn, Michigan), which processed the steel and glass and other parts for the cars that were assembled on its assembly line. A more recent example is the Benetton company, which operates its own retail shops to sell the apparel the company manufactures.

TABLE 1.2. Improved turnover tax for nonintegrated and vertically integrated business

	Nonintegrated	*Vertically integrated*
Mill sale to carpenter		
Taxable sale of $1,000 × 1%	**$10**	
Carpenter sale to retailer		
Taxable sale – $5,000* × 1%	**50**	
Credit for tax on purchases	**(10)**	
Retailer sales to consumers		
Taxable sale – $10,000** × 1%	100	
Credit for tax on purchases	**(50)**	
Carpenter sales directly to consumers		
Taxable sales – $10,000 × 1%		**$100**
Total tax imposed and collected	$100	**$100**

* The price would be $5,000 instead of $5,010 because the carpenter recovers the $10 tax on his taxable purchases.

** The sales prices would total $10,000 instead of $10,060 because the retailer would only be charged a pretax price of $5,000 and he would recover the $50 tax charged on the purchase of the tsables.

In Germany, Dr. Wilhelm von Siemens recognized the problems with turnover taxes and developed what he referred to as the "improved turnover tax" or "the refined turnover tax."[11] Thomas S. Adams discussed a value added concept in the United States in 1921.[12] The principle was to reduce the tax on sales by the tax already paid on business inputs to avoid the tax-on-a-tax effect and to remove the incentive to vertically integrate a business. The effect of this "improved" turnover tax for a nonintegrated series of businesses and a vertically integrated business is illustrated in Table 1.2.

This "improved" turnover tax is imposed and collected at each stage of the production and distribution of goods and services whenever there is a transaction, but the net tax liability represents only the tax on the value that has been added by the selling business at that stage. By granting a reduction in tax liability for the tax imposed on taxable purchases (the input tax credit), the tax base at each stage basically is limited to the value added by the employment of labor and capital. Before the widespread use of multistage VATs, some countries imposed single-stage consumption taxes. Single-stage taxes at the retail level are still used by almost all states

[11] C. Sullivan, THE TAX ON VALUE ADDED 12 (Columbia University Press 1965) [hereinafter Sullivan, Tax on Value Added], citing Gerhard Colm, "Methods of Financing Unemployment Compensation," **II** *Social Research 161* (May, 1935).

[12] Sullivan, Tax on Value Added, *supra* note 14, at 41, citing T. Adams, "Fundamental Problems of Federal Income Taxation," XXV *Quarterly Journal of Economics* 553 (1921). Adams referred to his proposal as a tax on "approximate net income" or "modified gross income" and recommended it to replace the direct personal income tax. *Id.*

in the United States and by several provinces in Canada. More commonly, a single-stage tax is imposed at the manufacturer's or wholesaler's level, but most of these have been replaced by VATs.

III. Direct and Indirect Taxes on an Income or Consumption Base

A. Direct and Indirect Taxes

Direct and indirect taxes can be imposed on an income base or consumption base. But what is the distinction between a direct and indirect tax?

Taxes customarily have been classified either as direct or indirect taxes. "A *direct tax* is one that is assessed upon the property, business or income of the individual who is to pay the tax. Conversely *indirect taxes* are taxes that are levied upon commodities before they reach the consumer who ultimately pay[s] the taxes as part of the market price of the commodity."[13] This distinction, based on the incidence of the tax, has been criticized because "modern economic theory" points out that income taxes (considered a direct tax) may be shifted.[14]

According to J. S. Mill's classic economic principles, the distinction between direct and indirect taxes relates to

> whether the person who actually pays the money over to the tax collecting authority suffers a corresponding reduction in his income. If he does, then – in the traditional language – impact and incidence are upon the same person and the tax is direct; if not and the burden is shifted and the real income of someone else is affected (i.e., impact and incidence are on different people) then the tax is indirect.[15]

In the field of international trade, an Annex to the World Trade Organization (WTO) agreement defines "direct taxes" as "taxes on wages, profits, interests, rents, royalties, and all other forms of income, and taxes on the ownership of real property" and "indirect taxes" as "sales, excise, turnover, value added, franchise, stamp, transfer, inventory and equipment taxes, border taxes and all taxes other than direct taxes and import charges."[16]

[13] *The Guide to American Law*, vol. 10:25 (1984) (defined by Schenk).

[14] See, for example, V. Thuronyi, Comparative Tax Law, 54–55 (Kluwer 2003).

[15] David Walker, "The Direct-Indirect Tax Problem: Fifteen Years of Controversy," 10 *Public Finance* 153, 154 (1955), citing John Stuart Mill, *Principles of Political Economy with Some of Their Applications to Social Philosophy*, Book V, ch. III (Ashley ed. 1848), new impression, Longmans, Green and Co. (London 1920).

[16] Agreement on Subsidies and Countervailing Measures, Annex I (Illustrative List of Export Subsidies), item (e), footnote 58. The SCM is Annex 1A to the WTO. Item (e) treats as an export subsidy the full or partial exemption, remission, or deferral specifically related to exports, of direct taxes or social welfare charges paid or payable by industrial or commercial enterprises, and footnote 58 to the term "direct taxes" includes the definitions in the text.

The direct versus indirect tax distinction has legal significance in countries subject to the WTO rules.[17] Under the Subsidies and Countervailing Measures (SCM) Agreement,[18] which is Annex 1 to the WTO, a contracting party is restricted in its ability to grant subsidies to exports or to impose more burdensome taxes on imports than apply to domestic goods.[19]

According to the WTO rules, border tax adjustments for indirect taxes do not constitute subsidies of exports or disadvantages to imports.[20] This WTO direct–indirect tax distinction apparently does not depend on who bears the tax.[21] The prohibition against export subsidies may affect the border adjustability of some of the federal taxes proposed in the United States to replace or supplement the federal income taxes, especially proposals for a sales-subtraction VAT that allows a deduction for wages paid.

[17] This direct–indirect distinction has been blurred in Canada. "In Canada, both the federal and provincial governments have the constitutional authority to levy sales taxes." N. Brooks, *The Canadian Goods and Services Tax: History, Policy, and Politics* 141 (Australian Tax Foundation 1993). The federal government has broad power to raise revenue with any mode or system of taxation, but the provincial governments are authorized to impose only direct taxes. Although a sales tax typically is considered an indirect tax, a 1943 Canadian Privy Council case held that a provincial retail sales tax was a direct tax for constitutional purposes. *Id.* at note 304. Professor Brooks quoted from the case: "[W]hen the purchase is made by an agent acting for his principal the tax nevertheless remains 'direct', being paid by the agent for and on behalf of his principal who really bears it." *Atlantic Smoke Shops Ltd v. Conlon*, [1943] A.C. 550, at 551.

[18] The Agreement on Subsidies and Countervailing Measures [hereinafter SCM Agreement], supplementing GATT, Arts. VI and XVI.

[19] The WTO, incorporating Article XVI of the original 1994 GATT agreement, provides the following: "[C]ontracting parties shall cease to grant either directly or indirectly any form of subsidy on the export of any product other than a primary product which subsidy results in the sale of such product for export at a price lower than the comparable price charged for the like product to buyers in the domestic market." Uruguay Round of Multilateral Trade Negotiations General Agreement on Tariffs and Trade, Apr. 15, 1994 [World Trade Organization, or WTO], encompasses, among other agreements, the General Agreement on Tariffs and Trade (GATT) 1994. The quote is from GATT 1994, Ad Art. XVI(4). *The Results of the Uruguay Round of Multilateral Trade Negotiations: The Legal Texts* (GATT Secretariat 1994) [hereinafter GATT], p. 509. If a contracting party grants or maintains any subsidy to increase exports or reduce imports, it is obligated to notify the other contracting parties "in writing of the extent and nature of the subsidization of the estimated effects … and of the circumstances making the subsidization necessary." *Id.* at Art. XVI.

[20] Whereas "government revenue that is otherwise due is foregone or not collected (e.g. fiscal incentives such as tax credits)" is a subsidy under SCM, *supra* note 18, Article 1.1(a)(1)(ii), a footnote to that item provides that "the exemption of an exported product from duties or taxes borne by the like product when destined for domestic consumption, or the remission of such duties or taxes in amounts not in excess of those which have accrued, shall not be deemed to be a subsidy."

[21] It is not clear if the direct–indirect tax distinction applies to imports. See letter from Leslie B. Samuels, Assistant Secretary for Tax Policy, U.S. Dept. of Treasury, to Senator Sam Nunn, February 1995.

B. Income and Consumption Base for Tax

Thomas Hobbes, in his *Leviathan*, advocated consumption as an appropriate base for taxation. In his view, people should pay tax on the basis of what they consume (withdraw from society's limited resources) rather than on what they earn in income (contribute to those resources through their labor). Both receive the protection from the government.[22]

Income and consumption can be viewed as different aspects of "consumption" in a broad sense. In this respect, income represents the potential power to consume and consumption represents the exercise of the power by consuming goods and services. An annual tax on individuals can be imposed on an income base or on a consumption base (the hybrid income-consumption base is used to impose the individual income tax in the United States).

As discussed earlier, taxes can be classified as direct or indirect. Direct taxes imposed on an income base include the familiar individual and corporate (or business) income tax and the payroll taxes. A direct tax such as the income tax imposed on individuals can be imposed on a consumption base by removing returns to capital (such as interest, dividends, and capital gains) from the tax base.[23] For example, a personal expenditure tax was used briefly in India and Sri Lanka and was proposed in the United States in 1995.[24] Many forms of indirect taxes can be levied on a consumption base, including selective excise taxes, a turnover tax, a single-stage sales tax (such as a manufacturer or a retail sales tax), or a multistage sales tax such as a value added tax.[25]

This book does not discuss the politics of raising revenue with an income-based tax or a consumption-based tax, or both, but includes the following thoughts on the importance of considering spending as well as taxation as part of fiscal policy.

One complaint about a VAT is that it is a regressive tax – the tax represents a larger percentage of the income of a low-income household than of a high-income household. One response to this argument comes from John Kenneth Galbraith, who focuses not only on the incidence of the tax but also on the combined effect of the tax and how its revenue is spent:

> The relation of the sales tax to the problem of social balance is admirably direct. The community is affluent in privately produced goods. It is poor in public services. The obvious solution is to tax the former to provide

[22] "What reason is there, that he which laboureth much, and sparing the fruits of his labor, consumeth little, should be charged more, than he that living idlely, getteth little, and spendeth all he gets: Seeing that one hath no more protection from the commonwealth than the other?" T. Hobbes, LEVIATHAN 184 (Dutton ed. 1914).

[23] See LESSONS OF TAX REFORM, at Box 2, pp. 24–25 (World Bank 1991) [hereinafter Lessons of Tax Reform]. On consumption tax, see the in-depth discussion in B. Fried, "Fairness and the Consumption Tax," 44 *Stanford Law Review* 961 (1992).

[24] See S.722, USA Tax Act of 1995, 104th Cong., 1st Sess., 141 Cong. Rec. S.5664 (Apr. 24, 1995).

[25] See discussion of Direct and Indirect Tax in Section III.

> the latter – by making private goods more expensive, public goods are made more abundant. Motion pictures, electronic entertainment and cigarettes are made more costly so that schools can be more handsomely supported. We pay more for soap, detergents and vacuum cleaners in order that we may have cleaner cities and less occasion to use them. We have more expensive cars and gasoline so that we may have more agreeable highways and streets on which to drive them. Food being relatively cheap, we tax it in order to have better medical services and better health in which to enjoy it.[26]

According to the staff of the Fiscal Affairs Department of the International Monetary Fund.

> Fiscal policy – taxation and spending – is a government's most direct tool for redistributing income, in both the short and the long run. However, the effect of redistributive tax policies, especially in the face of globalization, has been small. Policymakers should focus on developing a broadly based, efficient, and easily administered tax system with moderate marginal rates. Although the primary goal of the tax system should be to promote efficiency, policymakers also need to consider how to distribute the burden of taxation so the system is seen as fair and just.
>
> The expenditure side of the budget offers better opportunities than the tax side for redistributing income. The link between income redistribution and social spending – especially spending on health and education, through which governments can influence the formation and distribution of human capital – is particularly strong, and public investment in the human capital of the poor can be an efficient way to reduce income inequality over the long run.[27]

IV. Tax Structures in Developed and Developing Economies

This section includes some comparative data on the composition of tax regimes in developed countries. Many developing countries find it difficult to collect personal income tax in agricultural economies with a dispersed population. "As a result, the personal tax base [in developing countries] is often limited to public employees and employees of large firms, particularly multinational firms. ... Taxes on the income of large companies – including taxes levied on the profits of large mining operations and agricultural estates – present fewer administrative difficulties."[28]

In many developing countries, sales taxes at the retail or manufacturer level, complicated with numerous exemptions on imports and domestic

[26] John Kenneth Galbraith, *The Affluent Society* 238 (4th ed. Houghton Mifflin Co. 1984).

[27] Excerpt from "*Should Equity Be a Goal of Economic Policy?*" by staff of IMF's Fiscal Affairs Department, 35 Finance and Development #3, Sept. 1998, p. 4.

[28] See Lessons of Tax Reform, *supra* note 23, at 16.

TABLE 1.3. Total taxes as percentage of GDP

	1985	*2010*
Canada	32.5	31.0
France	42.8	42.9
Germany	36.1	36.1
Japan	26.7	27.6
New Zealand	30.9	31.5
Sweden	47.4	45.5
United Kingdom	37.0	34.9
United States	25.6	24.8
OECD Unweighted Avg.	32.5	33.8

OECD (2012), "Tax Levels and Tax Structures, 1965–2011," table 2, in *Revenue Statistics 2012*, OECD Publishing; http://dx.doi.org/10.1787/rev_stats-2012-4-en-fr.

sales, have been replaced by value added taxes, but unfortunately, they tend to bring many of the exemptions from the repealed taxes on consumption into their VATs.[29]

Developing countries must import a significant portion of the goods sold in the domestic market and raw materials and supplies used in domestic production. Taxes on imports (Customs duties and VAT) may represent a much larger percentage of revenue than taxes on domestic sales. The majority of VAT revenue will be collected by Customs and Excise personnel at the border. The remainder of VAT will be collected by the agency (if separate from Customs) responsible for the VAT.

Compared with developing countries, developed (or industrial) countries impose higher taxes as a percentage of gross domestic product (GDP) and tend to rely more heavily on direct personal income and payroll taxes.

In this book, we will concentrate on taxes imposed on goods and services. The tax on goods and services in the countries listed in Table 1.3 are depicted in Table 1.4. The data compare 1985 and 2010. Japan and the United States imposed the lowest tax on goods and services, as a percentage of GDP, in 2010.

Table 1.3 reveals that total taxes as a percentage of GDP remained fairly consistent, with total tax in some countries declining between 1985 and 2010. As a percentage of GDP, Table 1.4 shows that Germany, Japan, New Zealand, and Sweden increased their reliance on goods and services taxes, whereas Canada, France, the United Kingdom and the United States reduced their reliance on these taxes.[30] Although many assume that once

[29] See, for example, the Ghana Value Added Tax 1998, Schedule 1.

[30] "It is apparent that, over the longer term, the OECD member countries have relied increasingly on taxes on general consumption to provide their tax revenue." OECD

TABLE 1.4. Total tax on goods and services as percentage of GDP (the date in parentheses is the date VAT was introduced or became effective)

	1985	*2010*
Canada (1991)	10.3	7.5
France* (1968)	12.7	10.7
Germany (1968)	9.3	10.6
Japan (1989)	3.7	5.2
New Zealand (1986)	7.2	12.5
Sweden (1969)	12.6	13.4
United Kingdom (1973)	11.7	10.7
United States (no VAT)	4.8	4.5
OECD Unweighted Avg.	10.4	11.0

OECD (2012), "Tax Levels and Tax Structures, 1965–2011," table 23, in *Revenue Statistics 2012*, OECD Publishing; http://dx.doi.org/10.1787/rev_stats-2012-4-en-fr. Goods and services taxes include sales and value added taxes, excises and customs duties, and taxes on the use of goods such as motor vehicle taxes, and others.

* France introduced a form of VAT in 1954, but it did not become broadly based and imposed down to the retail stage until 1968.

enacted, the VAT rate only increases – and many have – the tax rate in some countries has in fact declined.[31]

V. The Value Added Tax

The VAT, as it is employed around the world, is two independent taxes that are joined with the credit for tax on purchases (including imports) against the tax imposed on sales. Indeed, the collection of the tax on imports and tax on domestic sales typically is administered by different departments of the tax authority – customs for imports and inland revenue (or a comparable department) for tax on domestic (including export) sales.

The First Council Directive on VAT, issued by the European Commission, includes a detailed definition of a VAT:

> The principle of the common system of value added tax involves the application to goods and services of a general tax on consumption exactly

CONSUMPTION TAX TRENDS 20 (OECD 2004). In part, this resulted from a "substitution of VAT/GST for [excises and] other consumption taxes." *Id.* at 23.

31 Of the countries with VATs listed in Appendix, 13 lowered their rates between 2006 and 2014, whereas 47 raised their rates. Canada reduced the GST rate from 7% to 6% and then 5%. See Governor General Michaelle Jean's speech from the Throne, April 4, 2006, in which she said in part: "[T]he Government will reduce the Goods and Services Tax by one percent. Cutting the GST will help all Canadians deal with the rising cost of living, put money back in people's pockets and help stimulate the economy .... The Government will continue with a responsible approach to lowering taxes for the benefit of Canadians and the Canadian economy, including a further reduction of the GST to five percent."

> proportional to the price of the goods and services, whatever the number of transactions which take place in the production and distribution process before the stage at which tax is charged.
>
> On each transaction, value added tax, calculated on the price of the goods or services at the rate applicable to such goods or services, shall be chargeable after deduction of the amount of value added tax borne directly by the various cost components.[32]

In recent years, developing countries searching for additional revenue or pressured by business to modernize their sales taxes have enacted value added taxes.

> To administer a full-fledged value-added tax properly is also not an easy task. Even a poorly-administered broad-based sales tax, however, can produce a lot of revenue with relatively few complaints from taxpayers. The revenue productivity of value-added taxes, even when relatively poorly administered, is undoubtedly one of their most attractive features to governments all over the world, in developing and developed countries alike.[33]

The promotion of a shift from income and payroll taxes to taxes on consumption accounts, in part, for the expansion of the countries that have adopted VATs over the past thirty years. The Organisation for Economic Co-operation and Development (OECD) has been active in the development of guidelines pertaining to VATs and goods and services taxes (GSTs). In 2009, tax policy officials from OECD countries, the European Commission, and nonmember economies issued the Lucerne VAT Conference Communique, suggesting that VAT may become even more important as a revenue source to deal with public debt imbalances.[34] In 2012, the OECD issued commentary on its International VAT Neutrality Guidelines.[35]

[32] First Council Directive of 11 April 1967 on the harmonization of legislation of member states concerning turnover taxes (67/227/EEC) (OJ P 71, 14.4.1967, p. 1301), Art. 2.

[33] R. Bird & O. Oldman, eds., *Taxation in Developing Countries* 368 (4th ed. Johns Hopkins University Press 1990).

[34] See http://www.oecd.org/dataoecd/19/12/43669264.pdf. The United States did not participate in the Communique.

[35] See OECD International VAT/GST Guidelines Draft Commentary on the International VAT Neutrality Guidelines, June 2012 (http://www.oecd.org/tax/consumption/50667035_ENG.pdf). This draft is part of the work of the Working Party No. 9 on Consumption Taxes of the Committee on Fiscal Affairs on the International VAT/GST Guidelines. The six guidelines are as follows:

1. The burden of value added taxes themselves should not lie on taxable businesses except where explicitly provided for in legislation.
2. Businesses in similar situations carrying out similar transactions should be subject to similar levels of taxation.
3. VAT rules should be framed in such a way that they are not the primary influence on business decisions.
4. With respect to the level of taxation, foreign businesses should not be disadvantaged nor advantaged compared to domestic businesses in the jurisdiction where the tax may be due or paid.

VI. The Proliferation of VATs

There are several reasons why VAT has become such a popular source of revenue. France adopted a primitive version of a VAT after World War II. In the Treaty of Rome (1957),[36] France and the other member countries agreed to share some of their national revenue (including revenue from VAT) to finance the operation of the European Economic Community, now the European Union. The treaty required member states to convert their turnover taxes (described earlier) to a harmonized VAT. All newly admitted members are likewise required to adopt the harmonized VAT.[37]

After World War II, many of the major industrialized countries became signatories to the General Agreement on Tariffs and Trade (GATT), now the WTO. They could not subsidize exports or tax imports more than domestically produced goods. When GATT was being negotiated, most of the European countries relied heavily on indirect taxes for their revenue. For many, international trade also represented a significant factor in their economies. In addition, it was easier to identify the indirect tax component in the price of exports and difficult, if not practically impossible, to identify any direct tax buried in product prices. It thus is not surprising that GATT permitted signatory countries (contracting parties) to rebate indirect, but not direct, taxes on exports. Contracting Parties assumed that they could rebate sales tax or VAT but not income or payroll taxes included in export prices.[38] The United States (a nation without a border-adjustable, federal broad-based consumption tax) did not object to this provision. Thus, countries that relied on turnover or value added tax had border-adjustable taxes; that is, they were able to rebate these taxes on exports and impose them on imports.

The International Monetary Fund (IMF) provides technical assistance in the area of finance to member countries. Over the past several decades, the IMF has assisted developing and transition countries to convert their

5. To ensure foreign businesses do not incur irrevocable VAT, governments may choose from a number of approaches.
6. Where specific administrative requirements for foreign businesses are deemed necessary, they should not create a disproportionate or inappropriate compliance burden for the businesses.

[36] See Treaty Establishing the European Economic Community, March 25, 1957, Art. 99, 298 U.N.T.S. 11, 76.

[37] The major EU document on the harmonization of the VATs in the Community is the VAT Directive (full citation and explanation is given in Chapter 3).

[38] GATT, *supra* note 18, at Annex I, Ad. Art. XVI, 8 U.S.T. at 1798–99, T.I.A.S. No. 3930, at 33, 278 U.N.T.S. at 218. This kind of tax on domestic consumption is acceptable under an annex to Art. XVI(4), which provides: "The exemption of an exported product from duties on taxes borne by the like product when destined for domestic consumption, or the remission of such duties or taxes in amounts not in excess of those which have accrued." It is considered impractical to identify the income or payroll tax included in the price of domestically sold products. The GATT rules reflect prevailing views that sales taxes like VAT are shifted forward and are borne by consumers, whereas income and payroll taxes are borne by owners and shareholders and employees.

turnover taxes, manufacturer's tax, retail sales tax, and other indirect taxes to VATs. This development was motivated both by the VAT's relative neutrality and its potential contribution to mobilize revenue.

In 1985, New Zealand adopted a European-style invoice VAT with a much broader base than had been adopted elsewhere. For example, NZ taxes certain government services and nonlife insurance. The NZ approach, referred to as the beginning of the "Modern VATs," has been copied, with modifications, in Canada, the Republic of South Africa and many other countries.

In 1989, Japan introduced its Consumption Tax, a VAT that differs from the European-style VAT in its calculation of net VAT liability and its use of invoices.[39] Canada's Goods and Services Tax became effective on January 1, 1991.[40] The Australian Goods and Services Tax became effective July 1, 2000.[41] The United States is now the only OECD country without a VAT. Although political leaders in some countries proposed to repeal the VAT, rarely does that threat become a reality.[42]

Not all countries are content with their VATs. For example, in 2010, the Philippine House of Representatives approved a bill to replace the VAT with a turnover tax. While removing credits for tax on purchases, the proposal would reduce the standard tax rate from the 12% VAT rate to a 6% VAST rate (a value simplified tax).[43] Russian leaders have discussed the possibility of replacing the VAT with a sales tax. Some, within the government, suggested that a sales tax is more suitable for Russia's natural resource-based export economy.[44] Other government activity dealing with

[39] After World War II, the Allied Mission to Japan recommended that Japan adopt a value added tax as a revenue source for the prefectures. The Diet (i.e. the legislature of Japan) enacted a national VAT with a delayed effective date. The effective date was postponed several times, and the VAT was repealed in 1954, without ever taking effect. The CT is Law No. 108, Part IV (1988) (Shohizei-ho). The English Translation is published in *Japan – National Consumption Tax Law: An English Translation* (CCH Int'l 1989).

[40] The Canadian GST is Part IX (and some Schedules to that part) of the Excise Tax Act, An Act to Amend the Excise Tax Act, the Criminal Code, the Customs Act, the Customs Tariff, the Excise Act, the Income Tax Act, the Statistics Act and the Tax Court of Canada Act, S.C. 1990, c. 45. It received Royal Assent on December 17, 1990. Canada has an unusual tax structure to accommodate the special status of an Indian or Indian band on certain First Nation (Indian band) land. The national GST does not apply to taxable supplies made on a reserve (land over which an Indian band exercises governmental powers) to an Indian. Several band councils or other governing bodies of a First Nation adopted the First Nation GST (FNGST). The FNGST is comparable to the Canadian GST and GST/HST. Where enacted, the FNGST, not the Canadian GST, applies to taxable supplies on First Nations lands. *Id.* at 5. In the case of alcoholic beverages, fuel, and tobacco products, the FNGST does not apply if the First Nation Tax applies to the sale.

[41] A New Tax System (Goods and Services Tax) Act 1999, No. 55 of 1999, assented to on July 8, 1999.

[42] See Philippine President Arroyo's plea to replace VAT with a tax simpler to administer and comply with. J. Gutierrez, "Philippine President in Collision Course with Country's Congress over Tax Package," *BNA Daily Tax Report*, Aug. 27, 2004, p. G-4.

[43] See, IBFD Tax News Service, Dec. 22, 2010. The bill was not enacted.

[44] See, J. Whalley & V. Kononova, "Recent Russian Debate on Moving from VAT to Sales Taxes and Its Global Implications," 1 *Journal of Globalization and Development* vol. 2, pp. 1–27 (2010).

VAT includes the decision by the South African government, in 2009, to allow qualified small businesses to pay a turnover tax instead of its obligations under the VAT, the income tax, the provisional tax, the tax on capital gain, and the secondary tax on companies.[45]

VII. Glossary of VAT Terms[46]

Accounts-based VAT. In an accounts-based VAT, the taxpayer computes his tax liability from data for each tax period taken from books of account. An accounts-based VAT typically will be an **addition** or **sales-subtraction VAT**. The alternative to this type of VAT is a transaction-based VAT such as the **credit-subtraction** VAT that relies on invoices (credit-invoice VAT). The **Japanese Consumption Tax (CT)** has features of a transaction- and accounts-based VAT.

Addition-method VAT. In an addition-method VAT, a taxpayer calculates value added by summing the value of certain factors of production (typically labor, rent, interest, and profits calculated for VAT purposes) that it uses in the production of taxable goods and services. For example, assume that a taxpayer hires employees at a cost of $400 to process wool purchased in the marketplace, pays rent for business premises of $100, and sells the processed wool at a profit for VAT purposes of $50. The value added by this firm, and thus the amount subject to the VAT, would be $550 ($400 + $100 + $50). Note that items included in value added do not include purchases that were taxed to prior suppliers, that is, VAT-paid inputs. It also assumes that interest and rent expenses are not subject to VAT. An alternative to an addition-method VAT is a **subtraction-method VAT.** Therefore, a VAT system would not rely on the additional method alone, but would only use it to complement another method that would capture the value represented by material input.

Consumption VAT. The tax base of a consumption-type VAT is the value of goods and services sold or transferred for personal consumption. For example, in a consumption, credit-subtraction VAT, a taxpayer typically claims an **input credit** for VAT paid on purchases of capital goods, as well as on inventory, and other **intermediate goods and services** used in the business. Almost all existing VATs are consumption VATs. The alternatives are a **gross-domestic-product VAT** and an **income VAT.**

Credit-method VAT. See **credit-subtraction VAT.**

Credit-subtraction VAT. In a credit-subtraction VAT, the taxpayer determines tax liability by subtracting the **input credit** from the **output tax.** For

[45] See Turnover Tax under section 48A of the Income Tax Act and http://www.sars.gov.za/home.asp?pid=43122.

[46] Some portions of this glossary were adapted from the glossary in A. Schenk, "Policy Issues in the Design of a Value-Added Tax: Some Recent Developments in OECD Countries," 1 *Tax Notes Int'l* 111, 124–125 (July 1989). The glossary in that article was prepared with the assistance of Michael J. McIntyre.

example, assume that T, the taxpayer, sells taxable garden tools for $100,000 during a taxable period. The VAT rate is 10% of sales, exclusive of the VAT. T makes taxable purchases of inventory and supplies of $65,000, and a VAT of $6,500 is paid by the seller on those purchases. T would pay net VAT liability of $3,500 ($10,000 output tax on sales less $6,500 input credit on purchases). The two credit-subtraction forms of VAT are the **credit-invoice VAT** and the **credit-subtraction VAT without invoices.** Most VATs are credit-subtraction VATs that rely on invoices. The Japanese CT is a credit-subtraction VAT that does not rely on invoices in the same way.

Credit-invoice VAT. A credit-invoice VAT is a **credit-subtraction VAT**, like the European VATs, that relies on invoices to verify tax reported on taxable sales by sellers and input credit claimed by purchasers on allowable taxable purchases.

Credit-subtraction VAT without invoices. The Japanese CT is the only major **credit-subtraction VAT** in use that does not rely on invoices like the credit-invoice VAT does. The taxpayer determines its **output tax** by multiplying taxable sales by the tax rate. In contrast to the treatment under the **credit-invoice VAT**, the **input credit** is usually calculated from company records for taxed purchases (at tax-inclusive prices) by multiplying the purchases by a fraction, the numerator of which is the tax rate and the denominator is 100 + the tax rate. To prevent the claim for unwarranted input credits, Japan requires CT taxpayers to retain documentation to substantiate claimed input credits.

Destination principle. In a VAT that defines its tax jurisdictional reach on the destination principle, the tax is imposed in the country of consumption – generally where the goods and services are delivered for personal consumption. Imports are subject to VAT and exports are free of VAT. Most nations with destination principle VATs tax only some imported services and zero-rate only some exported services. The alternative to the destination principle is the **origin principle.**

Exempt sale. An exempt sale is a sale that is not subject to VAT. The seller is not entitled to an **input credit** (or other adjustment) for VAT imposed on purchases allocated to the exempt sale. The alternatives to an exempt sale are a **taxable sale**, a **zero-rated sale**, and a **nontaxable transaction**.

Gross-domestic-product (GDP) VAT. The tax base of a gross-domestic-product VAT is goods and services included in gross domestic product, which includes personal consumption and capital goods (GDP also takes into account government consumption and gross investment, as well as the net of exports over imports). Taxpayers are not allowed an **input credit** (or other adjustment) for the VAT that they have paid on capital goods used in their business.

Income-style VAT. The tax base of an income VAT is the tax jurisdiction's net national income. Taxpayers are allowed an **input credit** (or other adjustment) for the VAT that they have paid on capital goods used in connection with their taxable business activity, but they must spread that credit over the useful lives of the capital goods through a depreciation-like allowance.

Input credit. An input credit is a credit that the taxpayer may take against output tax for the VAT that was paid (or is deemed to have been paid) on the purchases that qualify for credit under that type of VAT. In a **consumption VAT**, the taxpayer is typically allowed a credit for VAT paid on purchases of capital goods, inventory, and **intermediate goods and services** used in his taxable activities. An input credit is a feature of a **credit-subtraction VAT**. In an **invoice-based, credit-subtraction VAT**, the taxpayer determines the amount of the input credit by taking the sum of the VAT that appears on his purchase invoices. In a **credit-subtraction VAT** that does not rely on invoices (the **Japanese Consumption Tax**), the taxpayer typically determines the amount of the credit by multiplying his allowable purchases (deemed inclusive of VAT), as they appear in the books of account, by a fraction. The numerator of that fraction is the tax rate and the denominator is 100 plus the tax rate. The input credit is also referred to as the input tax credit.

Intermediate goods and services. Intermediate goods and services are goods and services that are purchased to produce other goods and services and are not used for personal consumption. Examples would be diesel fuel and accounting services purchased by a trucking firm as part of its business operations.

Invoice-based VAT. In an invoice-based VAT, the taxpayer computes his tax liability from the VAT shown on the invoices he receives on his allowable taxable purchases and the invoices he issues on his taxable sales. In practice, every invoice-based VAT is a **credit-subtraction VAT**. The alternatives to this type of VAT are a credit-subtraction VAT that does not rely on invoices (the **Japanese Consumption Tax**) and an **accounts-based VAT**.

Japanese Consumption Tax. See **credit-subtraction VAT without invoices**.

Nontaxable transaction. A nontaxable transaction (or a transaction that is not a sale for VAT purposes) is a transaction that does not come within the scope of the tax. For example, a transfer of an asset to a creditor as security for a loan is a nontaxable transaction. Tax on purchases allocable to the transaction may or may not qualify for the **input credit**. The alternative to a nontaxable transaction is either a taxable sale (at a positive or zero rate) or an **exempt sale**.

Origin principle. In a VAT that defines its tax jurisdictional reach on the origin principle, the tax is imposed in the country where goods are produced and services are rendered – where the value is added to those goods and services. To achieve a pure origin principle VAT, imports are not taxed and exports bear tax. The alternative to the origin principle is the **destination principle**.

Output tax. The output tax is the amount chargeable on a taxable sale and collected by the seller from the buyer. It constitutes the first step in computing the amount to be remitted by the seller to the government. Typically, the taxpayer (seller) calculates it by multiplying the price of taxable sales, exclusive of VAT, by the tax rate (or rates). With a VAT imposed at a single positive rate, the output tax may also be computed by multiplying taxable sales, inclusive of VAT, by a fraction, the numerator of which is the tax rate and the denominator of which is 100 plus the tax rate.

Sales-subtraction VAT. In a sales-subtraction VAT, the taxpayer pays tax at the applicable VAT rate on the difference between taxable sales and allowable (generally previously taxed) purchases, both inclusive of tax. For example, assume that T, a taxpayer, purchases wool in the marketplace for $1,000. That price includes the VAT collected by the seller of the wool. T processes the wool and then sells the processed wool to customers for a final price, after VAT, of $1,550. T would be subject to VAT on $550 ($1,550 minus $1,000). At a VAT rate of 10% applied to a **tax-inclusive** base, the VAT due would be $55 ($550 × 10%). This VAT is one type of **subtraction-method VAT**.

Subtraction-method VAT. In a subtraction-method VAT, a taxpayer pays tax either on the difference between taxable sales and allowable taxable purchases, or on the difference between the tax on taxable sales less the tax on taxable purchases. There are thus two types of subtraction-method VATs: a **sales-subtraction VAT** and a **credit-subtraction VAT**. The alternative to a subtraction-method VAT is an **addition-method VAT**.

Tax-deduction-method VAT. See **credit-subtraction VAT**.

Tax-inclusive base (TIB) and tax-exclusive base (TEB). To raise equivalent revenue, the rate applied to a tax-inclusive base (a base that includes the tax itself) is lower than the rate applied to a tax-exclusive base (a base that omits the tax itself). For example, a 10% rate on a TEB is equal to a 9.0909% rate on a TIB, calculated by the formula, rate on TIB = 1 / (1 + rate on TEB). Thus, if the rate on a TEB is 10%, the comparable rate on a TIB is 9.0909%, calculated as follows: TIB rate = 1/(1+10), or 1/11 = 9.0909%.

Value added tax (VAT). A value added tax (VAT) is a type of multistage sales tax imposed on goods and services that is collected in chunks at each stage of production and distribution of goods or the rendition of services in proportion to the value added by each taxpaying firm.

Zero-rated sale. A zero-rated sale is a taxable sale that is subject to a zero tax rate. The taxpayer does not report VAT on the sale and is entitled to an **input credit** for VAT imposed on purchases allocable to the sale. The goods or services sold are therefore free of tax.

VIII. Discussion Questions

1. A popular argument against sales and excise taxes is that they are not progressive as to income – that is, they are not based on the taxpayer's ability to pay. Can sales and excise taxes be made progressive? How? Does a higher rate of tax on luxury items make the sales tax progressive?
2. What does it mean to say that a sales tax distorts the pattern of consumption? Can a sales tax be neutral with respect to the pattern of consumption? How would you go about measuring distortion in the context of sales taxation? Why would you or should you do it?
3. Is a system of selective excise taxes preferable to a general sales tax in a developing country? In a developed country? Is it a question of having either excise taxes or a general sales tax, or is it a question of emphasis? Explain.
4. Assume that a country has chosen a system of *selective* excise taxes for administrative convenience but wants to design the tax system so that it will have a redistributive impact. Which goods and services should be tax exempt? Which should be subject to the normal rate of tax? Which should be subject to a high rate of tax?
5. Should capital goods be subject to sales taxation? Are there reasons why both developing and developed countries might wish to include capital goods in the base of a comprehensive value added tax? Might it be rational for a developing country to tax capital goods while at the same time selectively awarding extensive tax incentives for investment? See Richard Goode, *Government Finance in Developing Countries* 254 (The Brookings Institution 1984). Would the regressivity of a VAT be reduced by applying it to capital goods? See C. Sullivan, *The Tax on Value Added*, ch. 5 (Columbia University Press 1965).
6. A major problem of sales taxation is how to treat "small" firms – artisans, producers, independent contractors, itinerant vendors, small shops, owners of two- or three-family homes, family farms, and so on. Can they be "exempt" from filing tax returns without destroying or seriously distorting the tax base? What possible practical solutions can you identify?
7. What are the advantages and disadvantages of the various "national accounts" type bases (e.g., turnover or total transactions, gross domestic product, net product or income, or consumption)? If you assume both a comprehensive base and a single rate of tax, what are the implications of each of these bases for each of the following often mentioned goals of tax policy: revenue, computational simplicity, economic neutrality, income distribution, stabilization of prices, promotion of

exports, and the supply of cross-checking information for administrative purposes?

8. If, during an accounting period (1 year), a firm pays $100 for rent, $50 for interest, $500 for materials, $1,000 for wages, and $300 for salaries to managers and if the firm realizes a profit of $600, what is the firm's value added? To put the question another way, who adds value in each of these accounts to the economic output of the country? Who should be the taxpayer with respect to each item of value added?

2 Consumption Tax Forms and Base Alterations

I. Forms of Consumption-Based Taxes

A. Introduction

A direct tax on individuals that is measured by their level of consumption rather than their income is commonly referred to as a cash-flow or consumption-based income tax. Most taxes on consumption are indirect taxes. These taxes are collected by sellers of taxable goods and services and are expected to be borne by final consumers of those goods and services. The indirect tax on consumption may take the form of a single-stage tax such as the retail sales tax or a multistage tax such as a value added tax.

A value added tax is a generic name associated with a multistage tax that is levied on the value added by each business firm at every stage of production and distribution of goods and services. In part, the description of a VAT depends on the method used in calculating tax liability. In this chapter, there is a discussion of the addition, sales-subtraction, and credit-subtraction methods of calculating VAT liability.

The legislature may alter a VAT base by removing some sellers or some goods and services. This alteration of tax base is accomplished by providing an exemption for designated businesses (such as small businesses) or entities, such as units of government or nonprofit organizations. The legislature also can alter the tax base by granting exemption or altering the rate for particular goods and services, regardless of the nature of the seller. This chapter also discusses these various methods of providing special treatment under a value added tax.

B. Consumption-Based Direct Tax on Individuals

A consumption-based income tax was discussed by the British economist Nicholas Kaldor in his 1955 book, *An Expenditure Tax*.[1] Kaldor wrote that a

[1] N. Kaldor, *An Expenditure Tax* (George Allen & Unwin 1955) [hereinafter Kaldor]. Kaldor notes that the principle of taxing individuals on the basis of their expenditure rather than

progressive tax can be imposed on an expenditure base and still "advance towards an egalitarian society whilst improving the efficiency of operation and rate of progress of the economy."[2] In effect, Kaldor proposed an annual tax on personal expenditures at graduated rates.

Kaldor would rely on personal expenditures as the legal basis of the tax – the approach that satisfies "the requirements of equity and efficient administration."[3] Under Kaldor's approach, taxpayers would be required to declare their personal expenditures annually and pay tax directly to the government rather than pay tax to the sellers of goods and services as part of each sale, the so-called indirect consumption tax. In effect, the taxpayer is required to report all income and receipts for the year and then deduct all investment (carefully defined), the difference being consumption. Kaldor acknowledges that this approach to taxing annual consumption raises many difficult problems, such as the distinction between personal consumption and capital wealth (or investment), the treatment of gifts and bequests, and the need to set an annual exemption threshold for lower-income taxpayers, to name a few.

The debate on the feasibility and desirability of a cash-flow or consumption-based income tax includes the seminal article by Professor Andrews[4] that was expanded on by others.[5] Professor Andrews [6] criticizes the assumption in tax policy debate that the ideal tax system taxes "total personal gain or accretion, without distinctions as to source or use" – what he calls "an accretion-type personal income tax."[7] He claims that the individual income tax in the United States is inconsistent in its treatment of accumulations. According to Andrews, a cash-flow tax (a consumption-type tax) would produce net simplification in the income

income originated more than 300 years ago in a book by Thomas Hobbes in *Leviathan*, chapter XXX, and has been urged since then by John Stuart Mill, Alfred Marshall, and Arthur Pigou in England and Irving Fisher in the United States. *Id.* at intro. Kaldor notes in his book that Treasury Secretary Morgenthau proposed a form of expenditure tax in 1942 as an addition to the income tax. *Id.* at 16. He refers to *New York Times* reports on this tax proposal in the September 4–8, 1942, issues.

2 *Id.* at 15.

3 *Id.*

4 W. Andrews, "A Consumption-Type or Cash Flow Personal Income Tax," 87 *Harvard Law Review* 1113 (1974) [hereinafter Andrews, Consumption-Type or Cash Flow Personal Income Tax].

5 See, for example, M. Graetz, "Implementing a Progressive Consumption Tax," 92 *Harvard Law Review* 1575 (1979); W. Andrews, "Fairness and the Personal Income Tax: A Reply to Professor Warren," 88 *Harvard Law Review* 947 (1975); A. Warren, "Fairness and a Consumption-Type or Cash Flow Personal Income Tax," 88 *Harvard Law Review* 931 (1975); D. Bradford, "The Case for a Personal Expenditure Tax," in *What Should Be Taxed: Income or Expenditure* (J. Pechman, ed., Brookings Institution 1979); Advisory Comm. on Intergovernmental Relations, The Expenditure Tax (Information Report M-84 1974); and Institute for Fiscal Studies, "The Structure and Reform of Direct Taxation" (1978) (Meade Commission Report).

6 Andrews, Consumption-Type or Cash Flow Personal Income Tax, *supra* note 4, at 1113.

7 *Id.*

tax and result in a tax that is fairer and one that more efficiently distributes the tax burdens.[8]

The U.S. Treasury's Blueprints for Basic Tax Reform considered, as one option, the conversion of the individual income tax into a consumption-based income tax.[9] Blueprints concluded that a cash flow, consumption-based income tax was simpler than a comprehensive income tax (the latter merely broadened the income tax base). By including "*all* monetary receipts in the tax base, including the entire proceeds of sales of assets and gifts received, and allowing deductions for purchases of assets and gifts given, the annual consumption of a household could be measured without directly monitoring the purchases of goods and services."[10]

In 1995, U.S. Senators Nunn and Domenici proposed the USA Tax System to replace the existing federal income taxes. One portion of this proposal was to replace the individual income tax with a direct, personal, progressive tax on consumption (a consumption-based income tax) that would not tax savings and investment.[11]

It has also been proposed to institute a supplemental expenditure tax, targeted to wealthier taxpayers, in addition to the income tax, rather than replacing the income tax completely.[12]

C. Single and Multistage Sales Taxes

An indirect tax on consumption like a sales tax (or tax on goods and services) can be imposed at a single stage or at multiple stages of production or distribution. Single-stage sales taxes include retail sales taxes such as those imposed by most of the states in the United States or by some of the provinces in Canada. A single-stage tax can be imposed at the manufacturing level, such as the prior Canadian Manufacturer's Tax that was replaced by the Canadian Goods and Services Tax (a VAT), or at the wholesale level, such as the prior British Purchase Tax that was replaced by a VAT. A sales tax also can be imposed at more than one but less than all

[8] *Id.*

[9] U.S. Department of the Treasury, Blueprints for Basic Tax Reform, 2nd ed., 1984 [hereinafter Blueprints]. The primary work on Blueprints, by Deputy Assistant Secretary of the Treasury David F. Bradford, was issued on January 17, 1977. See also, David F. Bradford, *The X Tax in the World Economy: Going Global with a Simple, Progressive Tax* (AEI Press 2004). Bradford's X Tax is patterned after the Hall-Rabushka Flat Tax. See R. Hall & A. Rabushka, *The Flat Tax* (2nd ed. Hoover Press 1995).

[10] Blueprints, *supra* note 9, at 102.

[11] S.722, USA Tax Act of 1995, 104th Cong., 1st Sess., 141 Cong. Rec. S.5664 (Apr. 24, 1995) [hereinafter USA Tax Act], at Title II – USA Tax for Individuals, Ch. 1 – Unlimited Savings Allowance Tax for Individuals, §1. See also, H. Pepperell, "Thoughts on the Progressive Consumption Tax," 85 *Tax Notes* 529 (Oct. 25, 1999). This tax was proposed by Congressman English in 2003 as the Simplified USA Tax. H.R. 269, Simplified USA Tax Act of 2003, 108th Cong., 1st Sess. (Jan. 8, 2003).

[12] See Kaldor, *supra* note 1; W. Andrews, "A Supplemental Personal Expenditure Tax," in *What Should be Taxed: Income or Expenditure?* (J. Pechman, ed., 1980); and V. Thuronyi, *A Supplemental Expenditure Tax* (forthcoming).

levels of production or distribution. For example, the Louisiana sales tax is imposed at the wholesale and retail levels, with relief provided to retailers for the tax they paid on purchases from wholesalers.[13] The modern sales tax imposed at all levels of production and distribution is the VAT.

II. Overview of the Value Added Tax

A. In General

The value added tax is intended to tax personal consumption comprehensively, neutrally, and efficiently. The VAT has been the most pervasive tax reform throughout the world during the second half of the twentieth century (with stragglers following on thereafter) and has proved to be a major source of government revenue. The VAT is widely used in both developed and developing countries, at local, subnational, national, and even supranational (e.g., the European Union) levels of government. An occasional voice is even heard suggesting its use to finance a world infrastructure development fund or an international humanitarian relief fund.[14]

The base of the VAT – predominantly the personal consumption of individuals,[15] as measured by the price paid for goods and services – historically has been, in one form or another, an important source of government revenues. If, as is true in a growing number of jurisdictions, the rate of tax is uniform and the base is broad, the VAT will not interfere with patterns of consumption (that is, how consumers decide to divide their purchases among available choices), except for the choice between untaxed consumption (e.g., leisure) and taxed consumption. Nonuniform rates and extensive exemptions destroy neutrality and affect patterns of consumption, as well as patterns of production and distribution, while greatly increasing administrative and compliance costs.

Several different kinds of multistage consumption taxes can be described as VATs. A VAT can be described on the basis of the mechanical method used to calculate net tax liability for each tax period. The methods are the addition method and three forms of the subtraction method. The addition

[13] J. Due & J. Mikesell, *Sales Taxation: State and Local Structure and Administration* 6 (Johns Hopkins University Press 1983).

[14] See L. Speer, "French President Writes World Leaders Seeking Support for Global Development Tax," *BNA Daily Tax Report*, June 4, 2004, p. G-5, suggesting an international tax to finance human development. President Chirac suggested that the tax might be imposed on "international arms trade, cross-border financial transactions, or environmental emissions." France has been studying a global tax system to fund development projects. Professor Kaneko proposed an international humanitarian tax – a consumption tax on international travel to provide relief funds. H. Kaneko, "Proposal for International Humanitarian Tax – A Consumption Tax on International Air Travel," 17 *Tax Notes International* 1911 (Dec. 14, 1998), discussed in Chapter 7.

[15] Some VAT is borne by nonprofit organizations, units of government, small businesses, and others that purchase taxable goods and services and sell goods or services exempt from VAT.

method (the Michigan Single Business Tax and the New Hampshire Business Enterprise Tax rely on variations of the addition method for a state-level tax)[16] adds the components of value added by the firm for each tax period.[17] The subtraction methods are the sales-subtraction VAT (proposed in the United States and Canada but not in use), and two forms of credit-subtraction VATs. One credit-subtraction VAT relies on invoices (the almost universally used "credit-invoice" or "invoice" VAT) and the other does not rely on invoices (the originally enacted Japanese Consumption Tax). These methods are described in the next section of this chapter.

The definition of the tax base depends, in part, on the treatment of international transactions (origin versus destination principle tax), the treatment of the VAT itself (a tax-inclusive or tax-exclusive base), and the treatment of capital purchases (a gross domestic product, income, or consumption tax base). Each of these elements is briefly explained next, followed by a more detailed explanation of various methods of calculating VAT liability.[18]

B. Jurisdictional Reach of the Tax

Except for taxes levied on a global basis, tax legislation must define the extent to which a tax is imposed on cross-border transactions or activities. In a shrinking world marked by cross-border activities, it becomes critical to decide whether the VAT should exempt exports and tax imports, or tax exports and exempt imports. Virtually all VATs use the so-called destination principle under which personal consumption is taxed in the country of destination, which is assumed to be the country of consumption.[19]

[16] See discussion in Chapter 15.

[17] If landlords and banks are included among the firms paying tax, the addition method is simply the sum of payroll plus profits. If landlords and banks are not taxpayers, the addition method is the sum of wages, profits, rent, and interest.

[18] See generally, A. Schenk, *Value Added Tax – A Model Statute and Commentary: A Report of the Committee on Value Added Tax of the American Bar Association Section of Taxation* 1–2 (American Bar Association 1989) [hereinafter ABA Model VAT]; V. Thuronyi, ed., *Tax Law Design and Drafting* (IMF 1996) (several chapters provide a reference on VAT). For an extensive discussion of the elements of a VAT, see C. Shoup, *Public Finance* 250–266 (Aldine Publishing Company 1969) [hereinafter Shoup, Public Finance]; C. Sullivan, *The Tax on Value Added*, ch. 1 and 5 (Columbia University Press 1965); C. McLure, Jr., *The Value-Added Tax: Key to Deficit Reduction?* (American Enterprise Institute 1987) [hereinafter McLure, VAT], 71–102. See also C. Shoup, "Choosing Among Types of VATs," in *Value Added Tax in Developing Countries* (M. Gillis, C. Shoup, and G. Sicat, eds., World Bank, 1990) [hereinafter Shoup, Choosing Among VATs]; A. Schenk, "Value Added Tax: Does This Consumption Tax Have a Place in the Federal Tax System?," 7 *Virginia Tax Review* 207 (1987).

[19] The destination principle also has been adopted by the American states for their retail sales taxes, although the policy has not been articulated or debated the way it has in a VAT. The states typically have provisions that exempt from the sales tax goods shipped in interstate commerce, thus ceding taxation over "exports." The destination state will assert a use tax on the consumer. This pattern tends to assign the sales tax to the jurisdiction in which consumption is likely to occur.

There are some examples, however, of origin-based VATs, under which exports are taxed. Tax reform proposals in the United States sometimes have features of origin-based VATs.[20]

Under the destination principle, any VAT paid by the exporter on its purchases is refunded. In the terminology of a VAT, exports are zero-rated – that is, not only is the sale for export not taxed, but also a refund is given of VAT paid on inputs included in the exports.[21] Imports are taxed under the destination principle.

Most countries have detailed rules to identify the location of a transaction as a domestic sale, import, export, or foreign sale. These rules tend to limit a country's VAT jurisdiction under the destination principle to sales within the country, imports, and exports, although exports are free of tax.

New Zealand expanded its VAT jurisdiction beyond these conventional parameters. It also does not rely on the traditional detailed location of supply rules. South Africa and some other countries in southern Africa adopted the New Zealand approach. The jurisdictional reach of the New Zealand GST and South African VAT will be discussed more fully in Chapter 7.

C. Inclusion of VAT in Tax Base

A VAT can be imposed on a base that includes or excludes the tax itself. For example, assume that under a credit-invoice VAT, an umbrella sells for a pretax price of \$10. If the 10% VAT is imposed on a tax-exclusive base, the tax is 10% of \$10, or \$1, and the price to the consumer is \$11. If the 10% tax is imposed on a tax-inclusive base and the merchant is to get the same \$10 after remitting the tax imposed on the sale, the merchant will charge the consumer \$11.11 and the tax is 10% of that price, or \$1.11. Note that a 10% tax imposed on a tax-exclusive base yields exactly the same amount of tax revenue, namely, \$1 in the example, as a rate of 9.0909% does on a tax-inclusive base ($.090909 \times 11 = 1$). A transactional VAT such as the European invoice VAT can be imposed on either base. The same is true for an accounts-based VAT calculated under the sales-subtraction or addition method, which is imposed on the results of operations for a tax period, not on each sales transaction. The accounts can be adjusted to reflect a base that is tax-inclusive or tax-exclusive.[22]

[20] See, for example, the Shelby Flat Tax, S1040, Tax Simplification Act of 2003, 108th Cong., 1st Sess. (May 12, 2003), an origin-based tax on business activities.

[21] For a discussion of the origin and destination principles applied to international transactions in the context of GATT, see K. Messere, "Consumption Tax Rules," *IBFD Bulletin*, Dec. 1994, p. 665. See also Chapter 7.

[22] See EC Directive 98/6 of Feb. 16, 1998 requiring sellers to show "selling price" and "unit price," both of which include VAT.

D. Inclusion of Capital Goods in Tax Base

Looking at the VAT through concepts used in national income analysis aids thinking about how the tax works in practice. Gross domestic product is the sum of personal consumption expenditures, gross private domestic investment, net of exports over imports, and government consumption expenditures and gross investment. The modern VAT, as practiced, reaches only value added reflected in personal consumption (although it could, and some so advocate, reach further by seeking to tax net national product by including depreciation or to tax gross domestic product by including capital goods). To reach only personal consumption, those who draft the legislative structure of the VAT have to consider carefully the way in which value added reflected in inventory and in capital goods is treated in constructing the tax base and collecting the tax.

To put this range from gross domestic product to consumption into perspective, Table 2.1 illustrates the makeup of GDP for the United States for 2004, including a breakdown of personal consumption expenditures into categories of goods and services. A succinct but complex matrix and examples of bases and methods presented in Table 2.7 shows the calculation of tax under consumption, income, and GDP bases along with addition, subtraction, and credit methods of calculating tax liability.

The following material discusses the treatment of capital goods under a credit-invoice VAT. The same treatment can be provided under a sales-subtraction or addition method VAT.[23]

> The items that a firm purchases from other firms consist of raw materials, semi-manufactured goods, supplies used up in the process of manufacture or handling, services (e.g., banking, insurance, advertising), finished goods ready for resale to consumers (in the case of retailers), and finally machinery, equipment, and other capital goods. The treatment accorded to capital goods differs, however, depending on the type of value-added tax employed.[24]

Under a GDP VAT, the VAT on capital purchases is not recoverable as an input tax credit. This VAT is borne by the capital goods purchaser and, depending on competitive forces, may be shifted as a cost of doing business to its customers in the form of higher prices.

A national income (income) VAT allows the capital goods purchaser to recover the VAT on capital purchases, through a depreciation-like allowance, over the lives of the capital goods. A consumption VAT allows the capital goods purchaser to claim input credits for VAT on capital purchases immediately and in full in the period in which the capital goods are purchased. VAT on capital goods is treated the same as VAT on purchases of inventory, supplies, and other business inputs. To reduce the cash drain from refunds of excess input credits on capital purchases, some countries

[23] Shoup, Public Finance, *supra* note 18, at 258.

[24] *Id.* at 251.

TABLE 2.1. Gross domestic product and personal consumption data for 2011 (in billions)

Gross Domestic Product 2011		*$15,094.0*
Less:		
Gross private domestic investment	1,916.2	
Net exports of goods and services	(578.7)*	
Government consumption expenditure and gross investment	3,030.6	4,368.1
Personal consumption expenditures		10,725.9**
Categories of 2011 Personal Consumption Expenditures		
Durable goods		
Motor vehicles and parts	378.6	
Furniture and household equipment	253.4	
Recreational goods and vehicles	344.6	
Other	186.3	
	1,162.9	
Nondurable goods		
Food and beverages for off-premises consumption	808.6	
Clothing and footwear	350.3	
Gasoline, fuel oil, and other energy	428.2	
Other	896.6	
	2,483.7	
Services		
Housing and utilities	1,921.3	
Food services and accommodations	680.1	
Transportation	305.1	
Health care	1,730.4	
Recreation	400.5	
Financial services and insurance	804.8	
Final consumption expenditures of Not-for-Profit Organizations serving households	284.5	
Other	952.7	
	7,079.4	
Personal consumption expenditure	$10,726.0	

Bureau of Economic Analysis, U.S. Dept. of Commerce, Survey of Current Business, National Data, Tables 1.1.5 & 1.5.5 (July 2005).

* Do you understand the meaning of a negative figure on this line? (Hint: Think about the relationship among imports, exports, and personal consumption.

** Rounding difference. The table shows 10,726.0.

(particularly developing countries) require VAT-registered persons to carry forward excess input credits to a number of future tax periods and to use these credits to offset future VAT liabilities before any remaining credits are eligible for refund. "A carry forward to reduce a future year's positive value-added will not suffice, unless it is enlarged by an interest factor, since delay in tax relief is equivalent to reduction in tax relief."[25]

Although most VATs today are consumption-style VATs, a few countries are still in the process of converting their VAT to a consumption VAT.

As discussed, a multistage value added tax is described in part by the method employed to calculate tax liability. The next section provides a detailed discussion of the major methods of calculating tax liability for each tax period under a VAT.

III. Methods of Calculating VAT Liability

The special feature of the modern value added tax is the mode of collection.[26] This section discusses the widely used European-style, credit-invoice VAT; the Japanese-style credit-subtraction VAT that does not rely on invoices; the sales-subtraction VAT proposed but not enacted; and the addition-method VAT not used at the national level.

A. Credit-Invoice VAT

The most prevalent method of calculating VAT worldwide is the credit-invoice VAT (or invoice VAT) that relies on a tax-against-a-tax methodology. This form of VAT originated in Europe. Including the other elements in the description of the credit-invoice VAT, the European-style VAT reaches international transactions under the destination principle, imposes tax on a consumption base, and typically calculates output tax on tax-exclusive prices.[27]

With the almost universally used invoice method, the taxable firm calculates net tax liability for each tax reporting period (typically one month) as the difference between the tax charged on taxable sales (output tax) and the tax paid on imports and domestic purchases from other firms (input tax credits).[28]

Output tax (tax on taxable sales)

Less Input tax credits (tax on taxable imports and taxable domestic purchases)

Net tax liability for the period

[25] *Id.* at 254.

[26] For a thorough analysis of the advantage of the invoice VAT over the sales-subtraction VAT, see McLure, VAT, *supra* note 18. For another discussion of the various methods of calculating VAT liability, see A. Schenk, "The Plethora of Consumption Tax Proposals: Putting the Value Added Tax, Flat Tax, Retail Sales Tax, and USA Tax into Perspective," 33 *San Diego Law Review* 1281, 1305–1309 (1996).

[27] The EU VAT is discussed in Chapter 3, Section II.

[28] The European Union's VAT Directive, which lays down the fundamental structure and rules for member countries of the EU, describes the credit as a deduction from the tax collected on a firm's sales. Council Directive 2006/112/EC of 28 November 2006 on the common system of value added tax (OJ L347, 11.12.2006, p. 1 [hereinafter VAT Directive].

TABLE 2.2. No input credit on purchases from exempt small businesses

Output tax	
Taxable sales $100,000 × 10%	$10,000
Input credits	
Purchases from exempt small businesses $5,300	(00)
Taxable domestic purchases $60,000 × 10%	(6,000)
Taxable imports $10,000 × 10%	(1,000)
Net VAT liability for the period	$ 3,000

In this calculation, output tax = taxable sales multiplied by the tax rate, and input credits consist of both VAT on taxable imports listed on import documents and VAT on taxable domestic purchases listed on VAT invoices. Input credits for tax on imports and purchases are allowed only to the extent that the business inputs are used in making taxable sales. In some countries, such as sales within the EU, imports of goods are not taxed at the border but are reported and paid as output tax, generally with an offsetting input credit.

For example, if the final product is novelty shirts for sports teams, the final shirt passes through many different firms and processes, starting with the production of the cotton and ending with the sale by the retailer. At each step in the process, the shirt becomes more valuable. Each firm adds additional value to the shirt.

To illustrate just one stage of the VAT collection process, assume a VAT-registered retailer sold thousands of these shirts (taxable sales) in a tax period for $100,000 and makes taxable purchases of $60,000 and taxable imports of $10,000 (all at tax-exclusive prices). The imports and domestic purchases are all used in making the taxable sales. The VAT rate is 10%, applied to tax-exclusive prices. As shown in Table 2.2, the retailer's net VAT liability for the period is $3,000, calculated as follows.

The total VAT received by the government from all stages of production and distribution with respect to these shirts is $10,300, of which the dealer paid $4,000 ($3,000 with the VAT return and $1,000 on taxable imports), the retailer's suppliers other than the exempt small business paid $6,000, and, it is assumed, the exempt small business paid $300 of non-creditable VAT on its purchases. In short, except for the exempt small business, the share of the total tax that is paid by each firm is in proportion to the value each firm added to its taxable inputs.

A modern 10% VAT collects 10% of the value added at each stage in the process. In essence, the VAT can be looked at as a way of collecting in stages a retail sales tax. Analogous to income tax withholding, the VAT can be looked at as a form of withholding in the context of a retail sales tax. At each stage in the production and distribution process, part of the ultimate amount of the VAT is collected, just like part of the ultimate amount of the income tax is collected over the year through withholding. At the same time, however, each amount of VAT collected from one taxpayer is refunded to another (in the form of input credits), except for VAT collected on sales to final consumers.

The credit-invoice method is a tax imposed on transactions and links reported sales to the prices charged in market transactions. It does not easily handle some industries and transactions, such as secondhand goods acquired by a registered person from consumers for resale, financial intermediation services (including casualty insurance), and gambling.

The prompt recovery of tax by VAT-registered persons on business inputs is designed to remove VAT as a business cost and thereby remove VAT as an element in the tax-exclusive prices of taxable goods and services. To fully remove VAT as a business cost, a VAT-registered business should receive a prompt refund of any excess input credits for a tax period.

There have been a number of proposals in the United States to enact a European-style, credit-invoice VAT, starting in 1979, and refined in 1980.[29] A proposal by Graetz would use an invoice VAT to replace the individual income tax for taxpayers with income less than about $100,000.[30] No proposal has received serious legislative consideration.

B. Credit-Subtraction VAT That Does Not Rely on VAT Invoices

The credit-subtraction VAT without invoices is illustrated by the Japanese Consumption Tax (CT), as it was introduced in 1989.[31] Under that tax, tax on taxable sales (output tax) is calculated the same as under the credit-invoice VAT. Output tax is equal to total taxable sales for the period (exclusive of tax) multiplied by the tax rate. The CT did not require registered businesses to issue VAT invoices on taxable sales. The CT also allowed registered businesses to claim credits for CT on purchases from exempt small businesses as well as from registered suppliers. As a result, a registered business did not have any incentive to prefer a registered supplier. Input credits are denied for CT on purchases of exempt goods and services. Output tax is calculated on the basis of tax-exclusive sales prices of taxable goods and services, the same as under the European-style invoice VAT. Input credits are calculated from the tax-inclusive costs recorded in

[29] H.R. 7015, 96th Cong., 2d Sess., 126 Cong. Rec. 7481 (1980) [the Ullman Bill named after its proponent].

[30] See Michael Graetz, *The Decline (and Fall?) of the Income Tax* (W.W. Norton & Co. 1997); M. Graetz, *100 Million Unnecessary Returns* (Yale University Press 2008).

[31] Shohizei -ho [Consumption Tax Law], Law No. 108 of 1988, pt. IV [hereinafter Japanese CT Law]. The original Japanese VAT, adopted in 1950 but never implemented, calculated the tax by levying the tax rate on the difference between a firm's sales and its purchases. The evolving CT increased the substantiation requirements for input tax credits. The result is the movement of the CT closer to the European model that relies on invoices to verify output tax on taxable sales and input credit on domestic taxable purchases.

TABLE 2.3. Input credit available on purchases from exempt small businesses

Output tax		
Taxable sales $100, 000 × 10%		$10,000
Input credits*		
Purchases from exempt small businesses	$5,300	(482)
Taxable domestic purchases	$66,000	(6,000)
Taxable imports	$11,000	(1,000)
Net VAT liability for the period		$ 2,518

* Because imports and purchases are recorded at CT-inclusive prices, the input credits = the CT-inclusive prices multiplied by the fraction, the numerator of which is the tax rate (10%) and the denominator is 100 + the tax rate (110), even for purchases of otherwise taxable items from exempt small businesses. The actual Japanese CT rate is lower, but 10% was used to make the various calculations comparable.

purchase records, except for the cost of purchases exempt from CT. Input credit is equal to the tax-inclusive cost of allowable purchases and imports multiplied by the tax fraction. The tax fraction is the tax rate divided by 100 plus the tax rate. The retail firm in this example, if subject to the CT, has net CT liability for the period of $2,518, calculated as shown in Table 2.3.

Japan made significant changes in the CT, bringing the documentation required for input tax credits more in line with the invoice VATs in use elsewhere.

C. Sales-Subtraction VAT

The sales-subtraction method calculates net VAT liability by multiplying the tax rate by a base consisting of the difference between total taxable sales less total taxable purchases from other firms.[32] This information may be available from modified company sales and purchase records. Like an addition VAT, the sales-subtraction VAT is a period tax based on cumulative data for each tax period, not a tax imposed on individual transactions. The seller must price taxable goods and services inclusive of VAT. This VAT-inclusive data is used to calculate periodic VAT liability.[33]

[32] Finland relied on a sales-subtraction VAT, enacted in 1978, that had a base analogous to national income. See Shoup, Choosing Among VATs, *supra* note 18, at 14. Under existing value added taxes (although some modern American proposals are different), wages and salaries are not treated as a taxable purchase; that is, wage earners are not VAT taxpayers. If landlords and banks are subject to value added taxes (a number of countries tax the former but not the latter), then payment for those rental and financial services would also be subtracted from sales in computing a business firm's value added tax base.

[33] "[The legislature] ... could require disclosure of tax at the cash register or by a sign posted in retail stores indicating the tax rate that is included in the prices." O. Oldman & A. Schenk, "The Business Activities Tax: Have Senators Danforth and Boren Created a Better Value Added Tax?," 65 *Tax Notes* 1547, 1551 (Dec. 19, 1994) [hereinafter Oldman & Schenk, Business Activities Tax].

TABLE 2.4. Example of sales-subtractive VAT

Taxable sales		*$110,000*
Purchases allowable as deductions		
Purchases from exempt small businesses	5,300	
Taxable domestic purchases	66,000	
Taxable imports	11,000	
		$82,300
Tax base		27,700
Tax rate		9.0909%
Net VAT liability for the period		$2,518

The VAT liability for each period is the product of the tax base multiplied by the VAT rate. This method of calculating tax liability makes it difficult to impose more than one rate of VAT on taxable goods or services. The tax base is the difference between the total VAT-inclusive taxable sales and VAT-inclusive purchases. Although it is possible to deny deductions for VAT on purchases from exempt small businesses, for administrative reasons, these purchases may be deductible, in which case this VAT has been described as the "naïve" sales-subtraction VAT.[34]

To make the illustration comparable to the tables earlier in this chapter, for taxable sales and taxable purchases, Table 2.4 uses a 9.0909% rate on VAT-inclusive prices instead of the 10% rate applied to tax-exclusive prices. The retailer's net VAT liability for the period is the same $2,518 as under the Japanese-style, credit-subtraction VAT that does not rely on invoices. If it is administratively feasible to deny deductions for purchases from exempt small businesses, the net VAT liability would be the same: $3,000 payable under the credit-invoice VAT.

Several sales-subtraction VATs have been introduced in the U.S. Congress. One of the first was Sam Gibbons's proposal to replace many federal taxes with a sales-subtraction VAT and eliminate the individual income tax for incomes less than $75,000.[35] In addition to proposals for a pure sales-subtraction VAT, there have been proposals in the United States for a flat tax and coordinated consumption-based individual and business taxes.[36] The "flat taxes" are based on proposals by Robert Hall and Alvin Rabushka, for a sales-subtraction-style VAT that provides a deduction for wages paid. The wages then are taxed to the workers under a

[34] See McLure, VAT, *supra* note 18, at 71–79.

[35] Revenue Restructuring Act of 1996, H.R. 4050, 104th Cong., 2d Sess., 142 Cong. Rec. E1572 (Sept. 11, 1996).

[36] The most elaborate legislative proposal for a coordinated consumption-based individual and business tax was the Unlimited Savings Allowance (USA) Tax System. See S.722, USA Tax Act of 1995, 104th Cong., 1st Sess., 141 Cong. Rec. S5664 (April 24, 1995). See also, H.R. 269, Simplified USA Tax Act of 2003, 108th Cong., 1st Sess., Jan. 8, 2003.

consumption-based income tax that does not tax returns to capital, such as interest, dividends, and capital gains.[37] A panel established by President George W. Bush recommended tax reforms that would move the United States toward a consumption base.[38]

D. Addition-Method VAT

The addition-method VAT requires a taxable firm to calculate tax liability for each tax period by adding the firm's economic factors of production for the period (wages, rent and interest expense, and profit for VAT purposes) and multiplying the total by the tax rate. The Michigan Single Business Tax was a modified version of an addition-method VAT.[39]

The addition method has not been adopted as a national tax, except for Israel's taxation of financial institutions and insurance companies under a tax measured by the sum of the firm's wages and profits. This tax is administered by the income tax department, outside the VAT system.

Like the accounts-based sales-subtraction VAT (also a period tax), an addition VAT must be imposed at one rate because "company accounts do not usually divide sales by different product categories coinciding with different sales tax rates, and... they certainly never divide inputs by differential tax liabilities."[40]

If the "profit" portion of the addition-method VAT base is taken from data prepared for income tax purposes, this method of calculating VAT liability may be expected to be an income-based, not consumption-based, tax.[41] Because the tax base includes only the value added as measured by the economic factors of production employed at each stage, revenue lost at a prior stage is not recovered (as under the invoice VAT) at the next stage of production or distribution of goods or rendition of services. "As a period tax, an addition method VAT probably will be treated as a cost of production and included in the pricing structure of taxable goods and services. Since the VAT liability is not based on the ... sales price [of] ... goods, it is unlikely that the exact VAT, no more and no less, will be shifted to consumers."[42]

To make the calculation of net VAT liability for a tax period consistent with the example, it is necessary to add some assumptions. Sales and purchases listed in Tables 2.5 and 2.6 are at tax-inclusive prices and the tax rate in Table 2.6 is 9.0909%. Assume the retailer, in addition to the total purchases of $82,300 (including purchases from exempt small businesses), pays $17,000 in wages and $2,000 in interest and rent expense. The profit for VAT purposes is $8,700, calculated as follows.

37 Hall & Rabushka, THE FLAT TAX, *supra* note 9.

38 The President's Advisory Panel on Federal Tax Reform, Simple, Fair, and Pro-Growth: Proposals to Fix America's Tax System, Nov. 2005.

39 See also New Hampshire Business Enterprise Tax, discussed in Chapter 15, sec. VIII(B).

40 A. Tait, *Value Added Tax: International Practice and Problems* 5 (IMF 1988).

41 McLure, VAT, *supra* note 18, at 95. See also Shoup, Public Finance, *supra* note 18, ch. 9.

42 ABA Model VAT, *supra* note 18, at 6.

TABLE 2.5. Pro forma calculation of profit for VAT purposes

Taxable sales		*$110,000*
Expenses for VAT purposes		
Wages	$17,000	
Interest and rent expenses	2,000	
Purchases	82,300	
Total expenses		101,300
Profit for VAT purposes		$8,700

TABLE 2.6. Example of addition-method VAT

Wages	*$17,000*
Interest and rent expenses	2,000
Profit for VAT purposes	8,700
Tax base	$27,700
Tax rate	9.0909%
Net VAT liability for the period	$2,518

Applying the data in Table 2.5 to an addition-method calculation, the net VAT liability for the period is $2,518, the same as under the "naïve" sales-subtraction VAT.

Table 2.7 is a matrix presentation of the basic differences among these different kinds of VATs (addition, subtraction, and credit methods), combined with the three methods of handling purchases of capital goods (gross product, income, and consumption types, using national income account concepts).[43] For this purpose, the following data set for the firm are used.

Chart 2.1. Data set for Table 2.7

Current purchases	*300*	*Computation of profit:*		
Depreciation	40	Sales		1,000
Wages	400	Less costs:		
Rent	100	Purchases	300	
Profit	180	Depreciation	40	
Beginning inventory	100	Wages	400	
Investment in fixed		Rent	100	
Assets	50		840	
Sales	1,000	Change in inventory	(20)	
Closing inventory	120			820
		Profit		180

43 Table 2.7 is based on Shoup, Public Finance, *supra* note 18, at 257–260.

TABLE 2.7. Calculation of base under gross product, income, and consumption VAT

Base	*Addition*		*Subtraction*		*Credit*	
Gross Product	+Profit	180	+Sales	1,000	+Tax on sales	100
	+Depr.	40	– Purchases (current)	(300)	– Credit on purchases	(30)
	+Wages	400	+Increase in inventory	20	+Tax on invty increase	2
	+Rent pd	100				
	+Int. pd	0				
	VAT Base	720	VAT Base	720		
	Tax (10%)	72	Tax	72	Tax	72
Income	+Profit	180	+Sales	1,000	+Tax on sales	100
	+Wages	400	–Purchases (current)	(300)	–Credit on purchases	(30)
	+Rent pd	100	+Increase in inventory	20	+Tax on invty increase	2
	+Int. pd	0	–Depr.	(40)	–Tax on depreciable part of property	(4)
	VAT Base	680	VAT Base	680		
	Tax (10%)	68	Tax	68	Tax	68
Consumption	+Profit	180	+Sales	1,000	+Tax on sales	100
	+Wages	400	–Purchases (current)	(300)	–Credit on current and investment purchases	(35)
	–Increase in inventory	(20)	–Investment	(50)		
	+Depr.	40				
	–Investment	(50)				
	+Int. pd	0				
	+Rent pd	100				
	VAT Base	650	VAT Base	650		
	Tax (10%)	65	Tax	65	Tax	65

TABLE 2.8. Illustration of car rental firm renting only for personal consumption

Outlays		*Receipts*	
Purchase of car, Jan. 1	5,000	Rentals (20/day for 300 days/yrt	6,000
Labor – auto service and clerical	1,500		
Interest, office rent, and insurance	1,000	Sale of used auto at year end, Dec. 31	2,000
	7,500		8,000

Notes: Interest, office rent, and insurance paid by firm are part of firm's value added tax base. Capital goods transactions (office furniture, etc.) are omitted. Cars are inventory, not capital goods.

The addition method included in the first column of numbers in Table 2.7 is calculated under the gross product, income, and consumption treatment for capital goods. Rent and interest are accounted for in each block as part of the computation of value added by each firm. The assumption is that the provider of the leased premises or the loan is not a firm included in the VAT base. Hence, the value added by rent and interest as factors of production is included in the accounts of the firm paying the rent or interest (just as they would be imputed, or would increase "profit" if the firm used its own property or money).

In the Subtraction and Credit methods columns of Table 2.7, there is no mention of rent and interest. Do you see how they are nevertheless accounted for? They must be, of course, because all columns are based on the same data set preceding Table 2.7. Hint – look at the "spread" between sales (or tax on sales) and purchases (or tax on purchases) after adjustments for capital.

Tables 2.8 and 2.9 take a different approach. They illustrate how assumed tax-exclusive data from a firm that provides leasing services to consumers (Table 2.8) can be used to construct tax bases under a single-stage retail sales tax and under credit, addition, and subtraction method VATs (Table 2.9).

Assumptions: (1) General comprehensive VAT at single uniform 10% rate; (2) Profit is net income after depreciation and adjustment for inventory.

IV. Methods of Altering the Tax Base

In drafting an administrable VAT, tax policy makers must try to satisfy "the deep, widespread feelings of the people as to what is fair."[44] A normative base for a tax on consumption like the VAT is one that taxes final consumption of all goods and services. If the jurisdictional reach of the

[44] Gen. Headquarters, Supreme Commander for Allied Powers, Tokyo, 1 *Report on Japanese Taxation* 17 (1949) (four-volume report).

TABLE 2.9. Possible sales tax bases and tax payments (10% rate)

Base		*Tax*	*Description*
			Retail taxes
(a) Purchase of car	5,000 @ 10%	500	On goods
(b) Rentals	6,000 @ 10%	600	On services
(c) a + b		1,100	Double tax on goods and services
(d) Sale of used car	2,000 @ 10%	200	On used goods
(e) a + b + d		1,300	On goods and services and used goods
(f) b + d	8,000 @ 10%	800	Retail sales tax
			(consumption base)
(g) Tax on annual receipts	8,000 @ 10%	800	Credit-method VAT
Tax on purchase of car	5,000 @ 10%	500	
Tax due		300	
(h) Labor		1,500	Addition-method VAT
Interest, etc.		1,000	
Profit	8,000		
	−1,500		
	−1,000		
	−5,000	500	
Tax base		3,000	
Tax rate		10%	
Tax due		300	
(i) Annual receipts		8,000	Subtraction-method VAT
Tax paid purchases		5,000	
Net value added		3,000	
Tax rate		10%	
Tax due		300	

Note: Total tax collected in (f) is same as in (g), (h), and (i); however, in VAT, there is $500 tax collected before retail stage.

VAT is defined by the destination principle, the tax should be imposed on all imported goods and services and returned (by credit, or refund in the case of excess input credits) on all exported goods and services. In its pure state, the tax base would include services rendered by government; an isolated sale to a neighbor of a used refrigerator, toys, or an automobile; or the sale of a personal residence. For administrative as well as political or social reasons, no nation employs a VAT with such a broad base.

As a tax generally imposed on domestic consumption, a seller's quarterly or annual total sales activities should not be relevant. However, for administrative and compliance reasons, it is impractical to impose a collection and reporting requirement on every seller of any product or service. Every wage earner provides services and could be regarded as a taxable

TABLE 2.10. Effect of midstream exemption adapted from "The Value-Added Tax in Developing Countries"

	Purchases	*VAT at each stage*	*Sales (incl. VAT)*	*Sales (before VAT)*	*Gross tax*	*10% VAT Credit on purchases*	*10% VAT Net tax paid*	*If miller's sales exempt – VAT net*
Farmer	250	1,100	1,100	1,000	100	(00)	100	100
Miller	1,000	500	1,650	1,500	150	(100)	50	00
Baker	1,650	1,000	2,750	2,500	250	(150)	100	250
Retailer	2,750	1,500	4,400	4,000	400	(250)	150	150
		4,000					400	500

G. E. Lent, M. Casanegra, and M. Guerard, IMF Staff Papers, July 1973, p. 321. The table was adapted by Oliver Oldman.

supplier of them. No existing VAT does this. The quantum and nature of the sales activity therefore are used in most countries to define the persons or entities that are subject to VAT.

Most VATs apply to firms engaged in regular and continuous business activity, thereby removing from the VAT base isolated sales by an individual. A small business exemption removes a significant number of firms (but only a small percentage of value added) from the tax base. Government services and, in some countries, government purchases are not in the tax base.[45] Other exemptions, based on the nature of the seller, may be provided for charities and other nonprofits.

Multiple rates may be used to increase tax on luxuries or reduce the VAT burden on goods and services deemed necessities. Special treatment may be granted by exempting or zero-rating particular categories of goods or services. Some may be based on treaties or international agreements, such as diplomatic exemptions.[46] A lower VAT rate on labor intensive services has been suggested as a means to promote employment. The repealed Michigan Single Business Tax (a state-level addition-method VAT) included a tax concession to labor-intensive businesses.[47]

[45] "For example, some registered charities are exempt from [the Canadian] GST on their sales of property or services and they also can claim rebate for a portion of their non-creditable input tax on purchases attributable to their charitable activities." A. Schenk, GOODS AND SERVICES TAX: THE CANADIAN APPROACH TO VALUE-ADDED *Tax* 10 (1993), citing Canadian GST, Sch. V, Part VI, Public Sector Bodies.

[46] Saint Christopher and Nevis, Value Added Tax Act, 2010, No. 3 of 2010, sec. 63, provides that the minister may authorize the comptroller to refund VAT, instead of exempting or zero-rating acquisitions by diplomats and organizations covered by a technical assistance or humanitarian assistance agreement.

[47] Single Business Tax Act, PA. 1975, No. 228, MCL §208.1 et seq. (repealed).

As the VAT base is narrowed, especially by multiple rates and grants of exemptions and zero-rating, the costs increase for business to comply with and for the tax authorities to administer the tax. The methods of altering the VAT base are discussed in this section.

A. Entity Exemptions

There are two different kinds of entity exemptions granted under various VAT regimes. The first is the small business exemption, which does not depend on the kind of goods or services provided by the seller. The second is the exemption provided for all sales or particular sales made by an entity because of the nature of the entity. For example, the national government may be exempt from VAT, or only essential governmental services rendered by a unit of government may be exempt.

Typically, countries with VATs remove from the tax base firms with annual sales at or below the small business exemption threshold. This threshold varies among countries. For example, the threshold in Canada is Can.$30,000,[48] in the United Kingdom, £45,000,[49] and in Japan, ¥30 million.[50] Businesses exempt from tax do not report taxable sales and do not claim credit for tax on taxable purchases, and their customers generally are denied any VAT benefit from the cost of purchases from these exempt sellers.

A business making only sales that are exempt from tax would be treated the same as an exempt small business. In contrast, a business making both taxable and exempt sales would come within the VAT system for its taxable business activity and fall outside the VAT system for its exempt business activity.

There is a notable difference between the European-style VATs and the Japanese CT, but that difference is not inherent in the Japanese credit-subtraction VAT, which does not rely on invoices. A business subject to the CT can claim credit for implicit tax in the cost of purchases from exempt sellers such as exempt small businesses.[51] Thus, if a business subject to an 8% CT (currently 8% and scheduled to increase to 10% in October 2015) purchases a good for $1,050 from an exempt small business (assuming that the small business increased the price to cover his $50 CT), the business can claim an input credit for the full 8/108 of $1,050, or $77.78, even though, in this example, the purchase price does not contain that much CT. Under a European VAT, a credit cannot be claimed with respect to a purchase from an exempt supplier.

48 Canadian GST, subsection 148(1). The threshold for public service bodies is Can$50,000. There is no threshold for taxi and limousine operators and nonresident performers.

49 Value Added Tax Act 1994 [hereinafter VATA 1994], §3 and Sch. 1, ¶1(1) (United Kingdom).

50 Japanese CT Law, *supra* note 31, at Art. 9.

51 The Japanese CT denies input tax deductions for purchases exempt from tax, such as exempt medical supplies.

An exemption, based on the nature of the seller, may be provided for units of government and nonprofit organizations. These entities, even if outside the VAT registration system because all of their services are exempt, still must pay tax on their inputs and imports. Others may be taxable on services that compete with services rendered by the private sector.[52]

New Zealand treats activities of a public authority or local authority as taxable activities.[53] New Zealand exempts sales by a nonprofit body of donated goods and services.[54]

An exempt entity that is denied credit for VAT on inputs used in its exempt business activities (and for competitive or other reasons it cannot pass this cost on to its customers) may attempt to avoid tax on some purchased services by providing them in-house rather than purchasing them from outside taxable suppliers. To prevent this incentive toward vertical integration, some countries treat certain self-supplies by exempt entities as taxable sales to themselves, reportable on VAT returns, notwithstanding their general exemption from VAT.[55]

B. Zero-Rating[56]

Zero-rating is a mechanism for completely removing tax from a particular product or service or from a particular transaction. Under a credit-invoice VAT, a seller of a zero-rated item does not charge VAT on the sale. The sale is classified as a taxable sale subject to a zero-rate. Because the sale is taxable, the seller is entitled to recover as input credit the tax included in the cost of taxable purchases attributable to that sale.

[52] Under the VAT in the United Kingdom, tax applies "to taxable supplies by the Crown as it applies in relation to taxable supplies by taxable persons." VATA 1994, *supra* note 49, at section 41(1) (United Kingdom). Sales by government departments are not treated as sales made in "the carrying on of a business" (and therefore are not taxable) unless the Treasury so directs. *Id.* at section 41(2). In Japan, the complex provisions governing units of government and their eligibility for refunds of input tax are covered in Art. 60 of the CT. See Japanese CT Law, *supra* note 31.

[53] See New Zealand Goods and Services Tax Act 1985, No. 141, as amended, at section 6(l)(b). A public authority is any agency of government, including departments, but is not the governor-general, ministers, members of Parliament, or members of the Executive Council. *Id.* at section 2 definition of "public authority." A local authority is an authority included in section 2(1) of the Rating Powers Act 1988. *Id.* at section 2 definition of "local authority." Any payment by the Crown to the public authority is treated as a sale by the public authority that may be subject to GST. *Id.* at section 5(6).

[54] *Id.* at section 14(l)(b). A nonprofit body is an organization that is not conducted for profit or gain of a proprietor, member, or shareholder and that is prohibited from making distributions to any such person. *Id.* at section 2 definition of "non-profit body."

[55] VATA 1994, *supra* note 51, at §5(4)-(6) (United Kingdom).

[56] The material in subsections B–D is taken largely from Oldman & Schenk, Business Activities Tax, *supra* note 35, at 1557–1560, but it has been edited. In OECD countries, zero-rating is used more extensively in countries such as Canada, Ireland, and the United Kingdom. See Consumption Tax Trends 2012, VAT/GST and Excise Rates, Trends and Administrative Issues, Table 3.8 (OECD 2012).

Under a sales-subtraction VAT, zero-rating is accomplished by excluding the designated sales from gross receipts and allowing the business to deduct taxed purchases attributable to these zero-rated sales.

Under the destination principle, exports are zero-rated (regardless of the nature of the goods or services exported) because those exports will be consumed outside the taxing country. This zero-rating is not a preference. The export sales are merely beyond the jurisdictional reach of the tax.[57] The destination principle reflects the near universal understanding that in geographically assigning sales tax or VAT burdens and revenues, the country of consumption gets both; the country of production gets neither. Consistently most countries do not tax sales of goods located abroad for delivery abroad because these sales are beyond the scope of the VAT.[58]

Some countries include item or transactional zero-rating of particular goods or services for social or political reasons (such as sales of food). Some countries with credit-invoice VATs zero-rate a long list of goods and services.[59] For example, the United Kingdom zero-rates, among other items, certain food, water, books and other printed matter, recording aids for the blind and disabled, newspaper advertisements, news services, fuel and power, gold, and drugs and medicines.[60] Supplies by tax-favored industries or domestic industries, to be encouraged, may be granted a VAT status between exemption and zero-rating. For example, Brazil exempted supplies of goods in the field of information technology (IT) and exempted, on certain conditions, purchases of certain items to be used in manufacturing these products.[61] Some VAT systems zero-rate certain otherwise taxable domestic transactions between registered businesses both for administrative convenience and to avoid cash flow burdens on the parties to the transactions. The most common transaction in this group is the sale of a going business. This kind of transaction usually involves no net change in revenue to the government because the tax otherwise

[57] The zero-rating typically extends to transportation and other services directly attributable to the exported products. The zero-rating also may extend to the export of some other services.

[58] See VAT Directive, *supra* note 28, at Arts. 146–150. For example, transactions conducted outside the taxing jurisdiction (such as foreign sales of goods located outside the country), exports, export-related services, and international transport are zero-rated. New Zealand zero-rates exports of goods and allied services performed outside New Zealand, foreign sales of goods not located in New Zealand, services on property located outside the country, and services related to intellectual property to be used outside New Zealand. New Zealand Goods and Services Tax Act 1985, No. 141, §11 (other than §ll(c)). The Japanese CT zero-rates only export sales, including international transportation and telecommunications. See Japanese CT Law, *supra* note 31, at Arts. 7 and 8.

[59] Commonwealth of New Vatopia Value Added Tax Act, prepared by Alan Schenk, relying on his experience serving as technical advisor for the International Monetary Fund Legal Department, available at http://www.imf.org/external/np/leg. Go to Tax Law Drafting Samples: VAT [hereinafter New Vatopia VAT], appendix B, §17 and Sch. 1,¶2.

[60] See VATA 1994, *supra* note 49, at §30 and Sch. 8.

[61] Art. 9, Law 11,908, amending Art. 29 of Law 10,637 (IPI 2009), reported by Bruno Carramaschi, in cooperation with Linklaters LLP, in IBFD Tax News Service, March 20, 2009.

reportable by the seller is offset by an input credit or deduction to the purchaser or transferee.[62]

Some transactions are not subject to VAT because legal ownership to property is not transferred. Although they are not specifically zero-rated, the transactions receive treatment comparable to zero-rating. For example, Canada removes from the tax base transactions involving property seized or repossessed by a creditor to satisfy a debtor's obligation,[63] as well as transactions involving property transferred to an insurer in satisfaction of an insurance claim.[64] No tax is imposed on the repossession or transfer.

C. Transaction Exemption

If a sale of a particular good or service is exempt under a credit-invoice VAT, the sale is not taxed and the seller is denied an input credit for the tax paid on purchases used in that exempt activity. The grant of exemption for domestic sales substantially increases the administrative and compliance costs of a VAT, especially if a business makes both taxable and exempt sales. In the latter situation, the business must allocate credits between taxable and exempt activities because it is denied credit for input tax on purchases attributable to this exempt activity.

An exemption granted at an intermediate stage of production or distribution may increase the price paid by the final consumer and increase revenue to the fisc over the situations where this exemption is not provided.[65] A retail stage exemption reduces revenue and, to the extent the tax saving is passed on to consumers, reduces retail prices as well.

62 A purchaser of a zero-rated sale of a going business may be required to report tax on the purchase to the extent that the acquired assets are used in exempt activities. See New Vatopia, *supra* note 59, at §4(18) & (19). The United Kingdom treats the transfer of a going concern as neither a supply of goods nor a supply of services. Value Added Tax (Special Provisions) Order 1995 (SI 1995/1268, as amended), Art. 5.

63 These transactions are deemed to have been made for no consideration and therefore are not includible in the GST base. Canadian GST, Part IX of the Excise Tax Act, S.C 1993, c. 27, at section 183(l)(a),(b). These transactions nevertheless are treated as supplies. If the recipient has any purchases associated with this seizure or repossession, input tax on such purchases qualify for input credit.

64 These transactions also are deemed to have been made for no consideration. *Id.* at section 184(l)(a),(b).

65 "If … one or more of the earlier stages of value added are completely exempt, the tax-credit method fails to record the correct amount of cumulated tax paid unless either *(a)* the stage so exempted is the very first stage, typically the raw materials stage, or *(b)* either (1) at the exempt stage there is a refund of prior tax paid or (2) a shadow tentative tax is computed that can be shown on the invoice issued by the exempt seller and claimed as a credit by the one who purchases from him. If, no tax at all being due at the stage in question, no tax credit is taken by the exempt seller, all record of earlier tax paid is lost, and no account can be taken of it at later stages where taxation resumes. … Under the subtraction or addition method, exemption of the small firm at an intermediate stage does not give rise to over-taxation. On the other hand, revenue is always lost by the exemption; there is no catching up at a later stage, as there is under the tax credit for an

Under a sales-subtraction VAT, transactions are exempted by removing the sales from taxable gross receipts and by denying the deduction for the cost of purchases attributable to those exempt sales. Of course, the prices charged by sellers on exempt transactions may include tax paid by them on purchases used in that exempt sales activity.

Table 2.10 provides a graphic illustration of the effect of a midstream exemption under a credit-invoice VAT. The workings of a VAT may be illustrated by this simplified example based on the various stages involved in the production and sale of bread produced from, say, 500 bushels of wheat. The figures shown are in U.S. dollars.

It can be seen that a 10% tax is assessed at each stage of the process on the amount of sale, excluding the VAT, but that credit is taken for tax paid on purchases, leaving a net amount of tax chargeable on the value added at each stage. The cumulative tax – $400 – is equivalent to a rate of 10% on the $4,000 tax-exclusive retail sale of the product to consumers.

Although this book uses the terms zero-rating and exemption as explained earlier, EU VAT legislation (such as the VAT Directive) uses the concept of exemption with deduction (i.e., deduction of input credits) instead of zero-rating, although several member states use the term zero-rating in their VAT laws. The difference between "zero-rating" and "exemption with deduction" is just a matter of terminology.

D. Alteration of Base by Granting or Denying Credits

The tax base of a credit-invoice VAT or a credit-subtraction VAT without invoices (the Japanese CT) can be altered by granting extra input credits or denying otherwise available credits to promote some social, economic, or other nonrevenue goal. Existing VAT systems make only limited use of this device to alter the VAT base.

The VAT Directive provides that a member country may disallow otherwise allowable input credits on purchases for luxuries, amusement, or entertainment.[66] The Japanese CT, on the other hand, grants more input credit than can be accounted for (or was paid) with respect to some pur-

earlier-stage exemption. On balance, this failure to regain the revenue, equal to the tax rate times the value added by the exempt firm, seems less serious than the injustices that can occur under the tax-credit system. Apart from adding administrative complications, an exemption at any point along the cycle (except at the very beginning or at the ultimate stage) normally results in a break in the tax-credit chain, leading to an element of double taxation." C. S. Shoup, "General Sales Taxes: Retail Sales Tax, Value Added Tax," in PUBLIC FINANCE, 259–260 [hereinafter Shoup, General Sales Taxes, Retail Sales Tax, Value Added Tax].

[66] VAT Directive, *supra* note 28, at Art. 170. The disallowance of the input credits has the effect of taxing these expenditures as final consumption by those business firms (or the employees or customers who enjoy these purchases), but the tax-inclusive cost of these purchases will be included in the firm's pricing of its taxable output. The result is, of course, additional tax borne by the firm's customers.

chases. For example, the CT allows taxable businesses to claim input credit imputed from the full cost of purchases from exempt small businesses.

E. Multiple Rates

To achieve political or other nonrevenue goals, a nation may employ multiple VAT rates rather than grant exemption or zero-rating to particular categories of goods or services. A higher rate may be employed to discourage the consumption of particular goods (alcohol and tobacco) or to attempt to make the tax more progressive (luxuries). Many European countries impose lower positive rates on a variety of goods and services. For example, France imposes a lower 5.5 percent rate on chocolate.[67] The EU may make permanent a scheme under which a reduced VAT rate may be imposed by member states on some labor-intensive services. Argentina imposes a lower rate on the sale of camels and goats.[68]

> A tax credit method can be especially useful if it is desired to reduce the rate of the value-added tax at some stage in the productive and distributive process, say the raw materials or farm products stage, for administrative reasons, without reducing the total tax paid on total value added. The reduced tax at the earlier stage simply gives rise to an equally increased tax at a later stage. The determinative tax rate on the entire value of any commodity will be the tax rate applicable at the last stage, typically the retail stage. This result cannot be achieved under the addition or subtraction method.[69]

V. Discussion Questions

1. If the goal of a VAT is computational simplicity, which method of calculating tax liability (addition or one of the subtraction methods) is preferable for a consumption-type VAT?
2. Assuming the credit-subtraction method of calculating tax liability is used, is the GDP, income, or consumption VAT most compatible with the "simplified bookkeeping" used by some small firms? Why?
3. Is an income VAT using the addition method easier to administer than an income VAT using the sales-subtraction method?
4. If the tax base is to be measured by market sales transactions, rather than by the receipt of factor incomes or production during a given period, is a consumption-style VAT the logical choice?
5. If a firm builds a plant with its own labor force, how is the price (i.e., the value added) of this labor taken into account in the consumption-style VAT? In an income VAT? In a GDP VAT?

[67] See E. Cotessat, "Chocolate," 16 *Int'l VAT Monitor* 133 (March/April 2005).

[68] Law No. 25,951, effective Nov. 30, 2004, discussed in D. Calzetta, "VAT Rate on Camels and Goats," 16 *Int'l VAT Monitor* 37 (Jan./Feb. 2005).

[69] Shoup, General Sales Taxes, Retail Sales Tax, Value Added Tax, *supra* note 65, at 259–260 (footnotes omitted).

6. Under a single rate consumption-style VAT, which method of calculating tax liability is the best if a nation wants to exempt specific commodities, such as unprocessed food or medical drugs? Does the same reasoning apply if a higher rate is desired for luxury items?
7. What are the best ways to ease the compliance burden on farmers? On small retailers? On artisans who sell primarily to businesses?
8. How does zero rating differ from exemption? Is the concept of zero rating appropriate for any method of calculating tax liability other than the credit-invoice method? How would you describe the equivalent concept under the other methods, for example, the addition method?
9. Does adoption of the credit-subtraction method require the use of invoices for each transaction?
10. Reread footnote 65, an excerpt from Dr. Shoup's book on public finance. Do you agree with Dr. Shoup's last sentence in that footnote? Try to construct examples or point to examples in the reading. How does this analysis mesh with the effect of exemptions (especially the small business exemption) under the Japanese Consumption Tax?
11. A nation is considering the possible adoption of a national sales tax. Before it proposes specific legislation, it would like you to consider some of the basic issues that may affect the structure of the tax on consumption. The following are a few facts about the nation's economy and preliminary comments about the new tax.

    About 20,000 businesses account for about two-thirds of all production and distribution of goods and services in the country. There is a very large number of small retailers that sell goods and render services to final consumers. The remaining third is provided by more than 150,000 retailers and traders. Most of these, including street vendors and small shopkeepers, do not maintain detailed records of their operations.

    The strength of the nation's economy comes, in large part, from the export of both agricultural products and consumer goods. Its manufacturers also import significant amounts of raw materials and parts for goods that are consumed domestically and exported. The government wants the tax to be paid by consumers, but it is concerned about the effects that this new tax may have on the economy. The government also wants to encourage increased investment in new ventures and wants existing firms to modernize to remain competitive in the international markets.

    a. Should the government rely on a retail sales tax or a multistage VAT?
    b. Should the government adopt an origin or destination principle consumption tax?
    c. Politically, the government cannot set the tax rate above 5%. What difference does it make if it includes or excludes the new tax from the tax base?
    d. Should the government propose a gross national product, national income, or consumption-style tax?

12. Country X has a consumption-style, destination principle 10% European-style, credit-invoice method VAT levied on the tax-exclusive sales price of taxable goods and services and on imports. It provides a "small trader" exemption for businesses that have total taxable receipts less than $50,000 annually. In the current period, a distributor imports goods for $30,000 (before VAT) and pays $2,050 for services from a small trader exempt from VAT. This price includes $50 that the small trader paid in VAT on its purchases. The distributor sells to retailers all of its goods for $65,000 (before VAT). These retailers do not make any other purchases, and they sell these goods for $100,000 (before VAT). How much VAT does the government collect from the above transactions?
13. Nation A wants to provide special treatment for some suppliers of goods and services and for some specific goods and services. In the following statements, you should decide if the special treatment should take the form of zero-rating or exemption of the supplier and/or the particular goods and services.
    a. Nation A does not want to charge VAT on sales of goods or rendition of services by charities and units of government, but wants to deny them a refund for VAT paid on their purchases.
    b. Same as (a), except the charities and units of government shall obtain a refund for VAT paid on their purchases.
    c. Nation A does not want consumers who buy food at retail to bear any VAT on food.
    d. Nation A does not want to charge VAT on insurance premiums charged by insurance companies, but wants the insurance companies to bear VAT paid on their purchases.
14. Why do most nations that impose VAT zero-rate all exports of goods but zero-rate only limited categories of services?

3 Varieties of VAT in Use

I. Introduction

Several leading forms of VATs in OECD countries can be identified. This chapter describes the main VAT variants. The most influential is the harmonized VAT in the European Union (EU) member states. The EU model has the most extensive case law on VAT issues.

New Zealand departed from the EU model in a number of significant ways, including the expansion of the tax base for its Goods and Services Tax (GST) by limiting exemptions and zero-rating and by taxing many government services. South Africa modeled its VAT after the New Zealand GST but included some of its own unique features. For example, South Africa taxes all fee-based financial services. Australia's GST is also inspired by the New Zealand model, but there are significant departures.

Japan departed from the EU model by requiring registered firms to calculate periodic tax liability in a different fashion. Under the Japanese Consumption Tax (CT), taxable firms are not required to issue VAT invoices, which represent a central feature of other VAT regimes.

Canada has a national VAT (known as GST) and several provinces have harmonized VATs. The combined Quebec-national GSTs are administered by Quebec. The combined national and provincial HSTs (the Harmonized Sales Tax) are administered at the national level.

Non-OECD countries have been most influenced by the EU model, without adopting all its complexities. Many have adopted a simpler form of tax, involving only one rate and minimal exemptions. Several nonstandard features can also be found in various developing countries.

The VAT is called "value-added tax" in many countries, but other names are used as can be seen in the preceding discussion (for example, Goods and Services Tax or Consumption Tax). There is no particular policy significance to the differences in name, and we will refer generally to VAT to include all of these differently named VATs.

II. European Union: A Mature VAT Resistant to Change

A. VAT in the European Community

The EU's credit-invoice VAT is the most prevalent form of VAT in use today. The EU, formerly the European Economic Community, was created by the Treaty of Rome in 1957.[1] Article 93 of that treaty, as revised, requires the Council, "acting unanimously on a proposal from the Commission and after consulting the European Parliament and the Economic and Social Committee," to adopt provisions for the harmonization of turnover taxes within the Community.[2] Although there have been many attempts to change the rules governing approval of tax changes, tax directives still can be modified only with the unanimous consent of all member states. This unanimity requirement has stifled the modernization of the EU VAT.

As part of the Treaty of Rome, member states are required to harmonize their value added taxes, although rates among members can vary.[3] A convenient byproduct of this harmonization was the decision to use a portion of the VAT revenue to help finance Community operations.[4]

The VATs in place in member states define the jurisdictional reach of the tax on international transactions (outside the EU) under the destination principle. As a result, imports of goods from outside the Community are subject to VAT in the country of import. Exports to recipients outside the Community are zero-rated. The jurisdictional rules for transactions with

[1] The treaty establishing the European Economic Community (EEC) (later changed to the "European Community") was signed in Rome on March 25, 1957, and came into force on January 1, 1958. This treaty, commonly referred to as the Treaty of Rome, was revised many times, including the Treaty on European Union, signed in Maastricht on February 7, 1992, and entered into force on November 1, 1993, when the name was changed to the European Union. The Treaty of Amsterdam, signed on October 2, 1997, in force May 1, 1999, amended and renumbered the EU and EC treaties. The Treaty of Nice, entered into force on February 1, 2003, merged the Treaty of the European Union and the Treaty of the European Community. See http://europa.eu.int/abc/treaties_en.htm. See the consolidated version of the Treaty on European Union and the Treaty Establishing the European Community, 2002 (*Official Journal of the European Communities*, 2002/C 325/01) [hereinafter Treaty of Nice].

[2] *Id.*

[3] See Directive 2010/88EU, establishing a minimum standard rate of 15% until December 31, 2015. See also First VAT Directive of April 11, 1967 (67/227/EEC), requiring all member states to replace their indirect taxes with a common system of VAT.

[4] The VAT component is calculated by applying a rate (fluctuating between 1% and 1.4%) to an assessment basis that is capped at 50% of a member state's GDP. See Council Decision 70/243 of April 21, 1970, OJ1970, English Spec. Ed. (I), 224, discussed in P. Farmer & R. Lyal, *EC Tax Law* 87 (Clarendon Press 1994). See also B. Terra & P. Wattel, *European Tax Law* (2nd ed. Kluwer 1997). One proposal is to finance the EU with a 1% VAT imposed on a specified range of goods and services in all member countries. See Kirwin, "European Parliament, States Fail to Agree on Tax to Finance Budget," *BNA Daily Tax Report*, May 11, 2006, p. G-5.

individuals and businesses within the Community have been governed by a "transitional arrangement" that was to be replaced by 1997. The philosophy was to treat transactions across member states as transactions within a single country. The transitional arrangement is a hybrid origin-destination system. Sales to individuals resident in the Community generally are taxed in the country of sale (origin) regardless of the residence of the buyer.[5] Intra-Union business-to-business sales remain zero-rated, the same as sales outside the Community, at least until the transitional arrangement is completed. In 2010, the European Commission issued a Green Paper on "The future of VAT – Towards a simpler, more robust and efficient VAT system."[6] The EU agencies now recognize that the commitment to a "single market" that relies on the origin principle (the transitional system) is not politically achievable.[7] The Commission's view is the origin principle should be abandoned. The Council of the European Union invited the Commission to examine, with the member states, ways to implement the destination principle within the Union.[8] Consistent with the movement toward the destination principle, the EU is expanding the use of the "one stop shop" that currently provides that non-EU-based businesses supplying telecom, broadcasting, and e-services to consumers in the EU can register in only one EU member state and account for all supplies to consumers in the EU.[9]

The member states are required to harmonize their VATs in accordance with a series of VAT Directives issued by the Commission of the Community, most importantly the Sixth Directive. This, together with other directives, has now been consolidated into the "VAT Directive."[10] We will refer to the "VAT Directive" throughout the book, occasionally without detailed footnote citation (some of the cases will refer to the Sixth Directive, because they relate to a period before the VAT Directive replaced the Sixth Directive).

The influence of the VAT Directive extends beyond the EU. For example, the East European countries that recently became members or hope

[5] A resident of the Community that purchases goods in another member state generally is not subject to VAT on the purchases on his return home. There are exceptions covering (1) transport vehicles such as automobiles and (2) mail order sales within the Community. See http://www.eurunion.org/legislat/VATweb.htm.

[6] COM(2010) 695, Commission Staff Working Document, SEC (2010) 1455, 1.12.2010.

[7] See Communication from the Commission to the European Parliament, the Council, and the European Economic and Social Committee on the future of VAT towards a simpler, more robust and efficient VAT system tailored to the single market, 4.1, COM (2011) 851 final, Brussels, 6.12.2011

[8] The Commission has identified five options to implement the destination principle, promising further studies and proposals. See http://ec.europa.eu/taxation_customs/taxation/vat/future_vat/index_en.htm (Brussels, 30 October 2014).

[9] See the European Commission Press Release, Future VAT system: pro-business, pro-growth, IP/11/1508. On the registration of non-EU businesses, see Chapter 4.

[10] Council Directive 2006/112/EC of 28 November 2006 on the common system of value added tax, Official Journal No. L347/1 of 11.12.2006 [the VAT Directive]

to become part of the EU adopted the VAT Directive concepts in their VAT systems.[11]

Member states must adopt national legislation to implement the VAT directives. The directives bind "the Member States to achieve specific goals, leaving it up to the states to choose the form and the means for achieving them in national law."[12] The national courts interpret these national statutes in conformity with the VAT directives.[13] National VAT laws can be challenged if they are inconsistent with the Community directives. A national judge can refer a case involving the interpretation of a VAT Directive to the European Court of Justice (ECJ).[14] For example, a British court (such as a VAT Tribunal) may refer a VAT question to the ECJ to resolve an issue under the VAT Directive or a possible conflict between domestic law and the VAT Directive. Subject to some conditions, the Community action can take priority over the law of member states.[15] A VAT decision by the ECJ is binding on national courts of the member states. The following case illustrates the interplay between domestic VAT law and the VAT Directive.

W. G. Haydon-Baillie v. Commissioners of Customs and Excise[16]

The taxpayer, registered for VAT as a consultant, engaged as a sideline in the acquisition and restoration of a small number of ex-naval patrol boats of the 'Vosper Brave' class. He did this because they were a superb example of marine engineering and an important part of the British heritage. He sank some £750,000 into the work. He claimed that those costs should be treated as input tax and therefore VAT-deductible.

DECISION. This is the appeal of Mr. Wensley Grosvenor Haydon-Baillie against decisions of the Commissioners of Customs and Excise covering 1 July 1980 to 31 March 1984. The Commissioners claimed that the taxpayer was not entitled to credit for input tax because the relevant goods or services were not 'used or to be used for the purpose of any business carried on or to be carried on by him' within the meaning of the Value Added Tax Act 1983, section 14(3). The taxpayer

11 See Z. Kronbergs, "Survey of Latvia's VAT Legislation," 6 *Int'l VAT Monitor* 350 (Nov./Dec. 1995).

12 P. Mastrapasqua, "Current Status in Italy of EC Directives Regarding Taxation," 26 *Intertax* 413 (1998) [hereinafter Mastrapasque].

13 On the EU legal system, see A. J. Easson, *Taxation in the European Community* 89–95 (Athlone Press 1993).

14 *Id.* at 90.

15 The legal basis for this priority is in the Treaty establishing the European Community, Art. 5, ¶ 2; and Treaty on European Union, preamble, 12th recital and Art. 2, 2d paragraph. See note 1.

16 1986 VATTR 79 (United Kingdom) [edited by the authors].

claims that he is entitled to input credits under the test contained in Article 17 of the Sixth EEC Directive.

The taxpayer referred to the Value Added Tax Act 1983, section 14(3), and to the Sixth Council Directive of 17 May 1977, Title IV Article 4(1) and (2) and Title XI Article 17(1). The taxpayer's representative also referred the Value Added Tax Act 1983, section 47(1), which states:

> 'In this Act "business" includes any trade, profession or vocation.'
>
> He contends, and we accept, that 'business' has a wider connotation than trade, profession or vocation and that an activity may be a 'business' even though it would not for income tax purposes constitute a 'trade'. He contends that the future use of the craft for exhibition purposes and for chartering etc. will constitute the carrying on of a business by the appellant. He further makes the point that the preparation of the craft, from the period when it was acquired until the time when it will be ready for use, a period which includes the employment of many people for restoration, the sale of the engines from the boat, and the accumulation and in many cases the sale of spares and equipment, also constitute the carrying on of a business.
>
> [The Sixth Directive provides for deductions for input tax. ... The] taxpayer claims that he meets the Sixth Council Directive's description [in Article 4] of 'any person who independently carries on in any place any economic activity specified in paragraph 2 whatever the purpose or results of that activity', bearing in mind that paragraph 2 states that 'the economic activities referred to in paragraph 1 shall comprise all activities of producers, traders and persons supplying services. ... The exploitation of tangible or intangible property for the purpose of obtaining income therefrom on a continuing basis shall also be considered an economic activity.'

The Commissioners submit that the taxpayer had not demonstrated that his future 'museum' activities constituted a 'business' within the meaning of the Value Added Tax Act 1983, section 14(4). Those activities would be no more than a pleasant hobby. Alternatively any intention to turn the craft to pecuniary account in future is at present too vague to satisfy the words in section 14(4) 'business ... to be carried on.' The present activities should not be considered separately; they were merely preparatory to the future, non-business, activity. As respects the Sixth Directive, it is, in the present respect at least, superseded by the Value Added Tax Act 1983. This case depends on the meaning of section 14(4).

We deal first with the Sixth Council Directive. We have considered the decision of the Court of Justice of the European Communities in

Rompelman v. Minister Van Financien.[17] All that *Rompelman* really shows, in our view, is that a present input for a future economic activity may be a proper input. It leaves open the question whether the appellant's activities present or future are truly 'economic activities'.

Generally, had we to decide this matter by reference to the Sixth Directive and not to the Value Added Tax Act 1983, we should reach the same conclusion that we do reach by reference to the Value Added Tax Act 1983. However, we accept that the Sixth Directive was binding upon the United Kingdom legislature, who complied with it by making extensive amendments that are now incorporated in the consolidating statute, the Value Added Tax Act 1983. Consequently in our view, there is no further room for reliance on the Sixth Directive. The statute supersedes it.

[The Tribunal went on to consider whether the taxpayer's activities with respect to the restoration action was a business for purposes of the Value Added Tax Act 1983].

The work of restoration in itself is, we find, aimed at covering financial outgoings by receipts, so far as practical; and once restoration is complete, the uses to which the craft is likely to be put clearly differentiate it in character from a pleasure craft. This is a business, irrespective of whether the appellant hopes to, or eventually does, make an overall profit in income tax terms. The present activities constitute a business carried on by the appellant; and if we were wrong in that conclusion, we would nevertheless hold that the purpose of the present activities is to provide in the future a restored craft, which will then be the subject matter of a business 'to be carried on by' the taxpayer.

Held that since the relevant rule in the Value Added Tax Act 1983 [the VAT in the United Kingdom] echoed the intent of the Sixth VAT Directive there was no need to pay any further attention to the directive and the case should be decided on a construction of the English statute following English precedents, *that* the taxpayer's intention was to cover his financial outgoings by receipts from hiring out, exhibitions etc. *and that* this constituted a business under section 14 of the Act. Therefore the expenses were deductible as VAT input.

We therefore allow the appeal.

B. European Court of Justice

The European Commission (EC) or a member state may bring to the ECJ a claim "that a Member State has failed to fulfill an obligation under" the Treaty.[18] If a national court hearing a tax dispute involving EU legislation

[17] See Chapter 4 (IV)(C).

[18] Treaty of Nice, *supra* note 1, at Arts. 226 and 227.

(Community law) is not certain about the interpretation or validity of the Community law, the court may refer the issue to the ECJ.[19]

Most VAT cases come to the ECJ as a request for a preliminary ruling under Article 234 of the Treaty.[20] "The Court is not qualified to interpret domestic law."[21]

Advocates-general prepare nonbinding "opinions"[22] on cases brought before the ECJ and present them "with complete impartiality and independence."[23] The ECJ may sit to hear a case in a panel ranging from three to four, in a Grand Chamber, or the full court.[24]

The court issues "judgments" decided by a majority of the panel, with no dissenting opinions. Once the ECJ rules on the meaning of a word or term in the Sixth Directive, the national court decides the individual cases applying the ruling of the ECJ.[25]

C. Application of the EU VAT Directive

The Council of the European Union (the "Council") issues directives (tax directives must be approved by all member states). The directives usually require implementing legislation in the member states, although in some cases they may become directly effective.[26] There have been many directives dealing with VAT. The most significant was the Sixth Directive, orig-

[19] See *id.* at Arts. 220–245. The Court of First Instance was created in 1989 under the Single European Act to handle certain cases that are within the province of the ECJ *(id.* at Art. 225a of the Treaty of Nice).

[20] The ECJ has jurisdiction to give preliminary rulings on "(a) the interpretation of this Treaty; (b) the validity and interpretation of acts of the institutions of the Community and of the ECB; (c) the interpretation of the statutes of bodies established by an act of the Council, where those statutes so provide." *Id.* at Art. 234. The national court may bring the matter to the ECJ "if it considers that a decision on the question is necessary to enable it to give judgment" or where a question that the court can address by a preliminary ruling is raised in a court or tribunal of a member state and "there is no judicial remedy under national law" against a decision by that national court or tribunal. *Id.*

[21] Mastrapasque, *supra* note 12, at 414.

[22] Advocate-general "opinions" are published separately and may be incorporated as part of the court's "judgment." According to Art. 222 of the Treaty of Nice (see Treaty of Nice, *supra* note 1), the advocate-general shall "make, in open court, reasoned submissions on cases which, in accordance with the Statute of the Court of Justice, require his involvement."

[23] *Id.* See http://europa.eu.int/institutions/court/index_en.htm.

[24] The size of the panels may change as a result of the admission of ten new members. For example, until the change, the Grand Chamber consisted of thirteen judges, and the full court consisted of fifteen judges.

[25] See Case C-320/88, *Staatssecretaris van Financien v. Shipping and Forwarding Enterprise Safe BV* (Judgment of the ECJ 1990).

[26] A directive may be directly effective if the directive is unconditional or a member failed to comply with the implementation deadline, and other conditions are satisfied. *Id.* at 414.

inally issued in 1977.[27] The directives pertaining to VAT were consolidated into the "VAT Directive" in 2006.[28]

Despite the mandate from the EU to harmonize the rules regarding VAT, the VAT rules of the member states diverge on a number of topics. As a result, the EC has issued regulations to implement measures relating to the interpretation of some aspects of VAT, such as the place of a supply of services, the rules relating to invoices, and the definition of electronically supplied services.[29] They are designed to bring more consistency in the areas covered.

III. Japanese Consumption Tax

A. Credit-Subtraction VAT Without Invoices

Japan's first experience with VAT was unique. The Japanese Diet enacted a VAT in 1950 but deferred the effective date and modified its terms. In 1953, the Diet again modified it.[30] In 1954, the Diet repealed the VAT before it ever became effective. The VAT enacted in 1950 calculated tax liability under the sales-subtraction method.

In the 1980s, succeeding governments unsuccessfully tried to enact a VAT. A VAT (the Consumption Tax [CT]) ultimately was adopted in December 1988, effective April 1, 1989.[31] To accommodate political opposition from small businesses and others, the CT included an atypical method of calculating periodic tax liability. The CT did not require CT-registered firms to issue VAT invoices of the kind relied on in other VAT countries for the tax authorities to verify output tax to registered sellers and input credit to registered purchasers.

Although the CT was enacted as a tax-against-a-tax credit-subtraction VAT, the data for output tax and input credits is taken from accounting records for each tax period rather than from VAT invoices. The calculation of output tax liability mirrors the EU-style VAT. A registered seller multiplies taxable sales by the CT rate to arrive at output tax liability. If the taxable sales are recorded at CT-inclusive prices, the seller first calculates the CT-exclusive prices by multiplying CT-inclusive prices by the tax fraction. The tax fraction is the tax rate (originally 3% and now 8%) divided by

27 Sixth Council Directive 77/388/EEC of 17 May 1977 on the harmonization of the laws of the member states relating to turnover taxes, Common system of value added tax: uniform basis of assessment (OJ 1977 L145), 1.

28 Note 10 *supra*.

29 See, for example on a variety of issues, Council Implementing Regulation (EU) No. 282/2011 of March 15, 2011, laying down implementing measures for Directive 2006/112/EC on the common system of value added tax, vol. 54 L77, March 23, 2011.

30 This tax was recommended by the Shoup Mission after World War II as a revenue source for the subnational prefectures. See A. Schenk, "Japanese Consumption Tax: The Japanese Brand VAT," 42 *Tax Notes* 1625 (Mar. 27, 1989); C. K. SULLIVAN, THE TAX ON VALUE ADDED 134–139 (Columbia Univ. Press 1965).

31 Law No. 108, part IV (1988) (Shohizei-ho).

100 + the tax rate. For example, if CT-inclusive taxable sales are ¥1,080,000 and the tax rate is 8%, the CT-exclusive taxable sales are ¥1,000,000. The seller multiplies this amount by the 8% rate to arrive at ¥80,000 output tax liability. The rate is scheduled to increase to 10% in 2015.

The CT departs from the EU model VAT in calculating input credits. Data on taxable purchases are taken from the firm's purchase records. Assume the CT-inclusive cost of purchases qualifying for the credit is ¥648,000. The allowable input credit is ¥48,000 (648,000 × the tax fraction 8/108).

The Japanese CT departs from the European model in another way. To prevent discrimination against unregistered small businesses, registered sellers may claim input credits for CT on purchases of taxable goods and services, whether acquired from registered or unregistered suppliers. Input credit therefore is denied only for CT on purchases that are exempt from tax, such as postage stamps and certain medical services.[32]

Japan has special schemes for smaller businesses to calculate periodic CT liability. They will be discussed later in this book.[33]

Japan segregates one percentage point of its CT as prefecture (subnational) revenue. Under a revenue-sharing arrangement, the prefectures also receive a portion of the national government's CT revenue.[34]

B. Movement Toward Invoice-Method VAT

As the Japanese CT matured, the government increased the substantiation requirements for registered firms to claim input credits. Although formally a registered seller is not required to issue a VAT invoice (central to the EU-style credit-invoice VAT), as a practical matter, registered sellers are required to retain documentation to substantiate their claims for input credits, such as bills, receipts, statements of delivery, or other kinds of invoices that show the details of the transaction.[35] This documentation requirement allows the tax authority to deny credits if the taxpayer lacks adequate documentation, similar to the denial of credits without required VAT invoices under the European-style, credit-invoice VATs.

IV. New Zealand Goods and Services Tax

New Zealand's Goods and Services Tax (a VAT) was adopted on December 3, 1985, and became effective on October 1, 1986. The New Zealand GST has four features that distinguish it from earlier VATs, especially the EU VAT:

[32] *Id.* at §6.
[33] See Chapter 6 (VII).
[34] Schenk, "Japanese Consumption Tax after Six Years: A Unique VAT Matures," 69 *Tax Notes* 899, 911 (Nov. 13, 1995).
[35] *Id.* at 906.

1. The GST has a broader tax base with fewer categories of goods and services exempt from tax.
2. The GST is imposed on a broad category of services rendered by units of government.
3. The GST is imposed on casualty and other non-life insurance.
4. The jurisdiction to tax is based on the residence of the supplier, not the location of the supply.

Each of these features is discussed in this section.

A. Broad Tax Base

New Zealand exempts only limited categories of goods and services. It exempts financial services, the rental and some sales of a residential dwelling, fine metal, certain fringe benefits, and supplies of donated goods and services by a nonprofit body.[36] Absent from the list of exempt items are goods and services commonly viewed as necessities and exempt elsewhere, such as food, medical care, and education.

B. Taxation of Government Services

New Zealand indirectly taxes many services rendered by local units of government (local authorities). A local authority is deemed to make a taxable supply of goods and services to a person for consideration equal to rates (property taxes) the person pays to the local authority.[37] Many other charges the government imposes, such as road user charges, are specifically taxed under the GST.[38] There is increased interest in the appropriate taxation of government appropriations. Is the recipient of a government appropriation (whether another unit of government or a charity or business) making a supply to the government on receipt of an appropriation?[39]

C. Taxation of Casualty and Other Nonlife Insurance

Under current law, New Zealand imposes GST on premiums charged by providers of casualty and other nonlife insurance.[40] In addition to input

[36] See New Zealand Goods and Services Tax Act 1985, No. 141 [hereinafter NZ GST], §§14(1) and 21(I)(2).

[37] *Id.* at §5(7)(a). The same rule applies to council dues payable to the Chatham Islands Council. *Id* at §5(7)(b).

[38] *Id.* at §5(6)-(6E).

[39] For a discussion of this issue, see P. Pyanic and A. Fife, "GST Treatment of Appropriations – Where Are We Now and Is the Nature of the Payment Relevant?," 9 *Australian GST Journal* 105 (Oct. 2009).

[40] Premiums on life insurance contracts or reinsurance of life contracts are exempt financial services under §3. Other insurance is taxable under the definition of insurance under §2(1) that defines insurance as insurance that is not exempt under §3. Insurance is defined as "insurance or guarantee against loss, damage, injury, or risk of any kind

credits for GST on business inputs, these providers can claim input credits for the GST component in claims paid. Registered businesses that purchase taxable insurance contracts can claim credit for GST paid on the insurance premiums. If an insured business receives payment on an insurance claim, the claim received is treated as consideration for a supply of services.[41]

D. Global Reach of the New Zealand GST

Most countries impose VAT only on imports into the country and domestic sales within the country. These "territorial" countries have place of supply (or location) rules to determine whether a supply falls within the scope of the tax. If a supply takes place outside the country (such as a sale of goods physically located outside the country to be delivered outside the country), the supply is not subject to tax. It is the place where the supply occurs, not the "residence" of the supplier, that determines whether a supply comes within the scope of the tax. In these countries, foreign sales are beyond the scope of the tax. To relieve exports of tax, exports are treated as supplied within the taxing jurisdiction and are then zero-rated. Although the place of supply rules are relatively clear with respect to tangible goods, they are complex with respect to services.[42] It therefore is quite easy for a business to negotiate a contract for services to "place" the services outside a country and beyond the reach of the VAT.

New Zealand has different rules defining the scope of the tax. New Zealand imposes GST based on the residence of the supplier, not the place where the supply takes place. In theory, a supplier resident in New Zealand is subject to GST on its worldwide supplies.[43] The Act, however, narrows the scope of the tax considerably. The GST is imposed on a supply *in New Zealand* by a registered person in the course or furtherance of a taxable activity conducted by that person.[44] Goods and services are deemed supplied *in New Zealand* if the supplier is resident in New Zealand and are deemed supplied outside New Zealand if the supplier is not resident in New Zealand.[45] There are special rules treating certain supplies by nonresidents as supplied in New Zealand and treating certain supplies by nonresidents to registered persons (otherwise treated as supplied in NZ) as supplied outside New Zealand.[46] Certain exports of goods are zero-rated,

whatever, whether pursuant to any contract or any enactment; and includes reinsurance." See NZ GST, *supra* note 36.

[41] See generally *id.* at §5(13).

[42] See discussion in Chapter 7 (V and VI).

[43] There is some controversy as to whether New Zealand (and a few other countries, such as South Africa), in structure, have worldwide VAT systems. See, for example, R. Millar, "Cross-border Services," in *VAT in Africa* (R. Krever, ed., Pretoria University Law Press, 2008).

[44] NZ GST, *supra* note 36, at §8(1).

[45] *Id.* at §8(2).

[46] *Id.* at §8(3) and (4). A supplier may elect not to have the §8(4) rules apply.

even when made by residents. The New Zealand GST includes place of supply rules governing certain transactions. For example, there are special rules governing supplies of telecommunication services.

V. African Experience Expanding Base to Tax Financial Services

The South African VAT was modeled in part on that of New Zealand. South Africa adopted the New Zealand approach of taxing many government services. If a local authority imposes charges for electricity, gas, water, sewerage, and a few others, then the charges are subject to VAT. If the local authority does not charge for these services, then the rates on real property are taxable.[47]

South Africa expanded its VAT base beyond the New Zealand GST's broad base by taxing many financial services commonly exempt under most other VATs. South Africa taxes all fee-based financial services other than those services zero-rated as exports. Financial intermediation services for which there are no specific charges remain exempt from tax. In consultation with the banking industry, the South African Revenue Service developed a list of all banking services and classified them for VAT purposes as taxable, exempt, or zero-rated. This experimental system seems to be working well. Namibia and Botswana, South Africa's neighbors, adopted the South African approach that taxes fee-based financial services.[48]

[47] Value-Added Tax Act No. 89 of 1991, §10(15) (Republic of South Africa). Levies imposed by regional services councils, joint services boards, and transitional metropolitan councils are taxable. *Id.* at 8(6)(b) and 10(15), discussed in C. Beneke, ed., *Deloitte & Touche VAT Handbook* 55–57 (6th ed., Butterworth 2003).

[48] In recent years, Singapore and Australia adopted rules permitting financial institutions to recover some VAT on business inputs attributable to otherwise exempt intermediation services. These approaches are discussed in Chapter 11.

4 Registration, Taxpayer, and Taxable Activity

I. Introduction

Most VAT regimes require registered (or taxable) persons to file returns and remit tax. In most cases, a firm is required to register if it makes or expects to make at least the statutory minimum level of annual taxable sales in connection with its business or economic activity.

Not all sales by a person come within the scope of a VAT. For example, in most countries, an individual's casual sales do not constitute taxable business activity and are not taxed. Hobbies and similar activities that do not rise to the level of a "business" generally are not taxed. An employee could be treated as a person rendering taxable services to her employer and therefore a VAT taxpayer, but no country has done this.[1] This chapter discusses registration (including some required registration by nonresidents), who is liable for tax, and what economic activity subjects a seller to tax under various VAT regimes.

II. Registration

A. In General

Registration is part of a self-assessment VAT system that typically is reinforced with harsh civil and criminal penalties for noncompliance. Many VAT systems define a taxable person subject to the VAT rules as a person who is registered (a registrant) or is required to register. Nonresidents without a fixed location in the country may be subject to a different set of rules. The registration requirement generally is imposed on a person or firm that makes at least a threshold amount of taxable sales. The govern-

[1] The flat tax proposed, but not enacted, in the United States requires employees to file returns and pay tax on their wages and allows employers a flat tax deduction for the compensation paid to employees. See the Shelby Bill, S.1040, Tax Simplification Act of 2003, 108th Cong., 1st Sess. (May 12, 2003), and a fuller discussion in ch. 14 of Alan Schenk and Oliver Oldman, *Value Added Tax: A Comparative Approach* (CUP 2007).

ment may maintain a list of registered persons. The requirement to file returns is imposed only on those who must register.

An alternative, designed to provide the government with information on all firms engaged in business activity, is to require all businesses to register and to permit small firms with sales below a threshold amount to affirmatively request exemption from registration. This system does not by itself assure the tax authority that it has a record of all potential taxpayers and imposes substantial costs both on the requesting small business and on the government that must process these requests for exemption. For these reasons, this alternative generally has not been adopted.

B. Mandatory Registration

1. General Rules

Most VAT systems require persons engaged in regular business activity to register if their taxable sales in a given period (usually a year) exceed a threshold level.[2] The calculation of total taxable sales generally is on the basis of the value of sales determined under the nation's valuation rules for VAT purposes.[3] Businesses with low turnover may temporarily have taxable sales above the threshold as a result of sales out of the ordinary course of business. For example, a business may replace its worn out equipment or may sell in bulk some inventory as part of a program to terminate a product line. Such sales might be ignored in determining whether the business has taxable sales above the threshold.[4] Commentators have suggested that the threshold required for registration be based on the "value added" by the business (sales less defined purchases) rather than gross turnover.[5]

[2] Commonwealth of New Vatopia Value Added Tax Act, prepared by Alan Schenk, relying on his experience serving as technical advisor for the International Monetary Fund Legal Department, available at http://www.imf.org/external/np/leg. Go to Tax Law Drafting Samples: VAT [hereinafter New Vatopia VAT], §20. Canadian Goods and Services Tax, Part IX of the Excise Tax Act, An Act to Amend the Excise Tax Act, the Criminal Code, the Customs Act, the Customs Tariff, the Excise Act, the Income Tax Act, the Statistics Act and the Tax Court of Canada Act [hereinafter Canadian GST], §240(1). The Canadian GST is reproduced (with annotations) in D. M. Sherman, *The Practitioner's Goods and Services Tax Annotated, with Harmonized Sales Tax (HST)* (13th ed. 2003). See also *CCH Canadian Goods & Services Tax Reporter* (2004). There is no specific penalty for failure to register, but this violation is covered by §329(2), which includes the offence for failure to comply with any provision of the GST (such as §240) for which no other penalty is provided.

[3] New Vatopia VAT, *supra* note 2, at §11(3). The Vatopia valuation rules are covered in §16.

[4] See, for example, Value Added Tax Act, No. 1 of 2001 [hereinafter Botswana VAT], §16(3) (Botswana).

[5] See W. Turnier, "Accommodating to the Small Business Under a VAT," 47 *Tax Law* 963, 969 (1994) [hereinafter Turnier, Accommodating the Small Business], suggesting value added as a standard instead of sales turnover. New Vatopia VAT, *supra* note 2, §20(5).

Benefits as well as some VAT obligations may be limited to registered persons. For example, registered persons generally are entitled to recover VAT paid on business inputs (input tax credits) used in making taxable sales, and registered persons with excess input credits obtain refunds of the excess credits. The level of taxable sales may be calculated by looking back or looking forward, such as the past or the following future twelve months. To prevent a person from dividing up a single business into small parts to fall below the threshold required for registration, the VAT legislation may authorize the tax authority to aggregate sales by businesses owned by related persons.[6]

Failure to register and collect tax from customers does not relieve a person of the obligations to collect and remit tax. In fact, the tax authority may unilaterally register persons who fail to register.[7] Likewise, under some VAT regimes, the VAT authorities may refuse to register an applicant if the authorities determine that the person does not meet the registration requirements or, for persons who register voluntarily, if the authorities determine that the applicant will not maintain adequate records or comply with other obligations imposed on registered persons.[8]

Registered persons may be required to publicly post their certificates of registration in locations where they make taxable sales.[9] To reduce the opportunity for VAT fraud, including unwarranted use of certificates of registration, registered persons generally must notify the VAT authorities of any change in the name, location, or nature of the business activities they conduct.

2. Promoters of Public Entertainment

Music concerts and isolated athletic events such as boxing matches, circuses, and other shows to which the public is invited may be promoted by a sponsor operating within the country or by a nonresident who comes into the country for a single show or event. Unless the person regularly promotes events within the country, it may be extremely difficult for the tax authorities to locate the promoter and collect VAT chargeable on the sale of tickets for the event. Even if the promoter is a nonresident who promotes only one event in a twelve-month period, the grant of a small business exemption for this promoter may raise significant competitive inequities.

Some countries address this problem by requiring all promoters of public entertainment to register for VAT before they start selling tickets to an event, even if they do not expect to make annual taxable sales above the

6 See the discussion in Subsection (C)(3) on splitting a business and the related party rules.

7 See Grenada Value Added Tax Act, 2009, Act. No. 23 of 2009 [hereinafter Grenada VAT], §14(3). See also, New Vatopia VAT, appendix B, at §21(4).

8 Grenada VAT, *supra* note 7, at §13(2), *supra* note 2.

9 See *id.* at §14(11).

small business exemption threshold. To avoid unfair competition and to prevent tax avoidance by nonresidents who make taxable sales while in a country for a short time, Canada requires nonresidents to register before selling tickets to such events.[10] Canada imposes another obligation on these nonresidents to safeguard the revenue: a nonresident who is registered or required to register and who does not have a permanent establishment in Canada must provide adequate security for its tax liability.[11] Barbados has a strict rule on remittance of tax before the event. Before the scheduled event in Barbados, the promoter must remit 5% (the regular VAT rate is 15%) of the value of tickets printed for the event.[12] If tickets have not been printed, the promoter must remit an amount determined by the comptroller.[13]

3. Registration Regardless of Turnover

More generally, to prevent unfair competition or for other reasons, a nation with a small business exemption may require some sellers with low turnover to register. For example, in some countries, the state, state agencies, and local units of government are exempt from registration, regardless of turnover.[14] In other countries, the opposite is true. They must register if they conduct certain activities (typically in competition with the private sector) even if their taxable turnover is below the threshold.[15] Some countries require auctioneers to register regardless of taxable turnover.[16]

C. Registration Threshold and the Small Business Exemption

1. In General

A VAT could be imposed on all persons making sales of taxable goods and services, regardless of the dollar volume of sales. This definition of a person required to collect and remit tax would catch every casual sale by a consumer and all sales by street vendors and other occasional sellers.

10 This includes a place of amusement, a seminar, an activity, or an event. Canadian GST, *supra* note 2, at §240(2).

11 Canadian GST, *supra* note 2, at §240(6). The security must be provided in the amount and form acceptable to the minister. *Id.*

12 The Value Added Tax Act, Cap. 87, 1996, §34(8) (Barbados).

13 *Id.*

14 See A New Tax System (Goods and Services tax) Act 1999 [hereinafter Australian GST], §§149–10.

15 The United Kingdom subjects the state to VAT and local authorities making taxable sales must register, regardless of taxable turnover. Value Added Tax Act 1994, §§41(1) and 42 (United Kingdom). See also New Vatopia VAT, *supra* note 2, at §20(6).

16 See Canadian GST, *supra* note 2, at §177(1.2). See also New Vatopia VAT, *supra* note 2, at §§20(7) and 86(7).

Such a broad definition that caught sales of used toys to a neighbor or sales of used clothing at a lawn sale would impose an undue burden on both casual sellers and the government and would not raise any significant net revenue. "The quantum of business activity therefore is used in most countries to define the persons or entities that are subject to VAT."[17]

Countries typically include special VAT rules for small businesses. Certain small businesses may not be required to register and pay VAT, may be eligible for reduced tax liability, may be entitled to use simplified procedures to calculate tax liability, or may be subject to reduced record keeping requirements.[18]

Some countries reduce the compliance burden on small businesses by lengthening the accounting period (reducing the number of returns required each year) or permitting them to report on the cash or payments basis of accounting).[19] Others impose a turnover tax (at a rate lower than the standard rate but without any input credits to the supplier or purchaser) on very small businesses.[20]

Businesses exempt from tax on sales because of their low taxable turnover may be given the option to register and be taxable on their taxable sales. Most small businesses making domestic retail sales to consumers may still choose to remain exempt.

> Opting for registration may be a more rational choice for traders who contribute a smaller proportion of value-added to their supplies and either supply to registered traders, [export goods, or sell other zero-rated or lower-rated goods or services]. ... Registration effectively allows the supplier to pass on the value-added tax without an increase in the cost to the registered customer (who gets a credit for the tax charged and invoiced). In the case of zero-rated goods, the trader will, by registering, be able to obtain refunds of any tax paid on purchases.[21]

17 O. Oldman and A. Schenk, "The Business Activities Tax, Have Senators Danforth and Boren Created a Better Value Added Tax?," 65 *Tax Notes* 1547, at 1556 (1994).

18 Professor Turnier suggests five ways to accommodate small businesses. "First, small businesses either can be exempted or can be subject to taxation under special schemes. Second, the government may tax small businesses but may allow them to retain a percentage of the tax collected to compensate them for their substantially higher compliance costs. Third, rather than requiring small businesses to account for taxes under a variation of the accrual method typically used to calculate VAT liability, they can be allowed to employ the cash method. Fourth, one need not assign to the invoice the same critical weight that it has for larger taxpayers. Last, instead of requiring frequent periodic reporting of taxes (e.g., quarterly or bimonthly, small businesses can be permitted to report their taxes annually, with periodic payment of estimated taxes." Turnier, Accommodating the Small Business, *supra* note 5, at 963, 969.

19 See "Treatment of Small Businesses under VAT Systems," in CONSUMPTION TAX TRENDS 44 (OECD 1995) [hereinafter OECD].

20 For example, the People's Republic of China. See Chapter 14.

21 OECD, *supra* note 19, at 44.

It has been reported that some smaller firms register because they are embarrassed to admit to their customers (by not posting a certificate of registration) that their sales are below the registration threshold.

Small business exemption thresholds for resident businesses vary greatly.[22] The following is merely representative of the recent range. These thresholds tend to change frequently, especially outside the EU.[23] The basic range in Europe, expressed in Euros, is from no threshold in Spain to EUR 95,700 in the United Kingdom.[24] New Zealand's threshold is NZ$60,000 (US$25,300).[25] At the high end, Japan, for example, grants exemption for businesses with annual sales of ¥10 million (just over US$100,000[26]) and Singapore's threshold is $1 million (about US$800,000).[27] Some countries have different registration thresholds for different kinds of businesses.[28]

Smaller firms tend to be less efficient than their larger competitors. A high threshold may offer an undesirable subsidy and create some competitive inequities.[29] If the exemption extends to retailers, they "may obtain a competitive advantage over their taxable counterparts by selling at a lower tax-inclusive price to consumers who cannot claim input credits for the VAT element in their purchases."[30]

[22] For an analysis of the VAT registration thresholds in Europe, see F. Annacondia & W. van der Corput, "VAT Registration Thresholds in Europe," 2012 *International VAT Monitor* 422 (Nov./Dec. 2012). For thresholds in OECD countries, see *OECD CONSUMPTION TAX TRENDS: VAT/GST AND EXCISE RATES, TRENDS AND ADMINISTRATION ISSUES* (2004 ed., Table 3.6) (OECD 2005).

[23] Even in the EU, Belgium received authorization to increase its registration threshold from EUR5,580 to EUR25,000. COM (2012) 654 final of November 14, 2012.

[24] Annacondia and van der Corput, "VAT Registration Thresholds in Europe," 23 *International VAT Monitor* 422–425 (Nov./Dec. 2012). The *International VAT Monitor* publishes this data annually.

[25] See http://www.ird.gov.nz/yoursituation-bus/starting/registrations/starting-registeringfor gst.html (April 2013). The exchange rate on the New Zealand dollar was about $1.19 to the U.S. dollar in April 2013. See *New York Times*, April 6, 2013, p. B7.

[26] The turnover threshold was reduced from ¥30 to ¥10 million, effective April 1, 2003. See 14 *International VAT Monitor* 50 (Jan./Feb. 2003). That threshold remains. See http://www.nta.go.jp/tetsuzuki/shinkoku/shohi/otherinfo.htm. In April 2013, the exchange rate on Japanese yen was about 99 to the U.S. dollar. See *New York Times*, April 9, 2013, p. B9.In the Business Activities Tax proposed in the United States, the small business exemption applies to businesses with annual gross receipts of $100,000 or less. The Comprehensive Tax Restructuring and Simplification Act of 1994, 140 Cong. Rec. S. 6527, adding ch. 100 of new Subtitle K to the Internal Revenue Code of 1986, §10042(a),(d).

[27] See http://www.iras.gov.sg/irasHome/page04_ektd2546.aspx (April 2013); *New York Times*, April 9, 2013, p. B9.

[28] To prevent unfair competition between registered and unregistered taxi owners, Canada and Australia require all persons who conduct a taxi business to register the taxi business for GST purposes, regardless of the level of taxable turnover from the operation of the taxis. Canadian GST, *supra* note 2, at §§171.1 and 241(2); Australian GST, *supra* note 14, at §§144–145.

[29] One alternative is to limit the small trader exemption to retailers, especially if the exemption has a high threshold. C. E. McLure, Jr., THE VALUE-ADDED TAX: KEY TO DEFICIT REDUCTION (American Enterprise Institute Press 1987), at 115–117.

[30] A. Schenk, VALUE ADDED TAX – A MODEL STATUTE AND COMMENTARY: A REPORT OF THE COMMITTEE ON VALUE ADDED TAX OF THE AMERICAN BAR ASSOCIATION SECTION OF TAXATION 86–89 (American Bar Association 1989) [hereinafter ABA Model VAT].

The following chart shows, based on the assumptions stated, the VAT advantage to a consumer who buys from an exempt small business (SB) rather than a taxable business and the VAT disadvantage to a taxable business that buys from an exempt rather than a taxable supplier.

Chart 4.1. Illustration of the problem of small business under a credit-method VAT

*Exempt SB selling to consumer**	*Taxable (registered) SB selling to consumer*	
Purchases 100	Purchases	100
Input tax 10	Input tax	10
Margin or value added 50	Margin or value added	50
Sales (exempt) 160	Sales (before tax)	150
	Output tax	15
	Tax-inclusive sales price	165
	SB pays to government after getting input credit	5
Total VAT to government = 10*	Total VAT to government = 15*	
If customer from exempt SB is BB, then:	If customer from taxable SB is BB, then:	
BB	BB	
Purchases 160	Purchases	150
Input tax 0	Input tax	15
Margin or value added 240	Margin or value added	240
Sales (before tax) 400	Sales (before tax)	390
output tax 40	Output tax	39
	BB pays government	24
Total VAT to govt = 40 + 10 = 50**	Total VAT paid to government = 10 + 5 + 24, or 39**	

SB = Small business, trader, or farmer
C = Consumer who buys from SB for personal consumption
BB = Big business (big enough to be required to register under VAT)
* Note that C saves 5% by buying from an exempt small trader (retailer) rather than from a taxable trader (retailer). Exemption of the small business does not save the consumer the full tax of 15%.
** BB pays more by buying from exempt small business, government receives more, and consumer pays more if competitive considerations allow SB to shift tax.
*** With exemption, there is no tax on output and the small business must pay tax on business inputs.

A 2004 paper by Michael Keen and Jack Mintz attempts to provide a clear conceptual framework for setting VAT thresholds.[31] They first model the choice of the threshold as a matter of balancing the tax revenue lost by raising the threshold against the administrative and compliance costs saved by the tax authorities and taxpayer, taking the size distribution of firms as a given. Under this model, the social value of the revenue gained from each firm brought into tax by slightly lowering the threshold should

[31] M. Keen & J. Mintz, "The Optimal Threshold for a Value-Added Tax," 88 *Journal of Public Economics* 559–576 (2004).

equal, at the optimum, to the social costs of the additional administrative and compliance expenses incurred. One implication of this simple rule is that highly profitable or labor-intensive activities should be subject to relatively low thresholds.[32] They then consider the situation in which firms may adjust sizes according to where the threshold is set. Firms' responses to VAT thresholds are motivated by various considerations. Falling below the threshold may confer a competitive advantage to firms that transact with final consumers: even if they are unable to credit VAT paid on input purchases, they may be able to sell at VAT-inclusive prices (in markets where VAT-paying firms also make sales) without paying the VAT or paying less VAT. Moreover, they are able to save on compliance costs associated with VAT payments.

Keen and Mintz show that for any given threshold, the equilibrium distribution of firm size is characterized by a bunching of firms just below the threshold and an absence of firms for some distance above it. In particular, there are some firms that would produce above the threshold level in the absence of a VAT but choose to remain below the threshold to maximize after-tax profit. (These are neither the most productive nor the least productive firms.) Incrementally increasing the VAT threshold, therefore, may have the effect of allowing these firms to increase their production, which together with savings on administrative and compliances costs counteract the negative effects of lost revenue. Using Canadian data, Keen and Mintz perform simulations that suggest that optimal VAT thresholds may be considerably higher than implied by the simple model in which the distribution of firm size is taken as a given.

Using Japanese firm data from the period before and after the introduction of the Japanese VAT in 1989, Kazuki Onji found evidence that firms respond to the setting of VAT thresholds.[33] The response he studies is not limiting real production (as considered by Keen and Mintz) but splitting existing firms. He argues that because Japanese firms below the VAT threshold were subject to more favorable tax treatment than regular VAT payers, corporate groups had incentives to restructure their organizations by splitting some of their member corporations. Supporting the hypothesis was evidence that post-reform densities of firms at and below the threshold became thicker than the pre-reform densities, while a decline in densities in a range above the threshold was also observed.

Some influential reviews of VAT practices around the world document widely varying practices in setting VAT thresholds.[34] However, the comparisons offered can be cryptic and often contain incomplete and much

[32] However, according to country survey presented in their paper, countries that adopt different thresholds for manufacturing and services are just as likely to set higher thresholds for services as they would set lower thresholds.

[33] Kazuki Onji, "The Response of Firms to Eligibility Thresholds: Evidence from the Japanese Value-Added Tax," 93 *Journal of Public Economics* 766–775 (2009).

[34] See, e.g., L. Ebrill, M. Keen, J-P. Bodin, & V. Summers *The Modern VAT* (IMF 2001). R. Bird & P.P. Gendron, *VAT Revisited: A New Look at the Value Added Tax in Developing and Transitional Countries* Table 5.1 (USAID 2005).

conflicting information, suggesting either changing domestic law in the countries surveyed or missing details. Moreover, the conceptual discussion that accompanies these comparisons tends to abstract from the details. In Chapter 14, we examine the use of VAT thresholds in China and the policy issues they raise in some detail.

2. A Single Business and Related Person Rules

Under VAT regimes, it may be important to determine whether multiple businesses owned by a single person or members of a family must register and file separately or must file as a single VAT taxpayer. The question is whether each operation can be treated as a separate business for VAT purposes. This issue is significant if a person claims that a number of businesses controlled by that person qualify for the small business exemption, because the turnover of each business is below the registration threshold. As a general rule, all businesses operated by a single person are aggregated for VAT purposes. For example, if an individual operates two businesses as a sole proprietor, the turnover of one of which exceeds the registration threshold, then the person must register and the operations of both businesses are subject to VAT. On the other hand, if the person established separate legal entities to operate the two businesses, then only the legal entity whose turnover exceeded the threshold would have to register. In such a case, however, VAT laws may give the tax authority power to aggregate sales by related persons to determine whether the turnover exceeds the registration threshold or may mandate such aggregation under specified circumstances (for example, if two corporations have sufficient common ownership by the same person or related persons).

The concept of a "related person" raises difficult definitional issues, especially in countries where it is common practice for extended families to participate in the ownership and operation of retail shops.[35] The split of a single business into smaller parts owned by family members is illustrated by the British *Marner and Marner* case.

Commissioners of Customs and Excise v. Marner and Marner[36]

The appellants, a married couple, ran a public house in partnership. In addition the wife provided catering services at the public house as a separate venture, keeping the profits for herself, as she had done when the public house had been run by her father-in-law. The partnership was registered for value added tax purposes. The wife's catering services were not included with the taxable bar takings of the public

[35] See, e.g., New Vatopia VAT, *supra* note 2, at definition of "related person" in §2.

[36] 1 BVC 1060 (1977) (VATTR Manchester). *CCH British Value Added Tax Cases (1973–1983)* [edited by the authors].

house partnership nor was the catering business separately registered. The receipts from catering were below the registration threshold. The Commissioners decided that the catering services were taxable services rendered by the partnership. The appellants maintained that the catering was a separate business run by the wife alone and accordingly not taxable.

DECISION. Clearly in our view the catering element was a matter of assistance to the bar side of the premises, in that the probabilities and expectations would normally be that it would attract customers. This was a somewhat loose arrangement, such as one frequently finds where husband and wife are together concerned in business activities.

As a matter of law, if the catering is a separate enterprise by Mrs. Marner, the enterprise was neither registrable for the purposes of VAT nor would it be taxable. On the other hand if it was part of the general activities of the partnership then the catering receipts would be taxable activities and would be liable to be aggregated with the bar takings for the purposes of computation of VAT.

Again as a matter of law we regard it as perfectly feasible for a partner to indulge in business activities outside the partnership enterprise. Mr. Marner was perfectly well aware, as he could hardly fail to have been, of her activities and of the way in which she dealt with the financial aspect of payment for supplies and retention of profits for herself.

Referring to *Lindley on Partnership*, where a partnership agreement is not in writing, the intention must be derived from the words and conduct of the parties. It is, in our judgment, significant that in this case the catering activities had been carried on by Mrs. Marner prior to the formation of the partnership.

While the cost of utilities increased by the catering activities to an appreciable extent, it was substantially offset by the benefit to the bar trade by the catering activities. This was an activity in a rather loose business relationship between husband and wife, and we do not consider that this particular aspect carries sufficient weight to displace the general view which we have formed regarding the independence of the catering activities.

Had a receipt been asked for in respect of the bar sales it would by law have been required to carry the VAT registration number of the partnership. On the other hand Mrs. Marner said that she had been asked for catering receipts and that she issued these without a VAT registration number on them. That is, in our view, an indication in favour of severance.

The menus and bills were in the partnership name but that, in our view, is a rather loose way of putting it. We think that any customer consuming a snack or a meal would naturally assume that it was being supplied by the public house and would not be concerned to delve in any great detail into the question whether or not it was being supplied by one or other of the partners as a separate enterprise if, indeed, he was even conscious that the bar enterprise was being run in partnership.

A more serious item is however the consolidation of the trading and profit and loss accounts and balance sheet; this shows the catering purchases and sales consolidated with those of the bar takings and sales and it shows drawings in a composite sum which, as these were consolidated accounts, included also the drawings made by Mrs. Marner on her own account from the catering side of her enterprise.

It is perhaps unfortunate that separate accounts were not prepared for the two businesses but, having regard to the separation which has been achieved in the books of account and the working papers and in the dealings with the catering receipts, we do not consider that this is a factor which is sufficient to displace the conclusion which we have reached that the catering enterprise was a separate enterprise carried on by Mrs. Marner on her own account and that it was an entirely separate enterprise from the enterprise carried on by appellants in partnership; in respect of bar sales.

Held, allowing the taxpayers' appeal.

The British VAT Act was amended to make it easier to prevent the kinds of planning illustrated in the Marner and the following Jane Montgomery cases.[37]

3. Severing Value from the Business

To reduce the tax charged on supplies to consumers and others who cannot recover the tax, a business may try to avoid registration by splitting up (among a number of suppliers) the value of the services rendered to those customers. One approach is to treat the firm's employees as independent contractors. In that way, the owner removes the value of the employees' services from the employer's taxable sales. This approach was attempted

[37] VATA 1994, Sch. 1, para.1A (1) and (2), added by c. 16, sec. 31(1) (1997). "Paragraph 2 below is for the purpose of preventing the maintenance or creation of any artificial separation of business activities carried on by two or more persons from resulting in an avoidance of VAT.(2) In determining for the purposes of sub-paragraph (1) above whether any separation of business activities is artificial, regard shall be had to the extent to which the different persons carrying on those activities are closely bound to one another by financial, economic and organisational links." In *Commissioners of Customs and Excise v. Glassborow and Another?*, [1975] QB 465, [1974] 1 ALL ER1041, [1974] 2 WLR 851 (Queen's Bench Division), a husband and wife engaged in two distinct economic activities (as estate agent and as land developer) through two separate partnerships. The Queen's Bench held that the structure of the British VAT is to register "persons," not the businesses that persons engage in. The two partnerships consisting of the same partners are entitled to only one registration.

in the following *Jane Montgomery (Hair Stylists) Ltd* case in which a hair salon claimed that its stylists were self-employed so that the stylists' receipts from their customers were not reportable as receipts of the salon in determining whether the salon is above the registration threshold. The VAT Act was amended to reduce the opportunities for businesses to avoid registration. After the amendment, the government has been more successful in aggregating the turnover in cases like *Jane Montgomery*.[38]

Customs and Excise Commissioners v. Jane Montgomery (Hair Stylists) Ltd[39]

HEADNOTE. Jane Montgomery (Hair Stylists) Ltd (the company) operated a hairdressing salon. Its three hair stylists were first treated as employed by the company and payments received for the services they supplied were included in the company's turnover. In 1985 the stylists entered into franchise agreements with the company and thereafter they were treated as self-employed, their receipts were separated from those of the company. The commissioners issued a notice of compulsory registration for value added tax (VAT) and a penalty for late registration against the company on the basis that the receipts of the stylists fell to be aggregated with the receipts of the company with the result that the company's turnover had exceeded the VAT registration threshold. The company appealed contending that the hair stylists were self-employed and their receipts did not form part of the company's turnover. The tribunal considered that, although the degree of risk undertaken by the stylists was low, there were many factors which were incompatible with an employer/employee relationship and allowed the company's appeal. The commissioners appealed.

LORD MCCLUSKEY. The court is satisfied that this appeal raises no general question of law. The only issue is whether the supplies referred to in the appeal were made by the company and so constituted part of its turnover. If the turnover of the stylists must be added to that of the company's business then the turnover of the company's business becomes such that the business should be registered for VAT purposes.

In determining that question we must look at the substance of what has been established here rather than at mere matters of form. What is happening in these premises … is substantially the same as what was happening before the agreement took effect. [I]t cannot be said that on balance there has been any material and substantial change in the nature of the business carried on and the way in which it has been carried on. They have all engaged the same accountant; he was and

[38] See *Jones t/a DB Jones & Co.* [2001] BVC 4041 (United Kingdom).

[39] [1994] STC 256 (Court of Exchequer – Scotland) [edited by the authors].

> is the accountant to the company and it was he who was responsible for preparing the agreement and setting up the scheme which lies at the heart of this particular case. When the agreement was entered into blanks were left in it; and it was left to the accountant to fill in the blanks.
>
> By doing so he effectively determined the stylists' income from their work. That circumstance seems to us to yield the clear inference that the persons who had been employees were effectively ceding control over their remuneration, as well as many other things, to the accountant. The fact that they all employed the same accountant who was the accountant to the company clearly indicates that no one supposed that any conflict of interest could arise between the company's business and the work of the stylists. We also think it is significant that there is no finding at all that the stylists acted in ways that independent contractors would be expected to act in, for example, in relation to advertising their business or otherwise acting independently.
>
> The correct inference from the established facts is that, just as before the agreement was entered into, there was only one business which was being carried in the hairdressing salon. That was the company's business; and it follows that it was the company who made the taxable supplies provided by the stylists.
>
> Although there is no ground of appeal couched in quite the correct terms, we are satisfied that the proper course is to allow the appeal.

D. Voluntary Registration

A variety of businesses exempt from registration because their taxable sales are below the registration threshold can voluntarily register under many VAT regimes.[40] A person may voluntarily register if the person's customers are registered traders who prefer to purchase from registered sellers who issue VAT invoices for purchases that qualify for input credits. A new or expanding business also may voluntarily register to claim credit for VAT on its purchases of business inputs, including capital goods and inventory during that expansion phase. A person who registers

[40] Australia GST, *supra* note 14, at §23–10. Canadian GST, *supra* note 2, at §240(3)(a). "[A] non-resident person who in the ordinary course of carrying on business outside Canada regularly solicits orders for the supply by the person of tangible personal property for export to, or delivery in, Canada" may register voluntarily. *Id.* at §240(3)(b). A listed financial institution that is resident in Canada (exempt from GST on many financial services) may register voluntarily. *Id.* at §240(3)(c). A resident holding company (or company organized to acquire other corporations) that does not engage in commercial activity may voluntarily register if certain conditions are met. *Id.* at §240(3)(d). A. Schenk, *GOODS AND SERVICES TAX: THE CANADIAN APPROACH TO VALUE-ADDED TAX* [hereinafter Schenk, Canadian GST], 17. See New Vatopia VAT, *supra* note 2, at §20(5). See also, the discussions in Subsection E and Chapter 8 II(A).

voluntarily generally must remain registered for a minimum period, such as two years, and if registration then is cancelled, the person must recapture input credits claimed on goods that are on hand on the date the registration is cancelled.[41]

E. Cancellation of Registration

A registered person may cease to be registered if the person no longer meets the registration requirements or if the tax authority cancels the person's registration.[42] When registration is cancelled some or all of the input credits claimed on property held at that time must be repaid.[43]

A nation may provide a small business exemption because small businesses tend not to maintain adequate record keeping. If this is the rationale for the exemption, then once a business exceeds the threshold, and must keep required records, registration should be maintained even if that business' sales slip below the threshold. This decline may result from a drop in the firm's taxable sales or from the firm's shift in business from making taxable to supplying exempt sales. Australia adopted this principle.[44]

Another rationale for the small business exemption is that the compliance costs for a business with low turnover and the administrative costs for the government outweigh the tax liability payable by such businesses with low levels of value added. Countries such as Canada, favoring this rationale for the exemption, typically deregister the businesses whose taxable sales drop below the threshold.[45] Even if a business qualifies for deregistration because its turnover falls below the threshold, the person remains registered until the deregistration process is complete.[46] A business that registers voluntarily may be required to maintain registration for a minimum period, such as two years.[47]

[41] Under the British VAT, in *Marshall v. C&E Commissioners*, [1975] VATTR 98, a taxpayer who voluntarily registered his yacht charter business was taxed when he later sold the yachts and ceased to conduct business." Schenk, Canadian GST, *supra* note 40, at 17 and note 34.

[42] The New Vatopia VAT provides that the government may cancel a person's registration or a taxable person may request cancellation. New Vatopia VAT, *supra* note 2, at §22.

[43] See discussion in the next section of this chapter.

[44] See Australia GST, *supra* note 14, at §25–50. A VAT proposed in the United States is comparable. Revenue Restoration Act of 1996, H.R. 4050, 104th Cong., 2d Sess., 142 Cong. Rec. E1572 (1996) (Congressman Gibbons's bill was not enacted).

[45] Canadian GST, *supra* note 2, at §§148(1) & 242. There are special rules governing a person engaged in a business involving games of chance. See §148(l)(c) and 148(2)(c). Some sales are not included in calculating the $30,000 threshold. See §148(l)(a) and 148(2)(a) on sales of capital property and on financial services.

[46] See New Zealand Case R29 (1994), 16 NZTC 6,155.

[47] Canadian GST, *supra* note 2, at §242(2) has a one-year period. Unless the person ceases to engage in economic activity, Australia requires all registrants (whether mandatory or voluntary) to be registered for at least twelve months before deregistering. Australia GST, *supra* note 14, at §25–55. See New Vatopia VAT, *supra* note 2, at §13(8), providing for

Registration may be cancelled at the government's initiative. The government may cancel a person's registration if the business closes or no longer engages in taxable activity.[48] The cancellation prevents the person from issuing tax invoices and forces the person to recapture tax credits claimed on purchases of goods and sometimes services still on hand.

F. Transition to Registration and Cancellation of Registration

A previously unregistered person who is required to register or voluntarily registers may be eligible to claim input credits for VAT paid on previously acquired goods on hand when registration becomes effective, assuming that those goods will be used in connection with taxable activity.[49] For administrative reasons, it is less common for a VAT law (especially in countries that do not have sophisticated tax administration) to provide input credits for tax on services, rent, and capital goods on hand when registration becomes effective, even if these items are used by the newly registered person in making taxable sales. It is costly, in lost revenue, to expand the credit to cover these items. In addition, it is difficult administratively to verify that the business had unused services on hand when registration becomes effective. Nevertheless, many countries allow input credit for tax on pre-registration purchases.[50]

When a registrants deregister, they must repay tax benefits claimed while registered.[51] Otherwise, the deregistering persons would obtain a tax advantage over their competition. In Canada, a deregistering business generally must report as taxable sales the goods on hand immediately before it ceases to be registered.[52] In New Zealand, the recapture rules cover both goods and services.[53]

cancellation of registration for mandatory or voluntary registrants only after the expiration of two years from the effective date of the registration.

48 See, for example, Explanatory Notes to Bill C-62 as passed by the House of Commons on April 10, 1990, Department of Finance, May 1990 [hereinafter 1990 Explanatory Notes], 115.

49 See Canadian GST, *supra* note 2, at §171(1) and (2). Canada does not have a time limit. The input credit is not available with respect to assets on which GST was not paid, such as assets acquired before January 1, 1991, the date the GST became effective. See 1990 Explanatory Notes, *supra* note 50, at 60.

50 For example, Canada allows credits for tax on some services on hand when registration becomes effective. See Canadian GST, *supra* note 2, at §171(2)(a). Such input tax is not creditable if it is attributable to services provided before he becomes a registrant or to rents, royalties, or similar payments attributable to the pre-registration period. *Id.* at §171(2)(b).

51 Under the British VAT, in *Marshall v. C & E Commissioners*, *supra* note 41, a taxpayer who voluntarily registered his yacht charter business was taxed when he later sold the yachts and ceased to conduct business.

52 The assets include property acquired for consumption, use, or supply in the course of commercial activities. Canadian GST, *supra* note 2, at §171(3)(a)(i).

53 New Zealand requires the deregistering business to report the lesser of the cost or the market value of goods and services that are part of the assets of a taxable activity

G. Registration of Branches and Group of Companies

There are significant nontax reasons for VAT-registered businesses to file VAT returns (a) by branch or division of the company or (b) by consolidating operations for a group of related companies. For example, in a developing country with inadequate roads, postal services, and telecommunications, a company with branches in remote areas may find it almost impossible to collect branch data and file a single VAT return by the due date. If related companies engage in significant intercompany transactions, the filing of consolidated returns that disregard those transactions may significantly reduce VAT reporting obligations.

There also may be tax-motivated reasons for businesses to file by branch or by consolidating operations of related companies. Filing by branch does not (or should not) enable a business to come within the small business exemption. The calculation of taxable sales is made for the entire company. Consolidated reporting may allow a group of companies to ignore intercompany transactions and gain some cash-flow benefits. In addition, if one company has excess input credits that must be carried forward and a related company has net VAT liability that must be remitted to the tax authorities, consolidated reporting may allow the group to offset the excess credits against the net tax to reduce the tax payable in that tax period. Consolidated reporting gives the group a quicker recovery of excess credits than would be available if they reported separately because there generally is a delay (in some countries a significant time delay) in recovering refunds for excess credits. The EC recently issued a communication on the group option to encourage a more uniform application of the grouping schemes in member states.[54]

H. Electronic Commerce, Broadcasting, and Telecommunication Services

Generally, for a business to be subject to a country's registration and other VAT obligations, the business must be engaged in economic or business activity in the taxing jurisdiction. As a result of the competitive challenges faced by local businesses from nonresident firms rendering specified services or selling goods electronically, the EU departs from the general rules and requires those non-established firms to register (under certain conditions) in one of the member states.[55] The problem and the solution adopted in the EU and some other countries are discussed in Chapter 7 as part of the broader VAT issues governing cross-border transactions.

conducted by the person ceasing to be registered. New Zealand Goods and Services Tax Act 1985, No. 141 [hereinafter NZ GST], §5(3).

54 See COM (2009) 325 final, Brussels, 2.7.2009, Communication from the commission to the council and the European Parliament on the VAT group option provided for in Article 11 of the Council Directive 2006/112/EC of 28 November 2006 on the common system of value added tax, Official Journal No. L347/1 of 11.12.2006 [the VAT Directive].

55 See VAT Directive, *supra* note 54, at Art. 58, effective January 1, 2015; and Council Regulation (EU) No. 967/2012 of 9 October 2012, amending Implementing Regulation

III. Person Liable for Tax

A. General Principles

VAT generally is imposed on taxable domestic supplies of goods and services and on imports of goods and imports of some services. The person treated as the importer of taxable goods or the recipient of taxable imported services generally is liable for tax on those imports.[56]

On taxable domestic supplies of goods and services, the tax is imposed on, or must be accounted for by, the taxable (or registered) person making the supply.[57] The EU VAT Directive imposes VAT on taxable supplies by a taxable person. In the United Kingdom, South Africa, and in other countries the terms "taxable person" (or "vendor") and "registered person" are interrelated.[58] In the United Kingdom, subject to the VAT Directive rules, a taxable person is a person registered or required to register.[59] In Australia, the liability to pay tax is imposed on the person who makes taxable supplies,[60] and it is only a person who is registered or is required to register that can make taxable supplies.[61]

B. Person Treated as Seller

1. In General

Ordinarily, the person conducting business and making taxable sales is subject to registration and is liable for VAT. The identity of the seller is crucial. The identity is not obvious with Internet or auction sales, consignment sales, and services rendered by local units of government. Many of these transactions are discussed in this section.

(EU) No. 282/2011 as regards the special scheme for nonestablished taxable persons supplying telecommunications services, broadcasting services, or electronic services to non-taxable persons.

[56] See, for example, New Vatopia VAT, *supra* note 2, at §9(2)(b) and (c). The taxation of imports is covered in Chapter 7.

[57] Under the EU's VAT Directive, a taxable person is defined as "any person who independently carries out in any place any economic activity specified, whatever the purpose or results of that activity." VAT Directive, *supra* note 54, at Art. 9(1). "The [ABA] Model Act, section 4005(a), defines a taxable person as a person who engages in a taxable or nontaxable transaction in connection with a business, and a person who engages in a taxable casual sale under section 4003(a)(3); but the latter is a taxable person only with respect to the taxable casual sale." ABA Model VAT, *supra* note 30, at 31. Member states may "regard as a taxable person anyone who carries out, on a occasional basis, a transaction relating to" the specified activities. VAT Directive, *supra* note 54, at Art. 12(1).

[58] Value-Added Tax Act No. 89 of 1991 [hereinafter RSA VAT], §§1 definition of "vendor," 7(1) imposition of tax on vendors, 23 liability to register, and 28 liability of vendor to file returns and pay tax (Republic of South Africa). See also New Vatopia VAT, *supra* note 2, at §§6, 9, 23, and 24.

[59] Value-Added Tax Act 1994, §3(1) (United Kingdom).

[60] Australian GST, *supra* note 14, at §9–40. Botswana imposes tax on registered persons, who are required to file returns and pay tax. See Botswana VAT, *supra* note 4, at §§7(1)(a), 19(1), and 26(1).

[61] Australian GST, *supra* note 14, at §23–15.

If sales are made by a partnership, a club, or other unincorporated form of doing business, who is the supplier subject to the VAT obligations? Although a business may be an aggregation of its owners, to be administrable, the tax liability should be imposed at the entity level. For partnerships, it is the partnership, even in countries where a partnership does not have separate legal personality.

For administrative or other practical reasons, for some transactions a person other than the legal owner of property or other than the person rendering services may be treated as the supplier. Some of those special situations are discussed in the following subsections.

2. Services Rendered by Nonresidents

The recipient of a taxable imported service is the person liable for the tax on the service. The tax generally must be reported and paid by the recipient of the service under a reverse charge system. It is common for nations to tax imported services only if the importer is a person who cannot recover the tax on the import through the input tax credit. Although taxing the recipient of services under this self-assessment system may work when the recipient is a nonprofit organization, a unit of government, or a business making exempt domestic sales, it is not effective when the recipient is an individual consumer.

In the case of electronic commerce and telecommunications services, the EU solution – to require the non-established supplier to register, collect, and remit the tax on unregistered customers – is discussed in Chapter 7.

3. Auctions

There are several different kinds of auctions. Some are private auctions of goods in which the auction company serves as the agent for the owner selling the property being auctioned. The owners may be private individuals, registered businesses, or charitable or governmental organizations. Other auctions involve a unit of government of goods confiscated under authority of law (such as illegal contraband or goods seized or distrained to recover taxes or other obligations to the government). Goods repossessed on default by a debtor may be auctioned pursuant to a mortgage or other credit agreement.

In most or all of these situations, the "seller" at auction is the person who owns or is treated as the person with legal authority to sell, and the auction house serves as agent of the seller, receiving a commission for its services. Under the general rules in many VAT systems, the person making the taxable supply or sale is liable for VAT if the person is VAT-registered.[62] Generally, when an agent makes a sale on behalf of a principal, the supply

[62] See, as an example, New Vatopia VAT, *supra* note 2, at §9(2)(a) and the §2 definition of supplier.

is considered a supply by the principal.[63] As a result, without special rules governing auction sales, these sales would be treated under most VATs as sales by the principal (usually the owner of the goods). Auction sales by private consumers would escape tax, whereas sales of used goods by used goods dealers would be taxed. To remove this inconsistency, some VATs treat the auction house as the seller of the auctioned goods in connection with its taxable activity.[64] Under those regimes, the auction house must include the auction sales as part of its taxable sales.[65]

4. Local Government Services

Common practice is to exempt services rendered by local units of government.[66] Occasionally, services rendered by local (or even national) governments that compete with the private sector, such as electricity and water, are taxed. When they are taxed, the unit of government or parastatal is the seller.

New Zealand includes, in its GST base, services financed with real property taxes (local rates). New Zealand in effect treats rates as payments for the local public services provided with that revenue. Local government is the VAT-registered supplier. It adds the GST rate to the rates. South Africa taxes specified services financed by rates.[67]

IV. Business Activity Subject to VAT

A. Economic or Taxable Activity

As discussed earlier in this chapter, a person is a taxable person (or in some countries a registered person) if the person makes taxable sales above a threshold amount and such sales are made in connection with economic or taxable activity. The concept of economic activity is both expansive (covering a wide range of activity conducted on a regular basis) and narrowly focused (excluding activity by a business owner that is unrelated to the business). When an individual sells private-owned assets in multiple transactions, when does the activity change from isolated sales beyond the scope of the tax to continuous taxable sales that constitute economic activity subject to tax? An economic activity for VAT purposes generally is

[63] See *id*. at §5(1)(a).

[64] See *id*. at §5(3).

[65] If the VAT law gives registered sellers of used goods input credits attributable to used goods acquired in a transaction not subject to VAT, the auction house should be entitled to comparable credits when the auctioned goods are presumed to be acquired for auction in a transaction not subject to tax.

[66] See discussion in Chapter 9.

[67] RSA VAT, *supra* note 58, at §1 definition of "enterprise" and Government Notice No. 2570: Determination of category of businesses, October 21, 1991 (Republic of South Africa).

broader than the concept of trade for income tax purposes.[68] Some countries use the concept of "enterprise," not as a synonym for a business but as the kind of operation that gives the country jurisdiction to tax the activity. That concept is discussed in Chapter 7, Section V.

New Zealand relies on a concept of taxable activity that is based on factors such as continuity and frequency of activity. The New Zealand GST taxes a broad range of economic activity by defining taxable activity to include activities of governmental entities and activity conducted "continuously or regularly by any person, whether or not for a pecuniary profit."[69] New Zealand removes activities conducted "essentially as a private recreational pursuit or hobby" and activities conducted in an employment relationship, in a judicial capacity, or in a public administrative capacity.[70] In Canada, a person is not required to register for GST if the person's commercial activity is limited to real property sales not in the ordinary course of business.[71]

Early cases in the United Kingdom held that a business[72]

> must amount to a continuing activity which is predominantly concerned with the making of supplies to others for a consideration. There are, in effect, two parts to the test. First, for there to be an "activity" there must be sufficiency of scale to the supplies and they must be continued over a period of time. Second, the predominant concern of the person conducting the activity must be the making of supplies.[73]

The ECJ expanded on this concept in the *Hutchison 3G UK Ltd* case.[74] In that case, the United Kingdom allocated mobile telecommunication licenses to the successful bidders. The government took the position that these transfers were not taxable supplies incident to economic activity. If outside the scope of VAT, the bidders were denied credit for any portion of the amount paid for the frequencies. In discussing the concept of "economic activity" for VAT purposes, the ECJ wrote that activities must be of an economic nature. The issuance of these rights by a governmental

68 For a list of factors that can be used to determine whether an activity is the kind of activity that comes within the scope of a VAT, including continuity and value of the sales, profit, active control, and the appearance of a business, see A. TAIT, VALUE ADDED TAX: INTERNATIONAL PRACTICE AND PROBLEMS (IMF 1988) [hereinafter Tait, VAT], 368–369.

69 NZ GST, *supra* note 53, at §6(1).

70 *Id.* at §6(3).

71 Canadian GST, *supra* note 2, at §240(l)(b). A nonresident who does not conduct business in Canada also is not required to register. *Id.* at §240(l)(c). A nonresident may be deemed to conduct business in Canada if the person solicits orders for prescribed property to be sent to an address in Canada by mail or courier. *Id.* at §240(4).

72 See Value Added Tax Act 1994, §4 (United Kingdom); VAT Directive, *supra* note 54, at Arts. 9–13.

73 *The National Society for the Prevention of Cruelty to Children v. Customs and Excise Commissioners*, [1992] VATTR 417, at 422.

74 *Hutchison 3G UK Ltd and Others v. Commissioners of Customs and Excise*, Case C-369/04 [2007].

agency (which enables others to exploit the rights) is not the exploitation of property that qualifies as economic activity for VAT purposes.

In a United Kingdom case, the tax authority claimed that tax avoidance transactions did not constitute economic activity under the EU's Sixth Directive (now VAT Directive)[75] and, as a result, denied the seller input credits for VAT on acquisitions used to engage in those transactions. The ECJ ruled that transactions can constitute economic activity even if engaged in solely to obtain a tax advantage. It is for the national court to determine the substance and significance of any such transactions, and the national court can recast the transactions as if the abusive transaction had not been undertaken.[76] In an even more extreme case, the ECJ ruled that a person who, without the person's knowledge, participated in a carousel fraud was engaged in economic activity and was entitled to claim input tax credits.[77]

The ECJ, in the following case, addressed the distinction between private, occasional sales that are not within the scope of VAT and those that are conducted on a continuing basis and satisfy the VAT Directive's concept of economic activity. A related issue, in which a person who makes taxable supplies in connection with an economic activity and other supplies that are personal in nature, is discussed in the next subsection of this chapter.

JUDGMENT OF THE COURT (Second Chamber)

19 July 2012

In Case C-263/11, [2012] ECR I-0000
REFERENCE for a preliminary ruling under Article 267 TFEU from the Augstākās tiesas Senāts (Latvia), made by decision of 13 May 2011, received at the Court on 26 May 2012, in the proceedings
Ainārs Rēdlihs
v.
Valsts ieņēmumu dienests (VID, the Latvian State Revenue Service)

[75] VAT Directive, *supra* note 54, at Art.9(1). The United Kingdom also claimed that "a circular carousel fraud" (transactions, for example, going from Bob to Carl and back to Abel) is not economic activity; thus, the input credits are denied with respect to the sale. See14 *International VAT Monitor* 356 (July/Aug. 2003).

[76] *See Halifax pic, Leeds Permanent Development Services Ltd, County Wide Property Investments Ltd v. Commissioners of Customs & Excise*, Case C-255/02, Judgment on Feb. 21, 2006, [2006] ECR I-..., [2006] All ER (D) 283. In the *Optigen, Fulcrum, and Bond* joined cases, C-354/03, C-355/03, and C-484/03, *Optigen Ltd, Fulcrum Electronics Ltd and Bond House Systems Ltd v. Commissioners of Customs & Excise*, [2003] ECR I->»} OJ C 74, 25.03. 2006, p. 1 [hereinafter *Optigen, Fulcrum, and Bond*]. The ECJ ruled that an innocent person who is involved in a carousel fraud still is engaged in economic activity and his supplies remain supplies of goods and supplies of services.

[77] See Optigen, Fulcrum, and Bond, *supra* note 76.

Judgment

[Another question, not included in this excerpt, is whether the penalty for failing to register was excessive and violated the VAT Directive's principle of proportionality.]

European Union law

According to Article 2(1)(a) of the VAT Directive, which essentially reproduces the wording of Article 2(1) of the Sixth Directive, 'the supply of goods for consideration within the territory of a Member State by a taxable person acting as such … shall be subject to VAT'.

Article 9(1) of the VAT Directive, which is worded in terms which are essentially similar to those of Article 4(1) and (2) of the Sixth Directive, provides:

'"Taxable person" shall mean any person who, independently, carries out in any place any economic activity, whatever the purpose or results of that activity.

Any activity of producers, traders or persons supplying services, including mining and agricultural activities and activities of the professions, shall be regarded as "economic activity". The exploitation of tangible or intangible property for the purposes of obtaining income therefrom on a continuing basis shall in particular be regarded as an economic activity.'

Latvian law omitted

The dispute in the main proceedings and the questions referred for a preliminary ruling

During an inspection carried out by the VID, it was found that the applicant in the main proceedings had carried out 12 supplies of timber in April 2005 and 25 transactions of the same type over a period from May 2005 to December 2006. It was also found that the applicant in the main proceedings had not registered in the register of taxable persons for VAT purposes and had not declared any economic activity to the VID.

Mr Rēdlihs … submitted that the supplies of timber which he had carried out could not be considered to be an economic activity as they were neither systematic nor carried out independently. Those supplies were, he argued, of an exceptional nature inasmuch as they were effected, not for profit, but to alleviate the damage caused by a storm, which constituted a case of *force majeure*. … [I]t would not have been possible to sell in one lot all of the trees felled following that storm.

In the alternative, he submitted that he had acquired the forest at issue in order to meet his own personal needs and that the transfer of timber from that forest was for that reason not subject to VAT.

The questions referred for a preliminary ruling

By its first question, the referring court asks, essentially, whether Article 9(1) of the VAT Directive and Article 4(1) and (2) of the Sixth Directive must be interpreted as meaning that supplies of timber made by a natural person for the purpose of alleviating the consequences of a case of *force majeure* come within the scope of an 'economic activity' within the meaning of those provisions.

As regards the substance, it must first of all be pointed out that, under the VAT Directive, as under the Sixth Directive, the scope of VAT is very wide in that Article 2 of the former, which concerns taxable transactions, refers not only to the importation of goods but also to the supply of goods or services for consideration within the territory of the country by a taxable person acting as such (see Case C-86/09 *Future Health Technologies* [2010] ECR I-5215, paragraph 25 and the case-law cited).

[T]he fact that the supplies at issue were carried out to alleviate the consequences of an alleged case of *force majeure* does not in any way mean that those supplies were not carried out independently.

As regards, secondly, the concept of 'economic activity' within the meaning of Article 9(1) of the VAT Directive, it is settled case-law that that term is objective in character, in the sense that the activity is considered *per se* and without regard to its purpose or results (see, to that effect, Case C-223/03 *University of Huddersfield* [2006] ECR I-1751, paragraphs 47 and 48 and the case-law cited).

Consequently, the fact that supplies such as those at issue in the main proceedings were made in order to alleviate the consequences of a case of *force majeure*, that fact thus being related to the objective of the transactions carried out, has no effect on the question whether those supplies must be regarded as an 'economic activity' within the meaning of Article 9(1) of the VAT Directive.

[T]ransactions such as those at issue in the main proceedings must be regarded as 'economic activity' within the meaning of Article 9(1) of the VAT Directive if they are effected for the purpose of obtaining income therefrom on a continuing basis (see, by analogy, Case C-230/94 *Enkler* [1996] ECR I-4517, paragraph 22).

The issue of whether the activity at issue, namely the exploitation of a private forest, is designed to obtain income on a continuing basis is an issue of fact which must be assessed having regard to all the circumstances of the case, which include, inter alia, the nature of the property concerned (see, to that effect, *Enkler*, paragraphs 24 and 26).

That criterion must make it possible to determine whether an individual has used property in such a way that his activity is to be regarded as 'economic activity' within the meaning of the VAT Directive. The fact that property is suitable only for economic exploitation will normally be sufficient for a finding that its owner is exploiting it for the purposes of economic activities and, consequently, for the purpose of obtaining income on a continuing basis. On the other hand, if, by reason of its nature, property is capable of being used for both economic and private purposes, all the circumstances in which it is used will have to be examined in order to determine whether it is actually being used for the purpose of obtaining income on a continuing basis (*Enkler*, paragraph 27).

In the latter case, comparing the circumstances in which the person concerned actually uses the property with the circumstances in which the corresponding economic activity is usually carried out may be one way of ascertaining whether the activity concerned is carried on for the purpose of obtaining income on a continuing basis (*Enkler*, paragraph 28).

Thus, where the person concerned takes active steps in forestry management by mobilising resources similar to those deployed by a producer, a trader or a person supplying services within the meaning of the second subparagraph of Article 9(1) of the VAT Directive, the activity at issue in the main proceedings must be regarded as an 'economic activity' within the meaning of that provision (see, to that effect, Joined Cases C-180/10 and C-181/10 *Słaby and Others* [2011] ECR I-0000, paragraph 39).

... The fruits of tangible property, such as timber from a forest, may, by their very nature and depending on their characteristics and, in particular, their age, not be suitable for immediate economic exploitation, as a certain period of time may be objectively necessary before those fruits can become amenable to economic exploitation. Nevertheless, that does not mean that the supplies of timber which have taken place in the meantime, as a result of alleged *force majeure*, do not come within the scope of exploitation of tangible property for the purposes of obtaining income therefrom on a continuing basis within the meaning of the second subparagraph of Article 9(1) of the VAT Directive.

[T]he actual length of the period over which the supplies ... took place, the number of customers and the amount of earnings are also factors which, forming part of the circumstances of the case as a whole, may be taken into account, with others, when that question is under consideration (see *Enkler*, paragraph 29).

[T]he fact that [Mr Rēdlihs] ... acquired the tangible property in issue to meet his own personal needs ... does not preclude that property from being subsequently used for the purposes of the exercise of an 'economic activity' within the meaning of Article 9(1) of the VAT Directive.

On those grounds, the Court (Second Chamber) hereby rules:

Article 9(1) of Council Directive 2006/112/EC of 28 November 2006 on the common system of value added tax, as amended by Council

Directive 2006/138/EC of 19 December 2006, must be interpreted as meaning that supplies of timber made by a natural person for the purpose of alleviating the consequences of a case of *force majeure* come within the scope of the exploitation of tangible property, which must be regarded as an 'economic activity' within the meaning of that provision, where those supplies are carried out for the purposes of obtaining income therefrom on a continuing basis. It is for the national court to carry out an assessment of all the circumstances of the case in order to determine whether the exploitation of tangible property, such as a forest, is carried out for the purposes of obtaining income therefrom on a continuing basis.

B. Personal Sales

Taxable sales generally are limited to sales made incident to a taxable person's business or economic activity, not personal sales outside the scope of that activity.[78] When can sales by a person engaged in economic activity be treated as independent of the economic activity? In the United Kingdom, a person is entitled to claim input credits for tax only on purchases of "goods or services used or to be used for the purpose of any business carried on or to be carried on by him."[79] If a taxable person can establish that some sales are personal and independent of the person's trade or business, those sales are not subject to VAT. For example, where a farmer grew cannabis in a remote and inaccessible area of his farm, the New Zealand Taxation Review Authority held that it did not constitute part of the taxable farming activity and therefore was not subject to the GST.[80] This principle is illustrated in greater detail by the following *Stirling* case.

Stirling v. Commissioners of Customs and Excise[81]

The Appellant was registered for value added tax, and carries on the business of mixed farming, forestry, and the leasing of property and sporting rights, under his own name at Fairburn Estate. The Commissioners' assessment relates to the sale by the Appellant of part of a stamp collection and of furniture and other valuables contained in

[78] See New Vatopia VAT, *supra* note 2, at §6, incorporating the principles used in many VATs.

[79] Value Added Tax Act 1994, §24(l)(United Kingdom). For a Canadian case holding that a sale of an asset on which an input credit was denied is not a sale in the course of a commercial activity and therefore not taxable, see *Aubrett Holdings Ltd. v. H.M. The Queen*, [1998] Can. Tax Ct. LEXIS 509.

[80] Case T2 (1997) 18 NZTC 8,007, digested in *CCH New Zealand Goods and Services Tax Guide*, 196–145 (1997).

[81] [1985] VATTR 232, [1986] 2CMLR 117 (Edinburgh VAT Tribunal) [edited by the authors].

Fairburn House, which is part of the appellant's estate. [They claim] that these sales were made "in furtherance of" the businesses carried on by him.

The said estate, including Fairburn House, had been in the hands of the Appellant's family for nearly 100 years. He received it from his father in 1963. In 1979 the Appellant decided, in order to improve the profitability of his farming enterprise, to build a new dairy unit. The cost of the new dairy unit, due to unforeseeable causes, escalated to such an extent that by 1981 it reached £316,835. The financial problems were further aggravated by the sharp rise in bank rate. In 1977, Fairburn House (which had been empty since his father's death) was leased furnished for a period of 5 years in order to reduce the burden of rates [local real property taxes] and maintenance and in the hope that financially matters would improve. The most valuable portable items, including a number of paintings, were locked away in 2 storerooms. The remaining articles were large items such as paintings which could not be so stored and were therefore left for the Appellant's convenience in the tenanted rooms. During the currency of the lease the Appellant sold part of an inherited collection of valuable stamps, with the object of reducing the farm overdraft. In 1982, on the expiry of the lease, the Appellant could not service the interest payable on the farm overdraft from either branch of his business. He decided to sell Fairburn House and its contents, as well as other parts of the estate. The House was sold for a net price of £124,133, and the contents were sold by auction on 10 November 1982 for £280,000. The latter sum was paid into the farm's bank account and entered in the farm's account as capital injections into the business. The money was applied to reduce the overdraft to a manageable level. The Respondents' assessment relates to the said sales of stamps and the contents of the House.

Section 2(2) of the Finance Act 1972 provided that:

'Tax on the supply of goods or services shall be charged only where

(a) the supply is a taxable supply; and
(b) the goods or services are supplied by a taxable person in the course of a business carried on by him.'

The Finance Act 1977, with effect from 1 January 1978, substituted the following provision (which is now section 2(1) of the Value Added Tax Act 1983):

'Tax shall be charged on any supply of goods or services made in the United Kingdom, where it is a taxable supply made by a taxable person in the course or furtherance of any business carried on by him.'

The principal argument for the Respondents turned upon the meaning of the words "furtherance of any business" introduced by the 1977 Act. The supply was a taxable supply, not being an exempt supply. The Appellant was a taxable person. The sale of any goods by the

Appellant, whether or not they were connected in any way with his business, were taxable if made in furtherance of that business. It was not disputed that the purpose of the sales in question was to keep the Appellant's farming business from possible collapse by applying the proceeds of sale to a substantial reduction in the farm overdraft. The word "furtherance" could not be restricted to the disposal of assets belonging to the business, because section 45(6) of the 1977 Act (section 47(6) of the Value Added Tax Act 1983) provides that the disposition of assets of a business is a supply made in the course or furtherance of the business. Section 2(1) of the 1983 Act cast the net more widely than the wording of the original section 2(2) of the 1972 Act. The Respondents relied on *Alan Ridley v. Commissioners of Custom and Excise.* ... In that case the Appellant, who had acquired 1,600 acres of land on which he carried on the business of farming, later sold the sporting rights over the land in order to reduce his substantial bank overdraft....

[The Tribunal found that] ... the sale of the shooting rights in this case for the purpose of reducing the bank overdraft incurred in respect of the farming business assisted the finances of that business. In our judgment it follows from this that such sale was in furtherance of that business...

Counsel for the Appellant submitted that "furtherance" of any business meant that the assets sold had to be linked with the business activities of the taxpayer. In the present case the proceeds of sale had been entered as contributions to the capital accounts of the business; no input tax had been claimed on the commission paid for carrying out the sales; there had been no change in the structure of the farming business (apart from modernisation); and there was no reference in the accounts to the stamps and furniture as capital assets or stock in trade of the business. Further, the sales in question were an isolated transaction and not part of a continuing business.

No reference was made in the argument for either side to the provisions of the Sixth Council directive (VAT) of the European Economic Community (77/388) ..., but we are able to gain some assistance from its terms. Article 2 of the Sixth Directive charges the tax as follows:

'The following shall be subject to value added tax:

(1) [the supply of goods and services for consideration within the territory of a Member State by a taxable person acting as such].[82]

Article 4 provides:

(1) 'Taxable person' shall mean any person who independently carries out in any place any economic activity specified in paragraph 2, whatever the purpose or results of that activity.[83]

[82] VAT Directive, *supra* note 54, at Art. 2(1)(a) and (c).

[83] VAT Directive is basically the same. See Art. 9(1).

(2) The economic activities referred to in paragraph 1 shall comprise all activities of producers, traders and persons supplying services including mining and agricultural activities and activities of the professions....'

The said Act of 1977 was passed *inter alia* to give effect to the provisions of that Directive. The crucial phrase in the above-quoted Articles is the phrase 'acting as such' in Article 2(1). The supply of goods according to the Directive must exclude the supply by a taxable person who is acting in a personal capacity, and this is consistent with the description of a taxable person as a person who carries out the economic activities referred to in Article 4. In our opinion, the 1977 Act when it added the words 'or furtherance of any business to section 2(2) of the Finance Act 1972 did not intend, in defiance of the Sixth Directive, to extend the ambit of value added tax to supplies made by a taxable person who was not acting as such and was not carrying out an economic activity in terms of Article 4. In our opinion the purpose of the 1977 Act in adding the words 'or furtherance' was to ensure that all business activities were caught by the section, for example, fringe activities carried on separately from a main business; or transactions related in some way to the main business but which are different in character from the general run of the business, as where a retailer sells a delivery van. In the present case we reach the conclusion that the amended subsection does not result in the imposition of value added tax as the assets sold were not linked with the Appellant's business activities. The Appellant was merely selling personal assets which were in no way connected with his business. The leasing of the property, albeit at a low rent, was a business operation and the assets falling under the tenancy were business assets for the purposes of value added tax under section 47(6) of the 1983 Act, being a disposition of assets of the business in the course of the business. But such assets did not in the opinion of the tribunal include the stamps or the valuable items which were locked away in the house. Nor, in our opinion, were the valuable paintings and articles of virtu in the let rooms included in the lease, whose terms made no reference to such items and whose rent was much lower than it would have been if the inclusion of these items had been a matter of contract. On the other hand, the basic furniture supplied in the let rooms was an asset of the business, and on the evidence (as the parties agreed) this represented 15 per cent of the total proceeds of sale, resulting in a reduction of the Appellant's assessed liability to £4,761.

We accordingly allow the appeal to the extent of reducing the Appellant's liability to the said figure.

C. When Does a Business Begin?

A person who is organizing a business may incur preorganization expenses or purchase immovable property to be used in the business to be conducted in the future. In this situation, tax authorities may be concerned that the person will be claiming input credits for tax on assets that ultimately are not used in the business because the person decides not to enter into business. Chapter 6 discusses the allowance of input credits for tax on acquisitions made before a business opens or acquisitions related to activity after the firm stops making taxable sales. There is an overlap with this issue. This section focuses on the relationship between this early stage and the concept of "economic activity" for VAT purposes and discusses a person's eligibility or obligation to register before the person starts making taxable sales. In the *Inzo* case,[84] a company organized to turn sea water into drinking water commissioned a feasibility study, conducted other preliminary activities, incurred input VAT on purchases attributable to this phase of its operations, and later decided to abandon the project and liquidate before making taxable supplies. The ECJ held that once the tax authority accepted that the company intended to engage in economic activity and registered the person, except for cases of fraud or abuse, the authority could not retroactively remove that status and deny credits for input VAT, even if the company did not proceed from the study phase to the operational phase of making taxable supplies. The court in *Inzo* also held that once a business has the status of a VAT taxpayer (is registered), these preparatory activities are deemed to relate to the business's economic activity.[85]

In the following widely cited case involving the EU Sixth Directive, the ECJ examined the question of whether an investor's intent must be established by objective evidence before preliminary activities are considered economic activity and, therefore, make the person eligible to apply for registration if the registration threshold rules are satisfied.

Rompelman & Another v. Minister van Financiën[86]

The taxpayers, a husband and wife, acquired the right to future title to two units under construction that were expected to be used as showrooms, together with a usufructuary interest in the land. The

[84] *Intercommunale voor zeewaterontzilting (INZO) v. Belgium State*, Case C-110/94, [1996] ECR I-857 (ECJ 1996) [hereinafter Inzo].

[85] See Inzo, *supra* note 84.

[86] *Rompelman and Another v. Minister van Financiën* (judgment in Case No. 268/83), [1985] ECR 655, (ECJ 1985) [edited and summarized in part by the authors]. See also, Case C-280/10, *Kopalnia Odkrywkowa Polski Trawertyn P. Granatowicz, M. Wasiewicz spotka jawna v. Dyrektor Izby Skarbowej w Poznaniu*, [ECJ 2012], applying Rompelman where

taxpayers informed the inspector of taxes that the showrooms would be let to traders, and that the lessor and lessee would apply to be taxable on the leasing of the showrooms. They also applied under the Netherlands VAT to deduct the input tax on the instalments of the sale price payable by the taxpayers as building progressed.

On 18 October 1979 the taxpayers made a return claiming a refund of input tax, although title was not transferred until 31 October so the premises had not been let at the time the return was made.

The Supreme Court of the Netherlands sought a preliminary ruling on the question of whether "exploitation" within the meaning of the second sentence of Art. 4(2) of the Sixth Directive commenced as soon as a person purchased future property with a view to letting that property in due course and whether the purchase of such a right in future property might be regarded as an economic activity within Art. 4(1) of the Sixth Directive.

Before: Due (President of Chamber), Pescatore and Bahlmann JJ.

DECISION. The Rompelmans take the view that property is exploited as from the time of the acquisition of title to it. Such a preparatory act must be treated as part of the commercial activity since it is necessary in order to make that activity possible.

The Netherlands Government maintains that the moment at which an economic activity must be considered as having commenced precedes the date on which the property begins to yield regular income. In the present case, that means that a person who lets immovable property began to exploit it at the time when he bought it as future property. However, since an investment may, but does not necessarily, lead to the exploitation of property, exploitation must not be considered to exist until there is more objective evidence of the investor's intention. A declaration of intention must be confirmed by other facts and circumstances.

According to the Commission, it follows from Art. 17(1) of the Sixth Directive that the exploitation of immovable property will generally begin with the first preparatory act, that is to say with the first transaction on which input tax may be charged. The first transaction completed in the course of an economic activity consists in the acquisition of assets and therefore in the purchase of property. Having regard to those elements of the common VAT system it is necessary to consider the question whether the acquisition of a right to the transfer of the future ownership of a building which is still to be constructed in return for the payment of the purchase price in instalments as building progresses must in itself be regarded as the commencement of exploitation of tangible property and therefore as goods or as a service used for the purposes of taxable transactions, in this case for letting.

partners acquired capital goods and contributed them to the partnership before the partnership was registered for VAT purposes.

As regards the letting of immovable property, Art. 13B.(b) of the Sixth Directive provides that it is in principle exempt from VAT. However, since the Rompelmans apparently exercised the option provided for in Art. 13(c) to be taxed on lettings of immovable property, the letting in this case must be treated as a taxable transaction.

The preparatory acts, such as the acquisition of assets and therefore the purchase of immovable property, which form part of those transactions must themselves be treated as constituting economic activity.

The principle that VAT should be neutral as regards the tax burden on a business requires that the first investment expenditure incurred for the purposes of and with the view to commencing a business must be regarded as an economic activity. It would be contrary to that principle if such an activity did not commence until the property began to yield taxable income. Any other interpretation of Art. 4 of the Sixth Directive would burden the trader with the cost of VAT in the course of his economic activity without allowing him to deduct it in accordance with Art. 17 and would create an arbitrary distinction between investment expenditure incurred before actual exploitation of immovable property and expenditure incurred during exploitation.

THE COURT hereby rules:

The acquisition of a right to the future transfer of property rights in part of a building yet to be constructed with a view to letting such premises in due course may be regarded as an economic activity within the meaning of Art. 4(1) of the Sixth Directive. However, that provision does not preclude the tax administration from requiring the declared intention to be supported by objective evidence such as proof that the premises which it is proposed to construct are specifically suited to commercial exploitation.

D. Employee Not Engaged in Taxable Activity

Services provided by an employee to an employer are not taxable services under VAT regimes in use today. Individuals therefore are not, by virtue of their positions as employees, taxable persons subject to VAT. In some situations, there are disputes about the status of a person as an employee whose services are not taxable or an independent contractor whose services are taxable. For example, in the Netherlands, a managing director owning more than 50% of his company's stock was held to be independent.[87] As a result, the director's compensation was subject to VAT.

[87] The VAT Directive, *supra* note 54, at Art. 9(1), defines a taxable person as one who independently carries out in any place any economic activity, whatever the purpose or results of that activity. See Ravensberger and Heezen, "Managing Directors/Major Shareholders Are Taxable Persons," *VAT Monitor* 429 (Sept./Oct. 2002) (Netherlands); Gurtner, *VAT Symposium 2003, VAT Monitor* 474 (Nov./Dec. 2003) (Austria).

Typically, employers purchase tools and all other equipment used by employees and therefore get credit for tax paid on these items. Employees sent out to do work elsewhere, for example, plumbers, often furnish their own tools as a matter of efficient management practice.

> An employee may suffer a VAT disadvantage by not being treated as a taxable person. For example, if a musician must purchase her own expensive cello, a carpenter must purchase his own tools, or a guard must purchase his own uniform, the employee must bear VAT that cannot be offset by an input credit. … One alternative would be to enable the employee to claim credit for VAT charged on the purchases. An employee could be granted the option to file a VAT return and claim refund for VAT on an employment-related purchase. Alternatively, employers could be eligible to claim input credits for VAT on an employment-related purchase by employees. Each alternative presents administrative problems for taxable persons and for the … [government].[88]

V. Discussion Questions

1. Taxpayer A is a building contractor. To help his son (taxpayer B) start his own business, he gives him two used trucks and a crane. What will be the tax consequences? Would the situation be different if taxpayer B ceased his business and gave all the assets to his daughter?
2. To characterize the "taxable person," how do New Vatopia and the EU Sixth Directive take into account
   a. the nature of the activity performed;
   b. the place where this activity is performed;
   c. the aims of the activity;
   d. the legal status of the person carrying on the activity?
3. Can a person carrying on only exempt activities be a "taxable person" under the EU Sixth Directive? How does New Vatopia handle the ideas of exempt persons and exempt activities?
4. How are occasional transactions treated in the New Vatopia VAT and the EU Sixth Directive?
5. Under which circumstances are governments and other public law organizations deemed to be "taxable persons" under the EU Sixth Directive and the New Vatopia VAT?
6. Does either the receipt of rents from movable (personal) or immovable (real) property or the receipt of wages lead to the status of "taxable person" under either the EU Sixth Directive or the New Vatopia VAT?
7. Suppose you are drafting VAT legislation for your country. In defining the "taxable person" or "registered person," would you rely on
   a. the definition of business for income tax purposes;
   b. the definition of industrial and commercial activities, as this definition may be found in your private law;

[88] ABA Model VAT, *supra* note 30, at 32–33.

c. a completely independent definition for VAT purposes;
d. or, do you think you can do without the concept of "taxable person" and define the scope of the tax only by reference to the "taxable transactions"?

8. Is a merger between two companies a taxable transaction for VAT purposes? Is a special treatment provided in this case by the New Vatopia VAT and the EU Sixth Directive? Why?

5 Taxable Supplies and Tax Invoices

I. Introduction

Most VAT regimes impose VAT on a supply only if it is for consideration, and there is a clear connection between the supply and that consideration.[1] This chapter first examines the question, what is a supply for VAT purposes? It explores notions of supply, consideration, and the required link between a supply and the consideration received by the seller.

A sale for a single price may incorporate elements of multiple supplies that are taxed differently. For example, a portion of the supply, if independent, is taxable at a positive rate, and another portion, if independent, is exempt from tax. It is significant for VAT purposes if the transaction is respected as a single supply of these two components or is treated as two separate supplies. A major part of this chapter therefore focuses on resolving the perplexing question, what is "the supply"? In some cases, the VAT legislation and case law may draw a distinction between mixed supplies (with main and incidental elements) that are classified as a single supply of the main element and composite supplies that can be disaggregated and classified as multiple independent supplies.

Finally, a VAT invoice containing required information and issuable only by registered persons is considered central to a European-style invoice VAT. Some aspects of the VAT invoice are discussed in this chapter.

II. Supplies of Goods and Services

A VAT generally is considered a method of collecting in chunks a tax on the consumption of goods and services by final consumers. Most VATs, however, do not distinguish between consumer goods and services, on the one hand, and tangible goods held for investment and services related to the purchase of investments, on the other hand. Thus, a work of art

[1] See C. Amand, "When Is a Link Direct?" 7 *VAT Monitor* 3 (Jan./Feb. 1996) [hereinafter Amand, When Is a Link Direct?].

purchased as an investment commonly is included in the VAT base. The purchase of shares in a corporation is not included in the tax base, but the commission on the broker's services on the share acquisition generally is included in the base, unless those services are treated as exempt financial services. See the exemption for financial services in Chapter 11.

A. What Is a Supply for Consideration?

The domestic supply of taxable goods or services for consideration by a registered person, the import of taxable goods by anyone, and the import of taxable services by designed persons are taxed under transactional VATs like those in force in about 160 countries.[2] The domestic supply of goods and services generally includes sales, leases, and other transfers of rights.[3] The concept of a supply as broader than a sale is illustrated by the British case involving the taxpayer's sale of a known stolen car at auction. Although the sale may be void as a matter of local law, the Queen's Bench held that a supply "is the passing of possession in goods pursuant to an agreement whereunder the supplier agrees to part with and the recipient agrees to take possession" of the goods, even if, as in this case, the innocent purchaser at auction may have to give up the car.[4] Another British case held that serving a member a drink for a consideration in a nonprofit member's club was a supply for VAT purposes.[5] Selling is not a necessary prerequisite for a supply. "Supply," the term commonly used in VAT laws, is generally used in this chapter, but occasionally "sale" and "supply" are used interchangeably.

As mentioned, under most VAT regimes, tax is imposed on a supply of goods or services for consideration by a person registered for VAT. Does a registered person have to report, as a taxable supply, a "deposit" for a future supply of goods or services? There are two kinds of "deposits": deposits that can be applied to the amount charged for the goods or services supplied and deposits that are intended as security for the performance of an agreement between the parties. Generally, the receipt of a

2 See, for example, Council Directive 2006/112/EC of 28 November 2006 on the common system of value added tax, Art. 2 (OJ L347, 11.12.2006), 1 [hereinafter VAT Directive]; recasting Sixth Council Directive of 17 May 1977 on the harmonization of the laws of the members states relating to turnover taxes – Common System of Value Added Tax: Uniform Basis of Assessment (77/388/EEC), Art. 2 [hereinafter Sixth Directive]. See Commonwealth of New Vatopia Value Added Tax Act, http://www.imf.org/external/np/leg/tlaw/2003/eng/tlvat.htm [hereinafter New Vatopia], §9.

3 VAT Directive, *supra* note 2, at Arts. 5 and 6. In an unusual decision involving the Australian GST, the New South Wales Supreme Court, relying in part on the analysis of the Australian Tax Office, held that there was not a taxable supply if a registered business received compensation for expropriated property. See *CSR Ltd v. Hornsby Shire Council*, [2004] NSWSC 946, discussed in R. Krever, "Involuntary and Statutory Supplies – The Australian GST Base Narrows," 16 *Int'l VAT Monitor* 19 (Jan. /Feb. 2005).

4 *Customs and Excise Commissioners v. Oliver*, [1980] 1 All ER 353.

5 *Canton Lodge Club v. Customs and Excise Commissioners*, [1974] 3 All ER 798.

deposit that serves as security for the performance of an agreement is not a taxable supply at the time it is received. Although it may be difficult to determine, in some cases, whether a deposit fits in the first or second category, in this section, the discussion focuses on deposits that are prepayments for goods or services to be provided in the future.

Some commentators have suggested that the treatment of forfeited deposits (or forfeited full payments) should be based on the specifics of the contract between the supplier and the customer. Should the tax consequences depend on the vagaries of the terms of the agreement between supplier and customer?

There has been significant litigation over the tax consequences of prepayments for supplies (commonly services) in cases in which the person making the prepayment does not receive the benefit of the intended supply and the prepayment is forfeited. In fact, although many cases involve deposits, the controversy has expanded to cover the forfeiture of the entire payment for a supply. Some cases examine whether a forfeited prepayment is a supply "for consideration." If a sufficient link is not found, the court may conclude that a forfeited payment is not a "supply for consideration" and therefore not subject to VAT. On the other hand, the amount forfeited might be considered a payment for a right to receive services, perhaps during a specific time slot.

A related issue involves the timing rules (covered in Chapter 8). Under typical timing rules, a supply occurs on the date the invoice covering the supply is issued but may be accelerated if any payment is received before the invoice is issued.[6] If a deposit is treated as part of the consideration for a supply, the value of the entire supply must be reported in the tax period in which the supplier receives the deposit.

The following discussion focuses on transactions in which a deposit (or full payment) is forfeited and the customer does not receive the goods or services that were the subject of the supply. In 2007, the ECJ, in the *Société* case,[7] decided that a hotel's retention of a deposit on the client's cancellation of a hotel reservation was compensation to the hotel for the loss resulting from the client's default (a fixed cancellation charge). The ECJ decided that the forfeited deposit was not directly connected with (no direct link to) the supply of a service for consideration by the hotel and therefore not subject to tax under the Sixth Directive, Articles 2(1) and 6(1).[8] The Australian courts reached different conclusions.

6 Some countries require supplies to be reported in the earliest of the tax period in which an invoice is issued, accrual occurs, or any payment is received. See VAT Directive, *supra* note 2, Arts. 62–67. VAT is chargeable when goods or services are supplied, but member states can provide that VAT is chargeable no later than the time that the invoice is issued or the payment is received.

7 Case C-277/07, *Société thermate d'Eugénie-les-Baiins v. Ministère de l'Économie* (ECJ 2007).

8 Sixth Directive, *supra* note 2, at Art. 2(1) is comparable to the VAT Directive, *supra* note 2, at Art. 2(1)(a) and (c), and the Sixth Directive, Art. 6(1) is comparable to the VAT Directive, Arts. 24(1) and 25 (a)-(c).The VAT Directive, Art. 2(1)(c) taxes a "supply of services for consideration within the territory of a Member State by a taxable person acting as such."

In the *Reliance Carpet* case[9] (discussed in the following *Qantas* case), the Australian High Court held that the forfeiture of a deposit under a contract for the purchase of real property was a supply subject to GST. Qantas involves forfeited payments for flights that were not taken in which the customers were not able to obtain refunds for the unused tickets.

Commissioner of Taxation v. Qantas Airways Ltd[10]

High Court Australia 2012

GUMMOW, HAYNE, KIEFEL AND BELL JJ.

Introduction

The respondent ("Qantas") and its subsidiaries, including Jetstar Airways Pty Limited ("Jetstar"), provide domestic and international air travel but this litigation concerns only their domestic operations. Both Qantas and Jetstar supply classes of air travel with varying fare rules and conditions of carriage.

The amount in contest in this appeal is the GST on fares received from prospective passengers who failed to take the flights for which reservations and payment had been made. In accordance with the applicable conditions, some fares were forfeited while others were refundable on application within a stipulated period but no refund claim was made. [Under section 29-5(1) of the Australian GST, the] GST is attributable to the tax period in which there is received "any" of the consideration, being the fares paid, or, before that receipt, the invoice is issued.

The ... effect of the GST Act is that with respect to any particular transaction the GST is payable only once, at the end of the attributable taxation period. GST on the consideration received is not payable in each of the tax periods in which a series of events occur in performance of an executory contract; the GST is payable once, in the tax period of the first payment or invoice.

The fares were calculated to recover from the customer the GST payable on the amount of those fares. On payment of the fare the GST amount was recorded by the airline as a debt due to the Commissioner; the balance was credited to unearned income until the flight was taken or the fare was forfeited. The GST component of the fares for flights not taken was not refunded to customers.

[9] *Commissioner of Taxation v. Reliance Carpet Pty Ltd*, [2008] HCA 22; (2008) 236 CLR 342 (High Court Australia 2008).

[10] *Commissioner of Taxation v. Qantas Airways Ltd*, [2012] HCA 41 (High Court 2012) [edited by the authors].

The litigation

Qantas contended that GST was not payable on the unused fares and that the GST which had been paid on them should be refunded by the Commissioner. [The Commissioner issued an assessment. Qantas objected, the objection was disallowed, and the case was referred to the Administrative Appeals Tribunal ("the AAT"), which affirmed the disallowance. The case then went to the Federal Court of Australia. The Full Court held for Qantas.]
By special leave the Commissioner appeals to this Court against the whole of the judgment of the Full Court.

The decision of the Full Federal Court [in this case]

[The judges looked at the conditions of carriage between the airline and the booked passengers.] They concluded that it was plain that "what each customer pays for" is carriage by air and continued[11]:

"This is the essence, and sole purpose, of the transaction. The prospective supply is of air travel, [the relevant supply] … 'nothing more or less'.[12] [The purpose of the booking was air travel (that was the relevant supply), and the passenger did not take the flight. The airline retained the fare. There was no supply for which the consideration was paid.]

The legislation

The appeal turns upon the construction and application of [the operative provisions of the GST Act]. In particular, in the phrase "the supply *for* consideration" [emphasis added], which appears in the definition of "taxable supplies" in s 9-5(a) and is set out below, the word "for" is not used to adopt contractual principles. Rather, it requires a connection or relationship between the supply and the consideration.

Section 7-1 of the GST Act is identified as a "central provision." It relevantly states that GST is payable "on[13] taxable supplies." [The Act, in section 9-5, provides that a person makes a taxable supply if:]

"(a) you make the supply for consideration; and
(b) the supply is made in the course or furtherance of an *enterprise that you carry on; and
(c) the supply is connected with Australia; and
(d) you are registered, or required to be registered."

[11] (2011) 195 FCR 260 at 278.

[12] The reference is to a lower court decision, reversed by the High Court, in *Federal Commissioner of Taxation v. Reliance Carpet Co. Pty Ltd*, [2008] HCA 22; (2008); 236 CLR 342 at 347–348.

[13] The asterisks in the case were removed. They note that there is a definition of this word or term in the Australian GST Act.

The term "consideration" is defined in s 9–15 so as to include "any payment, or any act or forbearance, in connection with a supply of anything" (s 9–15(1)(a)), and "any payment, or any act or forbearance, in response to or for the inducement of a supply of anything" (s 9–15(1)(b)).

Sub-section (1) of s 9–10 states that a supply "is any form of supply whatsoever."

"Without limiting subsection (1), [sub-section (2) provides that] *supply* includes any of these:

(a) a supply of goods;
(b) *a supply of services;*
(c) a provision of advice or information;
(d) a grant, assignment or surrender of real property;
(e) *a creation*, grant, transfer, assignment or surrender of *any right;*
(f) a financial supply;
(g) *an entry into*, or release from, *an obligation*:
  (i) *to do anything*; or
  (ii) to refrain from an act; or
  (iii) to tolerate an act or situation;
(h) *any combination* of any 2 or more of the matters referred to in paragraphs (a) to (g)." [Emphasis added.]

The Commissioner relies upon the emphasised portions of pars (b), (e), (g) and (h).

With the distinction between "supply" and "taxable supply" in mind, the [High] Court observed in *Reliance Carpet*[14]:

"The composite expression 'a taxable supply' is of critical importance for the creation of liability to GST. In the facts and circumstances of a given case there may be disclosed consecutive acts each of which answers the statutory description of 'supply', but upon examination it may appear that there is no more than one 'taxable supply'."

That is not to deny that the one consideration may be received for more than one supply, although the GST will be payable once and will be attributable to the first tax period in which any of the consideration is received or invoiced.

The substance of the submission by Qantas, variously expressed, is that the Full Court [in this case] was correct because (i) the dealings between Qantas and Jetstar and prospective passengers were such that there was no more than one projected "taxable supply," namely the supply of air travel, (ii) this supply did not come to pass and (iii) no GST was exigible.

[14] [2008] HCA 22; (2008) 236 CLR 342 at 346.

Reliance Carpet

In *Reliance Carpet*,[15] the taxpayer entered into a land contract for real property. The purchaser paid a deposit of about 10% of the purchase price. The purchaser defaulted, there was rescission, and the taxpayer retained the deposit.

In *Reliance Carpet* the Full Court of the Federal Court [accepted the taxpayer's claim] that there had been no "taxable supply" because (i) the essential or principal supply was the single subject of the tax, (ii) in the instant case that single subject was a supply of real property and (iii) the contract had been terminated so that there had been no supply of real property and Div 99 [which deals with deposits] had no work to do. The Full Court said[16]:

"When the [taxpayer] entered into the contract for sale with the purchaser it entered into a contract for the supply of real property; nothing more and nothing less."

This Court reversed the decision of the Full Court. The Court said[17]:

"the use of the phrase 'nothing more and nothing less' appears to give insufficient weight both to the definition of 'real property' in the Act, and to the identity of the subject matter of the contract, in accordance with ordinary principles of conveyancing, as the title or estate of the vendor in a parcel of land rather than merely the parcel itself in a geographical sense,[18]"

and the Court also observed[19]:

"The circumstance that the deposit forfeited to the taxpayer had various characteristics does not mean that the taxpayer may fix upon such one or more of these characteristics as it selects to demonstrate that there was no taxable supply. It is sufficient for the Commissioner's case that the presence of one or more of these characteristics satisfies the criterion of 'consideration' for the application of the GST provisions respecting a 'taxable supply'. One of the characteristics of the deposit was that upon its payment on 5 February 2002 it operated as a security for the performance of the obligation of the purchaser to complete the Contract and was liable to forfeiture on that failure. That is sufficient for the Commissioner's case."

15 [2008] HCA 22; (2008) 236 CLR 342.
16 [2007] FCAFC 99; (2007) 160 FCR 433 at 445.
17 [2008] HCA 22; (2008) 236 CLR 342 at 348.
18 Cf. *Travinto Nominees Pty Ltd v. Vlattas*, [1973] HCA 14; (1973) 129 CLR 1 at 13; [1973] HCA 14; *The Commonwealth v. Western Australia*, [1999] HCA 5; (1999) 196 CLR 392 at 426; [1999] HCA 5; *Risk v. Northern Territory*, [2002] HCA 23; (2002) 210 CLR 392 at 418; [2002] HCA 23.
19 [2008] HCA 22; (2008) 236 CLR 342 at 352.

Division 99, ... was described by this Court[20] as a "wait and see" provision, whereby a deposit was taken to be consideration only when it was forfeited. The case provides no support for the proposition adopted by the Full Court in the present case that it was necessary to extract from the transaction between the airline and the prospective passenger the "essence" and "sole purpose" of the transaction.

The Commissioner's case [in the High Court]

[The Commissioner claimed] that the unused fares were received or invoiced in the assessed tax periods and that this was on or pursuant to the making of a contract between the airline and the customer under which the airline supplied rights, obligations and services in addition to the proposed flight. These rights, obligations and services comprised "payment ... in connection with a supply" thereof within the meaning of the definition of "consideration,"[21] so that there was a taxable supply attributable to that period.

The Full Court stated the following conclusions as to the effect of the Qantas conditions and the Jetstar conditions.[22] Using "Q" to identify the former and "J" to identify the latter:

"(1) A person can make a reservation (Qantas) or booking (Jetstar) without making any payment, but: if Qantas has not received payment for the ticket on or before the specified ticketing time, Qantas may cancel the reservation [Q 4.3] and, in consequence, travel will not be allowed [Q 4.2]; and, if Jetstar has not received payment, the person will not be carried, even if they have a booking [J 4.2].

(2) A person buys a Qantas ticket by paying the applicable fare, applicable fees or charges and all government taxes [Q 5.5]; a person does not buy, but only makes a Qantas reservation [Q 4.1]; a person both makes [J 4.1] and pays for a Jetstar booking by paying the applicable fare, applicable surcharges, fees or taxes, and any applicable amounts relating to changes to the booking [J 5.5].

(3) The fare covers the flight for the person and the person's Baggage Allowance from the airport at the place of departure specified on the Ticket (Qantas)/in the booking (Jetstar) to the airport at the place of destination specified on the Ticket (Qantas)/specified in the booking (Jetstar) [Q and J 5.1].

(4) A person may purchase a Qantas ticket without a reservation (an open-dated ticket), but the person will not be able to travel until the person makes a reservation in a specified class of service and on a specified date and flight [Q 4.2]. With Jetstar, a person cannot hold an open booking [J 6.2(a)].

[20] [2008] HCA 22; (2008) 236 CLR 342 at 354.

[21] Section 9–15(1)(a).

[22] (2011) 195 FCR 260 at 272.

(5) With Qantas, a person cannot fly without making a specified reservation, in a specified class of service and on a specified date and flight [Q 4.2]; with Jetstar, a person cannot travel without a booking on a specific flight [J 6.2(a)]."

The critical provision in the Qantas conditions is set out in cl 9.2, headed "Late or Cancelled Flights (Except in Circumstances Beyond Our Control)":

"*We will take all reasonable measures necessary to carry you and your baggage and to avoid delay in doing so.* In doing so and in order to prevent a flight cancellation, in exceptional circumstances we may arrange for a flight to be operated on our behalf by an alternative carrier and/or aircraft. [A list of exceptions follows. If the flight is cancelled or one of the other exceptions applies, the passenger has a number of options (the only remedies available), including a future flight or, in certain cases, a refund is available.]"

Conclusions

The Qantas conditions and the Jetstar conditions did not provide an unconditional promise to carry the passenger and baggage on a particular flight. They supplied something less than that. This was at least a promise to use best endeavours to carry the passenger and baggage, having regard to the circumstances of the business operations of the airline.[23] This was a "taxable supply" for which the consideration, being the fare, was received.

The GST payable for that taxable supply was attributable to and included in the calculation of the Qantas net amount for the tax periods in issue in this litigation and the assessments objected to were not shown to be excessive.

Orders

The appeal [by the Commissioner] should be allowed....

HEYDON J. [dissent]

The problem raised by the appeal can be answered in brief terms as follows. The expression "taxable supply" [in section 9-5] provides that a taxpayer makes a taxable supply if the taxpayer makes "the supply for consideration." A supply by a taxpayer implies that the taxpayer has supplied something to someone else.[24] The expression "supply

[23] See *Transfield Pty Ltd v. Arlo International Ltd*, [1980] HCA 15; (1980) 144 CLR 83 at 101, 107; [1980] HCA 15; *Hospital Products Ltd v. United States Surgical Corporation*, [1984] HCA 64; (1984) 156 CLR 41 at 64–65, 91–92, 116–117, 120, 137–138; [1984] HCA 64.

[24] *Westley Nominees Pty Ltd v. Coles Supermarkets Australia Pty Ltd*, [2006] FCAFC 115; (2006) 152 FCR 461 at 466.

for consideration" connotes a bargained-for exchange of value for performance. What, then, was the bargain?

The Full Court of the Federal Court of Australia said[25]: "what each customer pays for is carriage by air. This is the essence, and sole purpose, of the transaction"...[its] "legal substance" and "pith and substance,"[26] and its "direct object."[27]

The transaction was a contract of carriage by air – a conditional contract in numerous respects, but still a contract of carriage by air. Under that contract the respondent promised to supply the service of an air journey. Because the passengers with whom this appeal is concerned did not make themselves available to enjoy that service, the respondent did not supply them with any air journeys.

The Administrative Appeals Tribunal found as a fact that "the actual carriage of the passenger" was "obviously the purpose of each reservation."[28] In a sense the respondent supplied services or created a qualified right or entered a qualified obligation when it accepted the fare and made the reservation. But that stage of the transaction was incidental and preparatory to the central purpose, substance and object of the transaction – an actual air journey. What the intending passenger wanted was not so much a chose in action – a qualified promise to supply an air journey which it would be difficult to enforce legally. The intending passenger wanted the actual supply of an air journey. This, through no fault of its own, the respondent never supplied.

The parties agreed that there was only a single taxable supply. The respondent submitted that it made a conditional contract to carry the passenger by air, and that if no air journey took place, it had not supplied anything. On the other hand, the appellant submitted that when a passenger paid a fare, that passenger was supplied with a reservation in consideration of the fare paid. Thus the appellant concentrated on the making of a promise to supply an air journey. The respondent concentrated on the extent to which an air journey actually took place. The appellant concentrated on what was supplied when the seat was reserved and paid for. The respondent concentrated on what was not supplied when the passenger failed to attend at the time when the promised air journey was supposed to take place. The appellant said that the taxable supply was entering the contract to provide an air journey. The respondent said that the taxable supply was the actual provision, under contract, of an air journey.

25 *Qantas Airways Ltd v. Federal Commissioner of Taxation* (2011) 195 FCR 260 at 278 per Edmonds and Perram JJ (Stone J. concurring).

26 *Travelex Ltd v. Federal Commissioner of Taxation*, [2010] HCA 33; (2010) 241 CLR 510 at 524 per Heydon J.

27 *Travelex Ltd v. Federal Commissioner of Taxation*, [2010] HCA 33; (2010) 241 CLR 510 at 535 per Crennan and Bell JJ.

28 *Qantas Airways Ltd v. Commissioner of Taxation*, [2010] AATA 977; (2010) 119 ALD 199 at 205.

An interpretation of s 9-5 as fastening on the latter supply conforms more closely to practical reality. It prevents GST from being charged in relation to a promise to supply an air journey which the passenger's conduct prevented from being fulfilled and (in some instances) a promise to refund the fare which the passenger did not seek to have fulfilled. The fare was paid not to get a conditional promise to supply an air flight (which promise did take place) but to get an actual air journey (which never took place).

The respondent's position does have a superficially unattractive feature. The respondent seeks to acquire money paid by passengers who intended or expected that it would end up in the hands of the appellant, not those of the respondent. If the respondent's argument is correct, the passengers who have not claimed their fares back have left the respondent in a position to gain money which it was never meant to have. The lack of attractiveness in the respondent's position is not fundamental. So far as the contracts of passengers with the respondent did not give them any right to reclaim their fares, they have no cause for complaint. The position in which they find themselves is a result of their contractual choice. So far as the contracts of passengers with the respondent did give them a right to reclaim their fares which they have not exercised, they have no cause for complaint. The position in which they find themselves is a result of their failure to exercise their contractual rights to repayment. And the appellant cannot complain about not being able to retain money which the Act does not permit it to retain.

The appeal should be dismissed essentially for the reasons given by the Full Court.[29]

In some cases, the dispute is whether a transaction constitutes "a supply" within the VAT system and, if so, is a "supply of services" or a "supply of goods." Some of the cases relate to transactions involving ownership interests in business, such as a company's issuance of its own shares or a change in the partners in a partnership. Many countries treat these transactions as beyond the scope of the VAT. Because the issue typically arises in connection with the deductibility of input tax related to these transactions, those issues are covered in Chapter 6. The next subsections cover the taxability of an array of transactions, including the transfer of assets to an agent or appointed representative, and transactions, without monetary consideration changing hands, that may be "deemed" to be supplies for consideration for VAT purposes.

[29] AustLII at http://www.austlii.edu.au/au/cases/cth/HCA/2012/41.html.

1. Nonsupplies or Supplies Other Than in the Course of Taxable Activity

There is no uniform approach to the classification of transactions as "nonsupplies," which are not subject to VAT. If a VAT-registered business is denied an input credit for tax on the acquisition of an asset and the business sells that asset, the sale typically is not a supply subject to VAT.[30] Excluding such a transaction from the definition of supply is a drafting technique designed to impose tax only once in respect of the asset. For example, if a firm purchases an automobile for use in its business and is denied credit for tax on the automobile (as some VATs do), the sale of the automobile is not a supply under some VAT regimes.

In some transactions, there is no transfer of legal title. In others, the transfer of an asset may be to a person who holds the asset in a representative capacity.

A transfer of assets (or an entire business) to a legal representative generally is not treated as a supply subject to tax. For example, transfers of assets of a business to a receiver in bankruptcy commonly are not supplies and therefore do not attract tax.[31] Likewise, tax may not be imposed when the business assets of a person adjudged incompetent are transferred to a representative who then operates the ongoing business.[32]

A transaction treated as a nonsupply is in effect zero-rated if the transferor can claim credit for tax on purchases attributable to this transaction. The same transaction is in effect exempt if the transferor is denied credit for tax on purchases attributable to it. The following additional categories of transactions may be removed from the VAT base.

Asset Transfers to Creditors. When a debtor, as security for an obligation, transfers possession of, or grants a security interest in, an asset without transferring ownership of the asset, there is no supply for consideration that is subject to VAT. The same applies if an asset of a person under a legal disability is transferred to the person's legal representative.[33]

Business-to-Business Sales of a Going Concern. When a going concern is sold, the sale is not part of the process of production and distribution commonly included in a consumption tax base. The sale nevertheless is a taxable supply unless the law provides otherwise. When the sale is between VAT-registered businesses that make taxable sales, if it were taxable, the tax charged on the sale would be recoverable by the buyer as an input credit. The buyer's cost to finance the tax until it is recovered may

30 See Value Added Tax Act 1994, c. 23, Sch. 9, group 14 (United Kingdom) [hereinafter VATA 1994]; New Vatopia, *supra* note 2, at §4(17), treats this kind of sale as a supply "otherwise than in the course or furtherance of a taxable activity," and therefore as not within the scope of the VAT.

31 See VATA 1994, *supra* note 30, at §46, and SI 1995/2518, reg. 9 (United Kingdom). See New Vatopia, *supra* note 2, at §4(16).

32 VATA 1994, *supra* note 30, at §46(4), and SI 1995/2518, reg. 9 (United Kingdom).

33 See A. Schenk, *Value Added Tax – A Model Statute and Commentary: A Report of the Committee on Value Added Tax of the American Bar Association Section of Taxation*, 28 [hereinafter ABA Model VAT].

be significant, especially if excess credits must be carried forward for a period of months before they are eligible for refund. Aside from any cash flow benefit, the government would not receive any net revenue from the transaction.

The EU VAT Directive gives Member States the option to provide that no supply occurs on the transfer of a going concern, but the Members States may include rules to prevent the distortion of competition if the recipient is not subject to tax on all of its supplies.[34] By applying this rule, the Treasury in the United Kingdom has authority to issue an order removing transactions from the scope of the tax by treating them as neither supplies of goods nor supplies of services. Under this authority the Treasury ruled that the transfer of a business as a going concern is neither a supply of goods nor a supply of services.[35] Many VAT systems address this problem by either zero-rating the sale of a going concern[36] or excluding such a transaction from the definition of taxable supply.

2. Sales for Consideration

A supply is subject to VAT in most countries only if the supply is made for consideration.[37] If a supply is made and no consideration is explicitly charged or received, unless it is an exceptional situation, such as certain supplies between related persons, tax is not imposed on the transaction. For example, if a company operates a canteen and charges staff for meals but offers a meal to a business contact free of charge, the supply free of charge is not taxable.[38] Personal gifts generally are not VAT-able because they are not sales (they are not transferred for consideration) and they do not arise in connection with a business. Gratuitous transfers inter vivos to an individual or into trust thus would not attract VAT. Likewise, gratuitous transfers of personal articles, furniture, and other assets on death to an executor or administrator or directly to a beneficiary (or transfers by an executor or administrator to a beneficiary) would not be VAT-able. These transfers are not sales and they do not arise in connection with a business.[39]

34 See VAT Directive, *supra* note 2, at Art. 19. If an EU member state adopts this option, it cannot then restrict the "no supply" rule. For example, a member state cannot restrict the rule only to transfers to persons authorized to pursue the totality of the economic activity of the transferor. Case C-497/01, *Zita Modes SARL v. Administration de 1-enregistrement et des domains*, [2003] ECR 1–14, 393; [2003] All ER (D) 411.

35 SI 1995/1268, Art. 5. VATA 1994, *supra* note 30, at §49(1), generally requiring the transferor's records to be preserved by the transferee.

36 See New Zealand Goods and Services Tax Act, 1985, No. 141, §ll(l)(m) [hereinafter NZ GST]; New Vatopia, *supra* note 2, at §4(2), and Sch. I, ¶[2(o). Although many VATs zero-rate both a sale of an entire business as a going concern or a sale of a portion of a business capable of separate operation, Azerbaijan amended its VAT law to remove zero-rating for the transfer of an independent division of a business. See Alum Bati, "Azerbaijan: Transfer of Assets," *VAT Monitor*, 122 (Mar./Apr. 2005).

37 See, for example, VAT Directive, *supra* note 2, at Art. 2(1)(a).

38 See Case C-37/07, *Danfoss A/S AstraZeneca A/S v. Skatteministeriet* (ECJ 2008).

39 ABA Model VAT, *supra* note 33, at 26.

Implicit in the rule taxing only sales made for consideration is the requirement that there must be a sufficient link or connection between the sale and the consideration.[40] For some transactions, the VAT law may specifically provide that the transaction is a supply of goods or services for consideration. For example, in New Zealand, the local authority rates (local real property taxes) are treated as consideration for supplies of goods and services by a registered local authority.[41]

This subsection examines this requirement, that there must be a link between the sale and the consideration. In the following case, services were rendered and the recipient was not required to make any monetary payment.

Staatssecretaris van Financiën v. Cooperatieve Aardappelenbewarplaats G.A.[42]

[A cooperative association operated a cold storage warehouse for members to store their potatoes. Each member with shares in the co-op was entitled to store 1,000 kilograms of potatoes a year per share, and the co-op ordinarily imposed charges for the storage at the end of the season. In the years in issue, "pending the sale of the cold-store," the co-op decided not to charge members for potatoes stored in the warehouse. As a result, the value of the shares held by the members declined as the co-op incurred expenses to operate the warehouse.]

FACTS. Article 2 (a) of the Second Directive[43] on harmonization of turnover taxes provides that:

'The following shall be subject to the value added tax:

(a) The supply of goods and the provision of services within the territory of the country by a taxable person against payment';

and Article 8 provides:

'The basis of assessment shall be:

(a) in the case of supply of goods and the provision of services, everything which makes up the consideration for the supply of the goods or the provision of services, including all expenses and taxes except the value added tax itself.'

Finally Annex A point 13 regarding Article 8 (a) provides that:

[40] See Amand, When is a Link Direct?, *supra* note 1.

[41] NZ GST, *supra* note 36, at §5(7). See M. Pallot, "Local Authorities," 14 *Int'l VAT Monitor* 496 (Nov./Dec. 2003).

[42] Case 154/80, [1981] ECR 445, [1981] 3 CMLR 337 (ECJ 1980) [edited by the authors]. See New Vatopia, *supra* note 2, at §5(5).

[43] Second Council Directive, 67/228 of 11 April 1967.

> 'The expression "consideration" means everything received in return for the supply of goods or the provision of services, including incidental expenses (packing, transport, insurance, etc.) that is to say not only the cash amounts charged, but also, for example, the value of the goods received in exchange or, in the case of goods or services supplied by order of a public authority, the amount of the compensation received'.

But the Inspector thought that the co-operative had nevertheless charged its members something in return owing to the reduction in value of their shares owing to the non-collection of their storage charges and he therefore assessed what was received in return to be the storage charge ordinarily charged, namely 2 cents per kilogram of potatoes....

[The Netherlands Supreme Court referred the case to the Court of Justice to determine if there was ... "consideration" within Article 8(a) of the Second Directive.]

JUDGMENT. The co-operative claimed that it provided its services for no consideration because it had not required anything in return. The court held that VAT community law does not refer to the law of the Member States for its meaning, so the definition of terms may not be left to the discretion of each Member-State.

Services are taxable, within the meaning of the Second Directive, when the service is provided against payment and the basis of assessment for such a service is everything which makes up the consideration for the service; there must therefore be a direct link between the service provided and the consideration received which does not occur in a case where the consideration consists of an unascertained reduction in the value of the shares possessed by the members of the co-operative and such a loss of value may not be regarded as a payment received by the co-operative providing the services.

The consideration for services must be capable of being expressed in money. Such consideration is a subjective value since the basis of assessment for the provision of services is the consideration actually received and not a value assessed according to objective criteria.

Consequently a provision of services for which no definite subjective consideration is received does not constitute a provision of services "against payment" and is therefore not taxable within [Article 8(a)] ... of the Second Directive.

The relationship between the service and the consideration, as well as the existence of reciprocal obligations, is important, if not determinative.[44]

[44] Amand, When Is a Link Direct?, *supra* note 1, at 10. According to Amand, the core of the direct link requirement is the "principle of reciprocal obligation." *Id.*

Except where specifically included in the tax base,[45] a forced exaction in the nature of a tax presumably is not subject to VAT, even if the person making the payment receives some benefit from the services provided with the person's funds. The "link" requirement also arises in the case of grants made for research work. For example, under the Singapore GST, a grant is a supply for GST purposes only if the grantor obtains intellectual property rights or other benefits that arise from the work undertaken with the grant.[46]

In the United Kingdom, a VAT tribunal held that if a restaurant automatically added a service charge to its bills (and notified the customers of this fact on the menus), the service charge was part of the consideration for the meal and therefore taxable.[47] However, if customers were not informed on the menus or otherwise that a service charge would be added, a VAT tribunal held, in the *NDP Co.* case, that payments by customers for service were not part of the consideration for the meals (no direct link) and therefore not taxable.[48]

In the *Apple and Pear Development Council* case,[49] the Council (a body governed by public law) claimed that its activities funded with mandatory fees paid by its members were services provided for consideration, so the input tax on its purchases was recoverable.[50] The court held that a direct link was necessary between the service provided and the consideration received for a sale to be for consideration, a prerequisite for taxation under the VAT Directive.[51] The fees paid by each grower only indirectly benefitted the grower, and there was no relationship between the fees paid and the level of benefits received from the Council's promotional efforts. The ECJ therefore concluded that the Council's exercise of its functions with the funds provided by its members was not a supply of services for consideration within Article 2(1) of the VAT Directive.

The ECJ also relied on the "direct link" requirement to find that a street musician who solicited funds from pedestrians did not make sales for consideration under the Sixth Directive[52] and therefore was not subject to VAT on his receipts. According to the court in *Tolsma*, the musician played his barrel organ voluntarily, and those who deposited money in his tin did

[45] See Value Added Tax Act No. 89 of 1991 [hereinafter RSA VAT], §8(6)(a) (South Africa).

[46] See e-Tax Guide No. 1994/GST/2 (Singapore), discussed in *CCH Singapore Goods & Services Tax Guide*, ¶3–180 (2005).

[47] *Potters Lodge Restaurant Ltd v. Commissioners of Customs and Excise*, LON/79/286.

[48] *NDP Co. Ltd v. the Commissioners of Customs and Excise*, [1988] VATTR 40. Customers were not legally obligated to pay the service charge, and some refused to pay or paid only a portion of the listed service charge.

[49] *Apple and Pear Development Council v. Commissioners of Customs and Excise*, [1988] ECR 1443, [1988] 2 CMLR 394.

[50] By statute, the Council was authorized to impose and did impose mandatory annual fees on growers. The fees were used mainly for publicity and research.

[51] See VAT Directive, *supra* note 2, at Art. 2(1).

[52] *Id.*

not necessarily make payment in any relationship to the benefits that they may obtain.[53]

> The court [in *Tolsma*] considered that there was no agreement in that case between the parties, since the passers-by voluntarily made a donation, whose amount they determined as they wished. In addition, the court found that there was no necessary link between the musical service and the payments to which it gave rise, since the passers-by did not request music to be played for them. Moreover, they paid sums which depended not on the musical service but on subjective motives which might bring feelings of sympathy into play.[54]

Some transactions are taxable, even though they do not involve the transfer of an asset in return for consideration. To achieve this result, the law imputes a supply for consideration – a "deemed" supply.

3. Transactions or Transfers Deemed to Be Supplies for VAT Purposes

When a registered business deregisters but stays in operation, for the government to reclaim tax previously claimed on goods still on hand and prepaid services not used, the deregistration is treated as a supply of the goods (and possibly services) on hand when the person ceases to be a registered person. In addition, the diversion of business assets by a taxable person to the personal use of the owner or employees or the use of a taxable person's business assets for nonbusiness purposes commonly is treated as a supply for consideration.[55] If an asset used in making taxable supplies is converted to use in making exempt supplies, the change in use is a supply under many VATs. Finally, if a seller repossesses goods previously sold in a taxable sale, the repossession commonly is treated as a supply by the defaulting buyer. These "deemed" supplies are discussed next.

53 *Tolsma v. Inspecteur der Omzetbelasting Leeuwarden*, Case C-16/93), [1994] STC 509. The musician also knocked on doors of homes and shops to ask for funds.

54 *Id.* at 516, cited in *Customs and Excise Commissioners v. First National Bank of Chicago*, Case C-172/96, [1998], [1998] All ER (EC) 744, STC 850 (ECJ) [hereinafter *First National Bank*].

55 VAT Directive, *supra* note 2, at Arts. 16 and 26(1). Member states may change the rules with respect to services if it does not result in the distortion of competition. *Id.* at Art. 26(2). Self-supplies may also be treated as a sale for consideration in some circumstances. *Id.* at Art. 18. The self-supply rule may be "needed to treat a transaction as a taxable transaction in order to prevent the distortion of competition or VAT abuse in cases where persons engaging in exempt transactions can avoid VAT by vertically integrating their operations instead of purchasing property or services from outside vendors. ... Section 4037 treats certain self-consumption of property and services by a government entity or exempt organization as a deemed sale of property and services by it in a taxable transaction." ABA Model Act, *supra* note 33, at 38. See New Vatopia, *supra* note 2, at §4(6).

a. *Cease to Conduct Taxable Transactions*

A registered person claims input credits for tax on purchases of inventory, supplies, and other assets to be used in making taxable supplies. If that person deregisters (such as because the person's taxable sales fall below the registration threshold), the person will be holding goods and services free of VAT. Subsequent sales by the deregistered person will not attract VAT. As a result, in the absence of a rule that requires the clawback of previously claimed credits, the deregistered person will obtain a competitive advantage over registered or never registered competitors. Many VATs provide that a deregistering person is deemed to have supplied goods (and sometimes services) on hand on the last day that the person is registered.[56] The person may be required to report as taxable output the fair market value of the goods or services on hand.[57] The fair market value rule puts the deregistering person in the same position as that of an unregistered person who had purchased the goods or services at fair market value in taxable acquisitions.

Some VATs require the deregistering person to report the lesser of that person's cost to acquire the assets on hand or the open market value (fair market value) of the goods or services on hand.[58] The "cost" part of the rule places the person in the same position that the person would be in if she had not claimed credit for VAT on those goods and services. It may be administratively easier, however, for the person to use the fair market value rule rather than locating the original cost of items that may have been purchased long ago.

b. *Diversion of Business Assets to Personal or Employee Use*

If a VAT-registered business transfers goods or services acquired for use in the business to an owner, officer, or employee without charge, the transfer may represent compensation or a fringe benefit. The transfer may be an appropriate business expenditure, deductible for income tax purposes, but it provides the opportunity for VAT abuse. When the asset was purchased, the business claimed credit for tax on the acquisition. The business

56 See, for example, NZ GST, *supra* note 36, at §5(3), where the deemed supply occurs immediately before the person ceases to be a registered person, unless the business is continued by another registered person, such as on the zero-rated sale of a going concern; New Vatopia, *supra* note 2, at §4(21).

57 In New Zealand, the value of the deemed supply is the open market value. NZ GST, *supra* note 36, at §10(7A). See Singapore Goods and Services Tax Act, Cap. 117A, 2001 ed., Sch. 3, ¶8(2)(a) [hereinafter Singapore GST]. The deregistering person must account for output tax on goods on hand that are part of the business assets. See form GST F8, entitled Final Goods and Services Tax return, reproduced in *CCH Singapore Goods and Services Tax Guide*, ¶31–225. See also IRAS Circular, 2003/GST/4, cited *id.* at ¶3–455. The open market value is the price payable if the deregistering person purchased identical goods at that time. If that value is not ascertainable, the value for similar goods may be used. If the value for similar goods is not available, then the value is the cost to produce the goods. Singapore GST, Sch. 3, ¶[8(2)(b) and (c).

58 RSA VAT, *supra* note 45, at §§8(2) and 10(5).

therefore holds the asset free of VAT. If the transfer to the employee or other person was not VAT-able, the goods or services would be acquired by the owner, officer, or employee free of VAT. To avoid this result, these transfers without charge commonly are treated as supplies for consideration subject to VAT.[59]

c. *Change in the Use of Goods or Services*

If a VAT-registered business acquires an asset for use in making taxable supplies (e.g., $10,000 + $1,000 VAT), the business can recover the $1,000 tax charged on the acquisition of the asset as input credit against tax imposed on taxable sales. If the business acquires the same asset for use in making exempt supplies, the business cannot recover any of the $1,000 charged on the acquisition of the asset. If the business acquired that asset for use in making taxable supplies, recovering the $1,000 tax imposed, and then decided to use the asset in connection with its exempt activities, the VAT consequences should be the same as if the asset were originally acquired for use in making exempt supplies. To accomplish that result, many VATs include change-in-use rules that require the VAT-registered business to treat the change in use as a supply of the asset to itself in a taxable transaction.[60] In this example, the business must report taxable output of $10,000. The change-in-use rules can be quite complex, especially in a country such as Canada that has different rules for capital goods than for other assets.[61]

d. *Repossession of Goods Sold in a Taxable Transaction*

If a registered person makes a taxable sale of equipment for $10,000 plus $1,000 VAT, the seller reports the sale and remits the VAT to the government, even if the sale is on credit and none of the $11,000 tax-inclusive price has been received. The buyer, if VAT registered, claims credit for the $1,000 VAT in the accounting period the equipment was acquired. If the buyer defaults and the seller repossesses the goods, the transaction should be reversed for VAT purposes. The registered buyer should be required to report the repossession as a taxable supply of goods and repay the VAT

[59] VAT Directive, *supra* note 2, at Arts. 16 and 26. The NZ GST, *supra* note 36, at §211(1), generally imposes tax on a registered employer's provision of a fringe benefit (goods or services) to an employee. It is treated as a supply in the course of a taxable activity. The value of the supply is the value of the fringe benefit under the Income Tax Act 1994. See also *id.* at§§20(3A) and 23A. See New Vatopia, *supra* note 2, at §4(6).

[60] The change-in-use rules generally do not apply if a VAT-registered person was not entitled to claim credit on the acquisition of the asset. For example, the change-in-use rule would not apply to an automobile if the registered person were denied an input credit on the acquisition of the automobile, even if used in connection with taxable supplies.

[61] See, for example, Canadian Goods and Services Tax, Part IX of the Excise Tax Act [hereinafter Canadian GST], §206(3)-(5); NZ GST, *supra* note 36, at §21(l) et seq. To simplify the change-in-use rules, they could be limited to changes for assets above a threshold value.

previously claimed on the asset repossessed.[62] Consistently, the seller should recover the VAT charged, and remitted to the government, even though it was never collected.[63]

B. Supply of Goods versus Services

This subsection and Subsection C cover two somewhat interrelated questions. The first is whether a supply, about which there is some classification ambiguity, is a supply of goods or a supply of services. The second, and sometimes related, question is whether a transaction is a single, mixed, or composite supply – that is, whether a transaction, in the form a single transaction, should be broken down into multiple supplies or a transaction that, in form, contains multiple elements should be treated as a single transaction for VAT purposes.

In most cases, it is apparent that a supply is of goods or of services. Shoes are goods and having a lawyer prepare a will is a service. Nevertheless, for some transactions, there is ambiguity as to whether the supply involves goods or services. The distinction may be significant:

1. If there are different rules on the time and place of a supply of goods or a supply of services.[64]
2. If one classification, goods (e.g., food), receives a reduced rate but services (e.g., restaurant meals) are taxed at the regular rate.
3. If an import of goods is taxable but of services may not be taxed.

There are transactions (e.g., supplies of software provided over the Internet) that appear to be services but, if provided in the form of a tangible product, such as a compact disc, may be goods.

1. Supply of Goods – in General

The advantage of broad-based VATs is that they achieve more economic neutrality or less economic distortion. Ideally, VAT should be imposed on sales of all goods and services. If some items must receive special treatment, such as exemption or zero-rating, this treatment should be provided as exceptions to the general rule that all are taxed.

A "supply of goods" is not defined in a uniform manner in VAT statutes, but the EU VAT Directive is representative of the principles that broadly

[62] See NZ GST, *supra* note 36, at §5(2); New Vatopia, *supra* note 2, at §4(7). If the buyer was not entitled to claim credit for VAT on the asset when acquired, the buyer should not be required to report the repossession as a taxable supply of goods.

[63] These adjustments are made through rules requiring the issuance of tax credit and tax debit notes.

[64] For example, whereas the value of goods sold on the installment plan are taxable when the contract is entered into, if goods or property is leased, the tax is imposed on each periodic lease payment, on the earlier of the date of the receipt of payment or the date the payment becomes due. NZ GST, *supra* note 36, at §9(3).

define a supply of goods. According to the VAT Directive,[65] the supply of goods is the transfer of the right to dispose of tangible property as owner. While utilities, such as electricity, heat, gas, and air conditioning, may be classified as goods or as services,[66] the VAT Directive treats them as tangible property.[67] Member states have some discretion in classifying items as goods or services. For example, they can treat transfers of shares in a company that holds immovable property as transfers of tangible property.[68]

2. Supply of Services – in General

Services pose various problems under a VAT. First, because the same kind of professional may be used by the purchaser either for business or personal use, there is a risk that businesses may claim credit for tax on services used for personal purposes (the same problem arises with goods). Second, some services, such as financial services rendered by banks and insurance companies, are complex to tax under any VAT. Third, the location of a supply is critical for cross-border transactions. Because services are intangible, it is challenging to identify the location of services. The place-of-supply rules are discussed in Chapter 7. The taxation of hard-to-tax services is covered in more detail in subsequent chapters. This subsection covers issues relating to the identification of a supply as a supply of services.

Most VAT statutes define the supply of services as any supply that is not a supply of goods. This catchall definition is designed to prevent supplies from escaping tax by not falling within either the definition of goods or services.[69] In the early years of the introduction of VATs, a country may not have taxed the supply of services. According to Tait:

> There are at least four powerful reasons to ensure that the VAT includes services from the start. First, the contribution of the sector to gross national product is sizable and grows as the economy grows. Consequently, it may have a fairly large revenue potential. Second, failure to tax services distorts consumer choices, encouraging spending on services at the expense of goods

[65] VAT Directive, *supra* note 2, at Art. 14(1).

[66] For the Swiss treatment of electricity transactions under VAT, see R. Derks, "VAT Treatment of Electricity Transactions Under Swiss Law," 13 *Int'l VAT Monitor* 267 (July/Aug. 2002). Although the Swiss VAT treats electricity as a good, many transactions involving the international flows of electricity, such as the physical import of electricity, are treated as imported services. For contrast, see New Vatopia, *supra* note 2, at §4(l)(a)(iii), defining a supply of thermal or electrical energy, heat, gas, refrigeration, air conditioning, and water as a supply of goods.

[67] VAT Directive, *supra* note 2, at Art. 15(1).

[68] *Id.* at Art. 15(2).

[69] See A. Tait, VALUE ADDED TAX: INTERNATIONAL PRACTICE AND PROBLEMS (IMF 1988) [hereinafter Tait, VAT], at 387. "For instance, the sale of a racehorse is a supply of a taxable good, but the sale of a share in a syndicated racehorse would be the supply of a service. If all the shares were sold then, in essence, the horse is sold and that becomes a supply of goods. Either way, VAT is payable." *Id.* at 387–388. See New Vatopia, *supra* note 2, at §4(l)(b).

> and saving. Third, untaxed services mean traders are unable to claim VAT on their service inputs. This causes cascading, distorts choice, and encourages business to develop in-house services, creating further distortions. Fourth, as most of the services that are likely to become taxable are positively correlated with the expenditure of high-income households, subjecting them to taxation may improve equity.[70]

The principles in the EU VAT Directive are representative of the definition of a supply of services used under many VAT statutes. The VAT Directive provides a catchall classification rule that defines a supply of services as any transaction that does not constitute a supply of goods.[71] For example, the British VAT defines a supply of services as "anything which is not a supply of goods but is done for a consideration."[72] The New Zealand VAT defines services as "anything which is not goods or money."[73] Indeed, commonly a transaction in money is not a supply of goods or a supply of services and therefore does not come within the scope of a VAT.

If a person provides to another the use of tangible personal property or real property, retaining legal title and ownership, the transaction is a lease.[74] There is no uniformity of treatment of true leases for VAT purposes. Whereas the EU VAT treats the transfer of possession of goods (use of goods) as a supply of services,[75] the Canadian GST[76] and the South African VAT[77] treat leases as supplies of goods.

Under the EU VAT Directive, supplies of services may include transfers of intangible property and obligations to refrain from an act, such as under covenants not to compete.[78] If consideration received for an agreement to refrain from an act is a supply of services, then is a payment to a dairy farmer to discontinue milk production under a European Council Regulation[79] designed to reduce guaranteed global quantities of milk a supply of services for consideration taxable? The following excerpted case decides this issue within the EU.

[70] Tait, VAT, *supra* note 69, at 388.

[71] VAT Directive, *supra* note 2, at Art. 24(1).

[72] VATA 1994, *supra* note 30, at §5(2)(b).

[73] NZ GST, *supra* note 36, at §2.

[74] There also are classification issues when what in form is a lease in substance is actually a sale. Transactions respected as operating leases are treated as leases for VAT purposes. Installment sales or finance leases are considered sales for VAT purposes. VAT laws may provide statutory guidance to determine if the supply is a sale or lease. For example, see the definition of a "rental agreement" and an "instalment credit agreement" in RSA VAT, *supra* note 45, at §l.

[75] VATA 1994, *supra* note 30, at §5 and Sch. 4(1).

[76] Canadian GST, *supra* note 61, at §136(1), treats a "lease, licence or similar arrangement ... [for] the use or right to use real property or tangible personal property" as a supply of the real or tangible personal property.

[77] RSA VAT, *supra* note 45, §8(11). See New Vatopia, *supra* note 2, at §4(1).

[78] VAT Directive, *supra* note 2, at Art. 25.

[79] Council Regulation (EEC) 1336/86 of May 6, 1986.

Jurgen Mohr v. Finanzamt Bad Segeberg[80]

JUDGMENT. Mr Mohr was the owner of an agricultural holding on which he kept dairy cattle. In March 1987 he applied to the Federal Office for Food and Forestry for a grant for the definitive discontinuation of milk production (OJ 1986 L 119, p. 21) [and undertook] not to make any claim for a milk reference quantity under the common organization of the market.

On 23 September 1987 the Bundesamt upheld his application and granted him a single payment of DM 385 980. Subsequently, Mr Mohr sold his cattle and converted the business into a horse-riding centre, thus ceasing all milk production during that same year.

In his turnover tax [VAT] declaration for 1987 Mr Mohr did not mention the amount received by way of compensation for discontinuation of milk production. The Finanzamt decided to treat such compensation as consideration for a taxable supply, namely the discontinuation of milk production, and to make it subject to turnover tax.

Mr Mohr unsuccessfully challenged the Finanzamt' s decision before the Finanzgericht. He then brought the matter before the Bundesfinanzhof. The Bundesfinanzhof decided to stay the proceedings and referred the following questions to the Court of Justice for a preliminary ruling:

[In this reference,] the national court essentially seeks to ascertain whether Articles 6(1) and 11(A)(1)(a) of the Directive are to be interpreted as meaning that an undertaking to discontinue milk production constitutes a supply of services so that the compensation received for that purpose is subject to turnover tax.

According to Article 2(1) of the Directive, "the supply of goods or services effected for consideration within the territory of the country by a taxable person acting as such" is to be subject to value added tax.

Article 6(1) provides:

"Supply of services" shall mean any transaction which does not constitute a supply of goods within the meaning of Article 5. Such transactions may include inter alia: obligations to refrain from an act or to tolerate an act or situation.

Article 11(A)(1)(a) provides that the taxable amount is to be, "in respect of supplies of goods and services ..., everything which constitutes the consideration which has been or is to be obtained by the supplier from the purchaser, the customer or a third party for such supplies including subsidies directly linked to the price of such supplies."

Regulation No 1336/86 is part of a series of measures adopted by the Community with a view to limiting milk production. According to the third recital of the preamble to that regulation, in order to facilitate

[80] Case C-215/94, *1996 EC CELEX EEXIS 10783*; 1996 ECR I–959 (ECJ Judgment 1996) [edited by the authors].

the reduction of deliveries and direct sales involved in reducing guaranteed global quantities, a Community system should be established to finance the discontinuation of milk production by granting any producer, at the latter's request and provided that he fulfils certain eligibility requirements, compensation in return for his undertaking to discontinue definitively all milk production.

The German and Italian Governments submit that a milk producer who undertakes definitively to discontinue his production supplies a service for consideration within the meaning of Articles 2 and 6(1) of the Directive. Both Governments state in this regard that payment of compensation and an undertaking to discontinue milk production are mutually dependent, thus establishing the direct link between the service provided and consideration for it, as required by the case-law of the Court (Case 154/80 Staatsecretaris van Financien v Cooeperatieve Aardappelenbewaarplaats 1981 ECR 445 and Case C-16/93 Tolsma v Inspecteur der Omzetbelasting 1994 ECR 1–743). The service consists in an obligation to refrain from an act, within the meaning of the second indent of Article 6(1) of the Directive, namely to refrain from continuing milk production, and the compensation paid is in the nature of consideration for that undertaking, thus constituting a taxable amount within the meaning of Article 11(A)(1)(a) of the Directive.

That interpretation of the Directive cannot be accepted. According to Article 2(1) of the First Council Directive (67/227/EEC) of 11 April 1967 on the harmonization of legislation of Member States concerning turnover taxes (OJ, English Special Edition 1967 (I), p. 14), VAT is a general tax on the consumption of goods and services. In a case such as the present one, there is no consumption as envisaged in the Community VAT system.

In those circumstances, the undertaking given by a farmer that he will discontinue his milk production does not entail either for the Community or for the competent national authorities any benefit which would enable them to be considered consumers of a service. The undertaking in question does not therefore constitute a supply of services within the meaning of Article 6(1) of the Directive.

The answer to the questions referred to the Court for a preliminary ruling should therefore be that Articles 6(1) and 11(A)(1)(a) of the [Sixth] Directive [Articles 25 and 73 of the VAT Directive] must be interpreted as meaning that an undertaking to discontinue milk production given by a farmer under Regulation No 1336/86 does not constitute a supply of services. Consequently, any compensation received for that purpose is not subject to turnover tax.

3. Classification as Goods or Services – Predominant Element

In some cases, the distinction between goods and services depends on whether the predominant element of a complex transaction is a supply of goods or a supply of services. For example, in the following *Manfred Bog* case, under German VAT law, a supply of food and beverages for consumption on the spot is a supply of services that is taxed at the regular rate. There is a reduced tax rate on supplies of many kinds of prepared food. The reduced rate does not apply to services.[81] This case deals both with the issue discussed in this subsection (is the supply a supply of goods or a supply of services) and the issue covered in the next subsection (what is the supply, distinguishing among a single, mixed, and composite supply). The joined cases and the ECJ judgment follows.

Finanzamt Burgdorf v. Manfred Bog[82]

Mr Bog sold drinks and food prepared for consumption (in particular, sausages and chips) from three identical mobile snack bars at weekly markets. The mobile snack bars were equipped with a sales counter ... which could be used for the consumption of food on the spot .... In his turnover tax declaration for [2004] Mr Bog declared the turnover from the sale of drinks as subject to the standard rate of VAT, while the turnover from the sale of food was declared as subject to the reduced rate....

Case C-499/09

CinemaxX operates cinemas in various locations in Germany.

In the foyers of those cinemas, cinema-goers can buy, besides sweets and drinks, portions of popcorn and tortilla chips (nachos) in various sizes. There are no counters for consumption at the sales stands themselves, but in some cinema foyers there are varying numbers of tables to stand at, bar stools, and sometimes benches, chairs, tables, and counters along the walls. Not all of the above-mentioned furnishings are, however, present in all the cinemas. In some auditoria there are drink-holders attached to the seats.

In its turnover tax declaration for June 2005, CinemaxX declared the turnover from the sale of popcorn and tortilla chips as turnover subject to the reduced rate of VAT. The tax authorities contested the tax declaration and issued an assessment in which that turnover was subject to the standard rate....

[81] Council Directive 2009/47/EC of 5 May 2009 amending Directive 2006/112/EC as regards reduced rates of value added tax (OJ 2009 L 116, p. 18) authorizes member states to introduce a reduced rate for "restaurant and catering services." That directive was not yet in force, however, at the material time in the various main proceedings.

[82] Case C-479/09, Case C-499/09, Case C-501/09, and Case C-502/09, *Finanzamt Burgdorf v. Manfred Bog* (2011) ECR p. I-01457 (Judgment of the ECJ 2011) were joined cases [edited by the authors].

Case C-501/09

Mr Lohmeyer operated several snack stalls and a swinging grill from 1996 to 1999. There he sold food ready for consumption (fried sausages, sausages in curry sauce, hot dogs, chips, steaks, pork belly, skewered meat, spare ribs). He declared his entire turnover from the sale of food as turnover subject to the reduced rate of VAT.

The tax authorities established, however, that the stalls had counters, and considered that these were special facilities made available for the consumption of food on the spot, with the result that the transactions in question were in principle subject to the standard rate of VAT....

Case C-502/09

Fleischerei Nier is a limited partnership which operated a butcher's shop and a party catering service. The food which was ordered from the catering service was supplied hot in closed containers, while crockery, cutlery, tables for standing at and staff were also made available, according to the customers' wishes.

In its invoices Fleischerei Nier applied the standard rate of VAT to the charges for the provision of cutlery, crockery, tables for standing at and staff and the reduced rate of VAT to the charges for the food.

The tax authorities, however, considered that the supplies of food should also be subjected to the standard rate of VAT to the extent that they were combined with the provision of crockery, cutlery, tables or staff, and accordingly issued an amended tax assessment....

[T]he referring court is essentially asking the Court whether the various activities of supplying food or meals prepared for immediate consumption at issue in the four main proceedings constitute supplies of goods within the meaning of ... [Articles 14–19 of the VAT Directive] or supplies of services within the meaning of ... [Articles 24–29 of the VAT Directive], and what effect the additional elements of supply of services may have in this respect.

Preliminary observations

As a preliminary point, it must be established whether, for the purposes of VAT, the various activities at issue in the main proceedings are to be regarded as distinct transactions taxable separately or as single complex transactions comprising a number of elements.

According to the Court's case-law, where a transaction comprises a bundle of elements and acts, regard must be had to all the circumstances in which the transaction in question takes place in order to determine, first, whether there are two or more distinct supplies or one single supply and, secondly, whether, in the latter case, that single supply is to be regarded as a supply of goods or a supply of services.

The Court has also held, first, that it follows from … [Article 2 of the VAT Directive] that every transaction must normally be regarded as distinct and independent and, secondly, that a transaction which comprises a single supply from an economic point of view should not be artificially split, so as not to distort the functioning of the VAT system. There is a single supply where two or more elements or acts supplied by the taxable person to the customer are so closely linked that they form, objectively, a single, indivisible economic supply, which it would be artificial to split.

There is also a single supply where one or more elements are to be regarded as constituting the principal supply, while other elements are to be regarded, by contrast, as one or more ancillary supplies which share the tax treatment of the principal supply. In particular, a supply must be regarded as ancillary to a principal supply if it does not constitute for customers an end in itself but a means of better enjoying the principal service supplied.

In the present cases, in each of the disputes in the main proceedings, there is a combination of a supply of goods or several goods and a supply of various service elements, and the referring court considers that those supplies of goods and services form a single transaction for the purposes of VAT. There is nothing in the orders for reference or the observations submitted to the Court to show that that classification was not carried out in accordance with the above criteria.

In the case of supplies in connection with a party catering business such as that at issue in the main proceedings in Case C-502/09, it may be noted inter alia that the existence of a single transaction is independent of whether the caterer issues a single invoice covering all the elements or issues a separate invoice for the supply of the food.

Classification as a supply of goods or a supply of services

To determine whether a single complex supply … should be classified as a 'supply of goods' or a 'supply of services', all the circumstances in which the transaction takes place must be taken into account in order to ascertain its characteristic elements and to identify its predominant elements.

It should also be pointed out that the predominant element must be determined from the point of view of the typical consumer … and having regard, in an overall assessment, to the qualitative and not merely quantitative importance of the elements of supply of services in relation to the elements of supply of goods.

It should be noted in this respect that, as the marketing of goods is always accompanied by a minimal supply of services such as the displaying of the products on shelves or the issuing of an invoice, only services other than those which necessarily accompany the marketing of goods may be taken into account in assessing the part played by the supply of services within the whole of a complex transaction also involving the supply of a product.

The Court has held, more specifically, in Faaborg-Gelting Linien, paragraph 14, that restaurant transactions are characterised by a bundle of elements and acts, of which the provision of food is only one component and in which services largely predominate. They must therefore be regarded as supplies of services within the meaning of Article 6(1) of the Sixth Directive. The situation is different, however, where the transaction relates to food to take away and is not coupled with services designed to enhance consumption on the spot in an appropriate setting.

Thus in the case of restaurant transactions on board ferries, the Court observed that the supply of prepared food and drink for immediate consumption is the outcome of a series of services ranging from the cooking of the food to its physical service in a receptacle, while at the same time an infrastructure is placed at the customer's disposal, including a dining room with appurtenances (cloakroom etc.), furniture and crockery. People, whose occupation consists in carrying out restaurant transactions, will have to perform such tasks as laying the table, advising the customer and explaining the food and drink on the menu to him, serving at table and clearing the table after the food has been eaten (Faaborg-Gelting Linien, paragraph 13).

In the present cases, according to the information provided by the referring court, the activities at issue in the main proceedings in Cases C-497/09 and C-501/09 concern sales from mobile snack bars or snack stalls of sausages, chips and other hot food for immediate consumption.

The supply of such products presupposes that they are cooked or reheated, which constitutes a service that must be taken into account in the overall assessment of the transaction for the purpose of classifying it as a supply of goods or a supply of services.

However, since the preparation of the hot end product is limited essentially to basic standard actions, which for the most part are done not in response to an order from a particular customer but in continuous or regular fashion according to the demand generally foreseeable, it does not constitute the predominant element of the transaction in question, and cannot in itself characterise that transaction as a supply of services.

Moreover, with respect to the elements of supply of services that are characteristic of restaurant transactions, as described in the case-law summarised in paragraphs 63 to 65 above, it is clear that, in the activities at issue in the main proceedings in Cases C-497/09 and C-501/09, there are no waiters, no real advice to customers, no service properly speaking consisting in particular in transmitting orders to the kitchen and then presenting and serving dishes to customers at tables, no enclosed spaces at an appropriate temperature dedicated to the consumption of the food served, no cloakrooms or lavatories, and essentially no crockery, furniture or place settings.

The elements of supply of services mentioned by the referring court consist solely in the presence of rudimentary facilities such as counters to eat at, with no possibility of sitting down, enabling a limited number of customers to eat on the spot, in the open air. Such rudimentary facilities require only negligible human intervention. In those circumstances, those elements are only minimal ancillary services, and cannot alter the predominant character of the principal supply, namely that of a supply of goods.

The above considerations apply likewise to sales of popcorn and tortilla chips in the foyers of cinemas such as those at issue in the main proceedings in Case C-499/09.

According to the account of the facts given by the referring court, the preparation of popcorn, which coincides with its production, and the distribution of popcorn and tortilla chips in packagings form an integral part of the sale of those products, and are not therefore transactions that are independent of the sale. Furthermore, both the preparation of the food and its keeping at a certain temperature are performed regularly rather than to the order of an individual customer.

It should also be noted that the provision of furniture (tables for standing at, stools, chairs and benches), apart from the fact that it is not present in all the cinemas, is as a rule independent of the sale of popcorn and tortilla chips, and that the areas where this furniture is provided also serve as waiting rooms and meeting points. Moreover, in practice the food is consumed in the auditoria. For that purpose, the seats in some auditoria are equipped with drink-holders, whose purpose is also to ensure the cleanliness of the auditoria. The mere presence of those furnishings intended, not exclusively, possibly to facilitate the consumption of such food cannot be regarded as an element of supply of services such as to bestow on the transaction as a whole the quality of a supply of services.

Accordingly, with respect to activities such as those at issue in the main proceedings in Cases C-497/09, C-499/09 and C-501/09, the dominant element of the transactions in question, on an overall assessment of them, consists in the supply of food or meals ready for immediate consumption, with their summary and standardised preparation being intrinsic to them and the provision of rudimentary facilities to enable a limited number of customers to consume the food on the spot being of a merely ancillary and subordinate nature. Whether the customers use those rudimentary facilities or not is immaterial, since, as immediate consumption on the spot is not an essential characteristic of the transaction in question, it cannot determine its character.

With respect to party catering activities such as those at issue in the main proceedings in Case C-502/09, it should be noted, first, that

… several combinations of transactions are conceivable, depending on customers' wishes, ranging from the mere preparation and delivery of meals to the full service consisting in addition of the provision of crockery, furniture (tables and chairs), presentation of the dishes, decorations, provision of serving staff, and advice on the composition of the menu and if appropriate the choice of drinks.

Next, since what is concerned is a single supply, the classification of the transaction as a supply of goods or a supply of services will depend on all the factual circumstances, having regard to the qualitatively predominant elements from the point of view of the consumer.

As regards the food delivered by a party catering service, it must be observed that, unlike food supplied from snack stalls and mobile snack bars and in cinemas, it is not as a rule the result of mere standardised preparation but contains a distinctly greater aspect of the supply of services and requires more work and greater skill. Food quality, creativity and presentation are elements here which are most often of decisive importance for the customer. The customer is frequently offered the possibility not only of choosing the menu but even of having individual dishes made to order. This service aspect is moreover reflected linguistically, in so far as in everyday language one generally speaks of a catering 'service' and of food 'ordered' rather than 'bought' from the caterer.

The food is then delivered by the caterer in closed warmed receptacles or reheated by him on the spot. It is also essential for the customer that the food is delivered at the exact time he has specified.

Moreover, the supplies of a party catering service may include elements to enable consumption, such as the supply of crockery, cutlery or even furniture. Those elements, unlike the mere provision of a rudimentary infrastructure in the case of snack stalls or mobile snack bars and cinemas, require in addition a certain human intervention to deliver, collect, and if appropriate wash the items.

In the light of those considerations, it must be considered that, except in cases in which the caterer does no more than deliver standard meals without any additional service elements, or in which other special circumstances show that the supply of the food represents the predominant element of the transaction, the activities of a party catering service are supplies of services.

[T]herefore … Articles 5 and 6 of the Sixth Directive [Articles 14–19 and 24–29 of the VAT Directive] must be interpreted as meaning that:

– the supply of food or meals freshly prepared for immediate consumption from snack stalls or mobile snack bars or in cinema foyers is a supply of goods within the meaning of Article 5 [Articles 14–19 of the VAT Directive] if a qualitative examination of the entire transaction shows that the elements of supply of services preceding and accompanying the supply of the food are not predominant;

– except in cases in which a party catering service does no more than deliver standard meals without any additional elements of supply of services, or in which other special circumstances show that the supply of the food represents the predominant element of a transaction, the activities of a party catering service are supplies of services within the meaning of Article 6 [Articles 24–29 of the VAT Directive].

C. Single, Mixed, and Composite Supplies

This subsection covers the situations in which a transaction, which in form is a single transaction, should be broken down into multiple supplies for VAT purposes, and a transaction, which in form contains multiple elements (reported as multiple supplies), should be aggregated and treated as a single transaction for VAT purposes.

When a VAT system taxes some transactions at one or more positive rates and some at a zero-rate, while still others are exempt from tax, there may be an incentive for a supplier to bundle several independent supplies together as a single supply or disaggregate a single supply into separate component supplies to reduce the VAT borne by the purchaser on the transaction. The VAT incentive is greatest if the buyer, such as a consumer, cannot claim credit for VAT on the purchase. There also may be some incentive to combine or disaggregate elements of a transaction into supplies of goods and supplies of services to obtain the desired timing or place of supply rules for the various elements. The issue in these cases is "what is the supply?"

If a supply contains major and incidental elements, the VAT rules may classify the supply according to the major elements.[83] If a seller sells a machine for a price that includes the installation of the machine in the buyer's premises, the entire transaction may be treated as a supply of goods (the machine) if the installation services are merely incidental to the sale of the goods or as a supply of services if the installation services represent most of the value of the installed machine.

If a supply consists of multiple major elements and the supply is treated as a mixed supply, the supply must be disaggregated and taxed in conformity with those major elements. To analyze these transactions, initially they must be classified as either a single or mixed supply. The European Court of Justice decided a case involving multiple and composite supplies that is widely cited within and outside the EU. In *Card Protection Plan Ltd v Customs and Excise Commissioners*,[84] the company sold customers a credit card protection plan that indemnified them against financial loss and inconvenience if their cards were lost or stolen.[85] The company assisted customers by notifying the credit card issuers of the lost or stolen cards and providing their customers other services. To provide many of the

[83] New Vatopia, *supra* note 2, at §4(10)-(12).

[84] Case C-349/96, *Card Protection Plan Limited v. Commissioners of Customs and Excise*, [1999] STC 270, [1999] All ER (EC) 339 [hereinafter Card Protection Plan].

[85] In some cases, the company covered car keys, passports, and insurance documents.

services covered under the plan, the company purchased a block policy from an insurance company and listed its customers with the insurance company as the insured. The Commissioners claimed that the company provided a basket of taxable services,[86] not exempt insurance, because there was no direct contractual relationship between the company's customers and the insurance company. The company claimed that its services constituted an arrangement for insurance services and that there was a sufficient direct relationship between the customers and the insurance company to constitute exempt insurance services. Each side argued that there was a single supply, either of exempt insurance or taxable card registration services. In the request for a preliminary ruling, the ECJ was asked about "the proper test to be applied in deciding whether a transaction consists for VAT purposes of a single composite supply or of two or more independent supplies."[87] Applying the principles of the Sixth Directive [now VAT Directive],[88] the court held the following:

> Every supply of a service must normally be regarded as distinct and independent and ... a supply which comprises a single service from an economic point of view should not be artificially split. So as not to distort the functioning of the VAT system, the essential features of the transaction must be ascertained in order to determine whether the taxable person is supplying the customer, being a typical consumer, with several distinct principal services or with a single service.
>
> There is a single supply in particular in cases where one or more elements are to be regarded as constituting the principal service, whilst one or more elements are to be regarded, by contrast, as ancillary services which share the tax treatment of the principal service. A service must be regarded as ancillary to a principal service if it does not constitute for customers an aim in itself, but a means of better enjoying the principal service supplied.[89]

According to the European Court of Justice, the national court must determine, in light of the criteria set by the ECJ, whether transactions such as those in Card Protection Plan constitute two independent supplies or whether there is a principal supply to which the other is ancillary, so that both are taxed like the principal supply. The House of Lords decided "that the transaction performed by CPP for Dr. Howell is to be regarded for VAT purposes as comprising a principal exempt insurance supply and the

[86] The array of services provided by the company includes payment of indemnity for losses associated with the fraudulent use of cards, costs to find lost luggage or other items with the company's label previously attached, telephone advice on access to medical and other services, and repayable benefits such as cash advances and replacement of air tickets. *Id.* at paragraph 9 of the Judgment.

[87] *Id.* at paragraph 12 of the Judgment.

[88] Sixth Directive, *supra* note 2, at Art. 2(1) [VAT Directive, *supra* note 2, at Art. 2(1)(a) and (c)] imposes tax on "the supply of goods for consideration ... by a table person acting as such," and "the supply of services for consideration ... by a taxable person acting as such."

[89] Card Protection Plan, *supra* note 84, at paragraphs 30 and 31 of the Judgment.

other supplies in the transaction are ancillary so that they are to be treated as exempt for VAT purposes."[90]

The same single versus mixed supply issue has arisen in a number of subsequent cases. In *Purple Parking*,[91] referring to the *Card Protection* case, the ECJ order provided that the provision of off-airport parking and bus transportation to and from the parking to the airport constituted a single, indivisible economic supply of parking (the predominant part of the combined complex supply), denying zero-rating to the transportation portion of the supply. In the following *Plantiflor* case, the supplier tried to separate exempt postal charges for the delivery of its merchandise from the supply of taxable merchandise to be delivered to the customers.

Commissioners of Customs and Excise v. Plantiflor Limited[92]

LORD SLYNN OF HADLEY

My Lords,

[A customer, Miss Brierley, ordered some bulbs from "Bakker Holland," the name under which Plantiflor trade in the U.K. [hereinafter Plantiflor]. Plantiflor invoiced the bulbs and postage separately in order to reduce the VAT imposed on sales to its final consumers.] The invoice specified that the price of the goods [Miss Brierley] had ordered was £52.00. There were other charges of £2.50 ("Postage (£1.63) plus packing (£0.87)") and £0.25 transport insurance. The total was thus £54.75. The invoice acknowledged that she had already paid this sum. The total VAT was stated to be "£53.12 17.50% = £7.91." The difference between £53.12 and £54.75 is £1.63, the postage charged. Thus no VAT was charged on the postage. The commissioners however say that VAT was chargeable to Plantiflor on the postage. Plantiflor says it was not....

The contract between Plantiflor and its customers is to be found in a page in Plantiflor's catalogue and the order form filled in by the customer together perhaps with the invoice. The catalogue under the heading "Convenience of Delivery to Your Door" states:

"Bakker deliver every order, whether large or small, direct to your home. Everything neatly packed with the utmost care. You will also receive the latest Garden Review."

Under the heading "Collection and Delivery":

"Orders collected incur no handling charges. If you require delivery by carrier then a nominal charge is made to cover mail order packing and handling. We will happily arrange delivery on your behalf via

[90] *Card Protection Plan Limited v. Commissioners of Customs and Excise*, [2001] UKHL 4.

[91] Case C-117/11, *Purple Parking Ltd, Airparks Services Ltd v. the Commissioners for Her Majesty's Revenue Service* (ECJ 2012).

[92] [2002] UKHL 33 (House of Lords 2002) [edited by the authors].

Royal Mail Parcelforce if requested. In which case please include the postage and handling charge on your order. We will then advance all postal charges to Royal Mail on your behalf"....

Plantiflor is the subsidiary of a Dutch company and the group operates widely in Europe selling directly to the public. .... When orders are received ... they are forwarded to Holland where the goods are packed and sent by lorry to the United Kingdom. On arrival in the United Kingdom parcels go direct to Royal Mail Parcelforce, at the time a section of the Post Office. They are then delivered by Parcelforce....

Plantiflor entered into a contract with Parcelforce on 6 January 1994 in relation to the carriage of Plantiflor's products, the contract to remain in operation from 1 August 1993 until 31 August 1998. The agreement recited that "Plantiflor has agreed to send a certain number of items and Parcelforce has agreed to deliver them for Plantiflor at the prices set out below." Plantiflor's obligation was to send a minimum of 400,000 parcels a year....

On 21 September 1993 Plantiflor told Parcelforce that in Holland and Germany no VAT was charged on postage. This was on the basis that "providing we charge the customer the actual value of the postage paid to the PTT and that all contracts state clearly that we are receiving postage, and posting parcels on their behalf, we will no longer be the contract principal, merely the customers' agent." Plantiflor therefore proposed that Parcelforce should confirm that it delivered parcels "(a) for us as principal and (b) as agent of our retail customers"....

My Lords, it is clear that under the contract Plantiflor is to supply the goods packed and, if required, insured for the transport. A principal feature of its marketing is the "Convenience of Delivery to Your Door" that is really why "You'll Enjoy Ordering from Bakker" and the catalogue states "Bakker deliver every order, whether large or small, direct to your home." It is equally made clear that Plantiflor is not undertaking and does not intend to deliver the goods itself. What it is undertaking is to ensure that the goods are delivered. It will do this by arranging delivery via Royal Mail Parcelforce if so requested. The total payable for all this is in the present case £54.75. The sole question raised on this appeal is whether the "Postage (£1.63)" or that part of the "Contribution Towards Post and Packing £2.50" which relates to the postage cost is part of the consideration moving from the customer to Plantiflor for the relevant supply or whether it constitutes money handed to Plantiflor which is not part of that consideration....

Plantiflor's case relating to the transport in essence is that it made arrangements in September 1993 to act as agent for its customers and that it would receive the postage and pass it on to Parcelforce as such agent and that all services rendered by Parcelforce were rendered as principal to the customer. The consideration of £1.63 in fact moved from the customer to Parcelforce.

The Court of Appeal considered that the commissioners had conceded that there were two supplies – one of the sale of goods by Plantiflor and one of the service of arranging delivery of the goods via Parcelforce. There was also a supply of services by Parcelforce to the customer in the actual delivery of the goods. The judge thought this "concession" right. The Court of Appeal refused to allow the commissioners to go back on the concession and to argue that there was only one integral supply of the sale of delivered plants and that even if the delivery by Parcelforce was a supply by Parcelforce to the customer that there was still a supply of services by Parcelforce to the plaintiffs. The court, however, went on to say that these two arguments were in any event wrong, and to explain that delivery was quite separate from the sale and there were two supplies as the tribunal had accepted.

If, as I considered in *Customs and Excise Comrs v British Telecommunications plc* [1999] 1WLR 1376, 1382–1383, and as I still consider, the appropriate question is whether one act (here arranging the delivery) is "ancillary or incidental to another" (here the supply of bulbs) or is "a distinct supply," it seems to me on the contractual documents between Plantiflor and the customer which are before the House that these arrangements constituted a single supply. What the customer wanted and what Plantiflor agreed to provide was bulbs delivered to the home.

On the basis, however, that in the contractual documents between Plantiflor and its customer properly construed there were two supplies, the question arises whether the money received by Plantiflor for postage can constitute consideration received by Plantiflor or whether it is simply money that is channelled through Plantiflor but never became Plantiflor's property so that it cannot amount to consideration passing to Plantiflor.

It is contended by Plantiflor that there was no supply by Plantiflor to the customer in return for the postage. Properly analysed, Plantiflor was acting as agent for its customer and the only consideration received by Parcelforce (£1.63) for the only thing it did (delivering the parcels) was received from the customer. No consideration passed between the customer and Plantiflor for the delivery because Plantiflor did not deliver the goods and there was no consideration paid either in the postage charge or in the handling charge or in the price of the bulbs for arranging the delivery by Parcelforce.

As to the agency argument Plantiflor of course relies on the provision of the catalogue "We will … arrange delivery on your behalf. … We will then advance all postage charges to Royal Mail on your behalf." They insist that for this reason no consideration moved from Plantiflor to Parcelforce.

The tribunal [1977] V & DR 301, 322 accepted that "the role of Plantiflor in relation to delivery was that of agent or other intermediary."

This conclusion however does not take into account the terms of the agreement between Plantiflor and Parcelforce. It is plain from the terms of that agreement to which I have referred that Parcelforce was to deliver parcels "for Plantiflor." Parcelforce was to "charge Plantiflor" and Parcelforce was to pay invoices from Parcelforce by direct debit transfer. There is nothing in that agreement to express or even indicate that the two contracting parties were not acting as principals, in other words that Plantiflor was acting as agent for its customers. There is no link between Parcelforce and the customer. Since all that Parcelforce knew was the name of the addressee on the parcel (or perhaps even only the address), it might well not know the identity of the customer. Plantiflor agreed to pay postal charges; Plantiflor and not the customer was liable to pay Parcelforce. Even though Parcelforce supplied the service for delivery of the goods there was no consideration passing from the customer to Parcelforce. Plantiflor agreed to arrange delivery including paying Parcelforce for the postage and the customer paid Plantiflor for that.

It seems to me that looking at the written terms of both contracts (Plantiflor and its customer: Plantiflor and Parcelforce) it is not shown that this £1.63 or any other of the 400,000 sums of £1.63 became on payment to Plantiflor the property of Parcelforce. They are not sums earmarked for Parcelforce. They are part of the receipts by Plantiflor as part of its turnover.

For the reasons already given I would hold that VAT is payable in the sum of £1.63 in respect of postage and I would allow the appeal.

[Three other Lords would allow the appeal, with one writing a separate opinion, and one dissenting.]

The following cases provide additional examples of cases in this area. The British Court of Appeal held that a cable television fee could be separated from a zero-rated supply of a magazine to the cable subscribers, in part because there were two separate suppliers, even though the subscribers paid a single fee to the cable company for both and all subscribers received the magazine.[93] The connection of a cable in a customer's premises was held to be a supply independent of the supply of cable television services.[94] In another case, the court held that the purchase of automobiles with delivery charged separately was a single supply, not an independent sale of a car (on which no input credit was allowable) and separate

[93] *Telewest Communications pic and Another v. Customs & Excise Commissioners*, [2005] EWCA Civ. 102; [2005] STC 481 (Ct. App. Civil Div.).

[94] *DA Mac Carthaigh, Inspector of Taxes v. Cablelink Limited, Cablelink Waterford Limited and Galway Cable Vision*, [SC No 155 of 2003], [2003] 4 IR 510, Ireland Sup. Ct. The installation of the cable connection was a supply on immovable property that qualified for a lower VAT rate than the supply of the cable television services.

delivery services (on which input credit was allowable).[95] The delivery services were ancillary to the main supply of the car. If one element of a supply dominates the other elements, according to another UK case, the dominant element may be the one and only supply.[96]

In contrast, when a day train trip was coupled with "fine wine and dining," and the supplier emphasized the food, wine, and service in advertising for the trips, a British court held that the transaction was a mixed supply of transport and catering – the catering was an aim in itself, and each part was a separate supply.[97] A distance learning college that provided books and face-to-face teaching for a single fee for a course was allowed to treat the transaction as two supplies: a zero-rated supply of books and an exempt educational service. The court noted that the goods were physically dissociable from the education service.[98]

In some cases, such as *Canadian Airlines*,[99] the determination of when a transaction begins and ends can be critical to the single versus mixed supply question. Canadian Airlines offered all full fare business class passengers on trans-Atlantic flights free chauffer-driven limousine service to the airport for departure and from the airport on arrival. In the United Kingdom, the free service was limited to an 80-mile radius of the airport. There was no written contract with the passengers covering this service, and the fare was the same, whether or not the passengers used the limousine service.

The British VAT zero-rated:

"Transport of Passengers – …

(c) on any scheduled flight; or
(d) from a place within to a place without the United Kingdom or vice versa,

[95] *Commissioners of Customs and Excise v. British Telecommunications pic*, [1999] 3 All ER 961.

[96] *Customs and Excise Commissioners v. Wellington Private Hospital Ltd*, [1997] BVC 251 (United Kingdom), cited in Goods and Services Tax Ruling, GSTR 2001/8, Goods and services tax: apportioning the consideration for a supply that includes taxable and non-taxable parts, §51 (Australia) [hereinafter GSTR 2001/8]. See also *Dr. Beynon and Partners v. Customs and Excise Commissioners*, [2005] STC 55 (House of Lords 2004) (United Kingdom), holding that the administration of a drug by a doctor to a patient is a single supply of exempt medical care, not separate zero-rated drugs and exempt medical care. The case involved the ability of doctors under National Health regulations to provide pharmacy services if there was no pharmacy nearby.

[97] *Sea Containers Ltd v. Customs and Excise Commissioners*, [2000] BVC 60 (United Kingdom). In an earlier British case, *Customs and Excise Commissioners v. Professional Footballers' Association (Enterprises) Ltd*, [1992] STC 294, the Court of Appeal held that the presentation of trophies at an awards dinner was part of a single supply of the dinner function because of the link between the trophies presented and the price paid for the ticket to the dinner.

[98] *College of Estate Management v. Customs and Excise Commissioners*, [2004] STC 1471 (Ct. App. United Kingdom).

[99] *Canadian Airlines International Ltd v. the Commissioners of Customs and Excise*, LON/93/587A (1994).

to the extent that those services are supplied in the United Kingdom."[100]

When a reservation was made, it was not certain that the passenger would exercise this right for free limousine service. According to the Tribunal, "we consider it to be important that the limousines were not capable of being used at the same time as the flight. It seems to us that when an element is not contemporaneous with the main supply it is less likely to be incidental. We hold that the right to the limousine element was a separate supply." The portion of the air fare attributable to the limousine service was held to be for a separate supply and, hence, was not zero-rated.

A proposed Canadian policy addressing the single versus mixed supply issue borrowed principles from this jurisprudence. According to this proposed policy, each supply should be considered distinct and independent. An "economically" single supply should not be artificially split for tax purposes, and a supply is a single supply "where one or more elements constitute the supply and any remaining elements serve only to enhance the supply."[101] The thrust of the policy is that "two or more elements are part of a single supply when the elements are integral components; the elements are inextricably bound up with each other; the elements are so intertwined and interdependent that they must be supplied together; or one element of the transaction is so dominated by another element that the first element has lost any identity for fiscal purposes."[102]

Australia approaches this single, mixed, composite issue a little differently. In part, Australia distinguishes between mixed supplies that contain taxable and nontaxable parts and composite "supplies that appear to have more than one part but that are essentially supplies of one thing."[103] The focus is on elements of a transaction that may be combined or disaggregated to change the nature of the supply from taxable to nontaxable or vice versa. The Australian Tax Office (ATO) takes the position that the consideration for a mixed supply (with taxable and exempt parts that produce different tax consequences) must be apportioned, but not the consideration for a composite supply. "A mixed supply is a supply that has to be separated or unbundled as it contains separately identifiable taxable and non-taxable parts that need to be individually recognized."[104] In contrast,

[100] This provision does not reflect an exemption under the Sixth Directive but is a derogation under Art. 28(3)(b) during the transitional period.

[101] Policy P-077R2, entitled "Single and Multiple Supplies" (April 26, 2004) (Canada), at "Decision."

[102] *Id.* at "Discussion, General Comments."

[103] GSTR 2001/8, *supra* note 96. For a lengthy discussion of the ATO approach to mixed and composite supplies, see P. Stacey & W. Brown, "A Unifying Composite Supply Doctrine? An Australian View," 14 *Int'l VAT Monitor* 178 (May/June 2003). Additional articles by these authors explore the applicability of the composite supply doctrine in debt and equity streams. See P. Stacey & W. Brown, "GST Treatment of Debt and Equity Income Streams: An Australian View," 14 *Int'l VAT Monitor* 295 (July/Aug. 2003); *GST analyzing income streams – Part II*, 3 AGSTJ 41 (2003).

[104] GSTR 2001 /8, *supra* note 96, at ¶16.

if "a supply … contains a dominant part and the supply includes something that is integral, ancillary or incidental to that part, then the supply is composite."[105] According to the ATO, the distinction between separately identifiable and integral is a question of fact and degree that should be resolved by adopting a commonsense approach.[106] Expanding on the differences, the ATO position is that "a supply has separately identifiable parts where the parts require individual recognition and retention as separate parts, due to their relative significance in the supply."[107] In contrast, "a part of a supply will be integral, ancillary or incidental where it is insignificant in value or function, or merely contributes to or complements the use or enjoyment of the dominant part of the supply."[108]

In *Re AGR Joint Venture v. Commissioner of Taxation*,[109] the Australian Administrative Appeals Tribunal held, looking at the commercial reality of the transaction, a transaction that the taxpayer split into two parts was a single supply for GST purposes. In that case, the taxpayer sold coin blanks to the mint. It billed the precious metal used in the blanks separate from the fabrication cost for the blanks to claim the exemption for the metal content. The taxpayer did not physically deliver the metal, nor even give the mint an enforceable contractual right to identified metal until the blanks were fabricated.

D. Vouchers

A voucher typically represents the right to receive goods or services or to receive a discount on the acquisition of goods or services. The use of vouchers, such as gift certificates, transportation tickets, and prepaid phone cards, raises a number of VAT issues, with the prepayment for telecom services accounting for the largest segment of the voucher market. Nevertheless, the range of transactions involving the use of vouchers is so broad that it is difficult to treat all vouchers alike.

A supply may be treated as occurring on issuance of a voucher by a taxable person or not until the voucher is exchanged for taxable goods or services. Moreover, for some kinds of vouchers, delay until the time the voucher is exchanged may be necessary to determine the appropriate tax rate.

105 *Id.* at ¶17.

106 *Id.* at ¶20.

107 *Id.* at ¶52.

108 *Id.* at ¶59. Although South Africa does not have the same definition distinction between mixed and composite supplies, the Tax Court held that "passenger service charges" (airport charges) separately stated on airline tickets were part of the fare for international transport of passengers and therefore a single zero-rated supply. Income Tax Case No. 1775, discussed in M. Botes, "South Africa: Single Supply?," 15 *Int'l VAT Monitor* 470 (Nov./Dec. 2004).

109 [2007] AATA 1870.

Vouchers have been the subject of extensive review and analysis in Australia.[110] In Australia, "(a) voucher evidences a right or entitlement to receive supplies in the future, and the obligation to make supplies, on the exercise or redemption of that right or entitlement."[111] The issuance of a voucher under the Australian GST generally is a taxable supply.[112] However, the supply of a voucher may not be taxed until the voucher is redeemed if the voucher satisfies a series of conditions tied to the concept of a "face value voucher" (FVV) and meets the requirements in sections 100–25 and 100–5 of the Australian GST Act.[113]

A voucher that qualifies as a FVV is not taxed until the voucher is redeemed. A voucher meets the requirements of section 100–25 if the redemption of the voucher "entitles the holder to receive supplies in accordance with its terms." In addition, the voucher must have a single function or purpose (such as a bus ticket),[114] the voucher (such as a gift certificate) must be presented when it is redeemed for supplies, and the voucher must give the holder the right to supplies on redemption.[115] The supply of a voucher is not a taxable supply, even if it meets section 100–25, unless it also meets section 100–5. The supply of a voucher must otherwise be a taxable supply (e.g., it is supplied for consideration), and on redemption, the holder must be entitled to "a reasonable choice and flexibility of supplies"[116] with a value up to the monetary value stated on the voucher. For example, a voucher entitling the holder to a car wash and other services up to a $50 value (a choice of services) is a FVV that is not reportable for tax purposes until it is redeemed.[117] A voucher that entitles the holder only to a particular kind of supply (such as a particular kind of car wash) priced at $30 is taxable when the voucher is supplied because there is no choice.[118]

Where an employer provided retail vouchers to employees in return for giving up some of their salary payable in money, the ECJ ruled that the provision of a voucher was a supply of services for consideration for purposes of the Sixth Directive, Article 2(1).[119]

110 Goods and Services Tax: Vouchers, GSTR 2003/5 (Australia) [hereinafter GSTR 2003/5]. For an extensive examination of the taxation of telephone cards and its relationship to the taxation of vouchers, see R. Millar, "The Australian GST Treatment of Telephone Cards," 14 *Int'l VAT Monitor*, 365 (Sept./Oct. 2003).

111 GSTR 2003/5, *supra* note 110, at ¶7.

112 See, A New Tax System (Goods and Services Tax) Act 1999, No. 55 of 1999 at §9–5.

113 G5TR 2003/5, *supra* note 110, at ¶¶8 and 9. Even if the supply of a voucher is not subject to GST until it is redeemed, the supply of the voucher is taxed on issuance to the extent that the consideration received for the voucher exceeds its face value. *Id.* at ¶9.

114 *Id.* at ¶26. On redemption, the holder's right to receive supplies with the use of the voucher must terminate. *Id.* at ¶27.

115 *Id.* at ¶26.

116 *Id.* at ¶55.

117 *Id.* at ¶77.

118 *Id.* at ¶78.

119 Case C-40/09, *Astra Zeneca UK Ltd v. Commissioners of Her Majesty's Revenue and Customs.* Art. 2(1) of the Sixth Directive is comparable to Art. 2(1)(a) and (c) of the VAT Directive.

Prepaid telephone cards raise issues relating to vouchers that are included in the discussion of telecommunication services in Chapter 7, but in the context of "what is the supply" in this chapter, it is noteworthy that the ECJ ruled in the *Labera* case[120] that the sale of prepaid phone cards by a telecom service provider in the United Kingdom to a distributor in another member state, for resale by the distributor, was a supply of services by the issuer to the distributor and not a supply of services by the issuer to the end user who purchased at the end of the distribution chain.

A proposed EU Directive[121] defines three categories of vouchers:

1. A single-purpose voucher is a voucher carrying a right to receive a supply of goods or services where the supplier's identity, the place of supply and the applicable VAT rate for these goods or services are known at the time of issue of the voucher.
2. A discount voucher is a voucher carrying a right to receive a price discount or rebate.
3. A multipurpose voucher is any other voucher.

The proposed Directive regards the issuance of a multipurpose voucher and its redemption for goods and services as one single transaction,[122] VAT is not due until the time of redemption, and the tax consequences depend on the goods or services supplied for the voucher. When a multipurpose voucher is purchased by a distributor at below face value for resale, the distributor is taxed on the basis of the distributor's margin. Multiple-purpose vouchers involving supplies across borders are taxable when and where the goods or services are supplied. A prepayment on a single-purpose voucher is treated as a supply in the amount received.[123] In contrast, an advance payment on a multipurpose voucher is chargeable with VAT when the voucher is redeemed.[124] The person supplying goods or services in redemption of a multipurpose voucher is liable for VAT on the goods and services supplied.[125]

When the issuer of a discount voucher (e.g., a manufacturer) is different from the person who honors the discount on a supply of goods and services (e.g., a retailer), the latter is treated as making a supply to the issuer of the voucher in the amount of the discount.

120 Case C-520/10, *Labera Ltd v. the Commissioners for Her Majesty's Revenue and Customs* (Judgment of the ECJ 2012).

121 Proposal for a Council Directive amending Directive 2006/112/EC on the common system of value added tax, as regards the treatment of vouchers [hereinafter Proposed Directive].

122 VAT Directive, *supra* note 2, Art. 30b, as added by Proposed Directive, *supra* note 121.

123 VAT Directive, supra note 2, Art. 65, as added by Proposed Directive, *supra* note 121.

124 The value of a multipurpose voucher, related to its redemption, is covered in new Arts. 74a, 74b, and 74c of the VAT Directive, *supra* note 2, as added by Proposed Directive, *supra* note 121.

125 Proposed Directive, *supra* note 121, adding to Art. 193.

III. The VAT Invoice

A. Role of VAT Invoice

The VAT invoice is a central feature of the almost universally employed credit-invoice VAT system. Only a VAT-registered person can issue a VAT invoice, and only a VAT-registered person can claim credit against output tax liability for VAT imposed on acquisitions used in making taxable supplies. As a tax credit, the input tax credit allows the registered purchaser to reduce tax liability one dollar for each one dollar of VAT qualifying for the input credit. It is not surprising that severe penalties generally are imposed on anyone who improperly issues a VAT invoice.[126] The VAT invoice issued by the supplier serves as the audit tool to verify the supplier's reported taxable output from the supply and the purchaser's claimed input tax credit.[127]

B. Who Receives VAT Invoices?

In many VAT systems, a registered person must issue a VAT invoice for all taxable sales. In other systems, to reduce the opportunity for fraud resulting from trading in VAT invoices, VAT invoices can be issued only on taxable sales to other registered persons. In some countries, including the EU, a purchaser has the authority to issue a VAT invoice to himself with respect to an acquisition.[128]

The import declaration on imports of goods also serves as the equivalent of a VAT invoice to verify the importer's claimed credit for VAT on the import. Typically, there is no VAT invoice issued on imported services. Chapter 7 explains when VAT is imposed on imported services; the importer reports and remits tax on those imported services.

C. Contents of Required VAT Invoices

The centrality of the VAT invoice results in elaborate rules in VAT acts and regulations on the requirements related to the issuance of VAT invoices. In the EU, VAT invoices generally are issued in transactions between

[126] Goods and Services Tax (General) Regulations, Cap. 117A, Rg 10(1) (1993); and Singapore GST, *supra* note 57, at §64(2) imposing a civil penalty. See New Vatopia *supra* note 2, at §32(1).

[127] There is scant data that this cross-matching in fact occurs with any degree of consistency. Korea and Taiwan relied on an elaborate computer system of cross-matching copies of tax invoices sent to the government by the seller and the buyer. See China's Golden Tax Project for VAT administration in Chapter 14.

[128] See, for example, the United Kingdom's implementation of Council Directive 2010/45/EU (see note 130), in SI 2012 No. 2951, The Value Added Tax (Amendment) (No. 3) Regulations 2012, reg. 2(3), simplifying the provisions relating to self-billing.

registered persons. Sellers ordinarily do not issue VAT invoices on retail sales.[129] With the advent of electronic billing, the EU and other VAT regimes introduced and then expanded the rules governing electronic invoices.[130]

New Zealand has particularly detailed rules governing tax invoices.[131] A registered person who sells to a registered purchaser must, if the purchaser requests it, issue a tax invoice containing the following information:[132]

1. The words "tax invoice" placed in a prominent place
2. The seller's name and registration number
3. The recipient's name and address
4. The date invoice is issued
5. A description of items sold, including quantity or volume
6. A listing of tax-exclusive and tax-inclusive prices and amount of tax, or a statement of the consideration and that it includes tax

A tax invoice may contain less information if the consideration is below a certain threshold.[133] In limited situations, New Zealand allows the recipient to create a tax invoice for a taxable supply that it receives.[134] If a consumer sells secondhand goods to a registered recipient, the recipient will not receive a VAT invoice but must maintain records of the transaction, including much of the same information that is required on a VAT invoice.[135]

D. Waiver of Required VAT Invoices

For administrative reasons, in some countries, the tax administrator can waive the obligation to issue a VAT invoice in all transactions. This may be used in cases in which the law requires VAT invoices to be issued for all taxable sales and smaller retailers do not have the capacity or the retailer's sales are mainly to final consumers, so that the need to provide an audit trail for business-to-business transactions is not present. A policy

[129] See VAT Directive, *supra* note 2, at Art. 220. In the United Kingdom, the Commissioners by regulations may require taxable persons to issue VAT invoices that include particular information, such as whether VAT is chargeable on the supply, the amount of VAT chargeable, and the identification of the seller and the buyer. UK VATA 1994, *supra* note 30, *supra* note, at Sch. 11, ¶2A(1) and (2).

[130] See Council Directive 2010/45/EU of 13 July 2010 amending Directive 2006/112/EC [VAT Directive] on the common system of value added tax as regards the rules on invoicing, OJ L189/1, 22/07/2010. The Directive significantly revised and expanded the rules governing invoices, including electronic invoicing. See VAT Directive, *supra* note 2, at Arts. 217–240.

[131] NZ GST, *supra* note 36, at §24. See New Vatopia, *supra* note 2, at Sch. IV

[132] *Id.* at §24(1) and (3). The seller ordinarily can issue only one tax invoice for each taxable supply. If the original invoice is lost, the seller can issue a copy if it is clearly marked as such. *Id.* at §24(l)(a) and (b).

[133] *Id.* at §24(4).

[134] *Id.* at §24(2). The statute provides that if the seller issues a tax invoice governing the same sale, the recipient's invoice is deemed to be the tax invoice.

[135] *Id.* at §24(7).

alleviating the need for small businesses to issue VAT invoices may be motivated by the fact that small businesses tend to bear a disproportionate VAT compliance burden.

In New Zealand, some registrants are not obligated to issue a tax invoice or may be obligated to provide only limited information on a tax invoice. A supplier is not required to issue tax invoices if the consideration is below a stated threshold.[136] If the commissioner is satisfied that sufficient records are available on certain supplies or that requiring all of the particulars on tax invoices would be impractical, the commissioner may waive certain particulars or may waive the requirement to issue tax invoices, subject to conditions that the commissioner imposes.[137]

IV. Discussion Questions

1. In the cases discussed in this chapter, can you identify the value added or the item that can be regarded as adding value to the personal consumption being taxed at the end of the line – that is, the final retail sale?
2. Mr. Brown is a lawyer who has always kept the deepest attachment to the university where he graduated and gladly helps by rendering legal advice free of charge. Is there any provision in the EU VAT Directive relating to this situation? Should there be such a provision in a "model" VAT?
3. What are the main purposes of the distinction in the VAT Directive between goods and services? Could you draft a VAT Code without using this distinction?
4. Is the *Tolsma* decision correct for the reasons stated? Should the courts in cases like *Tolsma* decide if the payments made to the performer are for services or merely gratuitous payments made for altruistic or other reasons?
5. Do the New Vatopia VAT and the EU VAT Directive provide comparable VAT treatment for fringe benefits provided by employers to employees? See VAT Directive, Art 16. Is denial of employer's credit for inputs used in providing fringe benefits a technically sound solution to the problem or a compromise? What do you recommend and why?

[136] NZ GST, *supra* note 36, at §24(5).
[137] *Id.* at §24(6).

6 The Tax Credit Mechanism

I. Tax Credit for Purchases

A. Basic Input Tax Credit Rules

1. Allowance of Credit – General Rules

Under the credit or invoice VAT used almost universally, tax liability for each period is calculated as the difference between the tax chargeable on taxable sales (output tax) and tax charged both on taxable purchases and on taxable imports (input tax credit). Some credit-invoice VATs are worded so that the input tax is deducted from tax on taxable sales (output tax). In this book, input tax credit and input tax deduction are used interchangeably to mean the subtraction of input tax from output tax.

Unlike an income tax imposed on an income base that requires capital goods to be capitalized and depreciated and beginning and ending inventories to be taken into account in determining gross income from sales, VATs typically are consumption-based taxes that allow an immediate input credit for tax imposed on purchases of capital goods and inventory items. There are some exceptions discussed in this chapter.

The EU VAT Directive contains extensive rules on the availability of input tax credits (which the Directive refers to as deductions).[1] An input credit is available for tax on purchases of goods or services, imports of goods, or certain taxable self-supplies if these items are used for purposes of taxable transactions.[2] Taxpayers may engage in tax-motivated transactions in an attempt to convert assets used in making exempt supplies into assets used in making taxable supplies.[3]

[1] See Council Directive 2006/112/EC of 28 November 2006 on the common system of value added tax (OJ L347, 11.12.2006, p. 1) [hereinafter VAT Directive], Arts. 167–169 and 172. Limitations, restrictions, and adjustments to the right to deduct input VAT generally are included in Arts. 173–192.

[2] VAT Directive, *supra* note 1, at Art. 17(2).

[3] See, e.g., Case C-223/03, *University of Huddersfield Higher Education Corporation v. Commissioners of Customs and Excise* (ECJ Opinion 7 April 2005) (discussed in Chapter 10).

To claim credits for tax on goods acquired, the goods must exist. Although it seems self-evident, there are situations in which the existence of the goods may be in doubt. For example, in one case a business entered an agreement to buy containers to ship mud to oil rigs, immediately leased the containers without physically inspecting them, and received rent on some but not all of the containers. There apparently was fraud and some of the alleged containers listed on VAT invoices did not exist. The court held that if goods listed on invoices do not exist when the goods are to be transferred under the sale agreement, there is no supply unless the goods later come into existence, and therefore no input VAT is creditable.[4] In contrast, the ECJ ruled that a member state could not deny a taxable person a deduction for VAT listed on an invoice containing all of the required information unless the tax authority could establish, on the basis of objective evidence, that the purchaser knew or should have known that the issuer of the invoice or another person involved in the transaction (or series of transactions) giving rise to the deduction was connected with the fraud.[5] Likewise, where an unregistered person was issued a taxpayer identification number and issued an invoice with all of the required details, the person acquiring that item could not be denied deduction for VAT listed on that invoice.[6]

There are other cases of VAT fraud involving VAT invoices. A few are discussed here. In a Canadian case involving vehicles, *R. v. Prokofiew*,[7] the accused engaged in schemes involving purported sales to status Indians and resales by them (the purchases and sales were not subject to the Canadian GST) under circumstances in which the Indians were not intended to be the owners of the vehicles.[8] In South Africa, false export documents have been used to claim zero-rating for goods that are not exported, a seller and buyer have conspired to falsify invoices, and input VAT was claimed on falsified invoices covering services that cannot be physically investigated.[9] In the EU, the ECJ ruled that an innocent person who was an unknowing participant in a carousel fraud[10] still is engaged in

[4] *Howard v. Commissioners of Customs and Excise*, LON/80/457 (VATTR 1981)(United Kingdom).

[5] Case C-324/11, *Gábor Tóth v Nemzeti Adó- és Vámhivatal Észak-magyarországi Regionális Adó Főigazgatósága* (judgment of the ECJ 2012). See also the section on tax evasion in Chapter 10.

[6] Case C-438/09, *Boguslaw Juliusz Dandowski v. Dyrektor Izby Sharbowej w Lodzi* (judgment of the ECJ 2010).

[7] *R. v. Prokofiew (No. 1)*, [2004] GSTC 103 (Canada).

[8] See D. Sherman, "Five of Nine Accused Convicted in Huge GST Vehicle Fraud," 16 *Int'l VAT Monitor* 76 (Jan./Feb.2005).

[9] See L. Botes & M. Botes, "Money-Laundering in South Africa," 13 *VAT Monitor* 258 (July/Aug. 2002).

[10] "Carousel fraud" in simple terms may be as follows: Co. A in country A exports to B in country B and zero-rates the export, claiming credit for tax on its purchases. B sells to C in country B, charging VAT but not remitting it to the government. B disappears. C exports to A in country A, claiming credit for VAT B never reported or remitted. The goods start and end in country A, but government in B loses revenue on the defrauding

economic activity and making supplies of goods and supplies of services and, therefore, able to claim input tax credits with respect to those transactions. In the joined cases of *Optigen, Fulcrum, and Bond*, the court ruled: "The right to deduct input value added tax of a taxable person who carries out such transactions cannot be affected by the fact that in the chain of supply of which those transactions form part another prior or subsequent transaction is vitiated by value added tax fraud, without that taxable person knowing or having any means of knowing."[11]

If tax is paid on purchases used both for transactions qualifying for the input credit and for those that do not qualify, the input credit is available under the EU VAT Directive and most other VATs only for the portion attributable to the former.[12] For example, if, in a tax period, a registered business has $60,000 in taxable purchases directly attributable to taxable sales and $30,000 in taxable purchases directly attributable to exempt sales, the person can claim credit only for VAT on the $60,000 of purchases attributable to the taxable sales. As discussed in Part F of this chapter, in cases where inputs cannot be directly attributed to either taxable or exempt sales, an allocation formula must be used.

2. Credit for Input VAT on Capital Goods

Chapter 2 discusses the classification of a value added tax as a gross domestic product, income, or consumption VAT. The difference is the treatment of the input VAT on capital purchases. Most countries have a consumption-style VAT that provides an immediate credit for input VAT on capital purchases. There are a few exceptions. Some countries start with a GDP or income VAT as a transition to a consumption-style VAT.[13]

Some countries have elaborate rules covering the input credit on capital goods, especially on the acquisition of such property, on the change in the

company B. On VAT fraud generally, see M. Keen & S. Smith, "VAT Fraud and Evasion: What Do We Know and What Can be Done?" LIX *National Tax Journal* 861–887 (2006).

11 Joined Cases C-354/03, C-355/03, and C-484/03, *Optigen Ltd, Fulcrum Electronics Ltd and Bond House Systems Ltd v. Commissioners of Customs & Excise*, ECJ (Jan., 12, 2006). The EC issued a proposal for a Council Directive on a number of issues, including evasion of VAT. 2005 – COM (89), Countering tax evasion and avoidance. It has been estimated by the British Office for National Statistics that VAT fraud accounts for about 10% of UK exports. A. Seager, "Fraud Could Account for 10% of UK's Exports," *Guardian* (May 11, 2006), http://www.theguardian.com/business/2006/may/11/3.

12 VAT Directive, *supra* note 1, at Art. 173. See also Arts. 174 and 175 for the methods to be used to calculate allowable credits.

13 For example, Belarus went from a system providing for the recovery of input VAT on capital goods over a twelve-month period to a system allowing full input VAT credit at the time that capital (fixed) goods are put into operation. See Belarus Presidential Decree No. 1 of January 13, 2005, discussed in Strachuk, Belarus, IBFD Tax News Service, March 22, 2005. As part of its program to encourage industrial investment, Argentina is providing VAT refunds on capital purchases made during the period between November 2000 and November 2004, if the authorities are satisfied that the rebated VAT is reinvested into business expansion. Decree 379/2005, discussed in *BNA Daily Tax Report*, April 29, 2005, p. G-5.

use of capital goods from taxable to exempt activities, and on the disposition of capital goods.[14]

In the EU, there is an unusual feature relating to the treatment of input VAT on capital goods used partly in connection with taxable activities and partly in other activities. Two cases are discussed. *Eon Asset Management* involved two leased vehicles used to transport the managing director between home and work. The other, *Sandra Puffer*, deals with real property that is used for both business and personal purposes.

In *Eon Asset Management*,[15] the company leased one vehicle under a four-month operating lease[16] and leased another under a four-year finance lease.[17] The ECJ, relying in part on international financial accounting standards,[18] held that the national court must determine whether the finance lease is to be treated as the acquisition of capital goods. The VAT charged on the operating lease was deductible if there was a direct and immediate link between the leasing service received and the taxable person's economic activity. The referring court therefore must determine whether the vehicle to transport the managing director was used for Eon's business or the director's personal use.

In the EU, if a finance lease is classified as the acquisition of capital goods, the taxable person entering into this finance lease has three choices on how it should be treated:[19]

1. Allocate the goods to the assets of the business
2. Retain the goods wholly as private assets
3. Integrate the goods into the business only to the extent used for business purposes

If the capital goods are treated as within (2), the taxable person is denied deduction for input VAT charged on the finance lease. If the capital goods are treated as within (3) and the goods will be used 60% in connection with taxable activities, the taxable person can deduct 60% of the input VAT charged on the finance lease. No additional tax consequences generally are reportable until the person disposes of the asset.

14 See Canadian Goods and Services Tax, S.C. 1990, c. 45, as amended [hereinafter Canadian GST], §§195–211.

15 Case C-118/11, *Eon Aset Menidjmund OOD (Eon Asset Management) v. Direktor na Direktsia Obzhelvane I upravlenie na izpalnenieto – Varna pri Tsentralno upravlenie na Natsionalnata agentsia za prihodite* (Director of the Varna Appeals and Administration of Enforcement Office of the Central Office of the National Revenue Agency) (judgment of the ECJ 2012).

16 The lease was under a motor vehicle leasing contract.

17 The "lease" was under a financial leasing contract.

18 The International Accounting Standard 17 distinguishes between operating leases (which is the acquisition of services) and finance leases that transfer risks and rewards of legal ownership.

19 The ECJ cited Case C-291/92, *Armbrecht*, [1995] ECR I-2775; and Case C-434/03, *Charles and Charles-Tijmens*, [2005] ECR I-7037.

For capital goods treated as within (1) – that is, goods allocated to the assets of the business (acquired for purposes of economic activity) that are used both for purposes of taxed transactions and for other purposes – a taxable person can immediately deduct the entire input VAT on the acquisition of those capital goods. The person then must treat,[20] as a supply of services in each tax period, the portion of the goods covered by the finance lease that is used for "other" purposes – in the *Eon* case, private purposes. This rule (and the result in the *Puffer* case below) has now been reversed for immovable property (and other property as member states determine) under section 168a of the VAT Directive (added in 2009).

Under the prior rule (which may still apply to movable property except as countries provide otherwise), when a taxable person acquires a capital asset that is to be used partly for taxable economic activities and partly for personal or other purposes, and the person allocates that asset to business use, the taxable person may obtain an advantage not available, for example, to a non-taxable person or to a person acquiring the same capital goods and using them in making both taxable and exempt supplies. The following *Sandra Puffer* case explains that discrepancy.

Puffer (Sandra)
v.
Unabhängiger Finanzsenat, Außenstelle Linz[21]

[Note: This case raised several other issues of European law that are not included in this edited version that focuses on the input credit. The following excerpt includes references to the Sixth Directive. Most are in substance the same as the VAT Directive.]

Legal framework

Community legislation

Under Article 2 of the Sixth Directive[22] 'the following [transactions] shall be subject to [VAT]: ... the supply of goods ... for consideration within the territory of [a Member State] by a taxable person acting as such'.

Article 4(1) and (2) of the Sixth Directive state:

'1. 'Taxable person' shall mean any person who independently carries out in any place any economic activity ..., whatever the purpose or results of that activity.

[20] The ECJ cited Art. 26(1) of Directive 2006/112 [the VAT Directive, *supra* note 1].

[21] Case C-460/07, *Sandra Puffer v. Unabhängiger Finanzsenat, Außenstelle Linz* [2009] I-03251. Edited by the authors.

[22] Article 2(1) of the VAT Directive, *supra* note 1.

2. The economic activities referred to in paragraph 1 shall comprise all activities of producers, traders and persons supplying services including mining and agricultural activities and activities of the professions. The exploitation of tangible or intangible property for the purpose of obtaining income therefrom on a continuing basis shall also be considered an economic activity.[23]

Article 6(2)(a) of the Sixth Directive[24] treats the following as a supply of services for consideration: 'the use of goods forming part of the assets of a business for the private use of [a] taxable person or of his staff or more generally for purposes other than those of his business where the [VAT] on such goods [was] wholly or partly deductible'.

Under Article 11A(1)(c) of the Sixth Directive,[25] the taxable amount is to be: 'in respect of supplies referred to in Article 6(2),[26] the full cost to the taxable person of providing the services'.

According to Article 13B(b) of the Sixth Directive,[27] the Member States are to exempt 'the leasing or letting of immovable property', subject to certain exceptions which are not relevant in the present case. [The VAT Directive now gives member states the authority to reduce the scope of the exemption.]

Article 17 of the Sixth Directive, as amended by Council Directive 95/7/EC of 10 April 1995 (OJ 1995 L 102, p. 18) provides:

'1. The right to deduct shall arise at the time when the deductible tax becomes chargeable.
2. In so far as the goods and services are used for the purposes of his taxable transactions, the taxable person shall be entitled to deduct from the tax which he is liable to pay:
   a) [VAT] due or paid within the territory of the country in respect of goods or services supplied or to be supplied to him by another taxable person:[28] ...
5. As regards goods and services to be used by a taxable person both for transactions covered by paragraphs 2 and 3, in respect of which

[23] Article 9(1) of the VAT Directive provides:

1. 'Taxable person' shall mean any person who, independently, carries out in any place any economic activity, whatever the purpose or results of that activity.
   Any activity of producers, traders or persons supplying services, including mining and agricultural activities and activities of the professions, shall be regarded as 'economic activity'. The exploitation of tangible or intangible property for the purposes of obtaining income therefrom on a continuing basis shall in particular be regarded as an economic activity."

[24] Article 26(1)(a) of the VAT Directive, *supra* note 1.
[25] *Id.* at Art. 75.
[26] *Id.* at Art. 26.
[27] *Id.* at Art. 135.
[28] *Id.* at Arts. 167, 168(a), and 168a(1).

> [VAT] is deductible, and for transactions in respect of which [VAT] is not deductible, only such proportion of the value added tax shall be deductible as is attributable to the former transactions.[29]

This proportion shall be determined, in accordance with Article 19, for all the transactions carried out by the taxable person.... [30]'

Article 20 of the Sixth Directive, as amended by Council Directive 95/7/EC of 10 April 1995 (OJ 1995 L 102, p. 18), provides:

'1. The initial deduction shall be adjusted according to the procedures laid down by the Member States, in particular:
   (a) where that deduction was higher or lower than that to which the taxable person was entitled;[31]
   (b) where after the return is made some change occurs in the factors used to determine the amount to be deducted....[32]
2. In the case of capital goods, adjustment shall be spread over five years including that in which the goods were acquired or manufactured.[33] The annual adjustment shall be made only in respect of one-fifth of the tax imposed on the goods.[34] The adjustment shall be made on the basis of the variations in the deduction entitlement in subsequent years in relation to that for the year in which the goods were acquired or manufactured.[35]

By way of derogation from the preceding subparagraph, Member States may base the adjustment on a period of five full years starting from the time at which the goods are first used.[36]

In the case of immovable property acquired as capital goods, the adjustment period may be extended up to 20 years'.[37]

National legislation

Paragraph 12(2)(1) and 12(2)(2)(a) of the 1994 Law on Turnover Tax (Umsatzsteuergesetz 1994, BGBl. 663/1994; 'the UStG 1994'), in the version in force when the Republic of Austria acceded to the European Union, that is 1 January 1995, was worded as follows:

'1. Supplies or other services connected with the acquisition, construction or maintenance of buildings shall be regarded as being carried out for business purposes in so far as the consideration

[29] *Id.* at Art. 168(a)(1).
[30] See a not identical rule in *id.* at Arts. 174 and 175.
[31] *Id.* at Art. 184.
[32] *Id.* at Art. 185(1).
[33] See *id.* at Art. 187(1).
[34] *Id.* at Art. 187(2).
[35] *Id.* at Art. 187(2).
[36] *Id.* at Art. 187(1).
[37] *Id.* at Art. 187(1).

given for them constitutes operating costs or business expenses under the rules governing income tax.

2. Supplies or services shall not be regarded as being carried out for business purposes:
   (a) where the consideration does not consist principally of deductible expenses (costs) within the meaning of Paragraph 20(1), points (1) to (5), of the 1988 Law on Income Tax (Einkommensteuergesetz [1988], BGBl. 400/1988) or of Paragraphs 8(2) and 12(1), points (1) to (5) of the 1988 Law on Corporation Tax (Körperschaftsteuergesetz [1988], BGBl. 401/1988)'.

According to the order for reference, because Paragraph 20(1), points 1 to 5 of the 1988 Law on Income Tax excluded the deduction of living expenses, including those for accommodation, from taxable income, the effect of Paragraph 12(2)(1) and 12(2)(2)(a) of the UStG 1994 was that the VAT deduction was granted only in respect of the part of a building used for business purposes and not that used as a private residence.

Pursuant to the Tax Amendment Law of 1997 (Abgabenänderungsgesetz 1997, BGBl. I, 9/1998; 'the AbgÄG 1997'), first, Paragraph 12(2)(1) of the UStG 1994 was amended so that mixed-use buildings could be treated as forming, in their entirety, part of the assets of the business. Secondly, it was laid down in Paragraph 6(1)(16), in conjunction with Paragraph 6(2) and Paragraph 12(3), of the UStG 1994 that the use of parts of the building as a private residence was to constitute an 'exempt transaction' within the meaning of Article 13B(b) of the Sixth Directive,[38] thus excluding deductions.

According to the order for reference, by means of those amendments, the Austrian legislature wished to retain the exclusion of the VAT deductions for the parts of buildings used as a private residence, while recognising the possibility, deriving from Case C-269/00 *Seeling* [2003] ECR I-4101, of treating a mixed-use building as forming, in its entirety, part of the assets of the business.

The dispute in the main proceedings and the questions referred for a preliminary ruling

Over the period from November 2002 to June 2004, Ms Puffer built a single-family house with a swimming pool. From 2003, she used the house as a private residence, with the exception of one part, covering approximately 11% of the building, which she let for business purposes.

[38] *Id.* at Art. 135.

Ms Puffer treated the building as forming, in its entirety, part of her business and claimed the deduction of the full amount of input taxes charged on the construction of the building.

Pursuant to amended VAT assessment notices for the years 2002 and 2003, the Finanzamt (Tax Office), first, refused to take into account for deduction purposes the taxes paid on construction of the swimming pool. Second, in relation to the other building costs, it allowed a deduction of the input tax paid only to the extent of the use of the building for business purposes, that is, 11%.

Ms Puffer lodged an objection to those notices which was rejected by the Unabhängiger Finanzsenat on the ground, in particular, that when the Sixth Directive entered into force in Austria, the national legislation excluded the right to deduct input VAT payable in respect of the building costs of the parts of buildings used for private residential purposes and that the national legislature had not waived the option, provided for in Article 17(6) of the Sixth Directive, to retain that exclusion.

Ms Puffer then appealed against that decision to the Verwaltungsgerichtshof (Administrative Court). She claims, first, that the treatment of an asset as forming, in its entirety, part of the assets of the business confers a right, pursuant to the case-law of the Court, to the full deduction of VAT and, second, that the conditions set out in Article 17(6) of the Sixth Directive, allowing the Member States to retain an exclusion of the deductions existing when the Sixth Directive came into force, are not satisfied in the present case.

Having found that, contrary to Article17(2) of the Sixth Directive,[39] the Austrian legislation does not allow the full and immediate deduction of VAT on the building costs of a mixed-use building treated as forming, in its entirety, part of the assets of a business, the national court questions whether that provision is compatible with the general principle of equal treatment under Community law.

In that regard, the national court points out that the full and immediate deduction of VAT on the building costs of such a mixed-use building and the subsequent imposition of VAT on the expenses pertaining to the part of the building used as a private residence, spread over 10 years, have the effect of granting the taxable person, in respect of that period, an 'interest-free loan' not available to a non-taxable person.

Consequently, it asks whether the resulting financial advantage, quantified by it at 5% of the net costs of construction of the part of the building used for private purposes, gives rise to the unequal treatment of taxable and non-taxable persons and, within the category of taxable persons, between those who construct a building for purely private purposes and those who construct it, in part, for their business.

[39] *Id.* at Art. 176.

The first question, concerning the compatibility of Article 17(2)(a) of the Sixth Directive[40] *with the general principle of equal treatment under Community law.*

By its first question, the referring court asks, essentially, whether Articles 17(2)(a) and 6(2)(a) of the Sixth Directive[41] infringe the general principle of equal treatment under Community law by conferring on taxable persons, by means of a full and immediate right to deduct input VAT payable on the construction of a mixed-use building and the subsequent staggered imposition of that tax on the private use of the building, a financial advantage compared to non-taxable persons and to taxable persons who use their building only as a private residence.

Observations submitted to the Court

Ms Puffer claims that a trader may choose to treat mixed-use goods as forming, in their entirety, part of the assets of the business in order to maintain the possibility of deducting input VAT when the business use of those goods subsequently becomes more significant.

According to her, where the asset is initially allocated, even in part, to private use and is thereafter reallocated to business use, the Sixth Directive clearly no longer allows the deduction of the input tax. The immediate and full deduction of VAT and the subsequent staggered imposition of VAT on the private use of the goods follow from the scheme of the Sixth Directive and the Court has borne the implications of that scheme in mind in its case-law. Therefore, there is no reason to doubt the compatibility of that system with the general principle of equal treatment under Community law.

The Unabhängiger Finanzsenat points out that Article 17(2)(a) of the Sixth Directive[42] allows the deduction of input VAT only in so far as the goods and services are used for the purposes of the trader's taxable transactions. It follows that the Sixth Directive does not confer a right to deduct in respect of the proportion of private use of the goods.

According to it, in accordance with the clear wording of Article 17(2)(a) of the Sixth Directive,[43] the extent of the deduction permitted on the basis of the use of the goods for taxable transactions must first of all be established. Only thereafter is it necessary to verify whether private use of a part of goods initially allocated for use in taxable transactions must be treated as a supply of services for consideration under Article 6(2)(a) of the Sixth Directive.[44]

Consequently, according to the Unabhängiger Finanzsenat, neither the treatment of an asset as part of the assets of the business nor

40 *Id.* at Art. 168(a).
41 *Id.* at Arts. 168 and 176.
42 *Id.* at Art. 168(a).
43 *Id.* at Art. 168(a).
44 *Id.* at Art. 26(1)(a).

the status of trader can alone establish a right to deduct input VAT payable. Those are only two conditions among others which have to be met.

In particular, if those two conditions were sufficient, that would create circular reasoning and systemic inconsistencies. In that regard, the Unabhängiger Finanzsenat points out that traders who carry out only exempt transactions and who, therefore, may not deduct, as a rule, any input tax, could nevertheless claim deductions for goods subject to mixed use to the extent of their use for private purposes.

The Unabhängiger Finanzsenat also observes that traders carrying out partly exempt transactions and partly taxable transactions may deduct VAT from their taxable transactions only on a proportionate basis, in accordance with Article 17(5) of the Sixth Directive.[45] That proportion may differ considerably from the relative proportions of private and business use.

The Austrian Government concurred, at the hearing, with the interpretation of Article 17(2)(a) of the Sixth Directive[46] supported by the Unabhängiger Finanzsenat. That government takes the view that the wording of that provision authorises deductions only in respect of the part of a building intended for use in taxable transactions and not in respect of the part intended for private use. In short, it is not necessary, according to that government, to answer the first question, since, applying that interpretation, no problem of unequal treatment would arise.

The Commission states that the possibility for the taxable person to treat mixed-use goods, in their entirety, as forming part of the assets of the business, is based on the principle of fiscal neutrality which serves to guarantee the free and unhindered exercise of economic activities. The corresponding obligation, on the taxable person, to pay VAT on the expenses incurred in private use of the goods, treated as a service provided for consideration, aims precisely to ensure the equal treatment of taxable persons and non-taxable persons.

The slight financial advantage which taxable persons may retain under that system, first, is the result of their economic activity and their legal status which means that they collect and pay VAT to the tax authorities and, second, is the corollary of the fact that the business use of a mixed-use asset may increase in time. Thus, the existence of that advantage cannot permit the inference that there has been an infringement of the general principle of equal treatment under Community law.

It is only where any business use is ruled out at the outset, be it for objective reasons or because the taxable person himself has excluded

[45] See a somewhat different Art. 168(a)(1), VAT Directive, *supra* note 1.

[46] *Id.* at Art. 168(a).

such use, that allocation to business assets and the related deduction of input VAT are excluded.

In addition, the Commission considers that the principle of equal treatment is not infringed by the fact that a taxable person who has not elected to treat goods as forming part of the assets of his business cannot deduct input VAT payable, since the taxable person had that opportunity and did not use it. As the taxable person did not exercise that option, he cannot claim to have suffered unequal treatment.

Finally, the difference in treatment of taxable persons carrying out taxable transactions and those carrying out exempt transactions results, according to the Commission, in short, from the principle of neutrality [which] allows VAT to be deducted only in respect of taxable transactions.

Answer of the Court

First, it must be pointed out that it is settled case-law that, where capital goods are used both for business and for private purposes the taxpayer has the choice, for the purposes of VAT, of (i) allocating those goods wholly to the assets of his business, (ii) retaining them wholly within his private assets, thereby excluding them entirely from the system of VAT, or (iii) integrating them into his business only to the extent to which they are actually used for business purposes (Case C-434/03 *Charles and Charles-Tijmens* [2005] ECR I-7037, paragraph 23 and case-law cited, and Case C-72/05 *Wollny* [2006] ECR I-8297, paragraph 21).

Should the taxable person choose to treat capital goods used for both business and private purposes as business goods, the input VAT due on the acquisition of those goods is, in principle, immediately deductible in full (*Charles and Charles-Tijmens*, paragraph 24, and *Wollny*, paragraph 22).

However, it follows from Article 6(2)(a) of the Sixth Directive[47] that when the input VAT paid on goods forming part of the assets of a business is wholly or partly deductible, their use for the private purposes of the taxable person or of his staff or for purposes other than those of his business is treated as a supply of services for consideration. That use, which is therefore a 'taxable transaction' within the meaning of Article 17(2) of that directive[48] is, under Article 11A(1)(c) thereof,[49] taxed on the basis of the cost of providing the services (*Charles and Charles-Tijmens*, paragraph 25, and *Wollny*, paragraph 23).

Consequently, where a taxable person chooses to treat an entire building as forming part of the assets of his business and uses part of that building for private purposes he is both entitled to deduct the input VAT paid on all construction costs relating to that building and

[47] *Id.* at Art. 26(1)(a).

[48] *Id.* at Art. 168.

[49] *Id.* at Art. 75.

subject to the corresponding obligation to pay VAT on the amount of expenditure incurred to effect such use (*Wollny*, paragraph 24).

By contrast, if the taxable person chooses, when acquiring capital goods, to allocate those goods entirely to his private assets or to allocate only part of them to his business activities, no right to deduct can arise in relation to the part allocated to his private assets (see, to that effect, Case C-97/90 *Lennartz* [1991] ECR I-3795, paragraphs 8 and 9, and Case C-25/03 *HE* [2005] ECR I-3123, paragraph 43).

Equally, on that hypothesis, subsequent use for business purposes of the part of the goods allocated to private assets is not capable of giving rise to a right to deduct, because Article 17(1) of the Sixth Directive[50] lays down that the right to deduct is to arise at the time when the deductible tax becomes chargeable. There is no adjustment mechanism to that effect under Community legislation as it stands, as the Advocate General states in point 50 of her Opinion.

In the case of capital goods the mixed use of which varies over time, the interpretation of Article 17(1) and (2) of the Sixth Directive[51] supported by the Unabhängiger Finanzsenat and the Austrian Government could lead to the taxable person being denied deduction of VAT input tax payable for subsequent taxable business uses, despite the taxable person's initial wish to treat the goods in question, in their entirety, as forming part of the assets of the business, with future transactions in mind.

In such a situation, the taxable person is not relieved entirely of the burden of the tax relating to the item which he uses for the purposes of his economic activity and the taxation of his business activities would lead to double taxation contrary to the principle of fiscal neutrality inherent in the common system of VAT, of which the Sixth Directive forms part (see, to that effect, Case C-415/98 *Bakcsi* [2001] ECR I-1831, paragraph 46, and *HE*, paragraph 71).

In addition, even supposing that, after actual use for business purposes of the part of the building initially used for private purposes, a refund of the input tax due on the building costs was provided for, a financial charge would encumber the property during the period, which may sometimes be considerable, between the initial investment expenditure and the commencement of actual business use. The principle of the neutrality of VAT with regard to the taxation of the business requires that the investment expenditure incurred for the needs and objectives of a business be regarded as economic activities giving rise to an immediate deduction of input VAT due. The deduction system is meant to relieve the taxable person entirely of the burden of the VAT payable or paid in the course of all his taxable economic

[50] *Id.* at Art. 167.

[51] *Id.* at Arts. 167 and 168(a).

activities (see, to that effect, Case 268/83 *Rompelman* [1985] ECR 655, paragraphs 19 and 23).

Finally, contrary to what is contended by the Unabhängiger Finanzsenat and the Austrian Government, the interpretation of Article 17(2) of the Sixth Directive[52] deriving from the case-law does not give rise either to circular reasoning, as pointed out by the Advocate General in point 46 of her Opinion, nor to systemic inconsistencies.

Taxable persons who carry out only exempt transactions cannot deduct, under that provision, any input tax and also, therefore, cannot claim deductions concerning the use for private purposes of mixed-use goods.

Equally, with regard to taxable persons carrying out both exempt transactions and taxable transactions, there is no conflict between the proportions of private and business use and the proportionate deduction provided for in Article 17(5) of the Sixth Directive.

It follows from the scheme of Article 17 of that Directive[53] that if the taxable person chooses, when acquiring capital goods, to treat them, in their entirety, as forming part of the assets of his business, the immediate deduction of input VAT payable is permitted in relation to the part of the VAT which is proportionate to the amount relating to his taxable transactions. In so far as that proportion may subsequently vary over time, Article 20 of the Sixth Directive[54] provides for an adjustment mechanism. However, if the application of Articles 17 and 20 of that directive[55] results in the right to a partial deduction of VAT, the taxable person, like any person carrying out only taxable transactions, cannot avoid the staggered imposition of VAT on his private use of those goods.

Second, it should be borne in mind that, according to settled case-law, infringement of the general principle of equal treatment under Community law can arise through the application of different rules to comparable situations or the application of the same rule to different situations (see Case C-390/96 *Lease Plan* [1998] ECR I-2553, paragraph 34, and Case C-156/98 *Germany v Commission* [2000] ECR I-6857, paragraph 84).

It should also be borne in mind that the principle of fiscal neutrality is the reflection, in matters relating to VAT, of the principle of equal treatment (Case C-106/05 *L.u.P.* [2006] ECR I-5123, paragraph 48 and case-law cited, and Case C-309/06 *Marks & Spencer* [2008] ECR I-0000, paragraph 49).

Moreover, the Court has already held that, by treating the private use of goods treated by the taxable person as forming part of the

[52] *Id.* at Art. 168(a).

[53] *Id.* at Arts. 167, 168(a), and others.

[54] *Id.* at Arts. 184–192.

[55] *Id.* at Arts. 167, 168(a), 184–192, and others.

assets of his business as a supply of services for consideration, Article 6(2)(a) of the Sixth Directive[56] aims, first, to ensure equal treatment as between a taxable person, who was able to deduct the VAT on the acquisition or construction of those goods, and a final consumer, by preventing the former from enjoying an advantage to which he is not entitled by comparison with the latter who buys the goods and pays VAT on them, and, second, to ensure fiscal neutrality by ensuring a correspondence between deduction of input VAT and charging of output VAT (see, to that effect, *Wollny*, paragraphs 30 to 33).

However, with regard to the private use of mixed-use capital goods, it is possible, as the national court has pointed out, that that provision does not ensure, on its own, the same treatment of taxable persons and non-taxable persons or of other taxable persons who acquire goods of the same kind on a private basis and are, as a result of that fact, bound to pay immediately and in full the VAT imposed. It cannot be ruled out that the objective stated in … this judgment of relieving the taxable person entirely, by the mechanism laid down in Article 17(1) and (2) and Article 6(2)(a) of the Sixth Directive,[57] of the burden of VAT payable or paid in the course of all their economic activities, including any financial charge encumbering the property during the period between the initial investment expenditure and the commencement of actual business use, can give rise to a financial advantage with regard to the private use of those goods by those taxable persons (see, by analogy, *Wollny*, paragraph 38).

Thus, the possible difference of treatment of taxable and non-taxable persons results from the application of the principle of fiscal neutrality, the primary purpose of which is to ensure the equal treatment of taxable persons. That potential difference results, also, from the pursuit by those persons of their economic activities as defined in Article 4(2) of the Sixth Directive.[58] Finally, it is linked to the specific status of taxable persons provided for in the Sixth Directive, which results inter alia in the fact that, in accordance with Article 21 of that directive [no direct correlation in the VAT Directive], they are liable to VAT and must collect it.

Since those characteristics distinguish the position of taxable persons from that of non-taxable persons who do not exercise such economic activities, a possible difference in treatment results from the application of different rules to different situations, thus not giving rise to any infringement of the right to equal treatment.

The same applies to a taxable person who has allocated the capital goods, in their entirety, to his private assets, since he does not intend

[56] *Id.* at Art. 26(a)(1).
[57] *Id.* at Arts. 26(1)(a), 167, and 168(a).
[58] *Id.* at Art. 9(1).

> to use those goods to pursue his economic activities, but to use them for private purposes.
>
> Nor can a different view be reached as regards a taxable person who carries out only exempt operations, since such a taxable person is subject to the same VAT burden as a non-taxable person and his status thus largely similar to the latter.
>
> Finally, with regard to taxable persons carrying out both exempt and taxable transactions, the conclusions reached in … the present judgment show that they are treated, in respect of each category of their economic activities and in relation to the private use of their mixed-use goods, in exactly the same way as persons who exclusively pursue activities connected with one of those categories of activities or use.
>
> In the light of the foregoing, the answer to the first question is that Article 17(2)(a) and Article 6(2)(a) of the Sixth Directive[59] do not infringe the general principle of equal treatment under Community law by conferring on taxable persons, by means of a full and immediate right to deduct input VAT on the construction of a mixed-use building and the subsequent staggered imposition of that tax on the private use of the building, a financial advantage compared with non-taxable persons and with taxable persons who use their building only as a private residence.…

In 2009, the VAT Directive was amended by adding Article 168a, which reverses the result in *Puffer*, providing in the case of immovable property for an input credit on the basis of the proportion of business use.

3. Who Is Entitled to Claim Credit?

Generally, there is no dispute as to which person can claim credit for input VAT charged on the supply of goods or services in a two-party transaction. The recipient, who is responsible to pay the VAT on those goods or services, if a VAT-registered person, can claim credit if the acquisition is used in connection with the recipient's taxable activities. Controversy does exist, especially in the EU, in multiple-party transactions, where payment for a supply is made by a person other than the recipient. Can a third party making the payment take the input tax deduction? In *Redrow*,[60] a UK case, a house builder established a program to sell homes to people who had to sell their current home before buying a Redrow home. Redrow paid the fees of an estate agent who was successful in selling a potential Redrow customer's current home. The House of Lords held that the third party

[59] *Id.* at Arts. 26(1)(a) and 168(a).

[60] *Customs and Excise Commissioners v. Redrow Group plc* ([1999] STC 161, [1999] UKHL 4).

paying for the supply is entitled to the credit for the input VAT if the third party obtained a benefit (from the goods or services) for the purpose of a business conducted by the third party.[61]

Loyalty Management, combined cases on customer loyalty rewards schemes, covered Loyalty Management UK Ltd and Baxi Group Ltd.[62] In *Loyalty Management*, the customer with the loyalty rewards points redeemed the points with select merchants, and Loyalty Management, as the operator of the scheme, paid the merchant who redeemed the points. In Baxi Group, a third party operated the scheme, the customer redeemed the loyalty points directly with that operator, and Baxi, the sponsor of the scheme, paid the third party operator. The ECJ ruled that payment made by Loyalty Management to the merchants is consideration paid by Loyalty Management for the supply of goods or services to the customers (the customers do not issue VAT invoices and Loyalty cannot claim credit for any input VAT). The referring court is to determine whether those payments also include consideration for a separate supply of services to the merchants (to the extent it supplies services to merchants that are VAT-registered persons, it can claim credit for input VAT that the merchants charge on VAT invoices). It also ruled that payment made by Baxi Group (the sponsor) to the operator of the scheme is, in part, consideration paid by a third party (Baxi Group) for a supply of goods to those customers (the customers do not issue VAT invoices and Baxi cannot claim input tax credit) and, in part, consideration for a supply of services by the operator for the benefit of Baxi Group (the operator, if VAT-registered, can issue a VAT invoice and Baxi can claim credit for input VAT charged on that invoice).

4. Conditions to Claim Credit for Input VAT

Generally, a VAT-registered person can claim credit for input VAT on acquisitions (imports and domestic purchases) of goods and services used in connection with making taxable supplies. A registered person may be denied credit on acquisitions used for a mixed purpose – to use in making taxable transactions and for personal or other purposes. For example, credit for input VAT may be denied in whole or in part on purchases of automobiles that can be used both for business and for the personal use of officers, employees, or others. In China, a VAT-registered person who

[61] In *Her Majesty's Revenue and Customs v. Airtours Holidays Transport Limited*, [2010] UKUT 404, a company in financial difficulty paid Pricewaterhouse Coopers AG in Switzerland (PwC) for advisory services requested by financial institutions that were considering loans to Airtours; the British court held that the services were rendered primarily for the benefit of the financial institutions, not Airtours and denied Airtours the deduction for the input VAT paid on those services.

[62] Case C-53/09, *Commissioners for Her Majesty's Revenue and Customs v. Loyalty Management UK Ltd*, and Case C-55/09, *Commissioners for Her Majesty's Revenue and Customs v. Baxi Group Ltd* (judgment of ECJ 2010).

obtains a false invoice, even if unaware of its falsity, is denied credit for input VAT on the acquisition.

In some situations, the question is whether a transferee of goods or services, in a non-taxable or zero-rated transaction, is entitled to claim credit for input VAT paid by the transferor. As discussed earlier, and in a different context in the next subsection, the input VAT generally is creditable only by the VAT-registered person who acquires the taxable goods or services and uses them in connection with taxable activity. However, in *Faxworld*,[63] a partnership was established to assist in the creation of a capital company. The partnership purchased goods and services to be transferred to the newly created capital company. The transfer of the assets was a "non-supply" under the VAT Directive.[64] The ECJ held that the partnership was entitled to claim input VAT on its acquisitions "where its only output transaction ... was to effect ... the transfer for consideration" that was not a supply of goods or services.[65]

New Zealand limits the credit to purchases acquired by the person claiming the credit. In one case,[66] the taxpayer imported and paid tax on components that it stored and provided to a foreign manufacturer's New Zealand customers, even though it did not take legal title to the components. The taxpayer was paid by the foreign company for the storage and transfer of these components to the manufacturer's customers. The Tax Review Authority held that there was no taxable sale by the taxpayer for consideration, so the taxpayer did not acquire the components to make taxable sales. Therefore it was not eligible to claim credit for the GST on imports.

The input tax credit reduces tax liability. It therefore is not surprising that VAT statutes impose substantiation requirements to support claims for the input credit.[67]

The NZ GST requires a registered person to have an invoice or other supporting document in its possession to claim the credit.[68] In one case under this NZ statute, the taxpayer was denied input credits because of a lack of invoices to support its claimed credits. The Tax Review Authority found that the taxpayer was in the position to obtain and retain invoices as documentary evidence to support its claimed input credits.

In the following British case, the taxpayer was denied input credits for its estimates of input VAT not supported by VAT invoices for tax on petrol purchased for a vehicle admittedly used for business reasons.

[63] *Finanzamt Offenbach am Main-Land v. Faxworld Vorgründungsgesellschaft Peter Hünninghausen und Wolfgang Klein GbR*, Case C-137/02, [2004] ECR I-5547 [hereinafter Faxworld].

[64] See VAT Directive, *supra* note 1, at Arts. 19 and 29.

[65] *Faxworld*, *supra* note 63, at ¶43.

[66] Case T35 (Tax Review Authority 1996), 18 NZTC 8,235, digested in *CCH NZ GST Guide*, ¶96–162 (1998).

[67] See, for example, VAT Directive, *supra* note 1, at Art. 178.

[68] New Zealand Goods and Services Tax, 1985, No. 141 [hereinafter NZ GST], at §20(2). The registered person also must retain the required documents as required by §75.

Pelleted Casehardening Salts Ltd v. Commissioners of Customs and Excise[69]

The Appellant Company carries on business as a manufacturer of general chemicals and has since 1st April 1973 been registered for … [VAT]. Except in one area, which the tribunal will hereinafter consider in detail, its record in value added tax accounting and payment appears to have been immaculate.

The disputed portion of the assessment thus amounts to £405, being, £45 in respect of each quarterly accounting period. All of such quarterly claims to deduct input tax of £45 made by the Appellant Company were in respect of value added tax charged by suppliers of petrol which Mr Lindley alleges were supplied for the purposes of the business which was carried on by the Appellant Company. The Commissioners … contend that such deduction of input tax was incorrect in that the entitlement was claimed in respect of supplies which were not supported by the requisite documentation in the form of invoices.

[According to the VAT in effect at that time, a taxable person can claim input credits if] the goods or services supplied are used or to be used for the purpose of any business carried on or to be carried on by the taxable person making the claim.[70] I find it unnecessary to decide in this appeal whether or not the supplies of petrol in issue were for the purpose of a business carried on by the Appellant Company. I am prepared for the purposes of this appeal to assume that they were because, in my judgment, the only relevant issue herein is the sufficiency of the evidence whereby such supplies and the payment therefor are sought to be proved by the Appellant Company.

[R]egulations may provide, inter alia, for tax on the supply of goods or services to a taxable person … to be treated as his input tax only if and to the extent that the charge to tax is evidenced and quantified by reference to such documents as may be specified in the regulations or as the Commissioners may direct either generally or in particular cases or classes of cases. Regulation 55 provides, so far as relevant to be here stated:

'55(1) Save as the Commissioners may otherwise allow or direct either generally or in particular cases or classes of cases, a person claiming deduction of input tax under section 3(2) of the Act shall do so on the return furnished by him for the prescribed accounting period in which the tax became chargeable and, before so doing, shall if the claim is in respect of –

[69] VATTR (MAN/84/287), (1985) 2 BVC 205,192 (United Kingdom) [edited by the authors].

[70] A comparable rule is provided in the Value Added Tax Act 1994, ch. 23 (United Kingdom) [hereinafter VATA 1994], §24(1) [added by authors].

(a) a supply from another registered person, hold the document which is required to be provided under regulation 8....'

Such Regulation 8(1) provides that save as otherwise provided in those Regulations, or as the Commissioners may otherwise allow, a registered taxable person making a taxable supply to a taxable person shall provide him with a tax invoice. The particulars required in a tax invoice are contained in Regulation 9, but the stringency of those is controlled by Regulation 10 which provides:

10(1) Subject to paragraph (2) of this regulation [not relevant for the appeal], a registered taxable person who is a retailer shall not be required to provide a tax invoice, except that he shall provide such an invoice at the request of a customer who is a taxable person in respect of any supply to him: but in that event, if, but only if, the value of the supply, including tax, does not exceed £50, the tax invoice need contain only the following particulars:

(a) the name, address and registration number of the retailer;
(b) the date of the supply;
(c) a description sufficient to identify the goods or services supplied;
(d) the total amount payable including tax; and
(e) the rate of tax in force at the time of the supply.

The modified form of tax invoice specified in Regulation 10 may be demanded by the taxable recipient of a supply from a retailer and, in my judgment, upon the true construction of Regulation 55 he must demand such modified tax invoice if he is to comply with Regulations 55 and 8(1). The Appellant Company did not obtain any such tax invoices from its petrol suppliers and Mr Lindley now submits that such evidence was not required by law. I do not agree. It must be a matter of common – if not judicial – knowledge that petrol stations automatically issue modified tax invoices on any sales of petrol and in the event that they do not do so Regulation 10 enables a customer to demand such an invoice.

The only alleviation of the strict requirements of Regulations 55 and 8(1) seems to me to lie in the discretion of the Commissioners otherwise to allow or direct contained in the opening words of Regulation 55(1). I think that this is the submission which is inherently put forward in the argument of Mr Lindley. He says that in 1981 the Appellant Company was in precisely the same position of being assessed in respect of unvouched supplies of petrol and that the Commissioners then reduced that assessment by allowing input tax deduction of some £49 per quarter. He says that upon that precedent the Commissioners ought now to exercise a similar discretion in respect of an even greater sum of input tax than the sum of £45 per quarter which the Appellant Company claimed to deduct in its returns. In reply to this submission Mr CJM Peters, representing the Commissioners, referred the tribunal to a letter dated 5th May 1981 addressed to Mr Lindley on the occasion of the reduction of that assessment. Such letter states:

As a result of a review of the circumstances regarding the assessment for £442.41 notified on 26th January 1981 the Commissioners of Customs and Excise now reduce it to £63.00.

However I should like to point out that future claims of input tax may not be allowed unless some supporting evidence is provided e.g. a tax invoice. In relation to this matter I would like to draw your attention specifically to the paragraph entitled 'Evidence required to support claims to input tax'....

I enclose copies of the relevant notices for your purposes.

On production of this letter Mr Lindley drew the attention of the tribunal to the use of the word 'may' in the second paragraph thereof and said that in order to justify the instant assessment it should have read 'will'. That submission, in my judgment, does not require any comment from me. I regard it as a fair warning which could readily have been complied with by the requirement by the Appellant Company of a modified tax invoice from its petrol suppliers. It did not see fit so to require. I am unable to find, having regard to the warning contained in their letter dated 5th May 1981, that the Commissioners improperly exercised their discretion not to allow any evidence other than that required by [the Regulations].

DISPOSITION. Appeal dismissed.

What if a supplier fails to charge VAT in the honest belief that VAT is not chargeable and a court subsequently holds that the supply is taxable? The ECJ held that highway tolls are fees for services, not user taxes, and therefore are subject to VAT under the EU Sixth Directive.[71] Although France's highway operators started charging VAT on tolls, the trucking firms sought refunds for presumed VAT in tolls paid previously. The highest French court for administrative decisions held that the ECJ decision had retroactive application, so the toll road operators could issue retroactive VAT invoices.[72]

> A buyer [generally] is entitled to the input credit even if the seller does not remit the tax charged on its tax invoices. In this situation, the government's recourse is an action against the defaulting seller, not denial of the credit to the buyer who relied on the tax invoice and who either paid the seller in good faith or is liable to the seller.[73]

[71] Case C-260/98, *Commission of the European Communities v. Hellenic Republic*, [2000] ECR I-06537.

[72] *SA Etablissements Louis Mazet et autres v. Ministère d'Economie, Finances, et de l'Industrie*, Counseil d'Etat, No. 268681 (June 29, 2005), reported in Speer, "French Trucking Firms Demand VAT Refund from Highway Tolls," *BNA Daily Tax Report*, Oct. 7, 2005, p. G-4.

[73] A. Schenk, reporter, *Value Added Tax – A Model Statute and Commentary: A Report of the Committee on Value Added Tax of the American Bar Association Section of Taxation* 96 (American Bar Association1989) [hereinafter ABA Model Act].

In the EU, generally, this principle does not apply if the sale on which VAT was charged was a fraudulent sale, even if the purchaser was not aware of the fact that the sale was fraudulent.[74]

5. Purchases Not Used in Making Taxable Supplies

Some acquisitions are treated as personal consumption or represent such an inseparable aggregate of personal and business use that they are treated as nonbusiness, and therefore, to reduce the opportunities for tax abuse, VAT on those acquisitions is not creditable. In some countries, registered persons are categorically denied credit for input VAT on these acquisitions, whether or not the registered person can show that they were used partially or exclusively in making taxable supplies. Most commonly, especially in developing countries, these disallowance rules apply to passenger vehicles, entertainment expenses, and membership in country clubs and comparable facilities.[75] Canada denies 20% of the input credit on purchases of food, beverages, and entertainment, consistent with the 20% disallowance rule under the income tax for the cost of these items.[76] In the EU, the VAT Directive requires member states to deny deduction for input VAT on an "expenditure which is not strictly [a] business expenditure, such as that on luxuries, amusements or entertainment."[77]

A business that acquires an asset for use in taxable and other transactions can claim credit for tax on the proportion of the item used in taxable transactions.[78] For administrative reasons, credit for input VAT may be denied when most of the use is unrelated to the making of taxable supplies. A VAT may have a de minimis rule that denies the entire input

[74] See *Customs and Excise Commissioners v. Pennystar Ltd*, [1996] BVC 125. However, also see *Greenall* (1987) 3 BVC 1,320.

[75] See, for example, Value-Added Tax Act No. 89 of 1991, §17(2) (South Africa). South Africa removed from the disallowance rules vehicles used for certain game viewing. See Value Added Tax Act, sec. 1, paragraph (e) of definition of "motor car." Under this VAT rule, game viewing vehicles designed or converted for the transport of seven or more passengers in game parks and similar areas are deductible if the vehicles are used by registered persons in connection with making taxable supplies. M. Botes, "Game Viewing," 15 *VAT Monitor* 456 (Nov./Dec. 2004). See Value Added Tax Act, 2000, Act No. 1 of 2001, §20(2) (Botswana) and Commonwealth of New Vatopia Value Added Tax Act, IMF website at http://www.imf.org/external/np/leg. Go to Tax Law Drafting Samples: VAT [hereinafter New Vatopia VAT], §28.

[76] Canadian GST, *supra* note 14, at §236. This 20% is recaptured by adding this amount to the registrant's net tax. *Id.*

[77] VAT Directive, *supra* note 1, at Art. 176, first paragraph. There is a grandfather clause that allows member states to continue exclusions from the disallowance rules "[p]ending the entry into force of the provisions referred to in the first paragraph." *Id.* at Art. 176, second paragraph.

[78] VAT on the portion of a house purchased by a husband and wife and used in part to conduct economic activity is eligible for the input tax deduction in the EU if that portion of the home is allocated to the assets of the business. *Finanzamt Bergisch Gladbach v. Hans U. Hundt-Eßwein*, Case C-25/03, [2005] ECR I-3123 (judgment of the ECJ).

credit – for example, if 10% or less of an acquired asset is used in making taxable supplies. Other VAT systems deny any credit for input VAT unless the acquired asset is used principally in making taxable supplies. In New Zealand, for example, input tax on a purchase is creditable only if the tax is on "goods and services acquired for the principal purpose of making taxable supplies."[79] Thus, if an asset is devoted principally to personal use, no input credit is allowable, even if the asset may be used, for example, 20% in connection with taxable supplies. The EU frequently challenges a member state's input credit disallowance rule. Not surprisingly, this kind of disallowance rule requires a derogation granted only by the EC. Germany was authorized to deny deduction for input VAT on goods or services if they are used more than 90% for nonbusiness purposes.[80]

Tax authorities are more likely to challenge credits claimed for tax on purchases that may advance the taxpayer's personal rather than business interests. In *Ian Flockton*, the issue was whether the purchase was in fact used in the taxpayer's business. *Edmond Michael Alexander* involves expenses that may contain both personal and business elements.

Ian Flockton Developments Ltd v. Commisioners of Customs and Excise[81]

HEADNOTE. The taxpayer company was a manufacturing company of plastic mouldings and storage tanks and was registered for value added tax. The taxpayer company's customers were project engineers in chemical factories. The taxpayer company's orders were not sought by advertising but by personal contact and recommendation. At the material time the taxpayer company was anxious to find new customers and conceived the idea that the purchase and running of a racehorse would in some way advance the taxpayer company's business. The question arose whether for the purpose of value added tax the expenses relating to the purchase and upkeep of the racehorse were incurred wholly for the purposes of the business carried on by the taxpayer company. [The tribunal disallowed the input tax credits and the taxpayer appealed.]

[79] NZ GST, *supra* note 68, at §2(1) definition of input tax and at §3A(l)(a). In *Wairakei Court Ltd v. Commissioner of Inland Revenue*, 19 NZTC 15, 202, at 15, 206 (High Ct. NZ 1999), the court attempted to define the elements of this test. In determining the principal purpose, it is "necessary to consider both subjective and objective indicators … [and] make an overall evaluation of all relevant purposes. While the evaluation needs to be made on the basis that the principal purpose is to be ascertained at the time the goods and services were acquired, this does not mean purposes which will not be fulfilled until some time in the future should be automatically ruled out." *Id.*

[80] See COM (2004) 579 final of September 2, 2004, reported in *VAT Monitor* 442 (Nov./Dec. 2004). Austria also was authorized to deny input VAT on goods and services used more than 90% for nonbusiness purposes. H. Gurtner, "Austria: Deduction of Input VAT," 16 *VAT Monitor* 39 (Jan./Feb. 2005).

[81] [1987] STC 394 (Q.B. 1987) (United Kingdom) [edited by the authors].

Held – (1) The test to be applied in determining whether goods or services which were supplied to the taxpayer were used or to be used for the purpose of any business carried on by him was a subjective test. That meant that the fact-finding tribunal had to consider what was in the taxpayer's mind, and where the taxpayer was a company what was in the minds of the persons who controlled the company, at the relevant time in order to discover their object.

(2) Where there was no obvious and clear association between the taxpayer company's business and the expenditure concerned, the tribunal should approach any assertion that it was for the taxpayer company's business with circumspection and care and should bear in mind that it was for the taxpayer company to establish its case. It was both permissible and essential to test such evidence against the standards and thinking of the ordinary businessman in the position of the taxpayer company and, if the tribunal considered that no ordinary businessman would have incurred such expenditure for business purposes, that might be grounds for rejecting the taxpayer company's evidence. However, that should not be substituted as the test but only treated as a guide or factor to be taken into account when considering the credibility of the witness.

(3) The tribunal had found as a fact that the taxpayer company's object was to use the racehorse for the purposes of its business and accordingly the expenditure in question was incurred for the supplies of goods and services used or to be used for the purposes of its business.

DISPOSITION. Appeal allowed with costs.

Edmond Michael Alexander v. Commissioners of Customs and Excise[82]

Shortly after ... registration Mr Alexander submitted to the Commissioners ... a claim for relief in respect of tax which he alleged he had paid on 'clothes and ancillary items' required for his practice at the Bar. Subsequently on production of invoices the Commissioners conceded that Mr Alexander could deduct as input tax the amounts of tax charged to him on some items (including a gown, four collars, two bands and two shirts purchased from William Northam) and Mr Alexander withdrew his claim in respect of other items (including a

[82] [1976] VATTR 107 (London 1976) (United Kingdom) [edited by the authors].

wig purchased from another member of the Bar not registered as a taxable person). The foregoing leaves some 17 items still in dispute for us to consider on this appeal.

In evidence Mr Alexander stated that, as a manager before he entered Chambers as a pupil, he always wore a two-piece light coloured suit, that is to say, a jacket and trousers without a waistcoat. But it is a requirement of the Bar Council, the body which lays down the rules of etiquette which have to be observed by practising barristers, that members of the Bar appearing in court must wear a suit of a dark colour with a waistcoat. Accordingly, in order to meet such requirement he purchased … a dark navy-blue three-piece suit and … a black three-piece suit, for wearing in court. And, in order to wear such suits he bought the braces. … Next, it is also a requirement of the Bar Council that male members of the Bar in court should wear white shirts, butterfly collars and bands, necessitating the wearing of shirts with detachable collars. Accordingly, in order to meet such requirements he purchased … a white tunic shirt without a collar, … one dozen stiff white naval collars, … two more white tunic shirts without collars, and … front and back studs. Then, it was another such requirement that shoes worn by members of the Bar in court should be black. Previously, Mr Alexander stated, he had only worn brown shoes and so, in order to meet this requirement, he purchased two pairs of black shoes, … dark socks to wear with such shoes, [and] a suitcase which he had bought for the purpose of transporting his wig, gown, collars, bands, briefs and books to and from court in the course of his practice. Finally, … [he purchased] stationery, such as a folder, writing cards, book pads and ruled pads for use in Chambers and in court.

The provisions of the Act relating to input tax … permit the deduction as input tax of 'tax on the supply to a taxable person of any goods or services for the purpose of a business carried on or to be carried on by him'. This is of no assistance to Mr Alexander as he was not a taxable person at the time when the foregoing supplies of goods were made to him. [Under the Regulations, if a taxable person, after registration, claims deductions for tax paid on purchases made before registration], supported by such evidence as the Commissioners may require, they may authorise him to deduct, as if it were input tax, tax on the supply of goods to him before that date … for the purpose of a business which either was carried on or was to be carried on by him at the time of such supply.

At the time of the supplies Mr Alexander was not a taxable person and, as a result, was not entitled to require a supplier to give him a tax invoice for a supply. We consider that the till receipts and the oral evidence of Mr Alexander sufficiently establish to our satisfaction that he obtained such supplies …, and that all the suppliers, other than the Government Bookshop, were taxable persons.

So the foregoing involves two questions, first, whether the … items were supplies 'for the purposes of Mr Alexander's profession as a barrister and, secondly, whether at the time they were supplied, such profession was then to be carried on by him'. On this second point Mr Alexander in his addresses to the tribunal assumed that, as the items were supplied after he had formed an intention to practise at the Bar and were so supplied either shortly before starting, or during, his pupillage, they must all have been supplied at a time when such profession was 'to be carried on by him'. No argument to the contrary was advanced by Miss Bolt and accordingly we assume that the Commissioners accept that, in this case, the supplies were obtained by Mr Alexander at a time when the profession was 'to be carried on by him'.

On this appeal, in relation to the words in … the General Regulations, 'for the purpose of a business' Mr Alexander submitted that his claim should be allowed because the items supplied were necessary for the purposes of his intended profession. It was, he argued, necessary for him to buy the suits and other clothing and the shoes in order to practice at the Bar and appear in court properly dressed, and it was necessary for him to buy the suitcase for travelling to and from court. Miss Bolt contended that the test to be applied … [is] whether the clothing was of a specialised nature bought specifically for the purposes of the business, trade or profession. She argued that this covered such clothing as protective or working overalls for a doctor or surgeon and a wig and gown for a barrister, but not clothing of the type supplied to Mr Alexander in this case.

[The] test to apply is whether or not the … items were obtained by Mr Alexander for the purpose of enabling him to carry on his intended profession. This suggests to us that the test is a subjective one. Miss Bolt in this regard submitted that the proper test should be an objective, and not a subjective one. On this point we consider that the proper test should be a subjective one unless there is some provision of the Act or the General Regulations which provides or indicates to the contrary. In our view the use of the word 'purpose', in an Act of Parliament prima facie requires the application of a subjective test.

A supply may, of course, be obtained for more than one purpose or reason. Thus, in the present case it could perhaps be argued that a main reason for Mr Alexander purchasing the clothing items was to clothe himself decently, and his intention to practise at the Bar only affected the type of suits, shirts and other clothing which he bought. On this aspect we consider that, to come within the foregoing statutory provisions, the purpose of the business must be a main purpose, but not necessarily the only purpose, of obtaining the supply. If Parliament had intended to limit the provisions to supplies exclusively for the purpose of the business, it would have so provided expressly or by necessary implication.

Having regard to the foregoing we consider that, on this appeal, we must consider ... whether or not his main purpose, or one of his main purposes, in so doing was to enable him to carry on his intended profession as a barrister. In the light thereof we are satisfied that, in relation to ... three shirts, one dozen collars, one dark suit, a book pad and a ruled pad, Mr Alexander purchased the same for the purpose of his intended profession and that such purpose was his main purpose in obtaining such supplies. ... But we are not satisfied in relation to the remaining ten items.

This appeal is accordingly allowed as to part and dismissed as to part.

DISPOSITION. Appeal allowed in part.

The following British case involves input credits relating to the cost of an accounting firm's dinner dance.

KPMG Peat Marwick McLintock v. Commissioners of Customs and Excise[83]

KPMG Peat Marwick McLintock (hereinafter called 'the Appellants') carry on business as accountants. [The] Appellants had claimed input tax in respect of a business entertainment held annually in the New Year for members of their staff. The Commissioners decided that the claim for input tax in respect of these business entertainments should be disallowed.

[Although a taxable person may deduct input tax on "goods or services used or to be used for the purpose of any business carried on or to be carried on by him; ...,"[84] input tax on such expenditures generally is not deductible if it is attributable to business entertainment.]

Paragraph 2 of the 1981 Special Provisions Order [SI 1981 No. 1741] defines "business entertainment" as follows:

In this Order – 'business entertainment' means entertainment (including hospitality of any kind) provided by a taxable person in connection with a business carried on by him, but does not include the provision of anything for persons employed by the taxable person unless its provision for them is incidental to its provision for others.

The question at issue in this appeal has centred around the presence at the annual firm's dinner dance of not only employees (who by common consent come within the term 'persons employed by the taxable person') in respect of whom the expenditure on the provision of goods

[83] [1993] VATTR 118 (United Kingdom) [edited by the authors].

[84] A comparable rule is provided under VATA 1994, *supra* note 70, at §24(1) [added by authors].

or services would normally be an allowable input tax deduction, but also their spouses or partners who are not partnership employees and who, it is argued, by their presence at the dinner dance, are receiving hospitality from the firm and thereby constitute the function 'business entertainment' resulting in no deduction of input tax.

The Appellants are a firm of accountants providing a whole range of financial services to its clients. Because of the very nature of the business this often means that staff have to work unsociable hours and the success of the firm depends upon the commitment of the staff. In return for dedicated commitment the firm feels that it should show its appreciation by organising an annual staff dinner dance. The purpose of this event is to thank employees in a tangible way for their hard work throughout the year and to foster in them a feeling of belonging to an organisation as a whole. Many of the individual members of the firm have to work away from the office in outlying districts auditing company accounts and so forth. The purpose of the dinner dance is to bring them all under one roof once a year for social purposes and to encourage as many employees as possible to attend. Invitations are sent out only to employees but each one is given the opportunity of bringing a guest of his or her choosing – in many cases this will be the employee's spouse.

[The Appellants claimed that it] was a purpose of their business to care for their own staff, to encourage a good morale and to reward hard work and commitment. Thus, any expenditure laid out to achieve that purpose by means of the provision of hospitality was for the purpose of business. The provision here of goods and services (hospitality) was not for commercial or business reasons and was not provided to business customers or clients or other non-employees. It was provided to the staff or ... to "persons employed by the taxable person." In practice, of course, there may be occasions when hospitality is provided by a trader for customers or clients and upon which the trader's own employees are also present. In one sense the hospitality is provided to both employees and non-employees. The legislation involves a predominance test, as Counsel for the Appellants submitted. What was the paramount purpose of the entertainment or hospitality? If the paramount purpose is business entertainment then it matters not how the numbers are made up at the function. Even if "persons employed" greatly outnumber customers or clients, input tax deduction is not allowed. Conversely, if the paramount purpose is provision for "persons employed" by the taxable person it matters not that there are others who are not employed, input tax is deductible.

In the instant case the Tribunal has found as a fact that the use to which the Appellants put the goods or services which they provided was for the entertainment of their employees; that was not a use for the purpose of business entertainment as defined in the section. The presence of wives, husbands, partners or guests of employees at the dinner dance appears to the Tribunal to be purely incidental and wholly ancillary to the main purpose of the function – to have employees present with their permitted guests so that their participation in the entertainment provided might be directly facilitated....

For the foregoing reasons the Tribunal allows the appeal and holds that entertainment provided was not "business entertainment." The input tax in dispute is therefore deductible.

B. Pre-Opening Expenses and Post-Economic Activity

A general VAT principle entitles a registered person making taxable supplies to claim credit for input VAT on acquisitions used in making those taxable supplies. Consistent with that principle, a registered person entering business should be entitled to claim credit for input VAT on acquisitions used in connection with economic activity that directly relates to taxable supplies to be made in the future. Thus, tax on store fixtures, electrical services, painting, and other purchases made before a retail store opens for business should be creditable if the future sales by that store are taxable.

The opportunity for abuse in this area prompts many countries to restrict or impose conditions on the credit for input VAT attributable to acquisitions before the acquiring person starts making taxable supplies. A person may claim refunds for input VAT on purchases during the startup phase of a business and then may never make taxable sales. Thus, the tax authority may delay claims for refunds of excess credits until the person proves that the expenditures were made in connection with the subsequent business activity. On the other hand, if input VAT during the pre-opening phase is not eligible for credit, the VAT will not be economically neutral, and new businesses will be at a competitive disadvantage if they bear VAT on these costs.

The EU attempted to balance these concerns in favor of granting deductions for input VAT on pre-opening costs.[85] In *Rompelman*,[86] the ECJ treated a registered person as being engaged in business when the person acquired a right to a portion of a building to be constructed and leased. To avoid abuse, the court acknowledged the tax administration's right to demand proof that the property was suitable for commercial rental. In *Inzo*,[87] the

[85] Indeed, the ECJ ruled that domestic law in a member state cannot prevent a partnership from claiming credit for input VAT paid by a prospective partner on an asset acquired before the partnership was registered, assuming that the asset ultimately is used in the new partnership's economic activity. Case C-280/10, *Kopalnia Odkrywkowa Polski Trawertyn P. Granatowixz, M Wasiewiczspolkajawna v. Dyrektorizby Skarbowej w Poznaniu* (judgment of the ECJ 2011).

[86] See *Rompelman, supra* Chapter 4 (IV)(C).

[87] See Case C-110/94, *Intercommunale voor zeewaterontzilting (INZO) v. Belgian State*, [1996] ECR I-857 (ECJ 1996), discussed *supra* Chapter 4 (IV)(C).

ECJ allowed credit for input VAT on purchases related to a project that was abandoned and no taxable supplies were ever made. Consistently, where a company made improvements to land in preparation for making taxable supplies and the city then forced the company to exchange that improved land for other land so that the intended supplies were never made, the company was entitled to claim credit for input VAT on those improvements to the transferred property.[88] In fact, although EU member states can impose reasonable conditions to prevent fraud or abuse, they cannot establish a blanket denial of input VAT until a registered person commences economic or business activities.[89] The *Gabalfrisa* case[90] involved input VAT paid by entrepreneurs and professional practitioners before they started making taxable supplies. The Spanish VAT allowed this input VAT as a credit only when the individual commenced taxable activities. Under the Spanish VAT, the input VAT was creditable before the entrepreneurs or professional practitioners commenced taxable activities only for purchases other than land and then only if they met certain requirements. The conditions included the submission of a declaration of intent to commence business or professional activities before the input tax on purchases to be claimed as credit becomes due. The ECJ held that the Spanish legislation could not so restrict the right to deduct input VAT under Article 17 of the Sixth Directive (Articles 167, 173, and 176–177 of the VAT Directive).

Singapore has a procedure for an unregistered person to claim credits for purchases of taxable goods and services made before that person registers and engages in taxable activities. The Inland Revenue Authority of Singapore (IRAS) provides a checklist in a downloadable form[91] for a person to determine whether the person is eligible for a pre-registration input tax claim that can be made in the person's first GST return. To qualify, goods or services must have been purchased to make taxable supplies and must not be consumed or be related to goods consumed before the effective date of registration. For services, they must have been acquired not more than six months before registration and must not have been used in connection with services to customers before registration. Records must be maintained.

There are issues at the other end of the life of a business. Can a registered person claim credit for input VAT paid after the person ceases to

[88] *Belgium v. Ghent Coal Terminal NV*, Case C-37/95, [1998] All ER 223 (judgment of ECJ 1998).

[89] See F. Serrano, "VAT Deduction in Spain: The ECJ Against the Spanish Regime for Deduction of Input VAT Related to Transactions Prior to Carrying Out an Economic Activity," 11 *VAT Monitor* 157 (July/Aug. 2000), discussing *Gabalfrisa SL and Others v. Agencia Estatal de Administración Tributaria*, joined cases C-110/98 to C-147/98, [2000] ECR I-01577 [hereinafter *Gabalfrisa*].

[90] *Gabalfrisa, supra* note 89.

[91] The form is entitled "Pre-Registration Input Tax: Checklist for Self-review of Eligibility of Claim."

make taxable supplies? For example, where a person ceased to conduct a restaurant business but was obliged under the lease to pay rent on the restaurant premises after the business closed, the ECJ held that the input VAT was deductible until the lease expired.[92] The deductions presumably would not be available if the leased property were converted to a private purpose.

C. Impact of Subsidies on Allowable Input Credits

When a registered person making taxable and other supplies receives a subsidy, what is the effect of the subsidy on the calculation of allowable credits for input VAT? If the subsidy is directly linked to supplies, it may be treated as part of the taxable amounts of the supplies.[93] If not, it may be included in the allocation formula that determines the creditable portion of input VAT attributable to taxable supplies.[94] The initial problem in the EU is that the term "subsidy" is not defined in the VAT Directive. An advocate-general defined a subsidy in her Opinion as "a sum paid from public funds, usually in the general interest."[95]

The EU VAT Directive allows member states to treat subsidies the same as exempt supplies for purposes of the allocation formula that determines

[92] Case C-32/03, I/S *Fini H v. Skatteministeriet (Danish Ministry of Taxation)*, [2005] ECR I-1599. The ECJ ruled that "a person who has ceased an economic activity but who, because the lease contains a non-termination clause, continues to pay the rent and charges on the premises used for that activity is to be regarded as a taxable person within the meaning of that article and is entitled to deduct the VAT on the amounts thus paid, provided that there is a direct and immediate link between the payments made and the commercial activity and that the absence of any fraudulent or abusive intent has been established." *Id.* at ruling.

[93] See VAT Directive, *supra* note 1, at Arts. 11A(1)(a) and 26b(B)(3).

[94] According to the ECJ, for a subsidy to be included as part of the taxable amount of a supply, it must be paid "specifically to the subsidized body to enable it to provide particular goods or services." I. Arias and A. Barba, "The Impact of Subsidies on the Right to Deduct Input VAT: The Spanish Experience," 15 *VAT Monitor* 13, 15 (Jan./Feb. 2004) [hereinafter Spanish Experience with Subsidies], discussing the judgment in *ASBL Office des Produits Wallons v. Belgian State*, Case C-184/00, [2001] ECR I-9155. The authors suggest that some payments in the nature of subsidies should not be treated as subsidies for VAT purposes.

[95] *Keeping Newcastle Warm Ltd v Commissioners of Customs and Excise*, Case C-353/00 [2002] ECR I-5419, Opinion of February 5, 2002, cited in Spanish Experience with Subsidies, *supra* note 94, at 13. In the judgment of June 13, 2002, the ECJ held that the sum paid by the public authority to an economic operator such as Keeping Newcastle Warm (KNW) in connection with energy advice supplied by KNW to certain households was consideration for services supplied and therefore was part of the taxable amount of the supply of services. In Case C-204/03, *Commission of the European Communities v. Kingdom of Spain*, [2005] ECR I-8389 (judgment of the ECJ 2005), the court ruled that limiting the input tax deduction on the purchase of goods and services used to conduct only taxable transactions when those acquisitions were subsidized by the government violates Articles 17(2) and (5) and 19 of VAT Directive. In that case, the supplier received capital subsidies but made only taxable supplies.

the allowable credit for tax on business inputs.[96] The EC disagrees with France's practice of restricting input VAT on acquisitions of capital goods financed in part with subsidies.[97] The EC challenged Spain's practice of limiting deductions for input VAT, even when the subsidy was not linked to the price of supplies.[98]

There is another aspect of subsidized activities in some countries. In the Netherlands, for example, if a business performs sponsored research that is subsidized, the deductibility of input VAT depends on whether the supplier also conducts commercial activities for consideration. If the business conducts such commercial activities, it can also claim credit for input VAT related to its "non-commercial" research activities. If not, it is denied credit for input VAT attributable to those activities.[99]

D. Transactions Involving Shares of Stock

In EU countries, there has been litigation involving input tax on acquisitions related to transactions in stock. The *Kretztechnik* case is a significant case in this area.

Kretztechnik AG v. Finanzamt Linz[100]

The questions were raised in proceedings between Kretztechnik AG (Kretztechnik) and the Finanzamt Linz (Linz District Tax Office) concerning the latter's refusal to allow that company to deduct value added tax (VAT) paid by it on supplies relating to the issue of shares for the purposes of its admission to the Frankfurt Stock Exchange (Germany).

Article 13B(d)(5) of the Sixth Directive[101] provides that the Member States are to exempt from VAT transactions, including negotiation, excluding management and safekeeping, in shares, interests in companies or associations, debentures and other securities....

Article 17(2) of the Sixth Directive[102] provides:

[96] See VAT Directive, *supra* note 1, at Art. 174, paragraph 1.

[97] See 14 *VAT Monitor* 45 (Jan./Feb. 2003), citing IP/03/57 of January 16, 2003.

[98] In New Zealand, a grant or subsidy by a public authority to a registered person is part of the consideration for a supply to the public authority. See M. Pallot & D. White, "New Zealand: Public Authorities," 15 *VAT Monitor* 208 (May/June 2004).

[99] Decree No. BLKB 2011/64M of 25 November 2011, reported in IBFD Tax News Service, Dec. 29, 2011.

[100] Case C-465/03. [2005] ECR I- 4357; [2005] ECJ CELEX LEXIS 187 (judgment of the ECJ) [edited by the authors].

[101] Art. 135(1)(f) of the VAT Directive, *supra* note 1.

[102] *Id.* at Art. 168(a) has similar language. "In so far as the goods and services are used for the purposes of the taxed transactions of a taxable person, the taxable person shall be

In so far as the goods and services are used for the purposes of his taxable transactions, the taxable person shall be entitled to deduct from the tax which he is liable to pay:

(a) VAT due or paid in respect of goods or services supplied or to be supplied to him by another taxable person;...

The Sixth Directive was transposed into Austrian domestic law....

Kretztechnik is a company limited by shares established in Austria whose objects are the development and distribution of medical equipment. By resolution of its general meeting of shareholders of 18 January 2000, its capital was increased from EUR 10 million to EUR 12.5 million. With a view to raising the capital needed for that increase, it applied for admission to the Frankfurt Stock Exchange.

Kretztechnik was listed on that stock exchange in March 2000. Its capital was increased by the issue of bearer shares.

[The Finanzamt Linz claimed that issuing shares was exempt from VAT and therefore disallowed the input tax deduction for VAT paid by Kretztechnik on the supplies linked with its admission to the stock exchange.]

Kretztechnik challenged that tax assessment [and the court sought] ... a preliminary ruling from the Court of Justice.

THE FIRST QUESTION. [Kretztechnik claims that the issuance of new shares was to finance its business activities, not as a commercial activity of dealing in shares, and therefore] was not a supply for consideration within the meaning of Article 2(1) of the Sixth Directive.[103]

[The Finanzamt Linz maintains that] ... the issue of shares by a taxable person in order to increase its capital with a view to carrying on its economic activity constitutes a taxable transaction within the meaning of Article 2(1) of the Sixth Directive.

It is settled caselaw that the mere acquisition and holding of shares is not to be regarded as an economic activity within the meaning of the Sixth Directive. ... If, therefore, the acquisition of financial holdings in other undertakings does not in itself constitute an economic activity within the meaning of that directive, the same must be true of activities consisting in the sale of such holdings....

On the other hand, transactions that consist in obtaining income on a continuing basis from activities which go beyond the compass of the simple acquisition and sale of securities, such as transactions carried out in the course of a business trading in securities, do fall within the

entitled, in the Member State in which he carries out these transactions, to deduct the following from the VAT which he is liable to pay:

(a) The VAT due or paid in that Member State in respect of supplies to him of goods or services, carried out or to be carried out by another taxable person;"

103 *Id.* at Art. 2(1).

scope of the Sixth Directive but are exempted from VAT under Article 13B(d)(5) of that directive.[104]

[The VAT consequences do not depend on whether a company's issuance of shares occurs] in connection with its admission to a stock exchange or by a company not quoted on a stock exchange.

[U]nder Article 5(1) of the Sixth Directive,[105] a supply of goods involves the transfer of the right to dispose of tangible property as owner. The issue of new shares – which are securities representing intangible property – cannot therefore be regarded as a supply of goods for consideration within the meaning of Article 2(1) of that directive.[106]

The taxability of a share issue therefore depends on whether that transaction constitutes a supply of services for consideration within the meaning of Article 2(1) of the Sixth Directive.

In that connection the Court has already held that a partnership which admits a partner in consideration of payment of a contribution in cash does not effect to that partner a supply of services for consideration within the meaning of Article 2(1) of the Sixth Directive.[107]

The same conclusion must be drawn regarding the issue of shares for the purpose of raising capital.

As the Advocate General rightly observes ... a company that issues new shares is increasing its assets by acquiring additional capital, whilst granting the new shareholders a right of ownership of part of the capital thus increased. From the issuing company's point of view, the aim is to raise capital and not to provide services. As far as the shareholder is concerned, payment of the sums necessary for the increase of capital is not a payment of consideration but an investment or an employment of capital.

It follows that a share issue does not constitute a supply of goods or of services for consideration within the meaning of Article 2(1) of the Sixth Directive.[108] Therefore, such a transaction, whether or not carried out in connection with admission of the company concerned to a stock exchange, does not fall within the scope of that directive.

The answer to the first question must therefore be that a new share issue does not constitute a transaction falling within the scope of Article 2(1) of the Sixth Directive.[109]

THE THIRD QUESTION. [The third question is whether VAT on supplies attributable to a share issue is deductible under the Sixth Directive, Article 17(1) and (2).[110]]

[104] *Id.* at Art. 135(1)(f).

[105] *Id.* at Art. 14(1).

[106] *Id.* at Art. 2(1).

[107] *Id.*

[108] *Id.*

[109] *Id.*

[110] *Id.* at Arts. 167 and 168(a).

The Finanzamt Linz and the Austrian, Danish, German and Italian Governments maintain that, since a share issue associated with admission to a stock exchange does not constitute a taxable transaction within the meaning of Article 2(1) of the Sixth Directive,[111] there is no right to deduct the VAT levied on the supplies acquired for consideration for the purposes of that share issue. In the present case the inputs, which are subject to VAT, do not form an integral part of Kretztechnik's overall economic activity as a component of the price of the products that it markets. The expenses associated with those supplies are linked only to the admission of the company to a stock exchange and have no connection with its general business on which tax is paid.

Conversely, Kretztechnik, the United Kingdom Government and the Commission consider that, even if the inputs subject to VAT were connected not with specific taxable transactions but with expenses relating to the share issue, they could form part of the overheads of the company and constitute components of the price of the products marketed by it. In those circumstances, Kretztechnik has a right to deduct the input VAT on expenditure incurred in obtaining the supplies linked to the admission of that company to a stock exchange.

[A]ccording to settled case-law, the right of deduction provided for in Articles 17 to 20 of the Sixth Directive[112] is an integral part of the VAT scheme and in principle may not be limited.

It is clear … that, for VAT to be deductible, the input transactions must have a direct and immediate link with the output transactions giving rise to a right of deduction. Thus, the right to deduct VAT charged on the acquisition of input goods or services presupposes that the expenditure incurred in acquiring them was a component of the cost of the output transactions that gave rise to the right to deduct.

[The share issue was designed to increase capital for the benefit of its economic activity. VAT on the supplies associated with the share issuance is tax associated with its overhead and therefore constitutes] … component parts of the price of its products. Those supplies have a direct and immediate link with the whole economic activity of the taxable person.

The answer to the third question must therefore be that Article 17(1) and (2) of the Sixth Directive[113] confer the right to deduct in its entirety the VAT charged on the expenses incurred by a taxable person for the various supplies acquired by him in connection with a share issue, provided that all the transactions undertaken by the taxable person in the context of his economic activity constitute taxed transactions.

[111] *Id.* at Art. 2(1).

[112] Title X of the VAT Directive (Arts. 167–192), *supra* note 1.

[113] *Id.* at Arts. 167 and 168(a).

An earlier ECJ judgment in the *Polysar Investments* case[114] involved the claim of input VAT by a holding company whose only activities related to holding shares in subsidiary companies. The court held that the holding company was not a taxable person and therefore could not claim input VATs unless it was involved directly or indirectly in the management of the subsidiaries.[115] In the *Portugal Telecom* case,[116] the ECJ elaborated on activity by a holding company that went beyond the mere holding of shares in subsidiary companies. In that case, the holding company acquired services that it invoiced to the subsidiaries and deducted the input tax on the acquisition of those services. The ECJ held, largely applying Article 173(1), (2)(a) to (e) of the VAT Directive:

> [A] holding company such as that at issue in the main proceedings which, in addition to its main activity of managing shares in companies in which it holds all or part of the share capital, acquires goods and services which it subsequently invoices to those companies is authorised to deduct the amount of input VAT provided that the input services acquired have a direct and immediate link with the output economic transactions giving rise to a right to deduct.[117]

According to the ECJ, it is for the national court to determine whether the inputs are used for economic activities and for activities that give rise to a deduction.[118]

In the Netherlands, a company (the taxpayer) that held 50% of the stock in a subsidiary also rendered services to that subsidiary. When that company and the other 50% shareholder sold the subsidiary, a bank charged the taxpayer a fee plus VAT on the services related to that sale. The company claimed a deduction for that input VAT. The Dutch Supreme Court held that holding and selling shares in another company is not economic activity within VAT unless the shareholder is a professional dealer in securities or the shares (in a subsidiary) are held in connection with the shareholder's direct or indirect involvement in the management of the subsidiary. In

[114] *Polysar Investments Netherlands BV v. Inspecteur der Invoerrechten en Accijnzen, Arnham*, Case C-60/90, [1991] ECR I-3111; [1993] STC 222.

[115] *Id.* at ¶19 of the Judgment.

[116] Case C-496/11, *Portugal Telecom SGPS, SA v. Fazenda Publica* (ECJ 2012).

[117] Art. 17(5), VAT Directive, *supra* note 1.

[118] The ECJ went on to rule: "Where those goods and services are used by the holding company in order to perform both economic transactions giving rise to a right to deduct and economic transactions which do not, the deduction is allowed only in respect of the part of the VAT which is proportional to the amount relating to the former transactions and the national tax authorities are authorised to provide for one of the methods for determining the right to deduct in [Art. 173 of the VAT Directive]. Where those goods and services are used both for economic and non-economic activities, [Art. 173 of the VAT Directive] is not applicable and the methods of deduction and apportionment are to be defined by the Member States which, in exercising that power, must take account of the purpose and general scheme of the [VAT Directive] and, on that basis, lay down a method of calculation which objectively reflects the input expenditure actually attributed to each of those two activities."

that case, the court found that there was a direct link between the bank's services and the overall business activities of the shareholder, and therefore the input VAT attributable to taxable activities was deductible.[119]

Canada, by statute, allows the purchaser of stock of a company engaged in commercial activities to claim credits for tax on services related to the stock acquisition.[120]

E. Bad Debts

A seller who reports on the cash method generally reports sales as the sales price is collected.[121] If the purchaser defaults, no tax adjustment is necessary. Most VATs require most registered persons to report on the accrual or invoice method. Under those methods, the seller must report sales and remit VAT when the sale occurs or the invoice is issued, even if the VAT-inclusive price is paid later. "If the seller in a VAT regime serves as collection agent for the government (not the taxpayer that is to bear the VAT), and the buyer fails to pay the tax, the seller should recover the tax attributable to the bad debt."[122] The reason for this rule is that if merchants included the cost of uncollectible accounts and the VAT thereon in their pricing structure, they would recover the bad debt plus VAT from their paying customers. The VAT attributable to a bad debt therefore should be recoverable, so that it does not enter the pricing structure and result in VAT being imposed on the uncollected VAT shifted to paying customers. Many countries follow this model and allow sellers to claim credit (or reduce output tax) for the tax attributable to the bad debt.[123] This rule provides some opportunity for tax abuse, especially if the tax administration is not equipped to verify the propriety of these claimed credits for bad debts. As a result, some countries (especially developing countries) in effect make the seller the guarantor of the buyer's payment of VAT on purchases – or force the seller to collect the tax on the sale up front – and deny any VAT adjustment for bad debts.[124] In the United Kingdom, the

[119] Case 38,253 (Hoge Raad 14 March 2003) (Netherlands), discussed in *VAT Monitor* 266 (May/June 2003), and J. Bijl & J. Kerékgyárt, "Recovery of Input VAT Incurred on Costs Relating to the Sale of Shares," 14 *VAT Monitor* 209 (May/June 2003).

[120] Canadian GST, *supra* note 14, at §186(2) and (3).

[121] If a cash basis seller must report the sale and remit tax before receiving payment, such as with installment sales, the seller may be eligible for an input credit if the installment purchaser defaults and the debt is written off. See NZ GST, *supra* note 68, at §26(1).

[122] ABA Model Act, *supra* note 73, at 97.

[123] The VAT Directive, *supra* note 1, at Arts. 20(l)(b) and 11(C)(1), authorizes member states to provide relief for bad debts. The United Kingdom provides bad debt relief. VATA 1994, *supra* note 70, at §36. To qualify, the seller must meet several conditions, including the requirement that the debt be written off in the seller's books and the debt be outstanding at least six months since the sale. *Id.* at §36(1). State retail sales taxes [in the United States] typically authorize the seller reporting tax on the accrual method to deduct bad debts. See J. Due & J. Mikesell, SALES TAXATION: STATE AND LOCAL STRUCTURE AND ADMINISTRATION 40–42 (Urban Institute Press 1994).

[124] See Value Added Tax Statute, 1996, Statute No. 8, 1996, §§23 and 29 (Uganda).

supplier is not required to notify the debtor of his intention to claim bad debt relief, and a debtor loses the right to an input tax credit once a debt is more than six months overdue.[125]

Singapore takes a pragmatic approach to the allowance of credits for bad debts.[126] To qualify, the taxable person must have supplied the goods and accounted for and paid GST on the supply. The credit can be claimed no earlier than when the debtor became insolvent or twelve months after the supply if the supplier wrote off the whole or a portion of the consideration in the supplier's accounts as a bad debt. Certain records must be created and maintained, the supplier must agree to report any recovery, and certain other conditions must be satisfied.

F. Allocation of Deductions Between Taxable and Other Activities

Tax imposed on business inputs used in making taxable supplies is creditable, but not on inputs for other purposes. Especially for tax on inputs used for mixed purposes, rules are needed to determine the amount of tax that is creditable. Tax on inputs directly allocable to taxable activities is fully creditable. Tax on inputs directly allocable to exempt or other nontaxable activities is not creditable. It is inputs that do not fit into these two categories that raise most of the issues in this area.

There are several methods used to allocate input VAT between taxable and other activities. The EU rules on the allocation of allowable input VAT on taxable supplies go beyond a formulary allocation based on taxable to total supplies. For example, in appropriate cases taxpayers may allocate input VAT on the basis of the amount of floor space used in making taxable supplies.

Canada has elaborate rules that not only limit credits on individual purchases to the percentage of the asset used in commercial (taxable) activities. Canada disallows a portion or the entire credit on purchases that may contain business and personal consumption elements.[127] Tax credits are limited on vehicles and aircraft, club memberships, and certain food or entertainment.[128] In a case favorable to the taxpayer, a passenger ferry was exempt on transport charges and taxable on sales of food and other items

[125] These changes became effective January 1, 2003. See VATA 1994, *supra* note 70, at §26A, as inserted by FA 2002, §22(1). An input tax claimed on a purchase must be repaid if the supplier is not paid within six months of the later of (a) the date of the supply or (b) the date the debt became due. See SI 1995/2518, Value Added Tax Regs. 1995, reg. 172F, G & H, reported in *CCH British Value Added Tax Reporter* ¶18–917.

[126] It provides that a registered person who completes a downloadable form entitled Bad Debt Relief: Checklist For Self-Review of Eligibility of Claim and satisfies the conditions listed in that form, the supplier can claim credit for the GST element in the bad debt. The form does not appear to be numbered and is dated January 2005.

[127] See generally Canadian GST, *supra* note 14, at §169.

[128] See, for example, *id.* at §§170(1), and 202(2) and (4). For leases of certain vehicles or purchases of food, beverages, or entertainment, the registered person may be required

on board the ferry. The court held that the taxpayer's method of allocating input VAT on the basis of the square footage of the vessel used by passengers to access taxable items (25%) rather than on the percentage of taxable to total supplies (1.2%) was fair and reasonable, even if another method may have provided a better result.[129]

II. Treatment of Excess Input Credits – Carry Forward, Offset, or Refund

As discussed in detail in Chapter 7, most countries define the jurisdictional reach of their VATs under the destination principle. Applying the destination principle, exports are free of tax (zero-rated). As a result, exporters commonly report excess input VAT in their periodic VAT returns. In addition, even registered persons making sales taxable at a positive rate may experience occasional excess input VATs, such as when they make capital purchases generating substantial input credits or when they increase their inventory as part of an expansion of their businesses.

There is an implicit assumption in VAT systems that registered persons will recover input VAT used in making taxable sales so that the input VAT does not enter into the pricing structure for those sales. To accomplish that goal, a normative consumption-type VAT must grant registered persons the right to recover excess input VATs within a reasonable period of time after incurring the input tax.

Independent of the kind of rules discussed in this section, VATs may provide for quick refunds of tax on imports and domestic purchases, such as acquisitions by diplomats, or imports of goods by international organizations under a humanitarian or similar program.[130] These refunds may serve as an alternative to issuing exemption certificates to the eligible individuals or organizations because it is too difficult to control the appropriate use of such exemption certificates.

This section discusses some of the numerous variations employed for the recovery or the denial of recovery of excess input VATs. Legislatures and tax authorities are reluctant to grant quick cash refunds for excess credits because of the risk of fraud and the negative cash flow associated with that approach, while registered persons (and foreign businesses) are frustrated when they cannot predict when they will recover excess input VATs. Restrictions on refunds are common. As an extreme example, Hungary

to make year-end adjustments to recapture a portion of the claimed credits. *Id.* at §§235 and 236.

129 *Bay Ferries Ltd. v. The Queen*, 2004 TCC 663 (Tax Ct. Canada). The court in this case supported the use of alternative methods such as square footage over the percentage of taxable to total supplies. See *id.* at ¶55.

130 See New Vatopia VAT, *supra* note 75, at §47(1). For an analysis of the range of refund regimes, see Harrison & Krelove, "VAT Refunds: A Review of Country Experience," IMF Working Paper WP/05/218 (Nov. 2005).

attempted to deny refunds when the requesting person did not pay the full price for the acquired assets that formed the basis for the requested refund claim. The ECJ ruled that this condition violated Hungary's obligations under the VAT Directive. The Court stated that conditions to the grant of refunds of excess input tax deductions "cannot undermine the principle of fiscal neutrality by making the taxable person bear the burden of the VAT in whole or in part."[131] The longer the time interval between the time the excess input credits are reportable on a VAT return and the time when the person receives the benefit from the credit, the less the benefit from the recovery of excess credits.[132]

Commonly, the VAT law requires the government to refund excess credits within a prescribed period of time, unless the tax authorities institute an audit, in which case the refund can be delayed until a specified period of time after the audit is completed.[133]

There are three basic methods by which VAT systems provide for the recovery of excess input VATs. They can be illustrated graphically in Figure 6.1.

As the figure demonstrates, the excess input VATs can be recovered through an immediate refund procedure. This is quite unusual, except for input VAT attributable to exports and refunds to persons not in business in the country of purchase. In the European Union, refunds of input VAT on purchases may be claimed (1) by taxable persons established within the Community but not established in the country where the items are acquired,[134] or (2) by businesses not established in the EU, but acquired within the Community.[135] A person may not be established in a member country, for this purpose, even if it obtains services from a subsidiary of that person to engage in "non-supply" activity in the country.[136]

In many countries, the excess credits must be carried forward to a specified number of future periods ranging from three to six periods, after

131 Case C-274/10, *European Commission v. Republic of Hungary*, ¶45 (judgment of the ECJ 2011).

132 For example, in Cyprus, registered persons may have to carry forward some excess credits for three years. See Y. Tsangaris, "Refund of Input VAT," 15 *VAT Monitor* 34 (Jan./Feb. 2004).

133 For example, Romania does not issue refunds without an audit for certain specified categories of taxpayers, including new companies, those involved with alcoholic beverages, and those with a record of economic offenses. Other taxpayers can obtain refunds without an audit, including those with a low risk. For a discussion of the formula for the analysis of risk, see Ana-Maria Notingher, "New VAT Refund Procedure," 15 *VAT Monitor* 453 (Nov./Dec. 2004).

134 VAT Directive, *supra* note 1, at Art. 171(1).

135 *Id*. at Art. 171(2).

136 For example, in joined cases C-318/11 (*Daimler AG v. Skatteverket*) and C-319/11 (*Widex v. Skatteverket*), firms not established in Sweden engaged in research activity in Sweden, purchasing services for that activity from their Swedish subsidiaries. The ECJ ruled that the purchase of services from a wholly owned subsidiary did not result in the firms being "established" in Sweden.

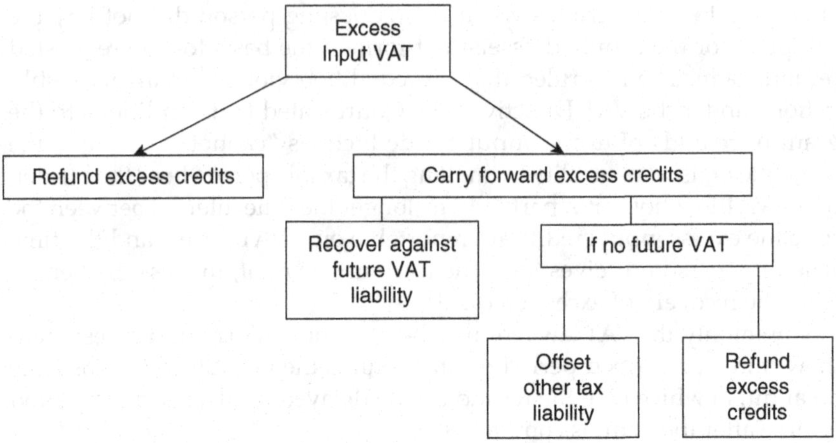

FIGURE 6.1. Recovery of excess input VATs.

which unused credits can either be used to offset the person's liability for other taxes[137] or refunded.[138]

There are variations that may be employed within these alternatives. For example, a registered exporter may claim a refund for excess credits attributable to exports when the exporter files the VAT return reporting the exports and may be required to carry forward other excess credits (attributable to sales taxable at a positive rate) for three to six months, after which those excess credits are eligible for a refund.[139] Another alternative may permit exporters to apply for a refund for excess credits attributable to the exports or to apply the excess credits in payment for other taxes owed by the exporter. This option, if granted, gives the business a more immediate benefit from its excess credits.[140] A third alternative gives taxpayers a prompt benefit from excess credits by allowing them to use these credits to pay VAT on their current taxable imports.[141] Some countries

137 In New Zealand, the tax authority may set off an available refund against a registered person's unpaid liability under other taxes. See NZ GST, *supra* note 68, at §46(6). In Hungary, any excess credits not already refunded may be refunded when a registered business is liquidated. See Hungarian VAT, discussed by M. Véghelyi, "Refund of Excess Input VAT," 14 *VAT Monitor* 137 (Mar./Apr. 2003).

138 See "Refunds of Excess Input Tax, Report on Bulgaria" in 13 *VAT Monitor* 402 (Sept./Oct. 2002).

139 See L. Tzenova, "Bulgaria: Excess Input Tax," 16 *VAT Monitor* 43 (Jan./Feb. 2005); see also "Slovak Republic, Refund of Input Tax," 14 *Int'l VAT Monitor* 343 (July/Aug. 2003).

140 There are also situations in which a refund occurs as a consequence of other rules. In Mexico, for example, customers purchasing some services are required to withhold and remit VAT chargeable on the services instead of paying the VAT to the supplier and claiming the VAT as an input credit. If VAT on these purchased services otherwise gives rise to refundable excess credits, the withholding system permits the purchasers, in effect, to get the immediate benefit from the recovery of the input VAT. See Serrano Salas, "Focus on Mexico," *VAT Monitor* 102 (Mar./Apr. 2003).

141 See the Ukraine procedure discussed in V. Yumashev, "Ukraine: VAT Promissory Notes Amended," 15 *VAT Monitor* 457 (Nov./Dec. 2004).

grant refunds of input VAT on capital goods that otherwise can be used only against output tax liability. Argentina did so as part of an investment promotion scheme.[142]

In the EU, the VAT Directive provides that if there are excess input tax deductions, "Member States may, in accordance with conditions which they shall determine, either make a refund or carry the excess forward to the following period. However, Member States may refuse to refund or carry forward if the amount of the excess is insignificant.[143] As a result of the complexity and cost associated with the VAT refund process and the time it takes to obtain refunds, in some situations, more than 50% of large firms in the EU do not apply for VAT refunds.[144]

An EU country's obligation to refund excess credits may not be satisfied by the issuance of government obligations to pay in the future. For example, the ECJ ruled that the issuance of government bonds by Italy does not satisfy Italy's obligation to make a refund "within a reasonable period of time by a payment in liquid funds or equivalent means. In any case, the method of refund adopted must not entail any financial risk for the taxable person."[145]

In the EU, there are two groups of nonresident, unregistered persons who can apply in a member state for refunds of input VAT paid. Taxable persons in one EU member state (A) that must pay VAT in another member state (B) are entitled to file for a refund of input VAT paid in member state (B) that is attributable to the requesting person's taxable supplies.[146]

Foreign persons not established in the EU also may be eligible to file for a refund of input VAT in a member state under a principle of reciprocity; that is, the refund is available if the country in which the foreign business is established does not impose a VAT-like tax or refunds VAT to businesses

[142] See, for example, the Argentina Law No. 25, 954 (Official Gazette of Sept. 6, 2004), discussed by D. Calzetta, "Accelerated VAT Refunds," 15 *VAT Monitor* 419 (Nov./Dec. 2004).

[143] VAT Directive, *supra* note 1, at Art. 183.

[144] Commission of the European Union, "Commission Staff Working Paper: European Tax Survey," SEC (2004) 1128/2, Oct. 9, 2004, p. 6.

[145] Case C-78/00, *Commission of the European Communities v. Italian Republic*, [2001] ECR I-8195, at ¶34 of the Judgment. A financial risk, for example, may entail a discount on the sale of the government bonds as a result of low interest payable on the bonds.

[146] Council Directive 2008/9/EC of 12 February 2008 laying down detailed rules for the refund of value added tax, provided for in Directive 2006/112/EC, to taxable persons not established in the Member State of refund but established in another Member State, OJ 2008 L44/23. The European Commission issued a proposal to allow traders to file a single electronic return and claim eligible refunds from other member states under the "one-stop shop" approach. See COM (2004) 728 final of 29 October 2004 and IP/04/1331 of 29 October 2004, discussed in R. Ainsworth, "The One-Stop Shop for VAT and RST: Common Approaches to EU-U.S. Consumption Tax Issues," 2005 *Tax Notes International* 693 (Feb. 21, 2005). The refund is not available if it is attributable to exempt supplies made by the requesting person in the member state where he is established. See *Etienne Débouche v. Inspecteur der Invoerrechten en Accijnzen*, Case C-302/93, [1996] ECR I-4495, discussed in J. Swinkels, "Tax Neutrality and Cross-Border Services," 16 *Int'l VAT Monitor* 94 (Mar./Apr. 2005.

that are resident in the granting state. To be eligible, the foreign person must meet the conditions imposed in the Thirteenth Council Directive and by the granting state.[147] The United Kingdom amended its VAT to deny input tax credits (or refund) for VAT paid on acquisitions in the United Kingdom by taxable persons established outside the United Kingdom if the credits relate to financial and insurance services supplied to customers outside the EU. In Case C-582/08, the ECJ ruled that the United Kingdom did not fail to comply with its VAT obligations by denying recovery of input tax incurred by an offshore supplier of insurance to insured persons outside the EU.[148]

New Zealand introduced similar rules on refunds available to nonresidents who register for GST and sell in business-to-business transactions in New Zealand.[149] As a result, there is no competitive disadvantage to those nonresident businesses. The change was effective April 1, 2014. Some countries provide for VAT rebates for foreign tourists where the country is satisfied that goods have been exported.[150]

III. Change from Exempt to Taxable or Taxable to Exempt Status

> [I]f a person making exempt sales (such as a person exempt from tax on sales under a [small business exemption] ...) purchases property and services, the VAT on such purchases is not eligible for the input credit. If the exempt seller becomes a taxable person, he then will charge VAT on all subsequent taxable sales and will be entitled to credit input tax on new purchases against this

147 See Thirteenth Council Directive of 17 November 1986, 86/560/EEC. Based in part on *Commission of the European Communities v. United Kingdom of Great Britain and Northern Ireland*, Case C-33/02, [2005] ECR I-1865, and on the Sixth, Eighth, and Thirteenth Directives, the British Revenue and Customs has liberalized the procedure under which a non-EU business can claim a refund of input VAT. See R. Ostilly, "UK's U-Turn," 17 *Int'l VAT Monitor* 95 (Mar./Apr. 2006). See also J. Swinkels, "VAT Refunds to Non-EU Banks," 16 *Int'l VAT Monitor* 105 (March/April 2005), discussing a Dutch case granting refunds to an Australian bank without a fixed establishment in the Netherlands that rendered services exclusively to non-EU customers. For an overview of thresholds for refunds available in European countries to registered businesses, foreign traders that are not registered in the EU, and nonresident tourists, see "Practical Information on VAT," 16 *Int'l VAT Monitor* 2–10 (Jan./Feb. 2005). This information has been updated annually.

148 *European Commission vs. United Kingdom of Great Britain and Northern Ireland* (judgment of the ECJ 2010). According to the Court, if there is an error in Art. 169(c) of the VAT Directive by not referring to the Thirteenth Directive and the UK law complied with the literal language of Art. 2 of the Thirteenth VAT Directive, the error should be corrected by the EU legislature (the European Commission), not the Court.

149 See NZ GST, *supra* note 68, at §54B giving nonresidents the opportunity to register for GST purposes. See also *id.* at §20(3L) giving the nonresident the right to claim input tax deductions.

150 See, for example, VATA 1994, *supra* note 70, at §30(6), on exported goods generally; and Sch. 9, zero-rating, Group 14, tax-free shops (United Kingdom); see also Canadian GST, *supra* note 14, at §252. Canada rebates the VAT on certain hotel accommodations for tourists as well. *Id.* at §252.1.

> output tax liability. To the extent that the taxable person sells inventory that was on hand when he became taxable, he is selling property that already bore noncreditable input tax. He will be charging VAT on the cost of this property a second time. If the taxable person were granted a credit for VAT attributable to the purchases of goods on hand when he switched to taxable status, he would be placed in the same tax position as if he acquired such property and services while he was a taxable person.[151]

To prevent a competitive disadvantage to a newly registered person, VAT systems may allow that person to claim credit, in the person's first VAT return, for tax on goods on hand that were purchased within a prescribed number of months before registration.[152] To prevent a competitive advantage to a deregistering person, VAT systems typically treat a deregistering person as having sold goods on hand immediately before the cancellation of registration becomes effective.[153]

IV. Used Property

A. Business-to-Business Sales of Used Property

A registered business making taxable sales claims credit for input VAT on assets (e.g., office furniture) acquired for use in making those taxable sales. The assets are held free of VAT. If the business sells this furniture after using it in its business for years, the sales are taxable, whether sold to a registered used-goods dealer or a private consumer. If the office furniture is purchased by a registered used-goods dealer for renovation and resale in a taxable transaction, the dealer claims credit for tax on the purchase and charges VAT on the resale price. Any consumer who purchases the refurbished used goods bears VAT only on the tax-exclusive prices of the used goods.

B. Sales of Used Property in Non-Taxable Transactions

A registered person may acquire goods in transactions not subject to tax. For example, a consumer may sell a used refrigerator to a used appliance dealer in a transaction not subject to VAT. If the acquired good is resold in a taxable transaction and some noncreditable VAT is buried in the selling price, the VAT is imposed more than once, resulting in some cascading of VAT.

151 ABA Model Act, *supra* note 73, at 100.

152 See Canadian GST, *supra* note 14, at §171(1). The Canadian credit is not limited to goods or services purchased within a given period before registration becomes effective.

153 See generally *id.* at §171(3)–(5).

> For example, assume that the first consumer bought a refrigerator for $1,000 plus $100 VAT (10 percent tax). After years of use, the consumer sells the used refrigerator to a dealer for $220, consisting of $200 plus the $20 VAT attributable to this portion of the original purchase price. The dealer resells it to a second consumer for $350, which includes the $20 VAT buried in the dealer's cost for the refrigerator. The only value [that is] added to this used property by the dealer is represented by the difference between this dealer's VAT-exclusive cost ($200) and VAT-exclusive selling price ($330), or $130. [Yet, if] the dealer charges $35 VAT on the [$350] selling price and does not obtain any VAT benefit from the $20 VAT element in the $220 purchase price, VAT will have been imposed a second time on the $200 VAT-exclusive cost of the used refrigerator (multiple tax), and VAT also will be imposed on the $20 VAT included in the dealer's $350 selling price (cascade effect). This multiple tax and cascade effect may further encourage the private sale of used refrigerators and similar products through [the Internet], newspaper advertisements or garage sales, thus creating a disadvantage for dealers in used consumer durable goods.[154]

The problem extends beyond these transactions. For example, in some countries, a registered business is denied credit for input VAT on automobiles. Because input VAT was not claimed on the acquisition of the automobile, the VAT Act may treat the sale of the used automobile to a used car dealer as a transaction not subject to VAT. In the absence of a special rule, the tax-exclusive price charged by the used car dealer would include some element of VAT. The same effect can occur if an unregistered small business sells used property (such as office furniture) to a used office furniture dealer who resells those goods.

Many VAT systems include rules to reduce or eliminate the cascading of VAT on secondhand or used goods. The scope of the covered goods and the method of calculating the tax by the reseller of the used goods differ. One approach is to calculate the taxable amount of the sale by the used goods dealer as the difference between the sales price and the dealer's cost for the used goods. In the EU, the VAT Directive requires member states to tax only the profit margin on supplies by a taxable dealer of secondhand goods, works of art, collectors' items, and antiques acquired from non-taxable persons; in certain exempt transactions; from an exempt small enterprise, or from another taxable dealer in a transaction reported under these rules.[155] The profit margin is the difference between the price charged for the goods and the purchase price.[156] Interpreting the scope of the term "secondhand goods,"[157] the ECJ held that a live animal (a horse in that case) purchased from a private individual, trained, and sold for a

[154] ABA Model Act, *supra* note 73, at 103.

[155] VAT Directive, *supra* note 1, at Arts. 313 and 314.

[156] VATA 1994, *supra* note 70, at §50A(4) [VAT Directive, *supra* note 1, at Art. 315].

[157] Secondhand goods are defined in the VAT Directive, *supra* note 1, at Art. 311, as "movable tangible property that is suitable for further use as it is or after repair, other than works of art, collectors' items or antiques and other than precious metals or precious stones as defined by the Member States."

specific use (a riding horse) may be considered a secondhand good subject to the profit margin rules.[158]

If the margin method is applied to the above example,

> the used property dealer would calculate the taxable amount of the sale of the used refrigerator by reducing the $350 selling price by the $220 cost. The dealer would charge $13 VAT on the $130 taxable amount, the value added by the dealer. [This approach] ... removes appreciation in the value of used property from the tax base if the used property is sold by the first consumer to the dealer for more than the consumer's purchase price.[159]
>
> Instead of providing a special rule to reduce the taxable amount of the resale of used property, the statute [could tax] ... the used property dealer's sale on the basis of the selling price of the used property (the same as in any other taxable sale), and grant the dealer a constructive input credit for the amount of VAT that would have been imposed on its purchase of the used property if such used property had been acquired in a taxable transaction.[160]

The Canadian GST allows a deemed credit for the cost of used goods purchased from an unregistered person.[161] Subject to conditions, the Australian GST grants the registered purchaser an input tax credit on purchases of secondhand goods acquired for sale or exchange in the ordinary course of business.[162] This credit has given rise to some tax-avoidance motivated transactions. For an extensive discussion of the Australian rules and some of the abuses, see the Australian Tax Office GST ruling in this area.[163]

> This constructive credit approach ... presents problems resulting from the break in the credit chain. The dealer in used property obtains an input credit without a tax invoice .... This break in the chain of tax invoices provides an opportunity for VAT evasion .... While the opportunity for evasion or avoidance can be reduced by requiring used property dealers to obtain receipts from consumers that sell them used property, it would be difficult for the

[158] *Forvaltnings AB Stenholmen v. Riksskatteverket*, Case C-320/02, [2004] ECR I-3509.

[159] For example, assume that the refrigerator was unique and that the consumer can sell it to the used property dealer for a VAT-exclusive price of $1,500. Because the dealer can reduce its tax base on sales by the full price paid for the refrigerator, if the market operates, the sales price should include all or most of the VAT that would be imposed if it were a taxable sale. The assumption here is that the selling price will increase to $1,650. The dealer resells it for a tax-exclusive price of $1,780. The price consists of the tax-inclusive $1,650 cost of the purchase plus $130 value added by the dealer. Because the reduction in the taxable amount of the sale is based on the dealer's entire purchase price, the government will never receive VAT on the $500 difference between the first consumer's $1,000 VAT-exclusive cost and his $1,500 tax-exclusive selling price. ABA Model Act, *supra* note 73, at 104.

[160] *Id.* at 105.

[161] Canadian GST, *supra* note 14, at §176. There are rules to prevent excessive credits on certain used goods.

[162] A New Tax System (Goods and Services Tax) Act 1999, §66–40 (Australia).

[163] GSTR 2004/D4 finalized, Goods and services tax: arrangements of the kind described in Taxpayer Alert TA 2004/9 – Exploitation of the secondhand goods provisions to obtain input tax credits.

government to verify the authenticity of these receipts because these consumers would not be subject to VAT audits.[164]

The opportunity for tax evasion has prompted some countries to go to the other extreme and tax the full selling price of used goods that were purchased in transactions not subject to tax, while not granting the seller any input credit or other adjustment to account for the input VAT paid by the seller to the secondhand goods dealer.[165]

If a sale to a dealer in used property is not a taxable transaction and the seller is selling for more than the seller's cost, the appreciation will go untaxed. It may be appropriate to leave this value out of the VAT base. The appreciation represents economic rent that will not affect the price of consumption.[166]

V. Post-Sale Price Adjustments and Refunds

A. In General

A rebate, return of merchandise, or adjustment of price may occur after a taxable sale has been completed and the tax invoice has been issued. These post-sale adjustments take a number of different forms. Commonly, the person making the adjustment must issue a debit or credit note to give notice of the adjustment to the recipient and provide an audit trail to verify that the adjustment has been properly accounted for by the parties.

The New Zealand GST has rules representative of those in other countries. If a supplier accounted for an incorrect amount of output tax on a tax invoice and possibly in a previously filed tax return because the supply was canceled, the nature of the supply was fundamentally changed, the consideration was changed, or some or all of the goods or services were returned, the supplier can adjust its tax liability as a result of this cancellation, return, or change.[167] If the adjustment resulted in a previous overstatement of tax liability, the correction is made by claiming an input credit and by issuing a credit note to the recipient of the supply.[168] If the adjustment resulted in a previous understatement of tax liability, the correction is made by reporting additional output tax liability and issuing a debit note to the recipient of the supply.[169]

If the registered recipient of the supply receives a credit note as described earlier, and it previously claimed an excessive input credit as a result of the tax reported on that purchase, the recipient must report

164 ABA Model Act, *supra* note 73, at 106.

165 See, for example, Value Added Tax Statute, 1996, Statute No. 8 1996, §§22 and 29(11) (Uganda).

166 Cui, Objections to Taxing Resale of Residential Property under a VAT, 137 Tax Notes 777 (2012).

167 NZ GST, *supra* note 68, at §25(1) and (2).

168 *Id.* at §25(2)(b) and (3)(a).

169 *Id.* at §25(2)(a) and (3)(b).

the tax adjustment as tax on a taxable supply.[170] If the registered recipient receives a debit note as described earlier and understated the allowable input credit as a result of the tax reported on that purchase, the recipient may claim an additional input credit to the extent listed on the debit note if that amount is otherwise creditable.[171]

The theft or destruction of property, including capital goods, may require a post-acquisition adjustment. The ECJ, however, ruled that an adjustment was not required where capital goods used to make taxable supplies were destroyed and replaced by capital goods to be used for the same purpose.[172]

B. Third Party Post-Sale Rebate to Final Consumer

A pre-retail registered producer may provide a cash rebate to a final consumer for various reasons, such as a sales incentive or to obtain information about a retailer or other final consumer of its products. For example, a manufacturer of a computer memory stick may offer retail customers cash rebates if they submit an invoice and a completed rebate form. The rebate does not alter the VAT imposed on the retail sales. Instead, the cash rebates reduce the consideration the manufacturer receives on its sales of memory sticks and the net consideration paid by the consumer. The VAT system should take account of that reduction in net consideration paid for the memory stick. If the manufacturer issues a consumer a cash rebate of $11.00 and the VAT rate is 10% on tax-exclusive prices, the manufacturer should be entitled to claim an input credit (or reduction in output tax) of $1.00 (rebate × tax rate/100 + tax rate, or 11 × 10/110).

VI. Casual Sales by Consumers

Even if a casual seller were treated as selling in connection with taxable activities, the annual sales likely will not exceed the small business exemption threshold used in most countries. However, even if the sale is of an item (such as a yacht) priced above the small business exemption threshold, most countries do not tax casual sales by consumers. Some countries make an exception for sales of real property.[173]

Casual sales by consumers tend to be of used items. If they are taxed, the tax consequences should follow the rules on used goods discussed earlier. If the casual seller is taxed only on the margin – the spread between

170 *Id.* at §25(4).

171 *Id.* at §25(5).

172 Case C-234/11, *Tets Haskovo AD v. Direktor na Direktsia 'Obzhalvane i upravlenie na izpalnenieto' – Varna pri Tsentralno upravlenie na Natsionalnata agentsia za prihodite* (Director of the Appeals and Management Directorate, Varna, at the Central Administration of the National Revenue Agency of Bulgaria) (judgment of the ECJ 2012).

173 A sale of a residential complex by an individual is taxable under the Canadian GST. See Canadian GST, *supra* note 14, at Sch. V, Part I, ¶9(d).

the sales price and the cost of the item sold – the seller should be required to substantiate the claimed cost with an invoice or other supporting document. To prevent possible abuse, if a casual sale is taxed, the seller should not be eligible for a refund of any excess input credits resulting from the sale.

One alternative may be to tax sales by unregistered persons if the sale exceeds a certain threshold amount. The Model Act developed in the United States by the American Bar Association tax section committee on VAT taxes high-priced casual sales. It allows the casual seller to claim a deferred input credit for VAT paid on the asset sold in a taxable casual sale.[174]

VII. Japan's System to Calculate Input Credits

The calculation of creditable input tax under the CT is unique. First, in form, a person registered under the CT calculates creditable input tax from company records rather than from VAT invoices. This form may not be substantively different from a European-style invoice VAT because the CT taxpayer still must substantiate its credits with "a bill, receipt, statement of delivery or other type of invoice that shows" the details of the transaction.[175] The CT taxpayer takes the total tax-inclusive cost of allowable purchases for the tax period and multiplies this total by the tax fraction, for a 7% CT–7/107, to arrive at the allowable input credits for the period.

The second difference, an accommodation to the small business sector in Japan, is that credits are available for the tax fraction of the cost of purchases from CT-exempt small businesses. Credits also are available for the presumed CT element in purchases of used goods from consumers. Purchases of items exempt from the CT do not qualify for credit.[176] "The input tax credit, therefore, is available for presumed tax on purchases from a business that does not charge CT on its sales because its turnover is below the small business exemption threshold,[177] but the credit is not available on the purchase of insurance that is exempt from the CT."[178]

[174] ABA Model Act, *supra* note 73, at §§4000 and 4019.

[175] See Beyer, Japan – National Consumption Tax Law: An English Translation (1989) [hereinafter Japan CT Law], 1994 Amendment Act, at Art. 30 amendment. This change is effective for purchases on or after April 1, 1997. *Id.* at appendix, Art. 7. See Beyer, Japan's Consumption Tax: Settled in to Stay, 2000 Worldwide Tax Daily 247–5, at 3 (Tax Analysts, Dec. 12, 2000).

[176] Japan CT Law, *supra* note 175, at Art. 30, and Art. 2(1)(9) definition of a "Transfer of Taxable Assets." For purchases of secondhand goods, the dealer in used goods can claim a credit on the basis of the dealer's purchase price of the goods from the consumer. For example, if a consumer buys a Picasso painting for 130 million yen and later sells it to an art gallery for 150 million yen, the gallery can claim an input deduction on the basis of the 150 million yen price.

[177] The 1950 Japanese VAT included a similar deduction for amounts paid on purchases from suppliers that were exempt from the VAT. C. Sullivan, THE TAX ON VALUE ADDED, 134–135 (Columbia University Press 1965).

[178] A. Schenk, "Japanese Consumption Tax After Six Years: A Unique VAT Matures," 69 *Tax Notes* 899 (Nov. 13, 1995), at 905–906.

VIII. Calculation of Tax Liability and Special Schemes

Most countries with VATs rely on the credit-invoice method of calculating periodic tax liability. Japan is an exception but has been moving to a method that relies increasingly on sales documents to verify output tax and input credits.

Registered businesses in most countries must report as output tax the tax on taxable sales taken from tax invoices. They claim as input credits the VAT charged on VAT invoices for purchases used in making taxable sales. Businesses with turnover below the registration threshold are outside the VAT system. To ease the compliance burden on businesses that are above the threshold but may not have sophisticated or computerized record keeping, the VAT, by law, regulations, or administrative practice, may authorize simplified schemes to minimize VAT record keeping and reporting obligations. For example, some countries rely on modified turnover tax regimes for businesses with turnover above the registration threshold. The United Kingdom provides an election for registered businesses to report under a flat-rate scheme.[179] Under the British scheme, participation must be authorized by the Commissioners, and electing traders are required to record sales.[180] The VAT liability is calculated on the basis of the appropriate percentage of the output for the trader's business category, including VAT, as listed in the regulations.[181] For example, under

[179] See, Value Added Tax Regulations 1995, SI 1995/2518, as amended, Part VIIA – Flat-Rate Scheme for Small Businesses, reg. 55 et seq. [hereinafter Flat-Rate Scheme]; Notice 733 Flat Rate Scheme for small businesses (August 2011).

[180] VATA 1994, *supra* note 70, at §26B. This scheme is in the VAT Regulations 1995, regulations 55A–55V, 57A, and 69A, and explained further in VAT Notice 733, Flat Rate Scheme for small businesses (April 2014). A taxable person is eligible to be approved for admission to the scheme only if the person's annual taxable supplies for the following year will not exceed £150,000, excluding VAT. Transactions involving capital goods are accounted for outside of this scheme.

[181] For example, from January 1, 2011, the appropriate percentage for select businesses were as follows.

Accountancy	*14.5%*
Agricultural services	11%
Computer and IT consultancy or data processing	14.5%
Entertainment or journalism	12.5%
Farming or agriculture not listed elsewhere	6.5%
Financial services	13.5%
Hotel or accommodation	10.5%
Lawyer or legal services	14.5%
Management consultancy	14%
Printing	8.5%
Repairing vehicles	8.5%
Retailing food, tobacco, children's clothing	4%
Retailing pharmaceuticals, medical goods, cosmetics or toiletries	8%
Secretarial services	13%
Sport or recreation	8.5%
Travel agency	10.5%
Wholesaling food	7.5%

the flat-rate scheme, if a trader has "relevant turnover," of £10,000 in a tax period and the appropriate percentage is 10%, the VAT for the period is £1,000. The UK system requires traders to calculate VAT liability on the basis of total turnover, with no reduction or credit for tax on purchases. The trader still issues VAT invoices on the trader's taxable supplies. The complex rules governing the conversion from the flat rate to the regular method of calculating VAT liability, when sales exceed the allowable limits, may deter some traders from electing the flat-rate scheme. There are restrictions on the use of the flat-rate scheme. For example, the scheme is not available to a tour operator.

IX. Discussion Questions

1. One might think that a consumption-type VAT system does not need any special treatment for input credits on capital goods. Explain why special treatment is provided by the VAT Directive and how this treatment operates.
2. What is the link between the tax credit mechanism and the concepts of self-supplies and self-services for business purposes under the VAT Directive, Arts. 18 and 27?
3. In a VAT system, there are two ways to prevent private consumption from escaping tax when such consumption takes place in a business context: (a) deny the input tax credit and (b) tax a deemed transaction between the taxpayer and himself or between the taxpayer and a third party. What use is made of these two models in the VAT Directive?
4. Would you expect that problems and solutions for casual sales, used goods, and trade-ins to be the same under a retail sales tax and a VAT? For the theory and practice in the state retail sales taxes (RSTs) in the United States, see R. Pomp & O. Oldman, "A Normative Inquiry into the Base of a Retail Sales Tax: Casual Sales, Used Goods, and Trade Ins," 43 *Nat'l. Tax J.* 427 (1990).

See Flat-Rate Scheme, *supra* note 179, at reg. 55K, as amended by S.I. 2010, No. 2940, Reg. 2, effective January 1, 2011.

7 Introduction to Cross-Border Aspects of VAT

I. Introduction to International Trade

For most countries with VATs, international trade is a significant component of their economies. A country with a VAT must define the jurisdictional reach of the tax. Should the tax reach global supplies or should it be limited to supplies within the country's territory? Whether global or territorial, should the tax be imposed on production within the country (an origin principle VAT), on domestic consumption (a destination principle VAT), or some combination of the two? Almost every country with a VAT imposes a territorial VAT that relies on the destination principle to define the jurisdictional limits of the tax. Under a pure destination principle, imports are taxed and exports are completely free of tax (zero-rated). With this system, it is important to identify the value of goods and services that are exported (and when they are exported) and identify the value of taxable imports and determine when they are taxable. This chapter discusses the rules that determine where a supply takes place, including the troublesome issues on cross-border transactions relating to the place where services are rendered and intangibles are supplied.

The location or place of the supply of cross-border services has become more significant with the advent of electronically supplied services.[1] If the place of supply rules applicable to the sale of goods and those applicable to the sale of services differ, the supplier must determine whether the sale is of goods or services, and this may be more difficult in the case of electronic commerce. For example, if computer software, music,

[1] See, for example, Working Party No. 9 on Consumption Taxes, Committee on Fiscal Affairs, OECD International VAT/GST Guidelines, February 2013, including "Draft Guidelines on place of taxation for cross-border supplies of services and intangibles to businesses that have establishments in more than one jurisdiction" and "Draft Guidelines on the implementation of specific rules for determining the place of taxation for cross border business-to-business supplies of services and intangibles." See also the EU VAT Directive and Regulations on place of supply discussed later in this chapter.

and videos are transmitted by electronic signals rather than in compact disks or other physical form, is the transaction a sale of goods or a sale of services?[2] Sales of standard packaged software have been treated as sales of goods, but sales of customized software have been treated as sales of services.[3]

Before we get to these issues, the next two sections discuss the vocabulary of international aspects of VAT and the jurisdictional reach of a VAT.

II. Vocabulary of Interjurisdictional (Cross-Border) Aspects of VAT

The following terms are used in this chapter and throughout the book. They relate to various VAT aspects of cross-border trade in goods and services.

- International – between countries or outside of a customs union or trading block
- Intrabloc – between member countries of a customs union or trading block (for example: the European Union (EU); North American Free Trade Agreement (NAFTA), Latin American Free Trade Association (LAFTA); and the Community of Andean Nations Agreement (CAN))
- Intranational – between states or provinces within a country, for example, in federal countries such as the United States, Australia, Brazil, Canada, and India
- Intrastate – between a state and local units of government, between municipalities, or within a state
- Location or place of supply – where a supply is treated as taking place for VAT purposes

The next section discusses the details of the two major methods of defining the jurisdictional reach of a VAT – the origin and the destination principles. It is possible to combine various elements of these two principles in defining the jurisdictional reach of a VAT.

Table 7.1[4] sets out the various options pertaining to the taxation of domestic transactions, exports, and imports and provides examples of their use in national or subnational sales or value added tax systems around the world. If a supply is not taxed and the supplier is entitled to recover input VAT, in this book, the supply is referred to as zero-rated. Under the EU VAT Directive, it is exempt with a right to deduct input tax. In Australia, it is "GST-free." If a supply is not taxed and the supplier is not entitled to recover input VAT, in this book, the supply is referred to as exempt from VAT. Under the EU VAT Directive, it is exempt with no

[2] See H. Lambert, "VAT and Electronic Commerce: European Union Insights into the Challenges Ahead," 9 *Tax Notes Int'l* 1645, 1646 (Nov. 23, 1998).

[3] *Id.*

[4] Adaptation by O. Oldman from 1979 lecture by C. S. Shoup.

TABLE 7.1. Options for the taxation of domestic and international trade

	Exports	*Domestic Trans's*	*Imports*	*Comments*
1	T	T	T	Rare, but Saipan made this proposal
2	T	E	T	Argentina formerly
3	T	T	E	Origin principle
4	T	E	E	Tax only on export of natural resources
5	E	T	T	Destination principle
6	E	E	T	See Surrey's* proposed surcharge on U.S. imports
7	E	T	E	German turnover tax in the 1920s**
8	E	E	E	United States at the national level

T = taxable transactions; E = exempt transactions

* Stanley Surrey was Professor of Law, Harvard Law School, and Assistant Secretary for Tax Policy in the U.S. Treasury Department from 1961 to 1969.

** See C.K. Sullivan, The Tax on Value Added 30 (New York: Columbia University Press 1965).

right to deduct input VAT. In Australia, it is "input taxed." If imports are exempt, they are completely free of VAT on import.

III. Definition of Tax Jurisdiction

A. Introduction

A country may impose VAT on transactions within its territory (a territorial VAT) or on transactions conducted all over the world (a global VAT). Whether the VAT is a global or territorial VAT, cross-border transactions can be defined under the origin or destination principle. This section explores these choices.

B. Territorial or Global Reach of the Tax

An income tax may be imposed only on income earned within the territory of the taxing jurisdiction (a territorial tax) or imposed on income earned worldwide (a global tax such as the U.S. income tax imposed on its citizens and residents), or some combination of both. The same may apply to a transactional tax on consumption, such as a VAT. A VAT can be imposed on the worldwide supplies of registered persons domiciled or residing in the taxing country (global), imposed only on domestic supplies[5] and imports (territorial), or on some combination of both.

[5] Zero-rated exports are deemed to be domestic supplies, so that they are eligible for input tax credits that otherwise are limited to domestic supplies.

New Zealand, South Africa, and a few other countries basically start with a VAT that has a global reach.[6] These countries impose VAT on registered "residents" on their worldwide supplies. The laws then narrow the tax base to resemble a territorial, destination principle VAT in use elsewhere, including the zero-rating of exports and the taxation of imports. As discussed later in the chapter, a taxpayer operating under a global VAT may find it more difficult to structure some foreign sales to avoid VAT jurisdiction.

Countries with VATs that are described in this book as global VATs historically did not include, in the VAT legislation, detailed place of supply rules on cross-border supplies because the imposition of tax did not depend on the place where the supply occurred. In contrast, most VAT systems in use today (territorial, destination principle taxes) are imposed only on the supply of goods or the rendition of services to be consumed domestically. The VATs in those countries need the place of supply rules discussed later in this chapter.

New Zealand's GST, described here as a global VAT, imposes tax largely on the basis of the residence of the seller. Supplies of goods and services by residents generally take place in New Zealand. Supplies of goods by nonresidents occur in New Zealand if the goods are in New Zealand when supplied. Supplies of services by nonresidents occur in New Zealand if the services are rendered in New Zealand. Imports of goods and some services are taxed.

The following *Wilson & Horton Ltd.* case illustrates the difficulty in identifying the location of advertisements placed by foreign customers under the NZ GST that did not include place of supply rules for the tax periods in question.

Wilson & Horton Ltd v. Commissioner of Inland Revenue[7]

HEADNOTE. Wilson & Horton Ltd (the objector) offered the service of publishing advertisements for its customers in its publications. This service was offered to people resident in New Zealand and overseas customers. In the case of advertisements placed by persons not resident in New Zealand, the advertisements were in five different categories, namely:

[6] See, for example, the New Zealand Goods and Services Tax Act 1985, 1985, No. 141 [hereinafter NZ GST], §8(2). Nonresidents are subject to the NZ GST if the goods supplied are located in New Zealand when the supply occurs or the services are physically performed in NZ by a person who is in NZ when the services are performed. *Id.* at §8(3). There are special rules in section 8 governing imported services and telecommunication services. Some commentators do not agree that countries such as New Zealand and South Africa have global VAT regimes that are modified to resemble territorial VATs. See R. Millar, "Jurisdictional Reach of VAT," in VAT IN AFRICA (R. Krever, ed.)175–214.

[7] [1996] 1 NZLR 26 (Ct. App. Wellington) [edited by the authors].

(Category 1)	Advertisements... which refer to services offered by New Zealand residents.
(Category 2)	Advertisements... which refer to goods situated outside of New Zealand which are offered by New Zealand residents.
(Category 3)	Advertisements... which refer to goods situated inside New Zealand offered by persons not resident in New Zealand.
(Category 4)	Advertisements... which refer to goods situated inside New Zealand which are offered by New Zealand residents.
(Category 5)	"Image" advertisements... for the promotion of a brand name or brand product, where the goods or services referred to in the advertisement are sold in New Zealand.

The Commissioner ... took the view that the objector had incorrectly zero-rated invoices sent to overseas customers. The Commissioner and the objector disagreed as to the proper treatment of invoices in the five categories referred to.

JUDGMENT: RICHARDSON J.[8] [Wilson & Horton publish advertisements for foreign clients in the *New Zealand Herald*. It consistently zero-rated these advertisements. The question on appeal was whether the five categories of supplies listed earlier were taxable at the standard 12.5% rate or were zero-rated under section ll(2)(e) of the Goods and Services Tax Act 1985.]

Section ll(2)(e) of the Act provides:

(2) Where, but for this section, a supply of services would be charged with tax under section 8 of this Act, any such supply shall be charged at the rate of zero per cent where –

(e) The services are supplied for and to a person who is not resident in New Zealand and who is outside New Zealand at the time the services are performed, not being services which are supplied directly in connection with –

(i) Land or any improvement thereto situated inside New Zealand; or
(ii) Moveable personal property ... situated inside New Zealand at the time the services are performed; ...

Much of the evidence and argument in the High Court was directed to the question of who benefited from the advertisements and, in particular, the manner in which New Zealand retailers of goods and services advertised and other persons in New Zealand benefited compared with any benefit to the foreign client. It is sufficient to note four features or implications of any comparative benefit assessment.

[8] The opinions of the other members of the panel were omitted.

First, many parties may benefit from an advertisement placed by a foreign client which advertises goods or services. For example:

(a) The foreign client which placed the advertisement (if the manufacturer or ultimate supplier of goods and services) will benefit from any increased sales to retailers;
(b) The retailers in New Zealand supplying the goods and services will also benefit from any increased sales arising from the advertisements;
(c) Wilson & Horton Ltd will receive a benefit from advertising revenue;
(d) Any advertising agency placing the advertisements on behalf of the non-resident client will receive a fee;
(e) Purchasers of the paper and members of the public reading the advertisements will benefit from an awareness of goods and services available in the market;
(f) Retailers and suppliers of related products may also benefit from cross-sales arising from the advertisements; and
(g) Investors in those businesses may benefit from increased sales arising from advertisements.

Second, there are obvious difficulties in measuring the benefits flowing to various parties from advertising activities.

Third, the newspaper office will neither know nor expect to be told what arrangements a foreign client has with its New Zealand franchisee or subsidiary whether for advertising of goods and services for supply in New Zealand or for image advertising of a brand, product or company, and for charging the franchisee or subsidiary for promotional activities.

Fourth, if New Zealand businesses benefit from the advertising by sales of advertised goods and services, those supplies are, of course, subject to GST.

Having regard to those considerations it is readily understandable why the benefit argument for the Commissioner in this Court was put on the basis that §ll(2)(e) was not satisfied unless the foreign client was the exclusive beneficiary of the advertisement it placed in the Herald.

THE SCHEME OF THE LEGISLATION. Liability for goods and services tax arises on "the supply ... in New Zealand of goods and services ... by a registered person in the course or furtherance of a taxable activity carried on by that person, by reference to the value of that supply" (§8(1)). Taxable activity, as defined in §6(l)(a), is directed to "the supply of goods and services to any other person for a consideration"; supplier "in relation to any supply of goods and services, means the person making the supply" (§2); and the recipient is "the person receiving the supply" (§2).

Those provisions are directed to the contractual arrangements between the supplier and the recipient of the supply. In keeping with the general statutory scheme in that respect §11, providing for zero-rating of supply transactions where the stated overseas element is present, follows that same pattern. It follows that where, as in the presently material §11 (2)(e), the provision refers to "services ... supplied ... to a person" the statutory dictionary applies and the phrase refers to the contractual position and so to the person who has provided the consideration. That is common ground between the parties, as it was in the High Court.

INTERPRETATION OF §ll(2)(e). To qualify for zero-rating under §ll(2)(e) the services supplied by Wilson & Horton in publishing advertisements in the Herald must satisfy two requirements.

First, the services must be supplied "for and to a person" who is not resident in New Zealand and who is not present in New Zealand when the services are performed. It is common ground that the latter elements, namely that the person concerned, the foreign client, was not resident in New Zealand and was not present in New Zealand when the advertisements were published in the Herald, were satisfied....

Section ll(2)(e) employs the composite expression "for and to a person."

While it is important to seek to give adequate meaning to all the words actually employed in the legislation, it is not realistic to expect that busy drafters or legislators will always ensure that each provision is tautly and precisely drawn without any surplusage. Also it is not uncommon for legislative drafting to convey emphasis through a combination of words. Some apparent repetition by the use of different or added words may be explicable for those reasons.

I am inclined to think that the framers of §ll(2)(e) employed both expressions to convey emphasis and perhaps to bring out the intent that the contract must be genuine and so the services must be supplied under that contract to and for the other contracting party.

Further, if one may read a flavour of benefit to the foreign client into the composite expression, that is met if it is apparent that the foreign client will benefit from the advertising, whether or not anyone else does. The obvious commercial inference is that the contracting party paying the bill expects to benefit from the services supplied. Equally obviously, in some cases others may benefit from any resulting sales. Paragraph (e) would surely have been worded differently had it been intended to exclude its application unless the foreign client was the only person who could benefit from the services supplied. It would either have been totally recast or, at least, have been prefaced by an adjective so as to read "the services are supplied exclusively for and to ...."

The statutory focus under §ll(2)(e) is on the contractual supply of services, not on non-contractual benefits. It is the foreign client to which the composite expression "for or to a person" relates. The statute is not in its terms concerned with whether, and if so, how the supply might affect other persons. Had Parliament intended to impose a separate benefit test calling for a comparative assessment of who might benefit from the content of particular advertisements, it could be expected to have said so explicitly rather than leaving it for implication. Had Parliament intended to exclude zero-rating wherever a New Zealand resident would benefit or might benefit from the advertisement (for example as a result of sales to readers of the newspapers) it would surely have said so. On a straightforward reading of §ll(2)(e) it is sufficient if the services are supplied for and to an overseas person, whatever benefits might probably or might conceivably accrue subsequently to others.

RESULT. The Court being unanimous the appeal is allowed, the orders made in the High Court are quashed and the question posed in the case stated, namely whether the Commissioner acted incorrectly in excluding from zero-rated supplies in the amended assessment of 22 March 1990 advertising undertaken by Wilson & Horton for persons who were not resident in New Zealand at the time of supply, is answered in the affirmative.

The global-territorial distinction may not be too significant in an island nation like New Zealand that can keep account of the international movement of goods. A similar approach, however, was adopted by the Republic of South Africa (RSA), whose businesses operate in contiguous and other geographically close countries. The RSA imposes VAT not on supplies made in RSA but on supplies by a vendor in the course of an "enterprise" conducted within or partly within the RSA.[9] It also taxes imports into the RSA.[10] Although worldwide supplies (a global approach) by an RSA business could be taxed, the scope of the VAT is not actually that broad. Foreign supplies by an RSA enterprise are not subject to the RSA VAT if the supplies are made through an operation (a branch or main business) outside the RSA. This reduction in asserted tax jurisdiction applies only if "the branch or main business can be separately identified, and an independent system of accounting is maintained by the concern in respect of the branch or main business."[11] For example, assume a business operating in the RSA has branches in Namibia and Zambia. The Namibian branch engages in significant sales activity there and maintains separate accounting records. The Zambia branch's supplies are too low to justify separate accounting. The Namibian supplies are not subject to the RSA VAT, but the South African Revenue Service could impose VAT on the RSA enterprise on sales in Zambia. If the Zambia supplies qualify as RSA exports, they will be

[9] Value-Added Tax Act No. 89 of 1991 [hereinafter RSA VAT], at §7(1).

[10] *Id.*

[11] *Id.* at proviso (ii) of §1 definition of enterprise.

zero-rated; otherwise, they are taxable at the standard VAT rate.[12] If the RSA enterprise sends an employee to perform services in Zambia, it may be more difficult to avoid the RSA VAT. The taxation of the importer of the services in Zambia depends on the rules governing imported services used or consumed there.[13]

The Australian GST basically is a territorial VAT, but it has a unique set of place of supply rules that makes it resemble a hybrid global/territorial system.[14] Like a territorial GST, a supply of goods is connected with Australia and therefore subject to tax or zero-rating if the goods are delivered or made available to the recipient in Australia, the goods are being removed from Australia, or the goods are being imported or installed or assembled in Australia. A supply of real property is connected with Australia if the real property or its related land is in Australia. Any other supply is connected with Australia if the thing (such as a service) is done in Australia or (resembling a global approach) the supplier makes the supply through an enterprise conducted in Australia.[15]

C. Origin or Destination Principle

1. In General

Whether a country defines the scope of its VAT as territorial or global, it must decide how to treat imports and exports. A country can define its jurisdiction to tax cross-border transactions under the origin or destination principle. Except for the remnants of the origin principle with respect to trade within the Commonwealth of Independent States (CIS) countries[16]

[12] See "South Africa: Place-of-Supply Rules," 16 *Int'l VAT Monitor* 140 (Mar./Apr. 2005).

[13] See the discussion of the reverse charge rules on imported services in section VI(C)(1).

[14] A New Tax System (Goods and Services Tax) Act 1999 [hereinafter Australian GST], §9–5. A supply of goods is connected with Australia if the goods are delivered or made available in Australia to the recipient of the supply, the goods are being removed from Australia, or the goods are being imported or installed or assembled in Australia. A supply of real property is connected with Australia if the real property or its related land is in Australia. Any other supply is connected with Australia if the thing (like a service) is done in Australia or the supplier makes the supply through an enterprise conducted in Australia. *Id.* at §9–25. A business or other activity apparently does not have to be conducted in Australia to be an enterprise, and therefore some supplies by a nonresident enterprise can be subject to the GST. See *id.* at §9–20 definition of an enterprise, which does not require that the business be conducted in Australia. Supplies of anything other than goods or real property that are not done in Australia are taxable only if the enterprise is carried on in Australia. *Id.* at §9–25(5). For this purpose, an enterprise is carried on in Australia if it is carried on through a permanent establishment (as defined in the Income Tax Act) or through a certain place that would be a permanent establishment if certain parts of the income tax definition of a permanent establishment did not apply. *Id.* at §9–25(6). Thus, supplies of services through a permanent establishment in Australia or services rendered in Australia appear to come within the scope of the GST, but most or all would be zero-rated.

[15] *Id.* at §9–25.

[16] The CIS countries are the Russian Federation and the former Soviet republics of Armenia, Azerbaijan, Belarus, Kazakhstan, Kyrgyzstan, Republic of Moldova, Tajikistan,

and the lack of complete zero-rating of the exports of goods by China,[17] all of the major countries of the world rely on the destination principle to define the scope of the VAT with respect to international transactions involving goods.[18] There is less consistency in the taxation of the international trade in services and intangibles.

Under the origin principle, VAT is imposed in the country of production, regardless of where the goods or services are consumed. Thus, imports are not taxed and exports bear tax on the full value of the exported items. As a result, there is no need for border tax adjustments. The VAT becomes a tax on domestic production of goods and the domestic rendition of services. On domestic consumption, the VAT component in the sales price and the VAT collected by the government will vary, depending on the amount of the value of the product added domestically and the value attributable to imports. This is particularly important if other countries rely on the destination principle to define the jurisdictional reach of the VAT and the country of production relies on the origin principle. For example, little revenue would be raised if a product is imported and only the value added by the retailer is included in the country's VAT base.

Under a pure destination principle, VAT is imposed on imports and rebated on exports. For this kind of VAT, the country imposing VAT must maintain "fiscal frontiers" (border tax adjustments). As implemented in most countries, under the destination principle, imports of most goods, imports of the value of services allocable to imported goods, and imports of some other services are taxed. The "other services" typically are services taxed under a "reverse charge" rule to a recipient who is not able to claim credit for tax on the import. For example, a university rendering exempt educational services that is denied credit for input VAT on domestic purchases may be taxed (under a reverse charge rule) on imports of architectural services to design a new building. In this way, the university is not encouraged to outsource those services to avoid non-creditable tax on architectural services obtained in the domestic market.

On the export side with a destination principle VAT, a country typically zero-rates

1. exports of most goods,
2. exports of services related to exported goods, and
3. exports of specified other services.

Turkmenistan, Ukraine, and Uzbekistan. CIS trade was formerly taxed on the origin basis but is now taxed on the destination basis, except for oil and gas exports. See OECD, Consumption Tax Trends 110–11 (2008).

17 See P. Chandra & C. Long, "VAT Rebates and Export Performance in China: Firm-Level Evidence," 102 *Journal of Public Economics* 13 (2013).

18 The EU has abandoned its goal of taxing transactions conducted within the EU under the origin principle. See Communication from the Commission to the European Parliament, the Council, and the European Economic and Social Committee on the future of VAT towards a simpler, more robust and efficient VAT system tailored to the single market, 4.1, COM (2011) 851 final, Brussels, June, 12, 2011.

TABLE 7.2. Example of destination and origin principles (inputs purchased domestically; 10% rate)

	Price	Destination principle	Origin pr.
Manufacturer's purchases from taxable supplier (taxable input)	4,000	+400	+400
Manufacturer's export sales	10,000*	00	+1,000
Less *input credit for tax on inputs*		–400	–400
Total tax to government		000	+600

* The total of sales made outside the country is $10,000. Under the origin principle, the value added within the country is taxable, resulting in $1,000 in VAT, consisting of $400 paid by the manufacturer's domestic supplier and $600 net paid by the manufacturer/exporter.

TABLE 7.3. Example of destination and origin principles (all inputs imported; 10% rate)

	Price	Destination principle	Origin pr.
Manufacturer imports its taxable inputs	4,000	400	00
Manufacturer exports its output	10,000	00	+600*
Less *input credit for tax on inputs*		–400	00
Total tax to government		000	+600

* The total of sales made outside the country is $10,000, but only the value added within the country is taxable, resulting in net $600 in VAT: no tax on imported inputs and $600 tax imposed on the $6,000 value added to the goods exported. A deemed credit must be provided so that the tax is not imposed on the value of the imports.

Notice that exports leave the country free of tax under the destination principle but bear tax only on the value added within the country under the origin principle.

As a result, the full value of goods and services consumed within the taxing jurisdiction is taxed, even if some of the taxable value is attributable to imported parts or the entire finished goods. Services rendered domestically also are taxed in full.

The origin and destination principles are illustrated in Tables 7.2 and 7.3. Table 7.2 is a company that purchases inputs domestically, manufactures goods, and exports all of its output. It is assumed that the VAT rate is 10%. Notice that the destination principle allows exports to leave the country free of tax and, in this example, treats exports like domestic sales.

2. Double Taxation of Consumer-to-Consumer Imports

The destination principle is designed to allocate tax jurisdiction to the country of consumption. The assumption and the typical result is that tax is not imposed more than once on the full value of final consumption.

However, if a consumer in one country exports used goods to a consumer in another country, and both countries rely on the destination principle, VAT may be imposed twice if the second country makes no allowance for the tax already paid to the first country and the first country fails to rebate any tax on the export by an unregistered consumer. The following EU case illustrates this problem of cross-border consumer-to-consumer transactions involving used goods. This case, but not the issue raised, may be limited to the EU because of an EU treaty principle that an import to a member state from another member state should not be taxed more heavily than a domestic supply of a similar product.

Staatssecretaris van Financïen v. Gaston Schul Douane-Expéditeur BV[19]

[The dispute relates to the amount of VAT imposed by the Netherlands on a consumer's import of a secondhand pleasure and sports boat that was purchased from a private person in France. The Netherlands tax authorities imposed VAT at the normal Dutch 18% rate on the purchase price of the boat. The boat was built in Monaco and taxed on import into France at 17.6% of its FF 269,571 value (FF 47,444.49).]

[T]he boat was sold to a Netherlands national residing in the Netherlands for FF 365 000, an amount which exceeded the price of the boat, including tax, at the time of its importation into France.

The [Dutch Regional Court of Appeal] ... took the view that ... the sum of the French VAT and the VAT payable on importation should not exceed the VAT charged in the Netherlands on a similar boat of equal value, net of tax, supplied to an individual on Netherlands territory. For that purpose the value on importation should be calculated by deducting the French VAT actually paid from the price on importation into the Netherlands; on that basis Netherlands VAT of 18 per cent should be calculated, and the French VAT paid should be deducted from the resulting amount.

[The Supreme Court of the Netherlands referred the following two questions to the ECJ for a preliminary ruling:]

'1. Where a Member State charges VAT on the importation, from another Member State, of a product which is supplied by a non-taxable (private) person, but does not charge VAT on the supply of similar products by a private person within its own territory, should that Member State, in order to prevent the tax from constituting internal taxation in excess of that imposed on similar domestic products as referred to in Article 95 of the Treaty[20] take

[19] Case 47/84, [1985] ECR1491, [1986] 1 CMLR 559 (ECJ 1985) [edited by the authors].

[20] Treaty of Rome, as revised by the Treaty of Amsterdam, May 1999, Art. 90 (ex Art. 95) provides: "No Member State shall impose, directly or indirectly, on the products of other

account of the amount of the VAT paid in the Member State of exportation that is still contained in the value of the product at the time of importation:

(a) in such a way that that amount is not included in the taxable amount for the purposes of VAT payable on importation and is in addition deducted from the VAT payable on importation, or else

(b) in such a way that that amount is deducted only from the VAT payable on importation?

2. How should the amount be calculated?'

In its first question the Hoge Raad [Supreme Court] asks essentially whether the residual part of the tax with which the imported goods are still burdened in the event of a sale by one private person to another must be taken into account solely in the calculation of the VAT payable on importation or also in determining the taxable amount. The second question is designed to ascertain how that residual part should be calculated.

The Commission states that the practical problems to be solved are in particular the following: by what method should account be taken of the VAT paid in another Member State without depriving the Member State of importation of tax revenue; how should the residual amount of tax contained in the purchase price be calculated; how can the authorities in the Member State of importation ascertain the rates of VAT applicable at the time of the initial purchase in the country of exportation; how should the amount of the residual tax contained in the sale price be calculated where different transactions have taken place in three or four different Member States; what form of proof should be required; what rule should be applied where the price of the second-hand goods is higher than the price of the goods new; and, lastly, should an exemption be provided for?

[The Commission's view was that if the goods increased in value while owned by the exporting private person, the exporting state should not refund any VAT and the importing state should tax only the difference between the import value and the original cost of the goods to the exporting seller. In other cases (when the value declined while owned by the exporting seller), the Commission's view was that the exporting state should refund to the exporter the tax based on the current value and the importing state should impose VAT on the same value.]

Those solutions can only be achieved by legislative means, that is to say by the amendment of the national laws concerning VAT payable on imports on the basis of a new Council Directive.

Member States any internal taxation of any kind in excess of that imposed directly or indirectly on similar domestic products. Furthermore, no Member State shall impose on the products of other Member States any internal taxation of such a nature as to afford indirect protection to other products."

[P]ending the adoption of a legislative solution, in charging VAT on imports account must be taken of the effect of Article 95 of the Treaty. It is therefore for the Court to lay down guidelines compatible with Article 95 of the Treaty, consistent with the general scheme of the Sixth Directive and sufficiently simple to be able to be applied in a uniform manner throughout the Member States.

The answer which must be given to the first question is therefore that where a Member State charges VAT on the importation, from another Member State, of goods supplied by a non-taxable person, but does not charge VAT on the supply by a private person of similar goods within its own territory, the VAT payable on importation must be calculated by taking into account the amount of VAT paid in the Member State of exportation which is still contained in the value of the product at the time of importation, in such a way that that amount is not included in the taxable amount and is in addition deducted from the VAT payable on importation.

The second question concerns the calculation of the residual part of the VAT paid in the Member State of exportation which is still contained in the value of the goods at the time of their importation.

The Netherlands and French Governments ... suggest that a rule should be applied whereby the tax charged in the exporting State is written off. To write off the tax on the basis of the useful life of the imported goods would be too uncertain to be acceptable, in view of the different practices in the various Member States and sectors concerned; therefore, an approach should be adopted similar to the system laid down in Article 20(2) of the Sixth Directive [VAT Directive, Art. 187] for adjustment of deductions in the case of capital goods which have been sold after being used. Such a system would involve writing off the goods over five years and would thus mean that the residual part of the VAT contained in the value of the imported goods would correspond to the VAT actually charged in the Member State of exportation less one-fifth per calendar year or part of a calendar year which had elapsed since the date on which the VAT was charged.

Schul considers that the amortization of the tax charged in the country of exportation will, in the majority of cases, be reflected by a reduction in the value of the goods. For that reason the residual part should in its view be calculated on the basis of the VAT rate applied in the Member State of exportation, provided that the resulting amount does not exceed the amount actually paid in that State. Where the value of the goods has increased, the residual amount will thus correspond to the amount actually paid.

Eventually, at the hearing, the Commission adopted the same opinion.

Having considered the various arguments, the Court shares that view. Any standard method, such as that suggested by the Netherlands and French Governments, would have the disadvantage of diverging

> too far from the rules of the Sixth Directive to be developed by judicial interpretation. Irrespective of its intrinsic merits, the method adopted by the [Dutch Regional Court of Appeal] stays close to those rules, whilst being practicable and observing the provisions of Article 95 of the Treaty.
>
> The method is consistent with Article 95 of the Treaty and the provisions of the Sixth Directive. It can be applied by the tax authorities without giving rise to serious practical difficulties since, in cases in which the value of the goods has decreased, the residual part of the tax that is still contained in that value at the time of importation is calculated by reducing the amount of VAT actually paid in the Member State of exportation by a percentage representing the proportion by which the goods have depreciated, whereas in cases in which the value of the goods has increased, that residual part simply corresponds to the amount of tax actually charged.
>
> In that connection it should be remembered that ... the burden of proving facts which justify the taking into account of the tax paid in the Member State of exportation that is still contained in the value of the goods on importation falls on the importer.

The result in this case may not be followed outside of the EU. Absent special legislation, it is likely that an import by a consumer from a consumer in the exporting country will be taxed at the full value on import, without reduction for any tax borne by the consumer in the country of export.

IV. Basic Place of Supply Rules for a Territorial, Destination Principle VAT

Most VAT regimes (territorial taxes) rely on the destination principle for their international transactions – exports are zero-rated and imports are taxed. Because the common structure is to limit input credits to acquisitions attributable to taxable supplies, zero-rated exports have to be treated as taxable supplies within the exporting country. Under most VATs, foreign sales of goods that are located outside the taxing jurisdiction at the time of sale are beyond the scope of the tax.[21] Consistent with

[21] If a nonresident sells goods or services within the taxing jurisdiction, under some VAT regimes, the sale may be treated as a foreign sale unless the nonresident seller conducts business within the country, the seller is registered for VAT purposes in the country, or the seller engages in activities for a short period of time and may otherwise avoid VAT liability. See Canadian Goods and Services tax, S.C. 1990, c. 45, §143(1). The last category covers nonresidents who charge admission to "a place of amusement, a seminar, an activity or an event." *Id.* at §143(l)(c). VAT paid on purchases attributable to these foreign supplies generally does not qualify for the input credit. The business making those purchases may be entitled to a refund of the tax paid in the foreign country. See, for example, Thirteenth Council Directive 86/560/EEC of 17 November 1986 on the

the destination principle, imports should be taxed. Whereas most VATs tax imports of goods, they generally tax only select imports of services. As a result, it is necessary to have rules to determine where a supply of goods and services occurs and where an import of services takes place. The EU changes in the rules governing the place of supply of services, discussed later, may prompt countries that follow the EU model VAT and countries with "Modern VATs" to follow the EU's lead.[22]

Supplies within the taxing country include supplies within the territorial boundaries of the country. Disputes may arise, for example, if a supply spans two countries[23] or occurs in territorial waters that extend beyond the limits recognized by neighboring countries or by international law.

The place of a supply of goods may depend in part on the terms of the supply. In the EU, if goods are to be delivered, the supply takes place where the goods are located when the shipment begins.[24] The location therefore can be altered by altering the place where the goods reside when they are shipped to the buyer. The UK VAT has a series of rules to determine the location of a supply of goods. If goods are not exported or imported, they are supplied in the United Kingdom if the goods are physically in the United Kingdom when supplied.[25] If the seller must install or assemble the goods, the supply takes place where the goods are installed or assembled.[26]

The following *RR Donnelley* case involves services rendered while goods are in a warehouse, raising a conflict between a rule taxing business-to-business services where the recipient is located and the rule taxing services connected with immovable property where the property is located.

harmonization of the laws of the Member States relating to turnover tax arrangements for the refund of value-added tax to taxable persons not established in Community territory [Official Journal L 326 of 21.11.1986].

22 For a discussion of "Modern VATs," see Chapter 1 (VI). Modern VATs are VAT regimes with tax bases much broader than those used in the EU and countries following the EU model.

23 How should the place of supply be determined for the construction, repair, and renovation of a bridge that connects two countries? In a contract covering a bridge over the Rodebach between Germany and the Netherlands, the two countries involved asked the European Council for authority to depart from the rules of the Sixth Directive and treat the construction site and the bridge after its completion as being on German territory. See COM (2005) 109 final, discussed in IBFD – EVD News: Terra/Kajus – 18 April 2005, p. 1.

24 See Council Directive 2006/112/EC of 28 November 2006 on the common system of value added tax (OJ L347, 11.12.2006, p. 1) [hereinafter VAT Directive], Art. 33. There are special rules, including those governing intra-Community supplies and supplies through distribution systems.

25 Value Added Tax Act 1994, ch. 23 (United Kingdom) [hereinafter VATA 1994], §7(2).

26 *Id.* at §7(3). There are additional rules governing sales involving other EU member states. *Id.* at §7(4)–(6). If a sale of goods is not governed by other rules and the goods are removed to or from the United Kingdom, the sale is located in the United Kingdom if they are removed from the United Kingdom and had not previously entered the United Kingdom. *Id.* at §7(7).

Minister Finansów v. RR Donnelley Global Turnkey Solutions Poland sp. z o.o.[27]

Judgment

Legal context

European Union law

Article 44 of the VAT Directive provides:

'The place of supply of services to a taxable person acting as such shall be the place where that person has established his business. However, if those services are provided to a fixed establishment of the taxable person located in a place other than the place where he has established his business, the place of supply of those services shall be the place where that fixed establishment is located. In the absence of such place of establishment or fixed establishment, the place of supply of services shall be the place where the taxable person who receives such services has his permanent address or usually resides.'

Article 47 of that directive provides:

'The place of supply of services connected with immovable property, including the services of experts and estate agents, the provision of accommodation in the hotel sector or in sectors with a similar function, such as holiday camps or sites developed for use as camping sites, the granting of rights to use immovable property and services for the preparation and coordination of construction work, such as the services of architects and of firms providing on-site supervision, shall be the place where the immovable property is located.'

[Polish law, omitted from this edited case, incorporates, in principle, sections 44 and 47 of the VAT Directive.]

The dispute in the main proceedings and the question referred for a preliminary ruling

As part of its business, RR provides to traders, who are subject to VAT and established in Member States other than the Republic of Poland, a complex service relating to the storage of goods. That service covers, inter alia, admission of the goods to a warehouse, placing them on the appropriate storage shelves, storing those goods, packaging the goods for customers and issuing, unloading and loading the goods. In addition, for certain contractual partners which are suppliers of goods to computer companies, the service at issue also includes the repackaging, into individual sets, of materials supplied in collective packaging. The provision of storage space is only one of several elements of the logistics process which RR manages. In addition, for the

[27] Case C-155/12 (Judgment of the ECJ 2013) [edited by the authors].

purpose of the service at issue, RR uses its own employees and packaging, the costs of which form an element of the consideration for the service. RR's contractual partners which order the storage services do not have established businesses in Poland and do not have a fixed establishment within Polish territory.

On 25 March 2010, RR submitted an application for individual interpretation concerning the determination of the place of the supply of a complex storage service for the purpose of calculating VAT. According to RR, the place where a supply of services of the kind which it provides is carried out must be the place where the service recipient is established. Consequently, RR argues, the services which it offers should not be subject to VAT in Poland. More specifically, the complex service relating to the storage of goods cannot be regarded as a service connected with immovable property as the intention of the parties is not to grant the recipients of the service at issue the right to use the storage area, but that service merely involves keeping the goods in an unaltered state and providing all additional services which are related to such a service.

In its individual interpretation, issued on 8 June 2010, the Polish tax authority, represented by the Minister Finansów, stated, however, that the services relating to the storage of goods were in the nature of services connected with immovable property and therefore came within [Article 47 of the VAT Directive]. In those circumstances, the place where those services were supplied was the place where the immovable property used for warehousing purposes was located.

RR brought an action against that individual interpretation, arguing that the interpretation . . . supported by the Minister Finansów departed from the wording and interpretation of Article 47 of the VAT Directive, that it was contrary to the principle of consistency of European Union law, and that it called into question the uniform application of that law in the Member States. In accordance with the provisions of that directive, the supplies of services connected with immovable property were, RR submitted, services which concerned such immovable property. That, it stated, was precisely not the case with regard to the supply of services at issue in the main proceedings.

By judgment of 25 November 2010, the . . . Regional Administrative Court, Łódź upheld that action, finding that the services provided by RR did not constitute a supply of services connected with immovable property. In particular, that court took the view that the services in question could not be categorised as services consisting in 'the granting of rights to use immovable property' in so far as the subject matter of the contracts concluded between RR and its contractual partners was the holding and active management of goods stored in RR's warehouses. Customers were given no right to use the immovable property in any manner whatsoever. The conclusive element of a supply of services such as that at issue in the main proceedings was, that court found, the handling of the goods in such a way as to enable the customer to market his goods in the most effective manner possible. In addition, that supply of services did not have a 'sufficiently direct connection with immovable property' within the meaning of the Court's case-law (Case C-166/05 *Heger* [2006] ECR I-7749), and therefore could not come under Article 47 of the VAT Directive. Consequently, when the services at issue are supplied to customers established outside Polish territory, they should not be subject to tax in Poland.

In support of the appeal on a point of law which he brought against that judgment before the Supreme Administrative Court, the Minister Finansów argued that, in the present case, the storage service is the principal and predominant service, as the other services offered by RR arise from the nature of the principal service. The close connection between that service and the immovable property specifically designated as a warehouse is, he argues, undeniable. Consequently, the place where that service is taxed must be determined in accordance with [Article 47 of the VAT Directive] and is therefore located in Poland.

In those circumstances, the Supreme Administrative Court decided to stay the proceedings and to refer the following questions to the Court of Justice for a preliminary ruling:

The referring court asks, in essence, whether Article 47 of the VAT Directive must be interpreted as meaning that a supply of complex storage services, ... constitutes a supply of services connected with immovable property within the terms of that article.

In order to provide a useful answer to the referring court, and having regard to the fact that the transaction covered by the question referred for a preliminary ruling consists of several elements, it is necessary to examine, in the first place, whether that transaction is to be regarded as consisting of a single supply or of several distinct and independent supplies which must be assessed separately from the point of view of VAT.

According to the Court's case-law, in certain circumstances several formally distinct services, which could be supplied separately and thus give rise, in turn, to taxation or exemption, must be considered to be a single transaction when they are not independent (Case C-425/06 *Part Service* [2008] ECR I-897, paragraph 51, and Case C-392/11 *Field Fisher Waterhouse* [2012] ECR I-0000, paragraph 15).

In this context, the Court has held that a supply must be regarded as a single supply where two or more elements or acts supplied by the taxable person are so closely linked that they form, objectively, a single, indivisible economic supply, which it would be artificial to split (see, to that effect, Case C-41/04 *Levob Verzekeringen and OV Bank* [2005] ECR I-9433, paragraph 22, and *Field Fisher Waterhouse*, paragraph 16).

That is also the case where one or more supplies constitute a principal supply and the other supply or supplies constitute one or more ancillary supplies which share the tax treatment of the principal supply. In particular, a supply must be regarded as ancillary to a principal supply if it does not constitute for customers an end in itself but a means of better enjoying the principal service supplied (see, to that effect, Case C-349/96 *CPP* [1999] ECR I-973, paragraph 30; Joined Cases C-497/09, C-499/09, C-501/09 and C-502/09 *Bog and Others* [2011] ECR I-1457, paragraph 54; and *Field Fisher Waterhouse*, paragraph 17).

Although it is for the national court to determine whether the taxable person supplies a single service in a particular case and to make all definitive findings of fact in that regard, the Court may, however, provide it with any guidance as to interpretation that will be helpful to it in disposing of the case (see, to that effect, *Levob Verzekeringen and OV Bank*, paragraph 23, and Case C-334/10 *X* [2012] ECR I-0000, paragraph 24).

[According to the advocate-general, in] her Opinion, in the main proceedings, the storage of the goods must, in principle, be considered to constitute the principal supply and that the reception, placement, issuing, unloading and loading of the goods amount to only ancillary supplies. For customers, these latter supplies do not, in principle, constitute an end in themselves, but are transactions which enable those customers better to enjoy the principal service.

However, with regard to the repackaging of the goods supplied in packaging in order to create individual sets, it should be added that this service, which is provided only to certain customers, must be considered to constitute an independent principal supply in all cases in which that repackaging is not absolutely necessary to ensure better storage of the goods at issue.

Having regard to the fact that it is not apparent from the file before the Court that, by its question, the referring court has referred to this second scenario, for the remainder of the reasoning it is necessary to take the view that the complex storage service at issue in the main proceedings constitutes one single transaction, the principal service of which comprises the storage of goods.

In those circumstances, it is necessary, secondly, to determine the location where that single transaction is deemed to be carried out.

In this regard, it must be stated that the VAT Directive ... [contains] both general rules for determining the place of taxation of such a service and particular provisions relating to the supply of specific services.

Accordingly, before being able to decide whether, in a given situation, a specific service supplied comes within Articles 44 and 45 of the VAT Directive, which set out general rules, it is necessary to deal with the question whether that situation is governed by one of the particular provisions set out in Articles 46 to 59b of that directive (see, by analogy with the Sixth Directive, Case C-327/94 *Dudda* [1996] ECR I-4595, paragraph 21).

In the present case, it is necessary to examine whether a storage service such as that at issue in the main proceedings is capable of coming within the scope of Article 47 of the VAT Directive.

With regard to the wording of that Article 47, ... it is clear that the storage services do not form part of the services expressly listed in Article 47, with the result that no useful conclusion for the purpose of answering the question referred can be drawn from the wording of Article 47.

However, it is apparent from the Court's case-law that only supplies of services which have a sufficiently direct connection with immovable property come under Article 47 of the VAT Directive (see, to that effect, *Inter-Mark Group*, paragraph 30). Such a connection is, moreover, characteristic of all supplies of services listed in that article (see, as regards Article 9(2)(a) of the Sixth Directive, *Heger*, paragraph 24).

As far as the concept of 'immovable property' is concerned, it should be borne in mind that the Court has already held that one of the essential characteristics of such property is that it is attached to a specific part of the territory of the Member State in which it is located (see, to that effect, *Heger*, paragraph 20).

Consequently, as the Advocate General noted ..., in order for a supply of services to come within the scope of Article 47 of the VAT Directive, that supply must be connected to expressly specific immovable property.

However, in so far as a large number of services are connected in one way or another with immovable property, it is, in addition, necessary that the supply of services should relate to the immovable property itself. That is the case, inter alia, where expressly specific immovable property must be considered to be a constituent element of a supply of services, in that it constitutes a central and essential element thereof (see, to that effect, *Heger*, paragraph 25).

It is clear that the supplies of services listed in Article 47 of the VAT Directive, which concern the use or the development of immovable property, or the management, including the operation and evaluation, of such property, are characterised by the fact that the immovable property itself constitutes the subject matter of the service.

It follows that a storage service such as that at issue in the main proceedings, which cannot be regarded as relating to the development, management or evaluation of immovable property, is capable of coming within the scope of Article 47 only on the condition that the recipient of that service is given a right to use all or part of expressly specific immovable property.

If ... it were to transpire that the recipients of such a storage service have, for example, no right of access to the part of the property where their goods are stored or that the immovable property on which or in which those goods are to be stored does not constitute a central and essential element of the supply of services – this being a matter for the national courts to determine –, a supply of services such as that at issue in the main proceedings could not come within the scope of Article 47 of the VAT Directive.

Consequently, the answer to the question referred is that Article 47 of the VAT Directive must be interpreted as meaning that the supply of a complex storage service, comprising admission of goods to a warehouse, placing them on the appropriate storage shelves, storing them, packaging them, issuing them, unloading and loading them, comes within the scope of that article only if the storage constitutes the principal service of a single transaction and only if the recipients of that service are given a right to use all or part of expressly specific immovable property.

What is the location of a broker's intermediation services related to the sale of a yacht when the buyer and seller reside in different countries? In one case in the EU, the broker in the Netherlands arranged a sale of a yacht located in and owned by a person in France to a buyer in the Netherlands. The sale was executed in France, where the yacht was located when the transport of the yacht began. The ECJ held that the broker's intermediation services took place where the transaction underlying the supply was carried out, not where the broker or customer resided.[28]

V. Goods Involved in International Trade

A. Imports of Goods

Under the destination principle employed almost universally, as discussed earlier, imports of goods and imports of some services are taxed. Imports of goods are taxable,[29] whether they are imported by VAT-registered persons or consumers. Goods generally are taxed when they "enter" the country for customs purposes. In practice, this means that the VAT is collected by customs at the border or at the post office when goods enter by post.[30] Services linked to the import of goods are taxed at the same time. Thus, insurance and freight generally are included in the value of taxable, imported goods.[31]

Some countries permit select importers to defer VAT on imported goods until they file VAT returns for the tax period that includes the date

[28] Case C-68/03, *Staatssecretaris van Financiën v. D. lipjes* (ECJ Judgment 2004).

[29] An import of money generally is not treated as an import of goods. See Australian GST, *supra* note 14, at §13–5(3).

[30] See generally *id.* at §33–15(1).

[31] The valuation rules are discussed in Chapter 8.

of the import. The deferral privilege varies by country. New Zealand has an optional deferred payment scheme that requires covered importers to pay duty within twenty-one working days after the end of the importer's billing cycle.[32] Likewise, in Australia,[33] a tax-compliant person, if approved for deferred payment, must pay GST on taxable imports "on or before the 21st day after the end of the month in which the liability for the GST arose."[34] The commissioner may refuse the application in specified circumstances, including the case in which the application is by a person convicted of a tax offense or the applicant owes prior taxes.[35]

Consistent with the WTO rules that prohibit discrimination against imports from member WTO countries, VAT legislation in a WTO-compliant country exempts an import of a good if that good is exempt or zero-rated when supplied domestically.[36] Thus, if the domestic sale of rice is zero-rated, the import of rice is not taxed. Contrary to this practice, Peru has taxed some imports that are not taxed if supplied domestically.[37] Goods placed in a bonded warehouse or imported directly into a duty-free zone may not be treated as imported for VAT purposes until they are withdrawn from the bonded warehouse or withdrawn from the duty-free zone for domestic consumption.[38]

B. Exports of Goods

Consistent with the destination principle, most countries zero-rate the exports of goods and typically, but not universally, grant quick refunds of excess input credits attributable to the exported goods.[39] The zero-rating has been the source of fraud significant in the EU. Some countries extend the zero-rating to the immediate prior stage on sales to exporters.[40]

Although the place of supplies on board transport vehicles is generally based on the port of departure, this rule does not apply when there are

[32] See Tax Information Bulletin Vol. 9, No. 11 (New Zealand).

[33] Australian GST, *supra* note 14, at §33–15(1)(b).

[34] A New Tax System (Goods and Services Tax) Regulations 1999 [hereinafter Australian GST Regs], Reg. 33–15.07.

[35] *Id.* at Reg. 33–15.04.

[36] See Marrakesh Agreement Establishing the World Trade Organization, Apr. 15, 1994,1867 U.N.T.S. 154.

[37] See Law 27, 614, effective December 30, 2001, discussed in 13 *Int'l VAT Monitor*, 226 (May/June 2002).

[38] See, for example, RSA VAT, *supra* note 9, at §13(1).

[39] Some countries require the excess credits, even if attributable to exported goods, to be carried forward to future periods and used to offset future output tax liability. China is one example of this approach. In many developing countries refunds are, in practice, not paid or are delayed, even if the law requires prompt payment.

[40] Those countries may impose some restrictions to reduce the opportunities for fraud. See the practice in Italy and Turkey; 2005 Financial Bill Law No. 311 of 30 December 2004 (Italy), discussed by A. P. Deiana, "Italy: Zero-rated Supplies Preceding Export," 16 *Int'l VAT Monitor*, 136 (Mar./Apr. 2005); B. Y. Soydan, "Simplifying Procedure for VAT Refunds in Turkey," 13 *Int'l VAT Monitor*, Vol. 13 21 (Jan./Feb. 2002).

stops outside the EU.[41] The *Antje Köhler* case involved sales aboard a cruise ship that began and ended its journey within the EU but also stopped outside the EU. The ECJ ruled that sales made during the stops outside the EU were not taxable in the EU.

VI. Services Involved in International Trade

A. Services Beyond the Scope of Tax in User's Jurisdiction

The place of supply rules developed in the EU (revised as discussed in section VI[D]) and adopted by many countries outside the EU locate the supply of many services at the supplier's place of business. This rule encouraged businesses to provide services through a place of business outside the country or countries in which they rendered services, so that the services were zero-rated exports from the country of their seat and the services were not taxed in the country where the customers used the services. For example, a South African company provided cable television services to subscribers in Uganda. The Uganda place of supply rule located the services where the services were rendered. The Uganda court held that the services supplied by the South African parent were rendered at the supplier's place of business outside Uganda and therefore were not taxable under the Ugandan VAT.[42] The Ugandan VAT law was amended after the tax year in question to provide that the supply takes place where the customer receives the signal or service.[43]

B. Imports of Services

Because of the intangible nature of most services, making them difficult to identify and tax, early VAT systems taxed only limited categories of imported services. These VAT systems imposed tax mainly on imported services attributable to imported goods by including the value of those services as part of the value of the imported goods. Even today, countries such as Australia define the value of a taxable import as the customs value plus certain taxes and duties, plus, to the extent not included in customs value, insurance and the amount paid or payable for transportation of goods to their place of consignment in Australia. As services became a larger proportion of the domestic economies of developed countries in particular, and domestic firms complained about the unfair competition from untaxed services from offshore providers, governments expanded the taxation of imported services.

[41] VAT Directive, *supra* note 24, at Art. 37.
[42] *Multi-Choice (U) Ltd. v. Uganda Revenue Authority*, Application No. TAT 1 of 2000 (Tax Appeals Tribunal Uganda).
[43] See Finance Act 1999, §17(5) (Uganda).

Much of the loss of revenue and competitive inequities from the non-taxation of imported services occurred in two situations:

1. Services imported by consumers
2. Services imported by businesses rendering exempt services because they could not recover VAT paid on comparable services purchased domestically

As a result, many countries started taxing services imported by these two groups. For administrative reasons, these recipients of imported services were taxed under a reverse charge rule.[44]

In *H.M. Revenue and Customs v. Zurich Insurance Company*,[45] PricewaterhouseCoopers AG in Switzerland (PwC), with its head office in Switzerland, rendered consultancy services related to the installation of SAP financial accounting software through its branch offices. The company's branch in the United Kingdom was a fixed establishment in the United Kingdom. The services were rendered by the UK staff (60%) and by PwC's Swiss staff in the United Kingdom (40%). The tribunal concluded that the supply took place at the company's home office in Switzerland, where the contract was entered into. On appeal, the court held that the services took place at the company's establishment in the United Kingdom, where the actual services were performed.

C. Exports of Services

Although there is substantial consistency among countries with a VAT in the zero-rating of exports of goods, there is a lack of consistency with respect to exports of services. The opportunity for abuse exists with respect to exported services because it is so difficult to audit, months later, whether services were in fact exported. In the EU, except for the special rules discussed in the next subsection, many exported services are zero-rated (exempt with the right to claim credit for tax on inputs). For example, zero-rated exports of services include services linked to a taxable person's export business;[46] services on specified goods to be exported;[47] and services related to certain foreign-going vessels and aircraft.[48] Some services rendered by intermediaries, which relate to transactions carried out outside the Community, are zero-rated.[49]

[44] See, for example, New Zealand's reverse charge rule to tax recipients of some imported services. The imported services are treated as supplied in New Zealand. NZ GST, *supra* note 6, at §§5B & 8(4B).

[45] [2006] EWHC 593 (Chancery Div).

[46] VAT Directive, *supra* note 24, at Art. 164(1)(b). A member state must consult with the VAT Committee to obtain this treatment.

[47] *Id*. at Art. 146(1)(d) and (e).

[48] *Id*. at Art. 148(c),(d),(f) and (g).

[49] *Id*. at Art. 153. A number of other transactions relating to international trade are zero-rated under chapter 10 of the VAT Directive. *Id*. at Arts. 154–166.

In Australia, services supplied to persons not established in Australia for consumption outside Australia are zero-rated (GST-free in the language of the Australian GST).[50] New Zealand zero-rates a list of exported services.[51]

In some cases, it is not clear whether a supply is of goods or services, and the classification may determine whether the supply is taxable or zero-rated. The following Canadian Tax Court case illustrates the link between the classification of a supply as a supply of services or a supply of goods, and its treatment as a taxable domestic supply or a zero-rated export.

Robertson v. The Queen[52]

The Appellant [taxpayer] ... resides in Yellowknife, Northwest Territories ("NWT"), [where he] ... operated a taxidermy business under the name "Robertson's Taxidermy."

In his taxidermy business, the Appellant receives from a hunter a bird, pelt, hide, skin, head, antlers etc. (the "Wildlife Part"). The Appellant performs certain processes to preserve the Wildlife Part and, where the customer requests, proceeds to prepare the Wildlife Part for display as a life-size mount, a rug mount, shoulder mount or an antler or skull mount (the "Processed Wildlife Part").

Once the Hunter kills the animal, ... he or she contacts the Appellant. The animal is then either shipped to or picked up by the Appellant.

Upon receipt of the animal and deposit, the Appellant fleshes out the animal skin and usually sends the hide to be tanned and processed by an unrelated, arm's length third party. Upon completion, the tanner returns the tanned head and hide to the Appellant and invoices the Appellant for the services rendered plus the applicable GST. The Appellant may also tan a hide himself if the animal is small.

The Appellant either creates or purchases the mannequins upon which the head and hide are mounted. Glass eyes, teeth, etc. are also utilized in the taxidermy process.

Once the Processed Wildlife Part is completed, it is then crated. For an "export sale," a U.S. transportation carrier is retained to ship the Processed Wildlife Part to the non-resident U.S. customer.

[50] Australian GST, *supra* note 14, at §38–190. See GSTR 2003/7, Goods and Services Tax: What do the expressions "directly connected with goods or real property" and "a supply of work physically performed on goods" mean for the purposes of subsection 38–190 of *A New Tax System (Goods and Services Tax) Act 1999* (Australia ATO)?

[51] The zero-rated services include services supplied directly in connection with (a) land outside New Zealand, (b) certain moveable personal property outside New Zealand when the services are performed, (c) goods supplied from outside New Zealand to a destination outside New Zealand, (d) services supplied to a nonresident who is outside New Zealand when the services are performed, and (e) several others. NZ GST, *supra* note 6, at 11 A(l).

[52] 2002 Can LII 910 (T.C.C.) [edited by the authors].

In order to export from the NWT the non-edible parts of a dead animal, the parts must meet the definition of a "manufactured product" under the *Wildlife Act*. The *Wildlife Act* defines a "manufactured product' as wildlife that is:

(a) prepared for use as or in an article to be sold as a garment, or
(b) preserved or prepared by a tanning or taxidermy process.

Counsel [for the Crown] submitted that at all material times, the Appellant did not supply tangible personal property to non-residents for export which would constitute a "zero-rated supply," by virtue of Schedule VI, Part V, section 7 of the [GST provisions of the Excise Tax Act] but rather provided a [taxable domestic] service related to tangible property located in Canada pursuant to sections 7(a) and 7(e).

He was asked to describe the process that he uses with respect to the polar bear mount. He said that they receive the hide, they remove the meat, fat and flesh. They wash it two to three times. The hide is salted and this requires 50 to 100 pounds of salt. This cures the skin and removes moisture. When the skin is dried it is perfectly preserved. The hide is then sent to the tannery where it may stay for six months. After its return from the tannery they soak it again. This loosens up the fibres and it can be restretched to its natural size. The article is then placed into the freezer.

He researches for the proper supply company to obtain the mannequin. When it is received it has to be altered. It has to fit the skin perfectly. The teeth and eyes are put into the article. The skin is stretched over the mannequin. They use approximately 20 pounds of glue to affix it to the mannequin and put it in place. The skin is then sewed up and the mount is groomed. It takes two to three weeks to dry before the finishing work is done.

He referred to a typical invoice ... [that] did not separate labour from the other items. The base and habitat are listed separately. The tanning is built into the price of the mount. Freight and crating are separate unless there is a flat rate agreed upon beforehand.

ANALYSIS AND DECISION. In the case at bar there is one main issue and there are several auxiliary issues. The main issue in this case is whether or not ... the Appellant was supplying a service in his taxidermy business (a contract for services) or whether the contract was for the sale of goods. In essence, counsel for the Appellant said that the taxidermist entered into a contract for the sale of goods whereas counsel for the Respondent says that in essence the taxidermist provided his services and that was what he was paid for.

[T]he Court is satisfied that the hunters in the case at bar did not transfer ownership of the Wildlife Part to the Appellant. Rather, the Appellant assumed possession of that Wildlife Part on behalf of the hunter. There is no doubt that in accordance with subsection 49(3) of the *Wildlife Business Regulations*, the holder of a tanner or a taxidermist licence obtains a proprietory interest, akin to a lien, against the Wildlife Part and was entitled to recover his costs by selling the Wildlife Part, if it was not picked up for a period of one year. When the Appellant returns the Wildlife Part to the hunter, in its final form, he is not providing "property" within the meaning of subsection 123(1) of the *Act*, to the hunter, at least in respect of that part of the final product which is composed of the Wildlife Part.

As agreed to in the Statement of Facts, the total cost of basic supplies and materials accounted for approximately 15 to 25 per cent of the total cost of the processed Wildlife Part to the customer. The remainder of the consideration was in the labour required to create the finished article.

In the case at bar, property in the total cost of the basic supplies and materials was transferred to the hunter as an addition to the Wildlife Part.

[O]f use in the present case, is a quotation from [*Crown Tire Service Ltd. v. R.* (1983), [1984] 2 F.C. 219 (Fed. T.D.)] ... in reference to the text, *Benjamin's Sale of Goods (London, 1974)*, in considering the distinction between a contract for the sale of goods and a contract for work and materials, where it is stated:

Where work is to be done on the land of the employer or on a chattel belonging to him, which involves the use or affixing of materials belonging to the person employed, the contract will ordinarily be one for work and materials, the property in the latter passing to the employer by accession and not under any contract of sale.

This Court is satisfied that the situation in the case at bar fits within the general principle as referred to in *Benjamin, supra*. There can be no doubt in the Court's mind that in the present case that the hunter retained ownership of the dead animal part throughout the process....

Counsel for the Respondent argued that ... [this case] dealt with the provision of services rather than a contract for the sale of goods. To that end he highlighted the high degree of talent possessed by the taxidermist in this case and the reputation that he enjoyed in the industry. Therefore, it was his position that customers hired the Appellant for his talent, skill and artistic ability, not for the materials that were incidentally provided during his service.

The [Crown argued that the] cost of the material that the Appellant affixed to the Wildlife Part was insignificant compared to the total cost that a hunter expends to obtain the final amount. The value of the trophy was derived principally from the Wildlife Part and not from the materials that the Appellant affixed to the part during the taxidermy process. Consequently, he argued, that the substance of the contract between the Appellant and the non-resident hunter was clearly one for services, not one for the sale of goods.

The Minister's administrative policy, with respect to section 7 of Part V of Schedule VI of the *Act*, provides that a service will be "in respect of" tangible personal property if the service is "physically performed on the tangible personal property" or if the service "enhances the value of the property." Again this interpretation is not binding on the Court, but it is indicative of the Minister's treatment of the matter.

[The] Court is satisfied that in accordance with subsection 7(e) of Part V of Schedule VI of the *Act*, during the appropriate period of time, the Appellant made a supply of a [taxable taxidermy] service to a non-resident person, which was, "a service in respect of tangible personal property that was situated in Canada at the time the service is performed" and consequently this subsection prevents the supply of that service from being zero-rated.

The appeal is therefore dismissed, with costs, and the Minister's assessments are confirmed.

D. EU's Revised Rules on Services

The EU recognized the significant changes in the pattern and level of services in developed nations, especially services rendered outside the country where a business may be established. The EU also abandoned its goal to implement the origin principle for supplies within the Community. The high level of fraud and lost VAT revenue no doubt contributed to the EU's focus on the international trade in services. The VAT Directive, as amended, revised the rules governing services. Regulations further clarified the place of supply rules included in the "VAT package," generally effective January 1, 2010.[53] This subsection covers those general rules. Telecommunications, broadcasting, and electronically supplied services, discussed later in this chapter, received special treatment.

The basic place of supply rules governing services are straightforward. Services rendered in business-to-business transactions (B2B) are taxed where the customer is located. Services rendered in business-to-consumer transactions (B2C) are taxed where the supplier is established. For this purpose, the regulations define the place where a business is established, where a fixed establishment is located, and when the business's location

[53] The so-called VAT package included Directives adopted at the ECOFIN meeting on January 12, 2008. The Directive discussed in this section is Council Directive 2008/8/EC of 12 February 2008 amending VAT Directive, *supra* note 24 [hereinafter Directive 2008/8/EC]. The regulations referred to most often in this section were issued later. See Council Implementing Regulation (EU) No. 282/2011 of 15 March 2011 laying down implementing measures for VAT Directive, *supra* note 24, OJ L77, 23.3.2011, p. 1 [hereinafter Reg. No. 282/2011], as amended by Council Regulation (EU) No. 967/2012 of 9 October 2012, as regards the special schemes for non-established taxable persons supplying telecommunications services, broadcasting services, or electronic services to non-taxable persons [hereinafter Reg. No. 967/2012]. For an in-depth examination of the place of supply rules in the EU, see the annual publication, B. Terra & J. Kajus, A GUIDE TO THE EUROPEAN VAT DIRECTIVES 2013 (IBFD 2013).

is respected for VAT purposes.[54] Many of the exceptions to the basic rules, discussed later, locate services where use and enjoyment take place. Most of those rules took effect January 1, 2010.[55]

1. Business-to-Business Services

Generally, in B2B transactions between taxable persons, the services take place where the recipient is established.[56] Even if a VAT-registered supplier also makes non-taxable supplies, for purposes of the place of supply rules, the supplier is treated as a taxable person with respect to all of the services rendered to him.[57] Any supplier who is a legal person (such as a corporation), whether or not a taxable person, is treated as a taxable person for purposes of these rules.[58]

2. Business-to-Consumer Services

Generally, in business-to-consumer (B2C) services within the EU, the services take place where the supplier established his business.[59] The services take place at the supplier's fixed establishment if the services are rendered from a fixed establishment that is not where the supplier established his business.[60]

3. Special Rules for Particular Situations

The Directive on the place where services are rendered lists ten cases that may or may not come within these general rules. Supplies of services by intermediaries acting for another person take place according to the general rules discussed in subsections (1) and (2).[61] Services linked to real property, such as hotel accommodations and services provided on a construction site, take place where the property is located.[62] While the transportation of passengers is a service located according to the distance covered,[63] intra-Community freight services rendered to non-taxable persons take place at the point of departure.[64]

Cultural, sporting, education, entertainment, and similar services take place where they are physically performed.[65] This rule applies when the

[54] Reg. No. 967/2012, *supra* note 53, at Arts. 10–13.
[55] See Directive 2008/8/EC, *supra* note 53, at Art. 2.
[56] See VAT Directive, *supra* note 24 (as amended by Directive 2008/8/EC) at Art. 44.
[57] See *id.* at Art. 43(1).
[58] See *id.* at Art. 43(2).
[59] See *id.* at Art. 45.
[60] See *id.*
[61] See *id.* at Art. 46.
[62] See *id.* at Art. 47.
[63] See *id.* at Art. 48.
[64] See *id* at Art. 50.
[65] See *id.* at Art. 53.

essential characteristic of the service is an admission to an event on payment in money or submission of a ticket.[66] Restaurant and catering services not rendered aboard modes of transport also take place where they are physically performed.[67]

4. Rules to Avoid Double Tax or Non-Tax

Member states have the option to change the place of supply for certain services.[68] For example, they can treat services physically performed within their territory (under the literal application of the place of supply rules) as taking place outside the Community if the effective use and enjoyment of the services occur outside the Community.[69] They also can treat services located outside the Community (under the literal application of the place of supply rules) as taking place in the EU if effective use and enjoyment takes place in the Community.[70] On the ECJ's sanction of a cross-border leasing scheme designed to take advantage of differences in the place of supply rules between two EU member states (with the result that the transaction was taxed nowhere), see *RBS Deutschland Holdings* discussed in Chapter 10 (II).

E. The OECD Project on Place of Supply for Cross-Border Services and Intangibles

According to a 2005 Organisation for Economic Co-Operation and Development report, consumption taxes should be imposed where goods or services are consumed, but for administrative reasons, countries may rely on proxies to determine where goods and services are consumed.[71] Internationally traded services and intangibles should be taxed in the

[66] See Reg. No. 282/2011, *supra* note 53, at Art. 32. This rule applies to ancillary services at the event, such as the use of the cloakroom. See *id.* at Art. 33.

[67] See VAT Directive, *supra* note 24 (as amended by Directive 2008/8/EC) at Art. 55. If rendered on board a ship, train, or aircraft, the restaurant or catering services take place where the passenger transport departs. *Id.* at Art. 57. Restaurant and catering services, although broadly defined, are limited to supplies where the services predominate. See Reg. No. 282/2011, *supra* note 53, at Art. 6. According to this regulation, the supply of prepared or unprepared food or beverages, or both, constitute restaurant and catering services if they represent only a component of the supply in which services predominate. The regulations define restaurant and catering services rendered aboard modes of transport that cross borders. *Id.* at Arts. 35–37.

[68] This special rule applies to services governed by VAT Directive, Arts. 44, 45, 56, and 59, as amended by Directive 2008/8/EC, *supra* note 53. They include B2B and B2C services covered by the general rules, short-term leases of transport, and services to non-taxable persons outside the Community.

[69] See VAT Directive, *supra* note 24 (as amended by Directive 2008/8/EC) at Art. 59a(a).

[70] See *id.* at Art. 59a(b). But see *id.* Art. 59b, applying to certain telecommunications, and radio and television broadcasting services.

[71] OECD, The Application of Consumption Taxes to International Trade in Services and Intangibles: Progress Report and Draft Principles (2005), ¶¶17 and 18.

jurisdiction of consumption.[72] On the basis of the principle that final consumers should bear the economic costs of VAT, according to the report, taxable businesses should not bear, as an economic cost, the VAT on goods and services used in making taxable supplies.[73]

In 2013, the OECD Committee on Fiscal Affairs, Working Party No. 9 on Consumption Taxes, as part of its project on the establishment of international VAT/GST guidelines, issued a draft for comments that includes

1. guidelines on the place of taxation for cross-border supplies of services and intangibles to businesses that have establishments in more than one jurisdiction, and
2. guidelines to determine the place of taxation for cross-border business-to-business supplies of services and intangibles.[74]

The working party intends to develop guidelines for cross-border supplies of services and intangibles to final consumers.

VII. Special Treatment for Particular Industries

A. Telecommunications, Broadcasting, and Electronically Supplied Services

1. Telecom and Broadcast Services

The international telecommunications,[75] broadcasting, and electronic services industries raise special problems. Electronic commerce, including electronically supplied services, conducted with the use of telecommunications and similar networks, raises related problems. They all can create competitive inequities and raise difficulties in identifying the place where services are consumed. For all of these services, tax administration and taxpayer compliance costs narrow the available choices. Restrictions on a nation's ability to collect tax from foreign sellers or to identify and collect tax from local consumers may require simple rules that foster voluntary compliance.

Telecommunication involves a wide range of services provided by transmitting and receiving signals and other data by radio, optical, and electromagnetic means, including access to the Internet and other information networks. Telecommunication services can be provided without

[72] *Id.* at ¶19.

[73] *Id.* at ¶20.

[74] Committee on Fiscal Affairs, Working Party No. 9 on Consumption Taxes, OECD International VAT/GST Guidelines, Draft Consolidated Version, invitation for comments, February, 2013. For the comments, see http://www.oecd.org/ctp/consumption/public-comments-international-vat-gst-guidelines.htm.

[75] For an interesting examination of the taxation of cable television, see note, "Taxation of Cable Television: First Amendment Limitations," 109 *Harv. L. Rev.* 440 (1995). Some countries, such as Singapore, zero-rate international telecommunications services. See "Singapore: International Telecommunications Services," 15 *Int'l VAT Monitor* 58 (Jan./Feb. 2004).

a central fixed location for the transmission and receipt of signals. For example, some services can be provided by satellite transmission. Services may be provided by a supplier that operates in or has working arrangements with companies in many countries. With mobile cellular phones, a customer of a telecommunications company in the United States can use his cellular phone in Europe or Asia. The phone customer controls the place where the service is used or enjoyed. A customer who purchases Internet access services in the EU may use that service to receive e-mail or telephone messages while on a business trip to South Africa.[76]

Rules developed before the explosion of new telecommunication services did not anticipate transactions such as those that straddle the line between the provision of information and the transmission of information, such as between processing data in connection with its transmission and the mere transmission of data in its original form.[77] The EU rules, in this section, cover three categories of cross-border services – telecommunication, broadcasting, and electronically supplied services.[78]

The general rules governing telecommunication and broadcast services are as follows:

1. Services rendered to a taxable person are located where the *customer* established his business.[79]
2. Services rendered to a non-taxable person are located where the *supplier* established his business.[80]

There are elaborate rules in the VAT Directive and regulations governing the status of a customer as a taxable or non-taxable person,[81] the "capacity

[76] These issues arise under state and local sales taxes in the United States. In 2000, Congress enacted the Mobile Telecommunications Sourcing Act. This act allocates jurisdiction to tax mobile phone services. It provides that charges for mobile phones can be taxed "by the taxing jurisdiction whose territorial limits encompass the customer's place of primary use, regardless of where the mobile telecommunication services originate, terminate, or pass through, and no other taxing jurisdiction may impose taxes, charges, or fees on charges for such mobile telecommunications services."

[77] P. Jenkins, "VAT and Telecommunications within the European Union," 6 *Int'l VAT Monitor* 286 (Sept./Oct. 1995).

[78] This section does not cover the special rules on other particular services. For the other particular provisions, see VAT Directive, *supra* note 24, at Arts. 46–57, including services supplied by intermediaries, services connected with immovable property, and cultural, artistic, sporting, scientific, and similar services.

[79] *Id.* at Art. 44. If the services are rendered to the customer's fixed establishment that is not where he established his business, the place of supply is at that fixed establishment. In addition, if the customer receives services other than where the business is established or where the person has a fixed establishment, the services are located where the customer has his permanent address or usually resides. *Id.*

[80] *Id.* at Art. 45. If the services are rendered at the supplier's fixed establishment that is not where he established his business, the place of supply is at that supplier's fixed establishment. In addition, if the supplier supplies services other than from the supplier's business establishment or fixed establishment, the services are located where the supplier has his permanent address or usually resides. *Id.*

[81] See VAT Directive, *supra* note 24, at Arts. 9–13 and 43, discussed in Reg. 282/2011, *supra* note 53, at Art. 17.

of the customer" who receives services exclusively for private use,[82] and the location of the customer.[83]

2. Electronically Supplied Services

This subsection discusses the EU's VAT Directive and implementing regulations governing electronically supplied services. These rules are designed to prevent EU consumers and unregistered EU public bodies from avoiding VAT by purchasing these services from suppliers outside the EU.

On electronically supplied services, the EU regulations provide that "electronically supplied services" include services rendered over the Internet or an electronic network. These services are rendered "essentially automated and involving minimal human intervention, and impossible to ensure in the absence of information technology."[84]

The EU has place of supply rules governing both inbound electronically supplied services when those services are rendered by taxable persons outside the Community to non-taxable persons in the EU, as well as the rules governing the export of electronically supplied and other services to customers outside the EU.

The VAT Directive rule on inbound services provides that the place of supply of electronically supplied services[85] rendered by a taxable person outside the Community[86] to a non-taxable person established (or who has his permanent address or resides) in a member state is at the customer's location (the user of the services) – that is, where that non-taxable person is established or has his permanent address or resides.[87] The rule governing outbound electronically supplied services is different. The supply to a non-taxable person established outside the Community is located where that person is established[88] or has his permanent address or usually resides.

[82] Reg. 282/2011, *supra* note 53, at Art. 19.

[83] *Id.* at Arts. 20–24.

[84] *Id.* at Art. 7(1).

[85] According to Annex II to the VAT Directive, *supra* note 24, an indicative list of electronically supplied services includes:

1. Web site supply, web-hosting, distance maintenance of programs and equipment;
2. supply of software and updating thereof;
3. supply of images, text and information and making available of databases;
4. supply of music, films and games, including games of chance and gambling games, and political, cultural, artistic, sporting, scientific and entertainment broadcasts and events; and
5. supply of distance teaching.

[86] This includes a taxable person with business established outside the Community or rendering services from a fixed establishment outside the Community (or who has his permanent address or usually resides outside the Community).

[87] VAT Directive, *supra* note 24, at Art. 58. The mere communication by the supplier and customer by electronic mail does not mean that the service is an electronically supplied service. *Id.*

[88] *Id.* at Art. 59. This rule includes a non-taxable person established or with his permanent address or usually resides outside the Community. The mere communication by the

3. Special Schemes for Non-Established Taxable Persons

The EU established special schemes, by regulation, for non-established taxable persons who supply telecom, broadcasting, or electronic services to non-taxable persons in the Community.[89] Under this regulation, there is a "non-Union scheme"[90] covering taxable persons not established in the Community and a "Union scheme"[91] for these services supplied by taxable persons established in the Community but not established in the member state of consumption. The Union scheme is not discussed here.

Effective 2015, telecom, broadcasting, and electronic services will be taxed in the member state where the customer is established, regardless of where the supplier is established. In the absence of the "non-Union scheme," a taxable person not established in the Community (a non-established person) who supplies covered services must register in each member state in which the person renders those services (where the services are consumed). Under the special non-Union scheme, which is optional, that person may register online in one member state and report and remit tax to that state on all these taxable services rendered to persons in all member states. That revenue is allocated by that "state of identification" to the state of consumption.

B. Electronic Commerce

Electronic commerce may involve goods or services. This distinction is blurred for transactions involving items such as software that can be downloaded (digital products) or provided in physical form. This area continues to be studied by the EU and other countries and examined by the OECD and commentators.

There have been proposals to apply technological developments to the collection and enforcement of VAT on electronic commerce. One commentator, Subhajit Basu, recommended the involvement of "the very technology that made the Internet and e-commerce possible." He relies on independent service providers (ISPs) to calculate, collect, and remit VAT and assumes that tax authorities (whether nations or subnational units of government) would enter into contracts with the ISPs to administer the tax collection system.[92] To make the system work, the necessary

supplier and customer by electronic mail does not mean that the service is an electronically supplied service. *Id.*

89 See Reg. No. 967/2012, *supra* note 53.

90 *Id.* at Art. 57a(1).

91 *Id.* at Art. 57a(2).

92 The Basu system requires uniform definitions of products and services and adequate tax compliance software. S. Basu, "Implementing E-Commerce Tax Policy," 1 *British Tax Review* 46, 68 (2004). Mr. Basu assumes that the tax authorities would bear the cost of building the system. *Id.* at 49. The identification of the parties to a sale and the classification of the seller as a registered person (for VAT or sales tax purposes) and the buyer as

tax information must be provided to the ISPs and retained and used without disclosure of private information. The mechanism may be digital certificates.[93]

The challenge is to bring e-commerce within the VAT or sales tax net without placing domestic businesses at a disadvantage compared with foreign competitors. Many of the place of supply, place of consumption, and tax administration and compliance issues pertaining to telecom services discussed earlier apply to e-commerce supplies as well. It is not surprising that some of the proposed solutions for the taxation of e-commerce resemble the revised EU rules on the taxation of telecommunications services, but the place of supply rules in the VAT Directive do not specifically include e-commerce as one of the "particular provisions."[94]

With the explosion of commerce over the Internet and the concern about the multiple taxation of sales conducted via electronic commerce, the U.S. Congress enacted a moratorium on taxes on Internet access and on multiple or discriminatory taxes on e-commerce. The Internet Tax Freedom Act's more expansive definition of e-commerce included "any transaction conducted over the Internet or through Internet access, comprising the sale, lease, license, offer, or delivery of property, goods, services, or information, whether or not for consideration, and includes the provision of Internet access."[95] The U.S. Congress extended the moratorium.[96] States

a business or consumer are other necessary elements of his proposal. Mr. Basu's position is that governments must relinquish some of their authority as "largely autonomous agents of taxation" and accept "higher levels of international coordination in the field of taxation." *Id.* at 68.

93 "Digital certificates (also known as electronic credentials or digital IDs) are digital documents attesting to the binding of a public key to an individual or entity. They allow verification of the claim that a given public key does in fact belong to a given individual or entity .... Such technology is mainly used on 'commerce servers.' These server IDs allow websites to identify themselves to users and to encrypt transactions with their visitors. Digital certificates go hand in hand with digital signatures. Digital signature work on key pairs, one of which is public and the other private. The private key is used to encrypt a document while the public key is used to decipher it. ... The digital certificate can be registered with a so-called 'trusted third party' such as a government agency or even a private company; the trusted third party can then act as a kind of bonding agency to ensure the veracity and accuracy of information given out by the digital certificates." *Id.* at 60–61.

94 VAT Directive, *supra* note 24, at Arts. 43–59b.

95 Internet Tax Freedom Act, 47 U.S.C. 151 note, §1004(3).

96 P.L. No. 108–435, Internet Tax Non-Discrimination Act, 118 Stat. 2615, 108th Cong., 2d Sess. (2003). This Act amended the Internet Tax Freedom Act, 47 U.S.C 151 note. "'Internet access service' does not include telecommunications services, except to the extent such services are purchased, used, or sold by a provider of Internet access to provide Internet access." *Id.* at §2(3) of the Internet Tax Non-Discrimination Act. There are a few other exceptions, including one that does not prevent states from taxing charges for voice or other similar services that use Internet protocol or any successor protocol. *Id.* at §5 of the Act. The law was extended again until November 1, 2014. P.L. 110–108, Internet Tax Freedom Act Amendment Act of 2007 (2007). Based on prior experience, this law may be extended again.

such as Wisconsin with existing Internet access taxes were exempt from the moratorium on taxes on such access.[97]

C. International Transportation Services

International transportation involves the physical movement of goods or passengers across national boundaries. International transportation raises issues about the proper allocation of jurisdiction to impose VAT among the countries with a connection to international freight and passenger travel by road, air, or water. Rules that allocate taxing jurisdiction according to the place where the services are rendered or the place where the services are consumed may cause confusion when transportation services include travel in international waters or in the air that goes beyond the jurisdiction of a single country.

In some situations, international transportation services avoid VAT entirely. The country of origin typically zero-rates these services as exports. For example, they are zero-rated in the EU.[98] A third country, whose borders are crossed during transit (in and out of the country), typically does not assert jurisdiction to tax the service provided within its borders. For goods, freight charges may be taxed by the importing country as part of the value of the imported goods.

In connection with the EC's basic principle that VAT should accrue to the country of consumption,[99] the Commission sought views from the public with respect to the value added taxation of transportation.[100] In that consultation paper, the Commission suggested that taxing intra-community passenger transport according to the distance covered in each country was impractical and difficult to apply. Instead, the Commission's alternative would locate this passenger transportation service at the place of departure.[101] With respect to intra-community transport of goods, the Commission suggested that the current rule continue – that is, the place of supply is also at the place of departure.[102]

Short-term leases of means of transport (cars, etc.) within the EU currently are located where the supplier has established his business. This has created opportunities for abuse. As a result, the Commission suggests that these short-term hires be treated as supplied where the transport is put at the recipient's disposal.[103] Long-term leases of means of transport would continue to be treated as supplied where the supplier is located.[104]

[97] *Id.* at §3 of the Act.

[98] See VAT Directive, *supra* note 24, at Art. 146(l)(e).

[99] COM (2000) 348 Final, 7 July 2000, "A strategy to improve the operation of the VAT system within the context of the internal market."

[100] Consultation Paper: VAT – The Place of Supply of Services to Non-Taxable Persons, European Commission, Brussels D (2005).

[101] *Id.* at point 4.2.2.

[102] *Id.* at point 4.2.3.

[103] *Id.* at point 4.2.5.

[104] *Id.*

VIII. Proposal to Fund Disaster Relief

Highlighting the pervasive under-taxation of international consumer travel among VAT regimes, Professor Hiroshi Kaneko proposed to impose a consumption tax on international air travel, with the revenue to be dedicated to the relief of disaster victims.

> I propose a personal consumption tax on international airfare. The revenues raised would go into an international fund dedicated to the relief of disaster victims. Currently, countries with a consumption tax impose it only on domestic consumption items. Should a product subject to the tax leave the country, the government refunds any taxes already collected. That refund follows, of course, from the very nature of the consumption tax. As a corollary, almost all these governments tax domestic but not international airfare. Unfortunately, this policy violates tax neutrality by skewing consumer choice away from domestic travel or other consumption. Importantly, for our rapidly expanding internationalizing age, my proposal would reduce that tax non-neutrality. The writer thinks that there is no limitation on the tax jurisdiction of a sovereign country to impose a consumption tax on international air travel as long as the ticket is purchased in its jurisdiction.
>
> A low tax rate would raise significant revenue. International air travel is a rapidly growing industry. Firms seem to add new routes monthly and new flights on existing routes daily. According to the statistics of the International Civil Aviation Organization (ICAO), total revenue from passengers of scheduled airlines of ICAO contracting states has been rapidly and drastically increasing and amounted to over US $200 billion in 1996. Though the revenue from personal passengers and that of business passengers are not distinguished in the statistics, it could be assumed that the former must also have been drastically increasing and has now reached a tremendously large amount. Therefore, as mentioned above, a modest tax on this base could also raise a correspondingly large amount of revenue. To use this revenue to help the victims of international disputes (perhaps for the removal of land mines as well) would be an important humanistic act. Most passengers would be glad to donate some money in the form of a consumption tax for people in misery.
>
> Implementing this proposal raises a wide variety of difficulties. Countries will need to cooperate in adopting the necessary legislation and appropriate and efficient administrative arrangements.[105]

[105] Kaneko, "Proposal for International Humanitarian Tax – A Consumption Tax on International Air Travel," 17 Tax Notes Int'l 1911 (Dec. 14, 1998).

IX. Discussion Questions

1. How should public (government-owned) domestic and international transportation services be treated under a VAT?
2. If international competitive pressures force the zero-rating of B2B international transportation services, will it be administratively feasible to apply VAT to consumer international transportation services? How?
3. Is it too far-fetched to envision a United Nations Development Program (UNDP) tax on value added in international air transportation (and perhaps other forms of transportation) that is now exempt or zero-rated? The question reflects the growing importance (value) of personal consumption of international transportation and tourism services and their absence from the base of value added taxes. How would input taxes paid by business under national VATs be handled? How could such a world tax be administered? How does this proposal compare with the Kaneko proposal for a humanitarian tax on air travel?
4. When the U.S. Supreme Court in the *Itel* case upheld Tennessee's retail sales and use tax on containers leased in Tennessee for international transportation, that result implemented a tax on the export of container services. VATs generally tax only the value of container services included in imports. Do you see a problem here? A solution? If the United States adopts a national VAT, how should it deal with Tennessee's tax on containers at the state level of government? See *Itel Containers Int'l Corp. v. Huddleston*, 113 S. Ct. 1095, 122 L. Ed. 421 (1993).

8 Timing and Valuation Rules

Timing (or tax accounting) rules are used to identify the tax period in which a taxpayer must pay tax on imports, report taxable sales, and claim deductions or credits for tax paid on allowable imports and domestic purchases. When a VAT is introduced or the rate is changed, effective date and transition rules are needed to identify which sales and purchases are subject to the old rules and which to the new or amended law.

VAT generally is imposed on the sum of the amount of money and the value of non-monetary consideration received for a taxable supply. Special valuation rules are provided for particular transactions. This chapter covers the timing, transition, and valuation rules.

I. The Timing Rules

A. Accrual, Hybrid, and Cash Methods – in General

This section discusses the rules governing the basic methods of accounting for VAT. It does not discuss the innumerable varieties of special schemes for retailers that are available in many countries.

Most taxpayers must use the accrual or a hybrid method of accounting to report sales and claim input credits under a credit-invoice VAT (like the European VATs). Under the accrual method, taxpayers generally report taxable sales when goods are sold or when services are rendered, subject to rules accelerating the reporting, and they claim input credits when the business acquires the goods or services eligible for the input credits.[1] Hybrid methods include the invoice method, under which sales are reportable when the sales invoice is issued, or a combination method whereby the sale is reportable on the earliest of payment, issuance of the

[1] See, for example, the VAT in the United Kingdom, Value Added Tax Act 1994, ch. 23 [hereinafter VATA 1994]. The UK rule provides that if goods are to be removed, the sale occurs on removal; otherwise, a sale occurs when goods are made available to the recipient. *Id.* at §6(2)(a) and (b). For a discussion of timing rules in the context of tax law design, see D. Williams, "Value-Added Tax," in 1 *Tax Law Design and Drafting* 164, 191–194 (V. Thuronyi, ed., IMF 1996).

invoice, or accrual. This combination method is the one most commonly prescribed by VAT laws. Some countries do not allow any person to use the cash method. Other countries permit registered persons who meet the statutory conditions (usually related to a lower level of taxable turnover) to report on the cash method.

The limits or prohibitions against the use of the cash method are imposed to prevent the mismatching that occurs if the seller can defer the payment of output tax to the government, yet the buyer can claim an immediate credit. The *Ch'elle Properties (NZ)* case, discussed in detail in Chapter 10, illustrates how one country relies on an anti-abuse rule to prevent taxpayers from mismatching methods of accounting. In that case, the cash basis (referred to in New Zealand as payments basis) seller reported sales on the installment basis and the accrual method buyer used refunds of input credits on installment purchases to finance those purchases. "Although the scheme conformed to the letter of the Act, [the mismatch between the invoice and cash method] departed from its fundamental objectives and therefore had the purpose and effect of defeating the intent and application of the Act."[2]

1. Imports

Imports are subject to VAT under uniform rules that generally do not distinguish between cash and accrual basis importers. In the EU, imports are taxable to the importer when goods are imported.[3] If imports are subject to customs duties or other import levies, the VAT generally is imposed when those duties become chargeable.[4] VAT on imports of goods generally is payable to Customs or the post office, not reportable on periodic VAT returns. The rule is different for cross-border supplies of goods in the EU between registered persons. In those transactions, the goods are received free of VAT, and the VAT imposed on the imported goods is reportable in the VAT return covering the period in which the goods are imported.

In most countries, a VAT-registered importer claims credit for allowable VAT on imported goods in the period in which the goods are imported.[5] To claim the credit, the importer also must have possession of the import documentation listing the VAT imposed.

There is a cash-flow cost if the tax on imports is paid before the importer obtains the benefit from the input credit. However, in countries such as New Zealand, the cash-flow cost is avoided. Customs issues a statement

[2] *Ch'elle Properties (NZ) Ltd v. Commissioner of Inland Revenue* [2004] 3 NZLR 274; 2004 NZLR LEXIS 12 (High Court N.Z. 2004). The decision was affirmed on appeal, [2007] NZCA 256.

[3] See Council Directive 2006/112/EC of 28 November 2006 on the common system of value added tax (OJ L347, 11.12.2006, p. 1) [hereinafter VAT Directive], Art. 70.

[4] See *id.* Art. 71.

[5] See, for example, New Zealand Goods and Services Tax Act, No. 141, §12(1) [hereinafter NZ GST].

to the importer that is the basis of an optional deferred payment arrangement. The importer must pay the duty and VAT within twenty-one working days after the importer's assigned billing cycle. The same statement serves as documentation to claim the offsetting input credits.[6]

The reporting rules on imports of services vary considerably by country because the taxation of imported services varies considerably.[7] The complexity increases where the classification of a supply as goods or services is ambiguous. Is computer software a good or a service?[8]

In some countries, imports of services are taxable under a reverse charge rule – that is, the importer treats the import of the service as a taxable supply by the importer to himself. In New Zealand, the import subject to the reverse charge rule is reportable at the earlier of the foreign supplier's issuance of the invoice or the importer's payment for the supply.[9] In countries requiring nonresident suppliers of specified imported services to register and charge and remit VAT, the recipient generally will claim the credit under the timing rules governing domestic supplies.

2. Accrual Method

The VAT rules under the accrual method may or may not be consistent with the taxpayer's method of reporting sales and purchases for income or financial reporting purposes.

For most firms in Japan, the timing rules for the Consumption Tax (a VAT) and income tax are consistent. Most Japanese businesses use the accrual method,[10] and they can follow their method of accounting used for income tax purposes in accounting for the Consumption Tax.

Under the European Union's VAT Directive, the tax is chargeable when the goods or services are supplied even though the time of payment may be deferred.[11] For businesses reporting on the accrual method, the chargeable event (when the conditions of the supply are fulfilled so that the tax is chargeable)[12] and the time the tax is chargeable coincide if goods are

[6] See *Tax Information Bulletin*, Vol. 9, No. 11 (Nov. 1997) (NZ).

[7] See discussion of cross-border transactions involving services, *supra* Chapter 7. Imports of services by registered persons generally are not taxed (see discussion, *supra* Chapter 7 [Section VI]). As a result, there will not be any timing issue. If any imported services are taxed (e.g., the services supplied over the Internet by a foreign supplier – treated as services rendered where used – are taxable and the supplier may be required to register in the EU and remit tax), the purchaser presumably can claim input credit under the timing rules governing domestic purchases.

[8] For example, in New Zealand, "shrink-wrapped" computer software is largely a service (intellectual property with respect to the contents). See the discussion in the text on the reverse charge rule applicable to some imports.

[9] NZ GST, *supra* note 5, at §§5B & 9(1). A special rule applies to supplies between associated (related) persons. *Id.* at §9(2).

[10] Special timing rules are provided in Japan for installment and deferred payment sales and for long-term construction contracts. See A. Schenk, "Japanese Consumption Tax After Six Years: A Unique VAT Matures," 69 *Tax Notes* 899, 910 (Nov. 13, 1995).

[11] See VAT Directive, *supra* note 3, at Art. 63.

[12] See *id.* at Art. 62(1) and (2).

delivered or services are performed before payment is received and before an invoice is issued. However, the tax point (the date a taxable sale is reportable) is accelerated to a date before the date of the supply if payment is received before the goods are delivered or the services are performed.[13] For example, if a sale is completed and an invoice is issued on July 1, but the purchaser makes advance partial payment on June 28, the tax point is June 28 in respect of the amount of the payment.

The timing rules for the purchaser to claim an input credit on a domestic purchase generally are linked to the rules governing the date the *seller* reports the sale. Thus, in the EU, the input tax on domestic purchases is deductible to the purchaser when the seller must report the sale.[14]

Instead of a basic tax point linked to accrual that is accelerated only for early payment, member states can require taxable sales to be reported on the earliest of the following three dates:

1. No later than the time the invoice is issued
2. No later than the time the payment is received
3. Where an invoice is not issued, or is issued late, within a specified period from the date of the supply[15]

Under the VAT in the United Kingdom, a sale of goods generally is reportable when the goods are removed from the seller's possession. However, if goods are shipped on consignment, on approval, on sale or return or comparable terms, the sale may not be reportable until the sale is certain.[16]

The British VAT adopts the VAT Directive's permissive three possible dates rule that a sale may be accelerated to a time before goods are delivered or services are performed (the accrual) if the seller issues a tax invoice or receives payment before that point.[17] The seller's receipt of payment accelerates the tax point for a sale if such payment discharges the buyer's liability (and the seller cannot sue for payment). See *C&E Commissioners v. Faith Construction Ltd* (1989) 4 BVC 111. If the seller receives prepayment and therefore reports the amount received as part of taxable sales, but the sale never takes place, the seller is entitled to a refund.[18]

[13] See VAT Directive, *supra* note 3, at Art. 65.

[14] See *id.* at Art. 167.

[15] See *id.* at Art. 66.

[16] To prevent lengthy deferrals of the tax point, some countries require these transfers to be reported not more than a fixed period after transfer by the seller. Goods sent on approval, on sale or return, or similar terms are subject to tax at the earlier of twelve months after removal or when it is certain that the sale occurred. VATA 1994, *supra* note 1, at §6(2)(c). However, in transactions not covered by §6(2)(c), if the supplier retains the ownership interests in goods until the goods are appropriated by the buyer, the supply generally occurs at the earliest of the date appropriated by the buyer, when the supplier issues an invoice, or the supplier receives a payment. SI 1995/2518, reg. 88. Under an exception, if an invoice is issued within fourteen days after the buyer appropriates the goods, the invoice date may govern. *Id.* and §6(5).

[17] *Id.* at §6(4).

[18] See VATA 1994, *supra* note 1, at §80 (United Kingdom) and discussion in N. Doran, "The Time of Supply Rules: How Far Do They Go?," 1998 *British Tax Review* 602.

In the United Kingdom, the tax point for a sale is not accelerated by payment if the payment represents only a security deposit.[19] If, by contrast, the deposit represents part payment, the deposit is reportable at the time of receipt. The following case involves deposits on vacation accommodations. In this case, the deposits were refundable if the customer did not use the accommodation and the company was able to lease the property to another tenant, but not if the company was unsuccessful in releasing the property.

Customs and Excise Commissioners v. Moonrakers Guest House Ltd[20]

Moonrakers Guest House Ltd (the company) ... carries on business in the provision of holiday accommodation, and the premises where this takes place are in the Isles of Scilly.

The booking form and 'Conditions of Tenancy'... are in the form of a letter to Mr and Mrs Gregory asking them to reserve a flat for a designated period at an identified rental. There then appears this passage:

> 'I enclose herewith Cheque/Cash by registered post/Postal Order/ Money Order for £... (25% of total rent) balance payable on arrival, and agree to abide by the attached Conditions of Tenancy.'
>
> The only relevant condition of tenancy is the last one.
>
> 'In the event of the cancellation of a booking, every effort will be made to re-let. However, if it is not possible to re-let the flat the full amount of rent exactly as if the accommodation had been occupied will be claimed.'
>
> [T]he position thus is that a 25% deposit is paid at the time when a booking is made. If the booking is taken up, the balance of the rental is payable at the time when the occupation of the property starts. If the booking is not taken up, efforts are made to relet the property. If the property is relet, the deposit is repaid, but if the property is not relet the customer remains liable under his contract for the full rental and the deposit is retained as part-payment.
>
> [T]he question at issue here relates to the timing of the liability. The commissioners contend, and contended before the tribunal, that the receipt of the deposit gives rise to a liability to value added tax at the time when the deposit is received. The tribunal rejected the commissioners' contention and it is submitted that the tribunal erred in law in reaching that decision.

The court must look at the facts as they are set out, particularly in the booking form to which I have already explicitly referred, in order to decide as a matter of law whether the money paid by way of deposit

[19] See Notice 700, The VAT guide, ¶14.2.3 (April 2002 ed.) [United Kingdom].

[20] [1992] STC 544 (Queen's Bench, UK) [edited by the authors].

could conceivably be said to remain the property of the payer. In my judgment it could not....

The statutory provisions governing the time of supply of service and thus the time when liability to value added tax arises are §§4 and 5 of the 1983 Act [now §6 of VATA 1994]. Section 4 reads as follows.

'[A] supply of services shall be treated as taking place at the time when the services are performed.'[21]

Then §5(1) states:

> 'If, before the time applicable under ... subsection (3) of section 4 above, the person making the supply issues a tax invoice in respect of it or if, before the time applicable under ... subsection (3) of that section, he receives a payment in respect of it, the supply shall, to the extent covered by the invoice or payment, be treated as taking place at the time the invoice is issued or the payment is received.'[22]

The commissioners in this case rely first and foremost on the simple and straightforward wording of §5(1) of the 1983 Act. The deposit is a payment received in respect of the supply of services. Furthermore it is received before the time applicable under §4(3). Accordingly to the extent covered by that payment (that is to say, 25% of the value of the supply) the supply is to be treated as taking place at the time when the payment is received. That is the commissioners' interpretation of the statute and, in my judgment, it is palpably correct.

What happened factually in the instant case was that those moneys went into the company's general account. They were not earmarked in any way in a separate account. They were not kept separate. They represented, in accordance with the written contract, a 25% payment of the total rental. It is perfectly true that the money would have been repaid if the property was relet, but that situation arose probably from an implied contractual term and from nothing else.

I turn lastly to what might happen if tax had been paid and if the customer did not take the accommodation. What would happen then, if the property was relet, would be that the customer would receive back his deposit and the company would be able to bring into account the value added tax in a future period, so that the company would not be the loser in the long run. That seems to me to be common sense and it is, in my judgment, the law.

In all the circumstances therefore this appeal must be allowed and the decision of the commissioners, namely that tax is chargeable on the deposits at the time they were paid, is upheld.

The input credit rules for a taxpayer who must report on the accrual method generally provide that input VAT is creditable in the tax period in

[21] This provision now is in VATA 1994, *supra* note 1, at §6(3).

[22] This provision included *id.* at §6(4) is substantially the same as §5(1) quoted in the text.

which the supply is made to him and he has a tax invoice for the purchase. Because most VATs require sellers to report taxable sales no later than the tax period in which an invoice is issued (even for a taxpayer reporting on the accrual method), the purchaser cannot claim input credits before the seller must report the sale. The following case resolves a dispute in the EU involving the time when an input tax deduction can be claimed, when services are received in one tax period and the invoice covering the services is received in a later period, and the law provides that a deduction cannot be taken until the purchaser has possession of the invoice.[23] The court was required to resolve differences between the German and the French and English language versions of the Sixth Directive.

Terra Baubedarf-Handel GmbH v. Finanzamt Osterholz-Scharmbeck[24]

THE COURT (Fifth Chamber)
JUDGMENT-BY. von Bahr

Community legislation

The first sentence of the first subparagraph of Article 10(2) of the Sixth Directive[25] provides:

'The chargeable event shall occur and the tax shall become chargeable when the goods are delivered or the services are performed.'

Article 17(1) and (2)(a) of the Sixth Directive[26] state:

1. The right to deduct shall arise at the time when the deductible tax becomes chargeable.
2. In so far as the goods and services are used for the purposes of his taxable transactions, the taxable person shall be entitled to deduct from the tax which he is liable to pay:
   (a) 'value added tax due or paid within the territory of the country in respect of goods or services supplied or to be supplied to him by another taxable person'.

Article 18(1) and (2) of the Sixth Directive state:

1. To exercise his right to deduct, the taxable person must:
   (a) in respect of deductions under Article 17(2) (a), hold an invoice, drawn up in accordance with Article 22(3); ...[27]
2. The taxable person shall effect the deduction by subtracting from the total amount of value added tax due for a given tax period

[23] See discussion *supra* for a discussion of the conditions that must be satisfied before an input tax can be claimed with respect to imports.
[24] Case C-152/02, [2004] ECR I- 5583, 2004 *ECJ CELEX EEXIS 151*.
[25] VAT Directive, *supra* note 3, at Art. 63.
[26] *Id.* at Art. 167.
[27] See *id.* at Art. 178.

the total amount of the tax in respect of which, during the same period, the right to deduct has arisen and can be exercised under the provisions of paragraph 1.[28]

Terra Baubedarf, a German company trading in building supplies, obtained supplies of services in 1999. However, the invoices relating to those services, although drawn up in December 1999, were not received by it until January 2000.

The [tax authorities] did not allow the deduction of the VAT paid by Terra Baubedarf for 1999 in respect of those services on the grounds that … the right to deduct could only be exercised in the case in point in respect of the year 2000, the year in which the relevant invoice was received.

Terra Baubedarf then brought an appeal [against an adverse decision by the tax office], claiming that a time-limit had been placed on its right to deduct the input VAT paid, in breach of the Sixth Directive.

The Bundesfinanzhof [the Federal Finance Court] observes that, according to the case-law of the Court, Terra Baubedarf's right to deduct arose in 1999 in accordance with Article 17 of the Sixth Directive, and that, in accordance with Article 18 of the Sixth Directive, that right could not be exercised until 2000, after receipt of the invoice.

'[The question referred to the ECJ is whether a taxable person can] exercise his right to deduct input tax only in respect of the calendar year in which he holds an invoice pursuant to Article 18(l)(a) of Directive 77/388/EEC or must the right to deduct always be exercised (even if retrospectively) in respect of the calendar year in which the right to deduct pursuant to Article 17(1) of Directive 77/388/EEC arose?'

[The taxpayer claims that the German language version of the Sixth Directive can be read as granting the deduction in the period in which goods or services are provided, and when a person receives the invoice for those items in a subsequent tax period, a literal reading of the VAT law requires the person to claim the deduction by amending the earlier return and claiming the deduction in that earlier period.] Technically, when the invoice is received after a tax period, immediate deduction can be guaranteed only through retroactive exercise of the right to deduct.

[The taxpayer claims] that, with regard to the rules governing the exercise of the right to deduct, that version does not establish clearly whether the period in respect of which the right to deduct may be claimed means the period in which the right to deduct arose or that in which the conditions referred to in the first paragraph of that article are satisfied in addition to the right to deduct. Other language versions enable that provision to be understood without ambiguity, however.

[28] *Id.* at Art. 179, when exercised in accordance with Art. 178.

[The argument in response is that] a retroactive right to deduct would result in significant additional work for both taxable persons and the tax authorities. Through the retroactive deduction of input VAT, provisional returns filed for a tax period would in fact have to be adjusted, in certain circumstances even several times in the same tax period, and the tax authorities would have to draw up correction notices.

By contrast, the interpretation upheld by the German Government guarantees a VAT system that can be applied and checked effectively as regards the deduction of input VAT.

The Commission cites the Italian and Dutch versions besides the French and English versions. It appears from those that the period concerned is determined by the concurrent existence of the origin of the right to deduct and possession of the invoice.

Reply of the Court

It must be noted first that Article 18 of the Sixth Directive relates to the conditions governing the exercise of the right to deduct, whilst the existence of such a right is covered by Article 17 of that directive.

It follows from Article 17(1) of the Sixth Directive that the right to deduct arises at the time when the deductible tax becomes chargeable. In accordance with Article 10(2) of that directive, that is the case as soon as the goods are delivered or the services are performed.

On the other hand, it is apparent from Article 18(l)(a), read in conjunction with Article 22(3) of the Sixth Directive,[29] that the exercise of the right to deduct referred to in Article 17(2)(a) of that directive is normally dependent on possession of the original of the invoice or of the document which, under the criteria determined by the Member State in question, may be considered to serve as an invoice.

[T]he German version of the first subparagraph of Article 18(2) of the Sixth Directive does not establish clearly whether the period in respect of which the right to deduct may be claimed means the period in which the right to deduct arose or that in which the conditions of possession of the invoice and the right to deduct are satisfied.

However, although the German version of that provision is ambiguous on that point, it is apparent from the French and English versions of the Sixth Directive that the deduction referred to in Article 17(2) thereof must be made in respect of the tax period in which the two conditions required under the first subparagraph of Article 18(2) are satisfied. In other words, the goods must have been delivered or the services performed and the taxable person must be in possession

[29] See *id.* at Arts. 209–216 and 243.

of the invoice or the document which, under the criteria determined by the Member State in question, may be considered to serve as an invoice.

THE COURT (FIFTH CHAMBER). In answer to the question referred to it by the Bundesfinanzhof by order of 21 March 2002, hereby rules:

> [The input tax deduction referred to in the Sixth Directive, Article 17(2) (a) and provided under Article 18(2) means] that the right to deduct must be exercised in respect of the tax period in which the two conditions required by that provision are satisfied, namely that the goods have been delivered or the services performed and that the taxable person holds the invoice or the document which, under the criteria determined by the Member State in question, may be considered to serve as an invoice.

3. Invoice Method

Many countries require businesses to report VAT on the invoice method of accounting for VAT – not a pure accrual method. Countries such as New Zealand and the Republic of South Africa rely on the invoice method. Under the invoice method, sales generally are reportable when the sales invoice is issued, but that tax point may be accelerated to the time consideration is received, if any consideration is received before the invoice is issued.[30] Moreover, input tax is deductible (the term used in South Africa) when the sale is made to the person claiming the deduction. Thus, the input tax generally is deductible when the supplier to the taxpayer issues the invoice or when the taxpayer makes a payment on the sale, whichever occurs earlier.[31]

4. Cash Method

> Taxable persons generally prefer to defer the tax point and payment obligation [on sales] as long as possible in order to invest and earn interest on VAT collected from customers. Since most sellers do not receive payment until after the sale is completed and income therefrom is properly accruable, taxable persons generally would prefer to base the timing rule (tax point) for sales on the cash rather than the accrual method.[32]

[30] See, for example, Value-Added Tax Act No. 89 of 1991, §9(1) (Republic of South Africa) [hereinafter RSA VAT], discussed in Chris Beneke, ed., DELOITTE & TOUCHE VAT HANDBOOK 6th ed. (Butterworths 2003) [hereinafter RSA VAT Handbook]. Special timing rules apply to particular transactions, such as installment sales.

[31] RSA VAT, *supra* note 30, at §16(3)(a).

[32] Excerpt from A. Schenk, reporter, VALUE ADDED TAX – A MODEL STATUTE AND COMMENTARY: A REPORT OF THE COMMITTEE ON VALUE ADDED TAX OF THE AMERICAN BAR ASSOCIATION SECTION OF TAXATION 136–138 (1989) [hereinafter ABA Model Act].

If, under the credit-invoice VAT, a business reports on the cash method, it reports sales when it receives the consideration and it claims credits for input tax when it pays for its purchases. A seller receiving property instead of cash as consideration must report the property when received.[33]

Countries commonly require businesses to report on the accrual or invoice method. Many, however, permit specified businesses to report VAT on the cash (or payments) method of accounting. The option to use the cash method usually is limited to firms with taxable supplies below a statutory threshold. For example, under the British VAT, a business can elect to use the cash method if its annual taxable sales do not exceed £350,000.[34] Some countries, such as New Zealand and South Africa, require an eligible business to obtain advance approval to use the cash method.[35]

In Case J 69,[36] decided under the NZ GST, a business challenged the commissioners' decision to deny use of the cash (payments) method. The business operated a bakery that made sales both at wholesale and retail. About 60% of the value of its sales (and 85%–90% of the number of sales) was cash sales, and the balance was sales on credit. Under the GST[37] in effect at the time, although taxpayers generally were required to use the invoice method, the Commissioner could allow taxpayers to use the payments method if the "Commissioner is satisfied that, due to the nature, volume, or value of taxable supplies made by that registered person and the nature of the accounting system employed by that person it would be appropriate for that person to furnish returns under this Act on a payments basis."[38] The court held that although accounting on the invoice method was not unduly burdensome, the taxpayer should be allowed to use the cash method.

B. Taxable Period

The cost for the government to administer and for businesses to comply with a VAT depend, in part, on the length of each taxable period and on the number and complexity of the returns required to be filed each year.

[33] In *A-Z Electrical v. Commissioners of Customs and Excise* [1993] VATTR 389, the seller subject to the British VAT was required to report as taxable sales the shares and loan stock received as payment, even though the issuer subsequently liquidated.

[34] See Value Added Tax (Cash Accounting) Regulations 1987 (SI 1995/2518), issued under VATA 1994, *supra* note 1, at §58 and Sch. 11, ¶2(7).

[35] NZ GST, *supra* note 5, at §19(2 (New Zealand)); RSA VAT, *supra* note 30, at §15(1) and (2). The cash (payments) method is available only for certain units of government and non-profit organizations and businesses with annual taxable sales not exceeding a threshold (2.5 million Rand in RSA). RSA also has an atypical rule requiring a business reporting on the payments method to report certain sales of more than 100,000 Rand on the invoice method, even if the business is authorized to use the payments method. RSA VAT, *supra* note 30, at §15(2A).

[36] (1987) 9 NZTC 1, 421.

[37] NZ GST, *supra* note 5, at §19(2)(c).

[38] The GST statute provides basically the same rule under NZ GST, *supra* note 5, at §§19(2) and 19A(l)(c).

1. Taxable Period – in General

For a newly registered person, a tax period starts on the date prescribed by statute (generally when registration becomes effective) or on the date specified by the tax authorities. Whether a person's first tax period starts at the beginning or in the middle of a period, the person must report only taxable supplies made on and after the effective date of the person's registration.[39] In Canada, the first tax period of a newly registered person begins on the day the person becomes a registrant and ends on the last day of the reporting period.[40] Under the Australian GST, the tax period starts at the beginning of a full reporting period, even if the person's registration takes effect within a reporting period.[41]

A tax period generally ends on the last day of a reporting period. If a person's reporting period is a calendar month, the tax period ends on the last day of each calendar month.[42] When a person ceases to be a registrant, in Canada, the person's last tax period as a registrant ends on the day before he ceases to be a registrant.[43] Australia has a special rule that terminates an individual or entity's tax period before the end of the reporting period. Under that rule, if an individual dies or becomes bankrupt, or an entity ceases to exist (such as on liquidation or being placed in receivership), the tax period ceases at the end of the day before death or other event.[44]

2. Variations in Length of Period

The length of a tax period varies considerably around the world, not only among countries but also within a country. "The length of the regular tax period should be determined by balancing the government's cost of processing and auditing returns, its desire to receive tax revenue as soon as possible, taxable persons' cost of filing returns, and their desire to avoid adverse cash flow. Longer tax periods may reduce tax administration and compliance costs for small businesses."[45]

[39] See the discussion of registration *supra* Chapter 4 (Section II). In Australia, where a person must apply for registration, registration generally takes effect on the date specified by the Commissioner. A New Tax System (Goods and Services Tax) Act 1999 [hereinafter Australia GST], §25–10.

[40] Excise Tax Act, R.S. 1985, Part IX Goods and Services Tax, S.C. 1990, c. 45 [hereinafter Canadian GST], §251(1)(b).

[41] See Australia GST, *supra* note 39, at §25–10 and Division 27.

[42] Some countries depart from this rule when the country's calendar departs from the Gregorian calendar. For example, in Ethiopia, the months of Nahase and Pagume are treated as one calendar month. See Value Added Tax Proclamation No. 285/2002, §2 definition of accounting period (Ethiopia).

[43] Canadian GST, *supra* note 40, at §251(2). For a person who becomes a bankrupt, there is a new tax period for activities as a bankrupt that begins the next day. *Id.* at §265(1)(g).

[44] Australia GST, *supra* note 39, at §27–40.

[45] ABA Model Act, *supra* note 32, at 136.

Most countries have standard tax periods of one, two, or three months. The shorter periods tend to be used in developing countries.[46] Countries with standard tax periods of two or three months generally grant registered persons the option to elect a one-month tax period and grant the tax authorities power to require a registered person to file monthly. A registered person with substantial zero-rated supplies (e.g., exports of goods) may elect a one-month tax period to obtain quicker refunds of excess input credits. A one-month period may be mandated for large taxpayers.[47] The tax authorities may impose a one-month tax period on persons who have a history of failing to comply with the VAT rules.[48]

At the other end of the spectrum, a tax period may be as long as a year. For example, in Australia a person not required to register may elect to register and adopt an annual tax period.[49] In the United Kingdom, a new business with annual taxable supplies of up to £150,000 can apply to file annually.[50] A business registered for at least twelve months with annual taxable supplies above the £150,000 threshold but not more than £600,000 can apply to file annually.[51] An annual filer in the United Kingdom must pay nine interim installments electronically.[52] In South Africa, a person engaged in farming activities can apply for a six-month tax period if the person's annual taxable supplies from farming do not exceed the statutory cap.[53]

Some countries specifically authorize persons to report on fiscal rather than calendar periods. Canada has elaborate rules providing for fiscal periods.[54]

To prevent abuse and the administrative cost for tax authorities, the VAT law may restrict a person's ability to change the length of the tax period frequently.[55]

3. Time to File Returns and Pay Tax

A VAT taxpayer generally pays its net tax liability at the time it files its periodic tax return. The return and payment generally must be submitted

[46] See Value Added Tax Act 2000, No. 1 of 2001, §25 (Botswana).

[47] Australia provides for a mandatory one-month tax period for persons with annual turnover of $20 million or more. Australia GST, *supra* note 39, at §27–15(1)(a) and (3).

[48] *Id.* at §§27–10 and 27–15.

[49] *Id.* at §151–5. To qualify for the annual tax period, the person must not have elected to pay GST in installments under §162–15. *Id.* at §151–5(b).

[50] Notice 732 Annual accounting (April 2003 ed.), ¶1.4 (United Kingdom).

[51] *Id.*

[52] Each installment is 10% of the expected annual liability. *Id.* at ¶6.1.

[53] RSA VAT, *supra* note 30, at §27(4). South Africa has a standard tax period of two months; a monthly tax period for large firms, electing persons, and those who repeatedly violated the VAT rules; and a twelve-month tax period for certain firms in the rental and management business. *Id.* at §27.

[54] Canadian GST, *supra* note 40, at §§243–250, as amended.

[55] For example, Australia prevents a person from withdrawing a one-month tax period election less than twelve months after the election took effect. Australia GST, *supra* note 39 at §27–20(2)(b).

within a month after the end of the tax period, although a longer delay such as two months may apply for persons with annual or other special accounting periods. If the tax period exceeds one month, taxable firms could be required to pay estimated tax liability between tax return due dates, with the interim payments credited against the tax liability for that tax period. This system designed to accelerate the payment of tax to the government has been used under federal excise and state retail sales taxes in the United States.[56]

C. Special Rules for Certain Sales

1. Installment or Deferred Payment Sales

VAT is imposed at the time taxable goods or services are sold, and generally VAT is imposed on the price charged. For cash or credit sales, this timing and valuation rule does not present any special problems. Although, under the accrual method, there may be some negative cash float (if the sales price is not collected before the tax on sale must be remitted to the government), the impact is manageable. If, however, the sale is an installment or deferred payment sale, the time lag between the sale and the collection of the sales price may be substantial.

In essence, an installment or deferred payment sale consists of two transactions – a cash sale and a loan. Viewed in this fashion, under the accrual method, VAT should be imposed on the cash price at the time of sale, no matter how the sale is financed. The loan should follow the rules governing financial intermediation transactions (invariably exempt from tax).

Most VAT regimes adopt this approach and impose tax on the cash price at the time of sale.[57] Timing and valuation problems arise, however, if the legislature accedes to trade group demands and allows the tax on sale to be deferred until installment payments are received.

Assume that a seller sells goods for $1,000, payable over ten years with interest payable on the unpaid balance. The installment sale generally is reportable for VAT purposes when the sale is made or when the invoice is issued, even if payment is deferred.[58] Financial services (including finance

[56] See J. Due & J. Mikesell, SALES TAXATION: STATE AND LOCAL STRUCTURE AND ADMINISTRATION 155–159 (Johns Hopkins University Press 1983). Although many of the federal excise taxes follow a common pattern for periodic deposits, the windfall profits tax provides a different payment schedule. See Internal Revenue Code of 1986, §4995(b) (United States).

[57] Although installment sales are taxable when the contract is entered into, rental or lease agreements become subject to VAT on the earlier of receipt of payment or payment becoming due. NZ GST, *supra* note 5, at §§9(3)(a) and (b). This rule can be quite onerous in the case of high-priced real estate sales. See *Aukland Institute of Studies Ltd v. Commissioner of Inland Revenue*, 20 NZTC 17,685 (High Ct. N.Z. 2002). There is an exception for progress payments covering the construction of a building or engineering work. See NZ GST, *supra* note 5, at §9(3)(aa)(ii).

[58] See VATA 1994, *supra* note 1, at §6.

or interest charges) usually are exempt from tax. Thus, separately stated finance charges on the installment sales are exempt from VAT. Under this scheme, the seller bears an interest cost whenever the seller must pay tax on the total installment sale price before the buyer pays the tax imposed on that installment sale. If market conditions permit, the seller could avoid this interest cost if the purchaser on the installment plan were required to pay the full VAT imposed on the sale when the sale occurs.

If a government permits installment sellers to report installment sales as each installment is received,[59] the government can be compensated for the deferral of the tax on these sales by imposing an interest charge equal to the finance charge the seller imposes on the buyer. The seller, in this case, is taxed on the entire installment payment (interest and principal).[60]

The Japanese CT does not adopt either of these two possible methods of reporting installment sales. The CT permits an installment seller to use the income tax reporting rules to report installment sales for CT purposes. Under the income tax rules, the seller can report installment sales when each installment is received, rather than the total sales price when the sale occurs. A seller who uses that installment method for income tax purposes therefore can also report installment sales for CT purposes as each installment is received. Financial services are exempt from CT. If the seller separately states the principal and interest charges on each installment of the installment sale, the seller reports only the principal portion of the installment for CT purposes. Thus, the CT rules permit installment sellers to defer their CT liability on installment sales without imposing an interest charge for the privilege of deferring the tax.

2. Goods Diverted to Personal Use

If an owner takes inventory off the shelf or uses other business property for personal use, the transaction may be treated as a taxable sale. When is such a transaction reportable? In the United Kingdom, a transaction like this – a self-supply – is treated as a taxable sale[61] reportable on the last day of the business's accounting period in which the goods are made available or used.[62]

59 "The cash price for durable goods often is described by economists as equal to the discounted present value of the stream of consumption that takes place over the lifetime of the goods. The tax on the cash price, therefore, is assumed to be equal to the sum of the discounted value of the taxes imposed on the annual value of consumer durable goods over their lifetimes." A. Schenk & O. Oldman, principal draftsmen, "Analysis of Tax Treatment of Financial Services under a Consumption-Style VAT: Report of the American Bar Association Section of Taxation Value Added Tax Committee," 44 *The Tax Law*, 181, 187.

60 *Id.* at 188.

61 VATA 1994, *supra* note 1, at Sch. 4, ¶5(4).

62 S.I. 1995/2518, VAT Regulations 1995, Reg. 81 (United Kingdom).

3. Other Special Cases

It is common for a VAT Act to include different timing rules for specific kinds of transactions. For example, under consumer protection legislation, door-to-door sales may be cancelled by the buyer within a specified number of days after the sale.[63] In some of those countries, a door-to-door sale may not be reportable until the cancellation period expires.[64] Some countries have complex rules governing the time when a supply with the use of a voucher, a stored value card, or other payment instrument is reportable for VAT purposes.[65]

II. Transition Rules

A. Introduction

This section provides an overview of some of the issues that arise when a country changes the VAT rate or makes other changes in the VAT law. It is not intended to provide a comprehensive review of the transition rules needed when a VAT replaces a sales tax. A more detailed analysis of transition rules is provided elsewhere.[66]

B. Change in Rates

VAT rates are changed relatively frequently. If the rate change is small, no special rules may be needed. The new (often higher) rate can simply apply to sales reportable after a specified date. Such a simple approach must, however, be reconciled with the accounting method or methods allowed under the law. For example, suppose that under current law a sale is reportable at the earliest of payment, invoice, or occurrence of the sale. If the rate is increased, consumers can take advantage of the lower rate in the case of a major item that is not delivered until after the effective date by arranging for the seller to issue an invoice before the effective date or by making a prepayment, which will be taxed under the lower rate in effect at the time of the prepayment. To forestall such maneuvers, the law might, for example, provide that the new rate is effective for supplies made after a specified date, even if an invoice is issued or payment is made earlier.

Even this approach may not be sufficient if the rate change is substantial. A substantially increased rate to be applied to sales occurring after a future date could encourage consumers to buy goods or services before

[63] The valuation of supplies door to door is discussed later in this chapter.

[64] See NZ GST, *supra* note 5, at §9(2)(b), where the supply occurs a day after the cancellation period expires.

[65] See Goods and Services Tax Ruling 2003/12 (Australia).

[66] See, for example, ch. 14 of A. Schenk & O. Oldman, *Value Added Tax: A Comparative Approach with Materials and Cases* (Transnational Publishers 2001).

the effective date. To avoid such a disruption of behavior, the rate change could be made applicable retrospective to the announcement date. Of course this can be difficult for taxable persons to carry out as a practical matter.

C. Other Amendments

Similar problems arise when an amendment removes or narrows an exemption or provision for zero-rating. Sales that were exempt or zero-rated will now be taxed. Again, the strictest measure to prevent abuse would be to make the new rules applicable concurrently with the announcement by the government of the new rules.

Removal of an exemption also raises problems for the input credit. With respect to items on hand at the time of the change in law, no input credit was taken (because the acquisition related to an exempt supply). If sales of these items are now taxed, the amount collected will be excessive. A possible approach would be to allow an input credit for the cost of the items in inventory, but even this will not be precise because input credit denied for indirect costs relating to the items will still have been denied.

D. Registration Requirement

VAT amending laws may change who is required to register for VAT. If the registration rules are expanded, there is not much of a problem. New taxpayers will simply face a registration requirement as of a specified date. If the registration requirement is contracted, however, some taxpayers registered under the old rules will not have to be registered under the new rules. The designers of the new rules must decide whether these taxpayers should be given the option to remain registered. This may depend on the structure of the voluntary registration rules. The deregistration rules generally tax the person on the goods on hand on the last day that the registration is in effect. See discussion in Chapter 4.

E. Pre–Effective Date Contracts Not Specifying VAT

Businesses may enter into contracts for the supply of goods and services long before the goods are to be delivered or the services are to be rendered. These contracts may set consideration at an amount that does not take into account possible future tax changes. Thus, a contract may not provide for a new tax rate, for the fact that the VAT prior to amendment did not tax the goods or services to be provided or that the supplier was not registered under the pre-amendment rules.

VAT laws commonly allow a supplier to collect tax on a VAT-able sale, even if the tax is not contemplated or provided for in the contract.

For example, the South African VAT gives the seller the right to recover the new VAT from the buyer, unless there is a specific provision in the agreement to the contrary.[67]

III. Valuation Rules

A. Taxable Amount or Value of a Supply – General Rule

The value of a taxable supply generally is the sum of the amount of money and the fair market value of property or services received as consideration. VAT statutes contain special rules to calculate the value of particular transactions. In some cases, the valuation is linked to value under income or other taxes. For example, the value of taxable fringe benefits provided to employees may be based on the value of these benefits under the income tax rules.[68]

The VAT Directive defines the taxable amount or value of a supply as "everything which constitutes consideration obtained or to be obtained by the supplier, in return for the supply, from the customer or a third party, including subsidies directly linked to the price of the supply."[69] For goods, this amount generally is the purchase price or cost; for services, the full cost of providing the services; and for other supplies under the VAT Directive, Art. 27, the open market value of services rendered.[70]

The taxable amount includes "(a) taxes, duties, levies and charges, excluding the VAT itself; (b) incidental expenses such as commission, packing, transport and insurance costs, charged by the supplier to the customer. Expenses covered by a separate agreement may be considered to be incidental expenses by the Member States."[71]

There was a dispute in the EU as to whether a credit or debit card handling fee paid by a merchant and acknowledged by the retail customer was an exempt financial service that could be deducted from the taxable amount of the retail sale.[72] Although the UK court ruled that the taxable amount could not be reduced by the fee, merchants in other EU countries continued to remove the fee from the taxable amount of their sales. An EC Council Regulation specifies that such fees do not alter the taxable

[67] RSA VAT, *supra* note 30, at §67(1).

[68] For example, see NZ GST, *supra* note 5, at §10(7).

[69] VAT Directive, *supra* note 3, at Art. 73.

[70] *Id.* at Arts. 73–77. Art. 76 defines open market value as "the full amount that, in order to obtain the goods or services in question at that time, a customer at the marketing stage at which the supply or goods or services takes place would have to pay, under conditions of fair competition, to a supplier at arm's length within the territory of the Member State in which the supply is subject to tax."

[71] *Id.* at Art. 78.

[72] *Debenhams Retail plc v. Revenue and Customs Commissioners*, [2005] EWCA Civ 892, [2005] All ER (D) 233 (Ct. App. July 18, 2005).

amount of the retail sale if the price the customer pays is not affected by how payment is accepted.[73]

In Singapore, grants received by a supplier generally are not treated as consideration for supplies made by the recipient. The grantee may be treated as making a supply if the grantor receives any value in return for the grant.[74] The dispute in the EU over the treatment of subsidies directly linked to the price of supplies as part of the value of a taxable supply was resolved in part by the ECJ in the following *Keeping Newcastle Warm* case.

Keeping Newcastle Warm Limited v. Commissioners of Customs and Excise[75]

Article HA(l)(a) of the Sixth Directive provides [in part]:

The taxable amount shall be: ... everything which constitutes the consideration which has been or is to be obtained by the supplier from the purchaser, the customer or a third party for such supplies including subsidies directly linked to the price of such supplies.

The Home Energy Efficiency Grants Regulations 1992 (hereinafter the Regulations) provide for the award of grants to improve energy efficiency in dwellings occupied by certain categories of persons.

In particular, Regulation 5 provides that a grant may be awarded for various kinds of work, including energy advice, which is defined as advice relating to thermal insulation or to the economic and efficient use of domestic appliances or of facilities for lighting, or for space or water heating.

KNW has for several years carried out work in the context of the grant scheme established by the Regulations, including the provision of energy advice. It has declared and paid VAT on the amounts paid to it by the EAGA [Energy Action Grants Agency] in the form of energy advice grants, in the amount of GBP 10 per piece of advice.

KNW brought proceedings before the VAT and Duties Tribunal for a refund of the VAT so paid by it between 1 April 1991 and 31 August 1996. KNW submitted that the grant for energy advice was not directly linked to the price of the supply, within the meaning of Article 11A (l)(a) of the Sixth Directive, and accordingly did not form part of the taxable amount for that supply. It claimed that the grant of GBP 10 was paid without reference to the price which would have

[73] Council Regulation (EC) No. 1777/2005 of Oct. 17, 2005, laying down implementing measures for Directive 77/388/EEC on the common system of value added tax, Art. 13, effective Jan. 1, 2006.

[74] A grant to scientists engaged in research is not a supply by the grantee if the grantor does not receive any rights over the results of the research or other benefits. *CCH Singapore Goods and Services Tax Guide*, ¶3–180 (2005), citing IRAS e-Tax Guide No. 1994/GST/2.

[75] Case C-353/00, 2002 ECR I–5419, 2002 ECJ *CELEX LEXIS 3571* [edited by the authors].

been charged for the energy advice if it had not been provided to the consumer for free.

The Commissioners submitted that the amount of GBP 10 was not a standard sum but was linked to the amount properly charged for the energy advice and that in any event it constituted the consideration for the supply.

[T]he VAT and Duties Tribunal, Manchester, pursuant to an order of the High Court, referred the following questions to the Court:

> Is a payment made by the Energy Action Grants Agency to the Appellant, which receives it in respect of energy advice given to an eligible householder, a subsidy within the meaning of that word in Article 11 A(l)(a) of the EC Sixth Council Directive?

KNW argues that the sum of GBP 10 awarded by the EAGA in respect of each piece of energy advice constitutes a subsidy, but one which is not directly linked to the price of the supply because the amount in practice always corresponds to the ceiling set for it. Furthermore, since the supply of energy advice to consumers is free, the grant is in fact in the nature of a flat-rate subsidy to the operating costs of KNW and is not directly linked to any cost. Accordingly, the grant does not form part of the consideration for the supply within the meaning of Article 11 A(l)(a) of the Sixth Directive.

Relying inter alia on the Court's judgments in Cooperatieve Aardappelenbewaarplaats (Case 154/80 1981 ECR 445) and Tolsma (Case C-16/93 1994 ECR I–743), the United Kingdom contends that the financial assistance at issue in the main proceedings constitutes consideration within the meaning of Article 11A(l)(a) of the Sixth Directive and that that concludes the dispute before the national court. In any event there is a direct link between the subsidy and the services supplied by KNW. The contract between KNW and the householder sets out the nature and cost of the work which KNW will carry out and deducts the amount of financial assistance available to the householder from the amount payable by the householder. But if for some reason the financial assistance is not forthcoming, the householder is obliged to pay KNW for the whole of the work.

The Commission submits that the purpose of Article 11A(l)(a) of the Sixth Directive is to ensure that the taxable basis includes the whole of the consideration paid in respect of the supply of goods or services, whether the consideration is paid by the recipient or by a third party, which may be a public authority. Accordingly, where a third party, including, as is the case in the main proceedings, a public authority, contributes a sum of money for a specific service provided to an individual, that sum is part of the taxable amount, irrespective of whether the payment constitutes a subsidy directly linked to the price of the supply. It does not follow from the fact that the sum paid systematically amounts to GBP 10 that the subsidy is not directly linked to the price.

It is clear that the sum paid by the EAGA to KNW is received by the latter in consideration for the service supplied by it to certain categories of recipient.

As consideration in respect of a supply, that sum forms part of the taxable amount within the meaning of Article 11A(l)(a) of the Sixth Directive.

Accordingly the answer to be given to the questions referred to the Court must be that Article 11 A(l)(a) of the Sixth Directive is to be interpreted as meaning that a sum such as that paid in the case in the main proceedings constitutes part of the consideration for the supply of services and forms part of the taxable amount in respect of that supply for the purposes of VAT.

In some cases, it is not clear what amount is charged for the item sold. For example, is the amount for a service charge (or tip) on a restaurant bill includible as part of the taxable amount of the sale? In the United Kingdom, the service charge is part of the taxable consideration if it is automatically included in the bill and the customer must pay it,[76] but it is not taxable if the service charge is added to the bill but is optional with the customer.[77]

In some financial transactions, the taxable amount may equal the spread between the bid and ask prices set by the trader.[78]

Sales of telephone cards, rail or bus passes, or other vouchers generally are not taxable if consideration of a stated value is indicated on the voucher.[79] The sale is taxable when the voucher or pass is used to pay for the service generally in the amount deducted from the voucher or pass for the service. However, tokens, stamps, or vouchers issued without a stated consideration may be taxed on issuance for the consideration paid if the voucher is exchangeable for a particular item, such as milk.[80] In that case, on redemption of this milk or other voucher, the value of the supply is treated as zero.[81]

In one case, a retailer sold its goods listed in a catalogue at its more than 300 showrooms. It sold vouchers (for its merchandise) to other businesses at a discount. The purchasers of the vouchers used them as incentives, but the persons who used the vouchers were not aware of the fact that they were originally issued at a discount. In a judgment issued by the

76 See *Potters Lodge Restaurant Ltd v. Commissioners of Customs and Excise*, LON/79/286.

77 See *NDP Co. Ltd v. Commissioners of Customs and Excise*, [1988] VATTR 40 (London). According to Customs and Excise in Canada, a tip added to a restaurant bill as a mandatory or suggested gratuity is subject to the Canadian GST. Revenue Canada, Customs and Excise, Information for the Food Services Industry (1990).

78 *Customs and Excise Commissioners v. First National Bank of Chicago*, Case C-172/96, [1998], [1998] All ER (EC) 744, STC 850 (ECJ).

79 See, for example, NZ GST, *supra* note 5, at §10(16).

80 *Id.* at §10(17).

81 *Id.*

European Court of Justice, the court in *Argos Distributors Ltd v. Customs and Excise Commissioners* ruled that the retailer must treat only the amount received on sale of the vouchers, not the face amount, as consideration for the supply:

> Article 11 (A)(1)(a) of the Sixth Directive must be interpreted as meaning that, when a supplier has sold a voucher to a buyer at a discount and promised subsequently to accept that voucher at its face value in full or part payment of the price of goods purchased by a customer who was not the buyer of the voucher, and who does not normally know the actual price at which the voucher was sold by the supplier, the consideration represented by the voucher is the sum actually received by the supplier upon the sale of the voucher.[82]

Abuses in the use of "face value vouchers" prompted the United Kingdom to amend its VAT Act in 2003. It now provides that the issuance of a "face value voucher"[83] generally is a supply for VAT purposes and therefore is taxable on issuance or subsequent supply.[84] In contrast, the supply of a "credit voucher"[85] generally is disregarded, "except to the extent (if any) that it exceeds the face value of the voucher.[86] If a face value voucher (other than a postage stamp) is supplied in a composite transaction with other goods or services and "the total consideration for the supplies is no different, or not significantly different, from what it would be if the voucher were not supplied," the supply of the voucher is deemed made for no consideration.[87]

What if a purchaser fails to pay the purchase price for a supply when due and, in litigation, the purchaser is required to pay an additional amount in the nature of interest? Does the taxable amount include the interest added to the consideration that the purchaser owes the seller? In *BAZ Bausystem AG v. Finanzamt München für Körperschaften*,[88] the European Court of Justice held that as the interest had no connection with the services and did not

[82] Case C-288/94, [1996] ECRI–5311,1996 ECJ CELEX LEXIS 10813.

[83] VATA 1994, *supra* note 1, at Sch. 10A, ¶1(1) defines a "face-value voucher" as "a token, stamp or voucher (whether in physical or electronic form) that represents a right to receive goods or services to the value of an amount stated on it or recorded in it."

[84] *Id.* at ¶2.

[85] *Id.* at ¶3(1) defines a "credit voucher" as "a face-value voucher issued by a person who – (a) is not a person from whom goods or services may be obtained by the use of the voucher, and (b) undertakes to give complete or partial reimbursement to any such person from whom goods or services are so obtained."

[86] *Id.* at ¶3(2). There is an exception if the person from whom the goods or services are obtained fails to account for VAT on the supply to the person using the voucher to obtain them. *Id.* at ¶3(3). Similar treatment is provided for the issuance of "retail vouchers." *Id.* at ¶4(l)-(4). The consideration received for the supply of a face-value voucher that is a postage stamp is disregarded, except to the extent that it exceeds the face value of the stamp. *Id.* at ¶5. Supplies of other face-value vouchers generally are supplies for VAT purposes. *Id.* at ¶6(l)-(5).

[87] *Id.* at ¶7(b).

[88] [1982] 3 CMLR 688 (ECJ) (Case 222/81). This case involved Council Directive No. 67/228, Art. 8(2).

represent part of the consideration in a commercial transaction, but merely represented compensation for the delay in payment, the interest was not part of the taxable amount within the meaning of Article 11A(a)(l) of the Sixth Directive.

B. Sales Free of Charge or for a Nominal Charge

A transfer of goods or services may be made for no charge or for less than fair market value for a number of reasons. The transfer may represent an arm's-length transaction undertaken for business reasons. For example, a company producing personal hygiene products may mail free samples of its toothpaste to consumers. Because VAT is imposed on sales for consideration and these transactions are not transfers for consideration, there is no taxable sale.[89] The company will factor the cost of these free samples into the sales price for its toothpaste. This cost will be taxed when the company sells its toothpaste. Of course, any related input tax is creditable.

If a seller receives services from his buyer as part of the consideration for the seller's sale, the value of the services received is included in the taxable amount of the sale, but only if there is a sufficient connection between the services received and the supply. In *Naturally Yours Cosmetics Ltd v. Customs and Excise*,[90] a wholesaler of cosmetic products marketed its products through independent contractors (exempt retailers selling through living room or hostess parties). The wholesaler sold its "retailers" "a pot of cream" for about 10% of its wholesale price as a "dating gift." In that case, the ECJ ruled that under the valuation rule in Article 11(A)(1)(a) of the Sixth Directive,

> where a supplier ('the wholesaler') supplies goods ('the inducement') to another ('the retailer') for a monetary consideration (namely a sum of money) which is less than that at which he supplies identical goods to the retailer for resale to the public on an undertaking by the retailer to apply the inducement in procuring another person to arrange, or in rewarding another for arranging, a gathering at which further goods of the wholesaler can be sold by the retailer to the public for their mutual benefit, on the understanding that if no such gathering is held the inducement must be returned to the supplier or paid for at its wholesale price, the taxable amount is the sum of the monetary consideration and of the value of the service provided by the retailer which consists in applying the inducement to procure the services of another person or in rewarding that person for those services the value of that service must be regarded as being equal to the difference between the price actually paid for that product and its normal wholesale price.[91]

[89] See, for example, Canadian GST, *supra* note 40, at §165(1), imposing GST on the value of the consideration for a taxable supply.

[90] Case 230/87, [1988] STC 879 (ECJ Judgment).

[91] See VAT Directive, *supra* note 3, at Art. [72], quoted at note 70.

In *Empire Stores Ltd v. Commissioners of Customs and Excise*,[92] a mail-order business gave "free" gifts to individuals who provided personal information about creditworthiness of themselves or other potential customers. The court held that if there is a direct link between the goods provided and the consideration received (the information about the customer), there is a taxable transaction with the taxable amount equal to the cost to the firm (not the retail value) of the goods provided in return for that information.

If a supply is made at below fair market value, the transaction generally is taxed at the price charged if it is made at arm's-length but not if the transaction is between related parties.

C. Discounts, Rebates, and Price Allowances

Under the EU VAT Directive, the taxable amount does not include "(a) price reductions by way of discount for early payment; (b) price discounts and rebates granted to the customer and obtained by him at the time of the supply; (c) amounts received by a taxable person from the customer, as repayment for expenditure incurred in the name and on behalf of the customer, and entered in his books in a suspense account."[93]

The taxable value of a cash sale is the cash price charged.[94] If the invoiced price is subject to a prompt payment discount or penalty for late payment, trade or quantity discount or other price allowance, or rebate available at the time of the sale, the value of the supply may not be so clear. In countries that exempt interest (financial intermediation services), the portion of the price representing interest should not be taxed.[95] This is the rule in the United Kingdom for unconditional prompt payment discounts. Unless the supply is an installment sale, the taxable amount is the invoice price less the discount, even if the discount is not taken.[96] Conditional discounts are treated differently.[97]

92 Case 33/93, [1994] 3 All ER 90 (Judgment of the ECJ 1994).

93 VAT Directive, *supra* note 3, Art. 79.

94 Canadian GST, *supra* note 40, at §153(l)(a).

95 "Modern billing procedures provide two amounts – the full price and the VAT, and the discounted price and the discounted VAT." A. Tait, *Value Added Tax: International Practice and Problems* [hereinafter Tait, VAT], 374 (International Monetary Fund 1998).

96 VATA 1994, *supra* note 1, at Sch. 6, ¶14(1) and 4(2).

97 If the discount is conditional, such as conditioned on the purchase of a certain quantity of the seller's goods, the United Kingdom ignores the discount. If the condition is satisfied, the seller can issue a credit note that includes a reduction in VAT. See Notice 700, *The VAT Guide*, ¶7.3.2(c) (April 2002 ed.) (United Kingdom). "Credit, or a contingent discount, can permit a purchaser to reclaim all the tax on the supply as an input tax. The scheme can operate in two ways. Both seller and purchaser can agree that the credit need not affect the original VAT (usually because the credit is going to be used in the near future and is not permitted to be used for a good with a different rate; that is, the credit will be used for a similar good to that originally purchased). Alternatively, the credit can be held for some time and allowed to be used for the purchase of some other good liable to a completely different VAT rate. In the latter case, both purchaser and seller should adjust the original VAT charge and a credit note should be issued to the purchaser with,

> Many businesses, both retail and other, indulge in promotional schemes to induce customers to trade with them. These are common in both developed and developing countries and, while understandable from a commercial point of view, they are an annoyance to the tax administrator. The basic point is clear; the VAT is liable on the price actually paid by the customer.[98]

What if a shop sells its products to customers with 0% financing? If the shop makes an arrangement with the finance company under which the finance company makes a loan to the shop's customer at the retail price and then pays the shop a discounted amount that represents the finance charges on the loan, must the shop report the retail price or the amount received from the finance company as the consideration for the supply? In *Customs and Excise Commissioners v. Primback Ltd*,[99] the ECJ ruled that the taxable amount of the sale is the full amount payable by the purchaser, not the net amount received by the shop from the finance company.

If a customer obtains a coupon from a newspaper or other advertising source or a customer receives a coupon on a package that entitles the customer to a discount on future purchases, must the seller include the face amount of the coupon in determining the taxable consideration for the sale of the merchandise sold at a price less the coupon discount? See *The Boots Company plc v. Commissioners of Customs & Excise*,[100] decided under Sixth VAT directive, Art. 11(A)(3)(b) [VAT Directive Art. 79(b)], in which the court held that certain price discounts and rebates allowed at the time of a supply are not includible as part of the consideration for a supply. They cover "the difference between the normal retail selling price of the goods supplied and the sum of money actually received by the retailer for those goods where the retailer accepts from the customer a coupon which he gave to the customer upon a previous purchase made at the normal retail selling price."[101]

D. Pledged Goods and Repossessions

> When a consumer borrows money from a pawn shop and gives property as collateral for the loan, the transaction is a loan with no VAT consequences. If the pawned article is redeemed, the repayment of the loan also has no VAT consequences, other than the tax on the intermediation services provided by the lender, the pawn shop [if intermediation services are taxed]. If, on the other hand, within the prescribed time period (such as six months), the

of course, the seller keeping a copy. The credit note shows the details of registration numbers and addresses, but also must show the total amount credited excluding the VAT and the rate and amount of VAT credited. When the purchaser receives a credit note which includes VAT, then he must reduce his input tax by the amount shown in the tax period when he receives the credit note." Tait, VAT, *supra* note 95, at 375.

98 *Id.* at 384.

99 Case C-34/99, [2001] 1 WLR 1693, [2001] All ER (EC) 714 (ECJ 2001).

100 Case C-126/88, [1990] ECR I-1235, [1990] STC 387 (ECJ 1990).

101 ABA Model Act, *supra* note 32, at 49.

> article is not redeemed or interest is not paid on the loan, the pawn shop generally acquires legal ownership and the right to sell the pawned article. … When the pawn shop acquires the right to sell the property, the shop … [should be] treated as having purchased the pawned article. When the pawn shop sells the article, VAT is imposed on the price charged.[102]

To avoid the double tax, the pawn shop should receive treatment similar to that available to used goods dealers who buy goods from consumers for resale. One option is to grant the pawn shop a deemed or constructive credit for the VAT implicit in the shop's cost for the pawned item.[103] An alternative is to define the taxable amount of the sale as the difference between the sales price and the loan amount on the pawned item.[104]

E. Post-sale Adjustments

> A seller may make a refund, rebate, or price adjustment after output tax on the sale is reportable. These post-sale adjustments should reduce the seller's output tax and the buyer's input credit. [One option is to grant the seller] … a credit for VAT deemed attributable to these post-sale adjustments, but only if the seller issues proof of the adjustment (a credit invoice)…. A rebate like an automobile manufacturer's rebate to the retail purchaser of a car … [may be] treated as a post-sale price adjustment. … The manufacturer sold the car to a dealer and charged VAT on the selling price. When the manufacturer later issues a check to a retail customer, it is not reducing the sales price to the dealer. Nevertheless, the net effect is to reduce the consideration the manufacturer received for the car and the retail customer paid for the car. The manufacturer therefore should rebate some VAT to the customer and should reduce its VAT liability. Assume VAT is imposed at a 10 percent rate and that the manufacturer wants to rebate $550 ($500 plus $50 VAT) to the retail customer. … [The manufacturer should be able to] claim a $50 credit.[105]

What are the VAT consequences of year-end rebates to members of a cooperative? Are they price discounts that reduce VAT liability or are they returns on the members' ownership interest in the coop that do not affect VAT liability? Under the Canadian GST, a patronage dividend is treated as a price adjustment, and a cooperative can elect one of several methods

[102] *Id.*

[103] See Canadian GST, *supra* note 40, at §176. See also NZ GST, *supra* note 5, at §2(1) definition of input tax and §20(3)(a)(ia).

[104] See VAT Directive, *supra* note 3, at Arts. 304(a), 305–307, 310–312, covering taxable dealers in secondhand goods and other items typically purchased from unregistered persons.

[105] The credit is equal to the amount rebated multiplied by the tax rate at the time of sale/100 plus the same tax rate. In the example in the text, the credit would be $550 × 10/110, or $50. ABA Model Act, *supra* note 32, at 49–50.

to calculate the GST reduction and to issue tax refunds to its members.[106] The following UK case represents a different approach.

Co-operative Retail Services Ltd v. Commissioners of Customs and Excise[107]

HEADNOTE. The Appellant, Co-operative Retail Services Ltd, owned and operated a substantial number of retail stores throughout the UK, selling a wide range of merchandise including food and also a travel agency. It was a member of the Co-operative Movement and was run on co-operative principles.

The Appellant was incorporated under the Industrial and Provident Societies Acts, its share capital being variable, depending on the amount invested with it by its members. A person became a member by investing money with it to a maximum of £10,000. Members received or were credited with interest on that capital and, in the case of qualifying members, with what the Appellant called a 'dividend'. Such dividend was calculated as a percentage of the aggregate amount of the members' respective purchases during a prescribed period, irrespective of any profit or loss the Appellant might make.

Under the Appellant's Shareholder Card Scheme, a [Visa] Shareholder Card was issued to qualifying members by the Co-operative Bank plc (an associated company). To obtain a card, a member with an investment of £50 or more must make application for a card and be subject to certain financial checks. In addition, a shareholder who retained the minimum investment of £50 for one year and remained a card holder, received a 'dividend' on his purchases (except food) of 5 per cent and on travel a dividend of 2.5 per cent. Every two months he received a statement showing how his purchases had qualified for a dividend. Once a year his total dividend was transferred to his Shareholders account where it earned interest.

The dividend was paid only at the end of January in each year and not at the point of sale, save in the case of travel agency business where the 2.5 per cent dividend was immediately deducted from the cost of the travel arrangements. The average amount of dividend paid in one year was between £70 and £90.

The 'dividend' was so called partly for historical reasons and partly because the Appellant considered that it would appear more attractive to potential shareholders than if it were called a 'discount' which many retailers offered.

106 Canadian GST, *supra* note 40, at §233. The GST deduction is taken during the period the dividend is paid. *Id.* at §233(2).

107 [1992] VATTR 60 (Manchester VAT Tribunal) [edited by the authors].

The Commissioners contend that those payments, known as 'dividends', are properly so called and represent distributions of profit.

The Appellant, on the other hand, contends that the dividends are in reality discounts, representing not a distribution of profit but a reduction in the price of the merchandise; and that the value of its outputs is to be calculated after deduction from the gross value of those outputs of the aggregate amount of the dividends paid to the relevant customers. The Commissioners acknowledge that if the Appellant's contentions are correct the assessment must be discharged.

[W]e have found nothing to identify the dividends as distributions of profit and have come to the conclusion that they are correctly to be regarded as rebates. We have found the decisive factor to be the contractual obligation upon the Appellant to make the payments regardless of the level of its profit – indeed, whether or not it makes a profit or a loss, and without any reference to the magnitude of that profit or loss. Such an obligation, we consider, is inconsistent with the payments being distributions of profit.

Accordingly we allow the appeal.

F. Related Party Transactions

If a taxable person transfers property or services to an unrelated purchaser for less than market value, the tax generally is imposed on the price charged. What about sales to related persons or to employees at below fair market value?

> While the "price charged" rule may facilitate tax administration and may not result in any significant revenue loss if the related buyer or the employee is a taxable person eligible to credit any input tax on the purchase, the rule does not work well where the related buyer or the employee is not a taxable person or is a taxable person that is not entitled to input credit for VAT charged on the purchase. For example, employers may distribute or sell consumer goods or services to employees free of charge or at a below market price.[108]

[108] ABA Model Act, *supra* note 32, at 55. To the extent that these items are used for personal consumption by the recipients, the basic valuation rule would permit avoidance of VAT. *In Hotel Scandic Gasaback AB (Scandic') v. Riksskatteverket*, Case C-412/03, [2005] ECJ CELEX LEXIS 34, [2005] ECR I–743 (ECJ 2005), the case involved the taxable amount of meals the company in the hotel and restaurant business provided in a company canteen at a fixed price to its staff. The price generally exceeds the company's cost, but a future price may be less than cost. The ECJ ruled that under Arts. 2, 5(6), and 6(2)(b) of the Sixth Council Directive [VAT Directive, Art.s 2(1), 16, and 26(1)(b)], a member cannot adopt a rule "whereby transactions in respect of which an actual consideration is paid are regarded as an application of goods or services for private use, even where that consideration is less than the cost price of the goods or services supplied."

Below-market sales of goods or services by a corporation to its shareholders may be undertaken to avoid VAT. "In these situations, the 'price charged' rule permits avoidance of VAT."[109]

To prevent this potential abuse in related party and similar transactions, the supplier may be required to value the sale at fair market value. For example, the Canadian GST uses the fair market value standard to value a sale to an unregistered person in a non-arm's-length transaction if the seller charges less than fair market value.[110]

G. Margin Schemes

There are a number of transactions that do not lend themselves to the credit-invoice method of calculating the taxable amount of a supply. The problem arises most frequently where the value of a supplier's service is represented by the margin or spread between the consideration received and payments made. The VAT treatment is complicated when some or all of the payments for business inputs are made to unregistered persons. Financial intermediation services, gambling and other games of chance, and insurance are illustrative. These are discussed in detail in Chapters 10 and 11.

Sales of used goods, works of art, collectors' items, and antiques raise similar issues relating to the calculation of the taxable amount of a supply.[111] Many countries have adopted margin schemes to account for sales of these goods. Absent a special scheme, the entire price charged for these previously owned items would be taxed.

Travel agent services pose a special problem in the calculation of the taxable amount of a supply. A travel agent may serve as a principal in providing travel services (such as organizing a convention for a business) or serve as an agent. When the travel company serves as principal, it generally is compensated an amount represented by the spread between the price charged for the travel services and the company's cost in obtaining the services from hotel and other travel service providers. The ease with which travel or tour companies can supply these services offshore or over the Internet has created competitive inequalities that are prompting countries to modify their VAT rules governing travel agents and tour companies.

In the EU, the VAT Directive provides a special margin scheme for travel agents,[112] if a travel agent deals with customers in his own name as principal and uses supplies of other taxable persons in providing the

[109] ABA Model Act, *supra* note 32, at 55.

[110] Canadian GST, *supra* note 40, at §155(1). There are some exceptions. See *id.* at §155(2).

[111] See discussion of used goods *supra* Chapter 6 (Section IV).

[112] See VAT Directive, *supra* note 3, at Arts. 306–310, applicable when a travel agent deals with customers in his own name and uses supplies of other taxable persons in providing the travel services. The ECJ ruled that the margin scheme applies to a company that organized an international study and language trip for high school and college students. *Finanzamt Heidelberg v. ISt internationale Sprach- und Studienreisen GmbH*, C-200/04, [2005] ECR I-8691.

travel services. In contrast, when a travel agent acts as agent of his customer (acts as an intermediary) or when the agent supplies the travel services using his own facilities, the special scheme does not apply. When the agent acts as intermediary, the agent will bill his customers for the amount paid to the suppliers of the travel services plus a commission and charge VAT on the total amount. The agent then will claim credit for VAT imposed on the agent's purchase of the travel services on behalf of the customer. When the agent supplies travel services using its own facilities (such as when the agent owns the hotel providing the accommodations), under the normal VAT rules, the accommodation and other travel services are taxable where the service is provided (where the hotel is located).[113] The unequal treatment of travel agents operating within the EU and those operating outside the EU but providing services either for persons within the EU or on travel within the EU prompted the European Commission to propose a Directive changing the special scheme for travel agents.[114]

H. Sales to Door-to-Door Sellers and Similar Independent Contractors

> Some businesses sell their products through independent contractors who resell to ultimate consumers door-to-door and not through a regular place of business. For VAT purposes, the door-to-door sellers may be considered retailers. Alternatively, the supplier may be considered the retailer; and the door-to-door sellers may be treated as agents. The reason this difference is important is that if the VAT statute provides a de minimis exemption for small traders, many of these door-to-door sellers would come within the exemption. The establishment of a network of independent contractors instead of employees may enable a distributor to sell its products to ultimate consumers without VAT on the value added by the door-to-door sellers, thus obtaining an advantage over its competitors that market their products through company-owned stores or through employees selling door-to-door. This marketing arrangement is similar to franchise operations where the franchisee is selling only the franchiser's products or services. Arguably, they should receive equivalent VAT treatment. There is, however, at least one significant difference. A franchisee typically sells to customers from a regular place of business.[115]

[113] K. Dewilde, K. Eeckhout, & C. Boone, "The Margin Scheme for Travel Agents: The European Commission's Proposal to Simplify the European VAT Rules," 14 *Int'l VAT Monitor* 7 (Jan./Feb. 2003).

[114] The proposal is part of a VAT strategy to improve the operation of the VAT system within the Internal Market (COM 2000) 348 final of June 7, 2000, discussed and cited in *id.* at p. 11. The proposal for the Council Directive was presented February 8, 2002. *Id.* To date, although there have been amendments by the European Parliament, the proposal has not become final. *Id.* at 13. The most recent action is a Proposal for a Regulation regarding supplies of travel services – COM (2003) 78 final/2 of March 24, 2003.

[115] ABA Model Act, *supra* note 32, at 57.

The potential abuse in this area can be minimized or eliminated if the small business exemption threshold is set at such a low level that these sellers (whether selling door-to-door or at living room parties) are caught in the VAT net. The problem with this approach, especially for developing countries without an adequate audit staff, is that it may substantially increase the number of tax returns that must be processed and may impose substantial compliance costs on small businesses that are not the target of the lower threshold, all without any significant increase in VAT revenue.

The alternative employed in some countries is to require the manufacturer or distributor who sells to these door-to-door sellers to report as the taxable amount of the sales the retail price of the items sold. The manufacturer and distributor know these prices because they generally set the recommended retail prices.

For example, in the EU, it is common for member states to prevent loss of revenue by providing that sales by producers or wholesalers to unregistered persons for resale be valued at retail, not the price charged the unregistered retailers. In *Gold Star Publications Ltd v. Commissioners of Customs and Excise*, [1992] 3 CMLR1 (Q.B. 1992), the taxpayer attempted to avoid this treatment under the UK VAT[116] by selling to unregistered intermediaries at catalogue prices less a 30% discount. The court held that the sales must be valued at the open market value, which in this case meant the value for a retail sale, not the value of the sale to the intermediaries.[117] In a similar case involving sales through unregistered agents, the court held that the Commissioners could order a mail-order company to use the catalogue prices as reasonable estimates of open market value, even if the agents often resold the products at less than the full catalogue price. See *Fine Art Developments plc v. Customs and Excise Commissioners*, 1993 British Value Added Tax Cases 21, at 33 (Q.B. 1993), in which the court stated, in part:

> Since it is impossible or excessively difficult to ascertain the actual prices at which these goods are sold to all the final consumers, the commissioners are entitled by Community law to use open market value as the basis for their assessments. What is the open market value in any case is a matter to be decided on the available evidence.

I. Self-Supply Transactions

When business assets or services are diverted to personal use, the business generally must report that diversion as a taxable supply. Under the VAT Directive,[118] the taxable amount of this diversion of business assets

[116] See VATA 1994, *supra* note 1, at Sch. 6, ¶2.

[117] By dictum, the court found that the 30% discount was not a discount as that term is meant in Sch. 6 of the UK VAT because the discount was the only compensation that the intermediary would receive for his or her efforts.

[118] VAT Directive, *supra* note 3, at Arts. 74 and 75.

or services to personal use generally is the purchase price of the goods or services, not the fair market value of such assets or services.

J. Taxable Amount – Imports

1. General Rule

Tax on imports generally is imposed on the customs value plus customs and other duties and taxes other than the VAT itself.[119] If insurance and freight are not included in customs value, they generally are added to the taxable value.[120] Some imports do not have a customs value or the customs value is not an accurate reflection of the value of the imports. The latter may occur if the invoice price is used as the customs value and the import comes from a related seller. In these situations, the taxable amount is the fair market value of the import. In the *Addidas* case,[121] the New Zealand court held that royalties paid by a NZ subsidiary to its foreign parent were includible in the VAT-able value of the goods imported by the subsidiary.

"Under United States customs law, dutiable value does not include any separately stated cost of transportation and insurance for the goods to the port of importation.[122] The European practice is to include these costs as part of the VAT-able value of imports."[123] In the United Kingdom, the value of imported goods from outside the EU includes, if not already included in customs value, the taxes, duties, and so on other than VAT, and incidental expenses such as commissions, packaging, transport, and insurance at least to the first destination in the United Kingdom.[124] New Zealand has a similar set of rules.[125]

2. Imports Placed in a Bonded Warehouse

Imports generally are taxed when they "enter" the country of import. If imports are placed in a bonded warehouse in the importing country,

[119] See, for example, NZ GST, *supra* note 5, at §12(2). "[Historically, customs duties were] ... imposed on imports to equalize foreign and domestic prices for goods, not primarily to raise revenue. It therefore would not be unreasonable to impose VAT on the customs duty-inclusive price of imports." ABA Model Act, *supra* note 32, at 47.

[120] See NZ GST, *supra* note 5, at §12(2)(c).

[121] *Addidas New Zealand Ltd v. Collector of Customs*, 1 NZCC ¶55–001 (1999).

[122] 19 U.S.C.A. §1401a(b)(l)(West 1980) (United States) provides that the value of imported merchandise generally is the price payable for the merchandise when sold for exportation to the United States, increased only by the packaging costs incurred by the buyer, any selling commission incurred by the buyer, the value of any assist, any royalty or license fee that the buyer must pay as a result of the import, and the proceeds of any subsequent resale, disposal, or use of the import that accrue to the seller. Dutiable value therefore does not include the cost of transportation and insurance.

[123] ABA Model Act, *supra* note 32, at 52.

[124] VATA 1994, *supra* note 1, at §21(1) and (2). There are special rules covering prompt payment discounts, works or art, antiques, and certain collectors' pieces. *Id.* at §21(3)-(6).

[125] NZ GST, *supra* note 5, at §12(2).

they generally are not treated as imported until they are removed from the bonded warehouse for domestic use or consumption. The value of the import should be based on the value at the point that they are removed from the warehouse, which may be the price paid or some other amount.[126]

3. Imports of Previously Exported Articles

> If a business sends goods to another business for repair, warranty work, assembly, manufacture, or other change and does not transfer ownership of the goods, the VAT consequences should be the same, whether the work is performed within or outside the ... [country]. Normally, if goods are shipped abroad by a business, the transfer is zero rated. If the same goods are re-imported, VAT generally is imposed on the import on the basis of the customs value. ... The importer may pay the import tax to Customs at the point of import and claim an input credit in the first return filed after the import. While the net result may be the same as having the work done ... [domestically], the importer may suffer some cash flow cost. The cash flow problem could be avoided by [not zero rating the export and] taxing the re-import on the amount charged for the repair or other work abroad.... If the goods are repaired under warranty free of charge, the import tax is zero.[127] A nontaxable person would not have any VAT consequences associated with the export for repair and would be subject to VAT on the amount charged for the repair of the imported article.[128]

The United Kingdom taxes only the value of the work done abroad on goods exported for such work and then reimported, assuming ownership of the goods has not changed.[129]

4. Imports from Unregistered Persons

When imported goods are purchased from a foreign, VAT-registered supplier, the foreign supplier's export sale generally is zero-rated (free of VAT) and the importer is subject to VAT on import. If the imported goods are purchased from an unregistered foreign person in a country with a VAT, the supplier likely was subject to VAT when he purchased the goods. The export by this unregistered person is not zero-rated, and therefore the price to the importer may include some embedded VAT. If the importing country taxes the full value or price charged for the goods, the goods will bear excessive VAT. In *Staatssecretaris van Financiën v. Gaston Schul Douane-Expéditeur BV*,[130] the ECJ interpreted the policies underlying the Treaty of

[126] See *id.* at §12. For a discussion of the British rules on fiscal warehousing, see VATA 1994, *supra* note 1, at §18A.

[127] Presumably, the buyer paid VAT on the value of the warranty that was included in the price of the product.

[128] ABA Model Act, *supra* note 32, at 53–54.

[129] Value Added Tax Regulations 1995 (SI 1995/2518), reg. 126 (United Kingdom).

[130] Case 47/84, [1985] ECR 1491. See discussion of this case, *supra* Chapter 7 (Section III(C)(2)).

Rome to reach a decision that prevented the imposition of VAT on the full value of the import if the import came from a consumer in another EU country.[131]

IV. Discussion Questions

1. How should VAT apply to credit sales and installment sales? Should the tax on the entire cash-equivalent sale price be collected by the seller at the time of the delivery of the goods or should the tax collection be based on each payment of part of the purchase price as received by the seller? Why? Compare the UK and the Japanese approaches (Section I(C)(1) of this chapter).
2. What are the advantages and disadvantages, to the government and to businesses subject to VAT, if businesses can use the same method of accounting for VAT purposes that they use for income tax purposes? What problems arise if a seller subject to VAT reports on the cash method and that seller's buyer subject to VAT reports on the accrual method, or vice versa?
3. Mr. Black is a furniture manufacturer. For his daughter's wedding, he gave her various pieces of furniture he manufactured. The cost of raw materials, supplies, and other items may be estimated at $1,000. The cost of labor may be estimated at $1,000. Mr. Black would sell this furniture to a wholesaler for $2,400 (including $400 profit). The wholesaler's price to the retailer would be $2,800, and the retailer's price to the consumer would be $3,300. Under the VAT Directive, is VAT chargeable on the gift made by Mr. Black? If you think that it is taxable, what is the taxable amount?

[131] In *Tulliasiamies and Antti Siilin*, Case C-101/00, [2002] ECR I–07487, [2002] ECJ CELEX LEXIS 3627, the ECJ reached a similar result with respect to the import of used cars from another member state.

9

Zero-Rating, Exemptions, and Exempt Entities

I. Introduction

This chapter covers exemptions and zero-rating. As discussed in more detail in Chapter 2, an exemption may be an "item" exemption limited to particular supplies of goods or services or an "entity" exemption applicable to all or most supplies by a particular kind of entity. Zero-rating generally is provided for exports of goods (regardless of the nature of the goods exported)[1] and exports of some services. In the case of supplies by a unit of government or nonprofit organization, an exemption may be provided for all supplies, restricted to certain supplies on the basis of the nature of the goods or services supplied, or provided for all supplies except those that compete with the private sector.

The next two parts of this chapter cover zero-rating and exemptions, with attention focused on the complexity resulting from borderline cases involving "item" exemptions or "item" zero-rating. Sections IV and V discuss cases in which two or more items with different VAT consequences are bundled to obtain the desired tax treatment and A-B-C transactions in which an upstream supplier wants to integrate its supply with a downstream supply to obtain the VAT treatment of the downstream supply. Section VI of this chapter discusses some of the special VAT problems associated with the nonprofit and governmental sectors and proposals to include more services by these sectors in the VAT base.

II. Zero-Rated Sales[2]

A. In General

A zero-rated sale is a taxable sale, subject to tax at a zero-rate. The supplier can claim credit against output tax for tax on purchases attributable to

[1] For an exception, see Value Added Tax Act 2005, Act No. 7 of 2005, Sch. II, ¶2(s) (exemption rather than zero-rating for "an export of unprocessed agricultural products") (Commonwealth of Dominica).

[2] Zero-rating is the term used in the United Kingdom and many other countries. Some VAT regimes describe these transactions as exempt supplies, with a right to recover tax

TABLE 9.1. Zero-rating only midstream or only retail stage

	Wholesale stage zero-rating		Retail stage zero-rating	
Manufacturer				
Sales $400,000	$40,000		$40,000	
No purchases	00		00	
Net VAT paid		$40,000		$40,000
Wholesaler				
Sales $1 million	$00		$100,000	
Purchases $400,000	(40,000)		(40,000)	
Net VAT paid (refund)		(40,000)		60,000
Retailer				
Sales $1.2 million	$120,000		$00	
Purchases $1 million	$00		(100,000)	
Net VAT paid (refund)		120,000		(100,000)
Total tax paid government		$120,000		$00
Consumers pay		$1,320,000		$1,200,000

that sale. The sale therefore is basically free of VAT.[3] If a sale at retail is zero-rated, the final consumer buys the item free of VAT. If the zero-rate applies only at an intermediate (such as wholesale) stage, and the retail stage was taxable, the tax not collected at the intermediate stage is recovered on the retail sale. Unlike exemption, zero-rating of an intermediate supply avoids cascading. In Table 9.1,[4] this distinction is illustrated for a 10% VAT.

Whereas many countries tend to limit zero-rating to exports of goods and related services, the United Kingdom and Canada zero-rate some food, and some countries zero-rate other specified supplies.[5] Some countries include a transactional zero-rating for the sale of a going concern

on business inputs. The EU approach is to list domestic supplies that are exempt or that member states can exempt. See Council Directive 2006/112/EC of 28 November 2006 on the common system of value added tax (OJ L347, 11.12.2006, p. 1) [hereinafter VAT Directive], at Arts. 135–142. It then allows a deduction for tax on inputs attributable to some exempt transactions (zero-rated) and denies deduction for other supplies that are exempt (exemptions). See VAT Directive, Arts. 168 and 169. Australia uses the term "GST-free supplies" in place of zero-rated and uses "input taxed" in place of exempt. See A New Tax System (Goods and Services Tax) Act 1999, Act No. 55 of 1999, Part 3-1, Div. 38.

3 Purchases from an exempt small business and other exempt purchases may include the seller's noncreditable VAT paid in its costs (inputs). This VAT therefore is included in the price of zero-rated sales.

4 See A. Schenk, Reporter, VALUE ADDED TAX – A MODEL STATUTE AND COMMENTARY: A REPORT OF THE COMMITTEE ON VALUE ADDED TAX OF THE AMERICAN BAR ASSOCIATION SECTION OF TAXATION [hereinafter ABA Model Act], 62.

5 For example, New Zealand zero-rates business-to-business financial services. See Goods and Services Tax Act 1985, 1985 No. 141 [hereinafter NZ GST].

between registered businesses. These transactions, if taxable, do not generate any net revenue to the government.

The tax advantage resulting from zero-rating encourages businesses to test the limits of zero-rating for particular goods or services. Litigation under the EU's VAT Directive and the Canadian GST is illustrative.

A UK VAT tribunal held that the zero-rating granted for equipment and appliances designed solely for use by a handicapped person was not available for a covered walkway constructed for the protection of students of a charity school providing VAT-exempt training and education services for disabled students.[6] The tribunal found that these walkways served as weather protection and were not designed solely for the use of handicapped students. Zero-rating goods sold to consumers reduces the prices they pay and reduces government revenue. To tailor zero-rating to particular food items, the United Kingdom zero-rates food, but makes exceptions for some food items such as confectionery, and then adds exceptions to these exceptions (so that some confectionery is zero-rated). It thus is not surprising that courts in the United Kingdom are asked to make fine-line distinctions among various food items. For example, in the following case, the court reviewed the trial court's finding that Pringles were similar to potato crisps, potato sticks, and potato puffs, and therefore were taxable.

Commissioners for Her Majesty's Revenue and Customs and Proctor & Gamble UK[7]

Lord Justice Jacob (giving the first judgment at the invitation of Mummery LJ):

Introduction

Are Pringles "similar to potato crisps and made from the potato?" [The decision involves] as much as £100m of tax for the past and about £20m a year for the future.

"Pringle" is the trade mark of a very successful product of the respondent, Procter and Gamble ("P&G"). It is a manufactured savoury snack product. We are concerned with the variety known as "Regular Pringles." The following [description] is taken from some of the findings of fact of the Tribunal:

> Regular Pringles are made from potato flour, corn flour, wheat starch and rice flour together with fat and emulsifier, salt and seasoning.

[6] This zero-rating now is included in the British Value Added Tax Act 1994, ch. 23 [hereinafter VATA 1994], Sch. 8, Group 12. If these items are purchased by a charity, they are zero-rated under Groups 12 and 15. *Portland College v. Commissioners of Customs and Excise*, MAN/92/226 (1993).

[7] [2009] EWCA Civ. 407. In the Supreme Court of Judicature, Court of Appeal (Civil Division) on appeal from the High Court of Justice, Chancery Division (2009) [edited by the authors].

> The precise percentages of each ingredient of Regular Pringles have varied from time to time and are not identical in the range of flavours because, for example, the flavouring may affect the salt content.
>
> Regular Pringles are manufactured by mixing the dry ingredients into dough with water and emulsifier, cutting shapes out of a dough sheet, frying it for a few seconds, adding oil and salt, cooling it and then adding flavours. A similar procedure applies to maize (in US parlance, corn) chips like tortillas. [T]he manufacturing process causes oil to go into the spaces throughout the texture of the product replacing the water content removed during the frying. This gives the "mouth-melt" feel when it is eaten. By contrast with potato crisps most of the fat stays on the surface.

Regular Pringles have a regular shape in the form of a saddle, which aids stacking them enabling high production speeds.

The recipe for Regular Pringles has varied somewhat. Of importance in this case is the amount of potato flour. In the final product this amount has hovered around 40% – sometimes a little more, sometimes a little less. Currently it is 42%.

Food products are generally zero-rated for VAT purposes; see Schedule 8, Group 1 of the VAT Act 1994. However there are some excepted items. Item 5 reads:

"Any of the following when packaged for human consumption without further preparation, namely, potato crisps, potato sticks, potato puffs and similar products made from the potato, or from potato flour, or from potato starch, and savoury products obtained by the swelling of cereals or cereal products; and salted or roasted nuts other than nuts in shell."

The question I posed at the outset is based upon item 5. The language of the question has its meaning to be derived from that context.

Art. 28.2 of the Sixth Directive (Art. 110 of the VAT Directive) permits zero rating in this case, but does not require it or provide any aid to construction. The only other possible aid to construction, one relied upon by Mr Roderick Cordara QC for P&G, emerges from Item 2 of the excepted items (see below).

The Tribunal answered the question "yes," so that Regular Pringles fell to be standard rated. On appeal, Warren J answered the question "no," so that the product would be zero rated. Arden LJ granted permission for this second appeal on the papers.

The Approach on a Second Appeal

[C]ounsel were agreed that what really mattered was whether the decision of the Tribunal was wrong in law. For it is the Tribunal which is the primary fact finder. It is also the primary maker of a value judgment based on those primary facts. Unless it has made a legal error in that in so doing (e.g. reached a perverse finding or failed to make a relevant finding) or has misconstrued the statutory test it is not for an appeal court to interfere.

The approach on appeal to value judgments of the primary decision maker

Often a statutory test will require a multi-factorial assessment based on a number of primary facts. Where that is so, an appeal court (whether first or second) should be slow to interfere with that overall assessment – what is commonly called a value-judgment.

In its full form the statutory question merely re-stated is whether Pringles are "similar [to potato crisps, potato sticks, potato puffs] and made from the potato, or from potato flour, or from potato starch."

[I]t is a composite question. So although it is convenient to ask separately whether Pringles are "similar" to potato crisps etc and whether they are "made from potato," one must also take into account the composite nature of the question. Moreover it is, to my mind, precisely the sort of question calling for a value judgment.

Before going further, I have this general observation. This sort of question – a matter of classification – is not one calling for or justifying over-elaborate, almost mind-numbing legal analysis. It is a short practical question calling for a short practical answer. The Tribunal did just that.

First, then, is a Pringle "similar to a potato crisp etc?" Or to be more precise was the Tribunal wrong in law so to hold? As I have said it made its primary findings of fact. Those findings are unchallenged. They include comparisons with corresponding aspects of a potato crisp (e.g. "This gives the 'mouth-melt' feel when it is eaten. By contrast with potato crisps [where] most of the fat stays on the surface"; and "they are a uniform yellow colour which is paler than a potato crisp.")

The Tribunal then went on to consider each side's arguments.

So it is [14] and [15] which contain the essential reasoning:

> [14] While we are aware of the potato content, the reasonable man may not be aware of the fact that a normal potato crisp has a maximum potato percentage in the 70s, the next largest ingredient being fat, or that Regular Pringles have a potato content of about 42 per cent because this is not required to be stated on the packaging. While the potato content of Regular Pringles is not advertised as such, a purchaser can see from the label that it does contain potato.
>
> [15] Standing back and taking all the factors of appearance, taste, ingredients, process of manufacture, marketing and packaging together (other than the ones we have stated above that we should ignore) and applying the reasonable man test, we consider that while in many respects Regular Pringles are different from potato crisps

and so they are near the borderline, they are sufficiently similar to satisfy that test.

I cannot see anything wrong, still less anything wrong in principle, with this. It was not incumbent on the Tribunal in making its multifactorial assessment not only to identify each and every aspect of similarity and dissimilarity (as this Tribunal so meticulously did) but to go on and spell out item by item how each was weighed as if it were using a real scientist's balance. In the end it was a matter of overall impression. All that is required is that "the judgment must enable the appellate court to understand why the judge reached his decision" and that the decision "must contain … a summary of the Tribunal's basic factual conclusion and statement of the reasons which have led them to reach the conclusion which they do on those basic facts" (*per* Thomas Bingham MR in *Meek v Birmingham City Council* [1987] IRLR 250). It is quite clear how this Tribunal reached its decision. In the words of Sir Thomas Bingham in *Meek* the parties have been told "why they have won or lost."

I should say a word about the Tribunal's reference to the "reasonable man." It may come from this court's use of him in *Ferrero*. The issue was whether the product concerned was "a biscuit" within the meaning of excepted item 2 of Schedule 8 Group 1. The Tribunal had used the test of "what view would be taken by the ordinary man in the street who had been informed as we have been informed." This Court accepted that approach.

To my mind this approach is saying no more than "what is the reasonable view on the basis of all the facts" – it does not matter if some of the facts would not be known to the "man in the street." That is why the test accepted as proper in *Ferrero* adds "who had been informed as we have been informed." The uninformed view of the man in the street is deliberately not being invoked.

So one can put the test for an appeal court considering this sort of classification exercise as simply this: has the fact finding and evaluating Tribunal reached a conclusion which is so unreasonable that no reasonable Tribunal, properly construing the statute, could reach?

The Tribunal here perhaps concerned itself a little too much with how much the man in the street would know about the potato content of Pringles. It does not matter – one of the factors to be considered in judging similarity is, to my mind, clearly potato content.

The Judge was persuaded that the Tribunal had misread the language of the statute. He thought one should disregard the potato content when considering the question of similarity. I cannot agree. As I have said similarity involves a question of degree and a multifactorial assessment of all the factors. One would not disregard the potato content if there were not the further requirement of "made of the potato." I do not see why adding it makes any difference.

There really is no more to be said about similarity.

The "made of potato" point is equally short. Mr Cordara's primary submission (rejected by the Judge) was that the product should be 100% made of potato or nearly so.

I reject these submissions. First the normal use of language does not compel that conclusion.

Secondly, not even potato crisps or potato sticks (no-one knew about potato puffs, even what they were) are 100% potato. So it is improbable that Parliament intended that a product, to be similar, must do so.

Thirdly the Item 2 "wholly or partly" point is not helpful. One can equally well say that when Parliament wanted to say "wholly" it said so. The different classes are essentially free-standing: so there is no reason to suppose that the draftsman trawls over each for an unnecessarily elaborate consistency between them.

If that point failed, Mr Cordara's alternative submission was that the product should have a sufficient content of potato to give it a quality of what he called "potatoness." Implicit in the submission was a challenge: if 100% potato is not called for, what is the lower limit?

I reject that submission too. As to "potatoness" I cannot think Parliament intended to invoke such an elusive test. It is an Aristotelian question: does the product have an "essence of potato." Moreover I have no real idea what the suggested test means: when pressed Mr Cordara could not provide any further elucidation.

What then of the lower limit challenge? I am reminded of what Justice Holmes wrote:

"When he has discovered that a difference is difference of degree, that distinguished extremes have between them a penumbra in which one gradually shades into the other, a tyro thinks to puzzle you by asking you where you are going to draw the line and an advocate of more experience will show the arbitrariness of the line proposed by putting cases very near it on one side or the other, *Law and Science in Law* Collected Legal Papers 1921, pp. 232–233."

Putting the point another way: you do not have to know where the precise line is to decide whether something is one side or the other.

The Tribunal said:

> [17] Here the potato flour content is over 40 per cent; it is the largest single ingredient by about 9 percentage points; and it is nearly three times larger than the other flours in the ingredients taken together. We have to give a yes or no answer to the question "are Regular Pringles [partly] made from the potato, from potato flour or from potato starch" and we are bound to say yes. There are other ingredients but it is made from potato flour in the sense that one cannot say that it is not made from potato flour, and the proportion of potato flour is significant being over 40 per cent. The fact that it is also made from other things does not affect this.

I cannot begin to see anything wrong with that, still less that that was not a conclusion which any reasonable Tribunal could reach. There is more than enough potato content for it to be a reasonable view that it is made from the potato.

The Judge thought that the statutory language required the potato content of the product concerned should be the same, or about the same, as that of a potato crisp etc (i.e. excluding the oil). I do not see why. Moreover as Mr Vajda pointed out, the potato content of crisps varies over a not insignificant range so the test is inherently uncertain.

To my mind the Judge's test (not advanced primarily by Mr Cordara before him or supported as his primary argument on this appeal) suffers from that wooliness objection, but the real objection is that it is just too elaborate. The statute is simply posing a kind of jury question "is it similar to a potato crisp etc and made of potato?" The question is not capable of elaboration or complex analysis.

Finally I should say a word about a decision of a differently constituted Tribunal concerning a product called Pringles Dippers (2003) VAT Decision 18381. It was decided that this was zero-rated. Part of the decision was devoted to the question of whether a Pringle Dipper was "made from the potato." It was held not, although the amount of potato was broadly the same as for a Regular Pringle. The present Tribunal took the view that the earlier Tribunal had erred in law [in] this respect, though there were other reasons (having no parallel with the present case) why the ultimate decision was justifiable. The present Tribunal were entitled to take that view – there is no rule of *stare decisis* between Tribunals of co-ordinate jurisdiction. Rightly it did so only when convinced the earlier decision was wrong – for broadly Tribunals should strive to achieve consistency amongst themselves. But once so convinced it was its duty to apply the law as it considered it to be. As far as we are concerned it was the present Tribunal which approached the question "made from the potato" correctly in law.

In the result I would allow this appeal.

The *Colour Offset Ltd* case[8] is another example of the kind of line drawing problems that result from the grant of zero-rating to particular goods or services. The law zero-rated books or booklets.[9] The court held that the supply of a blank diary and address book was not zero-rated.

[P]eople generally think of books as things to be read rather than as blank pages bound together. A filled-in diary of historical or literary interest may be a book because it is retained to be read or looked at. But a blank diary is not a book in the ordinary sense of the word. Likewise a blank address

[8] [1995] STC 85 (Q.B.Div.).

[9] Item 1 of Group 3 of Sch. 5 to the Value Added Tax Act 1983 [the same as Sch. 8, Group 3, item 1 of the VATA 1994, *supra* note 6].

book is not in the ordinary sense a book and it does not become one simply because its name includes the word 'book'.

The Canadian Tax Court held that "paan leaves" chewed to aid digestion and also used in Hindu religious ceremonies are not zero-rated "food for the purpose of human consumption."[10] In Canada, where "basic groceries" are zero-rated and catering services are taxable, the court held that a supply of prepared meals that required the customer to heat the food in an oven for thirty minutes or in a microwave for three minutes was zero-rated food, not catering.[11]

B. Zero-Rated Exports

Countries typically define the jurisdictional reach of their VATs under the destination principle – that is, goods and services are taxed in the country of consumption. As a result, exports are zero-rated and imports are taxed.[12] For administrative reasons, many countries zero-rate only defined categories of exported services (usually linked to exported goods).[13]

A country may rebate VAT paid on goods purchased by travelers if the goods physically accompany the departing tourists and can be inspected by customs officials at the airport or border post. This traveler rebate is not as prevalent as it once was.

C. Zero-Rating Other Transactions

Some business-to-business sales may appropriately be granted zero-rating if such treatment does not result in the loss of any net revenue and taxing such transactions may impose unnecessary cash and other burdens on the parties to the transactions. This applies in particular to sales of a going concern. EU countries typically zero-rate those transactions.[14]

[10] See *Kandawala v. The Queen*, [2004] GSTC 131 (Tax Ct. Canada), criticized in D. Sherman, Canada: Paan Leaves Are Not "Food" – But Why Exactly?, 16 *International VAT Monitor* 147 (Mar./Apr. 2005).

[11] See D. Sherman, "Canada," 14 *International VAT Monitor*, 441 (Sept./Oct. 2003), criticizing the analysis but not the result in *Complete Cuisine & Fine Foods to Go (1988) Ltd. v. The Queen*, [2003] GSTC 81 (Tax Ct. Canada Informal Procedure); and *Chef on the Run Franchise Division Ltd. v. The Queen*, [2003] GSTC 82 (Tax Ct Canada Informal Procedure).

[12] To fully implement the destination principle, exports should be zero-rated, even if the exporter comes within the de minimis exemption or otherwise is not a taxable person subject to VAT.

[13] Most countries include insurance and freight in the taxable value of imported goods. In addition, to prevent the distortion of competition between domestic and foreign suppliers of services, under a reverse charge rule, increasingly, countries tax recipients of imported services (such as financial and educational institutions) who cannot recover tax on their purchases. See discussion in Chapter 7.

[14] See, for example, VATA 1994, *supra* note 6, at §30(4) and Sch. 8. By zero-rating the transaction, the seller is entitled to claim credit for tax on purchases used in connection with the negotiation and sale of the business.

Absent conditions imposed on zero-rating of these transactions, there are opportunities for abuse. If the documents confirming the sale do not specify that the sale is zero-rated, the seller and the buyer may take inconsistent VAT positions with respect to the sale. The seller might claim that the sale is zero-rated (so that the seller does not have to report and remit VAT on the sale), and the buyer may claim that the purchase was taxable (so that the buyer can claim credit for the VAT component in the purchase price). To avoid the opportunity for the parties to take inconsistent positions on the nature of the transaction, some countries that zero-rate a sale of a going concern impose conditions.[15] The seller and the buyer may be required to file a form signed by both, specifying that the sale is being treated as a zero-rated sale of a going concern.[16] The authorities may refuse to recognize a seller's attempt to split a sale of a business into two transactions to obtain a tax or other advantage.[17]

What is the real justification for the zero-rating of the sale of a going concern? Does the same rationale apply to sales of other high-priced assets, such as the sale of aircraft and ships?

Zero-rating also has been provided in some business-to-business financial services in a number of countries (see Chapter 11 for details). Some transactions may be ignored for VAT purposes – that is, they are treated as nonsupplies or supplies other than in the course of a taxable activity. See discussion in Chapter 5 (II)(A)(1).

III. Exempt Sales

In exempt sales, the seller does not charge VAT or list VAT on sales documents, and as a result, the buyer will not have input credits on those purchases. In addition, the seller is not able to claim input credits for VAT on any of its purchases attributable to the exempt sales. Although exemptions on retail sales may be expected to reduce prices to consumers and reduce VAT revenue to the government, sales exemptions granted in the middle of the production-distribution chain that are followed by taxable sales by the purchasers of the exempt items actually increase consumer prices and VAT revenue over the amounts that would occur if those midstream sales were taxable. For example, with a 10% VAT,

> [i]f a wholesaler makes purchases of $400,000 plus $40,000 VAT, and makes sales of $1,000,000 exempt from VAT, the seller probably will shift the

[15] NZ GST, *supra* note 5, at §ll(l)(m); Value Added Tax Act No. 89 of 1991, §ll(l)(e) (South Africa) [hereinafter RSA VAT]. In South Africa, the requirements for zero-rating are discussed in practice No. 14, discussed in C. Beneke, ed., *Deloitte & Touche VAT HANDBOOK*, ¶7.43 (2003).

[16] NZ GST, *supra* note 5, at §§ 11(1)(c) and 24(1).

[17] In *re Debonne Holdings Pty Ltd v. Commissioner of Taxation*, 64 ATR 1154 (Admin. App. Tribunal 2006), the parties executed one contract as the supply of a going concern and another as a land contract, but the Tribunal held that there was only one transaction for GST purposes.

> $40,000 VAT into the prices for its products or services. Thus, if the selling prices in the absence of VAT would total $1,000,000, the seller would charge $1,040,000. The exemption in the middle of the production-distribution chain may result in a higher total tax burden on final consumers. Continuing the example, if a retailer made taxable sales of $1,240,000 ($1,200,000 plus $40,000 VAT built into the $1,040,000 cost of its purchases), the retailer will charge consumers $1,240,000 plus $124,000 VAT, or $1,364,000. The retailer does not receive any input credit because the wholesaler did not charge VAT on its sales.[18] If the wholesaler's sales were taxable, the retailer would have paid $60,000 more for its purchases ($1,100,000 VAT-inclusive price), but it could have claimed a $100,000 input credit and probably would have sold its goods to consumers for $1,200,000 plus $120,000 VAT, or $1,320,000 VAT-inclusive prices. The midstream exemption therefore increased the tax-inclusive prices to consumers by $44,000 over what they would have been if the sales were taxable at the wholesale stage, the $40,000 non-creditable VAT on the wholesaler's purchases and a $4,000 VAT at the retail level on this $40,000 cost buried in the retail prices.
>
> A retail stage exemption does not produce the punitive effect on consumers described above. The effect of an exemption from VAT on retail sales is to remove from the tax base the value added at the exempt retail stage. If, in the example, the wholesaler's sales were taxable and the retailer's sales were exempt, the retailer would charge customers $1,200,000 plus the non-creditable $100,000 VAT on its purchases, or $1,300,000. The $200,000 value added by the retailer would be exempt from the 10 percent ($20,000) VAT. These examples of exempt sales, expanded to cover sales to the wholesaler, are tabulated in the following chart[19] [see Table 9.2].

Businesses with low annual turnover may be exempt from VAT on all of their sales if they are covered by a small business exemption. The exemption has effects comparable to the effects just described for item exemptions. The small business exemption is discussed in Chapter 4.

The difficult line-drawing problems for zero-rated items, discussed earlier, exist for exemptions for specific items as well. For example, the United Kingdom exempts the "disposal of the remains of the dead."[20] The exhumation and reinternment of human remains to clear the former cemetery for redevelopment was held not to qualify for exemption.[21] The VAT Directive's exemption, incorporated into Belgium VAT, for the "supply" of human organs, blood, and milk[22] did not apply to the transportation of human organs and samples for hospitals and laboratories

[18] If the wholesaler's sales were VAT-able, the wholesaler would have charged $1,000,000 plus $100,000 VAT on its sales and would have obtained an input credit for the $40,000 VAT on its purchases. The wholesaler would have remitted the $60,000 net to the government.

[19] ABA Model Act, *supra* note 4, at 62–64.

[20] This service is exempt under VATA 1994, *supra* note 6, at Sch. 9, Group 8, item 1.

[21] *UFD Limited v. Commissioners of Customs and Excise*, [1982] 1 CMLR 193. The Tribunal held that the service was not supplied in the course of the service provider's business as an undertaker.

[22] VAT Directive, *supra* note 2, at Art. 132(1)(d).

TABLE 9.2. Exempting only midstream or only retail stage

Manufacturer	*Wholesale stage exemption*		*Retail stage exemption*	
Sales $400,000	$40,000		$40,000	
No purchases	00		00	
Net VAT paid		$40,000		$40,000
Wholesaler				
Sales if exempt are $1,040,000	$00			
Sales of $1,000,000 if taxable	00		100,000	
Purchases $400,000		00	(40,000)	
Net VAT paid (refund)				$60,000
Retailer				
Sales if wholesaler exempt = $1,240,000	124,000 00			
Sales if wholesaler taxable = $1,300,000			00	
Purchases if wholesaler exempt = $1,040,000		124,000	00	00
Purchases if wholesaler taxable = $1,000,000				
Net VAT paid				
Total tax to government		164,000		100,000
Consumers pay		$1,364,000		$1,300,000
Consumers would have paid if sales at all stages taxable		$1,320,000		$1,320,000

(a service), even though the sale of human organs was prohibited by local law.[23]

A principle of European Union VAT law is that member states must exempt imports that are exempt if supplied domestically. In *Commission of the European Communities v. Italian Republic*,[24] the court held that by imposing VAT on imports of free samples of low value, Italy violated this principle because comparable domestic supplies of free samples were exempt from VAT.

The EU VAT Directive lists activities that are eligible for exemption. A common problem in the EU is that member states adopt differing views on the scope of the authorized exemptions. The Directive, Art. 132(1)(m), exempts some services closely linked to sport or physical education by nonprofit-making organizations. The Netherlands exempted berths and moorings for vessels. The EC asked the Netherlands to abolish the exemption, claiming that it is not closely linked. In the following *PFC Clinic* case,

[23] See Case C-237/09, *Belgian State v. Nathalie De Fruytier* (Judgment of the ECJ 2010),

[24] [1990] 3 CMLR 718.

the Swedish tax authority denied a deduction for tax on purchases attributable to a variety of plastic surgeries and cosmetic treatments, claiming that the services were exempt under VAT Directive, Art. 132(1)(b) and (c).

Skatteverket v. PFC Clinic AB[25]

Judgment

This request for a preliminary ruling concerns the interpretation of Article 132(1)(b) and (c) of Council Directive 2006/112/EC of 28 November 2006 on the common system of value added tax (OJ 2006 L 347, p. 1) (the 'VAT Directive').

The request has been made in proceedings between the Skatteverket, which is competent, in Sweden, to collect value added tax ('VAT') and PFC Clinic AB ('PFC') concerning VAT due for the accounting period May 2007.

Legal context

The VAT Directive

Title IX of the VAT Directive is entitled 'Exemptions'. Chapter 1 of that title consists solely of Article 131, which is worded as follows:

> 'The exemptions provided for in Chapters 2 to 9 shall apply without prejudice to other Community provisions and in accordance with conditions which the Member States shall lay down for the purposes of ensuring the correct and straightforward application of those exemptions and of preventing any possible evasion, avoidance or abuse.'

Chapter 2 of Title IX is entitled 'Exemptions for certain activities in the public interest'. It consists of Articles 132 to 134.

Article 132(1) of the VAT Directive provides:

'Member States shall exempt the following transactions:

(b) hospital and medical care and closely related activities undertaken by bodies governed by public law or, under social conditions comparable with those applicable to bodies governed by public law, by hospitals, centres for medical treatment or diagnosis and other duly recognised establishments of a similar nature;

(c) the provision of medical care in the exercise of the medical and paramedical professions as defined by the Member State concerned;"

Article 133 of the VAT Directive provides that Member States may subject, on a case-by-case basis, the granting to bodies other than those governed by public law of the exemption provided for in, among

[25] Case C91/12 (ECJ 2013) [edited by the authors].

other provisions, Article 132(1)(b) thereof in respect of one or other of the conditions that it lays down.

Under Article 134 of the VAT Directive:

'The supply of goods or services shall not be granted exemption, as provided for in Article 132(1)(b) in the following cases:

(a) where the supply is not essential to the transactions exempted;
(b) where the basic purpose of the supply is to obtain additional income for the body in question through transactions which are in direct competition with those of commercial enterprises subject to VAT.'

In accordance with Article 173 of the VAT Directive, in the case of goods or services used by a taxable person both for transactions in respect of which VAT is deductible and for transactions in respect of which VAT is not deductible, only such proportion of the VAT as is attributable to the former transactions is to be deductible. The deductible proportion is to be determined, in accordance with Articles 174 and 175 of that directive, for all the transactions undertaken by the taxable person.

Swedish law

In accordance with Chapter 3(4) of Law 1994:200 on VAT (mervärdeskattelagen (1994:200), 'ML'), the supply of services which constitute medical care, dentistry or social care is exempt from taxation.

According to Chapter 3(5) of the ML, medical care means the medical prevention, examination or treatment of diseases, physical impairment and injuries and care in pregnancy and confinement, if the care is provided in a hospital or other institute operated by the public bodies or in the private sector institutes for inpatient care or if the care is provided otherwise by persons specially licensed to practise as medical professionals.

The dispute in the main proceedings and the questions referred for a preliminary ruling

PFC offers medical services in the field of plastic surgery and cosmetic treatments. At the material time, it provided services involving both cosmetic and reconstructive plastic surgery and also some skincare services.

PFC carries out procedures such as breast augmentation and reduction, breast lifts, abdominoplasty, liposuction, face lifts, brow lifts, eye, ear and nose operations and other plastic surgery. That company also offers treatments such as permanent hair removal and skin [rejuvenation] by pulsed light, anti-cellulite treatments and botox and restylane injections.

PFC claimed the refund of input tax for the period corresponding to May 2007. In response to that claim, the Skatteverket refused both the refund and the deduction of that tax. According to the Skatteverket,

VAT could not be refunded in respect of exempt transactions nor could a deduction of VAT be granted since cosmetic and reconstructive surgery constitute medical care exempt from taxation.

The Högsta förvaltningsdomstolen is unsure as to the manner in which the expressions 'medical care' and 'the provision of medical care' are to be applied in the context of medical services consisting in surgery and various treatments of the kind at issue in the main proceedings. That court asks in particular whether those expressions must be understood as including any type of plastic surgery or other cosmetic treatments carried out by doctors or other authorised healthcare professionals, or whether the underlying purpose of the acts [in] question is decisive for that purpose.

Consideration of the questions referred

By its questions, which it is appropriate to examine together, the referring court asks essentially whether Article 132(1)(b) and (c) of the VAT Directive must be interpreted as meaning that the supply of services such as those at issue in the main proceedings, consisting of plastic surgery and cosmetic treatments, are exempt from VAT.

Thus, by its second question, that court asks more specifically whether a preventive or therapeutic purpose for such services has any effect on the issue of whether they are exempt, which is the subject of the first question. If the answer is affirmative that court asks, by its third question, whether, in order to determine the existence of such a purpose, the subjective understanding the recipients of those services have of them must be taken into consideration. The fourth question asks what effect the fact that such services are supplied by licensed medical personnel has on the assessment to be carried out in the main proceedings.

With respect to those points, it must be recalled from the outset that the terms used to specify the exemptions in Article 132 of the VAT Directive are to be interpreted strictly, since they constitute exceptions to the general principle that VAT is to be levied on all goods and services supplied for consideration by a taxable person. Nevertheless, the interpretation of those terms must be consistent with the objectives pursued by those exemptions and comply with the requirements of the principle of fiscal neutrality. Thus, the requirement of strict interpretation does not mean that the terms used to specify the exemptions referred to in Article 132 should be construed in such a way as to deprive the exemptions of their intended effect (see by analogy, in particular, Case C86/09 *Future Health Technologies* [2010] ECR I5215, paragraph 30 and the case-law cited).

As regards medical services, it is apparent, by analogy, from the case-law on Directive 77/388 that Article 132(1)(b) and (c) of the VAT Directive, which have distinct fields of application, are intended to regulate all exemptions of medical services in the strict sense (see *Future Health Technologies*, paragraphs 26, 27 and 36 and the case-law cited). Article 132(1)(b) of that directive covers all services supplied in a hospital environment while Article 132(1)(c) thereof covers medical services provided outside such a framework, at the private address of the person providing the care, at the patient's home or at any other place (see, to that effect, Case C141/00 *Kügler* [2002] ECR I6833, paragraph 36, and *Future Health Technologies*, paragraph 36).

Accordingly, the concept of 'medical care' in Article 132(1)(b) of the VAT Directive and that of 'the provision of medical care' in Article 132(1)(c) are both intended to cover services that have as their purpose the diagnosis, treatment and, in so far as possible, cure of diseases or health disorders (see *Future Health Technologies*, paragraphs 37 and 38).

In that regard, it should be borne in mind that, whilst 'medical care' and 'the provision of medical care' must have a therapeutic aim, it does not necessarily follow that the therapeutic purpose of a service must be confined within a particularly narrow compass (see *Future Health Technologies*, paragraph 40 and the case-law cited).

Accordingly, it is clear from the case-law that medical services effected for the purpose of protecting, including maintaining or restoring, human health can benefit from the exemption under Article 132(1)(b) and (c) of the VAT Directive (see *Future Health Technologies*, paragraphs 41 and 42 and the case-law cited).

It follows, in the context of the exemption laid down in Article 132(1)(b) and (c) of the VAT Directive, that the purpose of the services such as those at issue in the main proceedings is relevant in order to determine whether those services are exempt from VAT. That exemption is intended to apply to services whose purpose is for diagnosing, treating or curing diseases or health disorders or to protect, maintain or restore human health (*Future Health Technologies*, paragraph 43).

Thus, services such as those at issue in the main proceedings, in so far as their purpose is to treat or provide care for persons who, as a result of an illness, injury or a congenital physical impairment, are in need of plastic surgery or other cosmetic treatment may fall within the concept of 'medical care' in Article 132(1)(b) of the VAT Directive and 'the provision of medical care' in Article 132(1)(c) thereof respectively. However, where the surgery is for purely cosmetic reasons it cannot be covered by that concept.

However, the Skatteverket states, in essence, that the examination of the purpose of the operation or treatment concerned would be extremely onerous for suppliers of services and the tax authorities and raises the possibility of 'serious problems of application and definition'.

It is true that, in situations such as that at issue in the main proceedings, it is possible that the same taxable person carries out both exempt activities under Article 132(1)(b) or (c) of the VAT Directive and activities subject to VAT.

However, such a situation is specifically envisaged by that directive and is governed by Article 173 et seq. thereof. In accordance with Article 173, in the case of goods or services used by a taxable person both for transactions in respect of which VAT is deductible and for transactions in respect of which VAT is not deductible, only such proportion of the VAT as is attributable to the former transactions is to be deductible. The deductible proportion is to be determined, in accordance with Articles 174 and 175 of that directive, for all the transactions undertaken by the taxable person acting as such.

As far as concerns whether the subjective understanding that the recipients of services, such as those at issue in the main proceedings, have must be taken into consideration in the assessment of the purpose of a specific intervention, which is the subject of the third question, it follows from the case-law that the health problems covered by exempt transactions under Article 132(1)(b) and (c) of the VAT Directive may be psychological (see to that effect, in particular, Case C45/01 *Dornier* [2003] ECR I12911, paragraph 50, and Joined Cases C443/04 and C444/04 *Solleveld and van den Hout-van Eijnsbergen* [2006] ECR I3617, paragraphs 16 and 24).

However, the subjective understanding that the person who undergoes plastic surgery or a cosmetic treatment has of it is not in itself decisive for the purpose of determining whether that intervention has a therapeutic purpose.

Since that is a medical assessment, it must be based on findings of a medical nature which are made by a person qualified for that purpose.

It follows that the fact, referred to in the fourth question, that services such as those at issue in the main proceedings are supplied or undertaken by a licensed member of the medical profession or that the purpose of such interventions is determined by such a professional, may influence the assessment of whether interventions such as those at issue in the main proceedings fall within the concepts of 'medical care' or 'medical treatment' within the meaning of Article 132(1)(b) and (c) of the VAT Directive respectively.

In order to give a complete answer to the questions referred, it must be recalled that, in order to determine whether services such as those at issue in the main proceedings are exempt from VAT, pursuant to Article 132(1)(b) or (c) of the VAT Directive, account must be taken of all the requirements laid down in Article 132(1)(b) or (c) and of the other relevant provisions of Title IX, Chapters 1 and 2 thereof (see by analogy, in particular, Case C262/08 *CopyGene* [2010] ECR I5053, paragraph 37), and not simply of the issue of whether such services fall within the concepts of 'medical care' and 'the provision of medical care' within the meaning of Article 132(1)(b) and (c) of that directive.

> Thus, as far as concerns, in particular, the exemption laid down in Article 132(1)(b) of the VAT Directive, where appropriate, in addition to the full text of that provision, Articles 131, 133 and 134 of that directive must be taken into consideration.
>
> In light of all of the foregoing considerations, the answer to the questions referred is that Article 132(1)(b) and (c) of the VAT Directive must be interpreted as meaning that:
>
> – supplies of services such as those at issue in the main proceedings, consisting in plastic surgery and other cosmetic treatments, fall within the concepts of 'medical care' and 'the provision of medical care' within the meaning of Article 132(1)(b) and (c) where those services are intended to diagnose, treat or cure diseases or health disorders or to protect, maintain or restore human health;
> – the subjective understanding that the person who undergoes plastic surgery or a cosmetic treatment has of it is not in itself decisive in order to determine whether that intervention has a therapeutic purpose;
> – the fact that services such as those at issue in the main proceedings are supplied or undertaken by a licensed member of the medical profession or that the purpose of such services is determined by such a professional may influence the assessment of whether interventions such as those at issue in the main proceedings fall within the concept of 'medical care' or 'the provision of medical care' within the meaning of Article 132(1)(b) and (c) of the VAT Directive respectively;
> – in order to determine whether supplies of services such as those at issue in the main proceedings are exempt from VAT pursuant to Article 132(1)(b) or (c) of the VAT Directive, all the requirements laid down in subparagraphs 1(b) or (c) thereof must be taken into account as well as the other relevant provisions in Title IX, Chapters 1 and 2 of that directive such as, as far as concerns Article 132(1)(b), Articles 131, 133 and 134 thereof.

The medical exemption in the EU also was tested in cases in which the medical professional did not render services for the purpose of diagnosis, treatment, or cure of a disease or health disorder.[26] In these cases, the ECJ strictly interpreted the exemption for "medical care."[27] Where a medical expert conducted biological tests at the request of an Austrian court to

[26] See generally, J. Swinkels, "VAT Exemption for Medical Care," 16 *International VAT Monitor* 14 (Jan./Feb. 2005). In the EU, although a member state has discretion to define paramedical professions exempt from VAT, it must ensure that it is treating comparable medical practitioners equally; thus, psychotherapists providing treatments like those of psychiatrists, psychologists, and others must be treated comparably. *H. Solieveld and J.E. van den Hout-van Eijnsbergen v. Staatssecretaris van Financiën*, Case C-443/04 and C-444/04 (ECJ April 27, 2006).

[27] See VAT Directive, *supra* note 2, at Art. 132(l)(c).

determine the "genetic affinity" of individuals, the ECJ ruled that the tests were not exempt from VAT under Article 13(A)(1)(c) because they were not done for the purpose of diagnosis, treatment, or cure of a disease or health disorder.[28]

The ECJ ruled consistently in two other cases. In the *Dr. Peter L. d'Ambrumenil* case,[29] doctors served as expert medical witnesses in legal cases involving medical negligence, personal injury, and disciplinary proceedings and claimed that some of their services were exempt from VAT. The ECJ found that the "purpose" of a medical service determines its qualification as an exempt medical service. A service is not exempt if the purpose is to "enable a third party to take a decision which has legal consequences for the person concerned or other persons."[30] In *Margarete Unterpertinger*,[31] the ECJ ruled that an expert medical report on the taxpayer's state of health to be used in litigation involving her claim for payment of a disability pension was not exempt from VAT.

Other exemptions under the EU's VAT have been the subject of extensive litigation. One is education. The VAT Directive, Art. 132(1)(i) exempts "the provision of children's or young people's education, school or university education, vocational training or retraining, including the supply of services and of goods closely related thereto, by bodies governed by public

[28] Case C-384/98, *D v. W* [2000] ECR 1–6795. In contrast, medical tests (to observe and examine patients for prophylactic purposes) conducted by a laboratory governed by private law were exempt. Case C-106/05, *L.u.R GmbH v. Finanzamt bochum-Mitte* (ECJ June 8, 2006).

[29] Case C-307/01, *Peter d'Ambrumenil and Dispute Resolution Services Ltd v. Commissioners of Customs and Excise*, [2003] ECR 1–13989.

[30] *Id.* at ¶[61]. The ECJ ruled that some services may be taxable and some exempt medical care under Article 13(A)(1)(c). The following medical services are exempt under Article 13(A)(1)(c):

- conducting medical examinations of individuals for employers or insurance companies,
- the taking of blood or other bodily samples to test for the presence of virus, infections or other diseases on behalf of employers or insurers, or
- certification of medical fitness, for example, as to fitness to travel,
- where those services are intended principally to protect the health of the person concerned."

The following medical services were not exempt:

- "giving certificates as to a person's medical condition for purposes such as entitlement to a war pension;
- medical examinations conducted with a view to the preparation of an expert medical report regarding issues of liability and the quantification of damages for individuals contemplating personal injury litigation;
- the preparation of medical reports following examinations referred to in the previous indent and medical reports based on medical notes without conducting a medical examination;
- medical examinations conducted with a view to the preparation of expert medical reports regarding professional medical negligence for individuals contemplating litigation;
- the preparation of medical reports following examinations referred to in the previous indent and medical reports based on medical notes without conducting a medical examination.

[31] Case C-212/01, *Margarete Unterpertinger v. Pensionsversicherungsanstalt der Arbeiter*, [2003] ECR I-13859.

law having such as their aim or by other organisations recognised by the Member State concerned as having similar objects." In a case the EC filed against Germany, Germany exempted from VAT the research activities conducted for consideration by state universities. The issue was whether these research services were "closely related" to university education for purposes of what is now VAT Directive, Article 132(l)(i). Strictly interpreting the exemptions as exceptions to the general principle that VAT is to be levied on all services supplied for consideration by a taxable person, the court held that the "closely related" concept was "designed to ensure that access to the benefits of such education is not hindered by the increased costs of providing it that would follow if it, or the supply of services and of goods closely related to it, were subject to VAT."[32] According to the court, the conduct of research projects for consideration, if subject to VAT, would not increase the cost of university education.[33] By exempting these services, Germany violated its obligations under what is now the VAT Directive.

In the following *Open University* case, the issue was whether the production and broadcasting of correspondence courses by the BBC to the university came within the exemption for university education.

Open University v. Commissioners[34]

HEADNOTE. In 1966 a report to Parliament recommended the establishment of a university which would present its courses through television and radio, programmed learning and audio-visual aids. [I]t was envisaged that such university would enter into 'an educations partnership' with the British Broadcasting Corporation ('the BBC').

[T]he Open University ('the University') was founded by Royal Charter dated the 23rd April 1969 having as its main object the advancement and dissemination of learning and knowledge by teaching and research by a diversity of means such as broadcasting and technological devices appropriate to higher education, by correspondence tuition, residential courses and seminars and in other relevant ways.

Each University course includes a number of television programmes which a student taking that course is expected to watch. At the beginning of a year the University sends to each student taking a course a printed guide to that course which summarises the television programmes included therein and indicates the work which he is expected to undertake during the year. At the same time it sends out printed and other material for the course. Students are required periodically to complete and submit assignments for evaluation and each summer to attend a six-day residential course. At the end of the year students must sit for an examination in their subjects.

[32] Case C-287/00, *Commission of the European Communities v. Federal Republic of Germany*, [2002] ECR I-05811, at ¶47.

[33] *Id.*

[34] [1982] VATTR 29 [edited by the authors].

[Under the Agreement between the BBC and the University:]

(a) the BBC would at the request of the University prepare and produce programmes incorporating such material as the course teams (on which the BBC should be represented) should nominate or approve;
(b) the BBC would provide adequate and suitable studio facilities for the production of the University programmes for broadcasting by television and by radio;
(c) programmes would be broadcast up to an eventual limit of thirty hours each week for a basic schedule of thirty-six weeks of the year, together with such additional supporting programmes as might be mutually agreed; and
(d) the University would pay to the BBC the actual costs ... to meet the requirements of the University as agreed by the BBC and the University....

[The University claimed that the BBC services were exempt] as 'the provision, otherwise than for profit, of education ... of a kind provided by a university', ... [or] as 'the supply of any ... services incidental to the provision of any education ... because, under the 'educational partnership' between the BBC and the University, the BBC provided the University education jointly with the University. Further, in the alternative the University contended that such services supplied by the BBC were exempt from tax under Article 13Al(i) of the Sixth [Directive, and the taxpayer could rely on it.] The Commissioners argued that the BBC merely supplied to the University the services and the facilities specified. They also argued that ... the University alone provided the education to the students.

JUDGMENT BY: TRIBUNAL. In our opinion, in making such supplies the BBC is not itself providing education. Education is provided by the University to its students in consideration of their fees. [T]he BBC is providing, in our view, the basic services of preparing, producing, presenting and reproducing the University's programmes on radio and television. ... It may be that members of the staff of the BBC are working on the course teams in the preparation of such programmes, but this does not result in the education, or any part thereof, being provided by the BBC, either alone or jointly with the University. However, in making such supplies the BBC is, in our opinion, supplying services 'incidental to the provision of any education' within item 4 of such Group 6. But, in our judgment, as the BBC is not itself providing the students with education, such services are excluded from the exemption....

We now go on to consider Article 13A1 (i) of the Sixth Council Directive (VAT) [VAT Directive, Art. 132(1)(i)]. In our view, [the] ... services and goods supplied by the BBC are, in the words of the subparagraph, 'closely related' to the supply of university education, but are

> not themselves university education. In our view the natural meaning to be given to the subparagraph, read as a whole, is that exemption is granted to supplies of services and of goods closely related thereto if made by the body governed by public law providing the education, vocational training or retraining.
>
> [T]he relevant services supplied by the BBC to the University are chargeable to tax at the standard rate. ... This appeal must be dismissed.

In some countries, the domestic transport of passengers is exempt. This exemption generally is included to reduce the VAT burden on lower-income households, especially where buses or minivans are used as transportation to work. Should the transportation in tour buses be included within the exemption?[35]

Some transactions claimed as exempt may be challenged as not within the purpose of the VAT Directive. See discussion in Chapter 10 (Section II).

IV. Allocation of a Single Price between Supplies with Different Tax Consequences

In some situations, a sale for a single price may represent both taxable and zero-rated components or both taxable and exempt components. In these transactions, should the supply be classified as a single supply or should the single supply be broken down into its component parts for VAT purposes? For example, if a sale is predominantly exempt and includes only an incidental component that is taxable, for administrative reasons, it may be treated as fully exempt. In *International Bible Students Association v. Commissioners of Customs and Excise*, [36] the Jehovah's Witnesses charged for food served at its annual religious convention. The court held that the catering was closely linked to "spiritual welfare" services conducted at the convention and therefore came within the exemption for such services under the Sixth Directive.[37]

The distinction between a single or composite supply, or in Australia, between a mixed and composite supply, is discussed in detail in Chapter 5 (II)(E). The discussion here assumes that a supply for a single price is split into two supplies, and each is taxed differently. The consideration must be allocated, for example, between the taxable and zero-rated supplies or between the taxable and exempt supplies. This problem is discussed in the *Rogers* case.

[35] In South Africa, game viewing drives are taxable at the standard rate, and tax on game viewing vehicles is creditable. See South Africa Revenue Service, Interpretation Note No. 42, sec. 5 (April, 2007), citing Value-Added Tax Act No. 89 of 1991, sec. 12(g).

[36] [1988] 1 CMLR 491.

[37] See VAT Directive, *supra* note 2, at Art. 132(1)(k).

Rogers v. Commissioners of Customs and Excise[38]

HEADNOTE. Appeal. The Appellant carried on business as a coach proprietor and tour operator. In the course thereof he sold and supplied package tours consisting of coach travel, hotel accommodation and meals at all-inclusive prices. For tax purposes supplies of transport are zero-rated whereas supplies of hotel accommodation and meals are standard-rated. [T]he Appellant accounted for the amounts paid for the package tours by valuing the standard-rated supplies of accommodation and meals provided by him at their cost prices as charged to him and attributing the balances of the amounts so paid to the zero-rated supplies of transport.

The Commissioners decided that some part of the Appellant's profit element should be attributed … to the standard-rated supplies of hotel accommodation and meals provided by him in the package tours. The Appellant thereupon appealed to the tribunal on the grounds that he had adopted a perfectly proper method of costing his supplies.

[The example in the case assumes that the taxpayer sells a tour package for £276. The cost to the tour operator of taxable hotel and meals is £61, the cost for zero-rated transport is £183, and the tour operator's profit is £32. These three items total £276. The taxpayer assumed that all of the profit was attributable to the zero-rated transport, leaving only £61 taxable. The Commissioners claimed that because hotels and meals account for one-quarter of the tour operator's cost for hotels, meals and transport, one-quarter of the £32 profit, or £8, should be attributed to hotels and meals, making the taxable supply £69 (£61 + £8)].

Held that the amounts received by the Appellant as the consideration for his package tours should be apportioned for tax purposes between the standard-rated elements and the zero-rated elements in proportion to their respective cost prices to the Appellant (and so that the costs of overheads should be similarly apportioned and not wholly added to the cost prices of the standard-rated elements of the package tours).

V. A-B-C Transactions

If the sale from B to C is exempt or zero-rated, can the sale from A to B receive the same treatment, especially if the goods actually are delivered by A to C? There is at least a cash-flow advantage if B can obtain the goods from A free of VAT. There is a balance between the desire to limit zero-rating to transactions that can be verified on audit and the fact that there is no net VAT to be gained by denying zero-rating to supplies that ultimately are exported by the purchaser. This issue was raised in the *Velker International Oil Company* case.

[38] [1984] VATTR 183 (Manchester) [edited by the authors].

Staatssecretaris van Financïen v. Velker International Oil Company Ltd NV, Rotterdam[39]

FACTS AND PROCEDURE. In November 1983 Velker International Oil Company Ltd NV, Rotterdam, a company incorporated under Antilles law (hereinafter referred to as "Velker") ["C" in the A-B-C-D chain of transactions], sold to Forsythe International BV, The Hague, (hereinafter referred to as "Forsythe") ["D" in the transactions] two consignments of bunker oil which it had previously acquired from Handelmaatschappij Verhoeven BV, Rotterdam, (hereinafter referred to as "Verhoeven") ["B" in the transactions]. Verhoeven had itself bought the first consignment of oil from Olie Verwerking Amsterdam BV (hereinafter referred to as "OVA") ["A" in the transactions]. The two consignments were supplied to Forsythe directly, the first by OVA on 5 November 1983 ["A" to "D"] and the second by Verhoeven on 11 November 1983 ["B" to "D"]. Forsythe ["D"] stored the consignments of oil in tanks rented from a storage firm and they were then loaded on to sea-going vessels engaged in economic activities other than inshore fishing; the first consignment was loaded on 6, 7 and 8 November 1983 and the second on 17 and 18 November 1983.

Such transactions, known as A-B-C transactions, are governed by Article 3(3) of the Wet op de Omzetbelasting, the Netherlands Law on Turnover Tax. Pursuant to that provision, where there is a chain of several persons undertaking to supply the same goods and in reality physical delivery takes place directly from the first person in the chain to the last, each person in the chain is deemed to have supplied the goods and thus to have effected a taxable transaction.

In this case each of the parties to the transactions applied a zero VAT rate [as] the supply of goods for the fuelling and provisioning of sea-going vessels engaged in economic activities other than inshore fishing [is] zero-rated.

However, the Netherlands tax authorities considered that the [zero-rating] was not justified in this case and issued an additional VAT assessment notice on Velker for 1983.

DECISION. Under the terms of Article 15 of the Sixth Directive[40]:

"Without prejudice to other Community provisions member states shall [zero rate] the following under conditions which they shall lay down for the purpose of ensuring the correct and straightforward application of such exemptions and of preventing any evasion, avoidance or abuse:

[39] Case C-185/89, 1990 ECR I-02561 (ECJ 1990) [edited by the authors].

[40] See VAT Directive, *supra* note 2, Art. 131.

> 1. the supply of goods dispatched or transported to a destination outside the territory of the country as defined in Article 3 by or on behalf of the vendor;
>
> 4. the supply of goods for the fuelling and provisioning of vessels: (a) used for navigation on the high seas and carrying passengers for reward or used for the purpose of commercial, industrial or fishing activities."

[T]he national court is asking whether the [zero rating] laid down by those provisions applies solely to the supply of goods to a vessel operator who is going to use those goods for fuelling and provisioning or whether it also extends to supplies effected at previous stages in the commercial chain on condition that the goods are ultimately used for the fuelling and provisioning of vessels.

The term "supply of goods for the fuelling and provisioning of vessels" is capable of bearing several literal meanings. It could refer to the supply of goods which the recipient will use for the fuelling and provisioning of his vessels or the supply, at whatever stage it takes place, of goods which will subsequently be used for that purpose.

In order to interpret the term recourse must therefore be had to the context in which it occurs, bearing in mind the purpose and structure of the Sixth Directive.

The provisions in the directive which grant … [zero-rating] must be interpreted strictly since they constitute exceptions to the general principle that turnover tax is levied on all goods or services supplied for consideration by a taxable person.

A strict interpretation is required in particular when the provisions in issue constitute exceptions to the rule that transactions taking place "within the territory of the country" are subject to the tax.

With regard to Article 15(4), it should be noted that the operations of fuelling and provisioning vessels mentioned therein are [zero-rated] because they are equated with exports.

[The zero-rating] applies only to the supply of goods to a vessel operator who will use those goods for fuelling and provisioning and cannot therefore be extended to the supply of those goods effected at a previous stage in the commercial chain.

According to [a submission by] the German Government, the [zero-rating] at issue is designed to allow administrative simplification, not to grant a fiscal benefit. In view of that objective, the [zero-rating] should, in its view, be extended to all commercial stages.

That argument cannot be accepted. The extension of the [zero-rating] to stages prior to the final supply of the goods to the vessel operator would require Member States to set up systems of supervision and control in order to satisfy themselves as to the ultimate use of the goods supplied free of tax.

[N]othing in the wording of the relevant provisions of Article 15(4), nor the context in which they appear, nor the objective which they pursue, justifies a construction of those provisions to the effect that storage of the goods after delivery and before the actual fuelling and provisioning operation causes the benefit of the exemption to be lost.

Article 15(4) of the Sixth Council Directive of 17 May 1977 must be construed to the effect that only supplies to a vessel operator of goods to be used by that operator for fuelling and provisioning are to be regarded as supplies of goods for the fuelling and provisioning of vessels, but there is no requirement that the goods should be actually loaded on board the vessels at the time of their supply to the operator.

In some EU countries, zero-rating on exports has been extended to sales made to the exporter. For example, in Italy, in a triangulation transaction, the sale of goods by an Italian supplier is zero-rated when it is made to another Italian supplier who exports the goods to a registered person in another EU country.[41]

VI. Governmental Entities and Nonprofit Organizations

A. Introduction

Services rendered by government entities and nonprofit organizations generally represent a substantial portion of a nation's GDP. Units of government and nonprofit organizations provide some services that may compete with the private sector.[42] There is tension between the desire to impose VAT on all personal consumption expenditures and the desire to provide some relief from the burden of VAT to very low-income households. The exemption for services of exempt organizations focused on poor consumers helps address the basic regressivity of a tax on consumption reasonably efficiently. Yet at the same time, an exemption for food benefits high-income households more in absolute terms than low-income households.

Some countries grant special VAT treatment to "charitable" and other "nonprofit" organizations. Some define NPOs as organizations that supply humanitarian aid. "[A criterion] for qualifying for special treatment

[41] See Emanuela Santoro, "Italian Tax Authorities Ruling on VAT Regime for Triangulation Scheme," Tax News Service, May 19, 2010, discussing Italian Tax Authorities Ruling No. 35/E, concerning the application of the exemption with credit VAT regime applicable to the intra-community sales of goods in a triangular scheme, where the exporter (B) acts on behalf of the supplier (A) in supplying the goods to a taxable customer (C) established in another EU country. The supplies by (A) and (B) both are zero-rated.

[42] The converse also occurs. Thus, for example, neighborhood groups may hire private security guards and trash collection companies to supplement the police and sanitation services provided by government.

under the VAT legislation depends upon the country's legal traditions and organizational structure."[43] In this chapter, unless noted to the contrary, activities of "nonprofit" and "charitable" organizations are used interchangeably.[44]

As discussed previously, VAT statutes generally deny credits for tax on purchases used in making exempt supplies. In a departure from these general principles, Norway grants refunds outside the VAT system for some input VAT attributable to VAT-exempt activities of nonprofit organizations.[45] Canada also refunds VAT paid on inputs by qualifying nonprofit organizations.[46]

The line-drawing problems associated with the grant of exemptions for specified supplies or particular entities were discussed earlier in this chapter. Similar problems apply for services rendered by nonprofits and units of government. For a variety of reasons, most countries exempt or zero-rate a range of these activities. Exemptions for activities of nonprofit organizations sometimes are granted because these organizations are providing services commonly provided by government. The following paragraphs mention some of the issues that arise when special treatment is provided for these activities. As a policy matter, should any activities of nonprofit organizations and government entities be granted special treatment? If it is desirable to grant special treatment to the "nonprofit-governmental" sectors, what activities should receive this special treatment, and should the special treatment take the form of exemption or zero-rating? For example, if it is desirable to reduce or eliminate the tax on necessities (such as residential housing) that represent a large percentage of the budget of low-income households, should the residential housing be exempt or zero-rated? Assuming exemption is selected, what residential housing should be exempt: sales of residential property or both sales and rentals? Should the exemption be limited to subsidized housing provided by a charitable organization or a unit of government, or should it be extended to market rate residential housing provided by anyone? If not all residential housing is exempt, should the accommodation portion of charges in hospitals and in university dormitories be exempt under this exemption or only if it fits within an education or medical care exemption?

[43] O. Gjems-Onstad, "VAT and Non-Profit Organizations," 5 *Int'l VAT Monitor* 69, 73–74 (March/April, 1994).

[44] Some countries draw a distinction between charities and nonprofit organizations. For example, under the Canadian GST, a "non-profit organization" includes certain government organizations at the federal or provincial level. Canadian Goods and Services Tax, Part IX of the Excise Tax Act, S.C. 1993, c. 27, as amended, §259(1) definition of nonprofit organization. A charity under this legislation "includes a non-profit organization that operates, otherwise than for profit, a health care facility." See §259(1) definition of "charity." A qualifying nonprofit organization is a nonprofit organization that receives at least 40% of its funding from the government. *Id.* at §259(2).

[45] The VAT base was expanded. The refund is available for VAT on services previously exempt from VAT. See O. Gjems-Onstad, "Refund of Input VAT to Norwegian NPOs," 15 *International VAT Monitor* 244 (July/Aug. 2004).

[46] See, generally, Guide RC 4034, GST/HST Public Service Bodies' Rebate.

The seller of exempt items (the government or nonprofit) cannot claim input credits for tax on its purchases attributable to the exempt sales. This effect may encourage nonprofits and government entities with exempt sales, for example, education or health services, to integrate vertically by, for example, hiring employees to clean and maintain buildings and equipment rather than paying a VAT-registered service company to provide these services.

If exempt services rendered by government entities and NPOs are sold at intermediate stages of production and distribution to taxable businesses (such as exempt tuition paid for employees), the supplies may produce the cascade effect described earlier in this chapter.[47] Some may argue that if the exempt items are sold to nontaxable purchasers (such as final consumers) and comparable items are sold by taxable businesses (if a public university's tuition is exempt and a for-profit university's tuition is taxable), the exemption may create some competitive inequities. On the other hand, a nonprofit organization may provide services that compete with private firms but charge lower prices because the service is subsidized with donations to the nonprofit. University-sponsored concerts and university sporting events are illustrative. A unit of government may subsidize the operation of public transport or may issue discount cards to students and senior citizens. Should these differences in form affect the tax treatment of transportation? The Ronald McDonald houses operated by a nonprofit organization provide subsidized or free accommodations near children's hospitals to parents of hospitalized children. Should these hotel services be subject to tax? If so, what is the taxable amount of the service?

A unit of government may receive cash or property to be used for a specified purpose. For example, land may be donated to a city to build a library or park. A nonprofit organization may receive cash or property from a variety of sources (government, a business, other nonprofits, or individuals) to provide a particular service. The tax consequences may vary, depending on whether the receipt is or is not linked to the provision of any goods or services. If it is linked to the provision of particular goods or services, then the tax consequences may differ if the services, for example, are welfare or other charitable services or are goods or services that are sold by and compete with private firms. A government may award a grant to a university to do medical research. Private pharmaceutical companies may be engaged in similar research. Should the government grant be taxable or exempt, if the research activities of a university generally are exempt from VAT?

A public radio station receives funds from a publisher to support the station. Should the taxation of the receipt depend on whether the station (a) does not publicize the name of the donor, (b) mentions the donor

[47] Because the exempt seller cannot issue a tax invoice listing VAT on the sale, the taxable purchaser cannot claim any input credit on the purchase. This cost (including any VAT embedded in the price) will be subject to VAT when the purchaser shifts this cost to its customers in the form of higher prices for its products or services.

during a broadcast, or (c) mentions the donor and the name of one of its recently released books during a broadcast? Should the VAT consequences depend on whether the publisher receives an income tax deduction for the donation?

This chapter explores a variety of approaches to the VAT treatment of services rendered by government entities and NPOs, especially in New Zealand and the EU. It includes a number of cases that illustrate the problems encountered with the EU approach. Some proposals to expand the taxation of these services are discussed. The chapter ends with a brief discussion of the VAT treatment of purchases by diplomats and international organizations.

B. Various Approaches to the Taxation of Governments and NPOs

Many countries exempt most sales of goods and services rendered by governments and NPOs, but may tax sales of specific goods and services. For example, in the EU, state, regional, and local government authorities and other bodies governed by public law are not subject to VAT on activities that they engage in as public authorities. Other activities conducted by the same entities and bodies may be taxed. The state or a local unit of government that renders taxable services may be required to register and charge VAT on its taxable supplies, regardless of the level of its taxable turnover. In other words, the threshold required to registration does not apply.

For years, commentators have suggested that a VAT could cover a much broader range of goods and services provided by governments and NPOs.[48] "If governmental units make sales of goods or services, there is no general justification for exclusion from tax simply because the vendor is a governmental unit. Only if there is some specific justification for the exemption of the service, whether provided by government or the private sector, is there a case for exemption."[49] New Zealand led in taxing government services by taxing the property taxes that are used to fund these services.

Commentary to a proposed model VAT for the United States suggested that for supplies made by the nonprofit-governmental sectors that are exempt from tax,

> the government agency or exempt organization can be treated either as the ultimate consumer or an agent for the group that ultimately will consume the goods or services. Under either theory, the sales *to* these entities should

[48] See A. Tait, VALUE ADDED TAX: INTERNATIONAL PRACTICE AND PROBLEMS 77–78 (International Monetary Fund, 1998) [hereinafter, Tait, VAT]; J. Due, INDIRECT TAXATION IN DEVELOPING ECONOMIES, 141–143 (Johns Hopkins University Press, 1970) [hereinafter Due, Tax in Developing Economies].

[49] Due, Tax in Developing Economies, *supra* note 48, at 141.

> be taxed. As consumers, the exempt organizations and government entities should not charge VAT on their sales nor be entitled to input credits for VAT on their purchases. With respect to items purchased for free distribution to beneficiaries, these entities may add little value. Where these entities hire employees to perform services that are dispensed without charge, however, the exempt organizations and government entities may add substantial value that would not be taxed under this scheme. [To] equalize the tax treatment for goods and services provided free of charge, VAT should be imposed on the salaries paid to employees.[50]

The following excerpt discusses the taxation of NPOs.[51]

> One characteristic trait of (parts of) the NPO sector, compared to the government and the for-profit sector, is that some of the services provided by the organization are performed by workers who do not receive compensation, i.e. volunteers. In Canada, supplies made by charities may be exempt from VAT if all functions of the NPO are performed exclusively (90% or more) by volunteers. It is an incentive for voluntary work and helps donations made in the form of unpaid work to remain untaxed.
>
> NPOs and especially charities make use of many special activities to raise money, for example fund-raising dinners, where donations and the supply of taxable goods are combined. [Theoretically, VAT should be imposed] on the actual portion of the price that relates to the taxable goods supplied.
>
> The supply of advertising is normally taxable. It may be difficult [such as with a "sponsorship"] to draw the line between taxable sales of advertising services and the tax-free receipts of donations. If services are provided to an NPO free of charge, should the provider be taxed for deemed supplies just as if the services had been sold for a consideration?
>
> Sales of donated goods, such as second-hand clothing and household items, which are sold in opportunity shops and similar retail outlets, may be exempt from VAT if the shops are run by nonprofit bodies. As private individuals will be able to sell their second-hand goods tax free, as is commonly the case under VAT legislation, allowing such sales by NPOs to be tax free may seem like a natural corollary. The price distortions which could occur between the sales made by a nonprofit opportunity shop and an ordinary business engaged in selling used goods may not be significant if these businesses are able to claim a credit for a notional input tax when buying second-hand goods from individuals. Without such a credit, ordinary businesses may effectively be excluded from competition.

C. Taxation in New Zealand

New Zealand can boast one of the broadest VAT bases in use today. Many of the principles in the EU study of the taxation of public sector bodies

[50] ABA Model Act, *supra* note 4, at 82–84. Footnotes have been omitted [edited by the authors].

[51] O. Gjems-Onstad, "VAT and Non-Profit Organizations," 5 *International VAT Monitor* 69–80 (March/April, 1994) [edited by the authors].

are incorporated in the NZ approach.[52] The broad NZ base extends to non-profits and government entities. Under the New Zealand GST,

> government departments, local authorities and other public bodies are treated as suppliers of goods and services both to the private sector and to the public sector. The value of supplies to the private sector is measured by the revenue received in fees and charges; the value of supplies to the Crown is represented by the Parliament's apportionment of funds.
>
> Public-sector bodies in New Zealand levy VAT on all goods or services sold to the private sector or other public-sector bodies and can reclaim VAT on all goods and services bought. For example, a New Zealand hospital will add VAT to the bill. Likewise the New Zealand police or armed forces can reclaim VAT on supplies bought from a private supplier or from other public-sector bodies. Local rates (a tax on real estate) are subject to VAT since they are not considered taxes but payments for local public services. And local authorities can reclaim VAT on their purchases.[53]

New Zealand still grants significant tax concessions for nonprofit bodies. It "effectively zero rate[s] such organizations to the extent that their activities are funded from donations."[54]

D. Taxation in the European Union

The EU VAT Directive has rules governing supplies by states, subnational government authorities, and bodies governed by public law. Under the VAT Directive, Article 13 (Article 4(5) of the Sixth Directive):

"1. States, regional and local government authorities and other bodies governed by public law shall not be regarded as taxable persons in respect of the activities or transactions in which they engage as public authorities, even where they collect dues, fees, contributions or payments in connection with those activities or transactions.

However, when they engage in such activities or transactions, they shall be regarded as taxable persons in respect of those activities or transactions where their treatment as non-taxable persons would lead to significant distortions of competition.

In any event, bodies governed by public law shall be regarded as taxable persons in respect of the activities listed in Annex I, provided that those activities are not carried out on such a small scale as to be negligible.

2. Member States may regard activities, exempt under Articles 132, 135, 136 and 371, Articles 374 to 377, Article 378(2), Article 379(2) or Articles 380 to 390b, engaged in by bodies governed by public law as activities in which those bodies engage as public authorities."

52 See discussion *infra*, this chapter.

53 J. Owens, "The Move to VAT," 2 *Intertax* 45, 50–51 (1996).

54 P. Barrand, "The Taxation of Non-Profit Bodies and Government Entities under the New Zealand GST," 2 *International VAT Monitor* 2–3 (Jan. 1991).

Commission of the European Communities v. Republic of Finland[55]

Judgment

By its application, the Commission of the European Communities seeks a declaration from the Court that, by failing to levy value added tax ('VAT') on legal advice services provided by public legal aid offices (that is, by public legal advisers employed by those offices) in return for part payment, as provided for in Finnish legislation on legal aid, while like services are subject to VAT when they are provided by private advisers, the Republic of Finland has failed to fulfil its obligations under Article 2(1) and Article 4(1), (2) and (5) of the Sixth Council Directive [VAT Directive, Art. 2(1), 9(1) & 13(1) similar].

Legal context

Article 2 of the Sixth Directive is worded as follows:

'The following shall be subject to [VAT]:

1. the supply of goods or services effected for consideration within the territory of the country by a taxable person acting as such;
2. the importation of goods.'

According to Article 4 of the Sixth Directive:

'1. "Taxable person" shall mean any person who independently carries out in any place any economic activity specified in paragraph 2, whatever the purpose or results of that activity.
2. The economic activities referred to in paragraph 1 shall comprise all activities of producers, traders and persons supplying services including mining and agricultural activities and activities of the professions. The exploitation of tangible or intangible property for the purpose of obtaining income therefrom on a continuing basis shall also be considered an economic activity."

States, regional and local government authorities and other bodies governed by public law shall not be considered taxable persons in respect of the activities or transactions in which they engage as public authorities, even where they collect dues, fees, contributions or payments in connection with these activities or transactions.

However, when they engage in such activities or transactions, they shall be considered taxable persons in respect of these activities or transactions where treatment as non-taxable persons would lead to significant distortions of competition.

[55] Case C-246/08, *Commission of the European Communities v. Republic of Finland*, [2009] ECR I-10605 (ECJ 2009) [edited by the authors].

Article 6(1) of the Sixth Directive provides:

'1. "Supply of services" shall mean any transaction which does not constitute a supply of goods within the meaning of Article 5.

Such transactions may include inter alia:

- assignments of intangible property whether or not it is the subject of a document establishing title,
- obligations to refrain from an act or to tolerate an act or situation,
- the performances of services in pursuance of an order made by or in the name of a public authority or in pursuance of the law.'

National legislation concerning legal aid

The legal aid scheme in Finland is based on four pieces of legislation adopted in 2002.

Article 1 of the Law on legal aid provides that legal aid, financed out of public funds, will be granted to any person who is in need of assistance with a legal matter but is unable, because of his financial situation, to meet the costs of dealing with his case. Legal aid may be granted both in legal proceedings and for non-contentious matters.

Under Article 8 of that law, legal aid is as a general rule provided by legal advisers employed by public legal aid offices ('public offices'). Those offices, of which there were 60 in 2008, employ around 220 advisers who are officials paid by the State. The operating costs of the public offices are met from public funds. Fees settled by recipients of legal aid are shown, however, as receipts in the accounts of each office and no public financing is made available in respect of operating costs covered in that way.

Article 8 of the Law on legal aid provides, however, that in the case of legal proceedings, a private adviser, namely an advocate or another private lawyer who has consented to act, may also be appointed. When the recipient of legal aid has himself proposed that he should be represented by a person who can show that he has the requisite professional qualifications, that person must be appointed, unless there are particular reasons why he should not be.

Article 17 of the Law on legal aid lays down rules concerning the fees of private advisers. It provides that a private adviser will be entitled to reasonable fees and to reimbursement of expenses, which are borne by the State and paid following deduction of any contribution owed by the recipient. Apart from that contribution, the private adviser may not receive any other payment or reimbursement from the recipient of legal aid.

The Government Decree on legal aid lays down in more detail the conditions under which the aid is granted.

Article 1 of the decree provides that legal aid is granted on the basis of the applicant's disposable income and assets and that it may, on that basis, be provided to him either free of charge or – which is one of the amendments made in 2002 to the legislation previously in force – in return for a part contribution borne by him. The decree distinguishes in that regard between a basic contribution ('perusomavastuu') and an additional contribution ('lisäomavastuu').

Under Article 5 of the Government Decree on legal aid, the basic contribution corresponds to a percentage of the fees and expenses of the adviser consulted, including VAT if it is included in the calculation of costs. The percentage is fixed by reference to the threshold of disposable monthly income.

Article 6 of the Government Decree on legal aid specifies that, in any event, aid will not be granted where disposable income exceeds EUR 1 400 for a single person and EUR 1 200 per person for a couple.

Under Article 7 of that Government decree, an additional contribution is required where the recipient has deposits or other similar assets which may easily be liquidated and whose value exceeds EUR 5 000. That contribution amounts to one half of the value of those deposits and assets in excess of EUR 5 000.

VAT legislation

Under Article 1 of the Law on Value Added Tax (arvonlisäverolaki (1501/1993)) of 30 December 1993, legal aid provided by a private adviser in legal proceedings is subject to VAT as a supply of legal services. By contrast, legal aid provided by the public offices free of charge or in return for a part contribution is not an activity which is subject to VAT.

The Pre-Litigation Procedure

On 13 October 2004, the Commission sent the Finnish authorities a letter concerning the fact that legal aid services of the same kind are treated differently, from the point of view of the VAT rules, depending on whether the services are provided by private advisers or by public offices. According to the information gathered by the Commission, the rules entailed a significant distortion of competition to the detriment of private advisers.

The Action

Arguments of the parties

The Commission makes clear that, in the present action, its sole complaint against the Republic of Finland is the fact that the latter does not levy VAT on legal aid services when they are provided by public offices in legal proceedings in return for a part contribution from the recipient of the service. Thus this action does not seek to challenge the fact that VAT is not levied on those services when they are provided by public offices free of charge, although the services provided by a private adviser are, for their part, in any event subject to VAT, with the State paying the fees and the VAT billed by the adviser. Indeed, the fact that public offices are not treated as taxable persons in those circumstances follows, in the latter case, from the fact that the services are provided to the recipient of legal aid free of charge, the only payment received by the lawyers employed by those offices being their normal salary. Accordingly, such services cannot be regarded as supplied for consideration, within the meaning of Article 2(1) of the Sixth Directive.

The Commission submits that when, conversely, public offices provide legal aid services in legal proceedings in return for a part contribution from the recipient, they are carrying out an economic activity within the meaning of the Sixth Directive. That economic activity gives rise to a supply of services effected for consideration within the meaning of Article 2(1) of that directive, since there is a direct link between the service supplied by the office and the consideration paid by the recipient.

In those circumstances, the Commission submits that it is necessary to consider whether the exceptions provided for in Article 4(5) of the Sixth Directive [VAT Directive, Article 13(1)] apply.

In any event, the Commission maintains that the fact that public offices are not treated as taxable persons in respect of legal aid services provided in return for a part contribution leads to significant distortions of competition within the meaning of the second subparagraph of Article 4(5) of the Sixth Directive. In view of the low level of the income and asset ceilings to which entitlement to the aid is subject, a difference of 22% in the payment to be made (corresponding to the applicable rate of VAT in Finland) appreciably distorts competition, all the more so since final consumers are not entitled to deduct the tax. That distortion of competition must be regarded as 'more than negligible' within the meaning of the case-law (see Case C 288/07 Isle of Wight Council and Others [2008] ECR I 7203, paragraph 79), since more than 4 000 people a year use legal aid services and pay a part contribution in return.

The Finnish Government contends that the legal aid services provided by the public offices form an indivisible whole which cannot be regarded as an economic activity within the meaning of Article 2(1) of the Sixth Directive [VAT Directive, Article 9(1)]. Those services are not supplied in such a way as to cover the costs to which they give rise but are mostly financed from public funds. The pursuit of those activities is therefore not accompanied by the economic risk characteristic of normal commercial activity. Furthermore, the contributions do not cover, even in part, the costs associated with such services. It is impossible to isolate – as a specific economic activity – an individual area of those offices' activities. Such a distinction cannot be justified either by the minimal contribution which must be paid by certain recipients of legal aid services depending on their financial situation or by the services themselves.

Findings of the Court

As a preliminary point, it should be stated that the Commission does not, by this action, challenge the failure to levy VAT on legal aid services provided by public offices when the supply of those services is effected (i) free of charge in legal proceedings and (ii) other than in such proceedings, whether free of charge or not.

The Commission's action concerns solely the failure to levy VAT on legal aid services provided by public offices in legal proceedings in return for a part contribution borne by the recipient where his disposable income exceeds the limit set for entitlement to free legal aid but does not exceed the ceiling barring all entitlement to legal aid. It is thus apparent that the Commission's action derives from the extension of the legal aid scheme in force in Finland, in return for a part payment by recipients, to persons with incomes which, whilst modest, are none the less higher than those of persons entitled to free legal aid. The reasoning which follows therefore relates solely to that part of the legal activities of the public offices.

It must be recalled that, although Article 4 of the Sixth Directive gives a very wide scope to VAT, only activities of an economic nature are covered by that tax [cases omitted].

According to Article 2 of the Sixth Directive concerning taxable transactions, together with the importation of goods, the supply of goods or services effected for consideration within the country is subject to VAT. Furthermore, under Article 4(1) of the Sixth Directive, 'taxable person' means any person who independently carries out an economic activity, whatever the purpose or results of that activity.

'Economic activities' are defined in Article 4(2) of the Sixth Directive as including all activities of producers, traders and persons supplying services, inter alia the exploitation of tangible or intangible property for the purpose of obtaining income therefrom on a continuing basis (see, in particular, Case C 465/03 Kretztechnik [2005] ECR I 4357, paragraph 18; and Hutchison 3G and Others, paragraph 27).

An analysis of those definitions shows that the scope of the term economic activities is very wide and that the term is objective in character, in the sense that the activity is considered per se and without regard to its purpose or results (see, inter alia, Commission v Greece, paragraph 26; and Case C-223/03 University of Huddersfield [2006] ECR I-1751, paragraph 47 and the case-law cited). An activity is thus, as a general rule, categorised as economic where it is permanent and is carried out in return for remuneration which is received by the person carrying out the activity (Commission v Netherlands, paragraphs 9 and 15; and Case C-408/06 Götz [2007] ECR I-11295, paragraph 18).

However, it follows from the case-law that the receipt of a payment does not, per se, mean that a given activity is economic in nature.

In order to determine whether the Commission's action is well founded, it is therefore appropriate to consider, in the first place, whether the legal aid services provided by the public offices in legal proceedings in return for a part payment constitute economic activities within the meaning of Article 2(1) and Article 4(1) and (2) of the Sixth Directive.

It must first of all be stated that, in view of the objective character of the term 'economic activities', the fact that the activity of the public offices consists in the performance of duties which are conferred and regulated by law, in the public interest and without any business or commercial objective, is in that regard irrelevant. Indeed, Article 6 of the Sixth Directive [see, for example, VAT Directive, Article 25(c)] expressly provides that certain activities carried on in pursuance of the law are to be subject to the system of VAT (Commission v Netherlands, paragraph 10,Commission v Greece, paragraph 28).

Moreover, it is established that the public offices provide the legal aid services in question on a permanent basis.

In those circumstances, it is appropriate to ascertain whether those services can be regarded as provided by the public offices in return for remuneration.

In that connection, it is clear from the case-law of the Court that, within the framework of the VAT system, taxable transactions presuppose the existence of a transaction between the parties in which a price or consideration is stipulated. Thus, where a person's activity consists exclusively in providing services for no direct consideration, there is no basis of assessment and the services are therefore not subject to VAT (see Case 89/81 Hong Kong Trade Development Council [1982] ECR 1277, paragraphs 9 and 10; and Case C 16/93 Tolsma [1994] ECR I 743, paragraph 12).

It follows from that, according to the Court's case-law, that a supply of services is effected 'for consideration' within the meaning of Article 2(1) of the Sixth Directive only if there is a legal relationship between the provider of the service and the recipient pursuant to which there is reciprocal performance, the remuneration received by the provider of the service constituting the value actually given in return for the service supplied to the recipient (see, inter alia, Tolsma, paragraph 14; Case C 2/95 SDC [1997] ECR I-3017, paragraph 45; and MKG-Kraftfahrzeuge-Factoring, paragraph 47).

Consequently, according to the case-law of the Court, a supply of services for consideration within the meaning of Article 2(1) of the Sixth Directive presupposes a direct link between the service provided and the consideration received (see, inter alia, Case 102/86 Apple and Pear Development Council [1988] ECR 1443, paragraphs

11 and 12; Case C-258/95 Fillibeck [1997] ECR I 5577, paragraph 12; and Commission v Greece, paragraph 29).

In this instance, the legal aid services with which the present action is concerned are not provided by the public offices free of charge and thus without any consideration, since the recipients of those services are required to make a payment to the public offices.

However, it is established that the payment concerned is only a part payment since it does not cover the whole amount of the fees set by the national legislation, by reference to the nature of the dispute, in respect of remuneration for legal aid services provided by public offices and private advisers. Indeed, the payment consisting in the basic contribution is a percentage, ranging from 20% to 75%, of that amount. Admittedly, that payment may, depending on the recipient's assets, be supplemented by an additional contribution. Nevertheless, the Commission does not maintain – and, as the Advocate General has noted, it is unlikely, in view of the income ceilings fixed by the national legislation for the grant of legal aid, – that the additional contribution could result in the recipient making a payment corresponding to the full amount of the fees set by the legislation concerned for the supply of legal aid services.

Although this part payment represents a portion of the fees, its amount is not calculated solely on the basis of those fees, but also depends upon the recipient's income and assets. Thus, it is the level of the latter – and not, for example, the number of hours worked by the public offices or the complexity of the case concerned – which determines the portion of the fees for which the recipient remains responsible.

It follows that the part payment made to the public offices by recipients of legal aid services depends only in part on the actual value of the services provided – the more modest the recipient's income and assets, the less strong the link with that value will be.

[T]he part payments made in 2007 by recipients of legal aid services provided by the public offices (which relate to only one third of all the services provided by public offices) amounted to EUR 1.9 million, whilst the gross operating costs of those offices were EUR 24.5 million. Even if those data also include legal aid services provided other than in court proceedings, such a difference suggests that the part payment borne by recipients must be regarded more as a fee, receipt of which does not, per se, mean that a given activity is economic in nature, than as consideration in the strict sense.

Therefore, in light of the foregoing, it does not appear that the link between the legal aid services provided by public offices and the payment to be made by the recipients is sufficiently direct for that payment to be regarded as consideration for those services and, accordingly, for those services to be regarded as economic activities for the purposes of Article 2(1) and Article 4(1) and (2) of the Sixth Directive.

The Commission has put forward no other evidence showing that the services in question constitute such economic activities. In particular, although the Commission maintains in its action that there is a direct link between the part payment made by recipients of legal aid services and the services supplied by public offices, it has not developed, in support of that claim, any specific arguments and has not produced any evidence capable of establishing that such a direct link exists, particularly in view of the fact that, for the purpose of determining that contribution, account is taken of the amount of the recipient's income and assets. According to settled case-law, in proceedings under Article 226 EC for failure to fulfil obligations it nonetheless falls to the Commission to prove the allegation that the obligation has not been fulfilled. It is the Commission's responsibility to place before the Court the information needed to enable the Court to establish that the obligation has not been fulfilled and in so doing the Commission may not rely on any presumptions (see, in particular, Case C 494/01 Commission v Ireland [2005] ECR I-3331, paragraph 41 and the case-law cited).

In those circumstances, since the public offices do not engage in an economic activity and since, for the first subparagraph of Article 4(5) of the Sixth Directive to apply, there must be a prior finding that the activity considered is of an economic nature, it is not necessary to consider, in the second place, the Commission's arguments concerning (i) the question whether those offices act as a public authority within the meaning of the first subparagraph of Article 4(5) when providing the legal aid services in question and (ii) whether the failure to levy VAT on that activity leads, in any event, to significant distortions of competition for the purposes of the second subparagraph of that provision.

In light of the foregoing, the present action must be dismissed.

The problem "is to define the activities in which public bodies act as public authorities, especially if their activities compete with similar business in the private sector."[56] "[While distortions of competition] may be clear, for instance, in the case of transport where state-owned buses compete with private buses, it is less clear if all the railways are state owned. In this instance, there would be no competition with any other railway, but there could be a significant tax advantage if privately owned buses and trucks were competing for passengers and freight and were taxed."[57]

In *Royal Academy of Music v. Commissioners of Customs and Excise*,[58] the Academy, a registered charity, claimed that the reconstruction work on its concert hall was zero-rated as the construction of a building for a relevant

[56] Tait, VAT, *supra* note 48, at 76. The changes were effective January 1, 1982.

[57] *Id.* at 77.

[58] [1994] VATTR 105, LON/92/2416.

charitable purpose, not "in the course or furtherance of a business."[59] The tribunal held that the Academy's charitable objective to promote music and provide music instruction did not prevent it from conducting economic activities. The provision of music education for tuition was the provision of services for consideration, the same as services provided by private businesses. Because the building therefore was used in part to conduct economic activities, the building was used in connection with business. The renovation was not entitled to zero-rating.

Exemptions under the EU VAT Directive include public postal services, certain medical care, the provision of human organs, blood, and milk, certain dental services and prostheses, certain services linked to welfare and social security work, certain goods and services to protect children and young persons rendered by bodies governed by public law, certain education, certain services related to spiritual welfare, certain services linked to sports or physical education rendered by nonprofit-making organizations, certain cultural services provided by public bodies or recognized cultural bodies, certain transport for sick or injured in special vehicles by duly authorized bodies, and noncommercial public radio and television.[60]

In *Lord Mayor and Citizens of the City of Westminster v. Commissioners of Customs and Excise*,[61] the provision of housing for homeless men at a nominal cost, rental of lockers to the men, service of simple meals to them, and sale of cigarettes and soft drinks through vending machines were held to be exempt as services closely linked to welfare services, consistent with the Sixth Directive. The tribunal noted that comparable services were not provided by the private sector.

Article 132(l)(n) of the VAT Directive exempts "the supply of certain cultural services, and the supply of goods closely linked thereto, by bodies governed by public law or by other cultural bodies recognised by the Member State concerned." VAT Directive, Article 133(b) gives member states the authority to subject some exemptions to certain conditions, including the condition that the body "must be managed and administered on an essentially voluntary basis by persons who have no direct or indirect interest, either themselves or through intermediaries, in the results of the activities concerned." Relying on that condition, the UK tax

[59] Zero-rating was claimed under VAT Act 1983, Sch. 5, Group 8A. VATA 1994, *supra* note 6, at Sch. 8, Group 5, provides that construction of a building for a relevant charitable purpose is zero-rated, but under note 6, a relevant charitable purpose means "otherwise than in the course or furtherance of a business."

[60] VAT Directive, *supra* note 2, at Art. 132(1). That Directive contains rules limiting the services of government and nonprofits that can be granted exemption by member states. Except for bodies governed by public law, member states can, in certain circumstances, deny the exemptions discussed next. For example, the exemptions may be available only (1) if the body does not systematically aim to make a profit, (2) if the body is managed essentially on a volunteer basis by persons without a direct or indirect interest in the results of the body's activities, (3) if the body's prices are approved by public authorities or do not exceed approved prices, and (4) if the exemption does not distort competition with taxable commercial enterprises. See *id.* at Art. 133.

[61] Case LON/87/564, [1990] 2 CMLR 81.

authorities challenged the Zoolological Society of London's claim for a refund of VAT paid on admission charges to its zoos. The Society consists of a governing body, the council, members, and honorary members. The council, consisting of a president, secretary, and treasurer, and nonoffice members who appoint the management boards, are not compensated. The director-general, the director of finance, director of personnel, and other employees are paid. The ECJ decided that the persons who are prohibited from having a financial interest "refers only to persons directly associated with the management and administration of a body and not to all persons working for reward in one way or another in its administration."[62] It is up to "competent national authorities" to determine if a person comes within the condition and therefore must not have a financial interest. It also is up to the competent national authorities to determine, by looking at the contribution of persons with a financial interest to the management of the body, if the essentially voluntary character of the management or administration of the body is met.

The ECJ ruled that the issuance by the competent national authority of licenses for radio frequencies reserved for telecom services is not an economic activity under [VAT Directive, Article 9(1)] and therefore is not within the scope of the VAT. The government cannot issue a VAT invoice for that transaction, and the purchasers are not entitled to deduct any VAT on the purchases.[63]

The rules under the EU VAT directives have spawned a number of cases involving a member state's power to limit or expand the authorized exemptions. The following case is illustrative.

TNT Post UK Ltd v. Commissioners for Her Majesty's Revenue and Customs[64]

Judgment

This reference for a preliminary ruling concerns the interpretation of Article 13A(1)(a) of Sixth Directive [VAT Directive, Article 132(1)(a)].

The reference was made regarding the legality of the exemption from value added tax (VAT) of postal services supplied by Royal Mail.

[62] Case C-267/00, *Commissioners of Customs and Excise v. Zoological Society of London*, [2002] ECR I-03353, at ¶19.

[63] Case C-284/04, *T-Mobile Austria GmbH and Others v. Republik Österreich*, [2007] ECR 1–5189 (ECJ 2007).

[64] Case C-357/07, (ECJ 2009) [edited by the authors and many cited cases deleted].

Legal context

Community legislation

Article 13A exemptions for certain activities in the public interest, provides:

1. Without prejudice to other Community provisions, Member States shall exempt the following under conditions which they shall lay down for the purpose of ensuring the correct and straightforward application of such exemptions and of preventing any possible evasion, avoidance or abuse:
(a) the supply by the public postal services of services other than passenger transport and telecommunications services, and the supply of goods incidental thereto;

Article 132(1)(a) of the VAT Directive is worded in identical terms to Article 13A(1)(a) of the Sixth Directive.

Directive 97/67/EC of the European Parliament and of the Council of 15 December 1997 establishes, pursuant to Article 1 thereof, common rules concerning, among other matters, the provision of a universal postal service within the Community and the criteria defining the services which may be reserved for universal service providers.

Recital 15 in the preamble to Directive 97/67 states:

'... the provisions of this Directive relating to universal service provision are without prejudice to the right of universal service operators to negotiate contracts with customers individually.'

Under Article 3 of Directive 97/67:

'1. Member States shall ensure that users enjoy the right to a universal service involving the permanent provision of a postal service of specified quality at all points in their territory at affordable prices for all users.
2. To this end, Member States shall take steps to ensure that the density of the points of contact and of the access points takes account of the needs of users.
3. They shall take steps to ensure that the universal service provider(s) guarantee(s) every working day and not less than five days a week, save in circumstances or geographical conditions deemed exceptional by the national regulatory authorities, [and details the minimums required]:
4. Each Member State shall adopt the measures necessary to ensure that the universal service includes minimum facilities.
5. The national regulatory authorities may increase the weight limit of universal service coverage for postal packages to any weight not exceeding 20 kilograms [but] shall ensure that postal packages received from other Member States and weighing up to 20 kilograms are delivered within their territories.

7. The universal service as defined in this Article shall cover both national and cross-border services.'

Article 7(1) of Directive 97/67 provides:

'To the extent necessary to ensure the maintenance of universal service, Member States may continue to reserve services to universal service provider(s). Those services shall be limited to the clearance, sorting, transport and delivery of items of domestic correspondence and incoming cross-border correspondence, whether by accelerated delivery or not, within [prescribed] weight and price limits.'

National legislation

The provisions intended to transpose Article 13A(1)(a) of the Sixth Directive are included in the Value Added Tax Act 1994, as amended by the Postal Services Act 2000 ('the Postal Services Act'), while the provisions seeking to transpose Directive 97/67 are included in the Postal Services Act.

Royal Mail was designated, in accordance with the Postal Services Act, as a universal service provider providing a universal postal service in the United Kingdom. No such notification has been given in respect of any other person.

On 18 February 2005, the Postal Services Commission issued a decision that, from 1 January 2006, it would grant a licence to any suitable applicant to convey any letter of any weight. As a result, the postal market in the United Kingdom was fully liberalised from that date but without affecting the status and obligations of Royal Mail as the only designated universal service provider in the United Kingdom.

Royal Mail licence contains the following obligations which apply only to Royal Mail: first, to provide the United Kingdom public with a universal postal service, including at least one delivery to every address every working day and one collection every day from every 'access point' within the United Kingdom, at affordable prices that are uniformly applied throughout the United Kingdom, and, secondly, to ensure that the United Kingdom public have ready access to that universal postal service through a sufficient number and density of access points.

On 20 January 2006, the Postal Services Commission granted a licence to TNT Post under Part II of the Postal Services Act, under which that company is authorised to convey any letter within the United Kingdom. That licence replaced an earlier licence issued on 23 December 2002.

The dispute in the main proceedings and the questions referred for a preliminary ruling

According to the referring court, Royal Mail, as the sole universal postal service provider in the United Kingdom, provides a large range of postal services to any undertaking or individual wishing to use its services. Those postal services are provided by means of an integrated national network which currently services around 27 million addresses six days a week subject to a public interest regulatory regime which is unique to Royal Mail amongst all postal operators. Letters and other mail are collected by Royal Mail from various locations, namely approximately 113 000 pillar boxes, 14 200 post offices and 90 000 business premises. Royal Mail employs approximately 185 000 persons in the United Kingdom.

TNT Post, which is part of the TNT Group which operates in more than 200 countries and employs over 128 000 people, provides postal distribution services for pre-sorted and unsorted business mail. Its business is the collection, provision of mechanised and manual sorting services (for unsorted mail), processing and delivery by road to a Royal Mail regional depot of its customers' mail. Those services are known as 'upstream services'.

On 6 April 2004, TNT Post entered into an agreement with Royal Mail under which Royal Mail agreed to provide 'downstream services', that is, to deliver the mail that TNT Post had collected, sorted and delivered by road to one of Royal Mail's regional depots. That agreement was made in accordance with the conditions of the licence held by Royal Mail, which requires it to provide access to its postal facilities to any postal operator or user seeking such access and to negotiate in good faith with a view to agreeing the terms of such access. TNT Post does not currently provide any 'downstream' services itself.

The referring court also states that the principal market for business mail, which accounts for 85% of TNT Post's United Kingdom mail volumes, lies in the financial services sector. Since financial institutions are unable to recover all the input VAT they incur, it is in TNT Post's commercial interest to minimise the amount of VAT it has to charge its customers.

The Value Added Tax Act 1994, as amended by the Postal Services Act, provides that the conveyance by Royal Mail of postal packets, which includes letters, is exempt from VAT, whereas the services provided by TNT Post (which, that company contends, are the same as those provided by Royal Mail) are subject to VAT at the standard rate of 17.5%.

Since it considered that the resolution of the dispute before it required the interpretation of Community law, the Queen's Bench Division (Administrative Court) of the High Court of Justice of England and Wales decided to stay the proceedings and to refer the following questions to the Court for a preliminary ruling:

'1. (a) How is the expression "the public postal services" in Article 13A(1)(a) of the [Sixth Directive] (now Article 132(1)(a) of Directive 2006/112) to be interpreted?

(b) Is the interpretation of that expression affected by the fact that postal services in a Member State have been liberalised, there are no reserved services within the meaning of [Directive 97/67] and there is one designated universal service provider that has been notified to the Commission pursuant to that directive (such as Royal Mail in the United Kingdom)?

(c) In the circumstances of the present case (which are as set out in (b) above) does that expression include

(i) only the sole designated universal services provider (such as Royal Mail in the United Kingdom) or

(ii) also a private postal operator (such as TNT Post)?

2. In the circumstances of the present case, is Article 13A(1)(a) of the [Sixth Directive] (now Article 132(1)(a) of Directive 2006/112) to be interpreted as requiring or permitting a Member State to exempt all postal services provided by "the public postal services"?
3. If Member States are required or permitted to exempt some, but not all, of the services provided by "the public postal services," ... by reference to which criteria are those services to be identified?'

The questions referred

The first question

By its first question, which must be dealt with as a whole, the referring court asks the Court how the term 'public postal services' in Article 13A(1)(a) of the Sixth Directive is to be interpreted, in particular in the present case where the postal services in a Member State have been liberalised.

In this connection, it is important to note, first of all, that the syntax of the whole phrase 'public postal services' clearly shows that the words in fact refer to the actual organisations which engage in the supply of the services to be exempted. In order to be covered by the wording of the provision, the services must therefore be performed by a body which may be described as 'the public postal service' in the organic sense of that expression (see Case 107/84 Commission v Germany [1985] ECR 2655, paragraph 11).

That interpretation is founded on the actual wording of Article 13A(1)(a) of the Sixth Directive. Furthermore, there is nothing to suggest that that interpretation would have been affected by facts such as the liberalisation of the postal sector, which has taken place since the delivery of the judgment in Commission v Germany.

On the contrary, the fact that Article 132(1)(a) of Directive 2006/112 is drafted in terms precisely identical to those in Article 13A(1)(a) of the Sixth Directive shows that the exemption provided for in the latter provision has been maintained in the form in which it was originally enacted, notwithstanding the liberalisation of the postal sector.

It follows that, in contrast to what is claimed by TNT Post and the Finnish and Swedish Governments, the exemption laid down in Article 13A(1)(a) of the Sixth Directive cannot be interpreted so as to cover, in essence, supplies of postal services, such as the reserved services within the meaning of Article 7 of Directive 97/67, regardless of the status of the provider of those services.

Secondly, the terms used to specify an exemption such as that set out in Article 13A(1)(a) of the Sixth Directive are to be interpreted strictly, since it constitutes an exception to the general principle that VAT is to be levied on all services supplied for consideration by a taxable person. Nevertheless, the interpretation of those terms must be consistent with the objectives pursued by those exemptions and comply with the requirements of the principle of fiscal neutrality inherent in the common system of VAT. Thus, the requirement of strict interpretation does not mean that the terms used to specify the exemptions referred to in Article 13 should be construed in such a way as to deprive the exemptions of their intended effect.

Thus, as the title which Article 13A of the Sixth Directive carries, the exemptions provided for in that Article are intended to encourage certain activities in the public interest.

That general objective takes the form, in the postal sector, of the more specific objective of offering postal services which meet the essential needs of the population at a reduced cost.

As Community law now stands, such an objective is the same, in essence, as that of Directive 97/67 to offer a universal postal service. Under Article 3(1) of that directive, such a service involves the permanent provision of a postal service of specified quality at all points in their territory at affordable prices for all users.

Therefore, notwithstanding the fact that it cannot be used as a basis for the interpretation of Article 13A(1)(a) of the Sixth Directive, the legal basis of which differs from that of Directive 97/67, the latter directive nevertheless constitutes a useful point of reference for the purposes of interpreting the term 'public postal services' within the meaning of that provision.

It follows that public postal services within the meaning of Article 13A(1)(a) of the Sixth Directive must be regarded as operators, whether they are public or private (see, to that effect, Commission v Germany, paragraph 16), who undertake to supply postal services which meet the essential needs of the population and therefore, in practice, to provide all or part of the universal postal service in a Member State, as defined in Article 3 of Directive 97/67.

Such an interpretation is not contrary to the principle of fiscal neutrality, which precludes economic operators carrying out the same transactions from being treated differently in relation to the levying of VAT.

As the Advocate General observes [in] her Opinion, the assessment of the comparability of the services supplied hinges not only on the comparison of individual services, but on the context in which those services are supplied.

As the facts in the main proceedings demonstrate, on account of the obligations described [earlier] in this judgment, which are required under its licence and connected with its status as the universal service provider, an operator such as Royal Mail supplies postal services under a legal regime which is substantially different to that under which an operator such as TNT Post provides such services.

Consequently, the answer to the first question is that term 'public postal services' in Article 13A(1)(a) of the Sixth Directive must be interpreted to cover operators, whether they are public or private, who undertake to provide, in a Member State, all or part of the universal postal service, as defined in Article 3 of Directive 97/67.

The second and third questions

By its second and third questions, which it is appropriate to deal with together, the referring court essentially asks whether the exemption provided for in Article 13A(1)(a) of the Sixth Directive applies to all of the postal services provided by the public postal services or only part of those services. In the latter situation, it wishes to know the criteria enabling the exempted services to be identified.

It must be observed in this connection that, under Article 13A(1)(a) of the Sixth Directive, the supply of services by the public postal services and supply of goods incidental thereto are exempted from VAT. Only passenger transport and telecommunications services are expressly excluded from the scope of that provision.

However, contrary to what is maintained by Royal Mail, the Greek and United Kingdom Governments and Ireland, it may not be inferred from that provision that all the supplies of services by the public postal services and supplies of goods incidental thereto which are not expressly excluded from the scope of that provision are exempted, regardless of their intrinsic nature.

It follows from the requirements referred to in this judgment that the exemption provided for in Article 13A(1)(a) must be both strictly interpreted and interpreted consistently with the objectives of that provision, that the supplies of services and of goods incidental thereto must be interpreted as being those that the public postal services carry out as such, that is, by virtue of their status as public postal services.

Such an interpretation is dictated, in particular, by the need to observe the principle of fiscal neutrality. The obligations on an operator such as Royal Mail, which – as is apparent [in] this judgment – distinguish the situation in which that operator supplies postal services from that in which an operator such as TNT provides such services, concern only the postal services supplied in its capacity as the universal service provider.

In the same way, it follows from the requirements set out in this judgment and, in particular, from the nature of the objective pursued by Article 13A(1)(a), which is to encourage an activity in the public interest, that the exemption is not to apply to specific services dissociable from the service of public interest, including services which meet special needs of economic operators.

The German Government and the Commission are therefore correct to submit that services supplied by the public postal services for which the terms have been individually negotiated cannot be regarded as exempted under Article 13A(1)(a) of the Sixth Directive. By their very nature, those services meet the special needs of the users concerned.

That interpretation is, moreover, confirmed by recital 15 in the preamble to Directive 97/67, from which it is apparent that the option to negotiate contracts with customers individually does not correspond, in principle, with the concept of universal service provision.

The exemption provided for in Article 13A(1)(a) of Sixth Directive 77/388 applies to the supply by the public postal services acting as such – that is, in their capacity as an operator who undertakes to provide all or part of the universal postal service in a Member State – of services other than passenger transport and telecommunications services, and the supply of goods incidental thereto. It does not apply to supplies of services or of goods incidental thereto for which the terms have been individually negotiated.

There have been other disputes between the EC and member states over the taxation of postal services. For example, in *Re VAT Postal Transport: EC Commission v. Germany*,[65] the ECJ ruled that charges for transportation for Deutsche Bundespost were not entitled to the exemption for postal services. On the other hand, the Commission challenged Sweden's decision to tax postal services rendered by operators required to provide universal postal services.[66] The Commission proposed that postal services be taxed, but the proposal was eventually withdrawn because of opposition by the United Kingdom and other countries.[67]

In light of the foregoing, it is not surprising that the EC has funded studies looking at alternatives to the current VAT treatment of public bodies and nonprofit organizations. An earlier study recommended substantial changes in the taxation of public sector bodies. It divided government activities into four groups:

1. Government transfer payments to redistribute income or wealth
2. The provision of goods and services that do not compete with private sector sales

[65] Case C-107/84, [1986] 2 CMLR 177 (ECJ).

[66] IP/06/484, 10 April 2006, VAT/ Postal services – Commission launches infringement proceedings against Germany, the United Kingdom, and Sweden.

[67] See House of Commons Library, VAT on Postal Services, Standard Note SN 3376 (July 15, 2013).

3. The provision of goods and services that compete with private sector sales but may not be priced at market rates
4. The provision of goods and services that may compete with the private sector and may be priced at market rates[68]

Although government transfer payments enable the recipients to consume, the money transfers themselves do not constitute the sale of goods or services and therefore should not be taxed. Activities in the second group, for which there is no direct link to individual users and therefore no consideration paid specifically for these services, generally are not taxable. They include the operation of the government and the provision of defense and similar services.[69] The third group of services that may compete with private sector sales, but may be subsidized, include services such as health care and education.[70] The fourth group includes postal services, telecommunications, electricity, gas, water, and passenger transportation.

Poddar, Aujean, and Jenkins propose a "full taxation system" that treats public sector bodies (predominantly governments) as intermediaries for VAT purposes that make sales to others, rather than treating them as final consumers of the goods and services they provide (the treatment under most VAT systems in use today). Consistent with this treatment, the authors suggest that governments collect tax on their outputs and claim credits for tax on their business inputs.[71] Even with this proposed full taxation system, the calculation of the value of a supply is complicated because governments collect revenue to fund their activities from explicit fees, levies, taxes, subsidies, borrowings, and other sources.[72] According to the authors, explicit fees, subsidies, and grant payments should be included as part of taxable consideration subject to VAT. The authors suggest that the full taxation model can be combined with zero or reduced tax rates for "merit services" such as "health, education, cultural activities and child care."[73]

The EC also funded a study of the VAT rules that apply to the public sector in member states and the study compared those rules with the VAT rules in a number of OECD countries outside the EU.[74] The study examines a full taxation solution in which VAT is charged on the core services studied, and the public entities can recover tax on business inputs attributable to those taxable services.

[68] See an article based on this study in Aujean, Jenkins, and Poddar, "A New Approach to Public Sector Bodies," 10 *International VAT Monitor* 144 (July/Aug. 1999).

[69] *Id.* at 144.

[70] *Id.*

[71] *Id.* at 146.

[72] *Id.*

[73] *Id.* at 148.

[74] VAT in the Public Sector and Exemptions in the Public Interest: Final Report for TAXUD/2009/DE/316 (March 1, 2011). The study was conducted as a collaboration with Copenhagen Economics and KPMG AG. They covered what was termed "core services" – that is, waste disposal, cultural services, education, hospital services, and broadcasting.

VII. Special Treatment for Diplomats, Embassies, and International Organizations

Nations vary in their treatment of sales to and imports by foreign diplomats, embassies, and international organizations. Special treatment may be provided for sales to international organizations (such as NATO or the World Bank) and their staffs that operate within the taxing nation. When special treatment is provided, it may be authorized under international agreements or domestic law other than the VAT statute. For example, exemption may be linked to special treatment provided under a country's laws concerning diplomatic privileges and immunities.

Under many sales taxes that were replaced with VATs, the exemption for diplomats and others was provided with the use of exemption certificates issued to the qualified organizations or individuals. The opportunity to use this exemption certificate for nonqualified purchases or by nonqualified purchasers resulted in abuses. When some of these countries converted their sales taxes to VATs, they retained the exemption certificate procedure. Others require eligible organizations or individuals to pay VAT on their domestic purchases and imports and submit invoices with documentation to support their requests for VAT refunds. The refund procedure reduces the opportunity for abuse but imposes the administrative burden on the agency to verify eligibility for refund and to issue the refunds.

Whether a nation relies on the exemption or refund system, it must identify the goods and services eligible for the special treatment. In the EU, member states zero-rate supplies "under diplomatic and consular arrangements," supplies connected with NATO forces and their civilian staffs, and many others.[75] Exemption also is provided for imports of goods under diplomatic and consular arrangements, imports by NATO and some other international organizations, and certain other imports.[76]

Developing countries that receive significant aid from donor countries and international organizations typically exempt (or provide a refund of VAT on) purchases directly linked to technical assistance or humanitarian assistance agreements. Exemptions of this kind also tend to open the door to evasion. New Zealand severely restricts diplomatic exemption and taxes goods or services acquired in New Zealand by diplomatic and consular staff.[77]

VIII. Discussion Questions

1. What are the different factors that make it difficult (or even impossible) for a VAT to reach all consumption expenditures? Is a direct expenditure tax likely to be more comprehensive in this respect?

[75] See VAT Directive, *supra* note 2, at Art. 151(1).
[76] See *id.* at Art. 143(1)(f)–(i).
[77] See N.Z. *Tax Information Bulletin*, Vol. 5, No. 11 (Apr. 1994).

Point out the problems related to the definition of the tax base – that is, final consumption – which are common to a VAT and to a direct expenditure tax.

2. In defining taxpayer, the VAT Directive takes into account neither the profit-making purpose nor the public nature of the organization supplying the goods or rendering the services, except for Art. 13. However, these two factors are many times made explicit conditions of the exemptions granted under Art. 132 of the VAT Directive. Is this consistent with the theory of VAT as a general consumption tax?
3. Suppose that you are drafting a VAT statute. Would you choose to tax or to exempt the following items?
   - Legal services
   - Medical care
   - Foreign travels
   - Education
   - Leasing and letting of immovable goods (RE)
   - Dues paid to nonprofit organizations (including museums, sporting and other private clubs, professional associations, trade associations, and so on)
   - Drugs delivered on prescription
   - Public transportation of persons
   - Sales to governmental bodies
   - Food
   - Newspapers and books
   - Insurance
   - Highway tolls
   - Veterinary surgery
   - Betting and gambling
   - Transportation of goods
4. Now that you understand the concept of a zero-rate of VAT, can you imagine the use of a negative rate of VAT – that is, consumption subsidy (temporary or selective)? How would such a system operate?
5. Is there any reason for nonprofits and units of government to register and report taxable sales on all taxable sales, even if they do not meet the registration threshold required for other businesses rendering taxable services?

   What is the justification for exempting NPOs from VAT? Evaluate this justification.
6. Would the use of an addition type VAT, rather than the credit method, be desirable with respect to NPOs? Explain how it might work.
7. What are the VAT consequences if an NPO exports goods or services?
8. If you have to choose among the approaches discussed to cover NPOs and governments under the VAT, which would you choose for the United States? For your own country?

10 VAT Evasion and Avoidance

I. Introduction

As with any tax, the VAT presents opportunities for tax avoidance and evasion. While some specific areas where avoidance and evasion occur have been discussed throughout this book, this chapter focuses on evasion and avoidance more generally. We use the standard terminology, with tax evasion meaning illegal behavior (usually involving fraud or concealment of facts from the tax administration) and tax avoidance meaning behavior that follows the letter but not necessarily the spirit of the law.

II. Avoidance

VAT avoidance transactions can take a number of forms. For example, a taxpayer may attempt to split a supply into several parts, some of which are exempt or zero-rated. A taxpayer carrying out both exempt and taxable supplies can carry out transactions aimed at manipulating the allocation of inputs to taxable supplies. If certain favorable treatment (e.g., the registration requirement or, as in the *Ch'elle* case discussed later, the requirement to use the accrual method) is based on a threshold amount of supplies, a taxpayer might fragment its business, so that each part of the business falls below the threshold.

To counter tax avoidance, the tax authority must of course first identify the tax avoidance transactions that it considers questionable. Although this takes some care, it is generally easier than uncovering tax evasion, because by definition tax avoidance does not involve the misstatement of facts or their willful concealment from the authorities. If that happens, then one enters the realm of tax evasion.

One means of reducing the extent of avoidance transactions is to design the law to minimize avoidance opportunities. For example, if exemptions are minimized, there will be fewer opportunities to characterize supplies as exempt (by splitting transactions or otherwise) or to manipulate input credits. Likewise, maintaining a single tax rate reduces the opportunity to characterize supplies as subject to a lower rate. In the case of registration thresholds, rules are needed to aggregate the supplies of related parties for purposes of the registration threshold. This is often done on the basis of a definition of related parties.

Some avoidance transactions can be dealt with by litigation. For example, if a taxpayer attempts to split a transaction into separate transactions, one of which is taxable while the other is exempt or zero-rated, a court might find that under VAT law there is only one taxable supply. This can come about by judicial interpretation of criteria in the law governing whether a particular transaction is to be treated as one supply or several separate supplies.

Normally, courts will be inclined to deal with an avoidance transaction by interpreting a specific statutory provision, rather than applying a general anti-avoidance rule. Some cases, however, cannot be disposed of in this manner, and recourse to a general anti-avoidance rule is needed. Most jurisdictions have a general anti-avoidance rule for VAT. In some countries, this is a judge-made rule, whereas in others it is codified by statute. Countries with a statutory rule may include the rule in the VAT law itself or in a general tax code or tax administration law. Although general anti-avoidance rules take different forms, they typically focus on transactions that are motivated mainly or entirely by tax avoidance and seek a tax advantage that is unintended by the statutory scheme.

The *Ch'elle* case provides an example of New Zealand's application of its general anti-avoidance rule in the VAT area.

CH'ELLE PROPERTIES Ltd v. COMMISSIONER of Inland Revenue[1]

Introduction

In this appeal the question was whether a claim for $9 million for GST credits by Ch'elle Properties (NZ) Ltd (Ch'elle) involved an arrangement which defeated the intention and application of the Goods and Services Tax Act 1985 (GST Act) contrary to s 76 of that Act....

The issue is: what is the intent and application of the GST Act and was it defeated in this case?...

Factual circumstances

In 1996 and 1997, Nigel Ashby incorporated a total of 114 companies. He was the sole director of all the companies and the shareholders were the trustees of his family trust. None of the companies had any assets or bank accounts. They were all administered under the

[1] Court of Appeal of New Zealand (June 25, 2007), [2007] NZCA 256 [edited by the authors].

umbrella of a management company, Queen Street Property Group, which was also controlled by Mr Ashby.

For GST purposes, each of the companies was registered on a payment basis.[2]

Michelle Wilson, a friend of Mr Ashby's former wife, incorporated the appellant, Ch'elle, in July 1998. She registered it the following month for GST on a monthly invoice basis.[3] Ch'elle declared its taxable activity was 'property trader'. It had no assets or bank accounts. Ms Wilson had no commercial experience or expertise relative to property trading.

In August 1998, Ch'elle entered into an agreement with M W Developments to purchase a property in Edgeworth Road in Glenfield. The transaction was initiated by Mr Ashby who was M W Developments' tax agent.

Ch'elle applied to the Commissioner in August 1998 for a private ruling under Part VA of the Tax Administration Act 1994 (TA Act) in relation to the GST implications of this transaction.

The letter seeking the ruling advised:

(a) Settlement would be deferred for 12 years;
(b) The purchase price (payable in 12 years) was $655,000;
(c) An immediate deposit of $100 was payable by Ch'elle with a further $64,900 payable upon receipt of the GST refund; and,
(d) Ch'elle was registered on an invoice basis.

Two similar transactions in relation to other properties on the North Shore were entered into later that year by Ch'elle also orchestrated by Mr Ashby.

On 5 November 1998, each of the 114 Ashby companies entered into a conditional contract to purchase from Waverley Developments Ltd a lot in a subdivision in Dominion Road, Papakura for $70,000. Each contract provided for a deposit of $10.00 on execution and the remainder was payable on the date for settlement specified in the contracts which was 31 August 1999.

On 21 May 1999 Ch'elle entered into conditional contracts with the 114 individual Ashby companies to purchase these properties for a total price of $80 million, in other words, an average of about $700,000 per contract.

Settlement was deferred for between 10 and 20 years. An initial deposit of $10.00 was payable on execution, with the balance of the deposit ($29,990) being payable subsequently. The vendor did not hold the deposits received as a stakeholder. During the deferred settlement period, the vendor company was to construct a house on each section.

[2] Ed. note: In other words, the cash method rather than the accrual method.

[3] Ed. note: In other words, the accrual method.

Each of the vendor companies issued an invoice to Ch'elle for the total ultimate price.

On 15 June 1999 the Commissioner issued a private ruling to Ch'elle in relation to the Edgeworth Road property. It was expressed to be applicable only to the one transaction and approved the payment of a GST refund. Because the Rulings Unit considered the sale and purchase agreement to be a credit contract, the refund was based on the present day value of the property rather than its estimated value at the date of settlement 12 years later.

Later that month, Ch'elle filed a GST return for the period ending 31 May 1999 claiming input tax credits of $398,333 in relation to 13 property transactions. These were the three transactions on the North Shore (including Edgeworth Road which was specifically covered by the private ruling) and ten of the 114 Papakura transactions.

In September 1999, the Commissioner paid Ch'elle $29,000 in relation to the Edgeworth Road transaction. That is not in issue in the proceedings.

On 20 October 1999 Ch'elle filed a further GST return for the remaining 104 properties claiming $9 million in input tax credits based on the estimated market value on the respective settlement dates 10 to 20 years into the future.

The Commissioner, on 14 March 2000, issued notices disallowing the claims. These were rejected by the appellant in May of that year.

On 12 September 2000, all 114 contracts between Waverley Developments and the companies were cancelled for failure to settle on the stipulated date of October 1999.

The dispute was considered by the Commissioner's Adjudication Unit. Following the release of its report, the Commissioner raised an assessment disallowing all input tax credits claimed other than those in relation to the three North Shore properties. Ch'elle then filed a notice of claim with the Taxation Review Authority. It held against Ch'elle. On appeal to the High Court, the same conclusion was reached although for slightly different reasons.

Was the scheme void because of tax avoidance?

Section 76(1) of the Act, which was in force at the relevant time, provides:

76 Agreement to defeat the intention and application of Act to be void –

(1) Notwithstanding anything in this Act, where the Commissioner is satisfied that an arrangement has been entered into between persons to defeat the intent and application of this Act, or of any provision of this Act, the Commissioner shall treat the arrangement as void for the purposes of this Act and shall adjust the amount of tax payable by any registered person (or refundable to that person by the Commissioner)

who is affected by the arrangement, whether or not that registered person is a party to it, in such manner as the Commissioner considers appropriate so as to counteract any tax advantage obtained by that registered person from or under that arrangement.

What was the arrangement between the parties?

Section 76(4) provided:

'Arrangement' means any contract, agreement, plan, or understanding (whether enforceable or unenforceable) including all steps and transactions by which it is carried into effect:

The steps and transactions that constitute the arrangement in this case were:

(a) The incorporation by Nigel Ashby of 114 companies (the Ashby companies);
(b) The registration of those companies for GST purposes on a payment basis;
(c) The incorporation of the appellant on 27 July 1998;
(d) The registration of the appellant for GST purposes on an invoice basis;
(e) The entry of the Ashby companies into conditional contracts to purchase from a third party Lots 1 to 114 in Dominion Road, Papakura on 5 November 1998;
(g) The entry by the appellant into conditional contracts with the 114 individual Ashby companies to purchase the 114 Dominion Road sections on 21 May 1999 and in particular terms stipulating that:
    (i) there be a deferral of settlement for between 10 and 20 years;
    (ii) an initial deposit of only $10 was required;
    (iii) that the vendor would not hold the deposits as stakeholders;
    (iv) an invoice for the full amount owing on settlement was issued at the time the contracts were signed;
(h) The submission by the appellant of a GST return in relation to 13 properties claiming input credits of $398,333; and
    (i) The submission by the appellant of a further GST return for the remaining properties claiming nearly $9 million in input credits on 20 October 1999.

Did the arrangement defeat the intent and application of the GST Act?

... [T]he appellant, contended that s 76 required a subjective intent.

This cannot be the case. This would lead to the anomalous situation where an identical transaction might in one case be sustainable, but in another struck down as tax avoidance because in the first instance the operator mistakenly, naively, unrealistically or opportunistically was of the view that what was being done was unassailable. The second, however, which involved a more confident person who thought it was worth "having a go" would be struck down. It is the objective assessment of the arrangement which will provide the answer as to whether it defeats the intention and application of the Act and is therefore void....

[The appellant] also argued that the various actions of the appellant were specifically allowed for under the GST Act, and therefore there could not have been defeating of the intent and application of the Act.

That submission overlooks the purpose and operation of the provision. As with all general anti-avoidance provisions, its purpose is to strike down arrangements that frustrate the taxing regime, despite the arrangement's technical compliance with substantive taxing provisions. Whatever might be said about separate items in a scheme of arrangement, s 76 provides for an overview and an assessment of the combined effect of the individual components....

In order to assess whether s 76 is triggered it is necessary to assess the scheme and purpose of the GST Act....

The general intent of the GST Act is to impose a broadly based consumption tax....

Section 19 outlines the three alternative methods upon which GST can be accounted for: invoice basis; payments basis; and hybrid basis. The method adopted determines when output and input tax is payable.

The essential distinction between the invoice and payments accounting bases is that an invoice basis requires GST to be returned pursuant to the accrual approach whereas the payments basis requires GST to be accounted for on a cash approach.

If an invoice basis is used the tax is normally brought to account for the return period in which the supply is deemed to be made. In most circumstances this will be the earlier of the time an invoice is issued/received or any payment is received/made: ss 9(1), 20(3)(a) and 20(4)(a). If the payment basis is adopted the tax is generally brought to account only when, and to the extent that, payment is made:

ss 20(3)(b) and 20(4)(b). Section 19(1) provides that the invoice basis is the standard method used. Under s 19A only certain defined persons will be entitled to account for GST on a payment basis namely:

(a) local authorities and non-profit bodies (s19A(1)(a));
(b) persons whose total value of taxable supplies had not exceeded $1 million in the preceding 12 months or was unlikely to exceed $1 million in the following 12 months (s 19A(1)(b)) ... or
(c) persons who satisfy the Commissioner that it would be appropriate for them to use the payment basis because of the nature, volume and value of their taxable supplies and the nature of their accounting systems (s 19A)(1)(c)). For example, dairy owners.

The operation of the different accounting bases means that there can be mismatches in terms of the timing between when an input tax credit is claimed on a particular supply and when the payment of output tax on that supply occurs: *Shell New Zealand Holdings Co Ltd v CIR* [1994] 3 NZLR 276 at 283 (CA).

In *Nicholls v CIR* (1999) 19 NZTC 15,233 (CA) Henry J said at [14]:

The Act distinguishes between taxpayers who are to account on an invoice basis, and those who are to account on a payments (or hybrid) basis. The need for consistency as between liability to pay output tax and the ability to deduct input tax within the same regime is obvious, and is reflected throughout the Act. There is however no need for consistency as between the two different regimes.

This Court stated in *Shell* at 283:

Heron J was influenced in his conclusion by a concern that there should be no difference in the timing of GST paid and GST refunded. However, given the different taxable periods available to registered persons (one month, two months, and six months – s 15) and the three bases of accounting for GST (invoice, payments and hybrid) inevitably there are numerous mismatches between times at which GST is paid by a recipient to a supplier and at which GST is refunded to the recipient.

The Act permits a degree of mismatching in terms of accounting methods; however, this does not mean that a gross mismatch in timing is irrelevant on a s 76 question. The Act seeks to limit the nature and degree of such mismatching. There are explicit restraints on a taxpayer's ability to register on a payment basis. For example, the $1 million annual turnover rule contained in s 19A(1)(b) is intended, in part, to prevent either singly high value supplies or multiple lower value supplies occurring between persons who are registered for GST on different accounting bases.

In this case the creation of the Ashby companies (which were entitled to register on a payments basis by virtue of the fact that the value of their proposed taxable supplies fell under the $1 million cap) effectively circumvented this limitation. As a result, the degree of mismatch contemplated and tolerated by the Act escalated to a level which could never have been intended.

We are satisfied that the arrangement triggered s 76 because:

(a) the invoices issued by the 114 Ashby companies were not going to be paid for 10 to 20 years (and consequently no output tax was payable) whereas Ch'elle was immediately entitled to input tax credits for the purchase of the properties . . .; and
(b) the proliferation of vendor companies had no rationale or utility beyond creating a mechanism to exploit a tax advantage by coming under the $1 million threshold. This mechanism operated to exploit the mismatch between the invoice and payments accounting bases and thereby defeated the intent and application of the Act. . . .

In the *Halifax* decision, the European Court of Justice developed a judge-made anti-avoidance rule under which transactions that are motivated solely by tax avoidance are not recognized for VAT purposes.

Halifax et al. v. Commissioners of Customs and Excise[4]

The main proceedings and the questions referred to the Court of Justice

Halifax is a banking company. The vast majority of its services are exempt from VAT. At the material time, it was able to recover less than 5% of its input VAT.

... Leeds Development is a property development company and County is a property development and investment company.

... Leeds Development and County, and another member of the Halifax Plc Group involved in the transactions at issue, Halifax Property Investments Ltd (hereinafter 'Property'), are each wholly owned subsidiaries of Halifax. Leeds Development and County are each registered separately for VAT, and Property is unregistered.

For the purposes of its business, Halifax needed to construct call centres on four different sites at Cromac Wood and at Dundonald in Northern Ireland, at Livingston in Scotland and at West Bank, Leeds, in the North-East of England, on which it held a lease with about 125 years to run or the freehold or a fee simple interest.

On 17 December 1999, Halifax initially contracted with Cusp Ltd, an arm's length property development and contracting company, for the development of the Cromac Wood site. By a novation agreement of 28 February 2000, Halifax then disengaged itself from that contract and its rights and obligations became those of County.

Between 29 February and 6 April 2000, Halifax, Leeds Development, County and Property entered into a number of agreements relating to the various sites. The order for reference shows that the transactions for each of the sites followed a similar course.

As regards the sites at Cromac Wood, Dundonald and Livingston, on 29 February 2000 Halifax entered into loan agreements with Leeds Development, under which it agreed to lend it sufficient amounts for Leeds Development to acquire an interest in and develop the sites, for a maximum total amount of GBP 59 million.

Halifax and Leeds Development also entered into an agreement for the carrying out of certain construction works on the sites. For those works, Leeds Development was paid a little over GBP 120 000 by Halifax, including VAT of almost GBP 20 000, and Leeds Development

[4] Case C-255/02 (ECJ 2006) [edited by the authors; citations to case law have been omitted, so readers interested in these should consult the full opinion on the ECJ website].

issued three receipted VAT invoices to Halifax for that amount. Halifax also entered into an agreement with Leeds Development to grant leases of the sites to the latter at a premium, each for a term of 20 years, with the lessee having an option to extend the term to 99 years.

On 29 February 2000, Leeds Development also entered into a development and funding agreement with County, under which the latter was to carry out or procure the carrying out of construction work on the Cromac Wood, Dundonald and Livingston sites, including the works which Leeds Development had agreed to carry out or procure under the agreement between it and Halifax.

On the same date, Halifax made the initial advances to Leeds Development under the loans together with payment for the works, amounting in all to GBP 44 815 000. That sum was paid into a bank account which was dealt with at the direction of Leeds Development. The latter instructed that an identical sum, including VAT of more than GBP 6 600 000, be paid to County by way of an advance payment for the works carried out or procured by the latter. That transaction was confirmed on the same day by the bank concerned and the funds were then placed on overnight deposit. On the same date, County issued a receipted VAT invoice to Leeds Development.

29 February 2000 was also the last day of Leeds Development's February 2000 accounting period. It submitted a return claiming recovery of VAT of almost GBP 6 700 000.

On 1 March 2000, the sum of GBP 44 815 000, plus accrued interest, was transferred to an account opened in County's name at another bank.

On 6 April 2000, pursuant to the agreement of 29 February 2000, Halifax granted to Leeds Development leases of the three sites at Cromac Wood, Dundonald and Livingston in exchange for premiums totalling around GBP 7 400 000, with each lease being treated as an exempt supply for VAT purposes. Each premium was funded by Leeds Development by a further drawdown under the initial loan agreements.

On the same date, Leeds Development also entered into an agreement to assign each of those leases to Property for a premium, with completion of each assignment to take place on the first working day after completion of the works and each being regarded as a VAT-exempt transaction. The premium was to be calculated by reference to a formula such that it was expected that Leeds Development would generate a total profit of GBP 180 000. Property in turn entered into agreements to under-let premises at Cromac Wood, Dundonald and Livingston to Halifax for a premium, in each case to be calculated by reference to the price paid by Property to Leeds Development for the assignment of the respective lease, plus a profit. The profit to be achieved by Property from those under-letting arrangements was expected to be GBP 85 000....

In order to carry out the works under the various agreements entered into with Leeds Development, County engaged independent main contractors and professionals ('the arm's-length builders') for each of the sites. It appears that agreements were entered into with the independent contractors by stages and that those agreements were accompanied by separate agreements to which Halifax was a party. Those agreements gave warranties to Halifax relating inter alia to the carrying out by the arm's-length builder concerned of its duties and obligations.

The referring tribunal states that the tax consequences of the above-mentioned agreements were as follows:

- Halifax could deduct the deductible proportion of input VAT on the works to be carried out under the agreements for works entered into with Leeds Development.
- Leeds Development could deduct for the February 2000 period the VAT shown on the County invoice of 29 February 2000, totalling more than GBP 6 600 000 and, for the March 2000 period, the VAT shown on the invoice of 13 March 2000 of about GBP 455 000.
- County would account for all the output VAT shown on those invoices and could deduct the input VAT paid for the works carried out by the arm's length builders.
- The agreements entered into by Leeds Development of 6 April 2000 in relation to the assignment to Property of the leases of the four sites would be exempt transactions. As they took place in a different year, those supplies would not cause any adjustments to Leeds Development' input tax recovery position for the February and March 2000 accounting periods, which fell within the year ending on 31 March 2000.

The referring tribunal also states that for that solution to be effective:

- Halifax, Leeds Development and County each had to be separately registered for VAT,
- throughout the first year in question, the standard-rated outputs of Leeds Development should be as high a proportion of its total outputs as possible. To that end, the exempt supplies of Leeds Development, made when it assigned its interests in the sites to Property, had to be delayed until a later year, and
- the property interests of Leeds Development in the sites had to be designed so that they did not rank as capital items. Otherwise the transfer of those rights to Property would affect the former's rights of deduction.

By decisions of 4 and 7 July 2000, the Commissioners refused Leeds Development's claims for deduction and those of County in relation to the VAT charged to it by the arm's-length builders.

According to the national tribunal, the Commissioners considered that:

- Leeds Development made no supplies of works to Halifax, nor did it obtain supplies of construction works from County – those transactions accordingly did not fall to be taken into account for VAT purposes.
- On a proper analysis of the arrangements as a whole, Halifax received supplies from the arm's-length builders and not from Leeds Development. Halifax could therefore deduct the VAT on those works, applying its normal recovery percentage.

Halifax, Leeds Development and County appealed against the Commissioners' decisions....

... [T]he national tribunal seeks essentially to ascertain whether the Sixth Directive must be interpreted as meaning that a taxable person has no right to deduct input VAT where the transactions on which that right is based constitute an abusive practice....

Findings of the Court

As a preliminary point, it must be noted that the problems raised by the questions submitted by the VAT and Duties Tribunal appear, at least in part, to stem from national rules which allow a taxable person who undertakes at the same time taxed and untaxed transactions, or only untaxed transactions, to transfer leases of immovable property to another entity under its control, which is entitled to opt for taxation of the letting of that property and thereby to deduct the total input VAT paid on construction or renovation costs.

Notwithstanding that finding, it must be borne in mind that, according to settled case-law, Community law cannot be relied on for abusive or fraudulent ends ....

The application of Community legislation cannot be extended to cover abusive practices by economic operators, that is to say transactions carried out not in the context of normal commercial operations, but solely for the purpose of wrongfully obtaining advantages provided for by Community law....

That principle of prohibiting abusive practices also applies to the sphere of VAT.

Preventing possible tax evasion, avoidance and abuse is an objective recognised and encouraged by the Sixth Directive....

However, as the Court has held on numerous occasions, Community legislation must be certain and its application foreseeable by those subject to it .... That requirement of legal certainty must be observed all the more strictly in the case of rules liable to entail financial consequences, in order that those concerned may know precisely the extent of the obligations which they impose on them....

Moreover, it is clear from the case-law that a trader's choice between exempt transactions and taxable transactions may be based on a range of factors, including tax considerations relating to the VAT system .... Where the taxable person chooses one of two transactions, the Sixth Directive does not require him to choose the one which involves paying the highest amount of VAT. On the contrary, ... taxpayers may choose to structure their business so as to limit their tax liability.

In view of the foregoing considerations, it would appear that, in the sphere of VAT, an abusive practice can be found to exist only if, first, the transactions concerned, notwithstanding formal application of the conditions laid down by the relevant provisions of the Sixth Directive and the national legislation transposing it, result in the accrual of a tax advantage the grant of which would be contrary to the purpose of those provisions.

Second, it must also be apparent from a number of objective factors that the essential aim of the transactions concerned is to obtain a tax advantage. As the Advocate General observed in point 89 of his Opinion, the prohibition of abuse is not relevant where the economic activity carried out may have some explanation other than the mere attainment of tax advantages.

It is for the national court to verify in accordance with the rules of evidence of national law, provided that the effectiveness of Community law is not undermined, whether action constituting such an abusive practice has taken place in the case before it....

To allow taxable persons to deduct all input VAT even though, in the context of their normal commercial operations, no transactions conforming with the deduction rules of the Sixth Directive or of the national legislation transposing it would have enabled them to deduct such VAT, or would have allowed them to deduct only a part, would be contrary to the principle of fiscal neutrality and, therefore, contrary to the purpose of those rules.

As regards the second element, whereby the transactions concerned must essentially seek to obtain a tax advantage, it must be borne in mind that it is the responsibility of the national court to determine the real substance and significance of the transactions concerned. In so doing, it may take account of the purely artificial nature of those transactions and the links of a legal, economic and/or personal nature between the operators involved in the scheme for reduction of the tax burden....

In any event, it is clear from the order for reference that the VAT and Duties Tribunal considers that the sole purpose of the transactions at issue in the main proceedings was to obtain a tax advantage.

... [I]t is only in the absence of fraud or abuse, and subject to adjustments which may be made in accordance with the conditions laid down in Article 20 of the Sixth Directive, that the right to deduct, once it has arisen, is retained ....

Accordingly, ... the Sixth Directive must be interpreted as precluding any right of a taxable person to deduct input VAT where the transactions from which that right derives constitute an abusive practice.

For it to be found that an abusive practice exists, it is necessary, first, that the transactions concerned, notwithstanding formal application of the conditions laid down by the relevant provisions of the Sixth Directive and of national legislation transposing it, result in the accrual of a tax advantage the grant of which would be contrary to the purpose of those provisions. Second, it must also be apparent from a number of objective factors that the essential aim of the transactions concerned is to obtain a tax advantage.

Question 1(b)

... Question 1(b) must be taken to mean that the national court seeks, essentially, to ascertain under what conditions VAT may be recovered where an abusive practice has been found to exist.

Observations submitted to the Court

The United Kingdom Government considers that it is necessary to examine the factors which demonstrate the true economic basis of the transactions and to determine whether or not the purposes of the Sixth Directive have been attained.

In this case, those factors are the ones established by the VAT and Duties Tribunal in its first decision, namely that:

(a) Halifax was the guiding mind behind the transactions;
(b) Halifax provided all of the funding for the transactions on an interest-free basis;
(c) Halifax remained in occupation of the sites throughout, so that the benefit of the construction works enured to it directly;
(d) Halifax had direct contractual links with the arm's-length builders in the form of the warranties; and
(e) neither County nor Leeds Development had any property interests of substance.

Those factors prompt the conclusion that Halifax is the recipient of the supply made by the arm's-length builders and thus give rise to a result that achieves the purpose of the Sixth Directive.

Findings of the Court

... [A] finding of abusive practice must not lead to a penalty, for which a clear and unambiguous legal basis would be necessary, but rather to an obligation to repay, simply as a consequence of that finding, which rendered undue all or part of the deductions of input VAT....

It follows that transactions involved in an abusive practice must be redefined so as to re-establish the situation that would have prevailed in the absence of the transactions constituting that abusive practice.

In that regard, the tax authorities are entitled to demand, with retroactive effect, repayment of the amounts deducted in relation to each transaction whenever they find that the right to deduct has been exercised abusively. . . .

However, they must also subtract therefrom any tax charged on an output transaction for which the taxable person was artificially liable under a scheme for reduction of the tax burden and, if appropriate, they must reimburse any excess.

Similarly, it must allow a taxable person who, in the absence of transactions constituting an abusive practice, would have benefited from the first transaction not constituting such a practice, to deduct, under the deduction rules of the Sixth Directive, the VAT on that input transaction.

It follows that the answer to Question 1(b) must be that, where an abusive practice has been found to exist, the transactions involved must be redefined so as to re-establish the situation that would have prevailed in the absence of the transactions constituting that abusive practice.

On those grounds, the Court (Grand Chamber) hereby rules:

1. Transactions of the kind at issue in the main proceedings constitute supplies of goods or services and an economic activity . . . provided that they satisfy the objective criteria on which those concepts are based, even if they are carried out with the sole aim of obtaining a tax advantage, without any other economic objective.[5]
2. The Sixth Directive must be interpreted as precluding any right of a taxable person to deduct input VAT where the transactions from which that right derives constitute an abusive practice.

   For it to be found that an abusive practice exists, it is necessary, first, that the transactions concerned, notwithstanding formal application of the conditions laid down by the relevant provisions of the Sixth Directive and of national legislation transposing it, result in the accrual of a tax advantage the grant of which would be contrary to the purpose of those provisions. Second, it must also be apparent from a number of objective factors that the essential aim of the transactions concerned is to obtain a tax advantage.
3. Where an abusive practice has been found to exist, the transactions involved must be redefined so as to re-establish the situation that would have prevailed in the absence of the transactions constituting that abusive practice.

[5] The portion of the opinion relating to this ruling has been omitted by the editors.

In the companion case to *Halifax*, the University of Huddersfield leased real property to a trust, which leased it back to the university.[6] Both leases were treated as taxable under duly made elections. The university incurred costs in renovating the property, which it claimed as input credit. Absent the lease arrangement, only a small portion of the VAT on the renovation would have been allowed as an input credit, given that most supplies of the university were exempt. On remand from the ECJ, the UK Lower Tribunal found that the lease arrangement was not abusive, because the tax advantage it allowed was not contrary to the VAT Directive.[7]

The House of Lords decision in the *Newnham College* case also involved a scheme by an educational institution to obtain input VAT credit for renovation expenses in a situation where otherwise little or no credit would have been available absent the scheme.[8] Newnham College was contemplating a renovation of its library. Because it provided exempt supplies, it could not have received input credit for the VAT on the materials and services involved in the renovation. Its advisers came up with a transaction under which a new entity was created to own the library. The college would pay this entity for the use of the library in the future. These payments would be taxable under the VAT. Accordingly, the new entity would be entitled to input credit for the VAT on the renovation costs. The tax authorities denied the input credit, citing a specific anti-avoidance rule that had been enacted with such transactions in mind. The House of Lords held, however, that the specific anti-avoidance rule did not apply, reading it rather narrowly. The court hinted that the tax authorities might have prevailed had they sought to invoke the abuse of rights theory established in Halifax. For some reason, the tax authorities adopted a litigation strategy of not invoking Halifax.

The Halifax decision was broadened by the ECJ in the following *Part Service* case.

Ministero dell'Economia e delle Finanze v. Part Service Srl[9]

Throughout 1987 Italservice and the leasing company IFIM Leasing Sas ('IFIM'), both belonging to the same financial group, were involved together in leasing arrangement transactions in connection, for the most part, with motor vehicles.

Those transactions were carried out under the following terms:

IFIM concluded a contract with a customer for the use of a motor vehicle with an option to purchase, in consideration of lease payments, the setting up of a surety corresponding to the costs of the vehicle

[6] ECR 1–1751 (ECJ 2006).

[7] [2013] UKFTT 429 (TC).

[8] *Principal and Fellows of Newnham College v. Her Majesty's Revenue and Customs*, [2008] UKHL 23.

[9] Case C-425/06 (ECJ 2008) [edited by the authors)].

not covered by the lease payments and the provision of an unlimited security.

Italservice concluded a contract with the customer under which it insured the vehicle against all risks except civil liability and guaranteed – by financing the surety and providing the unlimited security – the fulfilment of the obligations, in favour of IFIM, undertaken by that customer. In consideration thereof the customer paid, in advance, to Italservice an amount which reduced the total of the lease payments agreed between the customer and IFIM, reducing that total, in the majority of cases, to an amount barely above the cost of the vehicle, as well as a commission of 1% paid to a consultant.

The customer instructed Italservice to pay the amount financed to IFIM, on his behalf, by way of the surety provided for in the contract for use of the vehicle.

Italservice entrusted the performance of the contract with the customer to IFIM.

IFIM, as an intermediary, received additional remuneration from Italservice, and, in the event of default by the customer, an amount equivalent to that promised by Italservice to the customer, by way of refund, in the event of the customer fulfilling his obligations to make the lease payments.

... IFIM levied VAT on the customer's lease payments.

By contrast, ... the consideration paid by the customer to Italservice and by Italservice to IFIM was invoiced without VAT.

Following investigations carried out into Italservice the tax office held that, although the different agreements signed by the interested parties were contained in separate contracts, they together constituted a single contract concluded between three parties. According to that office, the consideration paid by the customer for the leasing arrangement had been artificially divided to reduce the taxable amount, as the role of lessor was split between Italservice and IFIM.

As a consequence, the tax office issued Italservice, on 1 September 1992, with an adjustment notice for VAT, in respect of the year 1987, in the amount of ITL 3 169 519 000, with interest and penalties of ITL 9 496 469 000.

Italservice contested that tax adjustment .... It claimed that it was not a single contract, but several linked contracts, that format having been chosen not for tax avoidance purposes, but for valid economic reasons associated with marketing (launching a new financial product with reduced premiums), with organization (separation of the risk management tasks: insurance, securities and financing confined to Italservice; management of a fleet of vehicles entrusted to operational companies) and the guarantee (financing serving as the guarantee deposit for fulfilling the obligations of the customer).

... [T]he Corte suprema di cassazione (Supreme Court of Cassation) ... is of the view that the decision to be taken requires resolution of the question whether the actions of the relevant parties, having regard to their reciprocal links, can be considered to be an abuse of rights or of legal form according to the definition given by Community case-law, notably in Case C-255/02 *Halifax and Others* [2006] ECR I-1609.

It considers that the division of the contracts has the effect of reducing the VAT burden to a lesser amount than that resulting from an ordinary leasing contract, since tax is levied only on the granting of use of the vehicle, the cost of which is practically equivalent to the purchase price of that vehicle.

It is therefore necessary to determine whether, for the purposes of VAT collection, with regard to the economic objective sought, the contracts must be held to constitute a unitary whole, or whether each contract remains autonomous and, accordingly, subject to its own particular tax rules.

In order to answer that question, it must be determined whether the fact that a financing transaction – regarded in economic practice and in national case-law as an essential component of a leasing contract – is regulated by a separate contract concerning the granting of the use of the goods, can constitute an abuse....

The first question

By its first question the referring court asks, in essence, whether the Sixth Directive should be interpreted as meaning that there can be a finding of an abusive practice when the accrual of a tax advantage is the principal aim of the transaction or the transactions in question, or if such a finding can only be made if the accrual of that tax advantage constitutes the sole aim pursued, to the exclusion of other economic objectives....

It must be observed that, in the context of the dispute in the main proceedings, the exemptions from VAT are under scrutiny and that, specifically in connection with those exemptions, Article 13 of the Sixth Directive requires Member States to 'prevent ... any possible evasion, avoidance or abuse'.

In paragraphs 74 and 75 of *Halifax and Others*, the Court first held that, in the context of interpreting the Sixth Directive, an abusive practice can be held to exist where:

- the transactions concerned, notwithstanding formal application of the conditions laid down by the relevant provisions of the Sixth Directive and the national legislation transposing it, result in the accrual of a tax advantage the grant of which would be contrary to the purpose of those provisions;
- it is apparent from a number of objective factors that the essential aim of the transactions concerned is to obtain a tax advantage.

When, subsequently, it provided the referring court with details for guidance in interpreting the transactions in the case in the main proceedings, the Court once again referred, at paragraph 81, to transactions essentially seeking to obtain a tax advantage.

Therefore, when it stated, in paragraph 82 of that judgment, that in any event, the transactions at issue had the sole purpose of obtaining a tax advantage, it was not establishing that circumstance as a condition for the existence of an abusive practice, but simply pointing out that, in the matter before the referring court in that case, the minimum threshold for classifying a practice as abusive had been passed.

The reply to the first question therefore is that the Sixth Directive must be interpreted as meaning that there can be a finding of an abusive practice when the accrual of a tax advantage constitutes the principal aim of the transaction or transactions at issue.

The second question

By its second question the referring court asks, in essence, whether, for the purposes of the application of VAT, transactions such as those at issue in the dispute in the main proceedings can be considered to be an abusive practice under the Sixth Directive.

By way of a preliminary point, it must be recalled that a trader's choice between exempt transactions and taxable transactions may be based on a range of factors, including tax considerations relating to the VAT system. Where the taxable person chooses one of two transactions, the Sixth Directive does not require him to choose the one which involves paying the highest amount of VAT. On the contrary, taxpayers may choose to structure their business so as to limit their tax liability (*Halifax and Others*, paragraph 73).

Nevertheless, when a transaction involves the supply of a number of services, the question arises whether it should be considered to be a single transaction or as several individual and independent supplies of services requiring separate assessment.

… [E]very transaction must normally be regarded as distinct and independent….

However, in certain circumstances, several formally distinct services, which could be supplied separately and thus give rise, in turn, to taxation or exemption, must be considered to be a single transaction when they are not independent.

Such is the case for example, where, in the course of a purely objective analysis, it is found that there is a single supply in cases where one or more elements are to be regarded as constituting the principal service, whilst one or more elements are to be regarded, by contrast, as ancillary services which share the tax treatment of the principal service …. In particular, a service must be regarded as ancillary to a principal service if it does not constitute for customers an aim in itself, but a means of better enjoying the principal service supplied….

It can also be held that there is a single supply where two or more elements or acts supplied by the taxable person to the customer are so closely linked that they form, objectively, a single, indivisible economic supply, which it would be artificial to split....

It is for the national court to assess if, the contractual structure of the transaction notwithstanding, the evidence put before the court discloses the characteristics of a single transaction.

In that context, it may find it necessary to extend its analysis by seeking evidence of indications of the existence of an abusive practice, which is the concept with which the question referred is concerned.

The Court, when giving a preliminary ruling, may, where appropriate, provide clarification designed to give the national court guidance in its interpretation (*Halifax and Others*, paragraph 77).

In the present case, the transactions at issue in the main proceedings, as described by the referring court, have the following characteristics:

- the two companies taking part in the leasing transaction are part of the same group;
- the service supplied by the leasing company (IFIM) is subject to a division, the financing element is entrusted to another company (Italservice) to be split into a credit service, an insurance service and a brokerage service;
- the service of the leasing company is therefore reduced to a service for renting a vehicle;
- the lease payments made by the customer are of an amount which is only slightly higher than the purchase cost of the vehicle;
- that service, considered in isolation, therefore seems to be economically unprofitable, so that the viability of the business cannot be ensured solely by means of contracts concluded with the customers;
- the leasing company receives the consideration of the leasing transaction only through the cumulative lease payments made by the customer and the amounts transferred from the other company of the same group.

In order to assess whether those transactions can be held to constitute an abusive practice, the national court must verify, first, whether the result sought is a tax advantage, the granting of which would be contrary to one or more of the objectives of the Sixth Directive and, then, whether that constituted the principal aim of the contractual approach adopted....

As regards the first criterion, that court can take into account that the anticipated result is the accrual of a tax advantage linked to the exemption, pursuant to Article 13B(a) and (d) of the Sixth Directive, of the services entrusted to the co-contracting company of the leasing company.

That result would appear to be contrary to the objective of Article 11A(1) of the Sixth Directive, namely the taxation of everything which constitutes consideration received or to be received from the customer.

Since the leasing of vehicles under leasing contracts constitutes a supply of services ..., such a transaction is normally subject to VAT....

As regards the second criterion, the national court, in the assessment which it must carry out, may take account of the purely artificial nature of the transactions and the links of a legal, economic and/or personal nature between the operators involved (*Halifax and Others*, paragraph 81), those aspects being such as to demonstrate that the accrual of a tax advantage constitutes the principal aim pursued, notwithstanding the possible existence, in addition, of economic objectives arising from, for example, marketing, organisation or guarantee considerations.

Therefore the reply to the second question referred must be that it is for the national court to determine, in light of the ruling on the interpretation of Community law provided by the present judgment, whether, for the purposes of the application of VAT, transactions such as those at issue in the dispute in the main proceedings can be considered to constitute an abusive practice under the Sixth Directive....

On those grounds, the Court (Second Chamber) hereby rules:

1. The [VAT] Directive ... must be interpreted as meaning that there can be a finding of an abusive practice when the accrual of a tax advantage constitutes the principal aim of the transaction or transactions at issue.
2. It is for the national court to determine, in light of the ruling on the interpretation of Community law provided by the present judgment, whether, for the purposes of the application of VAT, transactions such as those at issue in the dispute in the main proceedings can be considered to constitute an abusive practice under the Sixth Directive.

Another VAT avoidance fact pattern considered by the ECJ involved an insurance broker which set up transactions that in effect allowed him to obtain a full input credit for VAT on advertising services that he received.

Commissioners v. Paul Newey[10]

[D]uring the period at issue in the main proceedings, Mr Newey was a loan broker, established in Tamworth (United Kingdom). The broking services supplied in the United Kingdom by Mr Newey were,

[10] Case C-653/11 (ECJ 2013) [edited by the authors].

in accordance with Article 13B(d) of the Sixth Directive, exempt from VAT. By contrast, the advertising services supplied to Mr Newey in the United Kingdom, which were intended to attract potential borrowers, were subject to VAT, with the result that the tax borne by Mr Newey on the advertising costs was not recoverable.

In order to avoid that non-recoverable tax burden, Mr Newey incorporated the company Alabaster (CI) Ltd ('Alabaster'), which was established in Jersey, a territory in which the Sixth Directive does not apply, and granted that company the right to use the business name Ocean Finance. Mr Newey was the sole shareholder of that company.

Alabaster employed at least one person on a full-time basis and had its own management, natural persons resident in Jersey with no direct experience of broking who were suggested or recruited by Mr Newey's accountants and paid on the basis of the time devoted to Alabaster's business activities.

Under Alabaster's constitution and the law in force in Jersey, those directors were responsible for managing and exercising the powers of that company and Mr Newey played no part in its management.

The broking contracts were concluded directly between the lenders and Alabaster, with the result that the broking commissions were paid not to Mr Newey, but to that company.

However, Alabaster did not itself process the loan applications, but used Mr Newey's services for that purpose, which were provided, under a sub-contract ('the services agreement'), by his employees carrying on their business activities in Tamworth. That agreement contained a list of services Mr Newey was to provide which essentially covered all the processing tasks for the loan broking business. Under that agreement, Mr Newey also had the power to negotiate the terms of the contracts concluded between Alabaster and the lenders.

In return for those services, Mr Newey received fees fixed at 50% at the outset, and then at 60%, of the amount of the gross commissions immediately receivable in respect of each loan by Alabaster, plus certain expenses or disbursements.

In practice, potential borrowers contacted directly Mr Newey's employees in the United Kingdom who processed each file and sent the applications which satisfied the credit eligibility criteria to Jersey to Alabaster's directors for authorisation. The approval process generally took around one hour to complete and, in fact, no request for authorisation was refused.

As advertising aimed at potential borrowers was critical to the loan broking business, it represented a considerable part of the costs borne by Alabaster.

[T]he advertising services were provided by Wallace Barnaby & Associates Ltd ('Wallace Barnaby'), a company which was not connected with Alabaster and was also established in Jersey, under a contract concluded with the latter. Wallace Barnaby itself obtained those advertising services from advertising agencies established in the United Kingdom, in particular from the advertising agency Ekay Advertising. Under the law in force in Jersey, the payments made by Alabaster to Wallace Barnaby for those services were not subject to VAT.

Mr Newey was not entitled to use the advertising services on behalf of Alabaster and assumed no liability for the payment of the services provided by Wallace Barnaby to that company. However, he had the power to approve the content of the advertisements, regarding which he met with one of Ekay Advertising's employees working in the United Kingdom. Following those meetings, that employee made recommendations to Wallace Barnaby.

Wallace Barnaby, in turn, made recommendations to Alabaster's directors, who met each week after receiving those recommendations to determine the proposed advertising expenditure. In practice, none of those recommendations was rejected.

The Commissioners submit that, for VAT purposes, first, the advertising services concerned were supplied to Mr Newey in the United Kingdom and are therefore taxable in the United Kingdom and, secondly, the loan broking services were supplied in the United Kingdom by Mr Newey.

In the alternative, they submit that, if Alabaster has to be regarded as being, in Jersey, the recipient of the advertising services as well as the supplier of the loan broking services, the arrangements entered into for the purpose of bringing about this result are contrary to the principle of prohibition of the abuse of rights as stated by the Court in Case C-255/02 *Halifax and Others* [2006] ECR I-1609 and must be recharacterised.

Accordingly, on 27 September 2005, the Commissioners issued a VAT assessment to Mr Newey for the period 1 July 2002 to 31 December 2004 in the sum of 10 707 075 pounds sterling (GBP) in order to recover from him the VAT on the advertising services supplied to him during that period.

... [T]he referring court seeks, in essence, to know whether contractual terms are decisive for the purposes of identifying the supplier and the recipient in a 'supply of services' transaction ... and, if the answer is in the negative, under what circumstances those terms may be recharacterised.

It must be remembered first of all that the Sixth Directive establishes a common system of VAT based, inter alia, on a uniform definition of taxable transactions (*Halifax and Others*, paragraph 48).

Under Article 2(1) of the Sixth Directive, 'the supply of goods or services effected for consideration within the territory of the country by a taxable person acting as such' is to be subject to VAT. As regards, more specifically, the meaning of supply of services, the Court has repeatedly held that a supply of services is effected 'for consideration', within the meaning of Article 2(1) of that directive, and hence is taxable, only if there is a legal relationship between the provider of the service and the recipient pursuant to which there is reciprocal performance, the remuneration received by the provider of the service constituting the value actually given in return for the service supplied to the recipient....

It is also apparent from the case-law of the Court that the term supply of services is therefore objective in nature and applies without regard to the purpose or results of the transactions concerned and without its being necessary for the tax authorities to carry out inquiries to determine the intention of the taxable person (see, to that effect, *Halifax and Others*, paragraphs 56 and 57 and the case-law cited).

As regards in particular the importance of contractual terms in categorising a transaction as a taxable transaction, it is necessary to bear in mind the case-law of the Court according to which consideration of economic and commercial realities is a fundamental criterion for the application of the common system of VAT (see, to that effect, Joined Cases C-53/09 and C-55/09 *Loyalty Management UK and Baxi Group* [2010] ECR I-9187, paragraphs 39 and 40 and the case-law cited).

Given that the contractual position normally reflects the economic and commercial reality of the transactions and in order to satisfy the requirements of legal certainty, the relevant contractual terms constitute a factor to be taken into consideration when the supplier and the recipient in a 'supply of services' transaction within the meaning of Articles 2(1) and 6(1) of the Sixth Directive have to be identified.

It may, however, become apparent that, sometimes, certain contractual terms do not wholly reflect the economic and commercial reality of the transactions.

That is the case in particular if it becomes apparent that those contractual terms constitute a purely artificial arrangement which does not correspond with the economic and commercial reality of the transactions.

The Court has held on various occasions that preventing possible tax evasion, avoidance and abuse is an objective recognised and encouraged by the Sixth Directive (see *Halifax and Others*, paragraph 71 and the case-law cited) and that the effect of the principle that the abuse of rights is prohibited is to bar wholly artificial arrangements which do not reflect economic reality and are set up with the sole aim of obtaining a tax advantage....

In the main proceedings, it is not disputed that, formally, in accordance with the contractual terms, Alabaster provided the lenders with the supplies of loan broking services and that it was the recipient of the supplies of advertising services provided by Wallace Barnaby.

However, taking into account the economic reality of the business relationships between, on the one hand, Mr Newey, Alabaster and the lenders and, on the other hand, Mr Newey, Alabaster and Wallace

Barnaby, ... it is conceivable that the effective use and enjoyment of the services at issue in the main proceedings took place in the United Kingdom and that Mr Newey profited therefrom.

It is for the referring court, by means of an analysis of all the circumstances of the dispute in the main proceedings, to ascertain whether the contractual terms do not genuinely reflect economic reality and whether it is Mr Newey, and not Alabaster, who was actually the supplier of the loan broking services at issue and the recipient of the supplies of advertising services provided by Wallace Barnaby.

If that were the case, those contractual terms would have to be redefined so as to re-establish the situation that would have prevailed in the absence of the transactions constituting that abusive practice (see, to that effect, *Halifax and Others*, paragraph 98).

In the present case, the re-establishment of the situation that would have prevailed in the absence of the transactions at issue, if the referring court were to consider them to constitute an abusive practice, would, in particular, mean that the services agreement and the advertising arrangements concluded between Alabaster and Wallace Barnaby could not be relied upon against the Commissioners, who could legitimately regard Mr Newey as actually being the supplier of the loan broking services and the recipient of the supplies of advertising services at issue in the main proceedings.

In the light of the foregoing considerations, the answer to the [referring court's] ... questions is that contractual terms, even though they constitute a factor to be taken into consideration, are not decisive for the purposes of identifying the supplier and the recipient of a 'supply of services' within the meaning of Articles 2(1) and 6(1) of the Sixth Directive. They may in particular be disregarded if it becomes apparent that they do not reflect economic and commercial reality, but constitute a wholly artificial arrangement which does not reflect economic reality and was set up with the sole aim of obtaining a tax advantage, which it is for the national court to determine.

As has been the case generally with judicially developed or statutorily codified anti-avoidance doctrines in the direct tax area, it is often difficult for courts to apply such doctrines to specific cases, particularly where well-advised taxpayers have structured transactions in a way that is aimed at surviving judicial scrutiny. As a result, there is an inherent uncertainty as to how the anti-abuse doctrine will be applied. This is illustrated among other cases[11] by the RBS Deutschland decision, which upheld a tax arbitrage transaction (namely, a transaction designed to take advantage of inconsistent rules in two jurisdictions).

[11] Other cases in which the taxpayer succeeded in a tax planning transaction were the *Huddersfield* and *Newnham College* cases, *supra* notes 6 and 8.

Commissioners v. RBS Deutschland[12]

The dispute in the main proceedings and the questions referred for a preliminary ruling

RBSD is a company established in Germany carrying on business providing banking and leasing services. Since 31 March 2000, RBSD has been a member of the Royal Bank of Scotland Group. It does not have any place of establishment in the United Kingdom, but it is registered there for VAT purposes as a non-established taxable person.

In January 2000, Vinci plc ("Vinci"), a company incorporated in the United Kingdom, was introduced to RBSD with a view to RBSD supplying lease finance to Vinci. To that end, a number of agreements were entered into on 28 March 2001.

First, RBSD purchased motor cars in the United Kingdom from Vinci Fleet Services ("VFS"), a subsidiary of Vinci. VFS, which is also incorporated in the United Kingdom, had acquired those motor cars from car dealerships established in the United Kingdom....

RBSD also concluded a leasing agreement with Vinci for a term of two years, which could be extended, called the "Master Lease Agreement," under which RBSD was to act as lessor and Vinci as lessee in respect of the equipment identified in the schedules to that agreement, that is to say, motor cars.... Between 28 March 2001 and 29 August 2002, RBSD charged rentals of GBP 335 977.49 to Vinci and charged no VAT on those transactions....

The rental payments, received ... by RBSD ... were not subject to VAT in the United Kingdom since, under United Kingdom law, the transactions carried out under those leasing agreements were treated as supplies of services and consequently the United Kingdom tax authorities regarded them as having been made in Germany, that is to say, where the supplier had its place of business. Nor were those payments subject to VAT in Germany since, under German law, the transactions in question were treated as supplies of goods and were therefore regarded as having been made in the United Kingdom, that is to say, the place of supply.

Accordingly, no VAT was collected on the rental payments at issue in the main proceedings in either the United Kingdom or Germany....

Before the United Kingdom tax authorities, RBSD sought deduction in full of the input VAT of GBP 314 056.24 charged to it by VFS when it purchased the cars from that company. RBSD maintained, inter alia, that Article 17(3)(a) of the directive entitled it to deduct the input tax paid for the acquisition of those goods. Furthermore, RBSD maintained that the conditions governing application of the doctrine of abuse of rights were not met in this case, since these were leasing

[12] Case C-277/09 (ECJ 2010).

transactions conducted between three independent traders operating at arm's length.

The Commissioners refused to allow RBSD the VAT deduction claimed and demanded repayment of the input tax which had been credited to RBSD. The Commissioners contended that Article 17(3)(a) of the directive did not permit deduction of input VAT paid in respect of the acquisition of goods subsequently used for transactions which were not chargeable to VAT. The Commissioners pointed out, inter alia, that input tax could not be deducted or refunded if no output tax had been charged. Furthermore, it was argued, RBSD had engaged in an abusive practice because the legal arrangement which it had put in place had the essential aim of obtaining a fiscal advantage contrary to the purpose of the directive. The leasing terms were drawn up in order to enable it to exploit the differences in the ways in which the directive had been transposed in the United Kingdom and in Germany. . . .

Consideration of the questions referred

First question

By its first question the national court wishes to know, in essence, whether Article 17(3)(a) of the directive must be interpreted as meaning that a Member State may refuse to allow a taxable person to deduct input VAT paid on the acquisition of goods in that Member State, where those goods have been used for the purposes of leasing transactions carried out in another Member State and those output transactions have not been subject to VAT in the second Member State. . . .

It is common ground that, had the leasing transactions at issue in the main proceedings been carried out by a company having its place of business in the United Kingdom or by a company established in that Member State, they would have conferred entitlement to deduction of VAT, pursuant to Article 17(2)(a) of the directive, as regards the input tax paid on the purchase of the vehicles which were the subject-matter of the leasing.

In accordance with Article 17(3)(a) of the directive, the Member States are required to grant a taxable person the right to a deduction of VAT in so far as the input goods are used for the purposes of subsequent transactions carried out in another country, which would be eligible for deduction of tax if they had occurred in the territory of the Member State concerned.

The right to deduct input VAT for certain transactions in respect of other output transactions carried out in another Member State therefore depends, under that provision, on whether that right to deduct exists where all of those transactions are carried out within the territory of the same Member State.

... [T]his is indeed the case in regard to the circumstances of the main proceedings. RBSD may consequently, pursuant to Article 17(3)(a) of the directive, claim a deduction of the VAT paid on the purchase of the goods subsequently used for leasing purposes.

However, the Governments which submitted observations to the Court contended, in essence, that the right to deduct input VAT is conditional upon output VAT having been collected. In the main proceedings, since the German tax authorities did not collect VAT when the leasing transactions were carried out, RBSD cannot purport to be entitled, in the United Kingdom, to deduct the input VAT on the purchase of the vehicles.

The Court has indeed held that the deduction of input VAT is linked to the collection of output VAT .... [T]he Court stated that where goods or services acquired by a taxable person are used for purposes of transactions that are exempt or do not fall within the scope of VAT, no output VAT can be collected or input VAT deducted.

In the case in the main proceedings, however, the output leasing transactions carried out by RBSD were not exempt from VAT and came within its scope. They are therefore capable of giving rise to a right to deduct.

As regards the right to deduct under Article 17(2) of the directive, relating to the input VAT on the goods and services used by the taxable person for the purposes of his taxable output transactions, the Court has emphasised that the deduction mechanism is intended to relieve the trader entirely of the burden of the VAT payable or paid in the course of all his economic activities. The common system of VAT consequently ensures neutrality of taxation of all economic activities, provided that those activities are themselves subject in principle to VAT....

Accordingly, and in view of the facts of the main proceedings, the right to deduct VAT cannot depend on whether the output transaction has in fact given rise to the payment of VAT in the Member State concerned.

In so far as differences in the laws and regulations of the Member States continue to exist in this area, despite the establishment of the common system of VAT by the provisions of the directive, the fact that a Member State has not collected output VAT because of the manner in which it has categorised a commercial transaction cannot deny a taxable person the right to deduct input VAT paid in another Member State....

Consequently, the answer to the first question is that, in circumstances such as those of the main proceedings, Article 17(3)(a) of the directive must be interpreted as meaning that a Member State cannot refuse to allow a taxable person to deduct input VAT paid on the acquisition of goods in that Member State, where those goods have been used for the purposes of leasing transactions carried out in another

Member State, solely on the ground that the output transactions have not given rise to the payment of VAT in the second Member State.

The remaining questions

… [T]he national court asks whether, in the event that Article 17(3)(a) of the directive is interpreted as not entitling the tax authorities of a Member State to refuse to allow VAT to be deducted in circumstances such as those of the main proceedings, where a company established in one Member State elects to have its subsidiary, established in another Member State, carry out transactions for the leasing of goods to a third company established in the first Member State, in order to avoid VAT being payable on the sums paid as consideration for those transactions – the transactions having being categorised in the first Member State as supplies of rental services carried out in the second Member State, and in that second Member State as supplies of goods carried out in the first Member State – the principle of prohibiting abusive practices may influence the interpretation adopted.

At paragraphs 74 and 75 of *Halifax and Others*, the Court held, inter alia, that, in the sphere of VAT, an abusive practice can be found to exist only if, first, the transactions concerned, notwithstanding formal application of the conditions laid down by the relevant provisions of the directive and the national legislation transposing it, result in the accrual of a tax advantage the grant of which would be contrary to the purpose of the relevant provisions of the directive and, second, it is apparent from a number of objective factors that the essential aim of the transactions concerned is solely to obtain that tax advantage.

As regards the facts at issue in the main proceedings in the present case, it should be noted that the various transactions concerned took place between two parties which were legally unconnected. It is also common ground that those transactions were not artificial in nature and that they were carried out in the context of normal commercial operations.

As the national court has observed, the characteristics of the transactions at issue in the main proceedings and the nature of the relations between the companies that carried out those transactions contain nothing to suggest an artificial arrangement that does not reflect economic reality and the sole aim of which is to obtain a tax advantage …, since RBSD is a company established in Germany carrying on business providing banking and leasing services.

In those circumstances, the fact that services were supplied to a company established in one Member State by a company established in another Member State, and that the terms of the transactions carried out were chosen on the basis of factors specific to the economic operators concerned, cannot be regarded as constituting an abuse of rights. RBSD in fact provided the services at issue in the course of a genuine economic activity.

It is important to add that taxable persons are generally free to choose the organisational structures and the form of transactions which they consider to be most appropriate for their economic activities and for the purposes of limiting their tax burdens. . . .

On those grounds, the Court (Third Chamber) hereby rules:

1. . . . [A] Member State cannot refuse to allow a taxable person to deduct input value added tax paid on the acquisition of goods in that Member State, where those goods have been used for the purposes of leasing transactions carried out in another Member State, solely on the ground that the output transactions have not given rise to the payment of value added tax in the second Member State.
2. The principle of prohibiting abusive practices does not preclude the right to deduct value added tax, . . . in circumstances such as those of the main proceedings, in which a company established in one Member State elects to have its subsidiary, established in another Member State, carry out transactions for the leasing of goods to a third company established in the first Member State, in order to avoid a situation in which value added tax is payable on the sums paid as consideration for those transactions, the transactions having being categorised in the first Member State as supplies of rental services carried out in the second Member State, and in that second Member State as supplies of goods carried out in the first Member State.

III. VAT Evasion

Most VAT evasion, much like income tax evasion, consists in the failure to fully report taxable earnings. A business might keep two sets of books: one for the owners and one for the tax collector. The remedy for this kind of evasion – as for the income tax – is the use of risk management to identify firms to be audited and the conduct of audits designed to unearth this kind of noncompliance. This can be done through tools such as bank account analysis or indirect methods to estimate income, such as on the basis of inputs.

Tax can also be reduced by overstating deductions (or input credits). To obtain an input credit, an invoice is required. One way to police this kind of evasion is to check the validity of invoices. Some countries have undertaken ambitious programs to match invoices for input credits to output tax reported by the purported suppliers. Such an exercise can, however, be problematic, in part because many mismatches are a result of errors rather than evasion.

An extreme form of evasion is carousel fraud, involving a missing trader. This kind of scheme typically involves collusion between the supplier and customer (and the customer's application for a refund) while at the same time the supplier that issued the invoice disappears, failing to pay the output tax attributable to the invoice. This has been a huge problem in Europe. One partial solution has been to zero-rate supplies of goods or services that have been the object of carousel fraud abuse, for example, emissions permits,[13] so that there is no excess input tax to recover. Another is to deny an input tax credit to a participant in a fraud scheme. The following case examines the basis on which an input credit can be denied.

Belgian State v. Recolta Recycling[14]

Article 1131 of the Belgian Civil Code provides that 'an obligation with no basis or with a false or unlawful basis can give rise to no effect whatsoever'.

In the words of Article 1133 of the same code, 'the basis is unlawful when it is contrary to law, morality or public policy'....

Recolta bought from a certain Mr Ailliaud 16 luxury vehicles, which the latter had himself purchased from the company Auto-Mail. The purchases by Mr Ailliaud did not give rise to any VAT payable to the Treasury and Mr Ailliaud did not pass on to the Belgian State the VAT paid by Recolta, which resold the vehicles free of VAT to Auto-Mail under an authorisation for export sale.

The documents in the file show that, according to an investigation by the Special Inspectorate of Taxes, Mr Ailliaud and Auto-Mail had set up a scheme for 'carousel' tax fraud, of which the transactions with Recolta formed part.

On 26 October 1989, the Verviers VAT collector issued Recolta with a demand for payment of a sum in excess of BEF 4.8 million in respect of taxes and just over BEF 9.7 million in respect of fines (approximately EUR 360 000 in total).

Recolta brought opposition proceedings against that demand for payment before the Tribunal de première instance de Verviers. By a judgment of 1 October 1996, that court, after having found that there was nothing to suggest that Recolta and its directors knew or had any suspicion that they were involved in a major fraud scheme, declared that the demand for payment issued by the collector had no lawful basis and was therefore null and void. The case also gave rise to criminal proceedings, in the course of which the Tribunal correctionnel de Bruxelles (Brussels Criminal Court) made an order on 7 January 1994 discharging the manager of Recolta.

The Belgian State brought an appeal against that judgment before the Cour d'appel de Liège, submitting that the agreements on which

[13] See, e.g., HM Revenue and Customs, Revenue and Customs Brief 46/09 (July 30, 2009).

[14] Case C-440-04 (ECJ 2006), joined with *Kittel v. Belgian State*, Case 439/04 [edited by the authors].

those invoices were based were incurably void under domestic law because Mr Ailliaud's main purpose in entering into a contract with Recolta was to effect transactions which were contrary to the workings of VAT. As the transactions at issue had an unlawful basis, under Article 1131 of the Civil Code, the conditions required for entitlement to the right to deduct, inter alia that there should be a supply of goods, were not fulfilled.

The Cour d'appel de Liège upheld the judgment, whereupon the Belgian State appealed to the Cour de cassation.

The questions referred

The referring court … observes that, in domestic law, an agreement intended to defraud a third party, in the present case the Belgian State, whose rights are protected by public policy legislation, has an unlawful basis and is incurably void.

Since the matter concerns the general interest, it is enough that one party has contracted for unlawful purposes and it is not necessary for the other party to the contract to know of those purposes.

… [T]he Belgian State maintains, in support of its ground of appeal, that the VAT invoiced by a taxable person for the supply of goods is not deductible where the supply, albeit physically effected, took place under an agreement which was, in domestic law, incurably void, even if the purchase was made in good faith.

… [T]he referring court asks essentially whether, where a recipient of a supply of goods is a taxable person who did not and could not know that the transaction concerned was part of a fraud committed by the seller, Article 17 of the Sixth Directive must be interpreted as meaning that it precludes a rule of national law under which the fact that the contract of sale is void, by reason of a civil law provision which renders the contract incurably void as contrary to public policy on the ground that the basis of the contract is unlawful by reason of a matter which is attributable to the seller, causes that taxable person to lose his right to deduct that tax. That court asks whether the answer to that question is different where the contract is incurably void for fraudulent evasion of VAT.

The referring court also asks whether the answer to that question is different where the taxable person knew or should have known that, by his purchase, he was participating in a transaction connected with fraudulent evasion of VAT.

Findings of the Court

… [R]equiring the tax authorities to carry out inquiries to determine the intention of the taxable person would be contrary to the objectives of the common system of VAT of ensuring legal certainty and facilitating the measures necessary for the application of VAT by having regard, save in exceptional cases, to the objective character of the transaction concerned.

A fortiori, requiring the tax authorities, in order to determine whether a given transaction constitutes a supply by a taxable person acting as such and an economic activity, to take account of the intention of a trader other than the taxable person concerned involved in the same chain of supply and/or the possible fraudulent nature of another transaction in the chain, prior or subsequent to the transaction carried out by that taxable person, of which that taxable person had no knowledge and no means of knowledge, would be contrary to those objectives (Optigen, paragraph 46)....

The question whether the VAT payable on prior or subsequent sales of the goods concerned has or has not been paid to the Treasury is irrelevant to the right of the taxable person to deduct input VAT (see, to that effect, the order of the Court in Case C-395/02 *Transport Service* [2004] ECR I-1991, paragraph 26). According to the fundamental principle which underlies the common system of VAT, and which follows from Article 2 of the First and Sixth Directives, VAT applies to each transaction by way of production or distribution after deduction of the VAT directly borne by the various cost components (see, inter alia, Case C-98/98 *Midland Bank* [2000] ECR I-4177, paragraph 29; Case C-497/01 *Zita Modes* [2003] ECR I-14393, paragraph 37; and Optigen, paragraph 54).

In that context, as the referring court observed, it is settled case-law that the principle of fiscal neutrality prevents any general distinction between lawful and unlawful transactions. Consequently, the mere fact that conduct amounts to an offence does not entail exemption from tax; that exemption applies only in specific circumstances where, owing to the special characteristics of certain goods or services, any competition between a lawful economic sector and an unlawful sector is precluded (see, inter alia, Case C-158/98 *Coffeeshop 'Siberië'* [1999] ECR I-3971, paragraphs 14 and 21, and Case C-455/98 *Salumets and Others* [2000] ECR I-4993, paragraph 19). It is common ground, however, that that is not the case with either the computer components or the vehicles at issue in the main proceedings.

In the light of the foregoing, it is apparent that traders who take every precaution which could reasonably be required of them to ensure that their transactions are not connected with fraud, be it the fraudulent evasion of VAT or other fraud, must be able to rely on the legality of those transactions without the risk of losing their right to deduct the input VAT....

It follows that, where a recipient of a supply of goods is a taxable person who did not and could not know that the transaction concerned was connected with a fraud committed by the seller, Article 17 of the Sixth Directive must be interpreted as meaning that it precludes a rule of national law under which the fact that the contract of sale is void, by reason of a civil law provision which renders that contract incurably void as contrary to public policy for unlawful basis of the contract attributable to the seller, causes that taxable person to lose the right to deduct the VAT he has paid. It is irrelevant in this respect whether the fact that the contract is void is due to fraudulent evasion of VAT or to other fraud.

By contrast, the objective criteria which form the basis of the concepts of 'supply of goods effected by a taxable person acting as such' and 'economic activity' are not met where tax is evaded by the taxable person himself (see Case C-255/02 *Halifax and Others* [2006] ECR I-1609, paragraph 59).

As the Court has already observed, preventing tax evasion, avoidance and abuse is an objective recognised and encouraged by the Sixth Directive .... Community law cannot be relied on for abusive or fraudulent ends....

In the same way, a taxable person who knew or should have known that, by his purchase, he was taking part in a transaction connected with fraudulent evasion of VAT must, for the purposes of the Sixth Directive, be regarded as a participant in that fraud, irrespective of whether or not he profited by the resale of the goods.

That is because in such a situation the taxable person aids the perpetrators of the fraud and becomes their accomplice.

In addition, such an interpretation, by making it more difficult to carry out fraudulent transactions, is apt to prevent them.

Therefore, it is for the referring court to refuse entitlement to the right to deduct where it is ascertained, having regard to objective factors, that the taxable person knew or should have known that, by his purchase, he was participating in a transaction connected with fraudulent evasion of VAT, and to do so even where the transaction in question meets the objective criteria which form the basis of the concepts of 'supply of goods effected by a taxable person acting as such' and 'economic activity'.

It follows from the foregoing that ... where a recipient of a supply of goods is a taxable person who did not and could not know that the transaction concerned was connected with a fraud committed by the seller, Article 17 of the Sixth Directive must be interpreted as meaning that it precludes a rule of national law under which the fact that the contract of sale is void – by reason of a civil law provision which renders that contract incurably void as contrary to public policy for unlawful basis of the contract attributable to the seller – causes that taxable person to lose the right to deduct the VAT he has paid. It is irrelevant in this respect whether the fact that the contract is void is due to fraudulent evasion of VAT or to other fraud.

By contrast, where it is ascertained, having regard to objective factors, that the supply is to a taxable person who knew or should have known that, by his purchase, he was participating in a transaction connected with fraudulent evasion of VAT, it is for the national court to refuse that taxable person entitlement to the right to deduct....

Dubious VAT invoices were also at the heart of another ECJ case.

Maks Pen EOOD v. Direktor na Direktsia 'Obzhalvane i danachno-osiguritelna praktika' Sofia[15]

Maks Pen is a company registered under Bulgarian law which operates as a wholesaler of office supplies and advertising material.

The tax inspection to which it was subject ... led the tax authorities to contest the validity of the VAT deduction made on the basis of the tax included in the invoices of seven of its suppliers.

In respect of some of the suppliers themselves, or their sub-contractors, it was not possible to establish from the information requested of them during that inspection that they had the necessary resources to have made the supplies invoiced. Taking the view that either it was not proven, in respect of some of the sub-contractors, that the transactions in question had actually been carried out, or that those transactions were not carried out by the service providers referred to on the invoices, the tax authorities drew up an amended tax assessment notice contesting the deductibility of the VAT included in the invoices of those seven undertakings.

Maks Pen challenged that amended notice ... submitting that it possessed invoices and contractual documents in due form, that those invoices had been paid by bank transfer, that they were registered in the accounting records of the suppliers, that those suppliers had declared the VAT relating to those invoices, that there was therefore evidence that the supplies at issue had actually taken place and that, further, it was not disputed that Maks Pen itself had made supplies subsequent to the provision of those services.

The tax authorities submitted that it was not sufficient to hold invoices in due form to qualify for a right to deduct, where, in particular, the private documents presented in support of the invoices by the suppliers concerned were not reliably dated and had no probative value, and the sub-contractors had not declared the workers whose services they had used or the services supplied. Before the referring court, the tax authorities relied on new evidence, first, by challenging the validity of the signature of representatives of two of the suppliers and, secondly, by pointing out that one of them had not included in its accounting records or in its tax returns the invoices of one of the sub-contractors whose services it had used. While the tax authorities conceded that the services invoiced had been supplied to Maks Pen, they submitted that those services were not however provided by the suppliers mentioned in those invoices.

15 Case C-18/13 (ECJ 2014) [edited by the authors].

... T]t]he referring court asks, in essence, whether Directive 2006/112 must be interpreted as precluding a taxable person from deducting VAT on the invoices issued by a supplier where, although the supply was made, it is apparent that it was not actually made by that supplier or by its sub-contractor, inter alia because they did not have the personnel, equipment or assets required, there was no record of the costs of supplying the service in their accounts and the identification of persons signing certain documents as suppliers was shown to be inaccurate.

... [T]he prevention of tax evasion, tax avoidance and abuse is an objective recognised and encouraged by Directive 2006/112. In that connection, the Court has held that European Union law cannot be relied on for abusive or fraudulent ends. It is therefore for the national courts and authorities to refuse the right of deduction, if it is shown, in the light of objective evidence, that that right is being relied on for fraudulent or abusive ends....

While that is the position where tax evasion is committed by the taxable person himself, the same is also true where a taxable person knew, or should have known, that, by his acquisition, he was taking part in a transaction connected with the evasion of VAT. He must therefore, for the purposes of Directive 2006/112, be regarded as a participant in that evasion, whether or not he profits from the resale of the goods or the use of the services in the context of the taxable transactions subsequently carried out by him (see *Bonik*, paragraphs 38 to 39 and the case-law cited).

Accordingly, a taxable person cannot be refused the right of deduction unless it is established on the basis of objective evidence that that taxable person – to whom the supply of goods or services, on the basis of which the right of deduction is claimed, was made – knew or should have known that, through the acquisition of those goods or services, he was participating in a transaction connected with the evasion of VAT committed by the supplier or by another trader acting upstream or downstream in the chain of supply of those goods or services....

In that regard, if it were simply to be the case that, in the main proceedings, a supply made to Maks Pen was not actually made by the supplier mentioned on the invoices or by its sub-contractor, inter alia because they did not have the personnel, equipment or assets required, there was no record of the costs of making the supply in their accounts and the identification of persons signing certain documents as suppliers was shown to be inaccurate, that would not, in itself, be sufficient ground to exclude the right to deduct relied on by Maks Pen....

On those grounds, the Court (Seventh Chamber) hereby rules:

1. [The VAT Directive] must be interpreted as precluding a taxable person from deducting the value added tax included in the invoices issued by a supplier where, although the supply was made, it is apparent that it was not actually made by that supplier or by

its sub-contractor, inter alia because they did not have the personnel, equipment or assets required, there was no record of the costs of making the supply in their accounts and the identification of persons signing certain documents as the suppliers was shown to be inaccurate, subject to the twofold condition that such facts constitute fraudulent conduct and that it is established, in the light of the objective evidence provided by the tax authorities, that the taxable person knew or should have known that the transaction relied on to give entitlement to the right to deduct was connected with that fraud, which it is for the referring court to determine....

11 Gambling and Financial Services (Other than Insurance)

I. General Introduction

There are a group of services that pose particular problems under a credit-invoice VAT imposed on taxable transactions. They are gambling, transactions involving financial products that are priced to include implicit fees, and insurance (a particular kind of financial service). In all three cases, the value added by the service provider should be subject to a broad-based VAT, at least to the extent that it represents personal consumption expenditures. When early transaction-based, credit-invoice VATs were introduced in Europe and elsewhere, these kinds of services were difficult to include in the tax base because the credit-invoice VAT is based on charging tax on the consideration received by the supplier. For most financial services, the consideration is not explicitly stated. Moreover, financial services accounted for a much smaller percentage of personal consumption included in the VAT base than they do today.

Accordingly, it is not surprising that the default rule in early adopters of VAT was to exempt these services. Recently, some countries have been bringing gambling, more financial services, and casualty insurance into the VAT base. Many problems remain.

II. Gambling, Lotteries, and Other Games of Chance

In a typical transaction involving goods or services, a registered person remits to the government the difference between the tax on the price charged the customer and the tax on business inputs (such as inventory and supplies) used in making these sales. In a gambling transaction, whether a table game, a gaming machine, or a lottery, the gambler pays for the service (the chance to win) up front, and the value added cannot be calculated precisely until after winners are determined and winnings are paid out. Most, if not all, of the bets are placed and winnings are paid out to consumers who are not engaging in these transactions as VAT-registered persons. As a result, it is not important to devise a system of taxing gambling that provides input credits to the users of the services on a transaction-by-transaction basis.

Under most VAT systems, tax is imposed on the price charged for the service. If applied to gambling, the tax would amount to a turnover tax on gross receipts, not a value added tax imposed on the net value added by the casino – the margin. There are varying opinions on whether the appropriate tax base for gambling is the margin or something more. The differences, in part, depend on the value of the entertainment associated with a placed bet.[1]

The value added from the gambling activities of a casino, in countries that impose VAT on gambling, is measured under a margin method – that is, on the spread between bets placed and winnings paid out. New Zealand, for example, imposes VAT on lotteries calculated as the difference between the proceeds of ticket sales less winnings paid out.[2]

In the EU, a member state has discretion to tax or exempt gambling. Once a member decides to exempt gambling, it is not permissible to limit the exemption to certain suppliers of games of chance or gaming machines. Thus, Germany was precluded from exempting only gambling activities conducted in licensed public casinos.[3]

In the following case, the taxpayer claimed that when Germany taxed the operation of gaming machines, it could tax only the difference between the gross bets and the amount paid as winnings.

H.J. Glawe Spiel-und Unterhaltungsgeraete Aufstellungsgesellschaft mbH & Co. KG v. Finanzamt Hamburg-Barmbek-Uhlenhorst[4]

Judgment

Glawe installs and operates gaming machines in bars and restaurants. The operation of such machines is regulated by law. Before they are first put into service, the operator is required to fill the reserve

[1] See Y. Margalioth, *VAT on Gambling*, ch. 6; and A. Schenk, "Comments: VAT on Gambling," 217 in *VAT EXEMPTIONS: CONSEQUENCES AND DESIGN ALTERNATIVES* (Rita de la Feria, ed., Kluwer Law International 2013).

[2] New Zealand Goods and Services Tax Act, No. 141, §12(1) [hereinafter NZ GST], §10(14). Under the British VAT, the taxable amount attributable to payments to play a game of chance with a gaming machine is the amount paid by those playing the game less the amount received during the tax period by persons who won. Value Added Tax Act 1994, ch. 23, §13.

[3] Case C-453/02, *Finanzamt Gladbeck v. Edith Linneweber*, and Case C-462/02, *Finanzamt Herne-West v. Savvas Akritidis*, 2005 ECRI-1131, 2005 ECJ CELEX LEXIS 1.

[4] Case 38/93, *ECR 1994 p. I-1679* (ECJ 1994). The case was edited and some of the language was changed by the authors.

compartment holding the stock of coins from which winnings are paid out. When a player inserts a coin into the machine, it enters the cash box compartment if the reserve is full. If, following the payment of winnings, the reserve is no longer full, the coins inserted by players do not fall into the cash box but enter the reserve. When the operator opens the machine, he can only remove the contents of the cash box, and, before putting the machine back into service, he must replenish the reserve if it is not full. The machines must be set in such a way that they pay out as winnings at least 60% of the coins inserted by players (the stakes) after deduction of turnover tax, with the remainder, some 40%, being retained in the cash box.

In assessing Glawe' s VAT liability for the year 1991, the Finanzamt took as the taxable amount, for the purposes of the German legislation implementing Article 11 of the Sixth Directive [VAT Directive, Title VII Taxable Amount, Articles 73–82], the total stakes inserted into the machines in that year, less VAT....

Glawe believed that the Finanzamt should have taken as the taxable amount only the stakes actually remaining in the cash boxes of the machines, that is to say, the sums inserted, less both VAT and the winnings paid out to players. It therefore entered an objection against the Finanzamt's notice of assessment. When that objection was dismissed, Glawe brought an action before the Finanzgericht Hamburg, which has referred the following questions to the Court for a preliminary ruling:

"1. In the case of gaming machines offering the possibility of winning, is the taxable amount for the purposes of Article 11 A(1)(a) of the Sixth Directive [VAT Directive, Article 73] the total stakes inserted without deduction of the winnings automatically paid out to players?

2. If the winnings paid out must be deducted:

Does the principle of individual taxation require that winnings should be deducted only to the extent of the individual stake for a game or a series of games?

3. If Question 1 is answered in the negative:

Do the winnings automatically paid out constitute wholly or partly – to the extent of the individual stake for a game or series of games – rebates for the purposes of Article 11 A(3)(b) of the Sixth Directive [VAT Directive, Article 87(b)]?"

In answering those questions, it should be observed that Article 11 A(1)(a) of the Sixth Directive [VAT Directive, Article 73] provides that: "The taxable amount shall be: ... in respect of supplies of goods and services other than those referred to in (b), (c) and (d) below, everything which constitutes the consideration which has been or is to be obtained by the supplier from the purchaser, the customer or a third party for such supplies...."[5]

Under Article 11 A(3)(b) of the Sixth Directive the taxable amount is not to include price discounts and rebates allowed to the customer and accounted for at the time of the supply.

In its judgment in Case C-126/88 Boots v Commissioners of Customs and Excise [1990] ECR I-1235, at paragraph 19, the Court held that that latter provision is merely an application of the rule laid down in Article 11 A(1)(a) of the Sixth Directive, as interpreted, in particular, in the judgment in Case 230/87 Naturally Yours Cosmetics v Commissioners of Customs and Excise [1988] ECR 6365, at paragraph 16, according to which the taxable amount is the consideration actually received.

In the case of gaming machines such as those concerned in the main proceedings, which, pursuant to mandatory statutory requirements, are set in such a way that they pay out as winnings on average at least 60% of the stakes inserted, the consideration actually received by the operator in return for making the machines available consists only of the proportion of the stakes which he can actually take for himself.

Only those coins inserted into the machine which automatically enter the cash box are obtained by the operator, since those which enter the reserve are intended to replenish the money initially provided by him for the operation of the machine.

That interpretation is confirmed by an analysis of the destination, within the machine, of the stakes inserted by the recipients of the services provided, that is to say, the players. The stakes in fact divide into two parts: one serves to replenish the reserve, and thus to pay out winnings, and the remainder enters the cash box.

Since the proportion of the stakes which is paid out as winnings is mandatorily fixed in advance, it cannot be regarded as forming part of the consideration for the provision of the machine to the players, nor as the price for any other service provided to the players, such as giving them the opportunity of winning or the payment of winnings itself.

On those grounds,

THE COURT (Sixth Chamber) hereby rules:

Article 11 A(1)(a) of the Sixth Council Directive [VAT Directive, Article 73] must be interpreted as meaning that, in the case of gaming machines offering the possibility of winning, the taxable amount does not include the statutorily prescribed proportion of the total stakes inserted which corresponds to the winnings paid out to the players.

[5] Council Directive 2006/112/EC of 28 November 2006 on the common system of value added tax (OJ L347, 11.12.2006, p. 1) [hereinafter VAT Directive], Art. 73 language is similar. It provides: "In respect of the supply of goods or services, other than as referred to in Articles 74 to 77, the taxable amount shall include everything which constitutes consideration obtained or to be obtained by the supplier, in return for the supply, from the customer or a third party, including subsidies directly linked to the price of the supply."

III. Financial Services (Other than Insurance)

A. Introduction

A normative VAT imposed on all consumer goods and services may tax both explicit fees and implicit consideration for intermediation services. A challenge in designing a VAT base is to craft an administrable rule to tax financial intermediation services rendered by financial institutions and to give registered businesses, on a transaction-by-transaction basis, credits for input VAT attributable to the intermediation services.[6]

The following overview of the VAT treatment of financial services is designed to put customary practice and the array of current developments into perspective.[7]

A financial institution may charge fees for safety deposit boxes, financial advice, returned checks, and other services. Other entities may also provide financial services. For example, finance departments of retail stores provide financial services to their customers in the form of installment or hire-purchase sales.[8] A corporation may decide to raise funds for its

[6] For detailed discussions of the taxation of financial services, see *Consumption Taxation and Financial Services*, 57th Congress of the International Fiscal Association (Sydney 2003); Howell H. Zee, ed., *Taxing the Financial Sector: Concepts, Issues, and Practices* (IMF 2004); A. Schenk & H. Zee, "Treating Financial Services under a Value-Added Tax: Conceptual Issues and Country Practices," 22 *Tax Notes Int'l* 3309 (June 25, 2001); *Indirect Tax Treatment of Financial Services and Instruments*, Report of the OECD (Oct. 1998) [hereinafter OECD Report on Financial Services]; S. Poddar & M. English, "Taxation of Financial Services under a Value-Added Tax: Applying the Cash-Flow Approach," 50 *National Tax Journal* 89 (Mar. 1997) [hereinafter Poddar & English, Taxation of Financial Services]; A. Schenk, "Taxation of Financial Services under a Value Added Tax: A Critique of the Treatment Abroad and the Proposals in the United States," 9 *Tax Notes Int'l* 823 (1994) [hereinafter, Schenk, Taxation of Financial Services]. See also T. Neubig & H. Adrion, "Value Added Taxes and Other Consumption Taxes: Issues for Insurance Companies," 61 *Tax Notes* 1001 (1993); A. Schenk & O. Oldman, principal draftsmen, "Analysis of Tax Treatment of Financial Services under a Consumption-Style VAT: Report of American Bar Association Section of Taxation, Value Added Tax Committee," 44 *Tax Law* 181 (1990) [hereinafter Schenk & Oldman]; Y. Henderson [Kodrzycki], "Financial Intermediaries under Value-Added Tax," *New England Economic Review* 37 (July–Aug., 1988) [hereinafter Henderson]; V. Barham, S. Poddar & J. Whalley, "The Tax Treatment of Insurance Under a Consumption Type, Destination Basis VAT," 40 *National Tax Journal* 171 (1987) [hereinafter Barham, Poddar & Whalley]; L. Hoffman, S. Poddar & J. Whalley, "Taxation of Banking Services under a Consumption Type, Destination VAT," 40 *National Tax* 547 (1987) [hereinafter Hoffman, Poddar & Whalley].

[7] For a discussion of the application of VAT to the financial sector in the United States, see Schenk, "Taxation of Financial Services (including Insurance) under a U.S. Value-Added Tax" 63 *Tax Law Review* 409 (2010) [hereinafter Schenk, Taxing Financial Services under a U.S. VAT].

[8] Economists equate the cash price for durable goods with the discounted present value of the consumption of the durable goods that takes place over the lifetime of the goods. It therefore is reasonable to tax the cash price of durable goods at the time of purchase, whether the consumer pays the price out of personal savings, with a bank loan, or under an installment sales agreement. The finance charge on the bank loan or the interest portion of each installment under the installment sales agreement should follow the VAT

operations by issuing its own debentures through an underwriter instead of borrowing from a bank. Under principles of neutrality, a VAT should tax, not exempt, financial services.

The financial service sector accounted for almost 10% of U.S. GDP in 2008, depending on what is included as a financial service,[9] and about 25% of the GDP of many developed countries originates from the financial sector.[10] Although financial intermediation or margin services (taking deposits and making loans) are a significant portion of a bank's activities, fee income accounts for about 40% of the operating revenue of the twenty-five largest U.S. bank holding companies.[11] In this section, services based on margins and those based on explicit fees are explored separately.

The early VAT regimes, especially in Europe, exempted a wide range of services rendered predominantly to consumers because of the impact of a tax on consumption on low-income households or because the services (such as those rendered by nonprofits) were substitutes for services otherwise provided by government. Financial services are different.

Many financial services are rendered in B2B transactions and were exempt because it was considered too difficult to identify the value of those services (especially financial intermediation services) so that they could be taxed and, in B2B transactions, too difficult to identify the exact tax component in each transaction so that the customer could claim an input tax credit.

Some commentators question whether the value of financial services should be subject to VAT. They claim that to the extent users of financial services are trying to maximize their returns to savings, the value does not belong in a tax base measured by consumption.[12] There are persuasive arguments to the contrary. Financial services should be taxed if used to

treatment of interest. If the VAT could be paid on installment sales as each installment is paid, "then the base for the VAT must be the total of each installment payment including interest and related finance charges [This treatment results in the taxation of a sale and a lease alike, even in situations where it is difficult to distinguish a sale from a lease.] The tax on the interest component is the government's charge for its agreement to wait to receive the tax [footnote omitted]. It is not a tax on the portion of the interest paid on the loan to cover the purchase price." Schenk & Oldman, *supra* note 6, at 187–188 (some footnotes omitted or edited).

[9] See P. Merrill, "VAT Treatment of the Financial Sector," in *The VAT Reader: What a Federal Consumption Tax Would Men for America* 163 (Tax Analysts 2011). Peter Merrill includes rental and leasing services (other than real estate), accounting for 1.4% of GDP, as a financial service.

[10] H. Zee, "A New Approach to Taxing Financial Intermediation Services under a Value-Added Tax," 58 *National Tax Journal* 77, 78 (Mar. 2005) [hereinafter Zee, Modified Reverse Charge Approach].

[11] L. Radecki, "Banks' Payments-Driven Revenues," 5 *Economic Policy Review* 53 (July, 1999).

[12] See W. Jack, "The Treatment of Financial Services under a Broad-Based Consumption Tax," 53 *National Tax Journal* 841 (1999) (zero-rate intermediation services and tax fixed fees on financial services), and H. Grubert & J. Mackie, "Must Financial Services Be Taxed under a Consumption Tax?" 53 *National Tax Journal* 23 (1999).

purchase consumer goods and services.[13] There, therefore, is support for a rate of tax on financial services rendered to consumers at least as high as on the supply of consumer goods.[14]

When VATs expanded beyond Europe, the new VATs tended to follow the European exemption system. New Zealand and other countries adopting "modern VATs" explored broader-based VATs. The taxation of financial services received special attention, especially when financial institutions raised concerns about the cascading of VAT in B2B transactions and the potential competitive disadvantage that existed in global financial markets.

The changes from the customary exemption system include

1. the taxation of explicit fees for financial services,
2. the taxation of casualty insurance coverage,
3. the grant of partial input credit for purchases attributable to exempt financial services, and
4. the zero-rating of some BTB financial services.

Taking deposits and making loans are core bank services. In recent years, there has been an explosion in the number of different financial products offered by financial institutions and brokerage companies – some combining financial and nonfinancial products into a single product or combining multiple financial products into a single product.

This section focuses on the taxation of transactions involving money and other basic financial products. It is beyond the scope of this book to discuss other financial instruments and products that can reasonably be included within a broad definition of financial services, such as securitization arrangements,[15] derivatives, forward interest contracts, and interest rate or equity swaps. Transactions involving these instruments can be classified as supplies for VAT purposes, and they raise questions, such as who is the supplier, when does the supply occur, and what is the consideration for the supply.[16]

The next section explains why the early rationale for the exemption for this sector has lost force and explores the problems associated with the continued

[13] A. Auerbach & R. Gordon, "Taxation of Financial Services under a VAT," 92 *American Economic Review* 411 (2002).

[14] D. Rousslang, "Should Financial Services Be Taxed under a Consumption Tax? Probably," 55 *National Tax Journal* 281 (June 2002).

[15] For a general discussion of securitization arrangements and the VAT treatment of these arrangements under the Australian GST, see GSTR 2004/4, Goods and Services Tax Ruling: Goods and services tax: assignment of payment streams including under a securitization arrangement (ATO 2004). The ruling treats payment streams like these as financial services and therefore input-taxed (exempt from GST). In *Canada Trustco Mortgage Co. v. The Queen*, No. 2003–3554 (TCC 2004), the Tax Court held that in securitization transactions, the amounts attributable to the servicing of the mortgages and the mortgages themselves are treated as part of a single exempt financial services transaction.

[16] See P. Mason, "Solving the Issues of VAT and Financial Derivatives or It's VAT Jim, but Not As We Know It?" *Derivatives & Financial Instruments* 190 (July/Aug. 2000).

exemption today, including the difficult problem financial institutions have in allocating input credits between their taxable and other supplies.

B. Exemption for Most Financial Services

1. Early Rationale Has Lost Force

The accepted rationale for the exemption for financial services in the EU and elsewhere was that it is difficult to fit these services within a transaction-based, credit-invoice VAT. Although this rationale may still apply to financial intermediation services, where the value of the services is buried in interest charges on loans and interest paid on deposits, that rationale does not apply to services rendered for explicit fees. There are both administrative problems and economic distortions resulting from the exemptions maintained in the EU and in countries that followed the EU model.

2. Administrative Problems Associated with Exempting Financial Services

a. Importance of Certainty in Tax Treatment – Interpretation Problems

VAT is a tax imposed on transactions. It is important for a supplier of financial services to know in advance of rendering the services whether the services are taxable, exempt, or zero-rated. If a portfolio manager classifies a service as exempt and the revenue service successfully claims that the service is taxable, the supplier must pay the additional tax due and likely cannot recover that tax from its customers. In addition, the supplier must recalculate the allowable credit for input tax attributable to those earlier taxable services. The following *Deutsche Bank* case involving discretionary investment management services illustrates this problem.

Finanzamt Frankfurt am Main V-Höchst v. Deutsche Bank AG

Judgment[17]

The reference has been made in proceedings [involving the] exemption from value added tax ('VAT'), of the management of securities-based assets ('portfolio management') carried out by Deutsche Bank.

European Union legislation

[17] Case C-44/11, [2012] ECR I-0000 (ECJ 2012) [edited by the authors; many cited cases omitted].

Article 135 [of the VAT Directive] provides:

'1. Member States shall exempt the following transactions:

(a) insurance and reinsurance transactions, including related services performed by insurance brokers and insurance agents;...

(f) transactions, including negotiation but not management or safekeeping, in shares, interests in companies or associations, debentures and other securities, but excluding documents establishing title to goods, and the rights or securities referred to in Article 15(2);

(g) the management of special investment funds as defined by Member States;"

German legislation

Paragraph 4(8)(e) and (h) of the [Value Added Tax of 2005 in force at the time of the facts] UStG provides [in part]:

'... the following shall be exempt from tax:

(e) transactions in securities trading and the negotiation of such transactions, with the exception of the safekeeping and management of securities,...

(h) the management of investment fund assets under the Law on investment funds and the management of pension schemes under the Law on the supervision of insurance;'

The facts which gave rise to the dispute in the main proceedings and the questions referred for a preliminary ruling:

In 2008, Deutsche Bank provided, either itself or through subsidiaries, portfolio management services to client investors. Those client investors instructed Deutsche Bank to manage securities, at its own discretion and without obtaining prior instruction from them, in accordance with the investment strategy variants chosen by them and to take all measures which seemed appropriate for those purposes. Deutsche Bank was entitled to dispose of the assets (securities) in the name and on behalf of the client investors.

The client investors paid an annual fee amounting to 1.8% of the value of the managed assets. That fee consisted of a share for asset management amounting to 1.2% of the value of the managed assets and a share for buying and selling securities amounting to 0.6% of the value of the assets. The fee also covered account and portfolio administration and front-end fees for the acquisition of shares, including units in funds that were managed by undertakings belonging to Deutsche Bank.

At the end of each calendar quarter and at the end of each year, each client investor received a report on the progress of the asset management and was entitled to terminate the instruction at any time with immediate effect.

When it submitted its provisional VAT return for the May 2008 tax period, Deutsche Bank informed the Finanzamt that it assumed that the services supplied in connection with portfolio management were exempt from tax under Paragraph 4(8) of the UStG, if they were supplied to client investors in German territory and in the rest of the territory of the European Union. It also stated that it assumed, in accordance with Paragraph 3(4)(6)(a) of the UStG, that those services were not taxable if they were supplied to client investors established in third countries.

The Finanzamt rejected those arguments and, on 29 April 2009, issued a VAT interim payment notice for the May 2008 tax period in which it treated the transactions relating to the portfolio management for the client investors in question as taxable and non-exempt.

The Finance Court upheld the action brought by Deutsche Bank. The Finanzamt in turn appealed on a point of law to the Federal Finance Court against the judgment delivered by the Finanzgericht.

Since it has doubts, inter alia, as regards the categorisation of portfolio management with regard to VAT exemptions, the Bundesfinanzhof decided to stay the proceedings and to refer the following questions to the Court of Justice for a preliminary ruling:[18]

'1. Is [portfolio management], where a taxable person determines for remuneration the purchase and sale of securities and implements that determination by buying and selling the securities, exempt from tax:
- only in so far as it consists in the management of investment funds for a number of investors collectively within the meaning of Article 135(1)(g) of Directive [2006/112] or also
- in so far as it consists in individual portfolio management for individual investors within the meaning of Article 135(1)(f) of Directive [2006/112] (transactions in securities or the negotiation of such transactions)?

2. For the purposes of defining principal and ancillary services, what significance is to be attached to the criterion that the ancillary service does not constitute for customers an aim in itself, but a means of better enjoying the principal service supplied, in the context of separate reckoning for the ancillary service and the fact that the ancillary service can be provided by third parties?'

The second question

By its second question, which it is appropriate to examine first, the national court asks, in the context of defining, first, the principal service and, secondly, the ancillary service in a portfolio management service, namely where a taxable person for remuneration and on the basis of his own discretion takes decisions on the purchase and sale of securities and implements those decisions by buying and selling

[18] The third question, not significant for the principle being used in this case, is omitted.

the securities, what significance is to be attached to the criterion that the ancillary service does not constitute for customers an end in itself, but the means of enjoying the supplier's principal service under the best possible conditions, in relation to the separate charge in respect of an ancillary service and the fact that an ancillary service may be provided by third parties.

According to the case-law of the Court, where a transaction comprises a bundle of features and acts, regard must be had to all the circumstances in which the transaction in question takes place in order to determine, inter alia, whether that transaction consists of two or more distinct supplies or one single supply.

In that regard, the Court has held that there is a single supply, particularly where one element is to be regarded as constituting the principal service, whilst another is to be regarded as an ancillary service sharing the tax treatment of the principal service.

The Court has held that that is also the case where two or more elements or acts supplied by the taxable person to the customer, being a typical consumer, are so closely linked that they form, objectively, a single, indivisible economic supply, which it would be artificial to split.

[T]he Court considers that, by its second question, the national court seeks, in essence, to categorise, for VAT purposes, the portfolio management service at issue in the main proceedings, where a taxable person for remuneration and on the basis of his own discretion takes decisions on the purchase and sale of securities and implements those decisions by buying and selling the securities, and, in particular, to determine whether that activity must be regarded as a single economic supply.

It is true that those two elements of the portfolio management service may be provided separately. A client investor may wish only for an advisory service and prefer to decide on and make the investments himself. Conversely, a client investor who prefers to take the decisions on investments in securities and, more generally, to structure and monitor his assets himself, without making purchases or sales, may call on an intermediary for the latter type of transaction.

However, the average client investor, in the context of a portfolio management service such as that performed by Deutsche Bank in the main proceedings, seeks precisely a combination of those two elements.

In the context of the portfolio management service at issue in the main proceedings, those two elements are therefore not only inseparable, but must also be placed on the same footing. They are both indispensable in carrying out the service as a whole, with the result that it is not possible to take the view that one must be regarded as the principal service and the other as the ancillary service.

Consequently, those elements must be considered to be so closely linked that they form, objectively, a single economic supply, which it would be artificial to split.

The first question

By its first question, the national court asks, in essence, whether Article 135(1)(f) or (g) of Directive 2006/112 is to be interpreted as meaning that portfolio management, such as that at issue in the main proceedings, is exempt from VAT under that provision.

As regards the exemption provided for in Article 135(1)(g) of Directive 2006/112, it must be pointed out that the concept of 'management of special investment funds' is not defined in Directive 2006/112. The Court has however stated that the transactions covered by that exemption are those which are specific to the business of undertakings for collective investment.

In that regard, it is apparent from Article 1(2) of Council Directive 85/611/EEC of 20 December 1985 [as amended] on the coordination of laws, regulations and administrative provisions relating to undertakings for collective investment in transferable securities ... that they are undertakings the sole object of which is the collective investment in transferable securities and/or in other liquid financial assets of capital raised from the public, which operate on the principle of risk-spreading and the units of which are, at the request of holders, re-purchased or redeemed, directly or indirectly, out of those undertakings' assets.

In specific terms, what are involved are joint funds, in which many investments are pooled and spread over a range of securities which can be managed effectively in order to optimise results, and in which individual investments may be relatively modest. Such funds manage their investments in their own name and on their own behalf, while each investor owns a share of the fund but not the fund's investments as such.

By contrast, services such as those performed by Deutsche Bank in the main proceedings concern generally the assets of a single person, which must be of relatively high overall value in order to be dealt with profitably in such a way. The portfolio manager buys and sells investments in the name and on behalf of the client investor, who retains ownership of the individual securities throughout, and on termination of, the contract.

Consequently, the portfolio management activity carried out by Deutsche Bank, at issue in the main proceedings, does not correspond to the concept of 'management of special investment funds' within the meaning of Article 135(1)(g) of Directive 2006/112.

As regards the scope of Article 135(1)(f) of that directive, the Court has held that transactions in shares and other securities are transactions on the market in marketable securities and that trade in securities involves acts which alter the legal and financial situation as between the parties.

The words 'transactions ... in ... securities' within the meaning of that provision refer, therefore, to transactions which are liable to create, alter or extinguish parties' rights and obligations in respect of securities.

As has been stated in the present judgment, the portfolio management service at issue in the main proceedings consists basically of two elements, namely, on the one hand, of a service of analysing and monitoring the assets of client investors, and, on the other hand, of a service of actually purchasing and selling securities.

Although services of purchasing and selling securities may be covered by Article 135(1)(f) of Directive 2006/112, the same is not, by contrast, true of services of analysing and monitoring assets as the latter services do not necessarily involve transactions which are liable to create, alter or extinguish parties' rights and obligations in respect of securities.

However, it is not possible to regard the elements of which that service consists as constituting a principal service on the one hand and an ancillary service on the other. Those elements must be placed on the same footing.

In that regard, it is established case-law that the terms used to specify the exemptions referred to in Article 135(1) of Directive 2006/112 are to be interpreted strictly, since they constitute exceptions to the general principle that VAT is to be levied on all services supplied for consideration by a taxable person.

Consequently, since that service may be taken into account for VAT purposes only as a whole, it cannot be covered by Article 135(1)(f) of Directive 2006/112.

That interpretation is borne out by the scheme of Directive 2006/112. As stated by the German and Netherlands Governments, the management of 'special investment funds' by special management companies, which is exempt under Article 135(1)(g) of Directive 2006/112, refers to a form of management of securities-based assets. If that form of management of securities-based assets were already covered by the tax exemption in respect of transactions in securities laid down in Article 135(1)(f) of that directive, it would not have been necessary to insert an exemption with regard to it in Article 135(1)(g) of that directive.

Having regard to the foregoing, the answer to the first question referred is that Article 135(1)(f) or (g) of Directive 2006/112 must be interpreted as meaning that portfolio management, such as that at issue in the main proceedings, is not exempt from VAT under that provision.

There has been litigation over whether a supply is a financial service. For example, in New Zealand, one corporation issued redeemable preferred shares (membership shares) in a sister corporation that owned and operated a country club. The shares carried rights to use the country club facilities but, with limited exceptions, did not carry other rights to participate in corporate distributions. Shareholders also paid annual "subscriptions" to cover the cost of operating the country club. The court held that the supply of the shares was an exempt financial service,[19] not a taxable golf club.

b. Allocation of Input Tax Between Taxable and Exempt Supplies

i. Introduction

One of the most vexing compliance problems facing financial institutions is the allocation of the input tax on purchases between their taxable and exempt activities. The tax attributable to the exempt activities is not creditable against output tax liability on taxable sales.

ii. Methods of Allocating Disallowed Credits

The general principles applicable to the allocation of input VAT between taxable and other supplies are discussed in Chapter 6. The discussion here focuses on the special problems in allocating input VAT for a registered person rendering financial services that may be taxable, exempt, and zero-rated. Australia attempts to address this allocation issue in a GST ruling that includes an elaborate discussion of the issues involved and the various methods by which financial service providers may allocate input VAT under that GST.[20] The explanation that follows is taken in large part from this ruling.

Financial service providers first must allocate inputs that can be directly attributable to either taxable or other supplies. Under the direct attribution rules, the tax on inputs directly attributable to taxable supplies is fully creditable. Those directly attributable to exempt supplies are not creditable. "Where financial supply providers are unable to match individual costs with individual revenue streams, other apportionment methodologies may need to be used."[21] In Australia, if the direct method is not available or does not allocate all costs, the general formula for the indirect method (for mixed purpose acquisitions) is revenue/total revenue in which revenue includes taxable and zero-rated (GST-free) supplies and total revenue includes exempt supplies as well. In this formula, "revenue" is net revenue for financial supplies (such as the net of interest received and interest paid) and gross revenue for nonfinancial supplies (such as fees charged). Other acceptable indirect formulas include

[19] *Commissioner of Inland Revenue v. Gulf Harbour Development Ltd*, CA135/03 (N.Z. Ct. App. 2004).

[20] GSTR 2000/22 – Goods and Services Tax: determining the extent of creditable purpose for providers of financial supplies (Australia 18 December 2002) [hereinafter GSTR 2000/22]. See also the French tax administration Guideline 3 A-1-06, ignoring incidental exempt financial transactions and treating transactions as such if, in general, they are distinguishable from a taxable person's principal activity and not more than 10% of the taxable acquisitions are used in conducting the exempt financial transactions. See IBFD TNS Online, Feb. 24, 2006.

[21] GSTR 2000/22, *supra* note 20, at ¶58.

the number of transactions, floor space, profit, or hours spent on each activity.[22]

Mexico tried to abolish the kind of direct method available in Australia to reduce abuses in this area. Until 1999, Mexico found that reliance on the traditional method that permitted financial institutions to deduct fully any input VAT directly attributable to taxable activities gave creative tax planners the opportunity to claim excessive credits by classifying mixed purpose supplies as attributable to taxable activities.[23] Despite the fact that exempt activities represented about 80% of total activity, the banks did not try to allocate specific inputs to exempt activities.[24] Starting in fiscal year 1999, Mexico abolished direct attribution for input credits and, in most cases, required pro rata allocation to taxed and exempt activities on the basis of gross income (not net interest for financial institutions).[25] The banks challenged the law. The court struck down the denial of direct attribution on the grounds that taxpayers making only taxable sales should not be denied the right to attribute all of their input VAT to those transactions. In response, the Mexican Ministry of Finance administratively allowed full input credit for a list of items if they were "unequivocally" attributable to taxable activities but denied the use of net income in the pro rata allocation formula.

An amendment of the Mexican VAT in 2000 again allowed direct attribution to taxable and exempt activities, but only with respect to tangible goods, not services. Other than direct attribution for finance leasing and collection of loan collateral, a bank must apply annually for a ruling to obtain permission to use direct attribution. That ruling to a particular bank also addresses the method required to be used to apportion mixed purpose inputs.[26] The Mexican Ministry believed that abuses continued.[27] In 2001, the Mexican Banking Association proposed the taxation of all loans made by banks.

[22] *Id.* at ¶68–79.

[23] See R. Schatan, "VAT on Banking Services: Mexico's Experience," 14 *VAT Monitor 287* (July/Aug. 2003). "[T]he larger institutions invested substantial resources in reorganizing their cost centres in order to impute generous proportions of expenses to taxed activities." *Id.* at 289.

[24] *Id.* at 289. The author discusses other aggressive techniques used by the larger financial institutions to minimize or wipe out any VAT liability.

[25] "Net" was allowed for repossessions and transactions in stocks by financial institutions. *Id.* at 291.

[26] *Id.* at 292.

[27] In some cases, the Ministry takes a more conservative position than in other countries. For example, contrary to the South African decision to allows banks to claim full credit for input VAT on ATM machines, the Mexican Ministry reportedly takes the position that only "commissions paid by banks for cash withdrawals by their clients through ATMs that are operated by other banks can directly be attributed to taxed activities. The Ministry apparently takes the position that ATM services are not 'independent of the banks' efforts to obtain deposits from the public." *Id.* at 293.

3. Distortions Caused by Exemption of Financial Services

A number of economic distortions result from the broad exemption of financial services. They include the following:

1. "The undertaxation of the household consumption of financial services compared with the consumption of other goods and services because the value added by financial institutions is not taxed.
2. The overtaxation of the consumption of financial services by VAT-registered businesses because any VAT buried in the costs of financial services is not recoverable as input tax credits. There likely is a cascade of tax resulting when any VAT buried in these costs is included in the prices of goods and services sold by the business users of these exempt financial services.
3. The incentive for a financial service provider to vertically integrate and self-supply services in order to avoid some or all of the unrecoverable VAT on its purchases from registered domestic traders. Smaller financial service providers may be less able to vertically integrate than larger providers, creating another kind of non-neutrality.
4. The competitive advantage to an offshore financial service provider if it can render services to domestic household consumers or other domestic purchasers (such as units of government and other suppliers of exempt services) free of VAT."[28]

a. Vertical Integration

A financial service supplier is denied credit for input VAT on purchases attributable to exempt financial services. The supplier therefore has an incentive to provide more services in-house (vertically integrate) and thereby reduce noncreditable input VAT. For example, "instead of purchasing bank forms and stationery from an outside printer for $100,000 plus $10,000 in noncreditable VAT, a bank can operate its own print shop and reduce its costs [of doing business] if it can provide the same forms and stationery for less than the $110,000 tax-inclusive cost charged by the outside printer."[29] Vertical integration creates several problems, including discrimination against outside domestic suppliers of the services needed by these financial service suppliers and discrimination against smaller financial institutions that are not in a position to vertically integrate.

There are several methods available to offset this incentive for financial service suppliers to vertically integrate. The VAT law can include a rule that taxes such self-supplies. For example, if a bank establishes its own print shop to avoid noncreditable VAT on printing services purchased from outside suppliers, the bank can be treated as having supplied those printing services to itself in a taxable transaction. A second option, adopted by

[28] Schenk, Taxing Financial Services Under a U.S. VAT, *supra* note 7, at 418.

[29] Schenk, Taxation of Financial Services, *supra* note 6 at 830.

Australia, is to give financial service suppliers an input credit for a portion of services purchased from outside domestic suppliers if those purchases are used in making exempt financial supplies.[30]

b. Outsourcing

The classification of some services rendered to financial institutions as exempt financial services may give those institutions an incentive to outsource those services to foreign suppliers. If a bank or other financial institution obtains services domestically that are exempt from VAT, the cost of those services may include some disallowed input VAT. If the same services are imported and the country, consistent with WTO rules, exempts imported services that are exempt if supplied domestically, the import is completely free of VAT, especially if the foreign supplier operates in a country that zero-rates the export of those services (or, like the United States, does not impose a national VAT).

In many cases, the incentive to outsource services to foreign suppliers is minimized if the import is reportable (under a reverse charge rule) as a taxable supply by the importer. However, if the imported services would be exempt if provided domestically – if they constitute part of a complete financial function when done by a financial institution – the import is not subject to the reverse charge rule. The following *Datacenter* and *FDR* cases have expanded the scope of services that may be classified as exempt financial services in the EU and therefore may be imported free of the reverse charge rule. For these services, there is discrimination against domestic suppliers of the same services. The following are the facts in the *Datacenter* case, based on the exemption now covered in the VAT Directive, Article 135(1)(d) and (f).[31]

Sparekassernes Datacenter (SDC) v. Skatteministerie[32]

The main proceedings

SDC is an association which is registered for the purposes of VAT. Most of its members are savings banks. It provides to its members and to certain other customers who are connected to its data-handling

[30] See the input credit available for 75% of the cost of "reduced credit acquisitions," discussed in this chapter (III)(D)(3).

[31] VAT Directive, *supra* note 5, Art. 135(1)(d) and (f) is as follows: "1. Member States shall exempt the following transactions: (d) transactions, including negotiation, concerning deposit and current accounts, payments, transfers, debts, cheques and other negotiable instruments, but excluding debt collection; (f) transactions, including negotiation but not management or safekeeping, in shares, interests in companies or associations, debentures and other securities, but excluding documents establishing title to goods, and the rights and securities referred to in Article 15(2)."

[32] Case C-2/95, [1997] ECR I-03017 (ECJ Judgment) [edited by the authors]. An earlier British Value Added Tribunal held that cash collection and delivery, as well as credit checking services, were services normally performed by the Bank integral to its banking

network (hereinafter 'the banks') services relating to transfers, advice on, and trade in, securities, and management of deposits, purchase contracts and loans. SDC also offers services relating to its members' administrative affairs.

Before 1993 SDC provided the banks with services performed wholly or partly by electronic means. Those supplies of services were analogous to those which the biggest financial institutions carry out themselves using their own data-handling centres.

A typical SDC supply of service [consists] of a number of components which, added together, made up the service which a bank or its customers (hereinafter 'the customers') wished to have performed. SDC did not receive the remuneration for its supply of services from the customers but from the banks.

SDC performed services only at the request of a bank, a customer or other persons who were authorized, under a contract concluded with the customer, to require transactions such as payments to be effected. A customer could give information to SDC only after having been authorized to do so by a bank, in particular by the issue of a payment or credit card. SDC's name was not used.

According to the *Sparekassernes Datacenter* case, in the EU, it is the responsibility of the national court to determine, from the facts of each case, whether the operations carried out by the supplier qualify as specific and essential operations, or mere technical supplies. The status of services as exempt or taxable depends on the nature of the services, not the supplier. It is not essential for the exemption that there be a legal relationship between the service provider and the end customer.

The following *FDR* case held that credit card services provided by an outside supplier to banks constitute exempt financial services.

Customs and Excise Commissioners v. FDR Ltd[33]

FDR Ltd supplied credit card services to banks. Its clients were either 'issuers' (banks who issued credit cards to cardholders), 'acquirers' (banks who paid merchants, normally retailers, in exchange for vouchers accepted by those merchants in payment for goods or services), or banks who acted in both capacities.

In a typical credit card transaction, not involving FDR, a cardholder would hand his credit card to the merchant who then recorded the transaction, either manually or electronically. Before the transaction was finalised, the merchant could be required to obtain the

operations and therefore were exempt from VAT. *Barclays Bank PLC v. Commissioners*, 1988 VATTR 23.

[33] [2000] STC 672 (Ct. App. U.K.) [edited by the authors].

issuer's authorisation. The merchant would subsequently be paid by the acquirer, the acquirer would be paid by the issuer, and the issuer would be paid by the cardholder on presentation of a monthly account.

Some banks 'outsourced' their obligations in respect of such transactions to FDR. FDR maintained two accounts, the cardholder account and the merchant account. On being notified that a credit card transaction had occurred, FDR, after, if necessary, authorising the transaction, posted a credit to the merchant account and then made an entry on a magnetic tape which was supplied on a daily basis to BACS Ltd, an automated clearing house, instructing it to effect a credit in the merchant's own bank account and to create a corresponding debit in the acquirer's central accounts. FDR reconciled the accounts between issuers and acquirers on a daily basis by establishing the net position of each client bank and the net amount which needed to be transferred from or to that bank (the netting-off procedure). FDR made a payment out of its own funds to each client bank which was a net claimant and received (later the same day) a payment from each bank which was a net debtor. Those payments were made through the banking system using the CHAPS mechanism. FDR also posted a debit to the cardholder account (to which it also posted credit entries when the cardholder paid his or her monthly bill).

If the cardholder had arranged to pay his bill by direct debit, FDR also provided for BACS to debit the cardholder's ordinary bank account, and credit the issuer's account, with the relevant sum. For some of its clients, FDR also provided connected services which consisted of arranging for the credit card to be embossed with the cardholder's name and account number, preparing and sending to the cardholder periodic statements of his indebtedness to the issuer, and enclosing with the mailing any promotional leaflets or circulars required to be included by the issuer. FDR also calculated at the end of each month the aggregate fee which the merchant owed to the acquirer by way of commission on transactions, and sent a statement of the merchant account to the merchant. It would then make an appropriate entry on the BACS tape effecting a debit to the merchant's bank account in favour of the acquirer.

The commissioners considered that FDR's services were taxable at the standard rate. FDR appealed contending that the services were supplies falling within art 13B(d)(3) of [the Sixth Directive – VAT Directive, Article 135(1)(d)] which exempted from VAT 'transactions, including negotiation, concerning deposit and current accounts, payments, transfers, debts, cheques and other negotiable instruments'. The tribunal allowed the appeal. The commissioners appealed direct to the Court of Appeal.

JUDGMENT

FDR's case is that the supplies made by them in the course of their business, at any rate what has been called the 'core' or 'principal' supply, are exempt by force of art 13B(d)(3).

THE ISSUES

[On the facts, does] FDR make 'transfers' within art 13B(d)3)? [S]hould at least some of those activities be treated as a 'core' or 'principal' supply, and thus a single supply (so as to attract a unitary tax treatment for the purposes of VAT even though the same activities, if treated individually, would or might attract differing tax treatments), and, if so, how should the core supply be described? [I]f there is a core supply, what should its tax treatment be – taxable or exempt?

[W]e find that the principal service provided by FDR consists of processing all their card transactions and settling their liabilities and claims under these transactions in accordance with the obligations of the Issuers and Acquirers.

It is plain that ordinary accountancy services are not exempt from VAT, and that the exemptions granted by the provisions contained in art 13B(d) are much more narrowly confined. It is well recognised that commercial transactions whose essence involves the movement of money are in many cases, for conceptual reasons, ill-suited for the application of the VAT regime, and it seems likely that this is what lies behind the art 13B(d) exemptions.

[The court tests FDR's services against the reasoning in the *Datacenter* case in three areas], (a) transfers and BACS, (b) transfers and netting-off, and (c) transfers and the cardholder/Merchant accounts.

[I]t is in my judgment of the first importance to recognise that BACS for its own part exercises no judgment or discretion whatever. Once the relevant tape is prepared (and that is admittedly done by FDR) and delivered to BACS, the process is, as I have said, automatic. Moreover the inevitable outcome is a redistribution of the rights and obligations of payor and payee – a 'change in the legal and financial situation' – the very circumstances which in my judgment constitute a transfer of funds for the purposes of art 13B(d)(3). [I]t is a conclusion which conforms to the letter and spirit of art 13B(d) as it was explained in [the *Datacenter*] case.

The reality is that the netting-off process achieves precisely the same result as would be attained – unspeakably more laboriously – if, as between all the acquirers, issuers and payment systems, each debt owed by any one to any other were the subject of individual credit and debit entries in the bank accounts of the two of them. It cannot be right that the most inefficient way of doing X constitutes an exempt supply, but the most efficient way of doing it constitutes a taxable supply. On this issue the tribunal was in my judgment entirely right.

The truth is that to the extent that FDR indeed [effects] transfers of money, [it does so] by the CHAPS and BACS transactions. The former are admittedly transfers, and the latter I have found to be so.

There is a single supply in particular in cases where one or more elements are to be regarded as constituting the principal service, whilst one or more elements are to be regarded, by contrast, as ancillary services which share the tax treatment of the principal service. A service must be regarded as ancillary to a principal service if it does not constitute for customers an aim in itself, but a means of better enjoying the principal service supplied.

In my judgment the tribunal's conclusions (a) that there was here a single or core supply, and (b) that [the principal service provided by FDR consists of processing all their card transactions and settling their liabilities and claims under these transactions in accordance with the obligations of the Issuers and Acquirers] are well established.

I would have categorised the essential commercial activity here in very simple terms. It consists in the movement of money between cardholder, merchant, issuer and acquirer, for the convenience of the cardholder and the profit of the other three parties. Under the contractual arrangements which the tribunal examined at great length, that activity is essentially (with variations) 'outsourced' – a word not to be used without quotation marks – to FDR. So regarded, the supplies which FDR makes plainly fall within art 13B(d)(3).

C. Financial Intermediation Services – Services Measured by Margins

The following are a list of principles that could be used to develop a system of taxation of financial intermediation services.[34]

1. Subject to modifications justifiable for administrative or compliance reasons, the intermediation services rendered by financial institutions should be subject to the same tax treatment as other taxable goods or services, whether these financial services are imported, exported, or rendered for domestic consumption.
2. VAT should be imposed on the intermediation service component of finance charges on loans, and of interest payments on deposits, with appropriate value allocated to depositors and borrowers.
3. Businesses rendering taxable financial intermediation services should receive the same credit for VAT paid on their business inputs (on a transaction-by-transaction basis) as other businesses making taxable sales.

[34] These principles are taken, with some modification, from Schenk, Taxation of Financial Services, *supra* note 6, at 832–833.

4. Providers and users of financial intermediation services should enjoy the same cash-flow effects from the VAT that exist for providers and users of other taxable services.[35]
5. The value of financial intermediation services should be taxed only once – the cascading of VAT should be avoided. If any financial intermediation services are exempt from tax, to the extent that it is administratively feasible, the provider should not have any incentive to vertically integrate its operations to reduce the non-creditable VAT on its purchases.
6. The VAT regime for financial intermediation services should be able to accommodate to changes in the VAT rate.

Some banking associations and other providers of financial services have objected to the exempt status for these financial services and products. Banks may prefer to be taxable on their intermediation services, especially those rendered to taxable businesses for explicit fees, because the banks can deduct input tax on purchases attributable to taxable services, and the business users of these services can deduct input tax charged on such services.

The disallowance of input tax to the provider of exempt financial services (sometimes referred to as "blocked input tax") produces a cascade effect when these services are rendered to taxable businesses unable to claim input credits on the cost of these services.[36] Some countries proposed the taxation of financial services when they introduced VAT, only to back off as the VAT proposal proceeded through the political and legislative process.[37] The EU has been examining a possible alternative treatment for financial intermediation services.[38]

A transaction-based VAT imposed on explicit prices for each taxable transaction does not fit well when the value of a service is not represented by an explicit price. This occurs with financial intermediation services, where the value is measured by a margin or spread between charges for

[35] Under a credit-invoice VAT, the VAT ideally should not enter the pre-VAT pricing structure of goods and services supplied by the providers or taxable business users of financial services.

[36] Some economists claim "that in an open economy financial institutions cannot pass undeductable VAT on to their customers." J. Owens, "The Move to VAT," 2 *Interfax* 45, 49 (1996). On the forward shifting of a broad-based VAT, see C. Mclure, Jr., *The Value-Added Tax: Key To Deficit Reduction?* 30–32.

[37] When New Zealand and Canada issued their white papers on tax reform before enacting their VATs (their VATs are called Goods and Services Taxes [GSTs]), the governments indicated their intent to tax financial services. New Zealand ultimately enacted a GST that taxed only insurance services other than life insurance, and Canada enacted a GST that exempted domestic financial services and zero-rated the export of financial services.

[38] See Bureau of National Affairs, *Daily Tax Report*, June 15, 1993, p. G-5. The EC intends to make legislative proposals to modernize the taxation of financial services and insurance transactions. See Commissioner Kovacs speech at a conference May 11, 2006, IBFD EVD News: Terra/Kajus, May 15, 2006.

two or more items. For example, in the *First National Bank* case,[39] the bank served as a market maker in certain foreign currencies. The spread between the bank's bid and offer prices for a currency was the bank's gross profit from the currency transactions.

The ECJ, in an attempt to fit these currency transactions within the framework of a transactions-based VAT, held that the consideration for the currency transactions was equal to the net result of all of those transactions involving the purchases and sales of the currencies over a period of time. The following excerpts are from the Advocate General's Opinion and from the Judgment of the court:

> It is the customer who approaches the bank and asks for a service, namely the exchange of a foreign currency. The United Kingdom states that customers generally inquire at the bank about the two rates, that is to say about the spread. Customers therefore know by how much the selling price of foreign currencies exceeds the purchase price. Consequently, customers know that they are paying for the service and are aware of how much they are paying.
>
> It is also absolutely clear to the bank itself, which constitutes the other party to the reciprocal relationship, that its payment for the service of exchanging currencies results from its spread. This means that there is no doubt as between the supplier and the recipient of the service that the service is effected for consideration and that the consideration relates to the transaction in question. It remains to be noted therefore that, in the case of the rates at which the bank is prepared to purchase currencies from customers and to sell currencies to customers, the spread resulting from the difference in rates constitutes the payment for the service supplied by the bank.
>
> From the mere fact that no [explicit] fees or commission are charged by the bank upon a specific foreign exchange transaction it does not follow that no consideration is given. Moreover, any technical difficulties which exist in determining the amount of consideration cannot by themselves justify the conclusion that no consideration exists.
>
> To hold that currency transactions are taxable only when effected in return for payment of a commission or specific fees, which would thus allow a trader to avoid taxation if he sought to be remunerated for his services by providing for a spread between the proposed transaction rates rather than by charging such sums, would be a solution incompatible with the system put in place by the Sixth Directive and would be liable to place traders on an unequal footing for purposes of taxation.
>
> It must therefore be held that foreign exchange transactions, performed even without commission or direct fees, are supplies of services provided in return for consideration, that is to say supplies of services effected for consideration within the meaning of art 2(1) of the Sixth Directive [VAT Directive, Article 2(1)(a) and (c)]....

[39] Case C-172/96, *Customs and Excise Commissioners v. First National Bank of Chicago* [hereinafter First National Bank], [1998] All ER (EC) 744, STC 850 (ECJ); 1998 ECJ CELEX LEXIS 5819 (ECJ 1998).

So, the consideration, that is to say the amount which the bank can actually apply to its own use, must be regarded as consisting of the net result of its transactions over a given period of time.[40]

1. Deposits and Loans

Banks and other depository institutions take deposits and make loans. In this way, "they provide an intermediation service to both depositors and borrowers by channeling funds of person with certain preferences regarding risk and liquidity to other persons with different preferences."[41]

The services provided by the bank include the keeping of records and accounting for the depositors and borrowers' transactions. The banks combine the fee for these and other services with a charge for the pure cost of funds to calculate the amount imposed on borrowers as "interest." The percentage fee the bank would otherwise pay depositors as the pure cost of funds is reduced by the amount the bank charges for the bank's services to the depositors.

If the pure cost of funds is 2%[42] and the charge to make the loan (including keeping records), take the risk of a default, and make a profit is equal to an interest rate of another 2%, the bank will impose a 4% finance charge on the loans. If the charge to handle deposits and make a profit is equal to an interest rate of 0.5%, the bank will pay depositors 1.5% (2.0 less 0.5) on their deposits.[43] In this example, the 2% pure cost of funds represents the agreement by the depositor to defer consumption. It is not part of national income accounts and should not be in the VAT base.[44]

The value of intermediation services might be measured by the margin or spread between the interest charged on loans and the interest paid on deposits. However, this margin or spread may not represent an accurate measurement of the value of the intermediation services because these

[40] First National Bank, *supra* note 39, at ¶¶43–45 of the Opinion, and ¶¶30–34 and 47 of the Judgment [edited by the authors.]

[41] Henderson, *supra* note 6, at 37.

[42] Poddar and English use the rate the government pays on short-term obligations as the pure rate of interest. Poddar & English, Taxation of Financial Services, *supra* note 6, at 93 [added by authors].

[43] For a detailed analysis of the components of interest paid on deposits and finance charges on loans, see Henderson, *supra* note 6, at 185–187.

[44] "This example does not separate out the increase in the borrower's finance charge that is attributable to the risk that the borrower will default on the loan. Assume that the bank imposes a finance charge of 10 percent rather than 9.75 percent to cover the default risk. Arguably, the charge attributable to the risk of default should not be subject to VAT. [See Poddar & English, Taxation of Financial Services, *supra* note 6. The authors suggest that the charge attributable to the risk of default is a form of wealth transfer or redistribution of funds among the borrowers.] It may not be feasible, administratively, to calculate the charge attributable to the default risk on each transaction. There is an alternative, however. The charge for the risk of default (assumed to be 0.25 percent) can be taxed as part of the value of the intermediation services, and the bank can be allowed to claim an input credit for the tax attributable to bad debts." Schenk, Taxation of Financial Services, *supra* note 6, at 831–832 [footnotes renumbered].

services may be bundled with other services. Although banks may claim that costs and value are split equally between services to depositors and borrowers, banks may "cross-subsidize services to depositors," such as "'free' checking services."[45]

2. EU Approach

The prevailing practice is for countries to exempt the value of financial intermediation services, including finance or interest charges.[46] Although exemption generally is justified on administrative grounds, exemption does not necessarily simplify the VAT.[47]

The two most difficult aspects of any attempt to tax intermediation services are the lack of a mechanism for banks (1) to apportion their input credits between taxable activities and exempt intermediation services and (2) to allocate VAT on those intermediation services (if taxable) to business users on a transaction-by-transaction basis. Banks that currently render exempt domestic intermediation services, zero-rated exports of intermediation services, and other taxable financial services (such as investment advice) may battle the tax authorities over the proper allocation of input VAT between the exempt intermediation services, and the taxable and zero-rated financial services. "What is not known is the extent to which the tax authorities in the Member States vary in their willingness to accept aggressive approaches (1) to the direct allocation of inputs to taxable and to exempt supplies, and (2) the establishment of ratios of taxable to total supplies."[48]

The EU's VAT Directive defines the EU mandate for the exemption for financial services. In early 2008, after a lengthy study and public consultation process, the EC issued a Proposal for a Directive[49] and Proposal

[45] E. Hernandez-Pulido, "Alternatives for Taxing Financial Services through a VAT in Mexico" 42 (ITP/LL.M. paper at Harvard Law School May 1995).

[46] For a detailed analysis and justification for the exemption for financial intermediation services, see T. Edgar, "Exempt Treatment of Financial Intermediation Services under a Value-Added Tax: Assessing the Significance of Recent Challenges to an Imperfect Status Quo," 49 *Canadian Tax Journal* 1133 (2001). See also, PwC VAT Study: "How the EU VAT Exemptions Impact the Banking Sector: Study to Assess Whether Banks Enjoy a Tax Advantage as a Result of the EU VAT Exemption System" (October 18, 2011).

[47] See Canada's proposed Goods and Services Tax, Bill C-62, 2d Sess., 34th Parliament, 38–39 Elizabeth II, 1989–1990, as passed by the House of Commons, April 10, 1990, that includes complex input credit and other rules to implement the decision to exempt financial services, especially where a firm renders both exempt financial services and taxable services.

[48] See PriceWaterhouseCoopers LLP, Study to Increase the Understanding of the Economic Effects of the VAT Exemption for Financial and Insurance Services: Final Report to the European Commission ¶¶ 62 and 88 (Nov. 2, 2006). Schenk, Taxing Financial Services Under a U.S. VAT, *supra* note 7.

[49] Commission of the European Communities, Proposal for a Council Directive Amending Directive 2006/112/EC on the Common System of Value Added Tax, as Regards the Treatment of Insurance and Financial Services [Proposal for a Council Directive], in COM/2007/747 8 (Nov. 28, 2007). See also, TAXUD/2414/08, Directorate General Taxation

for a Council Regulation[50] designed to update the rules on the taxation of financial services and insurance services rendered by the "economic operators" – that is, by the insurance companies and financial service providers.[51]

Under current Article 135(1), member states must exempt the following services (including insurance and reinsurance) from VAT:

"(b) the granting and the negotiation of credit and the management of credit by the person granting it;
(c) the negotiation of or any dealings in credit guarantees or any other security for money and the management of credit guarantees by the person who is granting the credit;
(d) transactions, including negotiation, concerning deposit and current accounts, payments, transfers, debts, cheques and other negotiable instruments, but excluding debt collection;
(e) transactions, including negotiation, concerning currency, bank notes and coins used as legal tender, with the exception of collector's items, that is to say, gold, silver or other metal coins or bank notes which are not normally used as legal tender or coins of numismatic interest);
(f) transactions, including negotiation, but not management or safekeeping, in shares, interests in companies or associations, debentures and other securities, but excluding documents establishing title to goods, and the rights or securities referred to in Article 15(2) [certain rights and interests in immovable property];
(g) management of special investment funds[52] as defined by Member states."

and Customs Union, Harmonization of Turnover Taxes, Background Paper Requested by Council Presidency on Financial and Insurance Services, Brussels, 05/03/2008. Generally, a Directive takes effect when member states enact implementing legislation.

50 Commission of the European Communities, Proposal for a Council Regulation Laying Down Implementing Measures for Directive 2006/112/EC of 28 November 2006 on the Common System of Value Added Tax, as Regards the Treatment of Insurance and Financial Services 9, COM (2007) 747 final (Nov. 28, 2007), available at http://eur-lex.europa.eu/LexUriServ/LexUriServ.do? uri=COM:2007:0747:FIN:EN:PDF. The regulations are designed to increase legal certainty and reduce the administrative burden for operators and administrations. The regulations provide examples of services that come within and those that do not come within the exemption. For example, mortgage loans constitute the "granting of credit," but an installment sale agreement relating to a supply of goods or the provision of debit card services is not the "granting of credit." In the EU, a regulation "shall have general application. It shall be binding in its entirety and directly applicable in all Member States." Consolidated Version of the Treaty Establishing the European Community, Dec. 24, 2002, Art. 249, 2002 O.J. (C 325).

51 The Directive modifies the definition of the exempt services and, consistent with some decisions of the ECJ, applies the exemption to some discrete outsourced elements of the business of financial institutions, described as "the supply of any constituent element of an insurance or financial service, which constitutes a distinct whole and has the specific and essential character of the exempt service." Proposal for a Council Directive, note 49, at 10 (amending Art. 135, by inserting new paragraph 1a).

52 For a discussion of this exemption, with covered funds varying widely in different EU countries, see L. Nevelsteen & R. Van Den Plas, "Undertakings of Collective Investment and VAT in the EU," 14 *VAT Monitor* 456 (Nov./Dec. 2003).

Notwithstanding the preceding rules on exemption, Article 137 provides that member states can give taxpayers the option to be taxable on financial services described in Article 135(1)(b)-(g).[53]

Under the existing VAT Directive, some member states, including Germany, France, and Belgium, give taxpayers this option.[54] According to Cnossen,

> [b]etween Germany and France, the option may be used in respect of all financial institutions (Germany) or it may be restricted to specified financial institutions (France). The option may apply to individual transactions (Germany) or to all transactions (France). … The option may be restricted to financial services supplied to taxable businesses (Germany) or it may apply to financial services supplied to registered as well as non registered person (France). If the concern is with cascading, the German approach suffices. If the concern is with cascading as well as uniformity of tax-to-user price ratios, the French approach is preferable. Clearly, the German approach is the simplest to administer and comply with.[55]

Article 146(1)(d) and (e) of the VAT Directive (exempting services relating to customers outside the Community and services relating to the export of goods), combined with Article 169(b) granting input credits on those services, effectively zero-rates those financial services. Financial institutions that render zero-rated financial services must calculate the available input tax credits attributable to those financial services. Most non-EU countries with VATs that follow the EU model exempt financial intermediation and many other financial services.[56]

D. Departures from Total Exemption – Retain Exemption for Intermediation Services, But Tax Many Other Financial Services

1. Introduction

The EU practice of exempting many financial intermediation services, even if provided for explicit fees, spread to many other countries that adopted a VAT. Those countries have been reluctant to reform their treatment of financial services, in part because of reluctance to give up the revenue they currently collect from "blocked" input tax paid by financial institutions that is attributable to B2B transactions.

[53] The EU proposed revisions of the option to tax financial services. For an analysis of the various options available to EU member states to tax financial services, see report prepared for the European Banking Federation, "Design and Impact of the 'Option to Tax' System for Application of VAT to Financial Services" (Ernst & Young 2009).

[54] See Cnossen, "VAT Treatment of Financial Services," in International Studies in Taxation: Law and Economics – Liber Amicorum Mutén 91(G. Lindencrona, S. Lodin, and B. Wiman, eds., Kluwer 1999).

[55] *Id.* at 99.

[56] See Schenk, Taxation of Financial Services, *supra* note 6, at 833 [footnotes omitted].

In recent years, some countries departed significantly from the EU lead. These new approaches to the taxation of financial services attempt to reduce the supposed distortions caused by the exemption,[57] including the cascade effect of an exempt supply of financial services in B2B transactions, by expanding the scope of creditable business inputs or, like South Africa, by taxing fee-based financial services.

The major departures from the EU "total exemption" approach, enacted to date, fit in two major categories. Some countries tax all or most fee-based services. South Africa fits in this category. Some countries narrow the definition of a financial service and thereby reduce the scope of the exemption. Australia is illustrative. These two approaches are discussed next.

2. Taxation of Fee-Based Services – South Africa

The South African VAT originally exempted financial services but imposed VAT on services customarily taxed, such as safe deposit box rental and certain advisory services. Exports of financial services were zero-rated.[58] South Africa (RSA) then expanded the taxation of services rendered by financial institutions to cover most fee-based services.[59] Thus, currency exchange transactions, transactions involving cheques or letters of credit, transactions involving debt, equity, or participatory securities, and provisions of credit are taxable "to the extent that the consideration payable in respect thereof is any fee, commission or similar charge, excluding discounting cost."[60] The South African approach was adopted elsewhere.[61]

In South Africa, the banking industry and the tax authorities worked together to classify (as taxable, zero-rated, or exempt) an extensive list of services rendered by banks. Banking services provided to nonresidents, any transactions involving the collection of foreign bills or relating to

[57] Tim Edgar notes that these "supposed distortions have not been the subject of any systematic empirical study. T. Edgar, "The Search for Alternatives to the Exempt Treatment of Financial Services Under a Value Added Tax," in *GST in Retrospect and Prospect* 136 (R. Krever & D. White, eds., New Zealand: Brookers Ltd. 2007).

[58] Value-Added Tax Act No. 89 of 1991, Sec. 12(a).

[59] The Canadian GST taxes an extensive list of fee-based financial services but does not tax all such services. See Technical Information Bulletin B-060, *Listing of Taxable, Exempt and Zero-rated Products and Services of a Deposit-Taking Financial Institution* (August 1991).

[60] *Id.* at Sec. 2(1) proviso. In contrast, the OECD countries exempt many, if not most, of the services rendered for explicit fees. See OECD Report on Financial Services, *supra* note 6, at 7–10 and subsequent explanations.

[61] See, for example, Value-Added Tax: Banking Services Provided and Fees Which May Be Charged in Connection with Such Services, as prepared by Banker Association of Namibia and approved by the Ministry of Finance – Inland Revenue as Ruling 2/00 on Nov. 8, 2000, effective Nov. 27, 2000 (a similar document exists for the Botswana VAT); and Value-Added Tax: VAT Apportionment Method for Financial Services Industry, as prepared by Banker Association of Namibia and Approved by the Ministry of Finance – Inland Revenue as Ruling 3/00 on Nov. 8, 2000, effective Nov. 27, 2000.

letters of credit on imports and exports, and foreign guarantees in favor of or on behalf of a nonresident are zero-rated.[62]

Not intending to be exhaustive, the following list illustrates the expansiveness of the categories of fee-based services that have been taxable since October 1, 1996.[63] They include most fee-based services on checking and savings accounts, money transfers, off-site or electronic banking, credit and debit cards, foreign exchange transactions rendered in RSA for residents, mortgage loans, rental agreements, documentation and similar motor finance services, brokerage and underwriting transactions, registration of shares, custody of securities, investment advice, and safety deposit boxes. As a result, virtually all fee-based financial related services are taxable at a positive rate or zero-rated. Exemption is limited to interest charges or discounts that serve as interest charges or interest penalties.

As the list of taxable banking services expanded, the banks operating in South Africa could claim credit for a larger percentage of input tax on purchases, and registered businesses using these fee-based services could claim credit for VAT charged on these services. For example, the South African Revenue Services (SARS) ruled that input VAT on ATM machines is fully creditable because the machines generate taxable fees.

The banking industry and the tax authorities also established a standardized method for the financial services industry to apportion input VAT between taxable and exempt supplies.[64] Under the apportionment formula, the percentage input tax recovery rate is A/B x 100/1. In this formula, A is the total tax-exclusive value of standard and zero-rated supplies, and B is the total tax-exclusive value of all supplies. For purposes of this formula, some items previously the subject of disputes between the banks and the tax authorities are specifically included or specifically excluded from the numerator and/or denominator of the A/B fraction. For example, net interest,[65] gross profit or loss from dealing in financial assets, and insurance proceeds are included only in the denominator B;[66] defined gross rental receipts less interest payments, proceeds from the sale of repossessed goods, zero-rated supplies, and noninterest income are included in A and B. Specifically excluded from both A and B are

[62] This information was gathered from the schedule listing the tax status of banking services prepared by the Council of South African Bankers and approved by the Commissioner for Inland Revenue. It is Value-Added Tax: Banking Services Provided and Fees Which May Be Charged in Connection with Such Services, as prepared by COSAB and approved by the CIR on Aug. 15, 1996, effective Oct. 1, 1996.

[63] The list was updated as of March 1, 2006. The Indirect Tax Standing Committee of the Banking Association of South Africa – SARS, Banking Services Provided and Fees Which May Be Charged in Connection with Such Services, revised and approved March 2, 2006 (S. Africa) (effective March 1, 2006).

[64] See Practice Note, "VAT Apportionment Method for Financial Services Industry" (2003) (South Africa).

[65] For this purpose, interest receipts and interest paid excludes interest in respect of rental agreements.

[66] Any zero-rated portion of these items is included in A.

the cash value of installment credit agreements, bad debts, the deemed value of fringe benefits supplied, dividends, imported services, and a few other items.

3. Narrow Definition of Financial Services – Australia

Australia's GST exempts ("input taxed" in its GST terminology) transactions treated as financial supplies under the regulations.[67] The regulations designate supplies that are financial supplies (or incidental financial supplies treated as financial supplies) and those that are not financial supplies.[68] Some financial services rendered for a fee are taxable, whereas others (charges less than AUD1,000) are treated as exempt financial supplies.[69]

A registered person who renders exempt financial services is entitled to claim full input credits for tax on purchases related to the exempt supplies if the person does not exceed the "financial acquisitions threshold."[70] The inputs attributable to exempt financial services are not treated as attributable to *exempt* financial services if the supplier does not exceed that threshold, so long as the inputs relate to that supplier while carrying on its enterprise. The financial acquisition threshold is exceeded if the input credits related to the making of financial services exceed either AUD50,000,[71] or 10% of the input tax credits otherwise available in the current (or anticipated for the following) year.[72] If the registered person exceeds the financial acquisition threshold, the person may be able to claim credits for inputs attributable to exempt financial services under the "reduced credit acquisitions," which will be discussed.

A financial institution rendering exempt financial services has an incentive to self-supply services instead of outsourcing them. It would prefer to provide services in-house to avoid noncreditable GST on its

67 A New Tax System (Goods and Services Tax) Act 1999 [hereinafter Australia GST], §40–5.

68 A New Tax System (Goods and Services Tax) Regulations 1999 [hereinafter Australia GST regulations], Reg. 40–5.09 to 40.5.13. Schedule 7 to the regulations provides extensive examples of financial supplies, and Schedule 8 to the regulations provide extensive examples of supplies that are not financial supplies. There remain questions of the classification of some supplies as financial supplies or not financial supplies. For example, see the controversy over guarantees in P. Stacey "Guarantees: Multiple Supplies, Different GST Treatments," 15 *VAT Monitor* 398 (Nov./Dec. 2004). On the GST status of securitization transactions, see A. Joseph, "Securitization – The Position of SPVs under Australian GST," 16 *VAT Monitor* 109 (Mar./Apr. 2005). Australia treats the acquisition of securities (debt or shares) as the making of a financial supply to deny credits for costs incurred in making the acquisition. See R. Krever, "GST Legislation Plus 2005," annotation to GST Reg. 40–5.09.

69 See Australia GST regulations, *supra* note 68, at Reg. 40–5.09(4).

70 Goods and Services Tax Ruling 2002/2, Goods and services tax: GST treatment of financial supplies and related supplies and acquisitions, ¶3.

71 The regulations can provide for a different amount. *Id.* at ¶14.

72 *Id.*, based on Australia GST, *supra* note 67, at §§189–5 and 189–10. If the threshold is exceeded in the current or future period, the right to full credit is denied.

purchases of the same services from outside vendors. With self-supply, the financial service provider avoids GST on the labor and profit component of the service supplied to itself. For example, assume that a financial service provider purchased supplies for AUD25,000 plus an assumed 10% tax of AUD2,500, hired labor, and printed forms and stationery in-house for a total cost of AUD102,500. If the same printing services would cost AUD100,000 plus tax of AUD10,000 from an outside vendor, the financial service provider would save the extra AUD7,500 tax that the outside vendor would charge. Because any input tax paid to the outside vendor that is attributable to its exempt services would not be deductible for GST purposes in most countries, there exists a bias in favor of bringing the printing function in-house.

To offset this bias against self-supply, the Australian GST grants the financial service provider an input credit of 75% of the tax on "reduced credit acquisitions."[73] In the previous example, if the financial service provider purchased its forms and stationery from the outside supplier, it could claim an input credit of AUD7,500 (75 percent of the AUD10,000 tax on the purchase). In the example, the credit exactly offsets any benefit the financial service provider would obtain from providing its printing needs in-house.[74]

E. Departures from Total Exemption – Zero-Rate Financial Intermediation Services Fully or Partially

The second area of departure from the EU exemption approach is the zero-rating of many financial services, including financial intermediation services. Singapore and New Zealand fit in this group.

1. Singapore's Zero-Rating of Services to Taxable Customers

To reduce the cascading of VAT on financial services rendered to taxable businesses, the Singapore GST regulations include rules that effectively allow financial institutions to claim input credits for VAT attributable to certain exempt financial services.[75] For input VAT that is not directly attributable to taxable supplies or to exempt supplies, a financial service provider must allocate the input tax in proportion to the ratio of taxable

[73] Australia GST regulations, *supra* note 68 at Reg. 70–5.03. The regulations list acquisitions that are reduced credit acquisitions (Reg. 70–5.02). They include domestic purchases and certain offshore supplies (Reg. 70–5.02A).

[74] See the example in "The Application of Goods and Services Tax to Financial Services: Consultation Document," Honourable Peter Costello, M.P., Treasurer of the Commonwealth of Australia, Aug. 1999, appendix A, p. 13.

[75] For a claim that the generous input credit allocation rules reduce the administrative issues of the classification of currency exchange or forward contracts involving currency, see M. Vaughan, "Exchange of Currency," 13 *VAT Monitor* 363 (Sept. /Oct. 2002).

supplies to total supplies.[76] The regulations authorize the comptroller to approve a method of allocating input VAT that treats specified exempt financial services[77] supplied by a taxable person to another taxable person as taxable supplies.[78] As a result, those services are exempt, but the supplier can claim credit for input tax attributable to those services. These services are effectively zero-rated. Singapore also allows a percentage of input tax paid by exempt financial institutions to be recovered. This percentage is set annually for specified institutions.[79]

2. New Zealand's Zero-Rating for Some Services Rendered by Financial Service Providers

Effective January 1, 2005, New Zealand revised its treatment of financial intermediation services rendered to certain registered businesses and to other financial service providers.[80] The guidelines for the new elective zero-rating rules apply to businesses that supply financial services as part of their normal business activity.[81] The following explanation is taken from these guidelines.

If a financial service provider files the election, it may zero-rate financial intermediation services (otherwise exempt from GST)[82] rendered to a registered customer, but only if the *customer's* level of taxable supplies is 75% or more of total supplies for the period.[83] Financial services rendered to unregistered persons remain exempt from VAT.

To obtain this treatment, the financial service provider must satisfy itself that its customer is registered and meets the 75% test. To satisfy itself that the customer meets the 75% threshold, the financial service provider must either rely on information that it has on the customer or rely

76 Goods and Services Tax (General) Regulations (Rg 1) Part V, Reg. 29(2)(d) (Singapore).

77 *Id.* at Reg. 29(3), referring to exempt financial services under paragraph 1 of the Fourth Schedule to the GST.

78 *Id.* at Reg. 33, subject to Regs. 34 and 35.

79 See H. Zee, "VAT Treatment of Financial Services: A Primer on Conceptual Issues and Country Practices," 34(10) *Intertax* 458.

80 See NZ GST, *supra* note 2, at §§20(3)(h) and 20C, amended by (GST, Trans-Tasman Imputation and Miscellaneous Provisions) Act 2003. For a discussion of the government report leading up to these changes, see M. Pallot & D. White, "Improvements to the GST Treatment of Financial Services – The Proposed New Zealand Approach," 13 *VAT Monitor* 481 (Nov./Dec. 2002).

81 See "GST Guidelines for Working with the New Zero-Rating Rules," Inland Revenue Department, Oct. 2004 [hereinafter Guidelines to Zero-Rate Financial Services].

82 Zero-rating applies to paying or collecting interest, providing or brokering loans, issuing securities, providing credit, or exchanging currency. Zero-rating does not apply to "debt collection, equipment leasing, credit control, sales ledger and accounting services, investment guidance, fire and general insurance and the provision of advice." *Id.* at ¶7.

83 If the customer is part of a group, the services are zero-rated if the group meets the 75% threshold, even if the customer does not meet the threshold by itself. *Id.* at introduction. In calculating the 75% threshold, financial services that are zero-rated under these rules are omitted. In addition, imported services taxable under the reverse charge rule are excluded as well. *Id.* at ¶31.

on the Australian and New Zealand Standard Industrial Classification (ANZSIC) codes.[84]

Although the financial service provider is obliged to satisfy these conditions on a transaction-by-transaction basis, the NZ GST Act provides that an alternative method approved by Inland Revenue may be used to satisfy the conditions, if it "produces as fair and reasonable a result as identifying eligible customers on a transaction-by-transaction basis would."[85]

Under the NZ GST, if the principal purpose of a GST-registered person's acquisition of goods or services is to make taxable supplies, the input VAT on the acquisition is deductible in full.[86] For purposes of meeting the principal purpose test, the zero-rated financial services are counted as taxable supplies.[87]

Financial services rendered by a financial service provider to other financial institutions are not zero-rated because the customer will not meet the 75% test. As an alternative, an electing financial service provider can claim an input tax deduction attributable to financial services supplied to another financial service provider (direct supplier) who supplies financial services to businesses that would qualify for zero-rate treatment. The formula is provided in the guidelines.[88] The information necessary to calculate this deduction must be obtained from the direct supplier. This deduction is in addition to input tax otherwise deductible, "relates only to exempt supplies of financial services made to the direct supplier, and is limited to the extent that the direct supplier makes taxable supplies, including supplies of zero-rated financial services, to business customers that meet the 75 percent taxable supplies threshold."[89] Although New Zealand's new system effectively eliminates GST on registered business-

[84] Reliance on the codes satisfies the 75% threshold requirement. *Id.* at ¶40–51. The codes identify groupings of businesses that conduct similar economic activities. Some industry or business classifications (tables A and B) are either denied zero-rating or may be denied zero-rating unless there is proof that the 75% test is satisfied. See *id.* at ¶41 and 51. The list of codes is on the Statistics New Zealand Web site: http://www.stats.govt.nz/domino/external/web/carsweb.nsf/94772cd591085044c25-7e6007eec2c/5b3elb99a0d86615cc256cec007e6bl4?OpenDocument. *Id.* at 136. Inland Revenue provides guidance on how to determine eligibility per transaction or per customer account. *Id.* at ¶¶ 37–39.

[85] *Id.* at ¶10.

[86] See NZ GST, *supra* note 2, at §20(3)(a) and (b). An adjustment in the allowable input tax deduction is required to the extent that the registrant makes non-taxable supplies. *Id.* at §21.

[87] See Guidelines to Zero-Rate Financial Services, *supra* note 81, at ¶¶56–58. Special rules are provided to calculate the input tax deduction recovery ratio for financial service providers. *Id.* at ¶¶59–77.

[88] The formula is $a \times b/c \times d/e$, where a is the amount of input VAT deductible and nondeductible under §20(3) of the Act (other than 20(3)(h), if all financial services were taxable supplies; b is the total value of exempt financial services made to the other financial service supplier (direct supplier) for the period; c is the total value of supplies for the period; d is the total value of taxable supplies by the direct supplier determined under §20D of the Act; and e is the total value of supplies made by the direct supplier for the period under §20D of the Act. *Id.* at ¶78.

[89] *Id.*

to-registered business transactions, it leaves untouched the undertaxation of intermediation services rendered to final consumers.

F. Other Approaches to the Taxation of Financial Services

There are a number of other approaches to the taxation of financial services. Israel taxes more than the value of intermediation services, overtaxing many of the financial services. Under Italy's subnational IRAP (*imposta regionale sulle attivitàe produttive*), financial services are taxable under an income form of VAT, calculated under a subtraction method.

There have been proposals to tax financial services differently, but they have not been enacted in any country.[90] The Canadian approach was included in a Canadian White Paper that preceded the enactment of the Canadian GST. Two VAT bills were introduced in the U.S. Congress that departed from the EU model of taxing financial services. Satya Poddar and Morley English proposed a cash-flow approach to the taxation of financial intermediation services (modified by a tax calculation account [TCA] method). This proposal was pilot-tested in the EU. Howell Zee proposed a modified reverse-charging approach that taxes financial intermediation services on a transaction-by-transaction basis. Finally, Peter Merrill developed an interesting approach to taxing financial intermediation services.

1. Israel

Israel taxes financial services, including financial intermediation services rendered by banks and similar depository institutions, under a system that resembles an addition method VAT, but it is administered outside the VAT.[91] "First, banks pay and cannot recover VAT on their purchases of supplies, computers, energy, and other inputs that are used to provide their lending services.[92] Second, Israel requires banks to pay [tax] computed by the addition method on the total of their wages and profit."[93] In this way, Israel collects VAT on the bank's business inputs and collects tax on the value added by the banks. Combined, Israel taxes intermediation services rendered to businesses and consumers, overtaxing business users that cannot claim credit for any VAT embedded in the implicit charges for financial intermediation services.

[90] For a discussion of unenacted proposals, including some not discussed in this section, see P. Merrill, "VAT Treatment of the Financial Sector," in *The VAT Reader: What a Federal Consumption Tax Would Mean for America*, [hereinafter Merrill] (Tax Analysts 2011).

[91] In Israel, this tax on financial institutions and insurance companies is administered by the Income Tax Authority, whereas all other VAT is administered by the VAT Administration. See D. Gliksberg, "Israel's Value Added Tax Law," *VAT Monitor* 2 (July 1992).

[92] All countries that exempt financial services from the VAT deny banks input credits for VAT paid on their purchases used in the rendition of these services. Like Israel, these countries collect and keep VAT paid by banks on their taxable purchases.

[93] Schenk & Oldman, *supra* note 6, at 191.

2. Italy's IRAP

In 1997, Italy replaced a local income tax, a wealth tax, and social security taxes that financed national health with the IRAP. The IRAP is imposed at 4.25% (or a rate that may vary by one percentage point, as set by the regional authorities) on the net value of production in each Italian region. For the financial sector, the IRAP is a subtraction method, origin principle VAT.

The IRAP applies to the gross margin for the financial sector. It includes explicit fees and commissions and interest charges. The financial institution reduces this tax base by interest paid, the cost of intermediate goods and services, and depreciation on capital goods. As a result, the IRAP is an income form of VAT.

3. Canadian Flirtation with Taxation of Intermediation Services

The Canadian White Paper on Sales Tax Reform[94] that preceded the enactment of the Canadian GST discussed a few forms for a possible national VAT. The white paper recommended that the value of financial intermediation services be taxed under a subtraction method. The tax base for intermediation services would be the spread between specific financial receipts and the cost of funds.[95] A flaw in the white paper approach was that no input credit was provided for business users of the intermediation services.[96] In the final government proposal for the GST, financial intermediation services were exempt.[97]

[94] Tax Reform 1987: Sales Tax Reform 126–31 (June 18,1987).

[95] *Id.* at 130. The receipts are interest on bank loans, dividends on stock, foreign exchange gains, and other income from financial products. The cost of funds include interest paid to depositors and others and a return to the bank's shareholders. The return to investors "could be either in the form of a deduction for dividends paid or a prescribed allowance on equity." *Id.* For a discussion of the Canadian White Paper approach to the taxation of financial services, see Poddar and Greene's paper, "Taxation of Financial Services," presented at the International Institute of Public Finance, 44th Cong., Istanbul, August 1988.

[96] Henderson suggests a mechanism to grant input credits to business users for the VAT component in purchased financial services. See Henderson, *supra* note 6.

[97] "The Canadian government decided to exempt financial intermediation services for three basic reasons. First, the government claims that in practice it is extremely difficult to identify the price of intermediation services. Second, the government noted that there were technical problems translating the earlier White Paper proposal into an operational tax structure. Third, no country has successfully applied sales tax to financial intermediation services. See 1989 Federal Budget: Sales and Excise Tax Changes (Canada) April 27, 1989, *reproduced* in Can. Sales Tax Rep., Special Report No. 25, Extra Edition, at 47. The third point is questionable because Israel taxes intermediation services. The government statement may be implying that the Israeli approach is not successful because it does not provide credit for VAT paid by business on these services, but it does not so state. No doubt, the Canadian government had some concern about the effect of taxing financial services on the competitiveness of Canadian banks in the international marketplace, but this concern was not expressed as part of the official reasons for exempting financial intermediation services." Schenk & Oldman, *supra* note 6, at 191, note 36.

4. Proposals in the United States

An adaptation of a cash-flow approach to the taxation of financial services was included as part of a sales-subtraction VAT proposed but never seriously debated in the U.S. Congress.

> Senators Danforth and Boren's proposed [Business Activities Tax] BAT taxes "financial intermediation services" that include insurance, allows the financial intermediaries to deduct business purchases allocable to these taxable services, and treats purchases of these services as deductible purchases to the customers who use these services in connection with their taxable business activity.[98] The problem is that the BAT does not solve the most difficult problem. It does not include rules to explain how financial intermediaries should allocate the cost of implicit "financial intermediation services" rendered to businesses, so that they can deduct the cost if the services are used in connection with their taxable business activity.[99]
>
> To assure business users of taxable financial intermediation services that they can identify and deduct the cost of these services as business purchases, the BAT requires intermediaries to allocate and report fees for these services to business customers[100] within 45 days after the end of the taxable period in which the services are rendered.[101] The statute requires persons rendering

[98] See The Comprehensive Tax Restructuring and Simplification Act of 1994, 140 Cong. Rec. S6527 [hereinafter Danforth-Boren BAT], §§10034 and 10015(a)(2)(B), (d). The provisions that refer specifically to these financial and insurance services occupy more than 15% of the pages of the proposed BAT legislation. This figure demonstrates that "financial intermediation services" raise complex issues under a VAT.

[99] Taxable financial intermediation services, under the BAT, include a broad range of financial and insurance services: lending and insurance services, market-making and dealer services, and a catchall category of services rendered as an intermediary if the receipts come from "streams of income or expense, discounts, or other financial flows." (*Id.* at §10034(e)). The BAT uses a "cash-flow" or "flow-of-funds" approach to tax financial intermediation services rendered by financial intermediaries and insurance companies. This approach resembles the Poddar and English cash-flow approach that is designed to produce the same results as if a VAT were charged on the taxable intermediation services and the business users of these services received deductions for the tax-inclusive cost of such purchased taxable services. See Poddar & English, Taxation of Financial Services, *supra* note 6. The BAT base generally is equal to the difference between taxable gross receipts and deductible business purchases (which it should now be clear to the reader are in turn merely the supplier's taxable gross receipts). [Danforth-Boren BAT, *supra* note 98, at 10034(a)(2)]. For financial intermediation services, the statute substitutes financial receipts for gross receipts and adjusted business purchases for business purchases. Financial receipts are broadly defined to include all receipts attributable to these intermediation services, other than contributions to capital. The definition of adjusted business purchases is more elaborate. In addition to business purchases, as defined for other business activity, an intermediary can deduct principal and interest payments attributable to the firm's business activity, the costs and payments made under financial instruments (except for its own equity interests), payments of claims and cash surrender value in connection with insurance or reinsurance activity, and payments for reinsurance. *Id.* at §10034(c).

[100] See *id.* at §10034(d)(2), granting the Treasury authority to waive the notice requirement with respect to customers that are not receiving these services in connection with taxable business activity.

[101] *Id.* at §10034(d).

these services to allocate these fees on a reasonable and consistent basis, but it does not provide any guidance on how the calculation is to be made.[102]

An elaborate proposal to tax financial intermediation services under the subtraction method was included in another proposal for a U.S. VAT.[103]

5. The Poddar–English Proposal

One proposal to tax financial intermediation services under a European credit-invoice VAT is the flow-of-funds system advocated earlier and refined in a 1997 article by Satya Poddar and Morley English. It is the "truncated cash-flow method with tax calculation account [TCA] … that is designed to operationalize the cash flow method."[104] A basic cash-flow system taxes cash receipts and gives credits for cash outflows from intermediation services. The earlier proposal imposed tax on financial intermediation services under a pure cash-flow approach. Under that refined system,

> [c]ash inflows from financial transactions are treated as taxable sales (e.g., a bank would remit tax on a deposit), and cash outflows are treated as purchases of taxable inputs (e.g., a bank could claim an input tax credit on a deposit withdrawn). …To zero rate financial services rendered to nonresidents, transactions with nonresidents are ignored. … [A]ll input tax credits related to commercial activity are now claimable, not just those related to nonfinancial supplies. … [T]he results are the same as they would be if the financial institution were able to identify the value-added in each transaction, charge tax on it, and provide the appropriate invoice to allow business customers to claim input tax credits.[105]

It is difficult to apply the pure cash-flow approach to the taxation of financial intermediation services at the time a VAT is introduced or the tax rate of an ongoing VAT is revised.[106]

The EC commissioned Ernst and Young to pilot test a truncated Tax Calculation Account System, a modification of the TCA system developed

[102] *Id.* at §10034(d)(l)(A)(i). O. Oldman & A. Schenk, "The Business Activities Tax: Have Senators Danforth & Boren Created a Better Value Added Tax?" 10 *Tax Notes Int'l* 55, 69–70 (Jan. 2, 1995).

[103] USA Tax Act of 1995, S.722, 104th Cong., 1st Sess., 141 Cong. Rec. S5664 (1995). The Business Tax portion of the USA Tax attempts to tax all financial intermediation services. Assuming no loss carryover or transition basis deduction, gross profit of a financial intermediation business (an entity engaged in financial intermediation services for unrelated persons) is financial receipts less financial expenses. This calculation is designed to serve as a proxy to calculate the implicit charges for intermediation services.

[104] See Poddar & English, Taxation of Financial Services, *supra* note 6, at 89. See also Barham, Poddar & Whalley, and Hoffman, Poddar & Whalley, *supra* note 6. According to Poddar, this TCA system was pilot tested at ten major financial institutions and found to be "conceptually robust."

[105] Poddar & English, Taxation of Financial Services, *supra* note 6, at 92.

[106] *Id.* at 98–99.

earlier by Poddar and English of Ernst and Young.[107] Ten pilot studies were conducted.

> Under the TCA system, the tax base for margin services would be computed over the term of the financial contract, whereas the tax base under the normal VAT system is the explicit price charged for the goods or services. … [The] TCA allocates the total margin earned by the financial institution (being the difference between the interest rate charged on the loans and paid on the deposits) between the borrowers and depositors using the indexing rate as the benchmark. It is proposed that a short-term inter-bank rate (either 1-month or 3-month rate) be used for the indexing rate.[108]

To understand this system, it is helpful to review the financial flows in intermediation services rendered by banks. They include:

1. the transfer of funds from depositors to borrowers,
2. the pure interest charge for the depositor's agreement to defer consumption,
3. the premium charged for the risk that the borrower will default on the loan, and
4. the compensation to the bank to take deposits and make loans.[109]

Poddar and English's approach does not tax the pure interest or the risk premium in (2) and (3), and it nets out the transfers of capital by the bank from depositors to borrowers.

Even if the margin in (4) can be calculated to fully integrate this system into a credit-invoice VAT imposed on taxable transactions, it is still necessary to allocate the value of the services between the depositors and borrowers in order to notify the business users of the amount of input VAT on those services that is creditable.

Instead of taxing loan proceeds and giving credits for loan payments to borrowers, their truncated cash-flow method has the bank calculate and remit the net tax due on their intermediation transactions. Although this modified system corrects for the problems under a pure cash-flow approach, it imposes its own complicated compliance rules on financial institutions. The revised system includes a TCA. "The TCA is a tax suspense account" that handles "cash inflows and outflows of a capital nature."[110] It "allows deferral of tax on cash inflows and of tax credits on cash outflows. However, these deferrals are subject to interest charges at the government borrowing rate."[111] "The TCAs in the books of a business

[107] See http://europa.eu.int/comm/taxation_customs/publications/reports_studies/taxation/tca/TCA_system.htm.

[108] *Id.* at Executive Summary.

[109] See Poddar & English, Taxation of Financial Services, *supra* note 6, at 91–92.

[110] *Id.* at 99.

[111] *Id.* The (1) "tax payments on cash inflows … [are] debited to the TCA; (2) input tax credits on cash outflows … [are] credited to the TCA; (3) net balance in the TCA [is] subject to an indexing adjustment …; and (4) a balance in the TCA payable (or refundable …) periodically, after subtracting a notional amount equal to the tax rate times the value of the financial instrument at the end of the period." *Id.*

borrower or a business depositor are the mirror images of the TCAs for a loan or a deposit in the books of the bank. … [T]he TCA system eliminates any cash-flow problems by deferring tax payments and credits on capital transfers."[112] Issues remain such as the indexing rate and the frequency of indexing adjustments that are not fully addressed in the Poddar and English proposal. The other details of this proposed system are beyond the scope of this book.

6. Zee's Modified Reverse-Charging Approach

Howell Zee proposed a "modified reverse-charging" approach to the taxation of financial intermediation services (deposit-taking and lending activities) under a VAT.[113] One obstacle in taxing these services is that many of the bank inputs (deposits) come from unregistered final consumers who cannot issue VAT invoices. As part of his analysis, Zee notes that the reverse charge mechanism

> shifts the collection of the VAT on deposit interest from depositors to banks, in conjunction with the establishment of a franking mechanism managed by banks that effectively transfers the VAT so collected to borrowers as credits against the VAT on their loan interest on a transaction-to-transaction basis. The outcome ensures that the net VAT revenue to be remitted to the government by a bank is equal to the VAT rate on the bank's provision of intermediation services, while, at the same time, the VAT burden on such services is borne by final consumers either directly as bank borrowers or indirectly when they consume goods and services in which the intermediation services have been embedded.[114]

Zee acknowledges that a major issue in the development of a system to tax intermediation services is to provide a credit to business users on a transaction-by-transaction basis to integrate this system with the credit-invoice VATs used around the world. Under the proposed system, the bank will issue a VAT invoice to itself for its purchased inputs (from registered and unregistered depositors) and claim the same as an input credit against its output tax on interest collected from registered or unregistered borrowers. The business borrower can claim credit for VAT charged on the loan interest. Consistent with the destination principle, a reverse charge is applied to foreign deposits, and interest charged to foreign borrowers is treated as a zero-rated export.

The problem with this straight reverse-charge approach is that borrowers who are final consumers are overtaxed – they must bear VAT that exceeds the value of the intermediation services embedded in the loan. To correct this problem, Zee devised a system that uses the reverse charge on depositors

[112] *Id.* at 100.

[113] Zee, Modified Reverse Charge Approach, *supra* note 10. Zee suggests that the same approach can be extended to cover brokerage services and other services rendered for implicit fees. *Id* at 82–83.

[114] *Id.* at 78.

indirectly (a franking mechanism) to reduce the VAT paid by borrowers on a transaction-by-transaction basis, thus, the name – the modified reverse-charging approach.[115] The complexity in this approach is that the available credits are calculated after each deposit and loan in the franking account. Zee analogizes it to "a pooled account of depreciable assets under the declining-balance method" that must "maintain three running balances: (1) cumulated unlent deposits, (2) cumulated unclaimed reverse charges on the unlent deposits, and (3) unclaimed reverse charge per unit of unlent deposit. These balances are updated after each deposit or lending transaction, with the former giving rise to a credit entry and the latter to a debit entry"[116] The bank must account for the tax attributable to each borrower on these transactions and must issue a VAT invoice to such borrower for the net VAT payable.

In actual practice, deposits and loans are not closed out precisely at the end of each tax period. It therefore is necessary to treat all outstanding deposits as withdrawn and loans as fully paid at the end of each period and then redeposited and relent at the beginning of the next period at the same interest rates.[117] The audit for the tax authorities may be challenging, but computerized databases and other newer techniques may make such a system verifiable.

The described "modified reverse-charging approach" assumes that the intermediation services are consumed by borrowers and not depositors. Zee suggests that this approach can be extended to treat both depositors and borrowers as consuming a portion of the intermediation services rendered by the banks. It appears that the calculation of the value of the service rendered to depositors would be based on a presumed percentage. The VAT charged on deposits would be reported to depositors on their account statements and business depositors could claim this VAT as an input credit. The "net VAT paid by borrowers would be reduced by exactly the amount of the VAT paid by depositors."[118] Will a bank have an incentive to set the percentage to maximize the input VAT attributable to customers that can claim input credits?[119]

Zee compared the modified reverse-charge approach with the Poddar-English cash-flow approach. According to Zee, because the cash-flow approach includes the principal amounts of loans in the tax base, there will be cash-flow problems for borrowers and practical problems if the VAT rate changes over the life of individual loans and deposits,[120] but he acknowledges that the use of suspense accounts, the TCA accounts, maintained by the banks will track deposit and loan transactions by customer. On balance, Zee suggests that the TCA device "is unnecessarily

[115] *Id.* at 86.
[116] *Id.*
[117] *Id.* at 88.
[118] *Id.*
[119] The percentage merely determines the allocation of the VAT burden between depositors and borrowers. According to Zee, the allocation does not provide any inherent benefit to the banks, so setting the percentage could be left to the banks. *Id.* at 89.
[120] *Id.* at 90.

complex, because the tracking ... of inflows and outflows of the principal amounts of deposits and loans is superfluous for taxing financial intermediation services under an invoice-credit VAT."[121] His position is that the "modified reverse-charging approach removes an entire layer of administrative complexity [ignoring principal amounts] associated with the cash-flow approach that represents no value-added to resolving the problems entailed by the exemption approach."[122]

7. Some Thoughts

There have been other proposals such as Huizinga's simplified TCA method, supported by Merrill.[123] Under that system, B2B financial services are zero-rated, and financial services rendered to non-registered customers (B2C) would be taxed on an aggregate, not transactional basis. As an alternative to the TCA method on BTC transactions, Merrill suggests the use of the addition method that taxes wages and profit.

Most proposals, not enacted to date, to zero-rate B2B financial services and tax B2C financial services on an aggregate basis divide financial services into two categories – those rendered to registered and those rendered to non-registered customers. This separation does not take account of financial services rendered to registered customers that make both taxable and exempt supplies. This omission may be significant for supplies to customers such as hospitals and educational institutions that are VAT-registered but supply mainly exempt services.

It is worth noting that zero-rating, while reducing administration and compliance costs, if carried to an extreme, would produce a single-stage retail sales tax, not a VAT.

G. Islamic Finance

A key principle of Islamic law or the Shari'ah is the prohibition of interest (*riba*). Islamic finance, on the other hand, "does not reject the notion of time value of money. The capital provider is permitted an adequate return."[124] Instead of interest, "a yield from the deployment of money or capital generally arises in the form of profit and loss sharing."[125]

A number of countries have enacted or revised their VAT laws to be consistent with the Shari'ah. This trend reflects the growing importance of Islamic finance in the global financial services industry.

[121] *Id.* at 91.

[122] *Id.*

[123] H. Huizinga, Financial Services – VAT in Europe?,35 Economic Policy 499 (Oct. 2002); Merrill, *supra* note 90, at 180.

[124] "Islamic Financial Products: History and Concept," ch. 2, in *Law and Practice of Islamic Banking and Finance* (N.N. Thani, M.R.M. Abdullah, & M.H. Hassan), (Sweet & Maxwell Asia 2003).

[125] Islamic Finance, http://www.austrade.gov.au., p. 7.

Islamic financial transactions typically achieve virtually the same economic substance as a conventional loan transaction, while taking a different legal form. For example, under a *murabaha*, an Islamic Finance Institution (IFI) purchases an asset and then sells it to its client at a higher price with deferred payment terms. The interest that would ordinarily be paid by the client in a conventional loan – and which would constitute the bank's profit – is replaced by the difference between the purchase price and the sale price.

The challenge for dealing with such a transaction is to provide the same tax consequences as for conventional finance. In the case of a *murabaha*, the VAT law can do so by providing that the financial institution is deemed not to have acquired the asset and sold it to the client.[126]

Another example is the *Ijara*, which is essentially a sale-leaseback. In this case, the VAT law can provide neutrality vis-à-vis conventional finance by providing that the nominal lessee under an *Ijara* is treated as the owner of the property (and a portion of the lease payments is treated as if it were interest paid under a loan). If finance leases are generally treated as financing transactions for VAT purposes, there may not even be a need for a special rule concerning *Ijara*, as long as a typical *Ijara* transaction is covered by the finance lease rules.

In addition, the VAT law can specifically include Islamic finance transactions in the list of exempted financial services.[127]

A country without Shari'ah-specific VAT rules may achieve comparable VAT treatment for financial services by relying on judicial doctrines such as substance-over-form or economic substance.[128]

IV. Discussion Questions

1. Assume that Consumer borrows $1,000 from a friend to pay a MasterCard bill that was entirely for personal consumption items, namely, a new stereo music setup. In the current year, Consumer pays $100 interest on this loan. Should the interest collected by the friend be subject to VAT? If a corporation raises funds for its operations by issuing bonds for $1,000,000 and pays $80,000 interest to holders of the bonds, should the interest received by the bondholders be subject to VAT?
2. Consumer purchases a car for $13,000, paying a $3,000 cash down payment and financing the other $10,000. In the first year, in addition to the down payment, Consumer pays $1,000 principal and $1,200 interest on

126 For example, see South Africa VAT, Act 89 of 1991, as amended by Amendment Act of 2010, §8A.

127 Singapore Goods and Services Tax Act, ch. 117A, Act 31 of 1993, §14(1) and 22, and Fourth Schedule, Part I – Exempt Supplies, Finance 1.

128 See "Financial Institutions and Instruments – Tax Challenges and Solutions," Background Paper for the International Tax Dialogue Conference (Beijing 2009).

the car loan. If the goal is to tax value added in a manner that promotes administrative simplicity, how should the car sale and loan be treated? If, for political reasons, it is necessary to permit the sale to be reported as installment payments are received, how should the car sale and loan be treated?

3. Bank lends Consumer $1,000 and Business $10,000 from funds received from depositors. Bank collects $150 interest from Consumer and $1,000 interest from Business. Bank pays depositors $770 interest on deposits of $11,000. If the VAT is imposed on the value of financial intermediation services rendered by Bank, what should Bank's VAT base be and how should it be calculated?
4. If the VAT is imposed on the value of financial intermediation services, should the purchaser of those services receive an input credit for the VAT? If so, how should this credit be calculated?
5. Assuming that credit is granted for business purchases of financial services, should credit also be provided for those consumer-investors who obtain financial services to finance the acquisition of paintings, corporate stock, and gold bullion?
6. Underwriter charges Corporation $100,000 for its services in marketing $1,000,000 of Corporation's bonds (or alternatively 1,000 shares of Corporation's stock). Should the underwriting fee be subject to VAT? Any special problems? How would you handle "bought deals" and "swaps" where underwriting costs are built into the transaction price?
7. Are there tax policy or economic reasons to exempt from VAT the value of financial intermediation services?

   a. If these services are exempt, how should the exemption be provided? How should financial institutions calculate their VAT liability?
   b. If financial services are exempt from VAT, financial institutions have an incentive to provide internally some services previously purchased from outside vendors. For example, suppose that before VAT is enacted, Bank purchased cleaning services from a maintenance firm for $100,000. With the adoption of VAT, the maintenance firm would add $5,000 VAT (assuming a 5% VAT) to the Bank's bill. Bank cannot claim credit for the $5,000 VAT. How can the VAT statute prevent this incentive toward vertical integration? What purchases should be covered by this rule?

8. If financial services are exempt from VAT, how should the statute treat financial services used in connection with zero-rated exports of goods? (This question raises the problem of exempting items that relate to zero-rated exports. It is difficult to zero-rate financial services attributable to export sales under a regime that exempts financial services if the exporter cannot identify the VAT component in the exempt services.)

9. Bank takes deposits and makes loans. In addition, it provides checking accounts, safe deposit boxes, and estate and financial planning services to its customers. Assuming that financial intermediation services are exempt from VAT, how should the statute treat the provision of Bank's other financial services? If the value of checking account services is taxable, how should the value be calculated?
10. Should the existence of a competitive international market for financial intermediation services affect the decision to tax or exempt these services?

12 Insurance

I. Introduction

> An insurance company is a financial intermediary whose main line of business is the sale of a particular type of contingent contract, called an insurance policy. Under this contract, [in return for the premium], the insurer promises to pay some amount to the policy-holder, or to some other beneficiary, following the occurrence of an insured event.[1]

For VAT purposes, most countries lump together insurance and financial services rendered by financial institutions. The typical pattern is to include insurance within the definition of exempt financial services. There are some exceptions.

Israel does not tax insurance under its VAT. Rather, it taxes insurance companies under a system administered by the income tax department.[2] The Israeli tax is calculated under an addition method that includes wages and profits in the tax base and does not allow any deduction for VAT paid on business inputs.[3] In effect, Israel imposes tax on the full value of insurance services.

New Zealand taxes insurance other than life insurance under its GST. South Africa and several other countries follow the New Zealand pattern of taxing the value added by property and casualty insurance companies, on the basis of the margin between premiums received and claims paid.[4] Australia also is taxing property and casualty insurance under its GST

[1] D. Bradford & K. Logue, "The Effects of Tax Law Changes on Property-Casualty Insurance Prices," in *The Economics of Property-Casualty Insurance* 29 (D. Bradford, ed., University of Chicago Press 1998).

[2] See Chapter 11 for coverage of the Israeli approach to taxing banks.

[3] A. Schenk, "Taxation of Financial Services under a Value Added Tax: A Critique of the Treatment Abroad and the Proposals in the United States," 9 *Tax Notes International* 823 (1994) [hereinafter Schenk, Taxation of Financial Services].

[4] See, for example, Value-Added Tax Act No. 89 of 1991, §§1 definition of insurance, 2, 8(8), and 16(3)(c) (Republic of South Africa).

but departs from the New Zealand approach with respect to input credits available to insurers on claims paid.[5]

The following is a nonexclusive list of insurance-related transactions that may be taxed, zero-rated, or granted exemption from tax.

A. International Insurance Services
   1. Offshore insurance and reinsurance
   2. Insure foreign risks and foreign people
B. Domestic Insurance Services
   1. Insurance purchased as a separate policy from an insurance company
      a. Whole life or term insurance
      b. Risk or hazard (property-casualty) insurance – home, auto, personal injury, tour or travel cancellation
      c. Health and accident – treatment may be linked to treatment of medical care
   2. Reinsurance
   3. Services of agents, brokers, and claim adjusters
   4. Insurance protection provided by a supplier that is not a company licensed as an insurance company
      a. Credit card company protects purchases against breakage
      b. Automobile, equipment, or other rental company that charges separately for insurance or includes protection against damage in rental fee
      c. Insurance provided as part of a travel package
   5. Warranties provided through an insurance policy

A premium for property, casualty, or similar insurance coverage includes various elements. Part of the premium represents the fee for intermediation services rendered by the insurance company, including attracting customers, writing policies, investing the pooled funds to earn additional income to operate the business and pay claims, and finally, paying claims to the insured suffering covered losses. If the excess of the premium over the value of the intermediation services represents "protection against the loss, damage to, or destruction of the insured property, then, like the value of a warranty included in the price of a product, this component of the premium should be included in the VAT base."[6]

[5] A New Tax System (Goods and Services Tax) Act 1999 [hereinafter Australian GST], §78 (Australia).

[6] This portion of the premium may represent the present value of the right to acquire replacement property in the future or may represent the purchase of a service in the nature of a product warranty. As an example of the latter, assume a consumer purchased a one-year warranty for a television. The cost of the warranty represents consumption taxable in the period in which the warranty is purchased. When warranty work is performed in the future, the consumer will not be charged VAT on the value of that service. To be consistent, the company performing the warranty service should be entitled to claim input credit for purchases attributable to the warranty service. Schenk, Taxation of Financial Services, *supra* note 3, at 832.

In setting the premiums, the insurance provider considers the present value of the expected claims. For competitive reasons, the insurance company may reduce its premiums by a portion of the investment income earned on the pooled funds (or more accurately the net of investment income over investment expenses). In that case, to tax the value of intermediation services rendered by property or casualty insurance companies fully, the VAT base should include the net investment income. The value added tax base of a property or casualty insurance company therefore would be

Gross premiums
+ net investment income
– claims paid

No country includes net investment income as part of the taxation of nonlife insurance.

> Permanent life insurance contains additional elements. Permanent life premiums include "(1) a transfer element for claims paid to insured persons who die that year; (2) a savings element for additions to the insured's savings; and (3) a service element for administration and risk-taking by the insurance company."[7] Only the third element represents the intermediation service provided by the insurance company that should be included in the VAT base.[8]

To date, with the exception of Israel, no country taxes the intermediation services rendered by firms providing life insurance.

This chapter discusses the VAT consequences of insurance coverage (other than life insurance), first by discussing the possible inclusion of net investment income in the tax base. It then considers the exemption provided almost universally in the EU and elsewhere. Subsequent sections of this chapter discuss ways in which nonlife insurance coverage is taxed, with the primary focus on the New Zealand approach that is being copied in other countries. The Australian system and a U.S. proposal are then considered.

II. Broad-Based Tax on Casualty Insurance

As discussed earlier, to tax intermediation services rendered by casualty insurance companies (in some countries, referred to as "general insurance") fully, the tax base could include net investment income earned by the firms. This section explores this broader tax base.

The pro forma profit statement in Table 12.1, prepared for VAT purposes (not for income tax purposes and not in accordance with generally

[7] T. Neubig & H. Adrion, "Value Added Taxes and Other Consumption Taxes: Issues for Insurance Companies," 61 *Tax Notes* 1001,1006 (1993).

[8] Schenk, Taxation of Financial Services, *supra* note 3, at 832.

TABLE 12.1. Ideal Casualty Insurance Co. Pro Forma Profit Statement for VAT Purposes for the Year Ending December 31, 2013

Income	
Insurance premiums (VAT-exclusive)	$10,900,000*
Investment income	400,000
	$11,300,000
Expenses	
Wages	250,000
Investment expenses	200,000
Claims paid (VAT-exclusive)	10,200,000
Business purchases, including capital goods (VAT-exclusive)	400,000
Net VAT liability	**
Total expenses	11,050,000
Profit for VAT Purposes	250,000

* The premiums are priced to include $10,200,000 anticipated VAT-exclusive claims, $400,000 in VAT-exclusive cost of business inputs, $500,000 in value added by the business (wages and profits), less $200,000 in net investment income.

** The net VAT liability of $50,000, as calculated in Table 12.2, is not included in the data reported exclusive of VAT.

accepted accounting principles), shows income and expenses of a casualty insurance company. Figures taken from this statement can be used to prepare the VAT return (Table 12.2). Net investment income is treated as part of the receipts subject to VAT. The amounts in this statement (other than the tax itself) are shown exclusive of VAT. The tax rate is 10%, applied to a tax-exclusive base.

The tax liability for the period may be calculated under a credit-invoice VAT as the difference between

1. the tax imposed on both the premiums charged and the net investment income, and
2. the input credit attributable to the claims paid and the VAT on other business inputs used in making taxable sales of insurance services. Note that the claims paid to the insured are assumed to include the VAT. Therefore, to calculate the credit, this grossed-up VAT is multiplied by 10/110.

III. Exemption for Insurance Other than Life Insurance

The EU established the standard practice of including insurance within the definition of exempt financial services. The VAT Directive, in Article 135(1)(a), provides that member states shall exempt "insurance and reinsurance

TABLE 12.2. VAT Return Ideal Casualty Insurance Co. for the Year 2013

Output Tax	
Taxable premiums $10,900,000 × 10%	$1,090,000
Net investment income $200,000 × 10%	20,000
	$1,110,000
Input Tax Credits	
Claims paid (tax included) 11,220,000 × 10/110	(1,020,000)*
Taxable business purchases $400,000 × 10%	(40,000)
Total input credits	1,060,000
Net VAT Liability	$50,000

* If an insurance company can claim an input credit for the VAT component in the claims paid, it is expected that the insurance company will gross-up the claims paid.

transactions, including related services performed by insurance brokers and insurance agents."[9]

The practice in many countries that exempt insurance is to impose a separate insurance premium tax (IPT). In the United Kingdom, an IPT was imposed at a rate much lower than the VAT. To take advantage of this rate differential, suppliers of major household appliances set up their own insurance companies to structure service contracts on the appliances as insurance contracts. In response, the United Kingdom raised the IPT to the VAT rate, but only on premiums for insurance coverage on domestic appliances, motorcars, and certain travel. In a challenge by affected insurance and other companies offering these service contracts, claiming that the IPT is another turnover tax contrary to the Sixth Directive and claiming that the IPT nullifies the exemption for insurance provided in the Sixth Directive [now VAT Directive], the ECJ ruled that the higher rate was compatible with the Sixth Directive.[10] The following case involves the United Kingdom's attempt to limit the exemption for insurance to firms authorized to conduct the insurance business. In *Card Protection Plan Ltd (CPP) v. Commissioner of Customs and Excise*,[11] the taxpayer provided loss and theft coverage for credit cards, car keys, passports, and insurance documents. To cover its potential liability under its contracts with its customers, CPP purchased, through an insurance broker, block cover from an insurance company. The block cover policy lists CPP's customers as the insured parties. In addition to the insurance coverage, CPP provides its customers with other services, including the maintenance of a list of each

[9] Council Directive 2006/112/EC of 28 November 2006 on the common system of value added tax, Official Journal No. L347/1 of 11.12.2006 [VAT Directive].

[10] *GIL Insurance Ltd and Others v. Commissioner of Customs and Excise*, Case C-308/01, [2004] ECR I-04777.

[11] Case C-349/96, [1999] ECR I-973; 1999 ECJ CELEX LEXIS 2179.

customer's credit cards, a twenty-four-hour telephone line to report losses, and assistance in replacing credit cards. Under the UK VAT, exemption for insurance services is limited to insurance provided by firms permitted to conduct an insurance business under UK law.[12] The ECJ held that CPP, although not an insurance company, performed an insurance transaction entitled to exemption under Article 13B(a) of the Sixth Directive [VAT Directive, Article 135(1)(a)]. A member state, according to the court, cannot restrict the exemption to insurers authorized by national law to conduct the insurance business. According to the court, it is for the national court to determine if the exempt insurance supply and the taxable card registration services were two independent supplies (so that the insurance coverage was exempt and the card registration services were taxable) or a single supply, with the VAT treatment of a single supply linked to the consequences of the principal service rendered.

The incentive for banks to outsource services and claim that those purchases are exempt applies equally to insurance companies. The supplier of exempt services is attempting to reduce noncreditable input VAT on purchases used in rendering exempt services. For example, Chapter 11 discusses attempts by data processing firms and others to claim that their services provided to banks come within the exemption for financial services. The cases typically involve services that some banks provide in-house. Insurance companies want their suppliers to claim the "insurance" exemption for their supplies to insurance company customers that insurance companies sometimes provide in-house. The following cases are illustrative.

In *Staatssecretaris van Financiën v. Arthur Andersen & Co. Accountants,*[13] an insurance company outsourced some back office services to the accounting firm, and the service provider was claiming that the services were exempt insurance services. The ECJ, in part and edited, found the following.

> In that connection, it should be noted that it was indeed held, in relation to the Sixth Directive, that the professional activity described in Article 2(l)(b) of Directive77/92 'involves the power to render the insurer liable in respect of an insured person who has incurred a loss' (Taksatorringen, paragraph 45).[14]

[12] This case involved section 17 and Sch. 6, Group 2 of the Value Added Tax Act 1983, limiting exemption to insurance provided by companies permitted to carry on insurance business under the Insurance Companies Act 1982.

[13] Case C-472/03, [2005] ECR I-1719 (ECJ Judgment 2005).

[14] The VAT consequences of outsourced services also was the issue in *Assurandør-Societet, acting on behalf of Taksatorringen v. Skatteministeriet.* Case C-8/01, [2003] ECR I-13711 (ECJ Judgment 2005). In that case, the taxpayer was a member association of small- or medium-sized insurance companies. The taxpayer assesses damage to motor vehicles on behalf of its member companies. The taxpayer's services are allocated to members exactly in proportion to the member's share of joint expenses. The ECJ ruled that the services rendered by the taxpayer on behalf of its members are *not* exempt under the [now

However, as the Advocate General points out, it cannot be inferred from that case-law that the existence of a power to render the insurer liable is the determining criterion for recognition of an insurance agent within the meaning of [VAT Directive, Article 135(1)(a)]. Recognition of a person as an insurance agent presupposes an examination of what the activities in question comprise.

In that regard, irrespective of whether, as part of its activities, ACMC (Andersen Consulting Management Consultants) has a relationship with both the insurer and the insured parties, as required by the case-law for recognition as an insurance agent, it is apparent from the information contained in the order for reference, as supplemented by the information provided by the defendant in its written observations, that ACMC's activities consist in handling insurance applications, assessing the risks to be insured, determining whether a medical examination is required, deciding whether to accept the risk where such an examination is deemed unnecessary, issuing, managing and rescinding insurance policies and making amendments to contracts and modifying premiums, receiving premiums, managing claims, setting and paying commission for insurance agents and maintaining contact with them, handling aspects relating to reinsurance and supplying information to insured parties and insurance agents and to other interested parties, such as the tax authorities.

In the light of that information, it must be held that, although they contribute to the essence of the activities of an insurance company, the services rendered by ACMC to Universal Leven NV (UL), which are not insurance transactions within the meaning of [VAT Directive, Article 135(1)(a)], do not constitute services that typify an insurance agent either.

The services in question have specific aspects, such as the setting and payment of commission for insurance agents, the maintenance of contact with them, the handling of aspects relating to reinsurance and the supply of information to insurance agents and to the tax authorities, which, quite clearly, are not part of the activities of an insurance agent.

[E]ssential aspects of the work of an insurance agent, such as the finding of prospects and their introduction to the insurer, are clearly lacking in the present case. It is apparent from the order for reference – and the defendant has not disputed – that the activity of

VAT Directive, *supra* note 9, at Article 135(1)(a)] as insurance transactions *or* services related to those transactions by insurance brokers or insurance agents. [VAT Directive, Article 132(1)(f)] exempts services otherwise meeting the VAT exemption (for insurance) if provided for members, "provided that such exemption is not likely to produce distortion of competition." The ECJ ruled that the exemption "must be refused if there is a genuine risk that the exemption may by itself, immediately or in the future, give rise to distortions of competition. *Id.* at ¶76. It did not matter to the court that large insurance companies provided the same services in-house.

ACMC starts only when it handles the applications for insurance sent to it by the insurance agents through whom UL seeks prospects in the Netherlands life assurance market.

[T]he agreement between ACMC and UL must be regarded as a contract for subcontracted services under which ACMC provides UL with the human and administrative resources which it lacks, and supplies it with a series of services to assist it in the tasks inherent in its insurance activities. In that regard, it is important to note, that the staff of UL corresponds to only 2.9 full-time staff (FTS), whereas AIS has 17 FTS working on the 'back office' activities, and that the staff of AIS and UL share the same premises.

Consequently, the services rendered by ACMC to UL must be regarded as a form of cooperation consisting in assisting UL, for payment, in the performance of activities which would normally be carried out by it, but without having a contractual relationship with the insured parties. Such activities constitute a division of UL's activities and not the performance of services carried out by an insurance agent.

In the light of the foregoing, the answer to the question referred to the Court must be that [VAT Directive, Article 135(1)(a)] must be interpreted as meaning that 'back office' activities, consisting in rendering services, for payment, to an insurance company do not constitute the performance of services relating to insurance transactions carried out by an insurance broker or an insurance agent within the meaning of that provision.

The Canadian GST exempts financial services, including insurance.[15] In *Maritime Life Assurance Company v. HM The Queen*,[16] the taxpayer sold a variety of insurance products, including annuity contracts to provide retirement income. The contracts in issue require the taxpayer to invest the premiums in segregated funds, with the proceeds on maturity to be used to provide the annuity payments. Some of the policies provide additional insurance features, including guaranteed minimum value on maturity and guaranteed payment if the insured dies before maturity. The court found that the financial service features of the supply constituted more than 50% of the consideration for all of the services provided under the contracts; thus, the supply is an exempt financial service.

The Canadian GST includes as exempt insurance "the service of investigating and recommending the compensation *in satisfaction of a claim* [emphasis added] under an insurance policy," whether provided by the insurer or another person.[17] In *Mitchell Verification Services Group Inc. v.*

[15] Part IX of the Excise Tax Act, S.C. 1990, c. 45, as amended [hereinafter Canadian GST], Sch. V, Part VII.

[16] 1999 Can. Tax Ct. LEXIS 23.

[17] Canadian GST, *supra* note 17, at paragraph (j) of section 123(1) definition.

HM The Queen,[18] the court, in narrowly construing the exemption, held as taxable the service of investigating insurance claims and advising the insurance company that (a) it should conduct further investigation, (b) the claim submitted was excessive, or (c) the claimant was malingering, did not constitute the exempt service of investigating and recommending amounts for the settlement of claims. When a claim is received with respect to an exempt insurance service, the receipt of the claim or indemnity generally would be consideration for a supply that comes within the "insurance" exemption.

IV. New Zealand Taxation of Insurance

New Zealand developed its statutory scheme to tax insurance in consultation with accounting professionals and the insurance industry. It does not attempt to include net investment income in the tax base. Except for Australia and Israel, the New Zealand pattern is used in countries that tax nonlife insurance.

New Zealand taxes the gross premiums charged on the covered nonlife policies. It also zero-rates "exports" of insurance if the risk is located outside the country. New Zealand exempts life insurance.[19] Insurance providers can claim credits for tax on two categories of payments: input VAT on purchases attributable to taxable insurance and the tax fraction of claims paid (the "grossed-up" portion of claims paid).[20]

The tax consequences to an insured under a taxable insurance policy are linked to the status of the insured as a GST-registered or unregistered person. An unregistered person must bear GST charged on a taxable premium and does not have any GST consequences on receipt of an indemnity payment for a covered loss. The indemnity payment by the insurer is grossed-up to include GST, so that the insured has the funds to pay the GST-inclusive cost to replace the lost property or repair the damaged property.

If the insured is GST-registered and the coverage pertains to the insured's taxable activity, the tax paid on the premium is creditable. When the registered insured sustains a covered loss and receives an indemnity payment, the insured must report the GST component in the claim received as output tax "to the extent that it relates to a loss incurred in the course

[18] Can. Tax Ct. LEXIS 2275 (1998).

[19] Exempted life insurance includes insurance covering "the contingency of the termination or continuation of human life, marriage, civil union or de facto relationship, or the birth of a child." The exemption does not include entitlements "arising from fatal injuries." New Zealand Goods and Services Tax Act 1985, No. 141, as of January 1, 2014 [hereinafter NZ GST], section 3(2) definition of "life insurance contract."

[20] *Id.* at §20 generally and §20(3)(d) pertaining to insurance claims paid. There are many exceptions under the §20(3)(d) proviso, including the denial of credit if the claim relates to policies that are not taxable, policies that are taxable at a zero-rate, or payments in respect of the supply of goods or services or the import of goods. Credit also is denied if payment is made to an unregistered, nonresident.

or furtherance of the registered person's taxable activity."[21] Combining the input credit to the registered insurer with the output tax it reports on a received claim, the government does not receive any net GST revenue on insurance coverage provided to a GST-registered business that is attributable to its taxable activity.

Each consumer or unregistered business that is covered under a taxable premium bears GST on the gross premium, and not just on the value of the intermediation services rendered by the insurer. This treatment can be justified as follows.

> If the spread between the gross premium and the value of intermediation services rendered by the insurance company is viewed as a form of consumption similar to a warranty agreement, then New Zealand's taxation of this spread when the insurance invoice is issued is appropriate.
>
> If the taxation of the gross premium represents taxation of intermediation services and taxation of the present value of replacement property, then the tax regime still works even if the tax rate changes between the time that the premium is invoiced and the claims are paid.[22]

The New Zealand approach to the taxation of insurance departs from the basic invoice VAT principle that allows registered businesses to claim input tax credits only if supported by tax invoices from registered suppliers.[23] An insurance company subject to GST on its casualty or other taxable insurance premiums generally can claim input credit for the VAT element in its claims paid (grossed-up to include GST) on policies taxable at a positive rate, whether the claims are paid to registered or unregistered businesses or to consumers.[24]

Table 12.3 is a pro forma income statement for NZ GST purposes, assuming that net investment income is not included in the GST base. To compare the two approaches, the following discussion, as in Tables 12.1 and 12.2, assumes that the GST rate is 10%, not New Zealand's higher 15% rate. The pro forma profit statements of Tables 12.1 and 12.3 are identical. These examples do not take account of any changes to the NZ GST.

Applying the NZ GST formula, the casualty company's $30,000 tax liability is calculated in Table 12.4. The $20,000 tax difference between the broad base in Table 12.2 and the NZ base in Table 12.4 represents 10% tax on the $200,000 net investment income that is included in the broader tax base.

[21] *Id.* at §5(13), as amended in 2000. There are a few exceptions and limitations. For example, it does not apply if the insurance policy is not taxable at a positive rate. *Id.* at §5(13) proviso, §5(13B) and §20(3).

[22] Schenk, Taxation of Financial Services, *supra* note 3, at 834–836. Some footnotes omitted.

[23] This principle also is violated in a few other situations, such as where a VAT statute authorizes a dealer in used goods to claim a credit for a presumed VAT component in the purchase price of used goods acquired from a consumer.

[24] There are exceptions, as noted earlier.

TABLE 12.3. New Zealand Casualty Insurance Co. Pro Forma Profit Statement for GST Purposes for the Year Ending December 31, 2013

Income	
Insurance premiums (GST excluded)	$10,900,00
Investment income	400,000
	$11,300,000
Expenses	
Wages	250,000
Investment expenses	200,000
Claims paid (GST excluded)	10,200,000
Business purchases, including capital goods (GST excluded)	400,000*
Net VAT liability	**
Total expenses	11,050,000
Profit for GST Purposes	250,000

* The $40,000 GST paid on these business inputs is creditable against GST liability on premiums. It therefore is not included in this statement.
** The GST liability is not included in this data, which is GST-exclusive. The net GST liability is $30,000, as calculated in Table 12.4.

TABLE 12.4. GST Return New Zealand Casualty Co. for the Year 2013

Output Tax	
Taxable premiums	
$10,900,000 × 10%	$1,090,000
Input Tax Credits	
Claims paid (tax included)	
11,220,000 × 10/110	(1,020,000)
Taxable business purchases	
$400,000 × 10%	(40,000)
Total input credits	1,060,000
Net GST Liability	30,000

In this illustration, it is assumed that the casualty company reduces the premiums it charges its customers by the net investment income. In practice, this may or may not occur. The company has added value of at least $500,000 (wages and profits for GST purposes), but part of it is not taxed because net investment income is not included in the tax base. The government receives less revenue from the insurance company, equal to the tax on the net investment income.

In the following two subsections, the New Zealand approach to the taxation of casualty insurance is explained in more detail.

A. Application of the NZ Taxation of Casualty Insurance to GST-Registered Policyholders

We can disaggregate the casualty insurance company's total figures and look at the GST consequences to a group of customers who buy casualty insurance and to one customer who sustains a covered loss. Assume that ten GST-registered businesses purchased casualty policies for total GST-exclusive premiums of $10,900 and one of them (paying a premium of $1,090) suffered a loss of $11,220 (inclusive of GST).[25] Under the GST, the tax consequences to the registered purchasers of the casualty insurance policies and the one firm sustaining the covered loss are as follows:

To the casualty insurance company selling the 10 policies:

Output tax on premiums

$10,900 × 10% = $1,090

To the 10 registered policyholders purchasing the policies:

Input tax credit on premiums paid

$10,900 × 10% GST rate = <u>($1,090)</u>

Net revenue to government <u>00</u>

The government does not receive any net revenue as a result of the sale of policies to these ten GST-registered businesses – the output tax remitted by the casualty company is offset by the input credit claimed by the policyholders.

When the insurance company pays the covered claim, the GST consequences to the insurance company and the one loss-suffering, registered policyholder are as follows:

To the insurance company paying the claim:

Input tax credit on claim paid

$11,220 × 10/110 = ($1,020)[26]

To the registered policyholder receiving the claim:

Output tax on claim received

$11,220 x 10/110 = <u>$1,020</u>[27]

Net revenue to government <u>00</u>

[25] Assume that the claim is for $10,200 and, when it is grossed-up to include $1,020 of GST, the claim paid is $11,220.

[26] The insurance company will include the GST payable on the purchase of the replacement property because the NZ GST allows the insurance company an input credit for the GST component in that claim paid.

[27] The GST component in the claim received is reportable as output tax, the same as the GST component in any taxable receipt from sales by the policyholder.

Again, the government does not receive any net GST revenue because the input credit claimed by the insurance company is offset by the output tax reported by the policyholder.

When the GST-registered policyholder replaces the destroyed property for the GST-exclusive $10,200, he will pay $1,020 GST to the seller of this property, with the following consequences:

To the seller of the replacement property:

Output tax on taxable sale

$$\$10{,}200 \times 10\% = \$1{,}020$$

To the policyholder buying the replacement property:

Input tax credit on taxable purchase

$$\$10{,}200 \times 10\% = \underline{(\$1{,}020)}$$

Net revenue to government $\underline{00}$

In this final transaction, the government does not receive any net GST revenue. This is the correct result because in transactions between GST-registered insurers and the insured making only taxable sales, the government should not receive any net GST revenue. Net revenue should be collected only on sales to final consumers, exempt small businesses, or businesses making sales exempt from tax (collectively referred to in the following discussion as consumers).

B. Application of the NZ Taxation of Casualty Insurance to Policyholders Who Are Consumers

If we change this example and assume that all ten policyholders are consumers and that one of these consumers suffers the same covered loss assumed in that example, the NZ GST implications are as follows:[28]

To the casualty insurance company selling the policies:

Output tax on premiums

$$\$10{,}900 \times 10\% = \$1{,}090$$

To the ten consumers who purchase the policies:

GST-inclusive cost of insurance premiums (no GST refunds)

$$\$10{,}900 + 10\%\ \text{GST}\ (\$1{,}090) = \$11{,}990$$

The government receives $1,090 GST revenue on the gross premiums as a result of the sale of policies to these ten final consumers; the output tax remitted by the casualty company is not recoverable by the consumers.

[28] The same treatment applies to insured persons who are exempt small businesses or firms making sales exempt from GST.

When the insurance company pays the covered claim, the government should be returning some of the GST the insurer charged on the gross premiums, so that GST is collected only on the services rendered by the insurer measured by gross premiums less claims paid. The GST consequences to the insurance company and the policyholder claimant are as follows:

To the insurance company paying the claim:

Input tax credit on claim paid

$$\$11{,}220 \times 10/110 = (\$1{,}020)$$ [29]

To the policyholder receiving the claim:

$$\$10{,}200 \text{ grossed-up by } \$1{,}020 \text{ GST} = \$11{,}220$$ [30]

The government, at this point, returns some GST to the insured via the input credit provided to the insurer. The insurance company reimburses the insured for the GST that she will pay if she replaces the property for $10,200. The government has collected net revenue roughly equal to the taxed services rendered by the casualty insurance company to the policyholders.[31]

When the policyholder replaces the destroyed property for $10,200, she will pay GST to the seller of this property, with the following consequences:

To the seller of the replacement property:

Output tax on taxable sale

$$\$10{,}200 \times 10\% \text{ GST} = \$1{,}020$$

To the policyholder buying the taxable replacement property:

$$\$10{,}200 + \$1020 \text{ GST} = \$11{,}220 \text{ GST-inclusive price}$$

In this final transaction, the government receives $1,020 GST revenue on the sale of the replacement property to the consumer, like any taxable sale to a final consumer, and the consumer does not bear any net GST since the grossed-up claim includes the tax imposed on the replacement property.

C. Are Warranties "Insurance" in New Zealand?

In the Introduction to this chapter, there is a comparison between a warranty and the portion of an insurance premium that exceeds the value

29 The insurance company will include the GST payable on the purchase of the replacement property because the NZ GST allows the insurance company an input credit for the GST component in that claim paid, even when paid to a final consumer.

30 The GST component in the claim received is not taxable to the consumer.

31 These figures ignore the fact that the government received the revenue when the policies were sold and the government returns part of this revenue when the insurance company claims credits attributable to the claims paid.

of the intermediation services rendered by the insurance company. The warranty analogy is used as justification for the inclusion of this excess in a VAT base. If a warranty is included in a VAT base, so should this excess.

In *Suzuki New Zealand Ltd v. CIR*,[32] the foreign parent that manufactured vehicles gave warranties on the vehicles. The New Zealand distributor (the taxpayer) made the repairs covered by the warranties and was paid by the foreign manufacturer. The court held that the warranty payments made by the foreign parent to the taxpayer were taxable. The GST was amended to reverse that decision and zero-rate such warranty payments made by a non-registered foreign warrantor.[33]

V. Australia's Taxation of Insurance

In broad outline, both the NZ GST and the Australian GST tax premiums and provide, to some extent, input credits on claims paid.[34] Nevertheless, the details and the tax base for taxable insurance in these two countries diverge with respect to claims paid. The Australian GST taxes the premiums charged for general insurance (property and casualty) but not life insurance.[35] "Exports" of insurance on the international transport of goods and passengers and health insurance premiums are zero-rated.[36]

Generally, when a company in Australia pays a covered claim under a taxable insurance policy, the insurance provider is denied an input credit for any portion of the claim paid. A registered insured (unlike New Zealand) does not report the receipt of the claim as a taxable supply. Under an exception, the insurance company may be entitled to claim an input credit on the payment of a claim as provided under the Decreasing Adjustment Model in Division 78 of the Australian GST.[37] A credit is available to the extent that the insurer funds the GST component in the claim paid. The credit, contingent on the insurer including GST in the claim paid, is discussed next.[38]

If the insured can claim credit for GST on the premium, then the general rule applies and under Division 78, the insurer is denied a credit for the

[32] 20 NZTC 17,096 (Ct. App. 2001).

[33] See NZ GST, *supra* note 19, at §2(1) definition of "warranty," and §§5(2), 5(21), and 11A(l)(ma).

[34] See G. Chiert, *GST: Insurance and Financial Services* (2nd ed., Thompson ATP 2002); Joseph, "Insurance Transactions under Australian GST," 15 *VAT Monitor* 176 (May/June 2004) [hereinafter, Joseph].

[35] An Australian company issuing life policies that are exempt from VAT is denied input credits for VAT on purchases attributable to the exempt insurance. However, like any provider of exempt financial services, the life insurance provider can claim some input credits for "reduced credit acquisitions." See also the discussion in Chapter 11.

[36] Australian GST, *supra* note 5, at §38–3 55, item 6. See GSTR 2000/33, Goods and services tax: international travel insurance.

[37] See, generally, GSTR 2000/36, Goods and services tax: Insurance settlements by making supplies of goods or services (Australia).

[38] Australian GST, *supra* note 5, at §78–10.

claim paid. In contrast, if the insured is denied credit on the insurance premium (e.g., a consumer), then on the payment of a claim to that insured person, the insurer is entitled to a credit equal to the GST component in the claim paid (1 /11 in the case of the 10% Australian GST).[39] In between, if the insured can claim a partial credit for the GST on the premium, the insurer can claim a partial credit on the claim paid under a complex formula in Section 78–15 of the GST.

> To enable the insurer to determine the correct settlement payment, the insured is obliged to state the percentage of input tax that it can recover not later than the time of making the claim. … In effect, the insurer funds only the GST component of the repair cost that is not available to the insured as input tax.[40]

VI. A U.S. Proposal – The Nunn-Domenici USA Tax System

The Nunn-Domenici USA Tax System, a plan to radically revise the federal tax system in the United States, provides for the taxation of insurance. The treatment of insurance is under the Business Tax (BT) portion of that proposal. It includes the following basic elements:

1. Business loss and other nonlife insurance includes property and casualty, workers' compensation, corporate director and officer's (D&O) liability coverage, malpractice, health, disability, and business interruption policies.
2. A nonlife company's tax base includes not only intermediation services but also the warranty or protection services that are measured by the difference between the premiums and the intermediation services.
3. The BT applies a flow of funds approach that calculates the tax on insurance services under the subtraction method. An insurance company includes receipts, including premiums (but not equity contributions), and deducts business purchases (including financial expenses and claims). The resulting inclusion of principal transactions raises transition problems.
4. There are special rules governing international transactions, including special rules on the location of a supply of insurance. Insurance is provided where the provider is located (the location linked to the place where premiums are paid may be altered by regulations).
5. The international rules are as follows:
    a. Insurance provided outside the United States covering U.S. risks is treated as an imported service subject to the import tax. Payments of benefits are not imports.

[39] *Id.* at §78–15. The 10% rate is provided in §9–70.
[40] Joseph, *supra* note 34, at 179.

b. Insurance provided in the United States covering a foreign risk is treated as an exported service not subject to the BT. Payments of benefits are not deductible.

VII. Discussion Questions

1. What is the rationale of the New Zealand decision to tax property-casualty insurance but not life insurance?
2. If a legislature decides to tax some or all insurance services, what difference does it make to a business that purchases a taxable insurance policy if the legislature adopts the New Zealand or Australian approach?
3. Should a company selling property or casualty insurance charge VAT on the value of its intermediation services or on the entire premium? What does the difference between the premium and the value of intermediation services represent?
4. Explain the difference for VAT purposes between a warranty of a product's performance and insurance covering the product's loss by fire or theft.

13 Real Property

I. Introduction

One of the most complicated problems in designing a VAT base involves the taxation of real (immovable) property. Although in a sense real property is no different from many goods, in practical terms its extremely long life presents a number of difficulties.

If an economically idealized VAT base were envisaged, it would consist of personal consumption. Most goods and services are consumed shortly after purchase. For these, there is not much difference between this ideal "economic" tax base and the "legal" tax base as defined in VAT laws, namely, the value of goods and services supplied to final consumers.[1] For real property, however, personal consumption takes place over many years (the same is true for other consumer durables). One way of reconciling the legal tax base with the economic ideal is to reason that taxation at the time of first sale of residential real estate is a form of up-front taxation of the consumption value – that is, the legal tax base corresponds to the economic tax base in present value terms. However, the equivalence ceases to hold if the price of the property changes after its initial acquisition. One of the questions that has concerned VAT policy analysts is whether this suggests that there is something wrong with how residential real property is taxed, if tax is imposed only at the time of acquisition. As will be discussed further, it turns out that the answer is not as obvious as some might think.

A large portion of residential real property is financed. The financed portion is payable over many years. In contrast, tax imposed up front may significantly increase the down payment necessary to purchase that property. This raises political issues, especially when a new VAT is introduced.

Another challenge posed by real property has to do with mixed use. It is quite common for a building to be used for both taxable and exempt or

[1] See Sijbren Cnossen, "VAT Treatment of Immovable Property," [hereinafter Cnossen], in 1 *Tax Law Design and Drafting* 231 (V. Thuronyi, ed., International Monetary Fund 1996) for a discussion of the economic and legal viewpoints in taxing real property under the VAT.

personal purposes. Change in use is also frequent, given the long life of real property. Statutes differ in terms of the recapture period during which a change in use needs to be kept track of.

The form of transactions in which interests in real property can be transferred can also present a challenge for drafting. Real property can be sold or leased. The transfer of shares in a real property holding company is economically equivalent to the transfer of the property itself. If there are special rules for real property, as there inevitably are, there will also be a need to distinguish real property from personal property, and for this purpose reliance on property law will not always be appropriate for VAT purposes.

Many sales of real property involve used property that turns over infrequently. Sales of other used consumer durables also raise difficult practical problems under VATs, with many countries opting to tax the full value of previously taxed used goods resold by a taxable supplier.[2] This treatment results in the overtaxation of consumer durables. Resales of real property, especially by consumers, raise even more significant VAT problems.[3] Applying the normal VAT rules will mean that most resales of residential real estate will go untaxed, because they are not made as part of economic activity. The same piece of property may be sold more than once, and each subsequent sale may be at a higher price reflecting market appreciation. As a result, over the period of time that real property is held, the property may be consumed in part and appreciate in value as well – mixing the consumption and savings components of the property.

Real property may be sold or leased, held for commercial use or as residential property, or held for a dual purpose. In some cases, such as vacant land held for investment, the purchaser may not use the property at all. Focusing solely on the residential aspect of real property, a home or apartment may be owned or leased, may be leased without services or, like a hotel, may be provided with substantial services included in the daily, weekly, or monthly rate. Housing may be provided in a houseboat.[4]

II. Array of VAT Treatment of Real (or Immovable) Property

There are a significant number of possible combinations of treatment for commercial and residential property leased or sold. All real property (even owner-occupied housing) can be taxed, exempt, or zero-rated. There can be a combination of these approaches for different kinds of real property,

[2] See Chapter 6 (Section IV).

[3] For a comprehensive discussion of the taxation of residential property in South Africa from the purchaser's perspective that has application to many countries with VAT, see M. Botes, "VAT Implications of Buying Residential Property in South Africa," 14 *VAT Monitor* 450 (Nov./Dec. 2003).

[4] A houseboat has been held to constitute immovable property for VAT purposes. See *Leichenich v. Ansbert Peffekoven*, Case C-532/11 (ECJ Nov. 15, 2012).

such as taxing commercial real property and exempting residential property, whether leased or sold, or taxing new and exempting used residential property.[5] In some countries, the construction of a multi-unit building for rental or for either current or future sale of individual units (condominiums) complicates the VAT consequences of the transactions involving this property, especially if, like in Australia, sales of new residential units are taxable and sales of used residential units are exempt from tax.

In practice, there is probably less uniformity in the taxation of real property than in any other area of comparative VAT law. In very general terms, one can identify a "modern" approach (represented by countries such as Canada, Australia, and New Zealand), which involves taxing the first sale of residential real estate, otherwise exempting sales or leases of residential real estate, and generally taxing commercial real estate. Many countries simply exempt all residential real estate sales or leases. This latter approach does not, however, remove the tax burden on real estate, because input VAT for materials and building contractors is not creditable. The United Kingdom gets around this problem by zero-rating residential real estate, at the cost, of course, of removing this significant consumption item from the tax base. There is no uniform European approach, because the VAT Directive offers substantial flexibility.

Canada has complex rules governing the taxation of real property transactions. In part, Canada taxes sales and leases of new or used commercial real property and sales of new residential property, taxes repairs and building material on commercial and residential property, and exempts leases of residential real property and sales of used residential property if the seller or lessor paid and did not claim credit for GST on that property.[6]

Australia also has a complex set of rules governing real property. Australia zero-rates the grant of unimproved land by a unit of government (as a freehold or under a long-term lease).[7] It also zero-rates certain grants by a government agency of a freehold interest or grants of a long-term lease of land as potential residential land or for a farming business, if the land is subdivided from land on which a farming business was conducted for at least five years.[8]

[5] For example, Mexico exempts the supply of residential dwellings, except for hotels. See Serrano Salas, "Focus on Mexico," VAT Monitor *102* (Mar./Apr. 2003).

[6] The taxation of real property in Canada is more complex than suggested in the text. There is a tax rebate provided under section 256.1 of the GST to the landowner who leases land for residential purposes. See §§190–193, 206–211, Sch. IV, and Sch. V, part 1, and Sch. IX, part IV.

[7] A New Tax System (Goods and Services Tax) Act 1999 [hereinafter Australian GST], §38–445. The zero-rating covers a supply of a freehold or long-term lease by a unit of government, even if there was a prior zero-rated lease of the land and compliance with its terms entitled the recipient to this freehold or long-term lease. Leases preceding such zero-rated supplies of freeholds or long-term leases also may be zero-rated. *Id.* at §38–150. On the Australian GST, see R. Krever, *GST Legislation Plus* (Australian Tax Practice 2005).

[8] Australian GST, *supra* note 7, at §38–475(1)(a).

Australia exempts most real property used for residential purposes. A lease of residential premises (other than commercial residential premises) is exempt.[9] The exemption extends to a long-term lease of commercial residential accommodations, such as a long-term stay in a hotel.[10] A sale of residential premises is exempt if the property is to be used predominantly for residential accommodation.[11] The exemption on sale does not apply to sales of "commercial residential premises," or certain "new residential premises."[12] Long-term leases of residential premises are exempt, unless the lease is of property to be used by the lessee for sublease as commercial residential premises, or the lease covers certain new residential premises.[13] For example, the lease of a structure to be used by the lessee as a hotel is not exempt. Thus, except as noted earlier, sales of new residential premises and commercial residential premises (such as a hotel) by a registered person are taxable. Property serving multiple purposes is considered a mixed supply that must be apportioned. For example, the sale of a used building by a registered person with retail and residential premises is taxable to the extent that it is attributable to the retail premises and exempt to the extent it is attributable to the residential premises.[14]

Rules for taxing real property often exempt sales of existing structures but not new structures. This poses a problem when an existing structure is substantially renovated. For example, the ECJ had to consider a situation in which a building was partially demolished before sale but still occupied in part. It found that in that case the sale was of an existing building and, hence, was exempt.[15]

[9] *Id.* at §40–35(l)(a). Residential premises is land or a building (including a floating home) occupied as a residence, or intended to be, and capable of being occupied as a residence. *Id.* at §195–1 definition of residential premises. Commercial residential premises include hotels and similar establishments, accommodations at a school, a ship used in connection with a ship rental business or for entertainment or transport, marinas leased to ships used as residences, a caravan park or campground, or similar, but not premises used by students at an educational institution that is not a school. *Id.* at §195–1 definition of commercial residential premises.

[10] *Id.* at §40–35(l)(b).

[11] *Id.* at §40–65(1).

[12] *Id.* at §40–65(2). The exception does not apply to new residential premises that were used for residential accommodation before December 2, 1998. "Commercial residential premises" are discussed in note 8 *supra*. "New residential premises" is defined in §40–75 as residential premises not previously sold as residential premises and not previously the subject of a long-term lease. It also includes residential premises resulting from the substantial renovation of a building or built or containing a building that was built to replace demolished premises on the same land. Premises are not new after a period of five years in the circumstances provided in §40–75(2). If premises, as described earlier, are considered "new residential premises" because of substantial renovation or built to replace demolished premises, the land that is a part of the premises is also considered "new."

[13] *Id.* at §40–70. The denial of the exemption does not apply to new residential premises used for residential accommodation before December 2, 1998. *Id.* at §40–70(2)(b).

[14] See Australian GSTR 2003/3, ¶8.

[15] See *J.J. Komen en Zonen Beheer*, Case C-326/11 (ECJ July 12, 2012).

The following section discusses the EU approach to taxing real property.[16] It is followed by a section discussing a variety of proposals for the taxation of real property that depart from the EU model.

III. EU Approach to the Taxation of Real (or Immovable) Property

A. In General

The VAT Directive has a series of provisions covering the taxation of land and buildings. A building is any structure fixed to or in the ground, and building land is unimproved or improved land that is defined as such by a member.[17]

The VAT Directive, in principle, exempts leases and sales of residential and commercial real property. In contrast, new construction services and repairs and maintenance of existing structures (as well as building material) are taxable.[18]

The VAT Directive exempts "the leasing or letting of immovable property."[19] This exemption does not apply to hotel and similar accommodations, holiday camps, camp sites, parking sites, leases of permanently installed machinery and equipment, and leases of safes.[20]

Subject to an exception described next, the supply of a building (or parts of a building) and the land on which it stands is exempt,[21] as is the supply of unimproved land.[22] This exemption does not apply in the limited case in which a person making an occasional supply of real property is treated as a taxable person with respect to that supply. Although VAT generally is imposed on taxable sales by taxable persons who conduct economic activity, members may treat a person as a taxable person even if that person engages in an occasional transaction involving land and new buildings.[23] A member state may treat as a taxable person a person making an occasional supply before a building (or part of a building) has been occupied for the first time.[24]

In some cases, members are required to follow the directive; in other cases, the member has the option to treat real property transactions

[16] For an analysis of the disparate taxation of real property in the EU, despite harmonization, and the authors call for a more restrictive exemption, see C. Amand, G. Schellmann, and Rob Vermeulen, "Immovable Property and VAT – Lessons from Past Experience," 16 *International VAT Monitor* 325 (Sept./Oct. 2005).

[17] See Council Directive 2006/112/EC of 28 November 2006 on the common system of value added tax, Art. 12 (OJ L347, 11.12.2006, p. 1 [hereinafter VAT Directive].

[18] See *id.*, Art. 135(1)(j), (k), (l); Cnossen, *supra* note 1.

[19] VAT Directive, *supra* note 17, at Art. 135(1)(l). Members can restrict the scope of this exemption.

[20] See *id.* at Art. 135(2).

[21] *Id.* at Art 135(1)(j).

[22] *Id.* at Art. 135(l)(k).

[23] See *id.* at Art. 12(1).

[24] See *id.* at Art. 12(1)(a).

differently. Member states can give taxpayers the option to treat as taxable the lease of immovable property and other exempt real property transactions (and thereby claim input tax credits).[25] The member state can impose restrictions on the scope and impose other conditions on the use of this option to treat real property transactions as taxable.[26] In practical effect, the exception in the VAT Directive that gives member states the option to allow real property transactions to be taxable applies only to a person otherwise subject to VAT, not to a consumer.

The complexity of the rules governing real property predictably has generated substantial litigation. For example, in *Staatssecretaris van Financien (Secretary of State for Finance) v. Shipping and Forwarding Enterprise Safe BV (Safe Rekencentrum BV),*[27] the ECJ had to decide what kind of transfer of rights to property constituted a taxable supply. In that case (using letters to simplify the transaction), A gave B rights to property, including a power of attorney to transfer legal ownership of the property. Any change in the value of the property belonged to B. B[28] sold rights to the property to C, and A transferred title to the property directly to C. According to the court, a "supply of goods" in Article 5(1) of the Sixth Directive[29] includes the

> transfer of the right to dispose of tangible property as owner, even if there is no transfer of legal ownership of the property .... It is for the national court to determine in each individual case, on the basis of the facts of the case, whether there is a transfer of the right to dispose of the property as owner within the meaning of Article 5(1) of the Sixth Directive [VAT Directive, Article 14(1)].[30]

B. Exemption for Leasing and Terminating a Lease

1. What Is a "Lease" or "Letting" of Immovable Property?

The VAT Directive exempts the "letting of immovable property."[31] It includes the rental of "both water-based mooring berths for pleasure boats and land sites for storage of boats on port land."[32] The lease of a prefabricated building that is affixed to the land so that it cannot be easily dismantled or easily moved is the exempt lease of immovable property, even if the building is to be removed at the end of the lease and used at another site.[33]

25 See *id.* at Art. 137(1)(b), (c), (d).

26 See *id.* at Art. 137(2).

27 *Shipping and Forwarding Enterprise Safe BV*, Case C-320/88, [1990] ECR I–285, 1990 ECJ CELEX LEXIS 7163 (ECJ Judgment 1990) [hereinafter *Shipping & Forwarding*].

28 It was the trustee in bankruptcy of B's assets that made the transfer.

29 VAT Directive, *supra* note 17, at Art. 14(1).

30 *Shipping & Forwarding*, *supra* note 27, at ruling.

31 See VAT Directive, *supra* note 17, at Art. 135(1)(1).

32 *Fonden Marselisborg Lystbådehavn v. Skatteministeriet,*, Case C-428/02, 2005 ECJ LEXIS 74 (Judgment of the ECJ 2005).

33 *Rudolf Maierhofer v. Finanzamt Augsburg-Land*, Case C-315/00, [2003] ECR I–00563.

In some cases, the issue is whether an agreement constitutes a lease of immovable (real) property for VAT purposes. The *Sinclair Collis* case involved an agreement by the siteholder to allow the taxpayer exclusive rights to sell cigarettes through cigarette machines located on its premises in return for a share of the profits from the operation of the machines. The machines were freestanding or affixed to a wall. The Queen's Bench held that the machine occupied land. As such, the supply was a license to occupy land exempt under the UK VAT.[34] The House of Lords referred the question to the ECJ for a ruling on the interpretation of the Sixth Directive [VAT Directive, Article 135]. Sinclair Collis claimed that the use of space was not the lease of immovable property under the Sixth Directive. To qualify for the exemption, the taxpayer claimed that the tenant had to obtain "a right to occupy a defined piece or area of property as one's own and to exclude or allow access to others."[35] The ECJ ruled that the grant of the right to install and operate the machines for two years was not an exempt lease of immovable property:

> [T]he fundamental characteristic of a letting of immovable property for the purposes of Article [135(1)(l) of the VAT Directive] lies in conferring on the person concerned, for an agreed period and for payment, the right to occupy property as if that person were the owner and to exclude any other person from enjoyment of such a right.
>
> According to the information supplied by the national court, the subject matter of the agreement is not the passive provision of an area or space, together with the grant to the other party of a right to occupy it as though he were the owner and to exclude all other persons from the enjoyment of that right.
>
> That finding is supported, first of all, by the fact that the agreement does not prescribe any precisely defined area or space for the installation of the vending machines at the premises. [U]nder the agreement there is nothing to prevent the machines from being moved about, to a degree, as the site owner wishes.
>
> Secondly, the agreement does not confer on SC the right to control or restrict access to the area where the machines are placed. Whilst it is true that under the agreement SC retains an exclusive right of access to the machines to maintain them, keep them stocked with cigarettes and remove the cash inside, that right concerns only access to the machine itself, in particular its inner mechanism, and not access to that part of the premises where the machine is situated. In any event, according to the information provided by SC at the hearing, the right is restricted to the opening hours of the commercial establishment and cannot be exercised without the site owner's consent.

34 [1998] STC84KQ.B. 1998).

35 *Sinclair Collis Ltd v. Commissioners of Customs and Excise*, Case C-275/01, ¶17, ECR I–5965 (Judgment of the ECJ 2003).

> [T]he reply to the question referred should be that, on a proper construction of Article [135(1)(l) of the VAT Directive], the grant, by the owner of premises to an owner of a cigarette vending machine, of the right to install the machine, and to operate and maintain it in the premises for a period of two years, in a place nominated by the owner of the premises, in return for a percentage of the gross profits on the sales of cigarettes and other tobacco goods in the premises, but with no rights of possession or control being granted to the owner of the machine other than those expressly set out in the agreement between the parties, does not amount to a letting of immovable property within the meaning of that provision.[36]

In the following *Zinn* case, the British court considered whether fees paid for the right to occupy a particular seat in the Royal Albert Hall for 999 years were for an exempt license to occupy land.

Customs and Excise Commissioners v. Zinn and Another[37]

HEADNOTE: In order to raise funds to build and maintain the Royal Albert Hall, the corporation of the hall was empowered in 1866 by Royal Charter to grant subscribers to the funds permanent seats within the hall for the whole term for which the site of the hall was leased to the corporation. The lease was for a term of 999 years from 1867. The names of seat holders were entered in a register of members. Registered holders were permitted to transfer their seats by the use of a prescribed form in consideration of payment to them of an unspecified sum of money. The instrument of transfer was to be executed by both transferor and transferee. The transferor was deemed to remain the holder of the seat until the name of the transferee was entered in the register. The ability to enjoy performances was merely consequential upon and not the subject of an assignment of a seat. A value added tax tribunal decided that what had been granted originally had been a licence to occupy land for 999 years and that accordingly the money obtained by the taxpayers from sales of their seats had been obtained as a result of an assignment of a right to occupy land and accordingly was exempt from liability to value added tax by virtue of the Value Added Tax Act 1983, Sch 6, Group 1, item 1 [Value Added Tax Act 1994, c. 23, Sch. 9, Group 1, item 1]. The commissioners appealed contending that having regard to the real commercial purpose of the transaction, the sale of the seats was not a supply of a licence to occupy land but of a right to attend performances at the Albert Hall.

[36] *Id.* at ¶¶25, 27–31 [edited by the authors].
[37] [1988] STC 57 (Q.B. 1988) [edited by the authors].

JUDGMENT. The taxpayers maintain ... that the sale was an exempt supply by virtue of §17(1) and Item 1 of Group 1 of Sch 6 to the 1983 Act. Section 17(1)[38] reads:

'A supply of goods or services is an exempt supply if it is of a description for the time being specified in Schedule 6 to this Act.' Schedule 6, Group 1, Item 1[39] reads:

> The grant, assignment or surrender of any interest in or right over land or of any licence to occupy land, other than ... [and there is then set out a list of transactions to which the exemption does not apply].

The question at issue is whether the sale of the seats was an assignment of a licence to occupy land for the purposes of this provision. Counsel for the Crown submits that ... [w]hat the purchaser was paying for was the right to attend performances, and such rights of occupation of land as he might acquire were purely incidental. I must begin by setting out what is involved in a sale or assignment of what are called permanent seats at the Albert Hall. To do so I must go back to the year 1866 when the Corporation of the Hall of Arts and Sciences was incorporated by Royal Charter. By the 4th article of the charter it was provided:

> 'With a view to raise the required funds for the building and maintenance of the Hall, the Corporation may receive Subscriptions or Donations from any persons or societies desirous of giving the same and, subject to the rights reserved to Members of the Corporation by this Our Charter, may grant to the persons or societies giving such Subscriptions or Donations, such interests in the Hall as the Corporation deem expedient.'

The rights and obligations of subscribers and members were set out in the schedule referred to in the charter. The relevant paragraphs of the schedule are these:

'I. A register of Members shall be formed, and every person who has subscribed for, engaged to take, or is otherwise entitled to a permanent seat in the Hall, and whose name is entered on the register of Members, shall be a Member of the Corporation. ... 5. Every person who has engaged to take a seat in the Hall before the granting of this Charter, shall, on the payment of the first instalment due from him, be entitled to have his name inserted in the register of Members ... 7. The right of a Member to his seat shall continue for the whole term for which the site of the Hall is granted. 8. The interest of a Member in the Hall shall be personal estate, and not the nature of real estate ... 14. A certificate, under the Common Seal of the Corporation, specifying

[38] Value Added Tax Act 1994, c. 23, §31(1) [hereinafter VATA 1994] provides in part: "A supply of goods or services is an exempt supply if it is of a description for the time being specified in Schedule 9."

[39] *Id.* at Sch. 9, Group 1, item 1 provides in part: "The grant of any interest in or right over land or of any licence to occupy land, ..."

the seats belonging to any Member, shall be prima facie evidence of the title of the Member to such seats, and shall be given to any Member on payment of such sum, not exceeding Is., as may be determined by the regulations of the Corporation for the time being in force ... 24. A permanent seat in the Hall may be transferred by the registered holder thereof, and the transferee shall be registered as a holder of such seat in the place of the transferor

The forms of transfer or assignment giving rise to the money upon which value added tax is claimed are set out in the enclosures to the decision of the tribunal. They provide for the 'Seller' so-called 'in CONSIDERATION of the SUM of ', and then there follows the sum paid by the person referred to as the 'Buyer'. Then follow the words –

'... do hereby TRANSFER ... stalls ... of which I am registered as holder in the books of the "ROYAL ALBERT HALL" to hold unto the Buyer ... subject to the several conditions on which I HELD THE SAME at the time of the execution hereof.'

By a supplemental Royal Charter of 1887 and by various Acts of Parliament the rights of members over their boxes or seats were restricted. For example, the 1887 supplemental charter allowed the corporation to let the hall for, amongst other things, private meetings and to exclude members from the hall on the occasion of such meetings.

Counsel for the Crown submits [as the question to be resolved]: looking at the substance and reality of the matter, was this a purchase of seats or a right to attend performances albeit seated. He submits that it is the latter. Counsel for the taxpayer submits that the ability to enjoy performances is consequential upon the assignment of the seats but not the subject of the assignment.

Counsel for the taxpayer further points out that in this case, ... the vendor or supplier provided no services or facilities, nothing but the right to occupy the seat. ... Another difference in the present case is of course the very long term of years over which the seat licence extends. During that period it can, submits counsel for the taxpayer, like other items of property be exploited by its holder not merely for occupation and watching performances but also by sublicensing to others to whom the holder may sell tickets. The question at the end of the day is a short question, and answering it, I say at once that I prefer the arguments for the taxpayers. The agreement, and the only agreement, between the taxpayers and their assignees was that set out in the transfer document. Counsel for the Crown does not suggest that the transfer document is a sham. Yet he urges that it should be judged as if the consideration there set out was not the true or real consideration for the money paid.

The true consideration, he says, was the right to attend performances. But the taxpayers were under no obligation to provide the purchaser with performances, and no one suggests they could or would do so. Even the corporation is under no obligation to provide entertainment to its members, although no doubt it has a general obligation under the charter to make the Albert Hall available for performances. What is critical in my view is the nature of the consideration provided by the supplier. In law and in fact all that the taxpayers could and did supply in the present case was the licence to occupy [and therefore an exempt supply].

I would dismiss this appeal and hold that value added tax is not payable.

In one case, a taxable person tried to avoid the classification of a contract for the use of commercial space in a building as exempt "leasing or letting of immovable property." In *Belgium State v. Temco Europe SA*,[40] the taxable person (Temco) entered agreements with related companies that did not constitute rental contracts under Belgian law. Temco gave the transferees the right to conduct their operations in the property but without a fixed term or other usual attributes of a lease. Temco claimed input tax deductions for VAT paid on renovation work on the property. The ECJ ruled that the transactions with related companies constituted the exempt "leasing or letting of immovable property"[41] – that is

> transactions by which one company, through a number of contracts, simultaneously grants associated companies a licence to occupy a single property in return for a payment set essentially on the basis of the area occupied and by which the contracts, as performed, have as their essential object the making available, in a passive manner, of premises or parts of buildings in return for a payment linked to the passage of time, are transactions comprising the letting of immovable property within the meaning of that provision and not the provision of a service capable of being categorised in a different way.[42]

2. Disposition or Transfer of a Lease

If rent received on the lease of real (or immovable) property is exempt, does this exemption extend to consideration received by a lessee for the surrender of its rights under a lease? In *Lubbock Fine & Co. v. Commissioner of Customs and Excise*,[43] the ECJ treated "transactions with similar economic consequences … the same regardless of their legal nature."[44] This economic equivalence approach was subsequently rejected by the ECJ and replaced by a more literal approach in the *Mirror Group* and *Cantor Fitzgerald*[45] joined cases. *Mirror Group* is excerpted next.

[40] Case C-284/03, [2004] ECR I-11237 (Judgment of the ECJ) [hereinafter *Temco Europe SA*].

[41] VAT Directive, *supra* note 17, at Art. 135(1)(l).

[42] Temco Europe SA, *supra* note 40.

[43] Case C-63 /92,1993 ECJ CELEX LEXIS 3324 (Judgment of the ECJ).

[44] R. Teather, "Reverse Premiums and VAT – Return to the Beginning" 2004, vol. 1 *British Tax Review* 37 (2004).

[45] *Cantor Fitzgerald International v. Commissioners of Customs and Excise*, Case C-108/99, [2001] ECR I-7257, [2001] STC 1453 [hereinafter *Cantor Fitzgerald*].

Mirror Group pic v. Commissioners of Customs and Excise[46]

JUDGMENT

Background and the questions referred for a preliminary ruling

In 1993, Mirror Group, a company incorporated in the United Kingdom, was looking at various sites in London to which to move its newspaper publishing operations. According to the national court, it could expect favourable terms as an anchor tenant.

On 20 June 1993, Mirror Group entered into the following agreements with Olympia & York Canary Wharf Ltd (in administration) (O & Y):

- an agreement to lease floors 20 to 24 of One Canada Square, London (the building) (the principal agreement);
- the actual lease of those five floors;
- an option agreement giving Mirror Group an initial option, exercisable within six months, to take a lease or leases of up to four more floors of the building and – if that option was not exercised in respect of more than two floors during the six-month period – a second option, exercisable within 18 months thereafter, to take a lease or leases of one or two more floors (the option agreement).

The principal agreement stipulated that O & Y would pay Mirror Group a net inducement of £12 002 590, plus VAT, on or before 2 July 1993. That sum was described therein as consideration for the tenant entering into the agreement and as an inducement to it to take on the lease.

In accordance with the principal agreement, the following arrangements for payment were implemented:

- approximately £6.5 million (exclusive of VAT) relating to floors 20 to 24 of the building was paid into an escrow account and was released to Mirror Group in several instalments corresponding to when Mirror Group ceased to have a right to determine the leases and was thus obliged to take leases of those floors for the full 25-year period.
- approximately £5.5 million (exclusive of VAT) was paid to Mirror Group and was immediately placed by it, as it was required to do, in an escrow account by way of security. Mirror Group exercised its option only in respect of three further floors and thus retained only about £4.1 million.
- VAT of approximately £2.1 million was paid into an escrow account until 26 July 1993, on which date it was paid to the Commissioners.

46 Case C-409/98, [2001] ECR I–7175, [2001] STC 1453 [edited by the authors].

It was stipulated that no rent was payable in respect of floors 20 to 24 of the building for the first five years. Starting with the sixth year and until the end of the lease, rent was payable and increased progressively, but at no time did it amount to a full market rent. Provision was made for the leases of the additional floors, in respect of which Mirror Group exercised its option, to include essentially the same provisions about rent.

Under the principal agreement, Mirror Group was required to complete the fitting out of floors 20 to 24 of the building. It actually spent about £7.2 million on fitting out floors 20 to 24 and about £1.4 million on fitting out the additional floors, 17 to 19, in respect of which it exercised its option.

According to the VAT and Duties Tribunal, London (United Kingdom), the inducement was not, however, paid by O & Y to Mirror Group as consideration for the latter fitting out the premises.

Mirror Group claimed repayment of VAT of £2.1 million on the £12 million inducement, which the Commissioners refused by decision of 1 January 1997. It then appealed against the decision to the London VAT and Duties Tribunal.

In the Tribunal's view, the acceptance by Mirror Group of the terms of the principal agreement and its execution of the lease and the option agreement constituted things done in return for the inducement of £12 million. Therefore the Tribunal held that Mirror Group had made a supply of services for consideration.

As to the question of whether that supply of services was exempt, the VAT and Duties Tribunal pointed out that that would be the case only if the supply amounted to the leasing or letting of immovable property for the purposes of Article [135(1)(l) of the VAT] Directive. According to the Tribunal, it follows from paragraph 9 of the judgment in Case C-63/92 *Lubbock Fine* [1993] ECR1–6665 that a supply made by a tenant who has surrendered an existing lease to a landlord in return for a capital sum is an exempt supply.

In those circumstances, there was no proper reason for excluding from Article [135(1)(l) of the VAT] Directive a transaction resulting in a lease where, in contrast to the standard situation, it was not the tenant who paid a sum to the landlord in order to enter into the lease but, as in the main proceedings, the landlord who agreed to pay consideration to the tenant to ensure that the latter entered into the lease and subsequently complied with its terms. As regards the £5.5 million, the Tribunal found that it was an inducement payment relating solely to the options and that therefore it was not exempt.

Both Mirror Group and the Commissioners appealed against that decision to the High Court of Justice of England and Wales, Queen's Bench Division (Divisional Court). [T]hat court decided to stay proceedings and to refer the following questions to the Court for a preliminary ruling:

1. Following the decision of the Court in Case C-63/92 *(Lubbock Fine & Co. v Commissioners of Customs and Excise)*, does [Article 135(1)(l) of the VAT Directive] exempt from VAT a supply made by a person (the person) who does not initially have any interest in the immovable property, where that person enters into an agreement for lease of that immovable property with a landlord and/or accepts the grant of a lease by the landlord in return for a sum of money paid by the landlord?
2. Following the decision of the Court in Case C-63/92 *(Lubbock Fine & Co. v Commissioners of Customs and Excise)*, does [Article 135(1)(l) of the VAT Directive] exempt from VAT a supply made by a person (the person) who does not initially have any interest in the immovable property, where that person:
   a. enters into an option agreement in relation to leases of that immovable property in return for a sum of money being paid to the person, on terms that the money will remain in a special account as security for its obligations under the option agreement; and/or
   b. subsequently exercises the options under the option agreement and accepts the grant of leases of the immovable property in return for the release of the money in the special account to the person?

The first question

Mirror Group argues that the result of *Lubbock Fine* is that supplies of services which are directly linked to the creation, alteration, transfer or termination of a right to occupy immovable property fall within the scope of [Article 135(1)(l) of the VAT Directive]. Further, the supply of services made by a tenant as a result of entry into an agreement concerning the letting of immovable property cannot be treated any differently from a supply made by the landlord, given the requirement for a coherent application of the [VAT Directive] and respect for the principle of the neutrality of VAT.

The United Kingdom Government submits that the logic of the Court's reasoning in the judgment in *Lubbock Fine* was that payments for the renegotiation of a lease should be characterised in the same way for tax purposes as payments made for the lease as originally negotiated. That is not the situation in the case before the national court. Since Mirror Group had no title to the immovable property at the time of the transaction, it did not itself make a supply of leasing or letting services. However, the wording of [Article 135(1)(l)1 of the

VAT Directive] presupposes that there will be such a supply of services in order for that provision to apply.

According to the United Kingdom Government, the supply of services by Mirror Group consisted in entering into a lease or an agreement to enter into a lease. At the hearing, the Government pointed out that Mirror Group, by transferring its business to the building, attracted other tenants.

The German Government's analysis is, in essence, the same as that of the United Kingdom Government and it further takes the view that the supply of services made by Mirror Group should be likened to the supply made by an estate agent acting as broker for a lease to be entered into by the parties.

In its written observations, the Commission submits that Mirror Group made a supply of services for the purposes of [Article 24(1) of the VAT Directive] consisting in entering into a lease or an agreement to enter into a lease. That supply falls within the scope of [Article 135(1)(l) of the VAT Directive], if the Court's ruling in the judgment in *Lubbock Fine* is followed.

At the hearing, the Commission accepted that where, in a new building, a person becomes an anchor tenant, whose presence might attract other tenants, that could constitute a taxable supply of services to the landlord. It could amount to a form of advertising. However, such a supply of services is difficult to define. If there were no separate identifiable supply of services, it would be preferable to treat the payment at issue as an assessment of the value of the lease and, therefore, as a payment inextricably linked to the lease.

Findings of the Court

It must be borne in mind that, under [Article 2(1)(c) of the VAT Directive], a supply of goods or services effected for consideration within the territory of the country by a taxable person acting as such is subject to VAT.

It is not disputed that Mirror Group, when it entered into a contract relating to the lease of the building and agreed to take a lease of that building, acted as a taxable person but did not make a supply of goods. Therefore, it is necessary to consider whether Mirror Group, in acting thus, made a supply of services for consideration and, if it did, whether that supply falls within the leasing or letting of immovable property for the purposes of [Article 135(1)(l)13B(b) of the VAT Directive].

As to whether a supply of services was made, it must be noted that a taxable person who only pays the consideration in cash due in respect of a supply of services, or who undertakes to do so, does not himself make a supply of services for the purposes of [Article 2(1)(c) of the VAT Directive]. It follows that a tenant who undertakes, even in return for payment from the landlord, solely to become a tenant and to pay the rent does not, so far as that action is concerned, make a supply of services to the landlord.

However, the future tenant would make a supply of services for consideration if the landlord, taking the view that the presence of an anchor tenant in the building containing the leased premises will attract other tenants, were to make a payment by way of consideration for the future tenant's undertaking to transfer its business to the building concerned. In those circumstances, the undertaking of such a tenant could be qualified, as the United Kingdom Government in essence submits, as a taxable supply of advertising services.

In that context, it is appropriate to point out that it is for the national court, in the light of the guidance given by the Court, to ascertain whether, in the case before it, Mirror Group made a supply of services for consideration to the landlord and, if it did, what that supply was.

However, an operation such as that carried out by Mirror Group, if it does actually amount to a supply of services, cannot be qualified as a supply of services covered by the term the leasing or letting of immovable property.

In that regard, it has consistently been held that the terms used to specify the exemptions provided for by [Article 135 of the VAT Directive] are to be interpreted strictly, since they constitute exceptions to the general principle that VAT is to be levied on all services supplied for consideration by a taxable person.

The letting of immovable property for the purposes of [Article 135(1)(l) of the VAT Directive] essentially involves the landlord of property assigning to the tenant, in return for rent and for an agreed period, the right to occupy his property and to exclude other persons from it.

It is thus the landlord who makes a taxable supply of services and the tenant who, in return for the supply, pays consideration. That is not the case in the proceedings before the national court.

It is true that the Court ruled in *Lubbock Fine* that the leasing or letting of immovable property for the purposes of [Article 135(1)(l) of the VAT Directive] covers the case where a tenant surrenders his lease and returns the immovable property to his immediate landlord.

However, the Court must make clear that that judgment was given in respect of a tenant who had returned the immovable property leased to the landlord and who, consequently, for the purposes of taxation, had assigned his right to occupy the property back to the landlord by surrendering it. That is why the Court ruled … that the tenant's surrender of the supply of services made by the landlord, which involves a change in the contractual relationship, has to be exempt where the supply itself is exempt.

Those conditions are not met in the case before the national court. Mirror Group, as a prospective tenant, is not surrendering its right to occupy the property to the landlord.

Therefore, the answer to be given to the first question must be that a person who does not initially have any interest in the immovable property and who enters into an agreement for lease of that immovable property with a landlord and/or accepts the grant of a lease of the property in return for a sum of money paid by the landlord does not make a supply of services falling within [Article 135(1)(l) of the VAT Directive].

The second question

So far as the first part of the second question is concerned, the Commission rightly points out that a taxable person who merely enters into an option agreement of the kind at issue before the national court without a mutual exchange of supplies does not make a supply of services within the meaning of [Article 2(1)(c) of the VAT Directive].

The second part of the second question raises the same issues as the first question referred by the national court. It is necessary to consider whether, on the exercise of the option and entry into the lease by the tenant in return for a sum of money paid by the landlord, the tenant merely entered into the lease or whether it made a specific supply to the landlord. In the first case, there is no supply of services within the meaning of [Article 2(1)(c) of the VAT Directive]. In the second case, nothing points to the tenant making a supply of services falling within [Article 135(1)(l) of the VAT Directive]. Therefore, the answer to be given to the second question is that a person who does not initially have any interest in the immovable property and who enters into an option agreement such as the one before the national court in relation to leases of that immovable property in return for a sum of money paid by the landlord, on terms that the money will remain in a special account as security for its obligations under the option agreement, and who subsequently exercises the options under the option agreement and accepts the grant of leases of the immovable property in return for the release of the money in its special account, at no time makes a supply of services falling within [Article 135(1)(l) of the VAT Directive].

On those grounds,

THE COURT (Sixth Chamber),

in answer to the questions referred to it by the High Court of Justice of England and Wales, Queen's Bench Division (Divisional Court), by order of 15 October 1998, hereby rules:

1. A person who does not initially have any interest in the immovable property and who enters into an agreement for lease of that immovable property with a landlord and/or accepts the grant of

> a lease of the property in return for a sum of money paid by the landlord does not make a supply of services falling within [Article 135(1)(l) of the VAT Directive].
>
> 2. A person who does not initially have any interest in the immovable property and who enters into an option agreement such as the one before the national court in relation to leases of that immovable property in return for a sum of money paid by the landlord, on terms that the money will remain in a special account as security for its obligations under the option agreement, and who subsequently exercises the options under the option agreement and accepts the grant of leases of the immovable property in return for the release of the money in its special account, at no time makes a supply of services falling within [Article 135(1)(l) of the VAT Directive].

Cantor Fitzgerald International v. Commissioners of Customs and Excise[47] involved payment by a lessee on the transfer of an unfavorable leasehold interest to a sublessee. There, the rent payable for the remaining term of an existing lease on immovable property was above the fair rental value of the leased space. As a result, the taxpayer (sublessee) received from the lessee compensation to take over the lease, agreeing to be subject to all of the terms of the underlying lease. The lessee was not released of liability under the original lease. The Tribunal held that the receipt of this compensation was a supply exempt under Article 135(1)(l) of the VAT Directive. It did not matter that the consideration moved from the assignor to assignee rather than from assignee to assignor. Consistent with the *Mirror Group* case, the ECJ ruled: "[Article 135(1)(l) of the VAT Directive] ... does not exempt a supply of services which is made by a person who does not have any interest in the immovable property and which consists in the acceptance, for consideration, of an assignment of a lease of that property from the lessee."[48]

In Australia, the ATO issued an elaborate ruling covering the early termination of a lease.[49] The GST consequences depend in part on the reason for the termination. For example, a payment received by the lessor for an early termination of a lease that releases the lessee of its contractual obligations is a supply for consideration and, if connected with Australia, is a taxable supply.[50]

47 *Cantor Fitzgerald*, *supra* note 45.
48 *Id.*, *supra* note 45, at ruling.
49 GSTR 2003/11 (Australia).
50 *Id.* at ¶28.

C. Mixed Business–Personal Use and Change in Use

The following *Armbrecht* case, decided by the ECJ, involved the sale of a building used by the owner in part for business and in part as a private residence. He treated the residential portion as nonbusiness property. As a result, he did not charge rent and did not claim credit for input VAT on that portion of the property.

Finanzamt Uelzen v. Armbrecht[51]

HEADNOTE. The taxpayer, a hotelier, owned a building comprising a guest house, a restaurant and premises used as a private dwelling which he sold in 1981 for DM 1715m. German law exempted such a transaction from value added tax (VAT) pursuant to [Article 135(1)(j) of the VAT Directive], but also granted to taxable persons the right to opt for taxation on the transaction pursuant to [Article 137(1)(b) of the VAT Directive] where the transfer was made to another trader for the purposes of his business. The taxpayer opted for taxation on the transaction, but regarded only the sale of that part of the property which was used for business purposes as subject to VAT and accordingly invoiced the purchaser for [13%] VAT only on that part. Following an inspection, the tax office [took the position] ... that the taxpayer's property formed a single item in German civil law and should be treated as such for the application of the [VAT] Directive. The taxpayer challenged that decision in proceedings before the finance court, Lower Saxony, which allowed his appeal. The tax office appealed to the Bundesfinanzhof (the federal finance court), which stayed the proceedings and referred to the [ECJ the question of] ... whether the portion of an immovable property used for business purposes constituted a separate item of supply for the purposes of [Article 14 (1) of the VAT Directive].

DECISION: ...

The German government stresses that the taxpayer's property forms a single item in German civil law and is entered as such in the land register. It should therefore be treated as a single item for the application of the [VAT] Directive.

It is true that [Article 14(1) of the VAT Directive] does not define the extent of the property rights transferred, which must be determined in accordance with the applicable national law, but the court has held that the objective of the [VAT] Directive, which is to base the common system of VAT on a uniform definition of taxable transactions, would be jeopardised if the preconditions for a supply of goods, which is

[51] Case C–291 /92, ECR I–2775 (Judgment of the ECJ 1995) [hereinafter *Armbrecht*] [edited by the authors].

one of the three taxable transactions, varied from one member state to another. …

Consequently, the national law applicable in the main proceedings cannot provide the answer to the question raised, which concerns not the civil law applicable to supply but whether the transaction is subject to the tax.

The first question must therefore be understood as seeking to ascertain whether, where a taxable person sells property, part of which he had chosen to reserve for his private use, he acts with respect to the sale of that part as a taxable person within the meaning of [Article 2(1)(a) of the VAT Directive].

It is clear from the wording of [Article 2(1)(a) of the VAT Directive] that a taxable person must act 'as such' for a transaction to be subject to VAT.

A taxable person performing a transaction in a private capacity does not act as a taxable person. A transaction performed by a taxable person in a private capacity is not, therefore, subject to VAT.

Nor is there any provision in the [VAT] Directive which precludes a taxable person who wishes to retain part of an item of property amongst his private assets from excluding it from the VAT system.

This interpretation makes it possible for a taxable person to choose whether or not to integrate into his business, for the purposes of applying the [VAT] Directive, part of an asset which is given over to his private use. That approach concurs with one of the basic principles of the [VAT] Directive, namely that a taxable person must bear the burden of VAT only when it relates to goods or services which he uses for private consumption and not for his taxable business activities

As Advocate General Jacobs pointed out …, apportionment between the part allocated to the taxable person's business activities and the part retained for private use must be based on the proportions of private and business use in the year of acquisition. … The taxable person must, moreover, throughout his period of ownership of the property in question, demonstrate an intention to retain part of it amongst his private assets.

The right of option provided for in art [137], whilst making it possible to transform an exempted transaction into a taxable transaction and entitling the taxpayer to deduct input tax, does not enable a supply which does not fall within the scope of the tax as defined in the [VAT] Directive to be transformed into a taxable supply.

The answer to the first question must therefore be that, where a taxable person sells property part of which he had chosen to reserve for his private use, he does not act with respect to the sale of that part as a taxable person within the meaning of [Article 2(1)(c) of the VAT Directive].[52]

[The taxpayer prevailed.]

[52] This decision is consistent with *Stirling v. Commissioners of Customs and Excise* (1985) 2 BVC 205, excerpted in Chapter 4.

Contrary to the facts in the *Armbrecht* case, a taxable business in the EU may construct a building and treat the entire building as a business asset, even though a portion of the building is used for private residential purposes. What are the VAT consequences on the sale of that building?

In the EU, a taxable person can treat capital goods used both for business and private purposes as business goods and claim deductions for input tax on the acquisition of those goods.[53] The private use of the goods by the taxable person or his staff for nonbusiness purposes then becomes a supply of services for consideration equal to the *cost* of providing the services.[54]

In *Wolfgang Seeling v. Finanzamt Starnberg*,[55] the owner of a tree-surgery business constructed a building that he treated wholly as a business asset and used partly as a private residence, deducted all input tax on the building, and treated the personal use as taxable. Germany denied input tax on the personal use portion of the building, claiming that it was used for exempt "leasing or letting of immovable property." According to the ECJ:

> The letting of immovable property for the purposes of [Article 135(1)(l) of the VAT Directive] essentially involves the landlord of property assigning to the tenant, in return for rent and for an agreed period, the right to occupy his property and to exclude other persons from it.
>
> The private use by the taxable person of a dwelling in a building which he has treated as forming, in its entirety, part of the assets of his business does not satisfy those conditions.
>
> It is a feature of such use not only that no rent is paid but also that there is no genuine agreement on the duration of the right of enjoyment or the right of occupation of the dwelling, or to exclude third parties.
>
> It follows that the private use by the taxable person of a dwelling in a building which he has treated as forming, in its entirety, part of the assets of his business does not fall within [Article 135(1)(l) of the VAT Directive].[56]

There may be special rules for change in use of real property. For example, the United Kingdom zero-rates supplies of real property used for residential purposes and certain charitable purposes. If the use of the property changes within ten years, there is a self-supply. Thus, if a charity constructs a building, which is zero-rated, and within ten years changes the use to a business purpose, the change in use is treated as a taxable supply. This means that the charity is liable for output tax, but there is a corresponding input tax. If the business use is fully taxable, the two cancel each other out. If the business use is fully or partially exempt, the output tax will exceed the input tax credit allowed.[57]

53 See *Armbrecht*, *supra* note 51.

54 See VAT Directive, *supra* note 17, at Art. 26(1)(a), 75; Case C-97–90, *Lennartz v Finanzamt Muchen III*, [1991] ECR I-3795.

55 Case C-269/00, [2003] ECR I-04101.

56 *Id.* at ¶¶49–52, and Operative part (footnotes omitted).

57 See "Changing the Use or Disposing of Certificated Buildings," VCONST 21600, Her Majesty's Revenue and Customs Web site; VATA 1994, *supra* note 38, at Schedule 10; http://www.legislation.gov.uk/ukpga/1994/23/contents.

D. Tax-Motivated Transactions

To claim credit for input tax on real property that is, in substance, used in making exempt supplies, a taxpayer may engage in tax-avoidance motivated transactions designed to convert the real property into an asset used in making taxable supplies. For a detailed analysis of tax avoidance transactions, see Chapter 10. In one case, a British university leased newly renovated university buildings and then leased them back and opted to be taxable on the lease to claim credit for input tax on the renovations. A companion case involved a lease by a bank, designed to get around the fact that the bank would not have been entitled to input credit for construction costs. In judgments by the ECJ in the *University of Huddersfield* and *Halifax* cases discussed in Chapter 10, the court first rejected the argument that no input credit should be allowed in the case of transactions carried out solely to obtain a tax advantage, because such transactions should not be considered as carried out in the scope of economic activity (this part of the opinion is omitted). The court went on to rule that a taxable person is not entitled to deduct input VAT if the transactions constitute an abusive practice; in that case, the transactions can be restructured to eliminate the abuse practice. This important case established that the concept of abuse of rights applies for purposes of EU VAT law.

E. Interaction of Provisions

The following case illustrates the complex interaction of EU rules on real property, in a situation that at first glance seems fairly simple (a municipality that leases out sporting fields to several sports associations paid to have the fields covered with an artificial surface).

Staatssecretaris van Financiën v. Gemeente Vlaardingen,[58]

Judgment

Legal context

European Union ('EU') law

The Sixth Directive was repealed, with effect from 1 January 2007, by Council Directive 2006/112/EC of 28 November 2006 on the common system of value added tax (OJ 2006 L 347, p. 1). However, given the material time in relation to the facts, the main proceedings remain governed by the Sixth Directive.

[58] Case C-299/11 (ECJ 2012) [edited by the authors].

Under Article 2 of the Sixth Directive:

'The following shall be subject to [VAT]:

1. the supply of goods or services effected for consideration within the territory of the country by a taxable person acting as such;
2. the importation of goods.'

Article 4 of the Sixth Directive provided:

'1. "Taxable person" shall mean any person who independently carries out in any place any economic activity specified in paragraph 2 …
2. The economic activities referred to in paragraph 1 shall comprise all activities of producers, traders and persons supplying services …. The exploitation of tangible or intangible property for the purpose of obtaining income therefrom on a continuing basis shall also be considered an economic activity.
3. Member States may also treat as a taxable person anyone who carries out, on an occasional basis, a transaction relating to the activities referred to in paragraph 2 and in particular one of the following:
   (a) the supply before first occupation of buildings or parts of buildings and the land on which they stand; Member States may determine the conditions of application of this criterion to transformations of buildings and the land on which they stand.

Member States may apply criteria other than that of first occupation ….

"A building" shall be taken to mean any structure fixed to or in the ground;

   (b) the supply of building land.

"Building land" shall mean any unimproved or improved land defined as such by the Member States. …'

Title V of the Sixth Directive was entitled 'Taxable transactions' and comprised Articles 5 to 7 of that directive, respectively entitled 'Supply of goods', 'Supply of services' and 'Imports'.

Article 5 of the Sixth Directive was worded as follows:

'1. "Supply of goods" shall mean the transfer of the right to dispose of tangible property as owner. …
5. Member States may consider the handing over of certain works of construction to be supplies within the meaning of paragraph 1. …
7. Member States may treat as supplies made for consideration:
   (a) the application by a taxable person for the purposes of his business of goods produced, constructed, extracted, processed,

purchased or imported in the course of such business, where the [VAT] on such goods, had they been acquired from another taxable person, would not be wholly deductible;

(b) the application of goods by a taxable person for the purposes of a non-taxable transaction, where the [VAT] on such goods became wholly or partly deductible upon their acquisition or upon their application in accordance with subparagraph (a);

(c) except in those cases mentioned in paragraph 8, the retention of goods by a taxable person or his successors when he ceases to carry out a taxable economic activity where the [VAT] on such goods became wholly or partly deductible upon their acquisition or upon their application in accordance with subparagraph (a).'

Article 11 of the Sixth Directive provided:

'A. Within the territory of the country

1. The taxable amount shall be: …

(b) in respect of supplies referred to in Article 5(6) and (7), the purchase price of the goods or of similar goods or, in the absence of a purchase price, the cost price, determined as the time of supply; …'

Under Article 13(B) of the Sixth Directive:

'… Member States shall exempt …

(g) the supply of buildings or parts thereof, and of the land on which they stand, other than as described in Article 4(3)(a);

(h) the supply of land which has not been built on other than building land as described in Article 4(3)(b).'

Article 18 and Article 74 of Directive 2006/112 correspond, in essence, to Article 5(7) and Article 11(A)(1)(b) of the Sixth Directive.

Dutch law

Article 3 of the 1968 Law on Turnover Tax (Wet op de Omzetbelasting 1968), in the version applicable in the case before the referring court ('the Wet OB') is set out as follows:

'1. "Supply of goods" shall mean: …

(c) the supply of immovable properties by those who produced them with the exception of land which has not been built on other than building land …

(h) the use for business purposes of goods produced in-house in cases where, had the goods been acquired from a trader, the tax on the goods would not have been deductible or would not have been wholly deductible; goods which are produced to order, with the materials, including land, being provided, shall be treated as goods produced in-house; excluded from the application of this subsection is land which has not been built on other than building land ...'

Article 8(3) of the Wet OB states:

'With regard to the supply of goods as described in Article 3(1)(g) and (h), ... the consideration shall be the amount, exclusive of turnover tax, which would have to be paid for the goods if, at the time of supply, they were to be acquired or produced in the condition in which they are at that time.'

The dispute in the main proceedings and the question referred for a preliminary ruling

Vlaardingen owns a sports complex which includes a number of open air pitches. It rents out those pitches to sports associations, applying the VAT exemption laid down for such associations.

During 2003, Vlaardingen instructed contractors to cover the sports pitches, the surface of which was natural grass, with an artificial surface. After the completion of that work in 2004, Vlaardingen continued to rent out the same pitches, exempt from VAT, to the sports associations which had rented them previously.

After paying the invoices for that work, which amounted in total to EUR 1 547 440, including VAT in the amount of EUR 293 993, Vlaardingen was ineligible for a deduction of that VAT, as its activity in relation to the pitches at issue – namely, their renting out to sports associations – was exempt from VAT.

Following an audit of Vlaardingen's tax situation, the competent authority issued it with a notice of assessment, in respect of VAT for the year 2004, in the amount of EUR 116 099. According to that authority, Vlaardingen's application of the pitches at issue for its rental activity should be regarded as 'the use for business purposes of ... goods which are produced to order, with the materials, including land, being provided' within the meaning of Article 3(1)(h) of the Wet OB.

For the purposes of calculating VAT, the competent authority took into account both the costs of the transformation of the sports pitches concerned and the value of the ground on which those pitches lay:

Costs of transformation of the pitches: 1 547 440
Value of the ground: + EUR 610 940
Taxable amount: EUR 2 158 380
VAT at 19% on EUR 2 158 380: EUR 410 092
Deduction of VAT paid for the transformation: EUR 293 993
VAT payable: EUR 116 099.
Vlaardingen contested that levy ...

The Hoge Raad der Nederlanden (Supreme Court of the Netherlands) decided to stay the proceedings and to refer the following question to the Court of Justice for a preliminary ruling:

'Must Article 5(7)(a) of the Sixth Directive, read in conjunction with Article 5(5) and Article 11(A)(1)(b) of the Sixth Directive, be interpreted as meaning that, upon the occupation of immovable property by a taxable person for exempt purposes, a Member State may charge VAT in a case where:

- that immovable property consists of a (building) work completed on the taxable person's own land and to his own order by a third person for consideration, and
- that land was previously used by the taxable person for (the same) exempt business purposes, and the taxable person did not previously enjoy a VAT deduction in respect of that same land,

with the result that (the value of that) same land becomes included in the VAT charge?'

Consideration of the question referred for a preliminary ruling

As is apparent from the order for reference, the sports pitches at issue in the case before the referring court are owned by Vlaardingen and rented out by it to sports associations. That rental activity is an economic activity which is exempt from VAT.

It is also established that the supply of transformation works in respect of those pitches led to VAT being levied on that supply, payable by Vlaardingen. Without it being necessary to know whether that tax was levied pursuant to the rule laid down in Article 5(5) of the Sixth Directive or rather pursuant to one of the other rules laid down in that directive, it emerges in any event from the documents before the Court that the levying of that VAT – the legality of which, moreover, Vlaardingen does not dispute – did not primarily come about as a result of applying the option, available under Article 5(7)(a) of the Sixth Directive, of treating certain applications of goods as supplies made for consideration.

The option provided for under Article 5(7)(a) of the Sixth Directive did, on the other hand, lead to an assessment – disputed by Vlaardingen – according to which Vlaardingen had to pay, in addition to the VAT relating to the supply of transformation works in respect of its sports pitches, VAT relating to the value of the ground on which those pitches lie.

Consequently, the question referred must be construed as seeking to ascertain whether Article 5(7)(a) of the Sixth Directive, read in conjunction with Article 11(A)(1)(b) of that directive, must be interpreted as meaning that the application by a taxable person, for the purposes of an economic activity exempt from VAT, of sports pitches which he owns and which he has had transformed by a third person, can be subject to VAT calculated on the basis of the aggregate arrived at by adding to the transformation costs the value of the ground on which the pitches lie.

Article 5(7)(a) of the Sixth Directive concerned situations in which the mechanism for deduction provided for, by way of a general rule, under the Sixth Directive could not apply. In so far as goods are used for the purposes of an economic activity which is subject to output tax, it is necessary to deduct the input tax on those goods in order to avoid double taxation. On the other hand, where goods acquired by a taxable person are used for the purposes of transactions which are exempt, no input tax can be deducted. … As the Netherlands Government and the Commission pointed out, one of the situations concerned by Article 5(7)(a) of the Sixth Directive was that in which no deduction can be made, from the output VAT charged, of an amount paid by way of input VAT, since the output economic activity was exempt from VAT.

In particular, … Article 5(7)(a) of the Sixth Directive allowed Member States to develop their tax law in such a way that businesses which, owing to the fact that they are engaged in an activity which is exempt from VAT, cannot deduct the VAT that they have paid on acquiring their business goods are not placed at a disadvantage as compared with competitors engaged in the same activity who use goods which they have obtained without paying VAT, by producing the goods themselves or, more generally, by obtaining them 'in the course of [their] business'. In order to make those competitors subject to the same tax burden as businesses which have acquired their goods from a third party, Article 5(7)(a) of the Sixth Directive gave Member States the option of treating the application, for the purposes of the exempt activities of the business, of goods obtained in the course of business as a supply of goods made for consideration within the meaning of Article 2(1) and Article 5(1) of the Sixth Directive, and of making that application subject to VAT.

In order for it to be possible for that option, which was reproduced in Article 18 of Directive 2006/112, to be used in a way which truly eliminates all inequalities, in relation to VAT, between taxable persons who have acquired their goods from another taxable person and those who have acquired them in the course of their business, the terms 'goods produced, constructed, extracted, processed, … in the course of such business' must be construed – as the Netherlands Government and the Commission argue – as covering not only goods entirely produced, constructed, extracted or processed by the business concerned itself, but also goods constructed, extracted or processed by a third party with materials provided by that business.

A taxable person who, for the purposes of an activity exempt from VAT, applies goods which he owns and which he has had completed or improved by a third party could – but for the treatment option provided for under Article 5(7)(a) of the Sixth Directive – find himself in a situation in which only the work carried out by that third party would be subject to VAT. In order for such a taxable person to be subject, consistently with the aim of Article 5(7)(a), to the same tax burden as competitors who carry out the same exempt activity using goods which they have acquired in their entirety from a third party, it must be possible for the treatment option available under that provision to be extended to all goods completed or improved by the third party and, accordingly, to cause VAT to be levied on the basis of the overall value of those goods.

Consequently, it is open to the authorities of a Member State which makes use of the option available under Article 5(7)(a) of treating certain applications of goods as supplies made for consideration to hold that the tax burden, in terms of VAT, on a taxable person who rents out to sports associations pitches which it has had covered with an artificial surface must be at the same level as it would be for a competitor who rents out to sports associations pitches covered with artificial surfaces which have been purchased in their entirety from a third party.

In that case, those authorities must, in accordance with the rule laid down in Article 11(A)(1)(b) of the Sixth Directive, which has been reproduced in Article 74 of Directive 2006/112, calculate the VAT payable by that taxable person on the basis of a value which is determined at the time when the transformed sports pitches are applied – that is to say, at the time when they are put to use for the purposes of the exempt activity – and which corresponds to the market price for sports pitches of similar location, size and surface to the pitches at issue. In the light of those criteria, the aggregate of the value of the ground on which the pitches concerned lie and the cost of transforming those pitches may constitute an appropriate basis of assessment.

That being so, a taxation mechanism of that design cannot give rise to breach of the principles laid down in relation to VAT, which must at all times – including, therefore, when use is made of the treatment option referred to above – be respected by the Member State concerned.

In that regard, … the option of treating certain applications as supplies made for consideration, as interpreted above, cannot be used in order to charge VAT on the value of goods which the taxable person concerned has made available to the third party who completed or improved them, to the extent that the taxable person has already, in the context of an earlier tax period, paid VAT on that value. As the Commission stated, such repeated taxation would be incompatible both with the essential characteristic of VAT, referred to above, and with the aim of the above option, which is intended to enable Member States to make subject to VAT the application of goods for the purposes of activities exempt from VAT, but in no way authorises Member States to levy VAT several times on the same element of the value of those goods.

In the present case, it is for the referring court to ascertain whether, prior to the assessment at issue in the main proceedings, Vlaardingen had paid VAT on the value of the ground on which the sports pitches lie. If it transpires that this is indeed the position, it would have to be found that an assessment such as that made in Vlaardingen's case, in so far as it is based on the overall value of that land, goes beyond the option provided for in Article 5(7)(a) of the Sixth Directive and conflicts with the broad logic of that directive.

If it transpires that Vlaardingen had not, prior to the assessment at issue in the main proceedings, paid VAT on the value of the ground on which its sports pitches lie, it would also be necessary, before the VAT payable in accordance with that assessment could be declared compatible with Article 5(7)(a) of the Sixth Directive, to check that those pitches are not covered by the exemption provided for in Article 13(B)(h) of the Sixth Directive.

Under Article 13B(h) of the Sixth Directive, the supply of land which has not been built on, other than building land as described in Article 4(3)(b) of that directive, is exempt from VAT.

Accordingly, it is only if the sports pitches at issue in the main proceedings can be categorised as land which has been built on, or as building land within the meaning of Article 4(3)(b), that VAT would be payable on their application for the purposes of the business. It is sufficient to note in that regard that, where, pursuant to the option available under Article 5(7)(a) of the Sixth Directive, the application for the purposes of the business of land which is neither 'built-on-land' nor 'building land' is treated as a supply of that land made for consideration, that treatment causes Article 13(B)(h) of the Sixth Directive to apply, with the result that no VAT may be levied.

In the present case, it is for the referring court to check whether the application for the purposes of the business of sports pitches covered with an artificial surface may legitimately be treated as a supply of 'built-on-land' or 'building land'.

In the light of the foregoing, the answer to the question referred is that Article 5(7)(a) of the Sixth Directive, read in conjunction with Article 11(A)(1)(b) of that directive, must be interpreted as meaning that the application by a taxable person, for the purposes of an economic activity exempt from VAT, of sports pitches which he owns and which he has had transformed by a third person, can be subject to VAT calculated on the basis of the aggregate arrived at by adding to the transformation costs the value of the ground on which the pitches lie, to the extent that the taxable person has not yet paid the VAT relating to that value or to those costs, and provided that the pitches at issue are not covered by the exemption provided for in Article 13(B)(h) of the Sixth Directive.

IV. Proposals for the Taxation of Real Property

The following represents only a sample of the proposals on how real property should be treated under a VAT. Robert Conrad proposed that tax be imposed on all sales of new and used real property, with taxable purchasers eligible to claim input credits for VAT paid on the purchase. Except for a possible small business exemption, real estate agents and construction firms are taxable. Durable goods (such as refrigerators) should be taxed when sold for home improvement or home construction. Rentals should be taxed when provided by a taxable person. The first non-taxable purchaser (such as a consumer) bears the tax, which serves as a prepayment of future taxes, whether the future use is for investment or consumption. On resale, the non-taxable seller is expected to recover from the purchaser any remaining balance of the prepaid taxes. Any resale back to a taxable person triggers a restart of the input credit system.[59]

The model act developed by the American Bar Association Section of Taxation Committee on Value Added Tax taxes a broad range of transactions involving real property.[60] For administrative reasons, the committee decided not to tax the imputed rental value of home ownership. The committee compromise was to require a taxable person to charge VAT on sales, leases, and resales of land and improvements. A taxable person who sells or leases real property for residential or other nonbusiness purposes must charge VAT on those transactions, and the buyer or tenant cannot claim input credit for tax paid on the purchase or rental payments. A taxable person who purchases commercial real property can claim credit for tax on the purchase and must charge VAT on rentals. The model act includes an unusual provision that taxes casual sales by sellers who are not taxable persons, if the sales price exceeds the statutory threshold set for high-priced casual sales. To prevent the double taxation of real property disposed of in a casual sale, the model act provides a deferred credit for the tax paid when the property was acquired.[61]

The commentary to the American Bar Association Section of Taxation Model Act makes a novel recommendation to classify property, such as raw land, as property acquired for investment and therefore eligible for input credits. According to the commentary, special treatment can be provided for "investment assets placed in an investment custody account (ICA) if the investor's interest in the assets is limited to an intangible right to an investment return and the investor cannot obtain possession of

[59] See, generally, on VAT and real estate, R. Conrad, "The VAT and Real Estate," in *Value Added Taxation in Developing Countries* 95–103 (M. Gillis, C. Shoup, & G. Sicat, eds., World Bank 1990). See especially his discussion of Stock Value Added Tax (S-VAT) at 98–99.

[60] See A. Schenk, reporter, VALUE ADDED TAX: A MODEL STATUTE AND COMMENTARY, A REPORT OF THE COMMITTEE ON VALUE ADDED TAX OF THE AMERICAN BAR ASSOCIATION SECTION OF TAXATION 72–79 (American Bar Association 1989).

[61] *Id.* at 78.

the property."[62] The ICA would resemble a trust similar to an individual retirement account, but subject to income tax. VAT-able sales to an ICA trustee would be treated like purchases by a taxable business in connection with taxable activity and therefore eligible for an input tax credit. For example, if the trustee leases real estate placed in an ICA, the rents would be taxable as sales made in connection with business, and the input tax on the purchase of the property would be claimed as input credit. VAT would be imposed on any sale of the investment property or distribution of the property to the investor.

The Basic World Tax Code developed by the Harvard International Tax Program taxes a wide range of transactions involving immovable property within the VAT base.[63] All sales of immovable property are taxed, even if the sale is made by a consumer or the sale is not in the ordinary course of business. A taxable person is entitled to claim an input credit for tax on taxable purchases of immovable property if the property is used in connection with business. To prevent double taxation in the case of taxable sales of immovable property between non-taxable persons, the purchaser can claim a VAT refund to the extent the purchaser can establish the amount of tax previously paid on the sale to his seller. The code follows the common practice of taxing business leases and exempting nonbusiness leases; thus, input credit is allowed for tax paid on business leases but not for any VAT buried in the rent charged on nonbusiness leases.

Sijbren Cnossen supports the approach that fully taxes real property, including the rental value of owner-occupied housing.[64] He acknowledges the practical problems associated with the taxation of owner-occupied housing and notes that, if the residential rentals are taxed and the rental value of owner-occupied housing is exempt, home ownership is favored over residential rentals. The difficulty in taxing imputed rental led most countries to tax new construction and exempt residential rentals.[65] In an attempt to reduce the tax burden on housing occupied by low-income households, some countries exempt sales of small housing units.[66] For ease of administration, Cnossen suggests that all construction activity (including repairs and maintenance) should be taxed at a single rate.[67]

62 *Id.* at 182–184.

63 See excerpts from the Value Added Tax Law and Commentary portion of the Basic World Tax Code, 1996 edition, 123 and 289. The commentary criticizes the approach in some countries that exempt land and buildings but impose "high, cascading transfer taxes" instead. *Id.* at 289.

64 See Cnossen, *supra* note 1.

65 *Id.* at 242.

66 Turkey "exempt units up to 150 square meters. Presumably, some families are then tempted to buy two units and subsequently connect them." *Id.* at 242.

67 *Id.* at 245. Some countries do not follow this practice. For example, Ireland imposes a low rate on concrete; Italy taxes materials for the construction industry and repairs on old buildings at a low rate. The United Kingdom rules are even more inconsistent. Construction is taxed, but sales of new residential property is zero-rated, so allocation problems exist when renovation of a home is combined with the construction of a new adjoining structure. *Id.* at 239.

Cnossen's "second-best solution" includes the taxation of newly created houses, the exemption of residential rentals, and the exemption of housing services and sales of existing housing. Commercial sales and rentals of immovable property other than housing should be taxed. He opposes preferential rates because of the distortions and administrative complications they cause. Sales and leases of the same kind of property by the same kind of seller should be taxed alike. Cnossen recommends the abolition of transfer taxes on immovable property in the countries employing them and he recommends that they be replaced with a VAT.

Wei Cui has argued that the current practice of not taxing initial housing stock on introduction of a VAT and not taxing resales of residential housing is consistent with economic efficiency.[68] This is because if tax were imposed on the initial stock or on resales, this would simply result in imposing a burden on owners of housing, rather than affecting consumer prices, which are the relevant factor in evaluating whether VAT rules result in distortion of consumption. Under this argument, the approach taken by "modern" VATs under which new residential sales are taxed and commercial real estate sales or rentals are taxed but resales of previously occupied residential housing are not taxed is broadly appropriate.

V. Discussion Questions

1. Under the Basic World Tax Code or ABA Model approach to applying VAT to real estate, does every lessor (landlord) of rented property become a VAT taxpayer? Under the VAT Directive [previously Sixth Directive], does every seller of real estate collect and pay over VAT? What exceptions and why? How does the New Vatopia VAT handle real property?
2. How should a VAT treat the investment component of residential property as distinguished from the consumption component?
3. Suppose that A, the buyer of a new home, is required to pay VAT on the full price of land and building at the time of purchase. Suppose, further, that after ten years A resells the home to B at a greater price than A paid. What VAT consequences follow under the ABA Model? Under Conrad's S-VAT? Under the VAT Directive? What is the proper treatment in your view?
4. Many existing VATs around the world apply VAT to short-term rentals of living space – that is, hotels and other short-term lodging charges – but not to long-term residential rentals – that is, more than thirty, sixty, or ninety days. Can this be justified other than on the grounds of political or administrative expediency?
5. Does the purchase or rental of real estate by a business firm typically give rise to a VAT input credit? Even if the firm's output (or some of it) is exempt or zero-rated?

[68] W. Cui, "Objections to Taxing Resale of Residential Property under a VAT," 137 *Tax Notes* 777 (2012).

6. Consider the following proposal in conjunction with the ABA's proposed Investment Custody Account that would allow consumers who purchase investments to transfer those investments into a trust or similar account and thereby become eligible to claim credit for the input tax on such purchases. Homeowners would be allowed to put newly purchased homes into investment custody accounts. The trustee could rent to the owner at a market rent. The trustee would get full input credit and refund after purchase but would collect and pay the government the VAT on each rental payment. Is this proposal analytically sound? Is it workable?

14 An Anatomy of the Chinese VAT

I. Introduction

In 2013, the VAT in China yielded approximately the equivalent of USD 500 billion for the government, making it very likely the largest VAT in the world in terms of the dollar value of revenue generated. It is, however, not normally regarded as a paragon of VAT design and is perceived not only by international experts but also by Chinese tax policymakers and commentators themselves to be inferior to the VAT regimes adopted in advanced economies. The Chinese government has continuously attempted to "improve" its VAT in the last two decades, sometimes in part (but only in part) to make it conform more to common international practice. In this chapter, we present select aspects of the Chinese VAT, giving special emphasis to those features of it that contradict the normal recommendations for VAT design. We do this for three interrelated reasons.

The first is that many developing and middle-income countries and many transitional economies heavily rely on the VAT for revenue generation.[1] Many of them have "imperfect" VAT systems relative to policies recommended by standard public finance theory and practices adopted in developed countries.[2] However, from a comparative perspective, these systems (especially those found in large countries like China, India, and Brazil) are important in an obvious sense: they shape the understandings of large populations of taxpayers, tax professionals, and tax administrators about what the VAT is. For example, as discussed in this chapter, Chinese VAT taxpayers and tax administrators are accustomed to the fact that no refund for excess input credit will ever be given for domestic

[1] VAT design in developing countries has been the subject of numerous recent studies. See, especially, Richard M. Bird & Pierre-Pascal Gendron, *The VAT in Developing and Transitional Countries* (Cambridge University Press 2007); M. Keen, "What Do (and Don't) We Know about the Value Added Tax?" 47 *Journal of Economic Literature* 159–170 (Mar. 2009) (review of Bird and Gendron); and M. Keen, "Taxation and Development – Again," IMF Working Papers 12/220, International Monetary Fund (2012), and the works cited therein.

[2] For tax policy purists, they are even more "impure" than the impure, real-world VAT systems observed in advanced economies.

supplies. (The difficulty of issuing VAT refunds will resonate as a critical issue for those dealing with VATs in many, if not most, developing countries.) They also seem content with the absence of the concept of economic or business activity, supposedly central to the VAT laws of other countries. Relative to conventional portrayals of the VAT, these and other features of the Chinese VAT look quite unusual. However, it is useful for our comparative study to reflect some of this diversity of VAT law and design. Moreover, we may conclude, after careful analysis, that some of the supposedly "inferior" features of an impure VAT do not make enough of a difference in practice.

The second reason is that some aspects of VAT design that are infrequently discussed in the context of advanced economies take on greater importance in a less developed country like China. A clear example is the challenge of VAT administration in which the audit capacity is low and the risk of criminal VAT fraud high. Another is the taxation of small businesses falling below the VAT threshold. Yet, a third example is managing VAT policy transitions in which a government is continuously trying to "improve" its imperfect VAT. This chapter does not attempt to treat all these important topics but will try to convey a sense of the range of interesting issues that VAT law may be called on to address outside the developed country context.

Third and perhaps most controversially, some apparently unique features of the Chinese VAT are still understudied and poorly understood. One example is the adjustments of the rates of VAT refunds for hundreds of categories of exported products. Another is the adoption of the Golden Tax Project for VAT administration. These institutions have large impacts on the Chinese economy (and sometimes on world markets) and therefore have become the object of study by social scientists who are not tax specialists. VAT specialists, on the other hand, have tended to dismiss these institutions (without having undertaken much study) because they deviate from best VAT practice. This situation is awkward. This chapter thus presents some of these controversies in scholarly research.

II. Complementary Tax Base with a Turnover Tax on Services

The introduction of the VAT to China has been remarkably gradual. An early "value-added tax" was adopted for select manufactured goods in 1984 (when socialist economic planning still dominated the urban sector) and was so called only because it contrasted with the turnover taxes that had previously applied to such goods. A broader VAT came into effect in 1994 and applied to the sale of all goods except for intangible and immovable property, as well as to the provision of processing, repair, and replacement services. Very soon, this regime (call it "VAT Regime I") became the largest source of revenue for the government. However, it was not a comprehensive VAT, because a separate turnover tax, the Business Tax (BT), applied to the provision of other services and transfers of intangibles and immovable properties. Nor was the VAT (even where it was applicable) a "value added tax" in the normal sense of the term, because input tax on fixed asset purchases was not creditable against tax on output. This type of VAT was known in China as the "production-type" VAT, the idea being roughly that gross domestic production (of the VAT-able sectors), instead of domestic consumption (of VAT-able goods), formed the base of the VAT.[3]

VAT Regime I was replaced in 2009 as a result of a tax reform prompted by the global financial crisis:[4] input tax on fixed asset purchases became creditable. Under this new system (VAT Regime II), the co-existence of the VAT and the BT became the foremost difference between China's VAT and the comprehensive VAT on goods and services found in other countries. This coexistence of the VAT and a turnover tax that has its own large tax base has had a significant impact on the Chinese VAT. It means, for example, that breaks in the VAT chain are systematic and that incentives to join the VAT network so as to be able to pass on the input VAT credits are diminished. It also makes the analysis of the incidence of the VAT, as well as the design of quantitative measures of the performance of the VAT that have any economic significance, very difficult.

The Chinese Business Tax itself constitutes a remarkable system. For one, it applies to many of the sectors that were traditionally exempt from the VAT in European VAT systems, for example, financial services (including bank lending and various forms of insurance), the sale and rental of residential property, health care, and education. Although similar to VAT exemptions in that it breaks VAT chains, the BT directly collects a substantial amount of revenue (approximately USD 280 billion in 2013[5]). Clearly, the BT has a much broader base than most sales taxes or other turnover taxes found in other countries. The BT also applies to the cross-border flow of services.[6] In certain BT-able sectors of the Chinese economy, such as transportation and construction, where subcontracting is common and

[3] However, even VAT Regime I was more destination-based than it was origin-based in its international aspects. Given that as well as the regime's limited coverage, the term "production-type" VAT is more suggestive than it is an accurate description. Some have also claimed that VAT Regime I was of an income type. See J. Whalley & L. Wang, "Evaluating the Impure Chinese VAT Relative to a Pure Form in a Simple Monetary Trade Model with an Endogenous Trade Surplus," in *China's Integration Into the World Economy* (John Whalley, ed., World Scientific 2013)

[4] See W. Cui, "China's Tax Policy Response to the Global Financial Crisis," in *China and the Global Economic Crisis: A Comparison with Europe* 84–98 (J.P. Cabestan et al., eds., Routledge 2012).

[5] This may make the BT itself the second largest indirect tax in the world in terms of revenue yield – coming behind only the Chinese VAT. By comparison, for example, total sales or gross receipts taxes collected in the United States were less than USD 243 billion (see http://www.governing.com/gov-data/state-tax-revenue-data.html).

[6] See Wei Cui, "Taxing Cross-Border Services in China: The (Partial) Switch to Destination-Based Taxation," in *Value Added Tax and Direct Taxation: Similarities and Differences* 323–338 (M. Lang, P. Melz and E. Kristoffersson, IBFD 2009).

therefore "links" in the supply chain dense, the BT has even been designed to approximate a crude value added tax, so as to mitigate the effect of cascading. The Chinese BT thus displays certain superiorities over turnover taxes that were replaced by the VAT in other countries. At the same time, however, it weakens the Chinese VAT by creating pervasive breaks in VAT chains.

In 2011, the Chinese government announced a plan to replace the BT by the VAT in four years, so that a comprehensive VAT would apply to all goods and services by 2016. The manner in which this was to be accomplished was quite idiosyncratic by international standards but not entirely unfamiliar in the realm of Chinese policy implementation.[7] The city of Shanghai was chosen to carry out a "reform pilot" of replacing the BT with the VAT in certain transportation and "modern services" sectors, starting in January 2012. The reform pilot was geographically expanded to eight other provincial-level jurisdictions later in 2012 and to the entire country in the summer of 2013. The scope of the reform pilots (in terms of sectors covered) also slightly expanded in 2013. However, as of the beginning of 2014, the sectors that remain subject to the BT instead of the VAT both are the most important ones in terms of BT revenue historically generated and have the most noticeable effect on ordinary consumers (and therefore have the most political salience). These include residential and commercial real estate, construction, financial services, and many consumer services such as telecommunications, restaurant and hospitality, health care, education, and so on. These unreformed sectors generated more than 80% of BT revenue prior to the launch of the reform pilots. China thus seems destined to operate another interim regime – a "VAT Regime III" – before a comprehensive VAT is established. What is still not clear is how long this transitional regime will last, and what exact shape it will take.

VAT revenue in China is shared 25/75 between subnational governments and the national (central) government, according to where the revenue is collected. The determination of where VAT is payable within China, therefore, also decides which local government gets to take the 25% cut of the VAT. This 25% of VAT revenue is further divided by provincial and sub-provincial governments according to arrangements that vary from province to province. By contrast, BT revenue is almost entirely allocated to local governments and does not constitute a significant source of revenue for the central government. VAT on import is collected by the customs authorities and remitted entirely to the central government's treasury. Local governments, however, are partially responsible for financing VAT export refunds.[8]

Despite revenue sharing for the VAT and the fact that the BT generates revenue primarily for subnational governments, the basic legal frameworks governing the VAT and the BT respectively and the extensive body

[7] For an initial survey, see W. Cui, "China's Business-Tax-to-VAT Reform: An Interim Assessment," forthcoming in *British Tax Review* 2014(5).

[8] At the present, local governments are responsible for 7.5% of VAT refunds.

of administrative guidance implementing these frameworks are adopted at the national level. Provincial governments have discretion in setting VAT and BT rules only with respect to a few isolated, relatively minor items, such as choosing (within a nationally prescribed range) the minimal thresholds falling under which businesses are exempt from the VAT.[9] Sub-provincial governments generally have no discretion whatsoever in altering VAT or BT rules. In other words, the law governing the VAT and the BT is supposed to be uniform across the nation, and whatever variations in local practices there are emerge not as a result of subnational legislation but administratively, within grey areas left by national law. It should also be mentioned that even at the national level, VAT (or BT) law has not been made by the legislature but by the executive branch.[10] Indeed, most substantive rules governing the VAT and BT are set out not even in formal regulations but rather in administrative guidance that, strictly speaking, lack legal effect (i.e., they are not strictly binding on courts).[11]

Finally, it should be mentioned that the division of the Chinese comprehensive indirect tax system into the VAT and the BT has substantially shaped the structure of the Chinese tax administration. This structure itself is composed of two subsystems: the State Tax Bureau system and Local Tax Bureau system. The bulk of the former subsystem's resources is devoted to collecting VAT and the enterprise income tax from enterprises subject to the VAT. By contrast, the BT is the largest source of revenue for the Local Tax Bureau system, which also collects the enterprise income tax from most businesses subject to the BT.

III. Absence of the Business (or Economic) Activity Concept

From a comparative perspective, a notable feature of Chinese VAT law is the (at least apparent) absence of the concept of business (or economic) activity, including from the basic definitions of taxable supplies and taxable persons. As discussed in Chapter 4 (IV), this concept is ordinarily regarded as essential to the basic concept of a taxable person under the VAT: only a person making taxable supplies in connection with a business activity is a taxable person, and only a person engaged in a business activity is required to make a VAT registration. By contrast, under current Chinese VAT law (including regulations and administrative guidance), a taxpayer is simply an individual or organization that makes taxable sales. Individuals or organizations that make taxable sales of de minimis value are exempt from the VAT, and those that make sales of greater

[9] As discussed in Section IV, this is different from the threshold for VAT registration, which is set nationally.

[10] The law governing VAT crimes is an exception: legislative power with respect to criminal law is reserved to the National People's Congress.

[11] See, generally, W. Cui, "What Is the 'Law' in Chinese Tax Administration?" 19*Asia Pacific Law Review* 75–94 (2011).

value but still under the volume required for registration are subject to the simplified collection rules that will be discussed further. However, neither the definition of taxable persons nor the requirements of registration refer to engagements in business activities. Although in 2011, in regulatory guidance issued to govern the replacement of the BT by the VAT in pilot sectors, China introduced the notion of "non-business activities" in the definition of taxable sales for the pilot sectors, the notion still plays a limited, and arguably inessential, role.[12] This raises the question: Is the notion of business (or economic) activity essential to VAT law? If it is, then its absence from Chinese VAT law (at least until recently) must mean that the latter was deficient in some serious ways. What are these deficiencies?

This is an important question to reflect on because the notion of business (or economic) activity may not be amenable to very precise definition, and its consistent application to particular circumstances may depend on the availability of courts capable of setting precedents.[13] However, especially in developing countries (and in those civil law systems where the role of judicial precedents is still limited), the judiciary may be weak or in any case inactive in tax matters. To rely on the judiciary to elaborate on the meaning of a (purportedly) important legal concept may result in too little law, or in inconsistent or unreliable guidance. The reality of this concern is illustrated by the fact that even though Chinese income tax law (like the income tax laws of many other countries) has adopted the business activity concept, and even though the concept is certainly crucial to the income tax, it has received no known judicial interpretation and paltry regulatory guidance.

What could be amiss if a body of VAT law does not employ the concept of business (or economic) activity? That concept arguably plays two fundamental roles: one is determining whether VAT should be charged on a person's sales; the other is determining whether VAT paid on acquisitions can be credited or refunded. In both cases, the business activity

[12] Sales made in "non-business activities" are not taxable sales. The latest version of this provision is found in Art. 9 of the Implementation Measures for the "VAT in lieu of Business Tax" Pilot Reform, which is contained in appendix 1 of Ministry of Finance (MOF) and State Administration of Taxation (SAT), "Notice Regarding the Inclusion of Railway Transportation and Postal Service Industries under 'VAT in lieu of Business Tax' Pilot Reform" (Caishui [2013] No. 106). Nonbusiness activities (*fei yingyexing huodong*) are defined to include: (1) activities by nonbusiness organizations (*fei qiyexing danwei*) that involve collecting special governmental charges and administrative fees, (2) taxable services provided by employees to their organizational or individual proprietor employers; (3) taxable services provided by organizations or individual proprietors to their employees, and (4) other activities to be designated by the MOF and SAT. It should be clear that all of these exclusions from taxable sales could have been made without reference to the notion of business activities.

[13] For a review of case law under the European VAT Directives interpreting the economic activity concept, see Ben Terra & Julie Kajus, "A Guide to the European VAT Directives," 1 IBFD subchapters 9.2, 9.3, and 9.5 (2013). Alternatively, a tax administration that actively issues guidance on the application of the concept to disparate factual circumstances, e.g., through general rulings or published private rulings, is needed.

requirement plays a restrictive function, limiting the scopes of taxable sales and creditable acquisitions. In connection with the first role, it is debatable whether this restrictive function is necessary. In terms of the policy objective of taxing sales to individuals for consumption, a government may want to tax even "personal,"[14] "occasional," or "private" sales.[15] And any sale made to a purchaser for purposes other than consumption and related activities would not result in net taxation, anyway, assuming that the purchaser could claim an input tax credit. This suggests that the restrictive function of the business activity concept in determining taxable sales may be motivated primarily not by considerations of the proper tax base but by administrative considerations: if personal or casual sales were subject to the VAT, the cost of enforcement and compliance would increase, perhaps without a corresponding and sufficient increase in revenue to justify such costs. To put it differently, if taxable sales are not limited to those made in connection with business activities, there would be many taxable sales that taxpayers fail to report and tax agencies fail to monitor.[16]

How severe this administrative problem is may be open to debate. Some of it goes away if the government is willing to set a high enough VAT threshold. As will be discussed, China sets a high threshold for VAT registration but a low threshold for taxability and thus does not mitigate the consequence of not adopting the business activity concept in this manner. Another "solution" is for the government to adopt a clear administrative policy of non-enforcement, which taxpayers are unlikely to challenge. This may raise rule of law concerns, but it has not significantly undermined the operation of even sophisticated tax systems.[17]

The more serious problem of not deploying the business activity concept is likely associated with its function of restricting the claim of input credits. Acquisitions not made in connection with business activities may be used for personal consumption, and clearly one should not allow input credits or refunds for such purchases.[18] The issue here is not just administrative in nature but also a matter of delineating the correct tax base. Not surprisingly, most of the case law discussed in this book involving the application of the "economic activity" concept relates to the creditability/

[14] Consider the U.K. case *Stirling v. Commissioners of Customs and Excise* excerpted in Chapter 4 (IV)(B): a person who is already registered for VAT purposes sells valuable collectibles. Should such a sale not be included in the VAT basis if comprehensive consumption taxation is the goal?

[15] The question here is *whether* to tax such sales. *How* to tax such sales – especially if one wants to ensure that any previous VAT paid is relieved – is a separate matter.

[16] The non-enforcement of legally prescribed VAT obligations, especially if people become widely aware of it, may be undesirable in light of rule-of-law norms.

[17] For a discussion in the income tax context, see L. Zelenak, "Custom and the Rule of Law in the Administration of the Income Tax," 62 *Duke Law Journal* 829–855 (2012).

[18] Here the business activity concept under VAT law is very similar to the same concept used under income tax law, when the latter is used to determine the deductibility of expenses (a basic principle of income taxation is that personal expenses should not be deductible). Both the consumption tax and the income tax need to make the distinction between consumption and non-consumption.

refundability of input taxes. How does China deal with this issue without using the business activity concept?

The answer is twofold. First, a regulation categorically denies the right of individuals who are not registered as sole proprietors to register as "regular taxpayers" (see Section IV in this chapter), which is a prerequisite for claiming input credits. In other words, tax agencies rely on the regulatory apparatus of business registration (as sole proprietors) to determine which individuals may be eligible for input credits. One may argue that this as an implicit use of the business activity concept, instead of an example of its disuse.[19] Second, as discussed further in Section VI (A), at the present China generally does not permit any input tax refund other than in connection with exports. Input tax credit must be carried over and cannot be refunded even when a business liquidates. This means that situations adjudicated in cases like INZO and Rompelmans (discussed in Chapter 4 (IV)(C)), in which input credit arises during a period when a purported business has not yet commenced (or has decided not to commence) full activities would not transpire under the Chinese VAT. Presumably, however, China will abandon this unusual and fundamentally objectionable limitation on the ability to claim input credits/refunds and may therefore face the need to rely on rules that explicitly or implicitly use the business activity concept to a greater extent in the future.

Even so, insofar as the case law in the traditional VAT systems has moved toward a more liberal reading of the "business activity" requirement, so as to permit the claim of input credit in a broader range of cases, the restrictive function of "business activity" concept becomes less important.[20] Suppose that all acquisitions are creditable unless traceable to consumption, hobbies, or other similar personal activities by employees, owners, and so on. Then the restriction on input credit claims can be framed in terms of definitions of consumption or personal activities, without the need of the overarching business or economic activity concept.[21]

IV. The VAT Threshold and Small-Scale Taxpayers

The concept of the "VAT threshold" requires clarification in the Chinese context. What is called the "VAT threshold" under the basic VAT regulation applies only to individuals and not to other taxpayers engaged in

[19] However, note that VAT registration is legally tied to business registration only for individuals. For organizations and entities, there is no such tie. Moreover, it is not clear that the requirements of business registration reflect the concerns of VAT implementation that the "business activity" concept is supposed to reflect.

[20] In EU VAT Case Law 2011–2013 (forthcoming) for more recent EU case law.

[21] In this connection, it can be noted that even now, Chinese VAT law denies input credit for purchases used for individual consumption. Provisional Regulations on the Value Added Tax, Art. 10(1).

taxable sales (i.e., business and nonbusiness organizations) and is generally very low.[22] However, for all taxpayers above the threshold (or to whom the threshold does not apply), there is an important distinction between "regular taxpayers" and "small-scale taxpayers." Regular taxpayers apply the normal VAT and can both claim input credit and issue creditable VAT invoices to other taxpayers. Small-scale taxpayers, by contrast, pay "VAT" pursuant to a "simplified method" – which currently means a turnover tax at 3% – without being able to claim input credit or issue VAT invoices themselves to purchasers.[23] (However, they may request the tax bureau to issue special VAT invoices on their behalf at the 3% rate.) For this reason, one may regard the boundary between "regular taxpayers" and "small-scale taxpayers" as the "VAT threshold" in China.[24]

The choice of terminology aside, China is not unique in separating traders into three groups: the smallest firms that are categorically exempt from the VAT; somewhat larger firms that are subject to a "special regime" intended to generate lower administrative and compliance costs per taxpayer than regular VAT compliance; and a final group of firms that are subject to regular VAT mechanisms. Many other countries adopt some variation of this practice, differing in how the second group is chosen and the design of the "special regime" applicable to that group.[25] Yet this important type of practice has tended to receive only cursory mention in the academic literature. We discuss the following design issues in connection with Chinese rules: (1) who is included in the special regime; (2) the setting of the turnover tax rate; and (3) the overall incentive effects of the system, taking into account the option to register as a regular VAT payer and the ability to issue VAT invoices.

A. The Scope of the Small-Scale Taxpayers Regime

The line between "regular" and "small-scale" taxpayers under the Chinese VAT is drawn in part by the volume of annual sales:

1. For taxpayers either solely engaged in the production of goods or the provision of traditional taxable services,[26] or engaged principally

[22] For sales of goods, the threshold is monthly sales of CNY 5,000; for taxable services, monthly sales of CNY 3,000; and for tax assessed on a per transaction basis, sales per transaction (or per day) of CNY 200. In 2013, in coordination with the reform to replace the BT with the VAT, the monthly threshold was raised for all taxpayers to CNY 20,000. Individuals whose taxable sales fall below these thresholds are exempt from the VAT.

[23] Like other instances of "simplified collection" under the VAT, discussed in Section VII of this chapter, the 3% rate is called a "collection percentage."

[24] See Liam Ebrill et al., *The Modern VAT* 114 (International Monetary Fund 2001).

[25] M. Keen & J. Mintz, "The Optimal Threshold for a Value-Added Tax," 88 *Journal of Public Economics* 559–576 (2004), mentions Tanzania; Bird and Gendron, *supra* note 1, reports "simplified regimes" adopted in Belgium, Canada, France, Hungary, Italy, Korea, Portugal, and Spain.

[26] That is, services (such as repair and installation) that have been subject to the VAT prior to the effort to replace the BT by the VAT that launched in 2012.

(i.e., greater than 50% of annual sales) in the production of goods or provision of taxable services and also partially in the wholesale or retail sale of goods, annual sales of CNY 500,000 (approximately USD 81,967).
2. For taxpayers subject to the BT-to-VAT pilot,[27] annual sales of CNY 5 million (i.e., ten times the sales volume of the preceding category).
3. For other taxpayers, annual sales of CNY 800,000.

Note that the higher thresholds in categories (2) and (3) (non-manufacturing sectors) are contrary to the suggestion of some policy advisors that these sectors may involve higher value added and therefore justify lower thresholds. Another notable feature of the Chinese rules is that the annual sales amount is computed to include not only taxable but also exempt supplies, as well as any amount previously underreported but found under an audit or an assessment.

Individual persons that are not sole proprietors cannot be regular taxpayers even if their annual sales exceed the above amounts. Non-individual taxpayers that are not businesses, as well as businesses that engage in VAT-able transactions only infrequently, may elect to be small-scale taxpayers even if they generate sufficient sales in a year to qualify as regular taxpayers. Thus the category of small-scale taxpayers catches not only small businesses but also persons (individuals or entities) that are either not engaged in business or are engaged in businesses that are not yet subject to the VAT and make casual sales that are subject to the VAT.

Taxpayers with annual sales below the stipulated amounts may apply to be treated as regular taxpayers if they (1) can demonstrate "a sound accounting system" and provide accurate tax information and (2) have a fixed place of business. A person that has been determined to be a regular taxpayer generally may not be reclassified as a small-scale taxpayer.

It has been estimated that, nationally, 83% of VAT taxpayers were small-scale taxpayers.[28] Nonetheless, the amount of "VAT" revenue generated by this large population is small and has shown a consistent decline as a percentage of total domestic VAT revenue – to 2.69% of total VAT revenue in 2011.[29] Presumably, managing 83% of VAT taxpayers absorbs a far greater percentage of administrative resources than 2.69%, and from this perspective proposals that have been advanced within China to abolish the small-scale taxpayer system makes eminent sense. However, as we shall see, matters are more complex.

[27] See Section VIII.

[28] Wang Haiping, "Jiangsu Legislative Proposal: Small-Scale Taxpayer Regime Should Be Abolished in Reform," *21st Century Business Herald*, January 21, 2013.

[29] Computation based on data from the *China Tax Yearbook 2012*. Small-scale taxpayers contributed more than 83% of VAT remittance by sole proprietors.

B. The Setting of Tax Rates for Small-Scale Taxpayers

Before 2009, the VAT rate ("collection percentage") applicable to small-scale taxpayers was 6%.[30] The reduction of the rate to 3% was partially in response to calls by some prominent academics to "reduce the tax burden on medium and small enterprises."[31] Proponents of the reduction argued that the small-scale taxpayers were "discriminated against" relative to regular VAT payers subject to 17% tax on value added. However, it is a complex matter to compare the tax incidence of a low-rate turnover tax with the tax incidence of a VAT (perfect or imperfect). Moreover, at the expense of incurring greater compliance costs, Chinese small-scale taxpayers generally have the option of registering as regular taxpayers and thus avoid "discrimination." Finally, given differences in value added across sectors and firms, only a very low turnover rate can ensure that all small-scale taxpayers' tax remittance (as opposed to the average small-scale taxpayer's tax remittance) is not a greater proportion of their sales than for regular taxpayers. In any case, at the present 3% rate, the tax treatment of small-scale taxpayers is likely to be preferential compared to regular taxpayers. Thus when China lowered the sales volume requirement (i.e., the VAT threshold in the international sense) for regular taxpayer status in 2009, one municipal tax agency reported that only 20% of the businesses newly eligible for such status voluntarily elected such status, whereas 40% actually chose to deregister as business entities (presumably to reincorporate as smaller businesses).[32]

There are indeed a number of reasons for the turnover tax rate for anyone not electing to be a regular VAT payer to be set higher rather than lower. The first is that businesses have the option to register as a regular taxpayer to avoid any "excess" tax burden. Second, an important objective of subjecting small businesses to the turnover tax instead of exempting them altogether is revenue collection. Collecting the turnover tax from these businesses creates administrative and compliance costs, and the lower the VAT rate, the lesser the benefit to the government generated by such a tax.[33] Third, one benefit of imposing a turnover tax on small taxpayers is that it would allow the threshold for regular taxpayers to be set higher (because it compensates the revenue loss from setting the higher threshold).[34] A lower turnover tax rate means that the threshold for regular VAT compliance should also be lower.

30 For business engaged in distribution, this was administratively reduced to 4%, on account of lower average value added.

31 See, e.g., X. Ping et al., "A Study of the Welfare Effects of the VAT and the Business Tax (in Chinese)," 9 *Economic Research* 66–80 (2009).

32 Li Hong (Anyang State Tax Bureau, Henan Province), "Why Some Eligible Small Taxpayers Are Unwilling to Become Regular Taxpayers?" *China Taxation News*, Sept. 1, 2010, p. 7.

33 However, an increased turnover tax rate may increase the administrative cost of collecting it because of greater incentives for tax evasion.

34 Keen & Mintz, *supra* note 26.

Finally, one may even argue that, as a general matter, small businesses tend to display lower productivity, and it is unwise from a social perspective to offer tax preferences to unproductive firms. From this perspective, that small businesses bear proportionately higher tax compliance costs is simply an instance of the general phenomenon that small businesses are unable to benefit from economy of scale, and it is problematic for the government to intervene to subsidize such firms. Conversely, the lower the turnover tax rate applied to small-scale taxpayers, the greater incentive they may have for keeping their production under the regular taxpayer threshold.

C. Overall Incentive Effects

Chinese small-scale taxpayers have the right to request local tax bureaus to issue VAT special invoices to purchasers that reflect the 3% on their sales. Where this request is granted, the small-scale taxpayer is effectively subject to an exemption treatment on the relevant sale (i.e., it is still input-taxed). This treatment, however, is obtained through two additional layers of administrative cost: the cost of collecting the regular turnover tax and the cost for the seller to obtain a VAT invoice and for the purchaser to claim the input credit. Presumably, taxpayers will make this request when they are able to demand a higher VAT-exclusive price than otherwise from purchasers that are regular VAT payers, but only when the additional receipt is of a sufficient amount to justify the additional compliance cost. Consequently, the lower the turnover tax rate, the less frequently small-scale taxpayers would request tax authorities to issue special invoices on their behalf.

In recent years, maintaining the small-scale taxpayer system has been subject to some controversy in China; there have even been government internal proposals to abolish the system. Even though, as mentioned earlier, this seems to make sense from an administrative cost perspective, the behavior of small Chinese businesses under the simplified collection regime seems to suggest reasons for caution. First, small businesses subject to a low turnover tax should be more motivated to register as regular VAT taxpayers than businesses that are exempt. The extent of voluntary registration is not high in China even under the small-scale taxpayer system, and one might predict that voluntary registration would further diminish after the small-scale taxpayer system is abolished. Second, small businesses *already* could have obtained de facto exemption treatment by requesting VAT invoices issued on their behalf, but the level of use of this option appears not to be high, and instead the favored solution to "too high" a turnover tax rate is the legislative lowering of such rates. This may be either because it is administratively onerous to obtain tax invoices from local tax agencies[35] or because small businesses prefer not to report their sales to tax collectors. The latter possibility may confirm the suspicion,

[35] It is not clear how onerous this process truly is, and in any case it is likely to be much less onerous than achieving compliance as regular taxpayers through the Golden Tax Project, discussed in Section V.

held by opponents of the proposal to abolish the small-scale taxpayer system, that small businesses are less compliant than larger taxpayers and it would be unfair to allow them to get away with paying no tax. Finally, the abolition of the turnover tax on small businesses presumably would be accompanied by a lowering of the VAT threshold. This itself could lead to additional administrative and compliance costs, without any significant increase in revenue.

V. VAT Administration through the Golden Tax Project

China has adopted a unique technological system, the Golden Tax Project (GTP), for administering its VAT.[36] This administrative aspect of the Chinese system is arguably as important for understanding the Chinese VAT as recognizing the complementary tax bases of the VAT and the BT. It has had, and will continue to have, immense consequences for the development of the Chinese VAT and the VAT legal issues that arise. For example, the GTP crucially determines what input purchases are creditable (and when). Its administrative and compliance costs also inform the choice of the VAT threshold. The GTP is also extremely controversial. On the one hand, the Chinese government is heavily invested in further improving the system, seeing it as central to the future of Chinese tax administration. The large body of scholarly research in China also tends to endorse the GTP; arguments for its abolition are rare. On the other hand, the GTP has been summarily dismissed by international experts as a pariah in VAT design.[37] In this section, we describe the basic mechanics of the GTP and consider the controversy surrounding its evaluation.

The GTP was first developed in the mid-1990s, in response to rampant VAT frauds and evasion that emerged soon after the implementation of the VAT. Given the geographical and population size of the country, a rapidly changing economy, and the novelty of the VAT, tax agencies across the country found it very difficult to audit taxpayers effectively to prevent fraud and evasion. One instrument the government immediately adopted for dealing with this problem was criminal law, with high criminal penalties (including the death sentence) imposed on violations that involved only moderate amounts of tax evaded or defrauded. The other instrument

36 The development of the GTP has had several phases. The current, third phase of the project is expected to extend national tax administration technology beyond the VAT. In the following, our discussion of the GTP is confined to Phase II of the GTP, which is mainly devoted to VAT administration. See J. Winn & A. Zhang, "China's Golden Tax Project: A Technological Strategy for Reducing VAT Fraud," 4 *Peking University Journal of Legal Studies* 1–33 (2013).

37 See, e.g., M. Keen & S. Smith, "VAT Fraud and Evasion: What Do We Know, and What Can Be Done?" 59 *National Tax Journal* 861–887 (2006), p. 865, fn.5; G. Harrison & R. Krelove, "VAT Refunds: A Review of Country Experience," International Monetary Fund Working Paper WP/05/218 (2005), p. 27. These dismissals are discussed in Section IV(B).

that the government began to explore was standardizing VAT invoices. The invoice-credit VAT, after all, is supposed to create a paper trail that aids tax authorities in auditing transactions. If a system could be created in which all claims of input credits are necessarily traceable, through proper invoices, to reported sales, then tax evasion and fraud can be curbed. This logic is widely known in China as "controlling tax with invoices" and is embodied in the GTP system.

Two types of fundamental questions can be raised about the GTP system (and other systems for comprehensive cross-matching for a VAT[38]). First, what is the nature of the technological limitations that currently face such systems and prevent the fully effective curbing of evasion and fraud? Are these limitations temporary, which one can expect (or at least hope) to be overcome by technological progress, or are they inherent in any computerized system? That is, is there some fundamental reason why cross-matching technology is incapable of replacing tax audits? Second, are the costs of such systems justified? For example, is it wise to adopt a device that curbs the actions of a small set of criminals but imposes substantial compliance costs on all taxpayers? These questions should be borne in mind as we examine the Chinese GTP.

A. The Mechanics of the GTP

The GTP is normally spoken of as consisting of four subsystems: invoice generation, invoice authentication, cross-checking and inspection, and coordinated investigation. We discuss mainly the first three because coordinated investigation is largely a manual audit process triggered by findings in the GTP.

1. The Generation of VAT Invoices

Generally (but with numerous exceptions), "VAT special invoices" are required in China to support claims for input credits. To issue VAT special invoices to customers, each regular VAT taxpayer is required to obtain proprietary computer software from the State Tax Bureau as well as accessory hardware, in particular an IC (integrated circuit) card. The paper invoices themselves must also be purchased from the tax agency. When issuing an invoice, data must be entered into the GTP software, and an invoice will be printed stating the identities and tax registration numbers of the seller and the buyer, the name and industrial classification of the goods or services supplied, the taxable amount, VAT payable, the date of the invoice's

[38] Harrison & Krelove, *id.*, 27, cite South Korea, Indonesia, Bulgaria, Azerbaijan, and Albania as other countries adopting similar systems. Taiwan also adopts a cross-matching system (discussed briefly in Glenn Jenkins, Chun-Yan Kuo, & Keh-Nan Sun, *Taxation and Economic Development in Taiwan* 175, 179 (John F. Kennedy School of Government 2003).

issuance, certain other information,[39] and an identifying number for the invoice. In addition, an encrypted code (with either 84 or 108 digits) is generated and printed on the invoice, which reflects some of the data on the invoice. This encryption is later relied on to verify the authenticity of the invoice when the buyer uses it to claim input credit. However, because of limitations in the encryption technology, only the sales and tax amount, registration numbers, and the date and identifying number of the invoice itself are encrypted: a taxpayer may alter information on the invoice about the price, quantity, and nature of the goods and services supplied without the alteration being detected.[40]

The key function of the GTP in terms of seller compliance is that the information printed on VAT special invoices is also entered into the IC card installed on the seller's computer. The content in this IC card cannot be altered by the taxpayer,[41] and once a month the taxpayer must bring the IC card to the State Tax Bureau to upload its content to the bureau's system. (This uploaded information will then be used by the GTP system to perform cross-matching.) Thus, as long as the taxpayer files a return, the IC card ensures that all sales for which invoices were issued are accounted for on the tax return. Indeed, it is sometimes claimed that tax agencies are more interested in the content of IC cards than the content of VAT returns themselves, and the adequacy of VAT returns is assessed (at least preliminarily) only on the basis of their matching with the information in the IC cards, and not of their accurate reflection of business operations.

Of course, this component of the GTP system for ensuring seller compliance does not deal with unreported transactions for which no VAT invoice was issued (such invoices may not be needed by customers such as final consumers and producers who have no use for input credits). Its operation also assumes that the issuer of the invoice will be filing a tax return and account for the tax reported on invoices. Thus if the invoices and printing software come to be possessed by criminals, invoices might be issued but no tax paid. (This is analogous to missing trader fraud or carousel fraud in the EU.) To help prevent this kind of criminal activity, the government imposes legal obligations on taxpayers to safeguard their GTP accessories. Moreover, as we will see in Section VI(C), the system relies on the vigilance of purchasers to police VAT special invoices produced by criminals (as well as other more subtle forms of the issuance of "sham invoices"): it denies input credits to purchasers who rely on invoices that are classified as issued in suspect circumstances.[42]

[39] These may include the buyer's and seller's contact and bank account information.

[40] Fanghong Cai, "A Study of Problems of the VAT Invoice in the Golden Tax Project," *Proceedings of International Conference on Social Science and Environmental Protection* (2012) 470–472 (SSEP).

[41] This anti-fraud feature does unfortunately also imply considerable inflexibility: special procedures in the GTP system have to be designed for the correction of mistakes, the making of purchase price adjustments, etc., and correction of mistakes is not possible in all circumstances.

[42] See also the discussion of analogous legal regimes under EU VAT law in Chapter 10 Section III (Tax Evasion).

In the circumstance examined in the following court decision in the city of Nanjing in 2005, a taxpayer's computer with a GTP device installed on it was stolen by a burglar. The taxpayer was held to be negligent in failing to safeguard the GTP device and was fined. When this fine was challenged in court, two judicial tribunals agreed with the government (the defendant) that relevant administrative guidance required the taxpayer to put the GTP device in a safe box whenever not guarded by a person.

*****

Nanjing Shuangchao Trade Co. Ltd v. Xuanwu District State Tax Bureau, Nanjing Municipality (Judgment of the First Instance, Xuanwu District People's Court, Nanjing Municipality, Jiangsu Province (2005) Xuan Xing Chu Zi No. 70)[43]
Date of Decision: Oct. 28th, 2005
The plaintiff: Nanjing Shuangchao Trade Co. Ltd. ("Shuangchao Trade Company").
The defendant: Xuanwu District State Tax Bureau, Nanjing Municipality ("Xuanwu STB").

A. Complaints and Defenses in the First Instance trial:

1. The specific administrative act in dispute: on July 6th, 2005, the defendant made a determination to apply a tax administrative penalty to Shuangchao Trade Company, claiming that, in accordance with the provision in Item (5), Paragraph 1, Article 36 of the Measures for the Management of Invoices of the People's Republic of China, Shuangchao Trade Company's loss of its Tax Control Golden Tax Card to theft constituted an infraction, punishable by a fine of 400 Yuan.
2. The plaintiff argues that it has strictly guarded its Tax Control Golden Tax Card, in strict compliance with tax laws and regulations. On June 18th, 2005, the Golden Tax Card unexpectedly was stolen in a burglary incident; the plaintiff was not at fault, nor was it the case that it took inadequate measures to safeguard the Golden Tax Card, since the plaintiff company had installed security doors and security windows. Under such circumstances, it truly could not have been anticipated that the burglar would break the windows, and the plaintiff was also a victim. Therefore, the administrative penalty applied by the defendant is inappropriate and obviously unfair.
3. The defendant claimed that, according to the provisions of Article 30 of Measures for the Management of Invoices, Article 37 in

[43] Translated and edited by the authors. This first instance decision was upheld on the taxpayer's appeal in the Intermediate People's Court of Nanjing Municipality, Jiangsu Province on Jan. 9, 2006. (2005) Ning Xing Zhong Zi No. 167.

Administrative Measures for VAT Anti-Counterfeiting Tax and Invoice Control Systems adopted by the State Administration of Taxation (SAT), and Article 12 in "Provisional Rules on Strengthening the Management of Special Devices for VAT Anti-Counterfeiting Tax and Invoice Control Systems" adopted by the Jiangsu Provincial State Tax Bureau, the plaintiff company should strengthen security management in the purchase, installment, utilization and safe keeping of the special devices for business use of the VAT Anti-Counterfeiting Tax and Invoice Control System, so as to ensure the safety of invoice issuance devices. The invoice issuance device should be kept in a location protected by security facilities, and if the device is not in use, it should be kept in a special storage room or in a safe, and someone should be designated to be responsible for its management. However, the plaintiff failed to adopt effective methods to keep the special devices (including the Golden Tax Card) secure, did not keep the special devices in a special storage room or a safe according to relevant regulations when the device were not in use, which caused the special devices to be stolen on June 18th, 2005. As a result, the VAT Anti-Counterfeiting Tax and Invoice Control System could not properly function. According to Article 36 of Measures for the Management of Invoices and Article 43 in the SAT's Administrative Measures for VAT Anti-Counterfeiting Tax and Invoice Control Systems, the plaintiff who failed to keep the Golden Tax Card in accordance with the regulations and thus caused the malfunction of the system, shall be deemed to have failed to properly use and safeguard special invoices in accordance with relevant regulations and punished accordingly, and may be subject to a fine of less than 10,000 Yuan. The defendant determined a penalty of 400 yuan on the basis of clear facts and the correct application of regulation, and therefore requested the Court to uphold the defendant's administrative decision.[44]

[44] (Note by editors) On appeal, the taxpayer further argued "that the penalty applied by the appellee/defendant lacked adequate basis and displayed an incorrect application of the law. The defendant issued the penalty in accordance with Article 36 of Measures for the Management of Invoices, which however prescribes the penalty for the loss of invoices because of fault or negligence in invoice management. As the purpose of the legislation is to govern the loss of invoices resulting from the inappropriate management of invoices, the appellee's use of this provision is incorrect. Moreover, the safe-keeping requirements for the Tax Control Golden Tax Card in the "Provisional Rules on Strengthening the Management of Special Devices for VAT Anti-Counterfeiting Tax and Invoice Control Systems" of Jiangsu Provincial State Tax Bureau (i.e. that the card should be kept in special storage or a safe) apply only when the card is not in use. It does not apply when the card is in regular use. In fact, a Golden Tax Card in use cannot be dissembled freely by users, and there is no provision regarding the dissembling of the device in the above regulation."

B. Facts and Evidence Found in the First Instance Trial

Through open trial, Xuanwu District People's Court of Nanjing Municipality found the facts and evidence as follows. As a general taxpayer, the plaintiff company is an enterprise adopting the VAT Anti-Counterfeiting Tax and Invoice Control System. On June 18th, 2005, in a burglary at the office of the company, the Golden Tax Card (Card No. J31122204) was stolen along with computer which was used to issue VAT special invoices. After investigating and clarifying the above facts, the defendant claimed that the plaintiff did not utilize and keep the Tax Control Golden Tax Card according to relevant regulations, and thus this case is an instance of "system malfunction resulting from the inappropriate protection of devices" stipulated in the provision of Item (1), Article 43 in the SAT's Administrative Measures for VAT Anti-Counterfeiting Tax and Invoice Control System. According to [the provision of Article 43], where the enterprises using the VAT Anti-Counterfeiting Tax and Invoice Control System do not keep the special devices in accordance with relevant regulations, and thus cause the malfunction of the system, the enterprise shall be deemed to have failed to properly utilize and safeguard special invoices and be punished accordingly.

On July 2nd, 2005, the defendant issued the plaintiff the "Notice of Taxation Administrative Penalty", imposing a fine of 400 Yuan on the plaintiff and informing it of its right to argue and offer defense. The plaintiff did not make any argument or defense in writing. On July 6th, the defendant issued the Decision of Taxation Administrative Penalty, imposing a fine of 400 Yuan.

C. Reasons of First Instance Judgment

Based on the above facts and evidence, Xuanwu District People's Court holds that, the defendant Xuanwu STB has the right to inspect and punish any acts against the taxation regulations in its jurisdiction.

Tax Control Golden Tax Card is one of the special devices for enterprises adopting the VAT Anti-Counterfeiting Tax and Invoice Control System, which is part of the Anti-Counterfeiting Invoice Issue Subsystem of the country's Golden Tax Project, and is a special device for issuing VAT special invoice.

Article 37 in the SAT's "Administrative Measures for VAT Anti-Counterfeiting Tax and Invoice Control Systems" stipulates that, enterprises adopting the Anti-Counterfeiting Tax and Invoice Control System should take effective measures to keep the invoice issuance devices secure.

According to Article 12 in Jiangsu Provincial State Bureau's "Provisional Rules on Strengthening the Management of Special Devices for VAT Anti-Counterfeiting Tax and Invoice Control Systems", a general taxpayer should strengthen the security management of the enterprise special devices in the process of purchasing, installing, utilizing and keeping of the devices. The invoice issue devices should be placed in a site protected by security facilities, and if not in use, should be kept in a special storage or safe while managed by designated person. The Golden Tax Card, Tax Control IC Card and the VAT special invoices should be managed separately by three different persons.

As a general taxpayer and an enterprise adopting the VAT Anti-Counterfeiting Tax and Invoice Control System, the plaintiff company should bear the responsibility for the security of the special devices of the system that it uses. Therefore, though the plaintiff's devices were stolen in the office protected by anti-burglary facilities according to the plaintiff's statement, the plaintiff still bore the liability for inappropriate protection of the Golden Tax Card, which is one of the special devices for enterprises adopting the VAT Anti-Counterfeiting Tax and Invoice Control System. The defendant's determination regarding this liability is appropriate.

In accordance with Article 43 in the SAT's Administrative Measures for VAT Anti-Counterfeiting Tax and Invoice Control System, where the enterprises do not keep the special devices in accordance with relevant regulations, which results in one of several circumstances, the enterprise should be deemed to have failed to use and safeguard special invoices according to relevant rules and be punished accordingly. One of the circumstances is stipulated in item (1) as the malfunction of the system resulting from the inappropriate protection and management of the special devices or disassembling of the special devices without authorization.

In accordance with Article 17 in Jiangsu State Tax Bureau's "Provisional Rules on Strengthening the Management of Special Devices for VAT Anti-Counterfeiting Tax and Invoice Control System", a general taxpayer should be punished according to relevant regulations if his acts violate these Rules. Applying Paragraph 2 of Article 36 in Measures for the Management of Invoices, the defendant made an administrative penalty decision with correct application of law and regulation.

While the range of fine stipulated in Paragraph 2 of Article 36 of Measures for the Management of Invoices is any amount less than 10,000 Yuan, the defendant imposed to the plaintiff a fine of 400 Yuan based on the degree of liability of the plaintiff for the loss of the Golden Tax Card. The amount of the fine is not obviously unfair.

D. Conclusion

Xuanwu District People's Court of Nanjing Municipality adjudicated that the claim of Nanjing Shuangchao Trade Co. Ltd. should be rejected.

*****

2. Claiming Input Credit on the Basis of Invoices

To claim input VAT credit, purchasers must communicate with the local State Tax Bureau to have their special VAT invoices authenticated.[45] The authentication is based on the tax bureau's ability to decode the encryption on the invoice. As noted, limited encryption technology means that "authenticity" is a matter of degree: what is assured (assuming that the invoices are not issued with stolen accessories) is only that the invoice was issued by some identifiable taxpayer, on a given date, for a certain monetary amount of supplies and VAT charged.[46] That is, the transaction should be in the system for cross-matching.[47] Ironically, even for this limited amount of verification, the government's capacity to sustain the de-encryption system is so constrained (at least up until now) that taxpayers are required to submit invoices for authentication within one year of receipt. Any VAT special invoice that was not timely authenticated (for example, because it was misplaced) typically results in a permanent denial of the relevant input credit.

The management of VAT paper invoices for verification has been reported to be "very time consuming, labor intensive and costly."[48] Winn and Zhang, citing Chinese reports, state:

> [I]n 2003, the tax authorities had to certify around 300 million paper VAT Special Invoices, and the volume of paper invoices has increased since then. Tax authorities also bear the administrative cost of printing, selling and cancelling paper invoices. In 2006, PRC government research found that more than 40% of the costs incurred by Chinese taxpayers in relation to meeting their tax obligations could be attributed to handling VAT Special Invoices, and a significant amount of that cost is attributable to handling paper invoices.[49]

One can imagine the aggregate social cost of this aspect of VAT compliance in China to be large. However, what is even more remarkable is the rather limited advantage gained. As we will discuss in Section VI(C), the authentication of VAT invoices previously described by no means ensures that the content of the invoice matches the underlying transactions. A set of legal rules regarding the issuance of "sham invoices" that is independent

45 In the past, original paper invoices were taken to the local tax office for certification. It is now possible to scan paper invoices and transmit the electronic files to the government's certifying system. E-invoices per se are not yet permitted.

46 Thus, even a verified invoice may be "forged" in the sense that its content may have been altered.

47 One common critique of the invoice authentication subsystem is that it does not ensure that tax has been paid by the seller. See, e.g., Winn & Zhang, *supra* note 37, at 28. However, this is not the subsystem's intended function. Seller compliance is supposed to be secured by the VAT registration system and periodic reporting obligations of sellers and by the cross-matching system's ability to detect seller non-reporting and nonpayment.

48 Winn & Zhang, *id.*, 29.

49 *Id.*

of the GTP are needed for ensuring this latter type of matching.[50] Thus, the GTP system of special invoices serves to deter only a small set of criminals intent on blatantly forging invoices. However, it imposes significant compliance costs on everyone.

3. Cross-Checking and Inspecting VAT Special Invoices

In a third component of the GTP system, tax authorities compare transaction information submitted by sellers (through their IC cards) with information gathered from invoices submitted by purchasers in claiming input tax credits. Theoretically, if the information from seller and from purchaser fails to match, an investigation would be triggered. The task of cross-checking and investigation is carried out at the central government and provincial levels. How well this subsystem works is not well documented. Some have claimed that "the cross-checking and inspection functions are not performed in real time, but may take several weeks to complete. As a result of these time lags, some companies issued huge quantities of fraudulent VAT Special Invoices before shutting down."[51] Even if this is true, it only shows that the GTP has not stopped the most determined tax criminals (any more than such criminals have been effectively deterred in other countries[52]). And it seems to invite responses from advocates of the GTP that improvements in technology will address the criticism.

A different kind of critique of cross-checking through the GTP is that it may have crowded out real audits. The cross-checking of invoices is done at the national and provincial levels, but everyday VAT administration occurs at lower levels in China, mostly at the level of the county. The staff of county-level State Tax Bureaus and their audit divisions have direct contact with taxpayers, more firsthand knowledge of their business operations, and access to a variety of information that may potentially corroborate information shown in VAT returns. By contrast, information currently transmitted through the GTP is fairly impoverished (and may always remain so relative to the information possessed by local tax auditors). This suggests that cross-checking on the basis of such information is likely to be low yield and that cross-checking should at most complement, rather than substitute for, regular, non-GTP-based audits. However, because the GTP originated in the transitional decade of the 1990s when China had very limited tax audit capacity, an administrative culture may have emerged in which expanding the coverage of (and compliance with) the GTP, as well as improving the technology within that system, are seen as the most fundamental solutions to the needs of VAT administration. County-level VAT administrators thus handle IC cards, verify invoices,

[50] The enforcement of such rules also requires audit resources that are independent of the GTP.

[51] Winn & Zhang, *supra* note 37.

[52] See, generally, Keen & Smith, *supra* note 38.

and wait for instructions from higher-level bureaus to conduct field audits (on the basis of findings from the cross-checking subsystem). Real VAT audit capacity thus never develops.

B. Controversy Surrounding the GTP

The GTP has very strong advocates within Chinese tax administration, who firmly believe that China will remain an environment characterized by low compliance and high risks of tax fraud and evasion for years to come and that therefore a mandatory, highly restrictive invoicing system (accompanied by cross-checking) is a necessary instrument for the government.[53] There is voluminous commentary within China pointing out the system's imperfections both in terms of tax administrators' goals and in terms of the compliance costs it imposes.[54] However, few have argued for the system's abolition.

International experts on VAT design, by contrast, appear to find little to recommend in the GTP. They seem to hold this view on two grounds. The first is that the system of data gathering through the special IC cards of suppliers and invoice authentication of purchasers goes against the principle of self-assessment.[55] This is an insightful although not fully accurate observation:[56] because of the primacy given to the GTP system for determining the taxable sales of regular VAT taxpayers, and because generally input credits can be claimed only after the authentication of special VAT invoices, Chinese tax agencies do appear to systematically intervene in Chinese VAT taxpayers' tax reporting activities. According to authors from the IMF, because VAT return filings tend to be more frequent (e.g., done on a monthly basis) than filing for other taxes, the absence of self-assessment could significantly increase compliance and administrative costs of VAT collection. They also create all-too-frequent contact between

[53] Winn & Zhang, *supra* note 37, quote a Chinese official report that "the percentage of VAT Special Invoices that were verified for authenticity [in the second subsystem of the GTP] and suspected of non-compliance was reduced from 0.227% in January 2001 to 0.0002% in April 2007; the percentage of such invoices that were inspected [in the third subsystem of the GTP] and suspected of non-compliance was reduced from 8.5% in early 2001 to 0.031% in April 2007."

[54] Winn & Zhang, *id.*, summarize some of these critiques. They themselves argue that "the GTP is much more prescriptive than anything any tax authorities in Europe might ever have thought of implementing. With any technology-forcing regulation, there is a risk of lock-in to obsolete technologies and distortions in investment in technology. It will not be clear for some time whether the design of the GTP will impose such great obsolescence or distortion costs on Chinese enterprises that would outweigh the increased compliance benefits it seems likely to deliver."

[55] In Ebrill et al., *The Modern VAT*, *supra* note 25, at 139, China is identified as a country that introduced the VAT without self-assessment, presumably because of the GTP.

[56] As a matter of Chinese law, the VAT is self-assessed. A recent court decision elaborated on this point: *Zhejiang Longyou County Xikou Education Equipment Limited Company v. Longyou County State Tax Bureau*, Zhejiang Longyou County People's Court (2008) Qulongchuzi No. 10.

taxpayers and tax administrators, which decreases administrative effectiveness and increases the chance of corruption.[57] All of these comments are not inconsistent with Chinese experience.

The second ground for skepticism is that "large-scale cross-checking systems are a poor substitute for well-designed audit programs based on risk assessments, selective cross-checking, intelligence gathering, and targeted fraud investigation. The net benefits of large-scale crosschecking systems are yet to be proven, with associated costs to businesses and tax administrations continuing to be unacceptably high. Cross-checking should be directed at industries and taxpayer groups exhibiting the highest potential for invoice-related fraud, and should be applied on a sample basis or where a tax auditor has grounds for suspicion."[58]

VI. The Grant and Denial of Input Credits

The rules under the Chinese VAT governing the availability of input credits display some highly striking departures from international VAT norms. These departures have nonetheless persisted for more than two decades and have become quite entrenched; their reform is not on the Chinese government's near-term agenda. This section discusses three such features of the Chinese VAT: (1) the unavailability of refunds of input VAT other than in the context of exports; (2) restrictions on the refund of input credits for supposedly zero-rated exports; and (3) the denial of input credits for purchases accompanied by "sham invoices."

A. The General Unavailability of Refunds for Domestic Supplies

China adopts the unusual rule of generally disallowing the refund of excess input VAT credits that arise in connection with domestic supplies.[59] Excess input credits in any period can be carried forward, indefinitely, to offset VAT collected on future sales, but can never be refunded, not even when a business liquidates.[60] This imposes a significant cash-flow and sometimes permanent costs on business input purchases. It was reported that at the end of July 2012, there was more than 59 billion yuan (approximately USD 9.67 billion) of unused input VAT credit held by VAT taxpayers in the city of Beijing; this was equivalent to more than 60% of the total amount of domestic VAT (i.e., not counting VAT levied on imports) collected in

[57] Ebrill et al., *The Modern VAT*, *supra* note 25, at 141–142.

[58] Harrison & Krelove, *supra* note 38, at 28.

[59] China may not be unique in this regard. Ebrill et al., *The Modern VAT*, *supra* note 25, at 1 and 156, mentions this practice without naming specific countries

[60] As discussed in Chapter 6, the speedy refund of excess VAT input credits is a hallmark of an efficient VAT. Although numerous countries fall short of this best practice, it is relatively rare for VAT refunds to be delayed for more than a year.

Beijing during the year 2011.[61] This suggests that the magnitude of excess credit carryovers is likely to be significant across the country, although there appears to have been no systematic effort to quantify the aggregate scale of such carryovers.[62] Moreover, from a theoretical perspective, disallowing the refund of excess credits is objectionable not only when it results in actual financial burdens (in terms of cash flow or unrecoverable input tax) but also when it increases the risk facing businesses undertaking entrepreneurial activities: a business risks losing not only the investment it makes but also the VAT it will have paid on such investments.

The policy justification for not allowing VAT refunds for domestic suppliers is chiefly administrative in nature: VAT refunds create the most severe risks of VAT fraud. Fraudulently overstated input credits used to reduce VAT payable also deprives the state of revenue. However, for this latter form of fraud to be carried out, real sales have to be made and real output VAT have to be collected. By contrast, if VAT refunds are allowed, fraudsters can benefit from concocted input purchases without the need to make sales to customers. It might be argued, therefore, that by disallowing VAT refunds for domestic suppliers, China has limited the risk of the worst types of VAT fraud to the export sector. There, the economic cost of not refunding input VAT would put exporters at a much greater disadvantage than would be the case for suppliers to domestic customers. In other words, if we assume that the risk of fraudulent claims of refund is very high, it is conceivable that the cost (to the government) of allowing such refund may outweigh the benefit (to taxpayers) of allowing such refunds for domestic sales but be outweighed by the costs (to exporters) of not allowing such refunds for exports.

The important question, therefore, is how bad a burden is imposed on businesses by allowing only credit carryovers. In practice, Chinese taxpayers appear to complain more about the restrictions on the claim of input credits (including those that are imposed by the GTP) than about the absence of refund. Many of these former restrictions are imposed for administrative reasons, too, and not allowing refund of input credit may be among the less controversial devices the government has adopted to protect revenue. Even in its current push to modernize the Chinese VAT by expanding its scope to the service sector, the Chinese government has not signaled that it would change the credit carryover system.

[61] Data reported by the Beijing Municipal Finance Bureau and calculation based on *China Tax Yearbook 2012*. Because VAT on imported goods is collected by the customs authority as opposed to tax agencies, and the revenue from import VAT goes entirely to the national government, the Beijing municipal government may have no information about the amount of VAT collected from importers in Beijing.

[62] The Beijing municipal government gathered the preceding data on the eve of the reform of replacing the BT by the VAT in select sectors (see Section VI), because, as a result of different revenue sharing arrangements for taxable goods and for taxable services, carried-over input credits for the supply of goods would not be allowed to offset output VAT on services newly taxable under the VAT.

B. Reduced VAT Refunds for Exports

The Chinese VAT was originally designed in 1994 to apply zero-rating to exports and thus offer refunds of input credits to exporters. However, both the strain of VAT refunds on central and local government budgets and the high risks of VAT fraud led the government almost immediately (in 1995) to abandon zero-rating and limit export refunds. The government also soon began to adopt different rates of refund for finely differentiated categories of exported products, either to support or to discourage particular types of exports. These rates are frequently adjusted in response to conditions of international trade.[63] The combined effect of purposeful limitations on VAT refunds and limitations imposed by local budgetary conditions is thus highly complex and has become an important topic of investigation for researchers interested in trade policy. In the following paragraphs, we aim to situate this topic for readers primarily interested in VAT design.

We may begin with the basic design of VAT refunds for exported goods in China. The system not only produces incomplete refunds of input credits but also results in refund amounts that "are little connected to the taxes paid on material inputs."[64] Under the basic formula for export refunds, each enterprise engaged in export activity (possibly alongside making domestic supplies) calculates its VAT liabilities as

$$T = t * S - t * M - R,$$

where T is the VAT payable, t is the regular VAT rate applicable to input purchases and domestic supplies, S is the value of sales of enterprise, M is the value of material inputs of firm, and R is the refundable VAT on exports sales. R in turn is the product of the value of export sales (E) and a refund rate, r (i.e., $R = E * r$), where $t \geq r \geq 0$. The refund rate r may differ from exported product to exported product but does not depend on the nature of the input used. If we consider a taxpayer who is engaged only in exports,[65] the formula (after algebraic manipulation) is equivalent to $\Delta^*(t - r) - M * r$, where Δ is the value added of the exporter.[66] Thus if the exporter adds no value (i.e., $\Delta = 0$), his refund (i.e., negative tax liability) will be the value of his input multiplied by the refund rate: this may be lower than the regular VAT rate, and it is clear here why the refund

[63] For recent summaries of this history, see Whalley & Wang, *supra* note 3; P. Chandra & C. Long, "VAT Rebates and Export Performance in China: Firm-Level Evidence," 102 *Journal of Public Economics* 13–22 (2013); and Julien Gourdon, S. Monjon, & S. Poncet, "Incomplete VAT Rebates to Exporters: How Do They Affect China's Export Performance?" CEPII Working Paper, No 2014-05, February 2014 (http://www.cepii.fr/CEPII/en/publications/wp/abstract.asp?NoDoc=6584). According to Gourdon, Monion, and Poncet, "over the 2002–12 period, 87% of the products at the HS6 level underwent at least one change of their VAT refund rate, either upward or downward."

[64] Whalley & Wang *supra* note 3, at 205.

[65] For a taxpayer who is also engaged in domestic supplies, the system of rebate for exports may first reduce the VAT payable with respect to such domestic supplies and with any residual negative tax liability to be refunded.

[66] In the case of the taxpayer engaged only in exporting, $\Delta = S - M$.

of input credit is incomplete, compared to zero-rating. However, if the exporter does add value (i.e., $\Delta > 0$), then the refund of input credit is further reduced by the amount $\Delta^*(t - r)$. Indeed, it is possible that $\Delta^*(t - r) - M * r > 0$, so that an exporter with no domestic supplies and subject to "export refund" will owe a positive tax liability. To put it differently, the reduced rate of rebate for exports not only leaves a residual tax on input purchases but additionally taxes the exporter's value added.

As a matter of economic theory, incomplete rebates of input VAT for exported products constitute an implicit export tax.[67] The foregoing discussion shows that China's reduced VAT refunds for varieties of exported products impose an export tax that is more than implicit.[68] It may be intuited that such export taxes should have the effect of reducing the quantity of the types of products to which they apply. Some recent empirical research has indeed been devoted to confirming this intuition. Whereas some studies have supported the conclusion that China's adjustments of VAT refund rates have affected the quantities of the relevant exports in the predicted ways – that is, higher (lower) refund rates increase (decrease) the quantity of exports[69] – others claim that this effect holds only for products with competitive international markets and is less noticeable for products subject to less competition.[70] Overall, however, it appears that Chinese tax (and trade) policymakers have achieved some of their objectives despite adopting a highly unconventional and complex policy toward VAT refunds for exports.

Is it a good idea to control exports through VAT refunds in this way? Some economists have argued that it is. Whalley and Wang note that an ad valorem tax on all exports would be equivalent to an exchange rate adjustment (i.e., appreciation of the Chinese yuan). They argue:

> [I]n classical public finance analysis of the VAT, departures from a pure destination based consumption form would be regarded as distortionary and imposing welfare costs. However, in a model where the trade surplus is endogenously determined given the exchange rate and non accommodative monetary policy, such policies may instead be welfare improving compared to a pure VAT ... because they increase production costs for exports and lower the size of the trade surplus.... [Changes] in export rebate rates and exchange rate policy can be substitute instruments in terms of macro impacts on trade flows.[71]

[67] See Chandra & Long, *supra* note 64, at 14–15, for references to relevant theoretical literature.

[68] The authors of a study in Chinese also stress that to properly analyze the effect of the export rebate system, it is not enough to consider variations in the refund rate but also the amount to which it is applied (i.e., not just the value of inputs but also of value added). See C. E. Bai, X. Wang, & X. Zhong, "The Effect of Tax Rebate Policy Changes on China's Exports: An Empirical Analysis," 10 *China Economic Quarterly* 799–820 (2011).

[69] Chandra & Long, *supra* note 64; Gourdon, Monion, & Poncet, *supra* note 64.

[70] Bai, Wang, & Zhong, *supra* note 69.

[71] Whalley & Wang, *supra* note 3, at 200–201. These authors write that, generally, "particular features of policy structure in China which may strike those versed in classical theory

Refunds for exports will continue to be an area of active policy exploration (and empirical investigation) in China, not the least because, as a result of the expected replacement of the BT by the VAT for the taxation of services, exports of services will also gradually give rise to refunds.[72] Moreover, the expansion of the VAT to the service sector also means that there is more to refund – the removal of the cascading effects of the BT should lower the cost of production of many goods exported.

C. Denial of Input Credit for "Sham" Invoices

Just as limitations on tax agencies' audit capacity are known to have created delays in VAT refunds in many countries,[73] such limitations may pose obstacles to the claim of input credit: if confidence in the power of audits is lacking, VAT rules may be designed to impose stringent mechanical conditions on the claim of input credits, so as to reduce the risk of fraudulent claims. We have already seen that compliance with the GTP is a prerequisite in China for input deductions. However, the conditions for input credit claims are in fact even more restrictive. An important tool for combating VAT evasion in China is the concept of sham issuances (*xukai*) of VAT invoices. A "sham issuance" is distinguished from issuing forged invoices – the invoice issued is authentic (and passes muster with the GTP), it just does not correspond to actual transactions. An examination of the legal regimes surrounding sham issuances is necessary for understanding the true limitations on input credit claims in China.

"Sham issuance" has two distinct legal definitions, one for purposes of the Criminal Law and the other for purposes of civil sanctions. The sham issuance of a VAT invoice was made a specific crime under the Criminal Law early in the implementation of the VAT.[74] It is defined as issuing (for others or for oneself), allowing to be issued (for oneself), or mediating the issuance of invoices where there is no sale of goods or taxable services, where there is such sale or supply of service but the quantity or monetary amount shown on the invoices is untruthful, or where real business activities are undertaken but a different party is asked to issue the invoices on one's behalf.[75] A sham issuance of invoices with the tax amount shown of

as odd may make good sense given the overall policy system within which elements reside." *Id.*

[72] As of the beginning of 2014, only limited categories of exported services that are subject to the VAT are eligible for zero-rating. Pending the development of an administrative scheme for refunds to service providers, more categories of exported services are eligible for VAT exemption. It is not clear whether the reduced VAT refund concept will be used to discourage the export of any services.

[73] See Ebrill et al., *The Modern VAT*, *supra* note 25, chapter 15.

[74] Criminal Law (amended and adopted by the National People's Congress, March 14, 1997, effective as last amended in February 25, 2011), Art. 205.

[75] Fafa [1996]30, Interpretations Regarding Certain Issues in the Application of the Decision of the Standing Committee of the National People's Congress on Punishing the Crimes of Falsely Issuing, Forging and Illegally Selling VAT Special Invoices (Supreme People's Court, 17 October 1996).

more than 10,000 yuan, or leading to a tax underpayment of 5,000 yuan, may be sufficient to constitute a crime.[76] The punishment for the crime is extremely severe, leading to imprisonment or detention of up to three years for minimal amounts and up to ten years or even life imprisonment for greater amounts. It was only in 2011 that the death sentence for the crime was abolished. Also notable is the fact that when an entity is found to be guilty of the crime of sham issuance of VAT invoices, employees who are directly responsible for the crime are also criminally liable, with punishments that are potentially as heavy as those for individual perpetrators.

The Criminal Law definition of sham issuances is sufficiently broad that it may catch petty fraud or even what might be regarded in other countries as "VAT planning." One example is a chain of supplies from party A to party B (say for X dollars) and then from B to party C (say for Y dollars), where A and C are regular VAT taxpayers but B is not (B may be a small-scale taxpayer, an exempt taxpayer, or a taxpayer subject to the BT instead of the VAT).[77] Here, a sham issuance may involve A issuing a creditable invoice to C. The invoice may largely reflect the economic effect of the chain of transactions if the supply made by B to C is sufficiently similar to the supply from A to B (e.g., they are more processed versions of the same product), and A may properly report the tax reflected on the invoice.[78] The parties may have simply "repaired" a break in the VAT chain: the only amount of tax that the parties can be said to have evaded is the amount that would have resulted from the "cascading" over the break in the VAT chain. However, this arrangement would be treated as a sham issuance for which the participants bear criminal liability. Most relevantly for our purposes, C would not be able to claim an input credit if the arrangement is discovered.

As the Chinese economy and legal system become more developed, public prosecutors are often no longer willing to bring criminal cases against VAT infractions (as they were instructed to in the 1990s) like the one previously described, especially when there is no real revenue loss on the part of the government. Thus civil sanctions against sham issuances are now more important to tax administration. Although there are certain general, formally prescribed civil sanctions against sham issuances,[79] perhaps even more interesting is a set of administrative practices adopted by Chinese tax agencies that both expand the scope of the definition of

[76] *Id.*; generally, for there to be a crime, elements such as criminal intent must also be present.

[77] Such arrangements are described in *Linhai Industrial Lighting and Decoration v. Linhai State Tax Bureau* (People's Court of Linhai, Zhejiang Province, Linxingchuzi [2006] No. 2).

[78] A may be willing to issue the invoice for the dollar amount of Y instead of X if B or C covers the tax difference between the two.

[79] These were formalized fairly recently in the State Council's Measures for Managing Invoices, as revised by State Council Decree 587, 20 December 2010, and effective on February 1, 2011. According to this regulation, a sham issuance encompasses issuing, for oneself or for others, or allowing others to issue for oneself, invoices that are "inconsistent with actual business affairs." *Id.*, Art. 22. A sham issuance for an amount of no more than 10,000 yuan may attract a penalty of up to 50,000 yuan; a sham issuance for a greater amount may attract a penalty of between 50,000 and 500,000 yuan. *Id.*, Art. 37.

sham issuances and impose additional penalties, many of which arguably lack proper legislative authorization. In 1995, the State Administration of Taxation (SAT) took the position that any person who issued a sham invoice is responsible for paying the tax stated on the invoice – even if there is no underlying taxable transaction – and is deemed to engage in tax evasion (and subject to civil penalty as such) for failing to do so. During the same year, the SAT invented a "buyer strict liability" regime: any invoice that is the product of a sham issuance cannot be used to claim input credits, regardless of whether the buyer is aware of the sham issuance. In 1997, the SAT went further to provide that (1) anyone who knowingly uses invoices from sham issuances to claim input credit or export refunds is subject to a penalty of up to 500% of the tax underpayment; (2) if a buyer uses (for input credit or export refund) an invoice that names a different seller than the actual seller, or an invoice that is printed in a different jurisdiction from the one where the sale takes place, this constitutes per se the knowing use of sham invoices; and (3) even if no credit or refund is claimed, knowingly obtaining invoices that are sham (or that display incorrect sellers or place of sale) is punishable by fines. Such (actual or per se) uses or obtaining of sham invoices are punishable even if the invoices reflect a real supply received by the recipient of the invoice, and even if the quantities and amounts on the invoice are consistent with the actual transaction.[80]

These penalties effectively put the burden of detecting seller VAT fraud on buyers, which perhaps again reflects a lack of confidence in tax agencies' audit capacity. What is most remarkable, however, is that even innocent buyers, who receive VAT invoices from purported sellers who have delivered goods pursuant to real contracts with the buyers in which invoices correspond perfectly with the transactions from the buyers' perspectives, are denied input credit if the invoices turn out to be issued in a sham. This could happen if, for example, unknowingly to the buyer, the purported seller was not the owner of the goods sold and was simply acting on behalf of someone else (who is not able to issue VAT invoices). This position of "buyer strict liability" for the validity of invoices may seem harsh: it shifts the risk of VAT fraud from the government fisc to innocent private parties. Its application has been repeatedly litigated,[81] but the rule still stands today.[82]

[80] Compare this with the two cases excerpted in Chapter 10 Section III (*Belgian State v. Recolta Recycling*; and *Maks Pen EOOD v. Direktor na Direktsia 'Obzhalvane i danachno-osiguritelna praktika' Sofia*).

[81] See, e.g., *Qingdao Jiali Vegetable Oil Limited Company v. State Tax Bureau of the Qingdao Economic Technology Development Zone* (Qingdao Intermediate People's Court (2001) Qingxingzhongzi No. 113); *Wuxi Yixun Technology Limited Company v. Wuxi State Tax Bureau Inspection Bureau* (Wuxi Intermediate People's Court (2005) Xixingzhongzi No. 4); *Liaoning Liya Copper Processing Factor v. The Third Inspection Bureau of the Shenyang State Tax Bureau* (Shenyang Intermediate People's Court [2008] Shenxingzhongzi No. 16).

[82] If such innocent third parties are able to obtain valid invoices to replace previously obtained sham invoices, they may claim input credit on the basis of the new invoices. They are also not subject to interest or penalties for tax liabilities owed as a result of the denial of input credit for sham invoices.

One interesting question is how often these sham invoice rules are enforced. At least in the published judicial decisions, it appears that they tend to be enforced only when there is a nationally directed campaign targeting criminals conducting large fraud operations. Given that these campaigns are only periodic and reflect the initiative of the central SAT and not of the hundreds of thousands of State Tax Bureau administrators who routinely deal with taxpayers, one might conjecture that the likelihood of enforcement is not high. Sham issuances by definition cannot be caught by the GTP but only by real audits. And when the capacity for such audits is limited, putting indirect liability for VAT fraud on buyers can accomplish only so much.

In the following case from 2012, the taxpayer purchased goods from a seller that claimed it had procured a third party to make the sale on its behalf. Invoices issued by the third party were given to the taxpayer. The taxpayer took precaution to verify that the invoices were authentic. Nonetheless, it turned out that the invoices resulted from a "sham issuance." The taxpayer was subject to a heavy penalty for claiming both input VAT deduction and income tax deductions on the basis of these invoices. It disputed the fairness of the penalty in court. The first instance court held the penalty to be unfair, but that decision was reversed, and the government's position upheld, by a reviewing court.

*****

Inspection Bureau of Zhanjiang Municipal State Tax Bureau v. Shengjie Trading Co. Ltd., Zhanjiang Development Zone, The Intermediate People's Court of Zhanjiang Municipality, Guangdong Province, (2012) Zhan Zhong Fa Xing Zhong Zi No. 112 (September 13, 2012)[83]

The appellant Inspection Bureau of Zhanjiang Municipal State Tax Bureau ("Zhanjiang Inspection Bureau") refused to accept the administrative decision of the People's Court of Chican District, Zhanjiang Municipality, regarding the dispute over the administrative penalty applied to the appellee Shengjie Trade Co. Ltd., Zhanjiang Development Zone ("Shengjie Company"), and filed an appeal before the Court.

The first instance court identified the facts as follows: on Dec. 10th, 2008, and Dec. 17th, 2008, the plaintiff signed two purchase and sales contracts for industrial and mineral products with Shenghui Trade Co. Ltd., of Yixing Municipality, Guizhou Province ("Shenghui Company") ... and purchased a batch of manganese-silicon alloy products from Shenghui Company. In early 2009, the plaintiff received 413.64 tons of manganese-silicon alloy, and wire payments to Shenghui Company. Instead of providing invoices to the plaintiff, Shenghui Company informed the plaintiff that it was Shenzhen Shengdisen Company that

[83] Translated and edited by the authors.

supplied the 413.64 tons of manganese-silicon alloy, acting on behalf of Shenghui Company (but the plaintiff did not provide evidence to prove that the products were supplied by Shengdisen Company). On Feb. 26th, 2009, Pan Guohui, the legal representative of Shenghui Company, transferred 27 sets of VAT special invoices issued by Shengdisen Company to the plaintiff (the total invoiced amount is RMB 2,625,635.07 Yuan and the total tax payable is RMB 446,357.96 Yuan).

Upon receipt of the above VAT special invoices, the plaintiff filed an application for a special invoices authenticity certification to the Zhanjiang Economic and Technological Development Zone State Tax Bureau ("Development Zone STB"). On the same day, Development Zone STB issued a "Notice of the Result of Verification" to the plaintiff, which stated that "You have submitted 32 copies of input deduction forms of VAT special invoices issued by the Anti-counterfeiting Tax and Invoice Control System. It has been verified that the matched special invoices are 32 copies, and the tax payable is 694,365.46 Yuan. The verified input deduction forms of the special invoices are hereby returned to you. Please bind them with this notice together, and keep them on file for tax inspection. For further details about the verification, please refer to the list attached to this notice."

Based on this notice, the plaintiff believed that the invoices were qualified for the VAT deduction, and thus applied to the presiding tax authority for input VAT deduction of 446, 357.96 Yuan by submitting the 27 sets of VAT special invoices issued by Shengdisen Company.

A number of companies in Shenzhen (including Shengdisen Company) were suspected of criminal activities of issuing sham VAT special invoice for sales of gold. The Inspection Bureau of the State Administration of Taxation (SAT) issued a "Notice of the Collaborative Investigation on Shenzhen '917' Cases of Sham Issuances of VAT Special Invoice in Sales of Gold", which requested the relevant regional Inspection Bureaus of State Tax Bureaus to conduct investigations into local companies that may have obtained the sham VAT special invoices, collect the payment of the tax that had been deducted by such companies, and look into the relevant legal liabilities. According to the above notice, the defendant conducted an inspection between Nov. 15th and 25th, 2011, regarding the tax payments of the plaintiff. After investigating and collecting evidence, and consulting the plaintiff's statements and arguments while informing the latter of its relevant legal rights, the defendant issued a "Decision of Taxation Administrative Penalty" in Dec. 19th at the end of the inspection.

The Decision stated that the plaintiff Shengjie Company received 27 sets of VAT special invoices issued by Shengdisen Company on Feb. 26th, 2009, which collectively stated 2,625,635.07 Yuan in purchase price and 446,357.96 Yuan in tax. The total amount of price and tax is 3,071,993.03 Yuan. While the supplier is Shengdisen Company, the plaintiff made the payment to Shenghui Company.... The investigation by the Inspection Bureau of the Shenzhen State Tax Bureau confirmed that the 27 sets of VAT special invoices issued by Shengdisen Company were falsely issued. The plaintiff company claimed 2,625,635.07 Yuan of costs of sale of products for the year 2009, corresponding to the sum of the amounts stated on the above invoices. According to the provisions of the relevant tax legislations, regulations and administrative guidance, where the plaintiff over-deducts input VAT on the basis of sham invoices issued by third parties, the act constitutes tax evasion. The penalty is decided as follows: in addition of the collection of the VAT underpaid (446,357.96Yuan), a fine of 50% of the amount of VAT underpaid (223,178.45) is imposed; in addition of collecting the enterprise income tax underpaid (557,264.91) [as a result of the claim of purchases supported by sham invoices], a fine of 50% of the amount of underpaid enterprise income tax (278,632.45) is imposed. The total amount of fine is 501,811.43 Yuan.

The plaintiff refused to accept the Administrative Decision, and thus filed an application for administrative reconsideration to the Zhanjiang Municipal State Tax Bureau ("Zhanjiang STB"). Zhanjiang STB issued a Reconsideration Decision to uphold the decision of the Zhanjiang Inspection Bureau. The plaintiff refused to accept the reconsideration decision, and brought an administrative suit to the Court.

The Court also found that the Inspection Bureau of the Shenzhen Municipal State Tax Bureau issued to the defendant Zhanjiang Inspection Bureau a document entitled "Conclusions regarding the Nature of the Illegal Acts of Sham Issuance of VAT Special Invoices by Zechengxin Electronic Technology Co. Ltd. and 208 Other Shenzhen Companies" on Oct. 17th, 2011, and a "Notice of Confirmed Sham Issuances" on Nov. 3rd, 2011, which together confirmed that the 27 sets of invoices issued by Shengdisen Company were sham issuances.

The first instance court found that, according to Article 2 of the Notice of the SAT on the Issue of the Treatment of Taxpayers Receiving Sham VAT Special Invoices (Guoshuifa (1997) No. 134), while transacting in goods, if the buyer obtains from the seller special invoice issued by third parties, or obtains invoices printed in regions other than region where the good is sold, and either claims an input deduction or applies for a tax rebate for exports from the tax authority, the act should be treated as an act of tax evasion or fraudulent claims of export tax rebate. The underpaid tax should be collected, and a penalty of less than five times the amount of tax evaded or defrauded shall be imposed, all according the Law of Administration of Tax Collection and the relevant regulations. Article 2 of the "Supplementary Circular to the 'Notice on the Issue of the Treatment of Taxpayers Receiving Sham VAT Special Invoices'" (Guoshuifa [2000] 18) provides that, where the buyer receives VAT special invoices from regions other than the province where the supplier is located, it is a circumstance prescribed in Article 2 of [Guoshuifa (1997) No. 134].

In this case, the plaintiff Shengjie Company signed a contract with Shenghui Company regarding purchasing manganese-silicon alloy and remitted payment to Shenghui, but acquired from Shenghui VAT special invoices (confirmed to be falsely issued) that are issued by the third party, Shengdisen Company. It further claimed an input deduction to the tax authority. According to the aforementioned rules, the plaintiff's act is an instance of tax evasion, and thus the defendant's decision regarding the pursuit of payment of underpaid tax is made according to law. However, as the plaintiff was ignorant of the fact that the 27 sets invoice were sham invoices when claiming the tax deduction (and the invoices were verified by the Development Zone STB), the plaintiff did not act with a malicious intent. Therefore, the administrative decision made by the defendant regarding the imposition of a fine of 50% of the amount of underpaid tax on the plaintiff is obviously unfair and lacking factual support, and therefore should be reversed according to law. Nevertheless, as the plaintiff's act constituted tax evasion and should be punished, the defendant should reconsider the relevant facts concerning the plaintiff's tax evasion behavior, and determine the appropriate administrative penalty again. ...

Against the first court judgment, the Zhanjiang Inspection Bureau filed an appeal at the Court and claimed that ... the judgment of the first instance court is incorrect. It was acknowledged by all parties that the appellee purchased manganese-silicon alloy from Shenghui Company ... and made payments to the latter by bank transfer. The appellee obtained the 27 sets of VAT special invoices issued from Shengdisen Company through Shenghui Company. These invoices were obtained from Shenzhen Municipality of Guangdong Province, a region outside the place of sale, Xingyi Municipality of Guizhou Province, rather than issued by Shenghui Company. Having full awareness of this fact, the plaintiff still claimed a tax deduction to the tax authority. This amounts to an intentional act. The Notice of the Result of Verification issued by Zhanjiang Development Zone STB only verified the correspondence of the [encrypted] numbers on the certified invoices with the Arabic numerals in the taxpayer registration number, invoice number, price, quantity, sum of money, issue date, and other information stated on the invoices. It did not examine the Chinese characters such as name of product, issue unit etc., and did not certify the authenticity of the invoice. So the Development Zone STB bears no responsibility for the legitimacy or authenticity of the verified invoices. ...

This court holds that: … in this case, the appellee Shengjie Company entered into a manganese-silicon alloy purchase and sale contract with Shenghui Company, and remitted payment to Shenghui Company. However, Shenghui Company did not issue Shengjie Company invoices under its own name, but sent VAT special invoices issued by the third party Shenzhen Shengdisen Company. Adopting the invoices, Shengjie Company claimed tax deduction from the tax authority. The plaintiff thus failed to pay or underpaid tax through claiming tax deduction on the basis of sham invoices. According to the rules of the SAT cited earlier, the actions of the plaintiff constitute tax evasion. Therefore, the "Decision of Taxation Administrative Penalty" issued to Shengjie Company by the Inspection Bureau based on the above evidence is legitimate.

… The judgment made by the first instance court, that because the Shengjie Company was ignorant of the fact of the sham issuance of the invoices when claiming tax deduction to the tax authority, the decision regarding a fine of 50% amount of tax underpaid made by Inspection Bureau is obviously unfair and illegal, is incorrect as a matter of law and shall be corrected.

In summary, the "Decision of Taxation Administrative Penalty" made by Zhanjiang Inspection Bureau is legally valid. The first instance court ascertained the facts clearly, and conducted the trial procedure according to the law, but the law was incorrectly applied, so the first instance judgment shall be amended according to law. The appeal by the Zhanjiang Inspection Bureau is reasonable and shall be supported.… The judgments are as follows.

1. The judgment by Chican District People's Court shall be rescinded;
2. The specific administrative act, "Decision of Taxation Administrative Penalty" issued by the Zhanjiang Inspection Bureau on Nov. 19, 2011, shall be sustained. …

This judgment is final.

*****

VII. "Refund as Collected" and "Simplified Collection" Mechanisms as Tax Preferences

The Chinese VAT contains a formidable array of exemptions and preferences. This is partly the consequence of a basic political arrangement in which (1) the authority to grant such exemptions and preferences is delegated by the legislature and the Cabinet to the Ministry of Finance and State Administration of Taxation, and (2) these two agencies have exercised such authority without regard to formal rulemaking procedures and using policy instruments that lack the force of law.[84] This institutional arrangement also explains several characteristics of China's VAT exemptions and preferences: many are quite narrow and esoteric;[85] their policy rationales are often opaque; and it is sometimes unclear even how they actually benefit the taxpayers to whom they are targeted. Of course, the fact that China has made a transition to the market economy only recently and the government is accustomed to routine interventions in market activities also explains the multitude of tax preferences. Most of China's VAT exemptions do not match the OECD's list of typical VAT exemptions.[86]

We have already examined the workings and disadvantages of VAT exemptions in Chapter 9, and there is no need to revisit them here in the Chinese context. Instead, in this section, we consider two relatively unusual types of preferential VAT policy deployed in China: the refund of VAT paid and the application of low-rate turnover tax mechanisms to regular VAT taxpayers.

A. Refund of VAT Paid

The refund of VAT remitted is widely used in China as a form of preferential tax policy.[87] There are several types of such refunds that differ slightly in respect of the timing of the refund and the party from whom the rebate is claimed (e.g., a tax agency or a government finance department), but all of them have the following in common: a regular VAT taxpayer would charge VAT at the normally applicable rate on its sales and issue valid VAT invoices, which the purchasers could use to claim regular input tax deductions; however, the VAT remitted to the government by the seller would be returned to the taxpayer either in whole in part. We will label all such refunds as "refund as collected" (RAC) mechanisms. They have been deployed in China for a wide range of products such as software,

[84] This is why it would be seriously misleading to consult only the basic VAT legal framework for the list of VAT preferences. For example, the Value Added Tax Provisional Regulation lists only seven narrow categories of VAT-exempt supplies, whereas actual categories of VAT exemptions are many times that. For a discussion of informal rule-making by Chinese tax policymakers, see Cui, "What Is the 'Law' in Chinese Tax Administration?" *supra* note 11.

[85] The MOF and SAT have over time prescribed temporary or permanent exemptions for items ranging from material for scientific research, education, and science and technology development, to imported books, imported gold, construction materials with recycled elements, the supply of blood, agricultural machineries, fertilizers, animal feed, waste water processing, the repair of freight trains, the maintenance of rural electric grids, food sold at higher education institutions, donations to victims of natural disasters, materials used in national defense, materials used in building the National Theatre in Beijing, souvenirs sold at the Shanghai 2010 Expo, certain tea consumed by ethnic minorities, and so on.

[86] See OECD, *CONSUMPTION TAX TRENDS 2012: VAT/GST AND EXCISE 2012 RATES, TRENDS AND ADMINISTRATION ISSUES*, chapter 3. Many items on the OECD list, such as education, health care, financial services, and real estate sales, are subject to the BT in China instead.

[87] Note that this is not the refund of excess input credits: there has to be net VAT (output VAT reduced by input credit) paid for any refund to apply.

integrated circuits, nuclear-based electricity generation, products using specific forestry products or recycled material, fertilizers, mold used in manufacturing, specifically designated magazines and publications, aircraft maintenance, financial leases of equipment, pipeline transportation, and so on. The adoption of many of these preferences embodies some type of industrial policy, aimed at fostering the development of some particular industry, but they have also been used for social purposes such as poverty alleviation in specific regions and the encouragement of employment of disabled people.

As an accounting matter, all RAC rebates are treated as government subsidies. Their design often also reflects their nature as targeted subsidies. For example, they tend to be limited in duration (ranging from two to fifteen years) and could be very narrowly tailored, aimed not only at particular taxpayers but also at particular contracts that the taxpayers enter into.[88] They can be subject to policy-based caps, such as the rebate could not exceed a certain amount per disabled person employed. Sometimes even specific uses are prescribed for the VAT refund.[89]

RAC mechanisms may involve rebates (1) of 100% or a lower percentage of VAT remitted or (2) of the excess (if any) of VAT remitted over a certain percentage of sales revenue. To illustrate the workings of the latter type of RAC schemes, consider a scheme that was the cause of a formal complaint brought against China in the WTO: if a domestic VAT taxpayer produced and sold integrated circuits, and if the VAT actually paid by the VAT taxpayer with respect to such sales exceeded 3% of the sales price of the product, then the excess was refunded to the taxpayer by the government.[90] Thus, suppose that the value of the relevant input purchases made by the taxpayer is X, and the value of the output (an eligible type of integrated circuit) is Y, with $\Delta = Y - X$ being the value added. The standard VAT rate of 17% applies both to the input and output. Then a refund is due if the amount of VAT paid by the taxpayer ($17\% * Y - 17\% * X = 17\% * \Delta$) exceeds $Y * 3\%$. If there is such a refund, the effective tax rate on the supply would be $(17\% * Y - (17\% * \Delta - Y * 3\%))/Y = 17\% * (X/Y) + 3\%$. However, there would be no VAT refund if the value added by the taxpayer is sufficiently low – that is, if $\Delta/Y <= 3/17$ (or, equivalently, if the "mark-up", Δ/X, is less than or equal to 3/14).

China's RAC regime for integrated circuits came to international attention in 2004, when the United States (joined by the EC and Japan) requested a consultation under the WTO dispute resolution system regarding the consistency of the scheme with the GATT.[91] The parties reached a mutually

[88] For example, between 2006 and 2010, two Chinese ship builders received an RAC subsidy with respect to particular ship-building contracts.

[89] Thus for the years 2006–2008, products manufactured by digitally controlled machine tools received a 50% RAC rebate to be specifically used for technological improvement, environmental protection, energy use reduction, and certain R&D activities.

[90] See WTO Summary of Dispute DS309 China – Value-Added Tax on Integrated Circuits, available at http://www.wto.org/english/tratop_e/dispu_e/cases_e/ds309_e.htm.

[91] *Id.*

agreed solution and China agreed to eliminate the VAT refunds on integrated circuits. In reality, China may have had a good defense for the policy as a form of permissible producer subsidy under Article III.8(b) of the GATT. In any case, RAC preferences continue to proliferate in China.

From a tax policy perspective, RAC mechanisms are interesting because they are not subject to the typical objections directed at VAT exemptions – that is, they create tax cascading, encourage self-supply, and so on.[92] Instead, they are a form of VAT preference that does not break the VAT chain. Because the amount of VAT rebate depends on the value added, RAC mechanisms are a form of subsidy for types of value-creating input that is not subject to the VAT, for instance, capital and labor.[93] Even if they lead to price distortions, they do so in ways that differ from familiar VAT preferences such as exemptions and multiple rates.

B. "Simplified Collection"

In Section III, it was explained that more than 80% of all Chinese VAT taxpayers are categorized as small-scale taxpayers: they cannot claim input tax credit but are subject to a low-rate turnover tax pursuant to "simplified collection." It was also observed that when the rate of the low-rate turnover tax is set sufficiently low, some taxpayers can be expected to try to qualify for the turnover tax instead of regular VAT mechanisms. What may come as more surprising is that many types of transactions entered into by regular taxpayers are also subject to "simplified collection" in China. That is, the system either imposes a low-rate turnover tax on, or offers it as an option to, even taxpayers who are prepared for regular VAT compliance. The possible rationale for this reversion to the turnover tax deserves some examination.

The various simplified collection rules share the common feature that any VAT paid on input used to make supplies that are subject to low-rate simplified collection is not creditable.[94] They differ in terms of the applicable tax rate, whether they apply mandatorily or at the taxpayer's election, and whether creditable VAT invoices may be issued by the supplier.[95]

[92] Moreover, unlike VAT exemptions in Europe, these subsidies do not have a single historical origin but have continuously emerged over time and in different sectors, suggesting that they must in many cases result in tangible benefits to the targets of such policies.

[93] However, input purchases of exempt or low-rate supplies are also encouraged because they lead to a greater amount of net VAT paid and, therefore, a greater amount of refund.

[94] Otherwise we would have a form of reduced-rate supplies.

[95] For all supplies that are subject to simplified collection at the election of the taxpayer, and some supplies for which simplified collection is mandatory, suppliers are authorized to issue special VAT invoices that would allow the purchasers to claim input credits. Similar to the right of "small-scale taxpayers" to seek invoices issued on their behalf by tax agencies, the issuance of VAT invoices with respect to supplies subject to simplified collection makes such supplies similar to exempt supplies (i.e., the main consequence is that input tax credit is blocked for the supplier).

The supplies (by regular VAT taxpayers), which are subject to *mandatory* simplified collection, include the sale of many used fixed assets for which input tax credit had previously been denied.[96] The applicable tax rate to the sale of such used assets is 2%. Fixed assets for which input tax credit had been denied are extremely common in China for several reasons. The first is that China abandoned its "production-type" VAT, under which VAT paid on fixed asset input purchases is not creditable, on a nationwide basis only in 2009.[97] The second is that input tax credit would also be denied for fixed assets used for non-VAT-able supplies (i.e., the wide range of supplies subject to the BT), exempt supplies, or supplies otherwise subject to simplified collection. These two reasons imply that, until recently, input credits have been denied for *most* fixed assets. A third reason is that, before 2013, input purchases of yachts, motorcycles, and most automobiles were also denied input credit.[98] In all these cases, the original value of the fixed assets can be assumed to have been fully subject to the VAT. The taxation of the resale of such assets is thus clearly unjustifiable according to normal understandings of the VAT.[99] Nonetheless, the application of the low-rate turnover tax to such resale has been labeled by the government as "preferential."[100]

Another category of supplies subject to mandatory simplified collection is the sale of secondhand goods. The generally applicable tax rate here is also 2%, although if the goods are sold on a consignment basis by consignment shops, or by pawnbrokers, the applicable rate is 4%. As discussed in Chapter 6(IV), many VAT systems have adopted special methods for the sale of secondhand goods to deal with potential price distortions arising from unrelieved VAT embedded in purchases from individual consumers. These methods include notional input credits and margin schemes. The policy goal is usually to put used goods dealers on the same footing as private sellers. It is unclear whether China's simplified collection method for secondhand goods intends to achieve the same goal (the higher tax rate applicable to consignment shops and pawnbrokers rather suggests that it does not), and even if yes, how it accomplishes this purpose.

A variety of supplies are subject to simplified collection at taxpayers' election.[101] Here, simplified collection presumably *is* preferential (at least relative to the regular VAT, if not to any lower-rate turnover tax that other

[96] Fixed assets are defined as those to which accounting depreciation applies.

[97] See Section I *supra*.

[98] Since 2013, input credits generally became available for the purchase of these types of assets, despite the argument that they are likely to be used at least partly for consumption.

[99] Prior to 2009, the resale of such assets was "temporarily exempt" from the VAT if the resale value did not exceed the original price.

[100] SAT, Notice Regarding Applying Lower VAT Rates and Simplified VAT Collection Methods to Certain Goods, Caishui [2009] 9, Section 2.

[101] The election to apply the simplified method to such sales is usually for a minimum of thirty-six months.

taxpayers may be subject to) – otherwise taxpayers would simply not elect to use it. For instance, the simplified method and a 6% rate are available for the sales of certain self-manufactured goods, including electricity produced by small hydraulic power stations, a variety of earth materials used in construction, premixed concrete, tap water, and certain biological products. All biological products sold by authorized distributors and retailers of pharmaceuticals are eligible for simplified collection at 3%. Recently, "simplified collection" at the low 3% rate was made an option for many services that were previously subject to the BT and that are now newly VAT-able, under the reform to replace the BT with the VAT. These include public transportation (including taxis and long-distance transport); services related to the production of animation, the storage, transportation, and showing of film; and operating leases of equipment produced before the implementation of the VAT reform.

One may infer various policy considerations leading to the adoption of turnover tax mechanisms for these latter categories of supplies. One is that they are supplies predominantly sold to businesses that cannot claim input credits or to final consumers. For example, because the construction industry is still subject to the BT (itself a low-rate turnover tax), the sale of construction material could benefit from a low-rate turnover tax relative to the regular VAT. This may be called the "turnover tax creep," being the counterpart to the phenomenon of "exemption creep" observed in other countries.[102] The supplies may also be made primarily to final consumers (e.g., passengers in public transportation). Here, a low-rate sales tax without the ability to claim input credit by suppliers may still lead to a lower overall tax burden. Another possibility is that the low-rate tax serves as a form of transition policy, as shown in the case of operating leases of equipment purchased prior to the imposition of the VAT on leasing services.[103] In none of these cases is the primary justification of "simplified collection" the reduction of compliance costs.

However, the justifications commonly adduced by Chinese policymakers and commentators for the adoption of simplified collection tend to deviate from the above. One very-often-heard claim is that many suppliers do not have enough input credits for offsetting output tax and, therefore, would have to pay too much VAT.[104] This claim not only makes the assumption that

[102] If biological products tend to be sold to health care service providers (who are subject to the BT and not VAT), and electricity produced at small hydraulic power stations are sold primarily to tax-exempt rural electric grids, the application of simplified collection to these supplies can be explained similarly.

[103] Leasing services used to be subject to a 5% BT, which is not creditable by the lessee. Suppose that it is now subject to a 17% VAT, but the lessee cannot fully use the 17% input credit, whether because of limitations on the claim of input credits, the unavailability of refunds, or the increased tax cannot be fully passed on to final consumers. In this case, the conversion to the regular VAT may have a negative impact on the value of existing assets, which may be mitigated by the low-rate turnover tax.

[104] For an explicit statement of this justification in government guidance, see SAT, Notice Regarding Adopting Simplified VAT Collection for Premixed Concrete, Guoshuifa [2003] 37.

the burden of the VAT cannot be passed on to downstream suppliers and consumers (which may be true in some circumstances) but also, more puzzlingly, appears to assume that input credits can come "for free": if input credits are not available because no VAT has been paid on input purchases, the complaint about the lack of input credit is hard to understand. A more charitable interpretation of the claim is that the input purchases of the taxpayers have been subject to VAT, either directly or indirectly (e.g., because of buried input credit in goods sold by exempt sellers or sellers themselves subject to simplified collection), but such previous VAT cannot be properly documented, and therefore VAT input credits cannot safely be granted. It would then be easier for both the taxpayer and tax administrators to forego VAT mechanisms and opt for a low-rate turnover tax instead.

VIII. Managing the Transition from the BT to the VAT[105]

In this section, we examine the way in which China is currently managing the replacement of its BT with the VAT, to illustrate policy issues in *VAT transitions*, understood as policy changes that involve introducing the VAT, replacing turnover taxes with the VAT, or increasing (or decreasing) VAT rates. As discussed in Chapter 1, turnover taxes, as applied to transactions between businesses (B2B transactions), distort business' production decisions.[106] The removal of such inefficiencies is the fundamental motivation for China's current effort to replace the BT with the VAT. However, it is important to think about not just the "before" of turnover taxes and the "after" of the VAT but also about how to get from one to the other.

A. Some Economic Effects of VAT Transitions

Replacing a turnover tax with the VAT has several distinct types of economic effects. The first is the removal of actual and potential tax burdens on B2B transactions: the removal of actual burdens leads to revenue loss, and the removal of potential burdens (burdens that are already avoided by businesses but at the cost of making distortionary production decisions) improves production efficiency. A second type of economic effect is more complex. When the replacement of a turnover tax by the VAT applies to

[105] This section is based on Cui, "China's Business-Tax-to-VAT Reform: an Interim Assessment."

[106] In Section I, *supra*, we noted two important differences between the Chinese BT and turnover taxes commonly found elsewhere. First, the Chinese BT and VAT have complementary tax bases, whereas in most other jurisdictions the (same level of) government imposes either a VAT or a sales tax, but not both. Second, the BT is broad-based, covering, for example, the sale, resale, and lease of real estate and most services (including financial services and most common consumer services), whereas sales taxes in other countries leave many types of services out of the tax base.

transactions between businesses and final consumers (B2C transactions), the tax burden on such transactions may increase. In China this is because the common BT rates (3% and 5%) are significantly lower than the standard VAT rate (17%).[107] Although the lower BT rates were designed to take into account the BT's cascading nature, in sectors where the production chain is shorter (and therefore the extent of cascading lower) than average, the conversion to the VAT (if levied at the standard rate) means a real tax increase to consumers.

This tax rate increase may nonetheless be economically efficient for a couple of reasons. One is that the price increase for some services may merely reflect the fact that some consumed services were *under*-taxed relative to other consumer purchases and that relative prices among consumer goods and services were distorted by this under-taxation. Another is that the switch to a VAT shifts tax burdens from the return to capital to consumption, which also enhances efficiency under economic theory.[108] However, because tax and price increases are politically more salient than efficiency improvements, correcting under-taxation can be politically controversial.

Yet a third effect of replacing a low-rate turnover tax by the VAT may also generate political opposition. Insofar as there is an increase in the effective tax rate on sales to consumers, such a policy change economically has the effect of a one-time, lump-sum tax on the business assets used to produce such sales.[109] This effect can (if not anticipated) be efficient because it applies to an already existing set of assets and therefore does not lead to tax-induced behavioral distortions.[110] However, the owners of the relevant business assets may oppose the tax increase, and often political compromises are made through transition policies that alleviate the tax on existing capital. It should be noted that this effect – a lump-sum tax on existing capital assets – also exists whenever the general VAT rate increases. Such a VAT rate increase may occur as a result of introducing the VAT for the first time (i.e., the VAT rate goes from zero to positive), a tax reform to replace an existing cascading tax with the VAT, or simply within an existing VAT. Conversely, a VAT rate decrease, however it comes about, produces a "windfall gain" for existing assets.

In understanding the various economic effects of VAT transitions, it is sometimes also necessary to consider the *market structure* of the

[107] In other countries that convert a sales tax into a VAT, this problem arises often because the sales tax was not broad-based and effectively exempted many types of consumption purchases.

[108] In some populist political contexts, this may be portrayed as a policy of shifting the tax burden from businesses to consumers. This happened when the Canadian province of British Columbia tried in 2011 to replace its provincial sales tax with a VAT-like harmonized sales tax.

[109] See L. Kaplow, "Recovery of Pre-Enactment Basis under a Consumption Tax: The USA Tax System," 68 *Tax Notes* 1109–1118 (1995).

[110] See, generally, L. Kaplow, "Capital Levies and Transition to a Consumption Tax," in INSTITUTIONAL FOUNDATIONS OF PUBLIC FINANCE: ECONOMIC AND LEGAL PERSPECTIVES, (Alan Auerbach and Daniel Shaviro, eds., Harvard University Press 2009).

consumption goods affected. In a competitive market for a given good or service, who bears the economic burden of the VAT on the good or service depends on the price sensitivities ("elasticities") of producers and consumers. The supply of a good in a competitive market permitting new entrants tends to be very elastic in the long term, which means that the burden of a tax on the good is likely to be "shifted forward" mostly to consumers.[111] By contrast, in markets with imperfect competition and characterized by monopoly, oligopoly, or cartelization, the real burden of the VAT may be shifted in various ways and may sometimes be partially borne by producers.[112]

B. Special Challenges Facing China's Effort to Expand the VAT

Chinese policymakers, in planning the replacement of the BT with the VAT, faced important challenges, some but not all of which are unique to China. They also enjoyed certain special advantages relative to the circumstances for VAT reforms in other countries. One special advantage is that China already implements the VAT on the sale of goods. When the BT applies to services that are provided to VAT taxpayers, the breaks in the VAT chain imply blocked VAT credits (i.e., accumulated on VAT-able purchases by the service providers) and uncreditable turnover taxes. By applying the VAT to such services instead, input credits flow through and cascading is removed. This may lower the costs of production in a broad swath of the economy and lead to price decreases in competitive markets. It is relatively unusual for the introduction (or expansion) of the VAT to lead to price decreases. Another special "advantage" for Chinese policymakers is that several of the largest sectors of the economy to which the BT applies are real estate (more than 80% of which market in China is residential), financial services, health care, and education (including those provided by nonprofit or government-affiliated organizations). These are sectors that generally pose difficult questions of VAT design, which many advanced VAT systems have not adequately addressed.[113] If China simply delayed reforming these sectors and focused on extending the VAT to sectors where VAT design is simpler, it would still be able to move closer to "international norms."

There are also significant challenges to replacing the BT, however. One common challenge with efforts that have been made in other countries to replace turnover or sales taxes with the VAT is that many types of consumer services have been subject to low effective rates of tax. If the 17% VAT already applicable to the sale of consumer goods is extended to such

[111] See C. Carbonnier, "Who Pays Sales Taxes? Evidence from French VAT Reforms, 1987–1999," 91 *Journal of Public Economics* 1219–1229 (2007).

[112] Sometimes an imperfectly competitive market may see a price increase beyond the tax increase – the tax burden is "over-shifted" onto the consumer.

[113] See discussion in Chapters 9, 11 and 13.

services, price increases for the services are likely. This problem may be especially significant for extending the VAT to the housing sector, where prices are already very high in the largest cities. However, if one puts housing aside, price increases for some consumer services may be counterbalanced by price decreases for many consumer goods, and it is unclear that, overall, households would face higher prices if the 17% VAT applied to all goods and services (other than housing).

Another important political challenge to reform is that VAT revenue is currently claimed mostly (75%) by the central government, whereas the BT is claimed almost entirely by subnational governments. Replacing the BT with the VAT thus requires renegotiation of revenue sharing arrangements. This challenge, however, is not unique to China (as can be seen from the survey in Chapter 15), and it has been overcome in the past.[114]

Other challenges of VAT reform are more unique to China. One is that, as discussed in the earlier sections of this chapter, the Chinese VAT is highly "impure": there is no refund of excess input credits for domestic supplies; VAT refund for exports is limited; "simplified collection" applies widely to small businesses and even to many types of supplies made by regular VAT taxpayers; and the Golden Tax System and the stringent legal regime on sham invoices make the claiming of input credits a cumbersome and often uncertain affair. These features, plus the breadth of sectors for which the implementation of the VAT is delayed (e.g., construction and real estate, financial services, etc.), imply that there are many more business customers in China than in other countries who could not use input credits and therefore would prefer low, turnover taxes. This diminishes the significance of the advantage mentioned earlier of expanding the coverage of an existing VAT. It may even diminish the overall appeal of converting to the VAT from the BT, because some believe that it is overall unclear which is more distortionary, a low-rate turnover tax or a high-rate impure VAT.[115]

C. The Initial Approach to Replacing the BT: 2012–2013

In point of fact, China adopted a sector-by-sector approach for replacing the BT with the VAT. In 2012, it began the reform by extending the VAT to certain "pilot sectors" that are considered to involve "production-

[114] See, for example, Ehtisham Ahmad, Raju Singh, & Benjamin Lockwood, "Taxation Reforms and Changes in Revenue Assignments in China," IMF Working Paper WP/04/125 (July 2004), which predicted that revised revenue sharing was a prerequisite in China to abandoning the "production-type" VAT. This policy change (moving from VAT Regime I to VAT Regime II as discussed in Section I, *supra*) occurred in 2009 without any change in VAT revenue sharing.

[115] For an example of such skepticism, see B. Yang, "Extending the VAT to Services in China: Special Difficulties and Choices," 2 *Journal of Chinese Tax and Policy* 2–10 (February 2012). For a discussion of some commonly ignored welfare-reducing effects of VAT base-broadening, see J. Piggott & J. Whalley, "VAT Base Broadening, Self Supply, and the Informal Sector," 91 *American Economic Review* 1084–1094 (2001).

oriented services" and "modern services." These included ground and river transportation and aviation; equipment leasing; logistical services; R&D and technology services (including technology transfers and licensing); IT services; design, advertising, and IP-related services; the transfer of trademarks, copyright, and business goodwill; and accounting, tax, legal, management, and other consulting services. The government emphasized the "B2B' character of these services[116] – that is, they are predominantly intermediate input to businesses. *If* the government were able to identify only or primarily B2B transactions for the initial expansion of the VAT, then only the first set of economic effects discussed (a pure tax reduction combined with the elimination of distortions in production decisions) would be relevant. Whether it was wise to carry out the tax reform by thus choosing "easy" sectors first is a matter of political judgment. On the one hand, it may have put the reform on the political agenda with little opposition. On the other hand, it isolates the aspects of the conversion to the VAT that are more politically difficult (e.g., high tax on many consumer services and the lump sum tax on existing assets) and potentially makes policy trade-offs more difficult. The full benefit of the conversion to the VAT is also suppressed because many sectors of production still cannot use input credits.

A second aspect of China's approach in 2012 and 2013 to replacing the BT is the adoption of multiple rates, which is harder to rationalize. The VAT pilots deliberately introduced two new rates into the Chinese VAT: 11% for transportation services and 6% for services qualified as modern services.[117] Only the lease of tangible movable properties is subject to VAT at the regular 17% rate. This choice of multiple rates is mystifying especially in combination with the sector-by-sector approach. If reform sectors had been carefully chosen to comprise largely B2B transactions, *it should not matter* what the applicable VAT rate is: any VAT charged on the transaction to the purchaser will simply be credited by the purchaser against VAT on future outputs. Indeed, internationally, the deployment of multiple rates within VAT systems is mostly driven by the desire to offer favorable treatment for certain types of consumer goods (e.g., food and clothing), often on distributional grounds.[118] It is quite unusual for special VAT rates to be adopted specifically for B2B transactions.

As a result of the combination of the choice of sectors and the use of reduced rates for B2B transactions, China's reform to replace the BT has so far faced little opposition and is promoted by the government as a tax reform success. The main sector in which some resistance was encountered, namely transportation, is an illuminating example. The BT rate applicable to transportation had previously been only 3%, and providers of transportation services had been allowed to issue a special type of invoice that enabled customers to claim a deemed input credit, at the

[116] The government did not release any information regarding how much of each type of service is supplied to non-consumers. Clearly, some such services, e.g., passenger transport, are supplied to final consumers.

[117] Both rates are lower than the previous preferential rate of 13% under the VAT.

[118] See Ebril et al., *The Modern VAT*, *supra* note 25, chapter 7.

rate of 7% of value of the service.[119] Moreover, previous BT rules allowed, where there is subcontracting among transportation service providers, the 3% rate to apply to value added and not the full value of the contract (thus removing cascading). In other words, the BT treatment of the transportation sector already displayed certain VAT features. Thus it is not entirely surprising that expanding the VAT to transportation, even with an 11% rate, increased the tax burden on some businesses that apparently were unable to increase prices for their services.[120]

However, there are signs that much greater resistance to the expansion of the VAT is emerging. For example, the Chinese government originally announced the plan to expand the VAT to the telecommunications sector in 2013. This did not happen. Telecom services are until now subject to BT at a low 3% rate. It has been estimated that at least 80% of the value of telecom services provided in China represents individual consumption. And the telecom sector in China is dominated by three major state-owned corporate groups. The problem of reform is thus a matter of significantly increasing the tax rate of a consumer service in an oligopolistic market. The government had proposed to apply an 11% rate to telecom services on the conversion to the VAT. The major telecom operators objected that this would significantly increase their "tax burden" and that a 6% rate was more appropriate. Neither side has publicly discussed the prospect of increasing the tax-inclusive service prices to final consumers. Presumably, this is because neither side was interested in such a price increase.

With respect to consumer services provided in more competitive markets, any government-business negotiation would have to be more indirect. At the outset of the reform of replacing the BT, the government indicated an intention to apply "simplified collection" to "everyday" services. Given that, as explained in Section VII, "simplified collection" under the Chinese VAT is no different from the BT – except that the former may be set at an even lower (turnover tax) rate than the latter. This could be interpreted as an announcement that there would be no reform for such services. This would be manifestly bad policy, because it means maintaining the BT/VAT dichotomy with respect to a wide range of consumed goods and services. To avoid this outcome, both the government and the Chinese public will eventually have to face the fact (which holds also for the real estate sector) that the reform to replace the BT with the VAT is ultimately about adjustments in consumer prices.

In terms of revenue sharing, at least for the initial phases of the reform to replace the BT, all of the VAT revenue paid in connection with services newly subject to the VAT is assigned to the subnational jurisdiction in which the pilot businesses are located. By contrast, VAT payable in connection with goods and services previously subject to VAT is still shared 75%

119 The excess of this deemed credit over the actual BT charged may have been intended to remove some of the effect of input taxation (i.e., VAT paid on the purchase of vehicles).

120 Some subnational governments eager to promote the tax reform and support local businesses immediately offered subsidies to these businesses.

and 25% between national and provincial governments.[121] If a taxpayer was previously engaged in a VAT-payable business and has unused, carryover input credit, such input credit cannot be used against any new VAT payable as a result of transactions to which the reform of replacing the BT with the VAT applies. This rule is needed to prevent VAT payable to the pilot jurisdiction governments from being diluted because of the higher central government share of traditional VAT revenue. Moreover, the VAT payable by businesses engaged in both traditional and newly VAT-able supplies is allocated in proportion to the amount of the two types of taxable sales.[122]

IX. Discussion Questions

1. Does your country's VAT law use the "economic activity" or similar concept? If so, is it interpreted mostly administratively or judicially? Does it serve mainly to delimit the range of taxable supplies or to limit the capacity for the claim of input credit or refunds?
2. Are there different VAT thresholds in your country for different sectors? If so, what justifies these differences? Does your country's system tax businesses below the VAT threshold under a turnover or other tax regime? Does this make it more likely that they will elect to register for VAT purposes? How easy is it to elect VAT registration when a business falls below the VAT threshold?
3. The idea of systematic cross-matching in VAT administration is that for any claim of an input credit by a taxpayer, a computer system is to locate a matching report by the supplier of the transaction purportedly giving rise to the credit (and ideally, confirmation that the supplier has made a VAT tax payment or at least is likely to do so). Do you think such a system is feasible? Would it be desirable?
4. How does your country's VAT law deal with the example given in Section VI (C) (see text accompanying note 77 *supra*)? There is a chain of supply from A to B to C; B is an exempt supplier; to avoid the blocking of input tax created by B's exempt status, B arranges for A to issue a VAT invoice to C, as though the transaction was directly between A and C. Would C be able to claim an input credit on the strength of the invoice?[123]

121 State tax bureaus would collect VAT from pilot businesses in the pilot sectors and regions, whereas local tax bureaus would continue to collect BT.

122 The non-intuitive results of these rules can be shown in a simple example. If a business has 100 of carryover input credit, 20 of new input credit, 50 of new taxable supplies, and 50 of previously taxable supplies, then it would be able to claim 70 of input credit (20 of the new input credit and only 50 of the carried-over credit), and the VAT payable of 30 would be allocated half and half between central and provincial governments according to volume of the two types of taxable supplies.

123 Compare this with the "A-B-C transactions" discussed in Chapter 9 (V).

15 Interjurisdictional Aspects

I. Introduction

Almost all national-level (central-government) VATs rely on the destination principle to tax international transactions, with tax imposed on imports and removed from exports. The adoption at the subnational level of some form of VAT (see Table 2.7 for a review of the forms) is being debated or enacted in many countries.[1] There has been renewed interest in the problems of cross-border trade in the EU and within federal systems, especially in Canada, India, Brazil, and the United States. In addition to the long-standing problems faced by the EU and federal countries with cross-border trade, some of the recent attention to these issues has been propelled by the explosion of trade over the Internet (electronic or e-commerce). Indeed, the US Congress enacted a moratorium on subnational (state level) taxes on Internet access and on multiple or discriminatory taxes on e-commerce.[2]

Subnational units of government should control the revenue necessary to provide the services that they render. In any federal system, the fiscal authority and responsibility of subnational (referred to in this chapter also as regional) units of government must be established.[3] To possess ultimate fiscal autonomy, subnational units of government should have the authority to choose the taxes to be levied, define their tax bases, set their tax

[1] See R. Bird, *Subnational VATs: Experience and Prospects*, Proceedings, 93rd Annual Conference on Taxation of the National Tax Association 223 (2001) [hereinafter Bird, Subnational VATs]. See also R. Bird, "A Look at Local Business Taxes," 36 *State Tax Notes* 685 (May 30, 2005) [hereinafter Bird, Local Business Taxes.]

[2] See discussion of proposed reforms in the U.S. in Section VIII of this chapter.

[3] For an article covering the options and the effects of various forms of central and subnational sales and value added taxes, see C. E. McLure, Jr., "Tax Assignment and Subnational Fiscal Autonomy," 54 *Bulletin of the International Bureau of Fiscal Documentation* 626 (Dec. 2000) [hereinafter McLure, Subnational Fiscal Autonomy]. In this article, McLure examines each of the various options of imposing at one or more levels of government various sales and value added tax combinations, and tests each alternative against the principles of subnational fiscal autonomy.

rates, and administer the taxes they impose, but these elements can also be shared with national government.[4]

A recent body of literature addresses the sharing of revenue from a VAT between the central and local units of government, where there is only a central VAT or both a central and local VATs.[5] One option is for the central government to assign revenue to subnational governments by granting them power to impose their own taxes as just described. Alternatively, the central government could establish a harmonized tax applicable throughout the country and administered by the regional governments, or the central government could add a surtax on a national tax that belongs to the regional governments. A central government could enact a tax to be a shared source of revenue, with the central and regional units of government to share in a pre-established proportion.[6] Finally, the central government may impose its own tax and share the revenue with the regions (revenue sharing is not tax assignment).[7]

The delegation of legislative power may result in complicated tax regimes that create unintended effects on the national taxes. In Spain, the Spanish Autonomous Communities provided that some of their subnational taxes were linked to the national VAT; that is, some transactions were subject to the regional tax only if the VAT did not apply and other transactions were subject to tax if the transaction was subject to the national VAT. For example, a regional tax did not apply if the transaction (involving real property) was subject to VAT. As a result, sellers could elect to treat a real property transaction as VAT-able, notwithstanding the exemption generally applicable to the transaction, to avoid the regional tax. (An election of this kind is allowed under EU rules, as discussed in the chapter on real property.) Sellers generally made that election if the sale were to a registered buyer who could claim the input VAT as a credit.[8]

A significant administrative and political issue in designing an effective regional tax in a federal system or in a common market (or customs union) relates to the taxation of cross-border trade involving interregion or intra-Union transactions. There have been a series of proposals to address the

[4] *Id.* at 627.

[5] See, generally, R. Boadway & A. Shah, *Fiscal Federalism: Principles and Practice of Multiorder Governance* (Cambridge University Press 2009); Zee, "Aspects of Interjurisdictional Sharing of the Value-Added Tax," 36 *Public Finance Review* 147 (2008); McLure, Subnational Fiscal Autonomy, *supra* note 3. Zee discusses the range of possible sharing arrangements, depending in part on whether the base and rates are set by one unit or each has autonomy in setting rates and even bases. See also Zee's proposed VAT voucher system discussed in section III(C) in this chapter.

[6] Japan imposes a 5% CT, with 1% of the 5% dedicated as prefectural revenue. This revenue is apportioned to the prefectures on the basis of population. A portion of the remaining CT revenue goes to the prefectures as part of Japan's revenue sharing program. The rate increased to 8% in April 2014.

[7] McLure, Subnational Fiscal Autonomy, *supra* note 3, at 627–628.

[8] See R. Almendral, "Autonomous Communities Taking Advantage of the Mechanism to Ensure the Neutrality of VAT," 14 *Int'l VAT Monitor* 373 (Sept./Oct. 2003).

issues pertaining to cross-border trade within a federal system or common market. Some were developed for a specific country or union but may have broader application. Some were not designed for a particular situation but may or may not have general application.

The purpose of this chapter is to acquaint the reader with the problems and proposed solutions for subnational or intra-Union transactions. This chapter focuses on one common market, the EU. Other common markets do not have an obligatory set of detailed rules, comparable to the EU's VAT Directive, to harmonize the VAT rules within the market or union.[9] Intra-EU cross-border transactions resemble interstate transactions under subnational sales or value added taxes in federal systems. This chapter closes with a section discussing efforts to replace or reform state RSTs in the United States.

II. EU's Commitment to Intra-Union Borderless Trade

A. Introduction

The EU's problems in designing a system to tax intra-EU transactions are similar to the problems encountered in federal countries like Canada, Brazil, and the United States under subnational VATs or RSTs that allow for the free flow of goods without border controls.

The harmonized VAT in the EU began as a destination principle tax both for trade between member states and for trade outside the Community. The initial goal, announced in Community documents, was to work toward a system under which trade both within a member state and between member states would be based on the origin principle (the "definitive VAT regime" for the internal market) and trade with countries outside the Community would be governed by the destination principle. Under the origin principle generally, there are no border tax adjustments. Tax is imposed in the country where goods are produced and services are rendered, with no rebate of tax on sales intra-Union and no tax on intra-Union imports.[10] In contrast, under the destination principle, tax is imposed in the country where intra-Union goods and services are consumed, with a rebate of tax on export sales and the imposition of tax on imports. For subnational taxes, the origin principle allocates revenue to the jurisdiction of production of value added, rather than to the jurisdiction

[9] See, for example, Common Market for Eastern and Southern Africa (COMESA), Southern African Development Community (SADC), and [MERCASUR]. See, G. Glenday with collaboration from D. Hollinrake, Assessment of the Current State of Value Added Tax (VAT) Implementation in SADC Member States (2005), that describes the array of VAT rules within SADC (study available at https://fds.duke.edu/db/attachment/829).

[10] The problem with a pure origin-principle VAT is that products leave the taxing jurisdiction with tax, increasing their prices in the international marketplace.

of consumption. This makes the origin-based tax a competitive force in cross-border trade.

As early as 1963, there were recommendations for the adoption of the origin principle on intra-Community trade.[11] In 1989, the Council of the European Communities announced that the EU would terminate border controls for VAT within the Community, effective in 1993. In January 1993, an interim system was introduced. That system relies on the origin principle to tax sales to consumers and other unregistered persons, whether those purchasers reside within or outside the taxing country. A sale by a retailer in London either to a French tourist there or by mail to a consumer in France is taxed in London at the UK rate, with the revenue staying with the British Exchequer.[12] During the "transition" period, the destination principle applies for B2B supplies within the EU. A Spanish company shipping taxable goods to a VAT-registered German company will zero-rate the exported goods. The Spanish government will not receive any VAT revenue from this transaction. The imported goods are taxed in Germany.

The EU or Community (both are used interchangeably) was expecting to convert the VAT to an origin base for BTB and B2C supplies within the Union. Most of the proposals to implement the origin principle within the Union on B2B transactions, such as the "clearing house" scheme, have met with significant criticism or opposition on the basis of practical considerations.

In response to the lack of progress toward the definitive VAT regime, there were several proposals for alternative schemes to implement the origin principle, or a destination principle that does not involve significant risk of evasion. Before those proposals are discussed, the following material provides the background for the EU's commitment to move to a full origin principle for intra-EU trade. As will be discussed, the EU decided not to pursue the full origin principle, but the Council maintains its commitment to the exchange of information within the Community as an essential part of the establishment of the internal market. A 2003 Council regulation greatly expands the areas of administrative cooperation in the field of value added tax.[13]

[11] See "Report of the Fiscal and Financial Committee (Neumark Report)," in *The EEC Reports on Tax Harmonization* (IBFD), cited in R. Bird & P.P. Gendron, "Dual VATs and Cross-Border Trade: Two Problems, One Solution?" 5 *Int'l Tax and Public Finance* 429 (1998) [hereinafter Bird & Gendron 1998],

[12] *British Value Added Tax Reporter* (CCH Editions Ltd. 1999); B. Terra & J. Kajus, *A Guide to The European Vat Directives,* VOL.5A VAT AND SALES TAX RATES AROUND THE WORLD (International Bureau of Fiscal Documentation 1994/1995).

[13] Council Regulation (EC) No. 1798/2003 of 7 October 2003 on administrative cooperation in the field of value added tax and repealing Regulation (EEC) No. 218/92. The 2003 Regulation requires the administrative and competent authorities of member states to cooperate with each other and exchange information, respectively. Some information on intra-Community transactions, including services supplied electronically, must be provided by electronic means. *Id.* at Art. 1.

B. Selected Provisions of the Treaty Establishing the European Community[14]

Article 14 of the Consolidated Version of the Treaty Establishing the European Community provides for the establishment of the internal market by December 31, 1992 – a date not met.[15]

Article 90 imposes the nondiscrimination rule. No member can impose a higher tax on imports from another member than it imposes on domestic products or impose taxes on another member to protect its own products.[16] Article 91 prevents a member from subsidizing exports to another member by excessive refunds of internal taxes.[17] Article 92 prevents a member state from imposing charges or rebates on exports or imposing countervailing charges on imports from member states unless the European Council approves such measures for a limited time.[18] Article 93 gives the Council, by unanimous action, authority to harmonize indirect taxes to establish the internal market by the time (now delayed) specified in Article 14.[19] Article 94 gives the Council, by unanimous action, authority to issue directives related to the establishment and functioning of the common market.[20]

[14] Consolidated Version of the Treaty Establishing the European Community (originally the Treaty of Rome), OJ of the European Communities, C 325/33 of 24 December 2002, http://europa.eu.int/eur-lex/lex/en/treaties/dat/12002E [hereinafter Treaty Establishing European Community].

[15] Art. 14(2) provides: "The internal market shall comprise an area without internal frontiers in which the free movement of goods, persons, services and capital is ensured in accordance with the provisions of this Treaty." Treaty establishing the European Community (Nice consolidated version) Official Journal C 325, 24/12/2002 P. 0033 – 0184

[16] "No Member State shall impose, directly or indirectly, on the products of other member states any internal taxation of any kind in excess of that imposed directly or indirectly on similar domestic products. Furthermore, no Member State shall impose on the products of other member states any internal taxation of such a nature as to afford indirect protection to other products." *Id.* at Article 90.

[17] "Where products are exported to the territory of any Member State, any repayment of internal taxation shall not exceed the internal taxation imposed on them whether directly or indirectly." *Id.* at Article 91.

[18] "In the case of charges other than turnover taxes, excise duties and other forms of indirect taxation, remissions and repayments in respect of exports to other Member States may not be granted and countervailing charges in respect of imports from Member States may not be imposed unless the measures contemplated have been previously approved for a limited period by the Council acting by a qualified majority on a proposal from the Commission." *Id.* at Article 92.

[19] "The Council shall, acting unanimously on a proposal from the Commission and after consulting the European Parliament and the Economic and Social Committee, adopt provisions for the harmonisation of legislation concerning turnover taxes, excise duties and other forms of indirect taxation to the extent that such harmonisation is necessary to ensure the establishment and the functioning of the internal market within the time limit laid down in Article 14." *Id.* at Article 93.

[20] "The Council shall, acting unanimously on a proposal from the Commission and after consulting the European Parliament and the Economic and Social Committee, issue directives for the approximation of such laws, regulations or administrative provisions of the Member States as directly affect the establishment or functioning of the common market." *Id.* at Article 94.

Notwithstanding Article 94 and to achieve the objectives in Article 14, except as otherwise provided in the Treaty, Article 95(1) gives the Council authority to adopt nonfiscal measures[21] (according to Article 25(1)) "for the approximation of the provisions laid down by law, regulation or administration action in Member States which have as their object the establishment and functioning of the internal market."[22]

C. Timetable to Move Toward a Definitive VAT Regime

The EU, despite obligations under the 2006 VAT Directive,[23] did not implement the "definitive VAT regime." In 2012, the Council of the European Union conceded that the implementation of a full origin principle for intra-EU trade, as envisaged in the VAT Directive, Article 402 "remains unlikely to be politically achievable" and invited the Commission "to examine in detail the different possible ways to implement the destination principle."[24]

D. EU Member States Limited to One VAT

One aspect of the EU's commitment to a supranational VAT is the member states' obligations to eliminate and replace all national cumulative multistage taxes. This principle was carried over in the VAT Directive, Article 401, which "seeks to prevent the functioning of the common system of VAT from being jeopardized by fiscal measures of a member state levied on the movement of goods and services and charged on commercial

[21] Art. 95(2) provides that paragraph (1) does not apply to fiscal provisions. Treaty Establishing European Community, *supra* note 14.

[22] *Id.*at Art. 95, ¶6. According to Art. 95(6), the Commission has six months to approve or reject national provisions after determining if they arbitrarily discriminate or restrict trade between member states or provide an obstacle to the functioning of the internal market. If a member state is authorized to maintain or introduce a provision covered under Art. 95(6) that deviates from a harmonization measure, the Commission shall immediately examine whether to propose that the harmonization measure be adapted. *Id.* at Art. 95, ¶7.

[23] Art. 402 of the VAT Directive provides that the transitional arrangements in the Directive are to be replaced by definitive arrangements (the origin principle) for the taxation of supplies of goods or services within the Community. Council Directive 2006/112/EC of 28 November 2006 on the common system of value added tax, Official Journal No. L347/1 of 11.12.2006 [hereinafter VAT Directive]. Art. 404 of the VAT Directive requires the Commission, every four years, to "present a report to the European Parliament and to the Council on the operation of the common system of VAT in the Member States and, in particular, on the operation of the transitional arrangements for taxing trade between Member States. That report shall be accompanied, where appropriate, by proposals concerning the definitive arrangements."

[24] Council of the European Union, 3167th Council meeting on May 15, 2012, PRES 12/198, Brussels.

transactions in a way comparable to VAT."[25] This article prohibits taxes with the essential characteristics of a VAT.

Article 401 of the VAT Directive does not restrict a member state's right to impose a tax, duty, or charge, so long as it cannot be characterized as a turnover tax like the harmonized EU VAT and it does not impose border formalities with respect to trade between member states. Thus, for example, although this article permits a member state to impose a separate tax on betting and gambling (even though it is exempt from VAT under the VAT Directive), it prohibits such a tax if it can be characterized as a turnover tax like the VAT. A member state can have only one VAT, and that VAT must comply with the VAT Directive.

There have been a number of challenges to taxes in member states as violative of the one VAT principle (Article 33 of the prior Sixth VAT Directive), including subnational taxes. In 1998, Italy replaced a regional income tax, a tax on corporate dividend distributions, a net worth tax, and a payroll tax dedicated to a national health program with the *Imposta Regionale sulle Attività Produttive* (IRAP), a tax imposed in each region of Italy and collected by the central government.[26]

The IRAP has different rules for different business sectors. "For commercial and manufacturing enterprises, the tax base is the difference between the value of the production in the tax year (i.e. the gross proceeds plus any increase in inventory and work-in-progress) and the cost of production (i.e. the cost of raw and other materials and services, the depreciation of tangible and intangible assets, the reduction in the inventory of raw and other materials, provisions for risks, and miscellaneous costs)."[27] It is an origin principle tax at the subnational level that does not tax imports (imports are deductible), and tax attributable to exports is not rebated. The IRAP can be characterized as an income-type VAT, while the VAT Directive imposes a consumption-type VAT.

In the following *Banca Popolare di Cremona v. Agenzia Entrate Ufficio Cremona* case, the ECJ ruled that because the IRAP did not have all the essential characteristics of a VAT as imposed under the VAT Directive, it was a permitted tax.

[25] A. Philippart, "Cumulative Multi-Stage Taxes under Community Law," 14 *Int'l VAT Monitor* 83 (Mar./Apr. 2003), provides an excellent, in-depth discussion of the history of this rule, a discussion of the Article of the EC Treaty discussed next, and the ECJ case-law development in this area up to 2002. On the "subsidiarity" principle in the EU, see T. C. Hartley, *The Foundations of European Community Law*, 5th ed. (Oxford University Press 2003); Jeffcoat, *The Principle of Subsidiarity in European Community Law*, unpublished manuscript (University of Leicester School of Law 1999).

[26] Legislative Decree 446 of December 15, 1997. Apparently, there are similar taxes in France, Germany, Hungary, and Lithuania. See E. Lyman, "Regional Italian Governments May Be Liable to Pay Billions in Refunds for Corporate Tax," *BNA Daily Tax Report*, March 23, 2005, p. G-5.

[27] *Id.*

Banca popolare di Cremona Soc. coop. arl v. Agenzia Entrate Ufficio Cremona[28]

Judgment

This reference for a preliminary ruling relates to the interpretation of Article 33 of [the Sixth Directive, as amended by] Council Directive 91/680/CEE of 16 December 1991 (OJ 1991 L 376).

The reference was made in proceedings brought by Banca popolare di Cremona Soc. coop. arl ('Banca popolare') against Agenzia Entrate Ufficio Cremona concerning the levying of a regional tax on productive activities.

Legal context

Community legislation

Under Article 33(1) of the Sixth Directive[29]:

'Without prejudice to other Community provisions, in particular those laid down in the Community provisions in force relating to the general arrangements for the holding, movement and monitoring of products subject to excise duty, this Directive shall not prevent a Member State from maintaining or introducing taxes on insurance contracts, taxes on betting and gambling, excise duties, stamp duties and, more generally, any taxes, duties or charges which cannot be characterised as turnover taxes, provided however that those taxes, duties or charges do not, in trade between Member States, give rise to formalities connected with the crossing of frontiers.'...

National legislation

The regional tax on productive activities (imposta regionale sulle attività produttive, 'IRAP') was introduced by Legislative Decree No 446 of 15 December 1997 ....

The main proceedings and the question referred for a preliminary ruling

Banca popolare brought an action before the referring court against the decision of Agenzia Entrate Ufficio Cremona refusing to reimburse the IRAP paid in 1998 and 1999.

According to the applicant in the main proceedings, the legislative decree is not consistent with Article 33 of the Sixth Directive.

The referring court makes the following points:

- first, IRAP applies, in general, to all commercial transactions involving production or trade, relating to goods and services

[28] Edited by the authors.

[29] Substantially the same as Art. 401 of the VAT Directive *supra* note 23.

and arising from the regular exercise of an activity intended for that purpose, that is, through undertakings, trades and professions;
- second, although IRAP operates according to a different procedure from that for value added tax ('VAT'), it is levied on the net value deriving from production, or, more specifically, the net value 'added' to the product by the producer, with the result that IRAP is a value added tax;
- third, IRAP is levied at every stage of the production or distribution process;
- fourth, the total amount of IRAP collected in the various stages of the cycle, from production up to the final consumer, is equal to the rate of IRAP applied to the selling price of goods and services charged to the final consumer.

However, the referring court raises the question whether the differences between VAT and IRAP concern the essential characteristics which determine whether or not the taxes belong to the same category.

It is against that background that the Commissione tributaria provinciale di Cremona decided to stay proceedings and refer the following question to the Court of Justice for a preliminary ruling:

'Must Article 33 of [the Sixth Directive] be interpreted as meaning that it prohibits a charge to IRAP of the net value of production deriving from the regular exercise of an independently run activity whose object is the production of or trade in goods or the provision of services?'

The question referred for a preliminary ruling

By its question the referring court seeks essentially to know whether Article 33 of the Sixth Directive precludes the maintenance of a charge to tax with the characteristics of the tax at issue in the main proceedings.

In order to interpret Article 33 of the Sixth Directive it must be viewed against its legislative background. To that end it is useful to recall the objectives pursued by the introduction of a common system of VAT ....

According to the preamble to First Council Directive 67/227/EEC of 11 April 1967 on the harmonisation of legislation of Member States concerning turnover taxes (OJ, English Special Edition 1967 (I), p. 14, 'the First Directive'), harmonisation of legislation concerning turnover taxes should make it possible to establish a common market within which there is healthy competition and whose characteristics are similar to those of a domestic market, by eliminating tax differences liable to distort competition and hinder trade ....

Under Article 2 of the First Directive, the principle of the common system of VAT involves the application to goods and services, up to and including the retail trade stage, of a general tax on consumption exactly proportional to the price of the goods and services, whatever the number of transactions which take place in the production and distribution process before the stage at which tax is charged.

However, VAT is chargeable on each transaction only after deduction of the amount of VAT borne directly by the costs of the various price components. The procedure for deduction is so arranged ... that taxable persons are authorised to deduct from the VAT for which they are liable the VAT which the goods or services have already borne and that the tax is charged, at each stage, only on the added value and is finally borne by the ultimate consumer ....

In order to decide whether a tax, duty or charge can be characterised as a turnover tax within the meaning of Article 33 of the Sixth Directive, it is necessary, in particular, to determine whether it has the effect of jeopardising the functioning of the common system of VAT by being levied on the movement of goods and services and on commercial transactions in a way comparable to VAT.

The Court has stated in this regard that taxes, duties and charges must in any event be regarded as being imposed on the movement of goods and services in a way comparable to VAT if they exhibit the essential characteristics of VAT, even if they are not identical to it in every way .... Article 33 of the Sixth Directive does not, on the other hand, preclude the maintenance or introduction of a tax which does not display one of the essential characteristics of VAT ....

The Court has established the essential characteristics of VAT. Notwithstanding certain differences of wording, it appears from the case-law that there are four such characteristics: it applies generally to transactions relating to goods or services; it is proportional to the price charged by the taxable person in return for the goods and services which he has supplied; it is charged at each stage of the production and distribution process, including that of retail sale, irrespective of the number of transactions which have previously taken place; the amounts paid during the preceding stages of the process are deducted from the tax payable by a taxable person, with the result that the tax applies, at any given stage, only to the value added at that stage and the final burden of the tax rests ultimately on the consumer ....

In order to prevent outcomes which are inconsistent with the objective pursued by the common system of VAT ... any comparison of the characteristics of a tax such as IRAP with those of VAT must be made in the light of that objective. In that connection, particular attention must be paid to the need to safeguard the neutrality of the common system of VAT at all times.

In this case, as regards the second essential characteristic of VAT, it must first be observed that, whereas VAT is levied on individual transactions at the marketing stage and its amount is proportional to the price of goods or services supplied, IRAP is, in contrast, a tax charged on the net value of the production of an undertaking in a given period. Its basis of assessment is the difference appearing in the profit and loss account between the 'value of production' and the 'production costs' as defined by Italian legislation. It includes elements such as variation in stocks, amortisation and depreciation, which have no direct connection with the supply of goods or services as such. In those circumstances, IRAP cannot be considered proportional to the price of goods or services supplied.

Next, it must be observed, as regards the fourth essential characteristic of VAT, that the existence of differences in the method for calculating the deduction of tax already paid cannot exclude a tax from the prohibition laid down in Article 33 of the Sixth Directive if such differences are in fact technical in nature and do not prevent that tax from operating in essentially the same way as VAT. On the other hand, a tax levied on production in such a way that it is not certain that it will be borne, like a tax on consumption such as VAT, by the final consumer, is likely to fall outside the scope of Article 33 of the Sixth Directive.

In fact, whereas, through the mechanism of the deduction of tax laid down by Articles 17 to 20 of the Sixth Directive, VAT taxes only the final consumer and is completely neutral as regards the taxable persons involved in the production and distribution process prior to the stage of final taxation, regardless of the number of transactions involved ..., that is not the case with IRAP.

First, a taxable person cannot ascertain exactly the amount of IRAP already included in the purchase price of goods and services. Second, if, in order to pass on the burden of the tax due in connection with his own activities to the following stage in the distribution or consumption process, a taxpayer could include that burden in his sale price, the basis of assessment would then include not only the value added but also the tax itself, with the result that the IRAP would be calculated on an amount based on a sale price incorporating, in anticipation, the tax to be paid.

In any event, even on the assumption that a taxable person liable to IRAP selling to final consumers will take account, in fixing his price, of the amount of the charge included in its general expenses, not all taxable persons have the possibility of thus passing on, or passing on in full, the burden of the tax ....

It follows from all the foregoing considerations that, according to the legislation concerning IRAP, the tax is not intended to be passed on to the final consumer in a way that is characteristic of VAT ....

It follows from the foregoing considerations that a tax with the characteristics of IRAP differs from VAT in such a way that it cannot be characterised as a turnover tax within the meaning of Article 33(1) of the Sixth Directive.

The answer to the question referred for a preliminary ruling must therefore be that Article 33 of the Sixth Directive must be interpreted as meaning that it does not preclude the maintenance of a charge to tax with the characteristics of the tax at issue in the main proceedings.

III. EU Commitment to an Origin VAT: Its Problems and Proposals

A. In General and Early Proposals

The planned transition to a total origin-based VAT within the EU raised so many problems that it apparently has been abandoned. Although the origin principle has been implemented for sales to individuals who purchase goods and services for personal use, little progress has been made in developing rules for intra-Community trade between VAT-registered businesses. Under current rules, a VAT-registered person with tight cash flow has some incentive to purchase goods from a business in another member state rather than from a business in its home state. There is a cash flow advantage to the customer from intra-Community purchases, because intra-Community sales to registered persons are zero-rated. In contrast, a domestic purchase carries VAT, which is recovered only when the purchaser claims the input credit in the VAT return for the period in which the purchase is made.[30] (On the other hand, a business seller obtains a cash-flow advantage when it receives the VAT from a taxable domestic sale [output tax] rather than a zero-rated international sale because the seller does not remit that output VAT to the government until the tax for that period is due.)

The literature contains several proposals that address the taxation of intra-EU transactions under a VAT system that allows the free flow of goods among member states without border posts. One method proposed to handle the origin principle for intra-Community trade is the clearing system that taxes exports, allows input credit to the importer at the exporting country's VAT rate, and relies on consumption statistics or other data to allocate revenue on such trades between member states.[31]

Another proposal to implement the origin principle with little or no clearing system presupposes that (1) the Community will agree to impose a uniform regular (18%) and reduced (6%) rate on all intra-Community

[30] See, generally, Vanistendael "A Proposal for a Definitive VAT System: Taxation in the Country of Origin at the Rate of the Country of Destination, Without Clearing," 1 *EC Tax Review* 45–53 (1995) [hereinafter Vanistendael].

[31] See Commission of the European Communities, *A Common System of VAT: A Programme for the Single Market* (Brussels 1996).

transactions and (2) the member states will interpret and apply the VAT rules in a uniform manner. With these preconditions, Vanistendael suggested that VAT be imposed in the country of origin and paid in that country directly to an agent of the destination country located in the origin country. For example, an Italian firm selling goods to a French firm would charge VAT and remit the tax to the French VAT agent in Italy. In that way, the revenue will go directly to the destination country without any clearing system. He acknowledges that there still may be some clearing required because the rates in the origin and destination country may deviate from the uniform rates.[32]

A few other proposals are discussed in more detail in this section. Some are tailored to the EU (assuming an origin-based tax on trade within the Community) and others were designed to have broader applicability in federal systems and economic unions.

B. The Keen and Smith VIVAT for Intra-EU Trade

Some proposals rely on the destination principle for trade within the EU. The Keen and Smith Variable Integrated VAT (VIVAT) proposal retains the audit trail created with the invoice system and applies the destination principle for intra-Community transactions. It adds a clearing system that is required to allocate revenue from final sales to the consuming (or destination) jurisdiction. The term "province" is used to refer to member states (with respect to the EU) and to subnational states or provinces in federal systems. According to the Keen and Smith VIVAT, the provinces must set a single tax rate on intra- or interprovincial sales to registered persons, but can impose the local rate set by the province on sales to unregistered persons (e.g., consumers). As with VATs in use worldwide, sales outside the EU or federation are zero-rated, consistent with the destination principle. The VIVAT scheme therefore retains the audit trail through the use of tax invoices and relies on a clearing system to maintain the destination principle on interprovincial sales within the EU or federation. The clearing system takes the revenue received in the seller's state, gives it to the destination state, and allows a credit to the registered buyer in the destination state. In 2000, Keen expanded on the 1996[33] Keen and Smith proposal.[34] The following example is adapted from that article.

Assume that the tax rate on final consumption in the origin province is 8%, and in the destination province it is 12%. The uniform rate on sales between registered persons, wherever located within a union of provinces in a federal system, is 10%. A Corporation, a registered person, sells goods to B Corporation, a registered person in the same province, for $100. For

[32] Vanistendael, *supra* note 30, at 51–53. The author discusses the need to adapt the place of supply rules so that the "origin" country can easily be identified.

[33] See also M. Keen & S. Smith, "The Future of the Value Added Tax in the European Union," 23 *Economic Policy* 375 (1996).

[34] Keen, "VIVAT, CVAT and All That," 48 *Canadian Tax Journal* 409 (2000).

purposes of the example, assume that A does not have any inputs subject to VAT. B sells its entire output to C Corporation, located in another province, for $140, assuming that B does not have any inputs other than the purchase from A. C Corporation sells all of the goods domestically for $200. C's only inputs are the purchases from B. All of the figures are exclusive of VAT. The table shows that the VIVAT system taxes final sales under the destination principle (the destination province receives the VAT revenue) even with respect to interprovincial sales.

Chart 15.1. Illustration of VIVAT

A Corporation sale to domestic B Corporation	
A's intraprovince sale $100 x 10% uniform rate =	$10
A Corporation input tax	00
Net VAT paid to province	10
B Corporation export of goods from A	
B's interprovince sale 140 x 10% uniform rate	14
B Corporation input tax (from A Corporation)	*(10)*
Net VAT on interprovincial sales	$4
C Corporation (importer) domestic sales	
C's domestic sales $200 x 8% domestic rate	$16
C Corporation input credit (from B Corporation)	(14)
Net VAT paid to importing province	2
VAT collected by both provinces	$16
(based on an 8 percent rate on sales of $200 in destination province)	

According to Keen, the VIVAT is "equivalent to a common federal VAT levied at the intermediate [uniform] rate combined with a series of provincial retail sales taxes levied at rate[s] equal to the difference between the provincial VAT and the common intermediate rate."[35] VIVAT taxes inter- and intraprovincial sales to registered persons alike. The clearing system allocates the appropriate amount of revenue to the destination province. In the preceding example, the consuming province should receive revenue of 200 x the 8% provincial rate, or $16. It received only 2 on the sale by C Corporation and is entitled to the $14 that the other province collected with A and B's VAT returns. Keen notes that this clearing function can be accomplished more easily if a single agency collects and refunds the tax on the B2B transactions.

Unlike most VAT systems that treat all buyers (registered or unregistered) the same, the VIVAT treats registered buyers differently than unregistered buyers. The VIVAT follows the usual rule of zero-rating sales outside the federation (or EU). The seller, therefore, must separate sales into three categories: sales to registered persons within the federation,

[35] *Id.* at 418.

sales to unregistered persons within the federation, and sales for export outside the federation.

The VIVAT permits the free flow of goods within the union without border tax adjustments. It allows fiscal autonomy for member states to set their local VAT rates. The taxation (at origin state rates) of sales to consumers may reduce cross-border shopping to reduce VAT to the extent the origin and destination states impose VAT at comparable rates. A significant disadvantage is that the destination state must grant input credits for VAT paid to the origin state on intra-EU sales, and the destination state recoups this credit under the clearance system.

The VIVAT is designed with a single rate for sales to registered persons within the union. This will reduce the cost of clearing the tax among member states, but it requires clearance with its attendant costs.

There has been other significant scholarship that addresses subnational VATs in federal countries. The cross-border issues that confront national governments in the EU confront subnational governments in Canada that impose a national GST and provincial sales taxes or VATs and in other federal systems, such as Brazil, Argentina, and India.

C. Howell Zee's VAT Voucher System

Howell Zee,[36] considering the lack of progress in the EU and federal governments like Brazil, Canada, and India to develop a decentralized system that can apply the destination principle among jurisdictions (referred to as the states) without fiscal borders, proposed a voucher system to achieve this goal.[37] The idea is to develop a system that gives states (member states in the EU) independence in establishing their own VATs. To date, the zero-rating of exports within the state of origin (state of the supplier) and the deferred payment of tax by the purchaser in the destination state (the destination principle) has led to unacceptable levels of VAT evasion. The destination principle continues to be abused with the "missing trader" and "carousel" fraud.

The EU's initial goal to implement an origin principle for intra-EU trade has not been attainable. One problem with a proposal like the VIVAT system (an origin principle virtual VAT) is that it requires the supplier making intrastate sales to distinguish between intermediate and final sales and requires a clearing house to allocate revenue to the appropriate states.

Professor Zee's voucher system, in a federation or union without fiscal borders, gets the revenue, consistent with the destination principle, to the state where the goods or services are consumed. The supplier

[36] H. Zee, A VAT Voucher System for Origin-Based Taxation, 20(2) *EC Tax Review* 75 (2011) [hereinafter Zee, VAT Voucher System].

[37] *Id.* at 79.

charges tax on interstate sales at the rate in the origin state. The buyer gets credit for the VAT paid on the import at the destination state's rate, the same as any other purchase in the destination state. He describes his system as achieving an "origin-taxation-destination-revenue" outcome without "an over-arching fiscal authority" or "a central clearing arrangement and associated transfers of VAT revenue between jurisdictions."[38] "In this way, individual jurisdictions would be able to retain full autonomy in setting their VAT parameters in accordance with their own revenue needs, thus avoiding potential costly negotiations for reaching an agreement among all concerned jurisdictions on the VAT treatment of interjurisdiction trades."[39] His system provides incentives to both the exporting and importing state to enforce compliance with interstate sales, unlike other proposals to address interstate sales within a federation or union.[40]

The following are the central features of Zee's voucher system:

"(1) the use by importers in an importing jurisdiction of special VAT vouchers as means of payment for the VAT charged on exports by an exporting jurisdiction, and

(2) the acquisition of such vouchers by importers is predicated upon payment of reverse charges imposed on their imports at the applicable VAT rate(s) of an importing jurisdiction.

Moreover, to minimize potential abuse of the voucher system, it is proposed that the collection of reverse charges from importers and the issuance of vouchers – as well as the transmission of such vouchers to the suppliers of the importers[41] – be integrated into a single administrative process and executed by designated third party intermediaries, such as banks."[42]

38 *Id.* at 76 and 78.

39 *Id.* at 78.

40 "Since the VAT on exports is primarily paid in VAT vouchers issued by importing jurisdictions … [no] real revenue, the VAT authorities in exporting jurisdictions would have as strong an incentive as that under destination-based taxation in ensuring that all claims of VAT credits or refunds by their exporters are genuine. Likewise, the VAT authorities in importing jurisdictions would have a similarly strong incentive in ensuring that all imports are properly reversed charged [they generate revenue and determine input credits]. Compliance on the part of traders is equally incentive-compatible under the voucher system. Importers would have no incentive to evade reverse charges on imports, as they are subsequently creditable. [Exporters] would have little incentive to inflate their interjurisdiction relative to intrajurisdiction sales, as such actions would require documentary proof [in vouchers issued by intermediaries in their customers' jurisdictions]."

41 Presumably the actual transmission of vouchers could be carried out electronically.

42 The potential use of such financial intermediaries as VAT collection agents in general is already under study by the EU. See European Commission, Study on the Feasibility of Alternative Methods for Improving and Simplifying the Collection of VAT Through the Means of Modern Technologies and/or via Financial Intermediaries, TAXUD/2009/AO-05 (2009).

To impose tax in the origin state at the origin state's VAT rate and provide the revenue to the destination state at the destination's rate, "the VAT on exports in an exporting jurisdiction is being paid in the form of vouchers rather than real funds by importers in an importing jurisdiction. As such, voucher payments, unlike reverse charges, are not creditable against the importers' output VAT."[43] In addition, "VAT vouchers collected by exporters would be treated by their VAT authorities exactly like output VAT on their sales."[44]

The importer submits "a self-issued reverse-charge invoice," along with VAT at the importing state's rate, to the institution issuing the voucher. The vouchers, issued to the exporter by that institution issuing the voucher, are sent on behalf of the importer. The voucher, even if for a different amount of VAT, satisfies the buyer's obligation to the seller for the VAT listed on the seller's invoice.

The importer's VAT payment for VAT charged on the out-of-state seller's invoice does not go to the seller; rather, it is paid with the voucher submitted to that seller. In addition, the voucher issued by the buyer's bank does not represent an actual money payment.[45] The voucher is issued to the exporter and used by him to satisfy his output tax liability for the VAT charged on the export sale. The only output tax payable on this interstate sale is the amount paid on the reverse-charge when the importer requests the voucher to satisfy the VAT charged on the exporter's sales invoice.

VAT-registered importers who use the imports in making taxable sales offset this output tax with the input credit for the same amount, paying no net VAT on the import.[46] Professor Zee acknowledges that his system does not prevent cross-border shopping by unregistered traders who may buy from out-of-state suppliers operating in states with a much lower VAT rate and pay (in real money, not vouchers) the out-of-state supplier the VAT charged on the import.

For registered importers covered by the voucher system, the out-of-state supplier's VAT charged on the import and the VAT on the voucher submitted to the out-of-state supplier are noncash transactions. The VAT imposed on the exporter's invoice is satisfied (in the exporter's jurisdiction) with the VAT voucher issued by the bank to the exporter. The voucher from the importer's bank can be used as payment of the exporter's output tax on the export. The VAT on that voucher is not included in the importer's VAT return.

[43] Zee, VAT Voucher System, *supra* note 36, at 79.

[44] *Id.* at 79–80.

[45] The "only exceptions being imports carried out by unregistered traders who may elect to pay the VAT charged by exporting jurisdictions with real funds." *Id.* at 80. That VAT is not creditable in the importing state.

[46] Zee suggests that because of "mirror pair of documents" (the receipt showing payment of the reverse charge to the importer's bank and the voucher receipt sent to the exporter), the tax authorities in the export and import states could, by electronically cross-matching invoice numbers or otherwise, verify compliance.

IV. Canadian VATs and the Bird/Gendron Dual VAT

A. Introduction

The Bird and Gendron dual VAT has implications for the EU, but because it requires an understanding of the federal Canadian Goods and Services Tax, the provincial sales or value added tax, and the combined Harmonized Sales Tax (HST), the dual VAT is deferred until after the following discussion of the variety of VAT systems in operation in Canada.

In that federal system, the national GST defines the jurisdictional reach of the tax on international transactions under the destination principle. The subnational sales, value added tax, or HST also follow the destination principle on international transactions but may use the destination or a hybrid origin/destination principle on interprovincial transactions. The next section discusses the array of federal-provincial variations of the GST, HST, and provincial sales taxes.

B. Variety of Canadian Approaches

The taxation of interstate or interprovincial transactions (both referred to in this chapter as "interstate") is more complicated if a country relies both on a national and subnational sales or value added tax, each imposed on different tax bases. The rate for the federal part is 5% and the rate for the participating provincial parts vary from 8% to 10%. For example, Canada has a federal VAT (called the Goods and Services Tax), an HST for some provinces, and a variety of sales taxes in other provinces. The HST in effect in Ontario and other provinces is collected by the federal government, which remits the provincial portion of the tax to the appropriate provinces on the basis of a jointly developed formula using consumption patterns. The provinces have some flexibility in setting the provincial rate. Quebec administers the combined HST and remits the federal portion to the national government.[47] In most of the other provinces, the GST operates alongside existing provincial sales taxes (PSTs) imposed on tax bases that differ by province. With this configuration, the federal government administers the GST and the provinces administer their own PSTs on GST-inclusive bases. In Alberta, there is only a federal GST, no provincial sales tax.

The following covers some of the basic elements of the Canadian Harmonized Sales Tax. In October 1996, the federal government entered an agreement with Nova Scotia, New Brunswick, and Newfoundland

[47] Many of the differences between the HST and the Quebec Sales Tax are being eliminated. For example, the formerly zero-rated financial services now are exempt, effective January 1, 2013.

for the harmonization of the provincial sales taxes and the national GST – the HST. The "participating provinces" now include Labrador, Ontario, and Prince Edward Island. Ontario was added in 2010, and British Columbia, previously covered by the HST, withdrew as of April 1, 2013. There is a single federal administration of the HST.[48] The federal government provided revenue to newly participating provinces to offset some of the expected loss of provincial revenue resulting from the conversion to the HST.[49]

The HST incorporates the GST rules.

> [B]usinesses that are registered for the GST [are] required to collect and remit the tax at the HST rate ... on any taxable (other than zero-rated) supplies they make in the participating provinces. Similarly, businesses engaged in commercial activities anywhere in Canada that purchase goods and services in participating provinces that are taxed at the harmonized rate will be entitled to recover tax payable at the HST rate.[50]

Taxable businesses thus can claim input credits for the full HST on business inputs. This rule avoids the cascading of input tax when businesses in nonparticipating provinces purchase business inputs subject to the HST.[51] The HST revenue will be shared between the federal and provincial governments on the basis of "final consumption data provided by Statistics Canada."[52]

A central feature of the HST is the grant of input credits for the entire HST paid on business inputs used in providing taxable goods and services.[53] The credit for HST on business inputs is expected to benefit exports from participating provinces by eliminating the federal and provincial portions of the HST from the prices of those exports.

The HST attempts to resolve the intractable cross-border shopping problem that exists under state retail sales taxes (RSTs); that is, the HST is imposed on mail order and other interprovincial sales by businesses in Canada. All Canadian businesses registered under the GST or HST must collect and remit the HST "on goods or services sold into a participating province or shipped to a consumer in that province."[54]

[48] Dept. of Finance Canada News Release 96-075, "Sales Tax Harmonization: Detailed Agreements Reached," Oct. 23, 1996 [hereinafter News Release 96–075].

[49] See, for example, Dept. of Finance Canada News Release 96–039, "GST Harmonization and Adjustment Assistance," May 21, 1996.

[50] Dept. of Finance Canada News Release 97–003, "Governments Release Additional Guidelines for Tax-Inclusive Pricing Under Harmonized Sales Tax," January 17, 1997.

[51] In fact, a business outside the participating provinces may have some incentive to buy from businesses in participating provinces to recover the full HST. The PST it pays on like purchases from suppliers in its nonparticipating province would not be creditable against its GST liability. The shipping costs incurred when supplies are purchased from another province may offset some of the incentive just described.

[52] News Release 96–075, *supra* note 48.

[53] Technical Paper on Sales Tax Harmonization, Oct. 23, 1996, at 63–66.

[54] News Release 96–075, *supra* note 48, at An Overview.

C. Bird and Gendron Dual VAT Proposal

To handle the cross-border trade without border controls in a system consisting of a federal and subnational sales or value added taxes imposed at varying rates, Bird and Gendron advocate a two tier or dual VAT system. This dual VAT system is imposed on the destination principle with features of the Canadian federal GST and provincial Quebec Sales Tax (QST).[55] They suggest that the taxation of cross-border trade is alleviated if a nation has both a subnational and national VAT. Whereas by zero-rating interprovincial sales, the GST provides some opportunity for tax avoidance on mail order or e-commerce sales, the authors claim that the national VAT can be used to control or monitor interjurisdictional trade.[56] Indeed, they raise the possibility of using a "virtual VAT" in a place like the EU that does not have a central VAT.[57]

Bird and Gendron judge various alternatives for a dual federal-state VAT system by the following principles:

1. Harmonization should lead to simplification of the sales tax system, so that compliance and administration costs (and the related efficiency losses) are minimized.
2. Harmonization should respect provincial autonomy by allowing each province to choose its own sales tax rate.
3. There should only be one agency to administer and collect the sales tax.

On the basis of these principles, the authors concluded that the GST-QST combination[58] is a good model.[59] There is a single administration (at the provincial level), costs are reduced, and the province has autonomy in setting the tax rate. Interprovincial sales are treated like sales outside Canada – that is, the sales are zero-rated. Imports from another province are taxed at the next stage when the Quebec importer resells the imports. There is no clearing system required. A weak element in this approach is that unregistered persons must self-assess on purchases from Quebec.

To illustrate the dual VAT system, assume that the national GST rate is 20%, the QST rate is 8%, and sales to other provinces are zero-rated.[60] Assuming that the interprovincial sale is to a province with a provincial

[55] Bird and Gendron 1998, *supra* note 11. The authors emphasize in their 2000 article that the imposition of the subnational VAT on prices inclusive of the federal VAT provide the importing provinces with some incentive to apply the federal VAT properly. R. Bird and P.P. Gendron, "CVAT, VIVAT, and Dual VAT: Vertical 'Sharing' and Interstate Trade," 7 *Int'l Trade and Public Finance* 753 (2000) [hereinafter Bird and Gendron 2000].

[56] Bird and Gendron 2000, *supra* note 55, at 757 and 759.

[57] See *id.* at 754.

[58] The analysis was based on the Quebec Sales Tax that has been amended to more closely parallel the federal GST.

[59] The authors' preference for the GST-QST dual VAT system over the HST was based on earlier QST rules that gave Quebec a degree of fiscal autonomy to alter the tax base without unanimous consent from the participating provinces.

[60] The QST is imposed on a GST-inclusive base, so the effective combined rate is more than 15%. The example assumes each tax is imposed on a tax-exclusive base, so the combined rate is 15%.

sales tax (PST), not a VAT, it is assumed that the PST rate on sales to consumers is 8%. The GST-QST consequences (and the PST in the destination province) would be as follows:

Chart 15.2. Illustration of dual tax system

A Corporation intraprovince sale to B Corporation		
A's intraprovincial sale 100 × 28% GST-QST rate =	28	28
A Corporation input tax	00	00
Net VAT paid to Quebec (20 goes to national government)	28	28
B Corporation interprovincial sale to C Corporation*		
B's interprovincial sale 140 × 0% rate		00
B Corporation input tax (from A Corp)		28
Net VAT refund on interprovincial sales		28
C Corporation (importer) domestic sales		
C's domestic sales 200 × 20% GST rate		40
200 × 8% PST rate		16
C Corporation input credit (from B Corp)		00
Net VAT or sales tax paid to national and provincial government		56
Tax collected by national & provincial gov't & paid by final consumers	56	
National government 20% of 200 sales =	40	
Provincial government 8% of 200 sales = 56	16	
No revenue to the province of origin if all goods are exported to other provinces or countries.		

* Exports to buyers in other provinces or other countries are treated the same – both are zero-rated.

The Bird/Gendron dual VAT zero-rates interstate sales and taxes these goods, under the sales or value added tax in the buyer's state, when the buyer resells those goods (or incorporates them into goods or services subsequently sold). The tax treatment therefore is comparable to the deferral of tax on imports under a national VAT. This system may provide a cash flow advantage to a business that purchases goods interstate rather than domestically. The significance of the advantage, if any, depends on a number of factors, such as the interest cost (relating to VAT) that is incurred if a registered person must pay VAT on a domestic purchase before the person can receive a VAT benefit by claiming an input credit on the first VAT return filed after the purchase. This cost may be higher if the business is in an "excess credit" position and the state does not refund excess credits, but it requires that they be carried forward to future tax periods.

The Bird/Gendron dual VAT also requires a firm exempt from VAT that imports taxable goods to file a VAT return and pay tax on the import at the importing state's tax rate (like businesses subject to a state use tax in the United States for goods imported into the state).[61]

[61] Bird and Gendron acknowledge that none of the three proposals adequately address the taxation of interstate sales to final consumers. Except for automobiles and select other items, there is no attempt under the QST to collect provincial tax on consumer

V. Brazil and the Varsano "Little Boat Model"

A. Brazil's Tax Structure in General

Brazil's sales tax system is described in more detail because it is unique. Brazil does what Bird suggests: subnational governments finance their programs with subnational taxes.[62] Brazil has a multiple rate federal "excise tax" in the nature of a VAT imposed on imports and on raw materials and production up to the manufacturing stage (the IPI)[63] and a state VAT (state ICMS)[64] on agriculture, industry, and many services. The state ICMS is shared with municipalities. The national government establishes the main features of the ICMS, but within limits leaves the rate setting to the states. The services excluded from the ICMS are subject to the municipal tax, the ISS, that is imposed on the gross receipts (no input credits allowed) derived from a variety of industrial, commercial, and professional services.

To reduce the revenue disparity between producing and consuming states and, thus, give more revenue to the less developed states, the state ICMS adopts a part origin-part destination principle with respect to interstate transactions.[65] The central government sets the two low interstate rates (depending on the economic position of the destination state), so that the importing state can collect the difference between the interstate rate (applied on the origin principle) and the local rate in the consuming state.[66] There are some notable consequences of the ICMS treatment of interstate transactions. Assume that a sale from a firm in state A to a firm in state B is taxed at a 7% interstate rate. The buyer in state B sells the goods to a buyer

purchases from another province. Bird, "Rethinking Sub-National Taxes: A New Look at Tax Assignment," IMF WP/99/165, December 1999 [hereinafter Bird, Rethinking Sub-National Taxes].

62 See *id.*, discussed at section VII *infra.*

63 "*Imposto sobre productos industrializados*" is imposed on the manufacturing sector "on raw materials, intermediary products, packaging materials and finished goods with set-off for the tax paid at the earlier stage." M. Purohit, "Harmonizing Taxation of Interstate Trade under a Sub-National VAT – Lessons from International Experience," 13 *Int'l VAT Monitor* 169 (May/June 2002) [hereinafter Purohit, Harmonizing Tax under a Sub-National VAT]. Although generally there is no input credit on capital goods, an exception is made for "tax on machinery and equipment produced in Brazil forming part of fixed assets and used solely in the industrial process." *Id.* at 169.

64 The ICMS is the *Imposto sobre operações relativas à circulação de mercadorias e sobre prestações de serviços* (Tax on Operations Related to the Circulation of Goods and on the Provision of Interstate and Intermunicipal Transportation Services and of Communication Services) described in R. Varsano, "Sub-National Taxation and Treatment of Interstate Trade in Brazil," a paper presented to the Annual World Bank Conference on Development in Latin America and the Caribbean, Chile, 1999 [hereinafter Varsano, Sub-National Taxation].

65 The ICMS imposes lower than the standard rate on some specific goods and services. See generally, KPMG Issues and Insights, Brazil, VAT essentials, at http://www.kpmg.com/global/en/issuesandinsights/articlespublications/vat-gst-essentials/pages/brazil.aspx (March 2014).

66 The ICMS is the *Imposto sobre operaços relatives à circulaçâo de Mercadorias e services. Id.* ICMS is the Tax on Operations Related to the Circulation of Goods and on the Provision of Interstate and Intermunicipal Transportation Services and of Communication Services, described in Varsano, Sub-National Taxation, *supra* note 64.

outside Brazil. Under the current regime, the buyer in state B can claim an input credit for the 7% VAT paid to the firm in state A and reports no tax (a zero-rated sale) on the export sale. State A has, in effect, received VAT revenue from this eventual export sale. State B loses revenue by granting an input credit to the exporting firm in its state. Ordinarily, a state foregoes revenue on international export sales as a consequence of the destination principle, but, in this case, state B not only foregoes revenue but also suffers negative revenue because it did not receive any revenue from the import of the goods from state A.[67] This effect would not occur if the ICMS were imposed on the pure destination principle. Brazilian states can tax domestic and interstate sales, but not international exports.[68]

B. Varsano's "Little Boat Model"

Varsano developed a unique approach to the federal-state dual VAT dilemma that may be adaptable to the EU, Canada, and other federal systems. Varsano designed for his native Brazil the "little boat model," described by McLure as "ingenious and elegant" and that can have broad application elsewhere because it deals "with cross-border trade that is internal to a nation or to a group of nations that wish to form a single market without internal fiscal borders, such as the EU."[69] Bird added that Varsano's "little boat model" "may prove to be one of the key innovations in tax thought of the century."[70] McLure described his modification of the Varsano proposal as the Compensating VAT (or CVAT).

This subsection discusses the Varsano proposal. The following subsection explains McLure's modified CVAT.

The Varsano proposal was designed to replace Brazil's federal IPI, state ICMS, and municipal ISS with dual, consumption-style, destination-principle VATs. Brazil's origin-based state ICMS would be converted to a destination-based VAT.[71] To handle the tax avoidance or evasion resulting from zero-

[67] *Id.* at 16.

[68] The rates are prescribed by the National Public Finance Council (CONFAZ). Purohit, Harmonizing Tax under a Sub-National VAT, *supra* note 63, at 170. "The CONFAZ consists of all states' representatives with 27 councillors. Unanimity is required for any resolution to go through. The 1988 Constitution strengthened the legislative role of the CONFAZ." *Id.* at note 6.

[69] C.E. McLure, Jr., "Implementing Sub-National Value Added Taxes on Internal Trade: The Compensating VAT (CVAT)," 7 *Int'l Tax and Public Finance* 732 (2000) [hereinafter McLure, CVAT]. For a current brief, but comprehensive, survey and principled analysis of subnational revenues including the important place and role of value added taxes, see R. Bird, *Sub-National Revenues: Realities and Prospects*, reprinted from Decentralization and Accountability of The Pubic Sector 319–336Annual World Bank Conference on Development in Latin America and the Caribbean (S.J. Burki & G. Perry, eds., The World Bank 2000).

[70] See M. Marquez Roncaglia, "Brazil, Transfer of input ICMS," 14 *Int'l VAT Monitor* 66 (Jan./Feb. 2003).

[71] See *id.* The services currently under the ISS would be brought into the VAT to reduce the cascade effect of this tax and the attendant incentive toward vertical integration to avoid the tax.

rating interstate sales,[72] the Varsano proposal imposes, in essence, a second federal VAT that applies only to interstate transactions.[73]

The existing difference in ICMS rates on domestic and interstate sales has encouraged a tax scheme referred to as "invoice sightseeing," in which unregistered persons claim to be registered to avoid the tax on interstate purchases. The Varsano proposal assumes that the central government will set a standard ICMS tax rate that applies to interstate sales. The state ICMS rate, although fixed by each state, cannot vary from the standard rate, up or down, by more than 10%. If the standard rate were fixed at 20%, a state could set its ICMS rate within the range of 18% to 22%.

Varsano's proposal is for a tax imposed in each state on the origin principle to be converted to a destination principle tax when the revenue from interstate sales is allocated by the central government to the destination state. On interstate transactions, the "little boat model" uses the federal VAT to transport the state VAT across the border. The state VAT on cross-border transactions is reported on and paid with the federal VAT return, and the importer will claim the input tax credit on the interstate purchase on the federal VAT return. This scheme does not require interstate clearance of input tax credits. The exporting state does not receive the revenue from the interstate sale, and the importing state does not lose revenue resulting from the allowance of the input tax credit on the federal return. Goods shipped interstate enter the importing state free of the exporting state's VAT, so that the importer's only input credits (from the federal and state VAT) will be claimed on the federal VAT return.

Interstate sales to unregistered importers or consumers are reported on the federal VAT return and are subject to the federal and state VATs, like the B2B interstate sales described earlier. The central government then must allocate the state VAT revenue from this sale (no input credit allowed to the buyers) to the destination state. It is not clear how that revenue will be identified and allocated to the appropriate state.

The Varsano dual VAT requires registered persons to separate sales into four categories. To illustrate, it is assumed that the federal rate is 5%, the state rate is 15%, and the VAT imposed only on interstate sales and reported on the federal VAT return (the tax carried by Varsano's "little boat") is imposed at a 15% rate:

1. Intrastate sales reportable on the federal VAT return are taxed at the 5% federal rate and at the 15% state rate.
2. Interstate sales to registered persons (except for small traders subject to a special scheme) are zero-rated for state VAT purposes but reportable on the federal VAT return at a combined 20% federal and interstate VAT rate.
3. Interstate sales to unregistered persons, out-of-state households, and certain small businesses are zero-rated on the state VAT return. They

[72] Bird, Rethinking Sub-National Taxes, *supra* note 61.

[73] The success of a Varsano-type approach may depend on extensive exchange of tax information between the federal and state administrations and some uniformity in audits.

are reportable on the federal return and taxed at the combined 20% federal and interstate rates, but the interstate VAT is specially designated on the federal return (the explicit VAT), so that it can be allocated by the central government to the destination state.

4. Exports outside Brazil are zero-rated. Federal VAT on business inputs is creditable on the federal VAT return, and state VAT on business inputs is creditable on the state VAT return.

Some interstate transactions require special treatment. For example, some interstate sales are made to registered persons who make both taxable and exempt sales. The seller cannot be expected to know the extent to which the buyer will use the purchased items in each activity. The buyer will be denied input credits for the portion of the combined federal-state VAT rates paid on purchases used in the exempt activity. There must be some mechanism for the buyer to notify the central government (presumably on the federal VAT return) of the extent of the disallowance of state VAT, so that this portion of the state VAT is allocated to the destination state.

C. McLure's CVAT Modification of the Varsano Proposal

McLure modified Varsano's 1995 proposal for a subnational VAT that relies on an overriding federal VAT to handle interstate sales. Many of McLure's modifications were incorporated in Varsano's "little boat model" in his 1999 paper at the World Bank conference in Chile.

McLure named the modified Varsano proposal a CVAT, even though CVAT is only part of the system.[74] He promotes the CVAT particularly for use in countries without sophisticated tax administration, especially at the state level, although it has application in the EU and in other federal systems with sophisticated tax administration at the state level. The McLure CVAT consists of three separate taxes:

1. The federal VAT that relies on the destination principle for international trade.
2. The state VAT that taxes domestic sales, zero-rates interstate and international exports, and does not tax imports until they are resold.
3. The CVAT, which is imposed at a uniform rate and is administered as a separate part of the federal VAT return, handles only interstate transactions; that is, every registered person engaged in interstate trade must charge CVAT on interstate sales and remit the tax as part of its federal VAT return, and every registered person who imports from another state and uses the import in a taxable activity can claim CVAT charged on the purchase as an input tax credit on the CVAT portion of that person's federal VAT return.

McLure makes a number of significant assumptions in designing his CVAT. For example, he assumes that the federal government will administer the

[74] McLure, CVAT, *supra* note 69, at 724.

state VAT, the federal VAT, and the CVAT. He assumes that the tax bases for the federal and state VATs will be harmonized and the administration of the taxes will be uniform. To accommodate the EU situation, McLure treats the CVAT and the federal VAT as separate levies.[75] He treats state autonomy to set domestic tax rates as an important value, even at the sacrifice of administrative simplicity. McLure relies on the CVAT as a vehicle to handle "the digitized content over the internet," suggesting that, as it is so difficult to identify the location of the purchasers, these transactions could be covered by the CVAT.

To make the CVAT consistent with the Bird/Gendron Dual VAT example, assume in the following example that the federal VAT rate is 20%, the origin state imposes an 8% rate, the destination state is a 12% rate, and the CVAT rate is 10%.

Chart 15.3. Illustration of CVAT

A Corporation intrastate sale to B Corporation		
A's intrastate sale 100 × 28% federal-state rate =	28	
A Corporation input tax	00	
Net VAT paid	28	
On federal return: VAT of	20	
On state return: VAT of	8	
B Corporation interstate sale to C Corporation*		
B's interstate sale 140 x 30%		42
(20% federal rate, 0% state, and 10% CVAT)		
B Corporation input tax (invoice from A Corp)		(28)
(20 federal and 8 state)		
Net VAT payable		14
On federal return: VAT 28–20, or	8	
CVAT 10% of 140	14	
On state return: VAT 0–8, or	(8)	
C Corporation (interstate importer) domestic sales		
C's domestic sales 200 × 32% federal-state rate		64
C Corporation input credit (from B Corp) (federal return)		42
Net VAT paid with federal and state returns		22
On federal return: VAT 40–28, or	12	
CVAT – federal refund	(14)	
On state return: net VAT liability	24	
VAT collected by government and paid by consumer (200 × 32%) (Total of net paid by A, B, and C)		64

* Exports to buyers in other provinces or other countries are treated the same – both are zero-rated.

** McLure suggests that the federal VAT and CVAT could be combined for purposes of determining if the registered person is entitled to a refund.

75 For example, assume that the rate in state A on domestic sales is 17% and on interstate sales to state B is 7%. A seller in state A sells goods to a "buyer" (a wholesaler) in state B. The wholesaler in state B then resells the goods to a small business back in state A

Like the Bird/Gendron dual VAT, under the destination principle CVAT, the state of origin does not receive any net VAT revenue when all goods are exported to other states or countries. Registered persons subject to the state VAT must distinguish between sales to intrastate buyers and interstate buyers, regardless of the tax status of the buyers as registered or unregistered persons.[76] Assuming that the system works as planned, the CVAT collected from interstate registered sellers is returned (via input credits) to interstate registered purchases, resulting in no net revenue to the federal and state governments. The CVAT permits the free flow of goods interstate without border tax adjustments. A significant advantage is that it can handle consumer transactions by mail order or electronic commerce, thereby reducing incentives to engage in tax avoidance schemes. No clearing system is required, other than the CVAT itself. The CVAT adds another layer of administration (incorporated into the federal VAT) that is not expected to increase administration and compliance costs; indeed, these costs may decline with the CVAT. States retain fiscal autonomy to set local VAT rates. The state level VAT applies the destination principle to interstate sales, so that the destination state receives the revenue from goods and services consumed there.

For unregistered importers of goods traveling interstate, McLure suggests that CVAT reported on these sales can be allocated to states "in proportion to estimated intrastate sales to households and unregistered traders that are subject to VAT in each state."[77]

McLure pronounces the CVAT superior to the more complicated clearing system proposed for the EU by the European Commission. The clearing system requires interstate exporters to impose and remit tax on intra-EU transactions at the origin state rate to the origin state, the importing state to grant input credits for that tax, and finally the clearing house for the exporting state to reimburse the importing state for the credits given (the result under the destination principle for B2B sales).

McLure prefers the CVAT to the Keen-Smith VIVAT that is imposed at a uniform rate on interstate sales to registered persons and at the origin state rate on interstate sales to unregistered persons, with only registered persons who import goods interstate eligible to claim input credits for the VIVAT. McLure's disagreement is not only with VIVAT but also with the

and applies the interstate rate of 7%. Only invoices are exchanged, the goods in fact are shipped from the seller in state A to the small business in state A, and the small business in state A saves 10% tax. This is tax advantageous if the small business is exempt from the ICMS and cannot recover tax on purchases.

76 McLure claims that distinguishing between registered and unregistered buyers is not necessary because this difference does not have an impact on tax liabilities. *Id.* at 726. McLure acknowledges, however, that households and unregistered persons pay the CVAT, not the state VAT rate on interstate purchases. The incentive to engage in mail order shopping or e-commerce interstate depends on the disparity between the CVAT and destination state tax rates. The disparity also affects the number and dollar amount of CVAT refunds that would have to be paid. *Id.* at 729.

77 McLure, CVAT, *supra* note 69, at 431. This allocation presumably also could be used for services provided via electronic commerce.

European Commission's desire (on which VIVAT is based) to treat domestic and intra-EU transactions with registered persons alike. McLure thus does not support Keen and Smith's application of a uniform rate on all sales to registered persons within the EU (compliance symmetry), in part because the seller must distinguish between registered and unregistered buyers in the origin state. He finds it easier (except as noted on services) to treat all intrastate sales the same (whether the registered or unregistered persons) and subject interstate sales to the separate CVAT, not the origin state VAT.

McLure highlights the fact that the VIVAT weakens the audit trail of input credits on intrastate sales to registered persons (a point that Keen and Smith acknowledge) to the extent that the VIVAT rate is below the state VAT rate. McLure concedes that a similar problem may exist with CVAT, but with that system, the problem exists "only for interstate trade with registered traders in some states."[78] McLure also criticizes the requirement under VIVAT that the destination state must allow credit for tax collected by the origin state, necessitating interstate clearance of credits.

McLure does not support a hybrid CVAT/VIVAT system that limits CVAT to interstate sales to registered persons. McLure's major criticism is that the CVAT then would not apply to interstate sales to buyers claiming to be registered, which is the case, according to McLure, where CVAT is most needed. Under VIVAT, revenue from sales to unregistered persons (including households) also would go to the wrong state – that is, the origin state.

In a 2000 article, Bird and Gendron elaborate on the advantages of their dual VAT approach over the CVAT. The dual VAT patterned on the Canadian QST/GST at the time provided states with more flexibility than CVAT to depart from the national tax base, including the possibility that they can set their own rules on major aspects of the tax, such as the allowable input tax credits.[79] The flexibility is built into the state structure that zero-rates interstate sales. The Bird/Gendron dual VAT system relies on a single tax administration at the federal or state level, saving costs over the competing CVAT (two tax administrations).[80]

Bird and Gendron make an important practical point. The dual VAT, which accommodates the mixture of sales and value added taxes in Canadian provinces, may be more palatable politically than CVAT, which requires all participating states to adopt a uniform tax base.

D. General Comments

The preference for one system, or a combination of the features of more than one system, depends on a country's ranking of features that are

[78] *Id.* at 734.

[79] Bird and Gendron 2000, *supra* note 55, at 754. Quebec retained some restrictions on allowable input tax credits for large firms. Bird and Gendron 1998, *supra* note 11, at 434.

[80] Bird and Gendron 2000, *supra* note 55, at 757.

important to it, including an evaluation of which system will work with the level of its tax administration, especially subnational (referred to as state) tax administration.

Whichever system is selected, the system will be more likely to be successful if there is an extensive exchange of tax information among units of government, uniformity in audit procedures, uniform application of the VAT rules, and faith in the competence of the tax administration, especially at the state level. All commentators agree that it is preferable that the national and state level tax (in the EU, intra-EU transactions) should be administered by a single agency.

All of the proposals discussed here must contain a formula to allocate the revenue from interstate sales to the appropriate state when the buyer is denied input credit because it either is not registered or it is registered but uses some of the imports in an exempt activity.

VI. Subnational VATs in India

A. Enacted State-Level VATs

In January 2005, the Empowered Committee of State Finance Ministers in India issued "A White Paper on State-Level Value Added Tax."[81] The white paper reported on the consensus reach by state governments on the basic features of the state-level VAT. A large majority of the Indian states introduced a state-level VAT.[82]

The state-level VAT has harmonized design features that include minimum rates, but it provides some flexibility for states to depart from each other within given parameters.[83] The state VATs apply to intrastate sales.[84] The central government has the authority to tax interstate sales. In fact, it imposes an origin-principle Central Sales Tax (CST) on

[81] The Empowered Committee of State Finance Ministers, *A White Paper on State-Level Value Added Tax*, Constituted by the Ministry of Finance, Government of India on the Basis of Resolution Adopted in the Conference of the Chief Ministers on November 16, 1999 (New Delhi Jan. 17, 2005) [hereinafter White Paper on Indian State VAT].

[82] B. Doshi, "India: Introduction of State VAT," 15 *Int'l VAT Monitor* 204 (May/June 2005. According to Doshi, the states of Rajasthan, Madhya Pradesh, Gujarat, Jharkhand, and Chattisgarh announced that they will not introduce the VAT, and the states of Nadu and Uttar Pradesh announced that they will defer the introduction. The state of Haryana introduced its VAT previously. White Paper on Indian State VAT, *supra* note 81, at §1.7.

[83] See *id.* at §1.5.

[84] For a proposal to zero-rate interstate sales and administer that system through a rule that limits zero-rating to transactions in which the buyer can prove it paid tax to the destination state, see the proposal by Satya Poddar, that was presented in a paper and discussed at a tax reform conference in India in 1994. S. Poddar, *Reform of Domestic Consumption Taxes in India: Issues and Options* (National Institute of Public Finance and Policy New Delhi, 1994). He, along with Eric Hutton expanded on the proposal as part of a 2001 conference in the United States, Poddar & Hutton, "Zero Rating of Interstate Sales Under a Subnational VAT: A New Approach," 94th Annual Conference on Taxation of the National Tax Association (Nov. 2001).

interstate sales in goods,[85] but the states administer that tax and retain the revenue.[86] No input tax credit is allowed for the CST by any level of government.[87]

The state-level VAT is basically an origin-principle VAT within India that taxes sales within the state, does not tax imports into the state, and does not zero-rate sales to other states. It requires dealers with turnover over the threshold to register[88] and provides voluntary registration to those with turnover below the threshold.[89]

A registered manufacturer and trader can claim credits for input VAT on purchases, but the credit is limited. The input credit is available for sales made in state and out of state. Input credits are available for VAT paid on capital goods (except for a specified list of capital goods), but the input tax is creditable against tax on taxable sales, generally over a period of thirty-six months.[90] If a registered person has excess input credits, those credits must be carried over to the remainder of the current financial year and to the end of the next year. If any excess remain after that time, it is eligible for refund.[91] As is common in other VAT systems, exports of goods outside the country are zero-rated, and the exporter is entitled to a quick refund of input VAT attributable to the exported goods.[92]

B. Proposal for an Indian GST with an Integrated Interstate GST

A proposal, requiring constitutional and legislative changes, would create a trio of goods and services taxes (GSTs):

1. Central government GST (CGST)
2. State government GST (SGST)
3. Interstate GST (IGST)

[85] Central Sales Tax Act, 1956. The Central Sales Tax is going to be phased out. *Id.* at §4.3. The central government imposes the Central Value Added Tax that covers the manufacturing sector, including capital goods. B. Doshi, "India: Proposed Introduction of VAT at State Level," 13 *Int'l VAT Monitor* 309 (July/Aug. 2002.

[86] B. Doshi, "India: State Level," 15 *Int'l VAT Monitor* 445 (Nov./Dec. 2004).

[87] Satya Poddar & Shalini Mathur, "India," chapter 5 in *Gianluigi Bizioli and Claudio Sacchetto Tax Aspects of Fiscal Federalism: A Comparative Analysis* 198 (IBFD 2011) [hereinafter Poddar & Mathur].

[88] The threshold is annual turnover exceeding 500,000 rupees (US$11,468).

[89] White Paper on Indian State VAT, *supra* note 81, at §2.9. Dealers required to register (turnover above 500,000 rupees), but with turnover below 5,000,000 rupees, they can elect to pay a lower rate turnover tax (without any input credits) in lieu of the VAT. *Id.*

[90] *Id.* at §2.4. States can reduce the number of months over which the input credit on capital goods must be allocated.

[91] *Id.* at §2.3.

[92] *Id.* at §2.5. The refund is to be made within three months.

Both the CGST and SGST are to be levied on the basis of destination for international transactions. In the case of inter-state transactions within India, the state tax would apply in the state of destination, as opposed to that of origin. The proposed model does not envisage cross-utilization of input tax credit between CGST and SGST. Administratively, the union (federal) government and the states would have concurrent jurisdiction for the entire value chain and for all taxpayers, subject to common thresholds for registration prescribed for the states and the Centre. While the CGST and the SGST would be administered by the federal government and the states, respectively, various options are under consideration for harmonization of the two administrations.[93]

The unique part of this proposal is the IGST, the essential features of which are summarized by Poddar and Mathur as follows:

1. "Inter-state supplies of taxable goods and services are outside the scope of SGST .... Instead, they are made subject to IGST, which is a tax levied by the Centre at a rate equal to the sum of the CGST and SGST rates."
2. "The destination state allows the inter-state buyer/dealer in the state to claim a credit for the SGST portion of the IGST paid to the Centre. The destination state is reimbursed by the Centre for any such credits claimed/allowed."
3. "The inter-state seller remits IGST to the Centre, which then uses the funds to reimburse the destination state for the credits allowed to the inter-state buyer (i.e., for the SGST portion of the IGST)."
4. "To obviate the need for the inter-state seller to apply for a refund of the SGST paid on its inputs, the dealer is allowed to reduce the IGST payments by any such excess credits (i.e., input SGST in excess of output SGST). The Centre would then recoup the amount of any such SGST credits from the origin state."
5. "The mechanism requires the transaction details to be submitted to a central clearing agency which would verify the credits claimed by the inter-state seller and buyer and then inform the respective governments of the funds owing to or due to them."

> The success of the IGST model would be contingent upon a strong IT and complex accounting infrastructure and require a separate legislation for levy of IGST and rules for prioritizing the set off against CGST, IGST and SGST for its implementation. The model also involves complex accounting of input tax credit, apportionment between CGST and SGST and the consequent compliance and administrative burden. One important feature of this model is that any SGST on inter-state supplies to final consumers or exempt dealers (who cannot claim a credit for the tax charged by the inter-state seller) accrues to the Centre. Ideally, this revenue should flow to the destination state.[94]

[93] Poddar & Mathur, *supra* note 87.

[94] *Id.*

Poddar and Mathur suggest that the proposed IGST "could be viewed as a variant of the CVAT." They also describe an alternative proposal being considered in India,

> which provides for the collection by the seller of the SGST of the destination state and its remittance (after adjusting the input SGST) into a designated bank. The seller would issue a tax invoice to the buyer in the destination state, which would entitle the buyer to claim a credit for the tax in the same manner as for the tax paid on locally procured goods and services. The dealers would prepare returns showing inter-state and intra-state sales and purchases, which would be filed with the designated bank at the time of making the tax remittance. The central and state governments would jointly identify a nodal bank which would effectively act as a clearing house. It would host the IT infrastructure to perform the clearing house functions. The designated banks would transfer the tax payments and tax return information to the nodal bank, compute the tax amounts owing to or due from each of the States, and then debit/credit the amounts to their accounts.[95]

VII. Origin-Based Business Value Tax to Finance Subnational Government

Richard Bird urges subnational units of government to impose their own taxes to finance their programs. In a working paper of the IMF, Bird recommends that subnational governments adopt subnational origin-based VATs imposed on income,[96] not consumption (what he calls a Business Value Tax [BVT]), to finance the services they provide.[97] The BVT is levied on income (profits and wages), not consumption; imposed on production, not consumption (tax exports but not imports); and calculated on the basis of annual accounts (subtraction or addition), not on transactions.[98]

Regional or local government needs fiscal autonomy to meet its fiscal responsibilities. As government functions become decentralized, revenue

[95] *Id.*, at 209–211.

[96] See discussion *supra*, Chapter 1 (III). A key difference between an income and consumption base relates to the inclusion of capital goods in the tax base. Under an income base, the VAT on the acquisition of capital goods is recovered over the life of the goods, like depreciation under an income tax. Under a consumption base, the full VAT on the acquisition of capital goods is recovered immediately. See discussion in Chapter 1 (X)(E).

[97] R. Bird, Rethinking Sub-National Taxes, *supra* note 61. The concept of the BVT was discussed further in Bird, Subnational VATs: Experience and Prospects, *supra* note 1. See also R. Bird, Local Business Taxes, *supra* note 1, where the author considers the IRAP as the best example of an origin principle, accounts-based tax on value added by business firms by region, with the revenue retained by the region. For another analysis concluding that an origin principle, production VAT is a good replacement for the state corporate income tax and other business taxes, see W. Fox, L. Luna, and M. Murray, "Issues in the Design and Implementation of Production and Consumption VATs for the American States," Proceedings, 94th Annual Conference on Taxation, National Tax Association. 188 (2002).

[98] See R. Bird, Subnational VATs, *supra* note 1.

should be decentralized as well.[99] In many countries, either because of the tax base or the difficulty in administering the tax, the taxes assigned to subnational units of government, such as user fees and real property taxes, do not raise the level of revenue needed to finance the programs that are the responsibility of these local or regional governments. According to Bird, subnational governments should control their own revenue sources and tax rates.[100] They should not depend on revenue sharing or other methods by which national governments distribute a portion of the national taxes to the subnational units.

Bird claims that a subnational tax on business may be justified on a business benefit theory because businesses received valuable services from local government. Data from a study in the United States suggest that businesses may receive benefits equal to more than 10% of state and local expenditures.[101]

VIII. Reform of Subnational Taxes in the United States

There are many reasons why there is a need to reform subnational sales taxes in the United States. There is a patchwork of retail sales taxes in effect in most of the states (and the District of Columbia). There are forty-six different RSTs. Most states in the United States impose retail sales taxes (RSTs) that generally do not apply to interstate sales and impose use taxes on imports (but are not very successful in collecting them from consumers). The sales and use taxes are imposed on the destination principle. Consumers may avoid RSTs (of up to 9% or more in some locales) in both the state of sale and the state of destination by purchasing goods by mail order or on the Internet (electronic commerce).

Businesses that must comply with many state and local sales taxes devote substantial resources to this task. The sales tax base is shrinking, in part as a result of the expansion of services (generally not taxed), including the growing area of electronic commerce. For constitutional and other reasons, the states are not able to impose these RSTs and use taxes on most cross-border and mail order sales to consumers.

A recent development in the United States is the Streamlined Sales and Use Tax. A number of states have enacted legislation that would bring their sales and use taxes into compliance with the Streamlined Sales and Use Tax Agreement. Richard Ainsworth proposed a "digital VAT" that could also be used to harmonize sales taxes among the states in the United States.[102]

99 *Id.* at 16.

100 See, for example, McLure, Sub-national Fiscal Autonomy, *supra* note 3, referred to in Bird, Rethinking Sub-National Taxes, *supra* note 62.

101 R. Bird, Subnational VATs, *supra* note 1, at note 17, citing Oakland & Testa, "Community Development – Fiscal Interactions: Theory and Evidence from the Chicago Area," Working Paper Series, Federal Reserve Bank of Chicago (WP-1995/7).

102 R. Ainsworth, *The Digital VAT (D-VAT)*, 25 Va. Tax Rev. 835 (2006).

Some states in the United States have enacted or considered various forms of VAT or variations of VAT. Michigan had a Single Business Tax (SBT), an addition-method VAT. New Hampshire has a Business Enterprise Tax that some commentators refer to as a form of VAT. West Virginia and Minnesota considered but did not enact VATs. Other states, including Texas and Louisiana, have looked at a VAT. Texas enacted the Texas Margin Tax – a tax with some attributes of a VAT. Some of the subnational VATs proposed for other countries have been promoted as possible subnational VATs in the United States.[103]

The literature in the United States has begun to address the anticipated problems that likely would occur if Congress were to adopt a federal VAT or other federal tax on consumption that would have to coexist with state RSTs. In states with taxes that resemble VATs, the problems of coordination with a federal VAT would be somewhat different. The alternatives must be judged by objective criteria. Charles McLure proposed five characteristics of a well-designed sales tax system for this purpose.[104] Three of the characteristics are economic, one is administrative, and one is political:

1. "essentially all sales to consumers in a given jurisdiction would be taxed at a single rate;
2. essentially all sales to business would be exempt;
3. sales would be taxed under the destination principle . . .;
4. the first three objectives could be met without undue costs of compliance and administration; and
5. each level of government would have the power – and the responsibility – to set its own tax rate. (Note that compliance with the first two characteristics would essentially eliminate the power of each level of government also to determine its sales tax base.)"[105]

According to McLure, it will be difficult to coordinate defective state and local retail sales taxes (as they now exist) with even a federal VAT that meet his criteria for an ideal sales tax.[106] He and Richard Bird have come

[103] See Keen, "States' Rights and the Value Added Tax: How a VIVAT Would Work in the United States," Proceedings, 94 Annual Conference on Taxation, National Tax Association, 195 (2002), in which the author suggests that the VIVAT can tax interstate sales to final consumers under the destination principle at the rate in the state of consumption (he omits any consideration of the U.S. Constitutional issues with out-of-state sales).

[104] His conclusions will be discussed later in this chapter.

[105] Charles McLure, Jr., "Coordinating State Sales Taxes with a Federal VAT: Opportunities, Risks, and Challenges," 36 *State Tax Notes* 907 (June 20, 2005) (footnotes omitted). In a footnote, he leaves "open the possibility of exempting some sales to consumers (for example, of prescription drugs) and taxing some sales to business (for example, of luxury automobiles ostensibly used in business)." He does not consider state use taxes. "Taxation that is economically equivalent to a use tax is inherent in a destination-based sales tax." *Id.*

[106] *Id.* at 918.

to the conclusion that the best way for two levels of government to "levy sales taxes at reasonable costs is by agreeing on a common tax base and letting one level of government collect the tax for both."[107]

Alice Rivlin proposed a uniform state level tax to replace part of the revenue from state RSTs and raise revenue needed to finance services the states are obliged to provide. Although the article was written in 1990, it has vitality today. She recommended that this tax be administered by a central administrative agency, a feature that better handles interstate transactions by mail order or electronic commerce. She did not limit the state level uniform tax proposal to some form of VAT. In part, she wrote:

> The states should adopt a radical new approach to raising the revenues they urgently need. They should join forces to pass a new kind of tax, one that would be imposed by each state at a uniform rate. The money, which would be collected by some central agency, would then be distributed to each state on the basis of a formula, perhaps simply by population.[108]
>
> [I]f the formula for sharing the common tax favored less affluent jurisdictions, it would reduce disparities among states in the quality of public services. [This feature resembles the Brazil system (discussed earlier) that allocates more revenue on interstate sales to less developed states.]
>
> The increasing integration of the economy also makes a common tax attractive, both to states and to businesses. A rising share of business is now done by multistate and multinational corporations. Mail- and phone-order sales are exploding and largely escaping state sales taxes. The service sector, growing much faster than the goods-producing sector, is also becoming national and international, as legal, accounting, financial and advertising firms develop far-flung operations. Movement by the states to adopt common business taxes and share the proceeds could reduce the volume of business escaping taxation and cut the cost of administration for state governments and businesses alike.
>
> The states that enacted a uniform common tax could either establish their own agency to collect and distribute it or, perhaps, let the Internal Revenue Service do the job under contract to them.[109]

Some states have taken Ms. Rivlin's advice and have adopted legislation consistent with the Streamlined Sales and Use Tax Agreement, discussed later in this chapter.

[107] *Id.* at 918, quoting from Bird, "Cost and Complexity of Canada's VAT: The GST in International Perspective," 8 *Tax Notes Int'l* 37 (Jan. 3, 1994).

[108] Japan allocates part of the Consumption Tax (a VAT) revenue dedicated for the prefectures on the basis of prefecture population to reduce the disparity in resources available to affluent and poorer prefectures [added by the authors].

[109] Extract from Rivlin, "Wanted: A New State-Level Tax to Prepare Us for the 21st Century," *Governing* 74 (April 1990) [edited by the authors]. Ms. Rivlin, at the time this article was written, had been an economist at the Brookings Institution, and then was appointed director of the Congressional Budget Office. She subsequently served on President Clinton's Council of Economic Advisors and on the Federal Reserve Board.

A. Coexistence of Federal VAT and State Retail Sales Tax

There have been several proposals to impose VAT or other sales taxes in the United States, both at the federal and subnational levels of government.

> There have been a number of studies and commentaries suggesting that the states either move from their existing form of consumption tax (the state retail sales tax (RST)) to a broader-based consumption tax (the value-added tax)[110] or that the states shift from their state income tax and other taxes on business activity to a state VAT. States could follow Michigan's prior approach (subsequently repealed) and replace their income and other taxes on business activity with an apportioned tax like the Michigan Single Business Tax,[111] an addition form of value-added tax.[112]

Consumers in Canada experienced sticker shock at the cash register when the federal GST was imposed in addition to existing retail sales tax in many provinces. If the United States adopted a federal VAT, a sales-subtraction VAT (a period rather than a transactions tax) that is buried in product prices may be more compatible with existing state and local sales taxes than the European VAT.[113]

[110] See J. Due, "The Value-Added Tax: Possible State Use," 1 *State Tax Notes* 269 (1991), suggesting a possible origin-based state VAT. References in this article to state RSTs include local RSTs in those states that impose RSTs both at the state and local levels of government.

[111] See J. Francis, "A Closer Look at a State Invoice-Credit VAT," National Tax Association Annual Meeting, Oct. 1992, published in 3 *State Tax Notes* 804 (Nov. 30, 1992). In his article, Mr. Francis, director of tax research at the Florida Department of Revenue, argues that an apportioned state-level addition method VAT is inferior to the EC-style invoice VAT. He suggests that an EC-style VAT at the state level will tax consumption and not production, whereas an apportioned VAT such as the Michigan SBT taxes only the portion of final consumption produced within the taxing jurisdiction. Mr. Francis notes that an addition method VAT could be structured to tax consumption (by using a sales only allocation formula), but that the Michigan SBT does not do so.

[112] In June 1994, the Standing Committee on Finance (the "Committee") issued its Ninth Report, entitled "Replacing the GST: Options for Canada." In this report, the Committee recommended that Canada replace its GST with a National VAT and that provincial sales taxes be integrated with this national tax. The proposed National Tax would be buried in prices, but vendors that made sales that currently require GST disclosure on invoices would be required to disclose on invoices both their registration numbers and either the VAT rate or the amount of VAT payable on the sale. A. Schenk, "Federal Move to Consumption-Based Tax: Implications for State and Local Taxation and Insights from the Canadian Experience," 3 *State & Local Tax Law* 89 (1998) [hereinafter Schenk, Federal Move to Consumption Tax].

[113] See Schenk, Federal Move to Consumption Tax, *supra* note 114.

B. Subnational VATs in Use and Proposed for the United States

There are no classic VATs at the state level in the United States. The New Hampshire Business Enterprise Tax (BET) has been described as a form of VAT.[114] New York has a VAT structure for its multistage Hotel Room Occupancy Tax. "Room remarketers" charge tax on their sales of hotel rooms and can claim credit against that tax liability for the tax that they have to pay to the hotels providing the rooms.[115]

Michigan relied on a state-level VAT twice, first with a subtraction-method Business Activity Tax (BAT) from 1953 to 1967.[116] The BAT was replaced with income taxes, and then the corporate income tax and several other taxes on business were replaced with a SBT, an addition-method VAT. There was dissatisfaction with the SBT, in part because during economic downturns businesses still had to pay tax. The SBT was replaced in 2008 with the Michigan Business Tax, a two-part tax imposed on business income and gross receipts. That tax did not last long. Effective January 1, 2012, the state went back to a corporate income tax. The New Hampshire BET and the repealed Michigan SBT are discussed next, followed by a discussion of several proposed state level VATs, including a West Virginia SBT and Richard Ainsworth's proposed state level digital VAT.

1. New Hampshire Business Enterprise Tax

The New Hampshire BET is imposed at the rate of three-quarters of 1% of a business enterprise's taxable enterprise value tax base,[117] but only business enterprises with gross business receipts in excess of US$150,000 or enterprise value tax base greater than US$75,000 are required to file a return and pay tax.[118] The "taxable enterprise value tax base" is the "enterprise value tax base," as adjusted and apportioned to New Hampshire.[119] That base is calculated under the addition-method as the sum of compensation, interest, and dividends paid.[120] The adjustments reduce the base to

[114] For a discussion of the New Hampshire BET, see D. Kenyon, "A New State VAT: Lessons from NH," 49 *Nat'l Tax.* 381 (1996); V. H. Berghaus & W. Ardinger, "The Policy and Structure of the Business Enterprise Tax," *N.H. Bar* (Dec. 1993).

[115] See, R. Ainsworth, "New York Adopts a VAT," 61 *State Tax Notes* 223 (July 25, 2011); also available at http://ssrn.com/abstract=1868946.

[116] 1953 Mich. Pub. Acts 150.

[117] N.H. Rev. Stat. Ann §77-E:2 (2004).

[118] *Id.* at §77-E:5(I) (2004).

[119] *Id.* at §77-E:l(XV) (2004). The apportionment formula in §77-E:4, if applicable, is a three-factor formula that allocates compensation, interest, and dividends to New Hampshire. Dividends are apportioned on the basis of the average of the compensation, interest, and sales factors. If the apportionment "does not fairly represent the enterprise's business activity in this state," the enterprise can petition or the commissioner may require a different method of apportioning business activity to New Hampshire. *Id.* at § 77-E:4(II).

[120] *Id.* at§77-E:l(IX).

exclude such items as compensation that is retained for use in the business and dividends received from an affiliated corporation that was included in the payor's BET base subject to tax.[121]

Is the New Hampshire BET a tax on value added when it includes only dividends paid or amounts treated as dividends paid in the tax base, rather than the enterprise's profits as commonly defined for VAT purposes?[122] The predominant factor in the BET is compensation. A business subject to the BET is allowed to credit its BET liability against its liability under the separate New Hampshire business profits tax.

2. Michigan Single Business Tax

Michigan adopted a state-level modified addition-method VAT, its SBT, effective in 1975.[123] Despite its repeal, the Michigan SBT is discussed here because it is an example of an addition-method VAT, and it has been studied by other states that considered a state level VAT. Unfortunately, maybe in part because it resembled an income tax, the legislature could not resist pressure to add special rules so that, at the end, it was difficult to recognize it as a VAT.

In broad outline, a business calculated its SBT base by adding to "business income" the compensation paid to employees (including contributions to retirement plans), depreciation taken for tax purposes, and several other adjustments. The business then could deduct:

1. dividends, interest, and certain rent, royalty, and franchise fee receipts that are included in federal taxable income,
2. capital losses not deductible for federal tax purposes, and
3. a few other adjustments.

An apportionment formula then allocated a portion of the resulting tax base to Michigan.[124] The apportioned tax base then was adjusted by an investment tax credit that replaced, for years after 1999, a deduction for the apportioned cost of depreciable tangible assets physically located in

[121] *Id.* at § 77-E:3.

[122] Profits of noncorporate enterprises are taxed as are dividends, but undistributed corporate profits retained for use in the business are not taxed. For a claim that the BET is not a true VAT, see Schenk, "New Hampshire: Two Views on the Business Activity Tax (BET)," 5 *VAT Monitor* 234 (July/Aug. 1994).

[123] For a detailed discussion of the SBT, see B. Schwendener, Jr., 1650 T.M., Michigan Single Business Tax (1994 and supplement) [hereinafter, Schwendener, SBT]. The SBT was the Single Business Tax Act, P.A. 1975, No. 228, MCL §208.1 et seq.

[124] For tax years before January 1, 1997, for businesses other than transportation, finance, and insurance, the apportionment formula is 50% sales, 25% property, and 25% payroll. MCL §208.45. For tax years after 2005, the apportionment formula for these businesses will be 95% for sales, 2.5% for property, and 2.5% for payroll. 2005 Mi. P.A. 223, 2005 MI HB 4973, §45(a)(2). There is an option to allocate 100% on the basis of sales if the taxpayer does not own or rent real estate or tangible personal property associated with the taxpayer's business activities and gross sales in the state do not exceed $100,000. See MCLS §208.68(1).

Michigan and to be used in business activity in Michigan.[125] As an alternative to the special compensation deduction, a business could claim a deduction that in effect imposed tax on 50% of taxable gross receipts.[126] There was a variable annual exemption, and the legislature granted several tax credits, including a small business credit, for businesses subject to the SBT. The SBT rate[127] was scheduled to be phased out as economic conditions warranted.[128]

3. Proposed State-Level VATs

Eugene Steuerle's examination of the Michigan SBT concept and his exploration of studies of similar taxes in other states is illuminating.

> "[State value added taxes were] proposed by study commissions in both West Virginia and the District of Columbia and [were considered] in Minnesota and Texas. While no tax is without problems of defining the base or of enforcement, the potential for expansion of the single business tax [concept] is significant…
>
> In the case of West Virginia, its Commission on Fair Taxation bravely proposed reform that included the repeal of a wide range of distorting taxes that tended to "pick" on particular forms of activity or that simply were not worth the extra tax enforcement costs. These included the personal property tax that largely applied to business machinery, equipment, and inventory, the telecommunications tax, a health provider tax, an insurance premiums tax, an auto privilege tax, and a soft drink excise tax. The single business tax is also proposed to replace a business franchise tax, a corporate charter tax, a business registration tax, and a business and occupation tax. Many of these business taxes result in a double tax on different forms of income or consumption based mainly on organizational form or how many layers of business are involved in the final production. Such taxes are believed to be very distorting.
>
> The District of Columbia's case is somewhat unique in that so many services, particularly those of lawyers and other professionals, are produced by residents outside the District who then pay little or no tax on the income they earn inside the District on the value of services they provide. A SBT represents yet one more attempt to get at this issue.

125 See M.C.L. §208.35a. The available credit is based on a percentage of creditable investment expenditures, based on a two-step process. The percentage varies, depending on the level of the taxpayer's adjusted gross receipts.

126 Schwendener, SBT, *supra* note 123, at 1650–0012; MCL §208.22a.

127 P.A. 1975, No. 228, Single Business Tax Act, §31(1), as amended, P.A. 1994, No. 247, §1. The rate reduction started with a reduction from 2.35% to 2.30%, effective after September 30, 1994.

128 The rate is to be reduced by 0.1% in any year in which the comprehensive annual financial report of Michigan shows an ending balance of more than $250 million in the countercyclical budget and economic stabilization fund. The reduction occurs on January 1 following the end of the state fiscal year for which the report was issued. Mich. Stat. Ann. 7.558(31), §31(5).

> [A state level single business tax is not] some perfect form of taxation. None exists. Like many other areas of taxation that depend on geographical location, there are many border tensions as to whether income or consumption should be taxed by source or residence; even when one or another is chosen in theory, enforcement and implementation can be problems in practice. Transition problems can be significant. Like so many other state taxes such as the income tax, apportioning the tax base across jurisdictions is not only difficult but also threatened by inconsistent rules in different states. These rules cause some consumption or income to be taxed twice in two different jurisdictions; others to be taxed not at all.
>
> Whatever the future of the SBT, it could unwind only over a long period of time. Any expansion is likely to go hand-in-hand with a reduced reliance on other taxes. It could give states more elastic and stable tax sources. At the same time, it would raise new issues of tension across state boundaries, and it could even affect the federal government's own choices with respect to income and various forms of consumption taxes."[129]

Richard Ainsworth proposed a "digital VAT" or "D-VAT" as a method for the United States to harmonize e-solutions among tax jurisdictions (federal and state, and among states) and make them more comprehensive within each jurisdiction.[130] This proposed broad-based credit-invoice VAT is a "technology-intensive" VAT that incorporates electronic and third-party tax collection aspects of EU Council Directives and the U.S. Streamlined Sales and Use Tax Agreement.[131]

Under the Ainsworth proposal, certified service providers serve as collection agents.[132] All VAT documents (including invoices, returns, and notices) must be electronic, except for those permitted to use paper documents. Uniform digital identification of goods and services, similar to the EU's CN8 codes or the UNCPC codes, are required.[133] Mr. Ainsworth supports reliance on electronic data, on the basis that more than 99% of data generated worldwide in 1999 were computer generated.[134]

[129] E. Steuerle, "Will the Single Business Tax Catch On?" 81 *Tax Notes* 1013 (Nov. 23, 1998) [edited by the authors].

[130] Richard Ainsworth, *Digital VAT: A Proposal for the President's Advisory Panel on Federal Tax Reform*, President's Advisory Panel on Federal Tax Reform (Apr. 30, 2005), at http://comments.taxreformpanel.gov; reprinted as "A Digital VAT (D-VAT for the U.S.?" 108 *Tax Notes* 938 (Aug. 22, 2005) [hereinafter Ainsworth, Digital VAT]; Ainsworth, "Digital VAT and Development: D-VAT and Development," 39 *Tax Notes Int'l* 625 (August 15, 2005).

[131] R. Ainsworth, Digital VAT, *supra* note 130, at 2.

[132] "Software variations of this theme, certified automated systems (CASs) and certified proprietary systems (CPSs) will further facilitate administration and compliance." R. Ainsworth, Digital VAT, *supra* note 130, at 2. They all must be certified by the tax authorities. Based on the Streamlined Sales and Use Tax Agreement, §306, except for fraud, the users will be immunized "from liability for calculation or reporting errors." *Id.* at 4.

[133] The Combined Nomenclature in eight digits and the Central Product Classification, Version 1.0 are cited *id.* at 4.

[134] *Id.*

C. Streamlined Sales and Use Tax in the United States

Under current U.S. constitutional decisions, a seller cannot be required to collect sales taxes on interstate sales on behalf of the destination state unless the seller maintains a physical presence in the destination state.[135] In 2004, legislation was introduced in the U.S. Congress to give states that complied with the Streamlined Sales and Use Tax Interstate Agreement authority to require the out-of-state sellers to collect and remit sales tax on sales into that state.[136] To date, Congress has not enacted this or comparable legislation.

The Streamlined Sales and Use Tax Agreement[137] (different from the unenacted Interstate Agreement referred to previously) administered by the Streamlined Sales Tax Governing Board creates a unified state RST system for participating states that does not depend on federal congressional action to be effective. The agreement is designed "[t]o assist states as they administer a simpler and more uniform sales and use tax system."[138] This agreement imposes a series of requirements before a state can be certified as being in compliance.[139] Twenty-three states have been approved as full members. The system became effective on October 1, 2005.

The key features of this agreement emanating from the Streamlined Sales Tax Project are as follows. Each state that is a party to the agreement must establish a central state administration for all of its state and local sales and use taxes. Each participating state must adopt uniform definitions of key terms and a uniform base for its state and local sales and use taxes. A state can have only one general state sales and use tax rate (a different rate is permissible for food and drugs), and each sub-state jurisdiction can have only one tax rate per jurisdiction. States are required to maintain a database that will notify sellers of changes in rates or changes in the boundaries of tax jurisdictions within the state.[140] Although sellers must obtain information to support a purchaser's claimed exemption, the

[135] *Quill Corp. v. North Dakota*, 504 U.S. 298 (1992); *National Bellas Hess, Inc. v. Department of Revenue of Illinois*, 386 U.S. 753 (1967).

[136] See S. 1736, "The Streamlined Sales and Use Tax Act," 108th Cong., 1st Sess. (Oct. 14, 2003).

[137] See http://www.streamlinedsalestax.org.

[138] See *id.* at "Home."

[139] See Executive Summary, Streamlined Sales Tax Project, http://wwwstreamline-dsalestax.org (Apr. 2004). Sellers can use one of three technology models, including the use of a Certified Services Provider that is paid by the states. The Streamlined Sales Tax Project was established in March 2000, as a joint project of the National Conference of State Legislatures, the National Governors' Association, the Multistate Tax Commission, and the Federation of Tax Administrators. The project expects states to adopt the Uniform Sales and Use Tax Administration Act that allows the state to enter into an agreement with one or more other states and the Streamlined Sales and Use Tax Agreement that brings the state's sales and use tax laws in compliance with the principles discussed in the text.

[140] See Technology Implementation Guide, ch. 5, at http://www.streamlinedsalestax.org/uploads/downloads/TG%20Technology/TG13001%20Implementation%20Guide%20revised%202013.pdf.

burden related to the validity of a purchaser's exemption under the state sales and use tax law is on the purchaser.[141]

A series of issues remains. For example, a central registration system must be established and authority to maintain the system must be granted to an organization or entity. Sellers without a physical presence in a participating state are not required to collect sales and use taxes unless Congress adopts a law such as the Streamlined Sales and Use Tax Interstate Agreement that could require out-of-state sellers to collect for and remit the tax to the destination state. The governing board for the multistate compact is reviewing proposals from companies who are seeking contracts to collect and remit tax on behalf of registered retailers.[142]

IX. Discussion Questions

1. The main interjurisdictional issues in the context of federal countries are:
   a. dividing the VAT tax base among the jurisdictions while avoiding overlapping and underlapping;
   b. collecting the tax when transactions in goods and services cross borders; and
   c. coordinating definitions, rates, and administration among states and between a tax at the national level and corresponding taxes at the state level.

Is there a model solution for these issues for all federal countries? If so, what is it? If not, why not and what range of solutions exists? What other important interjurisdictional issues must federations face?

2. Are the issues in (1) the main issues for common markets? If not, what different problems do they pose?
3. Assume that in the United States the subnational units of government (states) are not willing to give up their power to define their tax base, their penalties, and so on, and therefore the states retain their diverse single stage retail sales taxes. What are the differences between federal adoption of an EU-style VAT (a transaction tax) and an addition or sales-subtraction VAT? Consider the effect on the RST base, the ease of operation of the federal alongside the state taxes, and the state's receptivity or opposition to the federal levy.
4. States in the United States and provinces in Canada derive a significant portion of the RST revenue (ranging from 15% to 33%) from tax on business inputs. How will this fact affect the state and provincial

[141] Purchasers are liable for the tax, interest, and penalties if they claim incorrect exemptions. *Id.*

[142] See D. Gregory, "Five Years in Making, Streamlined Sales Tax System Begins Official Business Oct. 1 Although Collections Will Start Later," *BNA Daily Tax Report*, Sept. 30, 2005, p. J-l.

governments' willingness to harmonize their RSTs with a European-style federal VAT?

5. If a single branch of government administers both a federal and state VAT, should the administrative function be given to the federal government, or the state governments, or divided between them?
6. What interstate competition problems are likely to arise if some but not all states in a federal system harmonize their RSTs with the federal VAT?
7. What are the administrative advantages and disadvantages associated with the imposition of a federal EU-style VAT alongside state RSTs?
8. If there is a federal–state integrated sales-subtraction VAT, with the states imposing varying tax rates, how can a business calculate its input credit for the state component of the combined VAT?

Appendix: VATs Worldwide[1]

No.	Country	Date VAT introduced	Standard rate
1	Albania	1996	20.0
2	Algeria	1992	17
3	Andorra		4.5
4	Angola		10
5	Antigua and Barbuda	2006	15
6	Argentina	1975	21.0
7	Armenia	1992	20.0
8	Australia	2000	10.0
9	Austria	1973	20.0
10	Azerbaijan	1992	18.0
11	Bangladesh	1991	15.0
12	Barbados	1997	17.5
13	Belarus	1992	20
14	Belgium	1971	21.0
15	Benin	1991	18.0
16	Bolivia	1973	13.0
17	Bosnia and Herzegovina	2006	17
18	Botswana	2002	12
19	Brazil	1967	20.0 (avg. IPI)
20	Bulgaria	1994	20.0
21	Burkina Faso	1993	18.0

(*continued*)

[1] VAT rates may change frequently. We cannot guarantee the accuracy of the information in this chart. We took the information from a number of sources written at different times. The list includes all UN member countries with a VAT, as well as Taiwan and West Bank Gaza. As of the beginning of 2014, about thirty-five UN member countries did not have a VAT and, therefore, are not on the list.

No.	Country	Date VAT introduced	Standard rate
22	Burundi	2009	18
23	Cambodia	1999	10.0
24	Cameroon	1999	19.25
25	Canada	1991	5.0
26	Cape Verde	2004	15.0
27	Central African Republic	2001	19.0
28	Chad	2000	18.0
29	Chile	1975	19.0
30	China	1994	17.0
31	Colombia	1975	16.0
32	Congo (Brazzaville)		18.00
33	Congo, Democratic Republic of the	1997	16.0
34	Costa Rica	1975	13.0
35	Côte d'Ivoire	1960	18.0
36	Croatia	1998	25.0
37	Cyprus	1992	18.0
38	Czech Republic	1993	21.0
39	Denmark	1967	25.0
40	Dominica	2006	15.0
41	Dominican Republic	1983	18.0
42	Ecuador	1970	12.0
43	Egypt	1991	10.0
44	El Salvador	1992	13.0
45	Equatorial Guinea	2004	15
46	Estonia	1992	20.0
47	Ethiopia	2003	15.0
48	Fiji	1992	15.0
49	Finland	1994	24.0
50	France	1968 (or 1948)	20.0
51	Gabon	1995	18.0
52	Gambia	2013	15.0
53	Georgia	1992	18.0
54	Germany	1968	19.0
55	Ghana	1998	17.5[a]
56	Greece	1987	23.0
57	Grenada	2009	15
58	Guatemala	1983	12.0
59	Guinea	1996	18.0
60	Guinea-Bissau	2001	15
61	Guyana	2007	16
62	Haiti	1982	10.0

No.	*Country*	*Date VAT introduced*	*Standard rate*
63	Honduras	1976	15.0
64	Hungary	1988	27.0
65	Iceland	1990	25.5
66	India	Service tax and some subnational VATs 2005	12.36–15
67	Indonesia	1985	10.0
68	Ireland	1972	23.0
69	Iran	2008	5
70	Israel	1976	18.0
71	Italy	1973	22.0
72	Jamaica	1991	16.5
73	Japan	1989	8.0
74	Jordan	1994	16
75	Kazakhstan	1992	12.0
76	Kenya	1990	16.0
77	Korea	1977	10.0
78	Kosovo	2001	16
79	Kyrgyz Republic	1992	20.0
80	Laos	2009	10
81	Latvia	1992	21.0
82	Lebanon	2002	10.0
83	Lesotho	2003	14.0
84	Liechtenstein		8.0
85	Lithuania	1992	21.0
86	Luxembourg	1970	15.0
87	Macedonia, FYR	2000	18.0
88	Madagascar	1994	20.0
89	Malawi	1989	16.5
90	Malaysia	2015 (announced)	6
91	Mali	1991	18.0
92	Malta	1995	18.0
93	Mauritania	1995	14.0
94	Mauritius	1998	15.0
95	Mexico	1980	16.0
96	Moldova	1992	20.0
97	Monaco	1963	20.0
98	Mongolia	1998	10.0
99	Montenegro	2003	17
100	Morocco	1986	20.0
101	Mozambique	1999	17.0
102	Myanmar	1990	5–100
103	Namibia	2000	15.0
104	Nepal	1997	13.0

No.	Country	Date VAT introduced	Standard rate
105	Netherlands	1969	21.0
106	New Zealand	1986	15.0
107	Nicaragua	1975	15.0
108	Niger	1986	19.0
109	Nigeria	1994	5.0
110	Norway	1970	25.0
111	Pakistan	1990	16.0–17.0
112	Palestine Autonomous Areas (West Bank Gaza)	1976	17.0
113	Panama	1977	7.0
114	Papua New Guinea	1999	10.0
115	Paraguay	1993	10.0
116	Peru	1973	18.0
117	Philippines	1988	12.0
118	Poland	1993	23.0
119	Portugal	1986	23.0
120	Romania	1993	24.0
121	Russia	1992	18.0
122	Rwanda	2001	18.0
123	St. Kitts and Nevis	2010	17
124	St. Lucia	2012	15
125	St. Vincent and the Grenadines	2007	15
126	Samoa	1994	15.0
127	Senegal	1980	18.0
128	Serbia	2005	20.0
129	Seychelles	2013	15
130	Sierra Leone	2009	15.0
131	Singapore	1994	7.0
132	Slovak Republic	1993	20.0
133	Slovenia	1999	22.0
134	South Africa	1991	14.0
135	Spain	1986	21.0
136	Sri Lanka	1998	12.0
137	Sudan	2000	17.0
138	Suriname	1999	8.0–10.0
139	Swaziland	2012	14.0
140	Sweden	1969	25.0
141	Switzerland	1995	8.0
142	Taiwan	1986	5.0
143	Tajikistan	1992	20.0
144	Tanzania	1998	18.0

No.	*Country*	*Date VAT introduced*	*Standard rate*
145	Thailand	1992	7.0
146	Togo	1995	18.0
147	Tonga	2005	15.0
148	Trinidad and Tobago	1990	15.0
149	Tunisia	1988	18.0
150	Turkey	1985	18.0
151	Turkmenistan	1992	15.0
152	Uganda	1996	18.0
153	Ukraine	1992	20.0
154	United Kingdom	1973	20.0
155	Uruguay	1968	22.0
156	Uzbekistan	1992	20.0
157	Vanuatu	1998	13.0
158	Venezuela	1993	12.0
159	Vietnam	1999	10.0
160	Zambia	1995	16.0
161	Zimbabwe	2004	15.0

[a] Ghana's 17.5% rate includes the 2.5% National Health Insurance Levy.

Index

Printed in the United States
By Bookmasters